# The Gender Reader

EVELYN ASHTON-JONES
*University of Idaho*

GARY A. OLSON
*University of South Florida*

**ALLYN AND BACON**
**BOSTON LONDON TORONTO SYDNEY TOKYO SINGAPORE**

Executive Editor: Joseph Opiela
Series Editorial Assistant: Amy Capute
Editorial-Production Service: Editorial Inc.
Cover Administrator: Linda Dickinson
Composition and Manufacturing Buyer: Louise Richardson



**Library of Congress Cataloging-in-Publication Data**

The Gender Reader / Evelyn Ashton-Jones, Gary A. Olson.
p. cm.
ISBN 0-205-13068-2 (recycled, acid-free paper)
1. Sex role. 2. Sex discrimination against women. 3. Sexism.
I. Ashton-Jones, Evelyn, date. II. Olson, Gary A., date.
HQ1075.G465 1991
305.3—dc20 90-14446
CIP

This textbook is printed on recycled, acid-free paper.

**Credits**

Pages 4–11. Virginia Adams, "Male and Female: Differences Between Them," *Time* Magazine, Vol. 99, no. 12. Copyright 1972 Time Inc. Reprinted by permission.

Pages 12–21. Pamela Weintraub, "The Brain: His and Hers," *Discover* Magazine, April 1981. (Pamela Weintraub/© 1981 by Discover Publications.)

*Credits continued on page 557, which constitutes an extension of the copyright page.*

Printed in the United States of America

10 9 8 7 6 5 4 3 2 1 95 94 93 92 91 90

# Contents

# Preface

According to a Pakistani proverb, "Woman's place is in the home or the grave." A similar North American saying decrees that a woman should be kept "barefoot, pregnant, and in the kitchen." These popular expressions reveal an attitude we have come to call "sexist." But like many frequently repeated words and phrases, the word *sexist* has almost become a cliché; it has lost the power of its meaning. As many authors of the selections in this text suggest, sexism is the counterpart of racism. Just as *racism* refers to the doctrine that inherent differences among races make the people of one race superior to those of another and thereby justify the mistreatment and even abuse of the "inferior" race, *sexism* refers to the doctrine that perceived inherent differences between men and women make one sex (almost always men) superior to the other and thereby justify discrimination toward and abuse of the "inferior" sex. Like racism, sexism—as the proverbs cited above suggest—is a kind of hatred, a degrading of an entire group of people based solely on their sex or, in the case of racism, skin color. In both cases, the "inferior" group is treated as an underclass.

Just as the second half of this century has witnessed a growing consciousness of and sensitivity toward racial prejudice, so too have we become more conscious of the effects of sexual discrimination. The women's movement has led the struggle to educate society to reexamine attitudes about gender. Consequently, the roles of men and women—indeed, our very notions of gender—are in transition. What *is* "woman's place"—her role? What is man's role in society? *The Gender Reader* explores these complex and fascinating questions as well as numerous other issues related to gender relations.

This text is appropriate for students taking courses in composition or women's studies or anyone else who is thinking and writing about questions of gender. The sixty-one essays in the collection represent a wide range of perspectives on numerous important issues. Although most of the selections were published in the last few decades, several are historical pieces that provide a sense of continuity with the past.

We like to think of these selections as voices in an age-old "conversation" about the nature of men and women and their social roles. Like any conversation among multiple participants, it is characterized by agreement and disagreement, consensus and dissension, bickering and debate, reasoned argument and emotional pleading. As a whole, however, the conversation itself is enlightening because it awakens consciousness, stirs dormant emotions, forces people to become involved, to take issue, and, we hope, to enter the conversation themselves.

The metaphor of voices in a conversation is especially apt, we believe, because not only does it frame the subject as an organic, ever-changing, *human* activity (rather than as a dualistic right-or-wrong search for truth), but it also alludes to a key feminist theme: that throughout the ages male-dominated social and legal institutions have conspired to "silence" women, to prevent them from participating in society's largest, most important "conversations." Most germane to our present purposes, however, is that seeing this subject as a continuing discussion may help students discover that they too have voices, that they too can participate in this conversation, that they need not be intimidated by the essays in this collection simply because they were written by "published authors" and "great thinkers." We invite you and your students to join the discussion.

The conversation begins in Part I, "Gender Roles: Difference and Change," with an exploration of differences between men and women and a debate over the source of these differences. The participants also discuss changing notions of femininity and masculinity. Part II, "Women's Role: Historical Perspectives," presents voices from and about the past, examining previous views of women as well as their role and status in society. The authors represented in Part III, "Language and Sexism," analyze the nature and effects of sexist language, and those in Part IV, "Gender and Social Institutions," talk about gender relations in the educational system, the home, and the family.

Part V, "Gender and Public Policy," presents several sometimes passionate debates about comparable worth, pornography, and abortion. "Sexism and the Status of Women," Part VI, examines economic discrimination and social powerlessness. Part VII, "Additional Readings," contains discussions of issues relevant to gender studies, from the treatment of women in Middle Eastern countries to the connections between racism and feminism.

Together, these sixty-one voices provide but a sampling of the larger conversation, but they illustrate, we trust, several crucial gender issues and suggest the range of perspectives on them. The writings provide ample background for rich classroom discussion and thoughtful student essays on the intricacies of gender relations.

Each selection is followed by two sets of questions: "Reflecting on Meaning" and "Exploring Rhetorical Strategies." We call the first set "Reflecting on Meaning" because these are challenging discussion questions that often transcend the text itself, asking students not only to analyze the text but also to make connections beyond the text with their own experience. The questions in this section are demanding, and they are not meant to be "answered" as, for example, "homework" questions. Rather, they are intended to stimulate critical thinking and classroom discussion; and, of course, they may suggest topics and themes that can be explored in an extended way in formal essays. The questions called "Exploring Rhetorical Strategies" will help students examine the essays *as pieces of writing.* We avoid strictly formalistic questions, though, asking students instead to examine how the authors use rhetorical devices to further meaning. Again, the focus is on critical thinking and discussion.

Following each of the six main parts of the book is a section called "Taking a Stand: Questions for Consideration." These critical thinking questions are "intertextual," asking students to make connections and compare assumptions and evidence among several essays in each part of the book. Through analyzing and synthesizing essays from various sections, students can begin to formulate their own reasoned opinions and assumptions about the subject—a necessary step in preparing to make their own voices heard, both in and out of writing.

As you and your students listen to the voices recorded in *The Gender Reader,* we hope that you become angry and pleased, outraged and optimistic, disturbed and comforted—so much so that you become impatient to add your own voices to this age-old conversation.

We'd like to recognize Joseph Opiela at Allyn and Bacon, who had the vision and courage to take a chance in producing this text, as well as our project editor, Rowena Dores. Thanks are due also to several readers who examined and commented on early versions of this book: Rebecca E. Burnett, Carnegie-Mellon University; Kathleen Shine Cain, Merrimack College; Cyndia Clegg, Pepperdine University; Susan Gabriel, Southern Illinois University at Edwardsville; C. Jeriel Howard, Northeastern Illinois University; Mary Lay, Clarkson University; Susan Miller, University of Utah; Louise Z. Smith, University of Massachusetts–Boston; and Judith Stanford, Rivier College. Finally, we'd like to thank Marlyne S. Olson and Joseph D. Olson for their assistance in this project.

Evelyn Ashton-Jones
Gary A. Olson

# Foreword for Students

When my father came to my forty-eighth birthday party, he put a damper on the occasion by solemnly declaring, "My mother died when she was your age." Then he added wistfully, "And she was an old woman." And, indeed, she probably was. She had given birth to ten children, had never lived in a home with running water, and, during the winter months when her schoolteaching husband was away in any small town that would give him a job, she had been a single parent who ran the family farm, who kept her children fed, clothed, and in school, and who served as a nurse and midwife in the small isolated community where she lived in northern Arizona. She died from pneumonia that developed after she walked through a snowstorm to care for a sick neighbor.

There at my birthday party was a seventy-eight-year-old man standing Januslike between two generations—his mother and his daughter—and pondering the differences. I had given birth to only three children, the last when I was twenty-six years old. When my grandmother died at forty-eight, her youngest child was only eight years old; on my forty-eighth birthday, my youngest child was twenty-two years old and away at college. My house not only had running water but also an automatic washing machine and dryer, a dishwasher, a vacuum cleaner, and a microwave oven. But more important, I had a good chance of living a productive and useful life for another *thirty* years, according to statisticians.

The differences between my grandmother's life and my own are fairly typical, and they underlie and motivate today's feminist movement. We've probably all heard some variation of this statement: If women would just quit complaining, then this whole feminist movement would go away and we could settle down and concentrate on more important issues. But my birthday-party story suggests that the feminist movement is not bringing the changes. Rather, they have come from outside, and they are forcing people to react in new ways and choose from options never before available.

Technological advances have brought many of these changes. Better medical care for women means that they live longer and healthier lives. This same improved medical care means that their children also have a better chance for survival; consequently, women no longer feel they need to have ten children in hopes of raising five or six. Nor do families feel they need five or six children to work the family farm. And better methods of birth control allow women to decide how many children they will have.

Technology also helps protect us from the elements and makes our daily work easier. When my father was a child, most men in his community were engaged in hard physical labor; although a schoolteacher, his own father couldn't provide food for a large family without a farm. Ranching, farming, and building all require physical strength, and these men's wives would have been at a disadvantage had they been doing the same jobs their husbands did. But today in my community, most men are engaged in jobs based on intellectual work; they are teachers, lawyers, sales representatives, computer programmers, doctors, business people, bankers, and engineers. My women friends and I have the physical strength to do the jobs our husbands do; in fact, today many husbands and wives are in similar professions, as the phrase "dual-career couple" suggests.

In industrialized nations, power machinery and conveyor belts do much of the lifting and hauling that used to require "manpower." Even war has changed: as it has moved away from hand-to-hand combat, women have become involved. This change results at least partly from the difference in women's and men's physical strength, which dissipate when the strength of a human being—male or female—is compared to the power of an airplane or a tank.

Technological changes in the last sixty years have changed women's lives more than men's. Both men's and women's life expectancies have increased over the last three generations, but the increase for women has been almost twice as great, primarily because women are the ones who give birth to children, a health-related area that has improved tremendously. Women's lives have also changed more because of technology's "push-pull" effect: women are pushed from their homes by electricity and modern appliances that make housework for today's smaller families less than a full-time job; and they are pulled into the work force because today's economy requires more workers and because most jobs—including those requiring physical labor—are jobs that women can do.

Echoing earlier times when physical strength was a primary value, many jobs today are still sorted into "male" and "female" categories—but on the basis of prestige rather than physical labor. For example, the male pilot of a large passenger plane exerts less physical energy than does a female stewardess who serves drinks and dinner to 150 passengers during a three-hour flight. Nor does a male grocery-store manager expend as much physical energy as does a female cashier who every day lifts thousands of pounds of groceries from shopping carts, passes them in front of the register as she rings up the prices, and bags them on the other side. In a similar way, a male school principal does not exert the same physical effort as do teachers, especially those teaching very young or handicapped children who often must be lifted and moved.

Because the most profound changes have come to women's lives, women were the ones who first noticed and began talking about "consciousness raising" and then about "woman's liberation," "the women's movement," and "feminism." But people soon realized that men, too, were being affected by the same kinds of changes and by what was happening to the women in their lives. These changes influence every aspect of modern living so intimately that all of us—whether male or female—are being forced to think about their effects. This change explains why this book is entitled *The Gender Reader* and why it was written for men as well as women students.

Social systems are complex sets of agreements—some so subtle that we aren't aware of having bought into them. Nevertheless, these agreements determine our attitudes, values, and behavior. When a society is stable, most of its members have little trouble "fitting in" because they model their own behavior after their parents' and friends' behavior. But changes bring new pieces to an old puzzle, and as we try to make these new pieces fit in, we inevitably have some bumping and shoving. Sometimes this bumping is literal. When a man and a woman both approach a door at the same time, the old system required that the woman always stand back and wait for the man to open the door, but today either or both may reach out to open it.

The way in which we address business letters provides another example. We used to automatically begin such letters with "Dear Sir" or "Gentlemen," but now we're forced to stop and think about the matter. On eighty letters of application for a professor's job at the university where I work, most writers avoided the old masculine greetings, but they weren't sure what else to use. As a result, they relied on twenty forms, including "Good Morning," "Dear Reader," "Dear Selection Committee," "Dear Sir/Madam," "Dear Colleagues," "Gentlepeople," and "To Whom It May Concern." Ten years from now we will probably settle down to one or two nonsexist options, but for now we're confused.

At the grocery store the other night, I had an experience that illustrates how clever people can take advantage of a social system in change. When the bagger, a petite young woman, took one of my shopping carts to the car, I asked her if it had been difficult to get a job as a "carry-out boy." She laughingly explained, "Oh, no. The manager looks for carry-outs like me because when I offer to take people's groceries out, most say they'll do it themselves. That way I can take care of all the lines. But if we have athletic-looking boys, everyone says yes, and it takes three or four of them to keep the customers happy."

Although these examples are taken from the simplest levels, they illustrate the extent to which changes have upset the system, and that people are groping for solutions to what used to be non-problems. To understand how we are being affected and what we need to do to benefit our lives and society, we must undergo many such experiences. But it isn't enough just to have these experiences. We need to ponder and discuss and see how our reactions fit with other people's reactions. Before laws can be made, we have to arrive at group decisions through consensus. And because many of the attitudes and behaviors involved are too subtle to be controlled by laws, they will always be subject to informal group consensus.

I might end this foreword with the cliché, "Happy reading!" But that would be less than honest. Change makes people insecure and uncomfortable, and this is a book about change. Therefore, it isn't likely to provide you with the kind of happy feeling you can get from reading a wish-fulfilling romance or a sports story. Nevertheless, I'm confident that you will enjoy the book because it's exciting to study cultural change and to participate in determining how change will occur. That's what *The Gender Reader* is about. As you read, ponder, think, write, discuss, and even argue, remember that you are playing a role in shaping society for the 1990s as well as for the year 2000 and beyond.

Alleen Pace Nilsen
*Assistant Vice President for Academic Affairs*
*Arizona State University*

# Part I

# Gender Roles: Difference and Change

Are the qualities we most commonly associate with gender—with femininity and masculinity—a function of our biological makeup, or are they a product of social forces? That is, is our "femaleness" or "maleness" inherent within each of us—a product of our genes—or are these roles *constructed* by the assumptions, values, and prejudices of our culture? These two perspectives frame the debate among scholars, researchers, and commentators interested in gender studies, a debate that became especially active (and heated) during the seventies and eighties as our traditional notions of masculinity and femininity began to change. The essays in Part I address these issues from a number of perspectives.

In the first group of essays, "Gender Differences: Sociology or Biology?" the authors explore the differences between men and women. In doing so they enter, consciously or not, the sociology-biology debate. Virginia Adams begins the section by reviewing scientific research that attempts to establish exactly what the differences between men and women are. Similarly, Pamela Weintraub surveys research into the physical differences between the male and female brains. Prudence Mackintosh reports on her attempt to raise her sons in a nonsexist environment and thereby overcome the cultural stereotypes that derive from these differences. Dorothy Sayers argues that any attempt to place human beings into two classes—women and men—is unjust. And Lucy Gilbert and Paula Webster state outright that gender roles are indeed created by powerful social forces, as is the notion that femininity is inferior to masculinity.

Perhaps any discussion of the differences between women and men is difficult because our very definitions of femininity and masculinity are changing radically. In the section "Masculinity in Transition," Alan Alda parodies the traditional "macho" male and, in doing so, implies that the emerging male role is quite different. Herb Goldberg argues that contrary to current popular opinion the male condition is not one of privilege—that men, too, are oppressed by society's expectations of their gender roles. In fact, writes Harold Rosenberg, the "masculine ideal" has almost vanished. Nevertheless, says Marc Fasteau, traditional notions of manliness hold powerful sway over most men, preventing them, for example, from forming close personal bonds with other men. Our conceptions of maleness and femaleness *are* changing, however, and, what is emerging, according to Noel Perrin, is a new kind of gender: androgynes, people who cannot be conveniently cubbyholed into neat categories of "male" or "female." Finally, Edmund White makes us closely examine our preconceived assumptions about gender when he defines "gay" and "straight" culture. All six of these essays provide perspectives not only on masculinity in transition, but on the changing idea of gender itself.

The third group of essayists in Part I, "Femininity and Sisterhood," probe the concept of "femininity" and the bonds that unite women in a common cause. Simone de Beauvoir suggests that what leads to women's oppression is that women are defined as "other"—that is, not as individuals equal to men but in contradistinction to men; men represent the norm, women the variance from the norm. Naomi Weisstein shows how the field of psychology has helped to "construct" what it means to be female. Susan Brownmiller, also interested in psychology, explores the kinds of emotions "appropriate" for each gender, and concludes that society looks negatively on so-called feminine expressions of emotion. Finally, Gloria Steinem describes the shared experiences and feelings that unite all women regardless of age, class, or race.

All the essays in Part I explore in one way or another the question of gender roles, but together they provide only a glimpse of the complexity of this central issue. In their struggles to understand gender, these authors present many views for us to consider.

# Chapter 1

## GENDER DIFFERENCES: SOCIOLOGY OR BIOLOGY?

### Male and Female: Differences Between Them

VIRGINIA ADAMS

*"Are women immutably different from men?" In the following essay, Virginia Adams poses and attempts to answer this question by surveying research in the natural and social sciences. She suggests that differences do indeed exist—some a result of social conditioning, but others fundamentally biological in origin and thus "immutable." Nevertheless, she concludes, "most women are capable of doing whatever they want."*

"The Book of Genesis had it wrong. In the beginning God created Eve," says Johns Hopkins Medical Psychologist John Money. What he means is that the basic tendency of the human fetus is to develop as a female. If the genes order the gonads to become testicles and put out the male hormone androgen, the embryo will turn into a boy; otherwise it becomes a girl: "You have to add something to get a male," Money notes. "Nature's first intention is to create a female."

Nature may prefer women, but virtually every culture has been partial to men. That contradiction raises an increasingly pertinent question (as well as the hackles of militant feminists): Are women immutably different from men? Women's Liberationists believe that any differences—other than anatomical—are a result of conditioning by society. The opposing view is that all of the differences are fixed in the genes. To scientists, however, the nature-nurture controversy is oversimplified. To them, what human beings are results from a complex interaction between both forces. Says Oxford Biologist Christopher Ounsted: "It is a false dichotomy to say that this difference is acquired and that one genetic. To try and differentiate is like asking a penny whether it is really a heads penny or a tails penny." As Berkeley Psychologist Frank Beach suggests, "Predispositions may be genetic; complex behavior patterns are probably not."

The idea that genetic predispositions exist is based on three kinds of evidence. First, there are the "cultural universals" cited by Margaret Mead. Almost everywhere, the mother is the principal caretaker of the child, and male dominance and aggression are the rule. Some anthropologists believe there has been an occasional female-dominated society; others insist that none have existed.

## Sex Typing

Then there is the fact that among most ground-dwelling primates, males are dominant and have as a major function the protection of females and offspring. Some research suggests that this is true even when the young are raised apart from adults, which seems to mean that they do not learn their roles from their society.

Finally, behavioral sex differences show up long before any baby could possibly perceive subtle differences between his parents or know which parent he is expected to imitate. "A useful strategy," says Harvard Psychologist Jerome Kagan, "is to assume that the earlier a particular difference appears, the more likely it is to be influenced by biological factors."

Physical differences appear even before birth. The heart of the female fetus often beats faster, and girls develop more rapidly. "Physiologically," says Sociologist Barbette Blackington, "women are better-made animals." Males do have more strength and endurance—though that hardly matters in a technological society.

Recent research hints that there may even be sex differences in the brain. According to some experimenters, the presence of the male hormone testosterone in the fetus may "masculinize" the brain, organizing the fetal nerve centers in characteristic ways. This possible "sex typing" of the central nervous system before birth may make men and women respond differently to incoming stimuli, Sociologist John Gagnon believes.

In fact, newborn girls do show different responses in some situations. They react more strongly to the removal of a blanket and more quickly to touch and pain. Moreover, experiments demonstrate that twelve-week-old girls gaze longer at photographs of faces than at geometric figures. Boys show no preference then, though eventually they pay more attention to figures. Kagan acknowledges the effect of environment, but he has found that it exerts a greater influence on girls than on boys. The female infants who experienced the most "face-to-face interaction" with their mothers were more attentive to faces than girls whose mothers did not exchange looks with them so much. Among boys, there was no consistent relationship.

## Internal Organs

As some psychologists see it, this very early female attention to the human face suggests that women may have a greater and even partly innate sensitivity to other human beings. Perhaps this explains why girls seem to get more satisfaction from relationships with people.

Even after infancy, the sexes show differential interests that do not seem to grow solely out of experience. Psychoanalyst Erik Erikson has found that boys and girls aged ten to twelve use space differently when asked to construct a scene with toys. Girls often build a low wall, sometimes with an elaborate doorway, surrounding a quiet interior scene. Boys are likely to construct towers, façades with cannons, and lively exterior scenes. Erikson acknowledges that cultural influences are at work, but he is convinced that they do not fully explain the nature of children's play. The differences, he says, "seem to parallel the morphology [shape and form] of genital differentiation itself: in a male, an external organ, erectible and intrusive; internal organs in the female, with vestibular access, leading to statically expectant ova."

In aptitude as well as in interest, sex differences become apparent early in life. Though girls are generally less adept than boys at mathematical and spatial reasoning, they learn to count sooner and to talk earlier and better. Some scientists think this female verbal superiority may be caused by sex-linked differences in the brain. Others believe it may exist because, as observation proves, mothers talk to infant girls more than to baby boys. But does the mother's talking cause the child to do likewise, or could it be the other way round? Psychologist Michael Lewis suggests the possibility that girls are talked to more because, for biological reasons, they respond more than boys to words and thus stimulate their mothers to keep talking.

Evidence that parental behavior does affect speech comes from tests made by Kagan among poor Guatemalan children. There, boys are more highly valued than girls, are talked to more and become more verbal. In the U.S., Psychiatrist David Levy has found that boys who are atypically good with words and inept with figures have been overprotected by their mothers. Psychologist Elizabeth Bing has observed that girls who excel at math and spatial problems have often been left to work alone by their mothers, while highly verbal girls have mothers who offer frequent suggestions, praise and criticism.

While girls outdo boys verbally, they often lag behind in solving analytical problems, those that require attention to detail. Girls seem to think "globally," responding to situations as a whole instead of abstracting single elements. In the "rod and frame test," for instance, a subject sits in a dark room before a luminous rod inside a slightly tilted frame, and is asked to move the rod to an upright position. Boys can separate the rod visually from the frame and make it stand straight; girls, misled by the tipped frame, usually adjust the rod not to the true vertical but to a position parallel with the sides of the frame.

In another experiment, children are asked to group related pictures. Boys again pay attention to details, perhaps putting together pictures that show people with an arm raised; girls make functional groups of, for example, a doctor, a nurse and a wheelchair.

In all such differences, environmental influence is suggested by the fact that children who think analytically most often prove to have mothers who have encouraged initiative and exploration, while youngsters who think globally have generally been tied to their mothers' apron strings. In Western society, of course, it is usually boys who are urged toward adventure. Herein, perhaps—there is no proof—lies an explanation for the apparent male capacity to think analytically.

In IQ tests, males and females score pretty much alike. Since this is true, why do women seem less creative? Many social scientists are convinced that the reasons are cultural. Women, they say, learn early in life that female accomplishment brings few rewards. In some cases, women cannot be creative because they are discriminated against. In other instances, a woman's creativity may well be blunted by fear of nonconformity, failure or even success itself. Unlike men, Kagan says, women are trained to have strong anxiety about being wrong.

To many psychoanalysts, however, the explanation lies in the fact that women possess the greatest creative power of all: bringing new life into being; thus they need not compensate by producing works of art. Men, it is theorized, are driven to make up for what seems to them a deficiency. That they feel keenly, though unconsciously, their inability to bear children is shown in dreams reported on the analyst's couch, in the behavior of small boys who play with dolls and walk around with their stomachs thrust forward in imitation of their pregnant mothers and in primitive rites and ancient myths. According to these myths, presumably conceived by males, Adam delivered Eve from his rib cage, Zeus gave birth to Athena out of his head, and when Semele was burned to death, Zeus seized Dionysus from her womb and sewed him up in his thigh until the infant had developed.

There are personality differences between the sexes too. Although no trait is confined to one sex—there are women who exceed the male average even in supposedly masculine characteristics—some distinctions turn up remarkably early. At New York University, for example, researchers have found that a female infant stops sucking a bottle and looks up when someone comes into the room; a male pays no attention to the visitor.

Another Kagan experiment shows that girls of twelve months who become frightened in a strange room drift toward their mothers, while boys look for something interesting to do. At four months, twice as many girls as boys cry when frightened in a strange laboratory. What is more, Kagan says, similar differences can be seen in monkeys and baboons, which "forces us to consider the possibility that some of the psychological differences between men and women may not be the product of experience alone but of subtle biological differences."

## Female Passivity

Many researchers have found greater dependence and docility in very young girls, greater autonomy and activity in boys. When a barrier is set up to separate youngsters from their mothers, boys try to knock it down; girls cry helplessly. There is little doubt that maternal encouragement—or discouragement—of such behavior plays a major role in determining adult personality. For example, a mother often stimulates male autonomy by throwing a toy far away from her young son, thus tacitly suggesting to him that he leave her to get it.

Animal studies suggest that there may be a biological factor in maternal behavior: mothers of rhesus monkeys punish their male babies earlier and more often than their female offspring; they also touch their female babies more often and act more protective toward them.

As for the controversial question of female "passivity," Psychoanalyst Helen Deutsch believes that the concept has been misunderstood. "There is no contradiction between being feminine and working. The ego can be active in both men and women," she says. It is only in love and in sex that passivity is particularly appropriate for women. As she sees it, passivity is no more than a kind of openness and warmth; it does not mean "inactivity, emptiness or immobility."

Another controversy rages over the effect of hormones. Militant women, who discount hormonal influence, disagree violently with scientific researchers, who almost unanimously agree that hormones help determine how people feel and act. So far, there have been few studies of male hormones, but scientists think they may eventually discover hormonal cycles in men that produce cyclic changes in mood and behavior. As for females, studies have indicated that 49% of female medical and surgical hospital admissions, most psychiatric hospital admissions and 62% of violent crimes among women prisoners occur on premenstrual and menstrual days. At Worcester State Hospital in Massachusetts, Psychologists Donald and Inge Broverman have found that estrogen sharpens sensory perception. They believe that this heightened sensitivity may lead more women than men to shy away from situations of stress.

## Fierce Bulls

One trait thought to be affected by hormones is aggressiveness. In all cultures, investigators report, male infants tend to play more aggressively than females. While scientists think a genetic factor may be involved, they also observe that society fosters the difference by permitting male aggression and encouraging female adaptability. Some suggest that females may be as aggressive as men—but with words instead of deeds.

The definitive research on hormones and aggression is still to be done. However, it has been established that the female hormone estrogen inhibits aggression in both animal and human males. It has also been proved that the male hormone androgen influences aggression in animals. For example, castration produces tractable steers rather than fierce bulls.

The influence of androgen begins even before birth. Administered to pregnant primates, the hormone makes newborn females play more aggressively than ordinary females. Moreover, such masculinized animals are usually aggressive as long as they live, even if they are never again exposed to androgen.

According to some experts, this long-lasting effect of hormones administered or secreted before birth may help explain why boys are more aggressive than girls even during their early years when both sexes appear to produce equal amounts of male and female hormones. Other observers have suggested that the spurt in male-hormone production at puberty could be one of the causes of delinquency in adolescent boys, but there is no proof that this is so.

Will there some day be a "unisex" society with no differences between men and women, except anatomical ones? It seems unlikely. Anatomy, parturition and gender, observes Psychologist Joseph Adelson, cannot be wished away "in a spasm of the distended will, as though the will, in pursuit of total human possibility, can amplify itself to overcome the given." Or, as Psychoanalyst Therese Benedek sees it, "biology precedes personality."

"Nature has been the oppressor," observes Michael Lewis. Women's role as caretaker "was the evolutionary result of their biological role in birth and feeding." The baby bottle has freed women from some of the tasks of that role, but, says University of Michigan Psychologist Judith Bardwick, "the major responsibility for child rearing is the woman's, even in the Soviet Union, the Israeli kibbutz, Scandinavia and mainland China." Furthermore, though mothering skills are mostly learned, it is a fact that if animals are raised in isolation and then put in a room with the young of the species, it is the females who go to the infants and take care of them.

"Perhaps the known biological differences can be totally overcome, and society can approach a state in which a person's sex is of no consequence for any significant activity except childbearing," admits Jerome Kagan. "But we must ask if such a society will be satisfying to its members." As he sees it, "complementarity" is what makes relationships stable and pleasurable.

Psychoanalyst Martin Symonds agrees. "The basic reason why unisex must fail is that in the sexual act itself, the man has to be assertive, if tenderly, and the woman has to be receptive. What gives trouble is when men see assertiveness as aggression and women see receptiveness as submission." Unisex, he sums up, would be "a disaster," because children need roles to identify with and rebel against. "You can't identify with a blur. A unisex world would be a frictionless environment in which nobody would be able to grow up."

The crucial point is that a difference is not a deficiency. As Biologist Ounsted puts it, "We are all human beings and in this sense equal. We are not, however, the same." In the opinion of

John Money, "You can play fair only if you recognize and respect authentic differences."

Though scientists disagree about the precise nature and causes of these differences, there is no argument about two points: society plays a tremendous part in shaping the differences, and most women are capable of doing whatever they want. Only in the top ranges of ability, says Kagan, are innate differences significant; for typical men and women, "the biological differences are totally irrelevant." Psychiatrist Donald Lunde agrees. "There is no evidence," he asserts, "that men are any more or less qualified by biological sex differences alone to perform the tasks generally reserved for them in today's societies."

---

## REFLECTING ON MEANING

1. Adams surveys numerous research studies that examine differences between men and women. What have these studies concluded? What specific differences have they identified? Do these studies attribute differences to biology, psychology, or sociology? What differences have they *not* been able to verify?
2. Adams cites several scientists about the likelihood of a "unisex" society in the future. How does Adams define this society? Do the scientists think that such a society will come about? Why or why not? How do they feel about such a society? How do their feelings about the differences between men and women influence their feelings about a unisex society? Do you agree with Kagan and Symonds on the value of gender differences? Why or why not?
3. What "answer" to the question of difference can you derive from the information Adams provides? Are gender differences innate? Are they a result of socialization? What does her concluding paragraph suggest about differences and their origins? Do you agree that "most women are capable of doing whatever they want"?

## EXPLORING RHETORICAL STRATEGIES

1. Adams's essay appeared in *Time* magazine in 1972 as part of a special issue dedicated to women's issues and the achievements of the women's movement. Is it possible that *Time*'s editorial

policies influenced Adams as she planned and composed her essay? In what ways? What concerns might her audience—*Time*'s readership—have presented for her?

2. Adams's second paragraph places her essay in the context of the debate over gender differences. What three voices in the debate does she distinguish? Which voice does she encourage her audience to identify with? How does she accomplish this goal? Is this rhetorical tactic a fair one? Why doesn't she identify with the other voices?

3. Adams twice uses the adjective *militant* to describe women with feminist viewpoints, and she claims that these militants "disagree violently with scientific researchers." Why does she characterize feminists in this way? Is her characterization valid? Are men who "disagree violently" considered militant, or have the women she is describing violated a social model of behavior? Which model? What does Adams's word choice tell you about her concerns as a writer and as a woman?

# The Brain: His and Hers

## PAMELA WEINTRAUB

*Pamela Weintraub surveys research on the brain in order to offer a firm answer to the question of difference: "Yes," she states, "male and female brains do differ." Drawing on diverse scientific disciplines to support her assertion, Weintraub suggests that physical differences in the brain may account for differences in women's and men's thinking and behavior. She concludes that scientific research to establish biological explanations for difference will not undermine women's efforts to achieve social equality; rather, it can prove beneficial for men and women alike.*

Are the brains of men and women different? If so, do men and women differ in abilities, talents, and deficiencies? A scientific answer to these questions could affect society and culture, and variously shock, intrigue, delight, depress, and reassure people of both sexes. Now an answer is coming into sight: Yes, male and female brains do differ.

That men and women think and behave differently is a widely held assumption. Generations of writers have lavished their attention on these differences, proclaiming, for example, that aggressiveness and promiscuity are natural to the male, that domesticity is the legacy of the female. Today's feminists acknowledge some differences, but hotly dispute the notion that they are innate. They stress that it is society, not nature, that gives men the drive to dominate and keeps women from achieving careers and power. But proof that behavioral and intellectual differences between the sexes are partly rooted in the structure of the brain, that women are inherently superior in some areas of endeavor and men in others would in no way undermine legitimate demands for social equality. Instead the result could be a better, more realistic relationship between the sexes.

The evidence suggesting differences between male and female brains comes from research in behavior, biochemistry, anatomy, and neuropsychology. The most recent study deals with the long-established fact that skill in mathematics is far more common among men than women. Feminists—and many scientists—blame sexual stereotyping. But psychologists Camilla Benbow and Julian Stanley, at Johns Hopkins University, challenged that interpretation after testing 9,927 seventh and eighth graders with high IQs. As Benbow told *Discover* reporter John Bucher, of the students who scored 500 or better on the math part of the Scholastic Aptitude Test, boys outnumbered girls by more than two to one. In other words, the psychologists argue, male superiority in math is so pronounced that, to some extent, it must be inborn.

This finding follows several recent studies proving that male and female brains, at least in animals, are physically different. From the hypothalamus, the center for sexual drive, to the cerebral cortex, the seat of thought, scientists have found consistent variations between the sexes. The causes of these differences, they say, are the sex hormones—the male androgens and female estrogens and progesterones that are secreted by the sex glands and carried through the blood stream to distant parts of the body, where they control everything from menstruation to the growth of facial hair.

Basic to all the studies of gender and the brain are the facts of sex determination. When a child is conceived, each parent contributes a sex chromosome, either an X or a Y (so-called for their shapes). When two X's combine, the fetus develops ovaries and becomes a girl. An X and a Y produce a boy; the Y chromosome makes a protein that coats the cells programmed to become ovaries, directing them to become testicles instead. The testicles then pump out two androgens, one that absorbs what would have become a uterus, and another, testosterone, that causes a penis to develop.

Though scientists have not yet been able to pinpoint any physiological differences between the brains of men and women, they think that the development of the brain parallels that of the genitals. If the fetus is a boy, they say, the testosterone that produces the penis also masculinizes tissue in the hypothalamus and other nearby structures deep within the brain. New data suggest that if the fetus is a girl, estrogen secreted by the ovaries feminizes brain tissue in the surrounding cerebral cortex. Scientists cannot dissect living human brains, but they have found ingenious ways to test their theories. The major approaches:

## Human Behavior

To shed light on the sexuality of the brain, endocrinologist Julianne Imperato-McGinley of Cornell Medical College in New York City studied 38 men in an isolated part of the Dominican Republic who, because of a genetic disorder, started life as girls. They stayed indoors playing with dolls and learning to cook while boys fought and shouted outside. At the age of eleven, when the breasts of normal girls began to enlarge, the children studied by Imperato-McGinley showed no change. But at twelve, most of them began to feel stirrings of sexual desire for girls. At puberty, their voices deepened, their testicles descended, and their clitorises enlarged to become penises.

These children came from a group of families carrying a rare mutant gene that deprived them of an enzyme needed to make testosterone work in the skin of their genitals. For this reason, their external genitals looked female at birth. But at puberty their bodies were able to use testosterone without the enzyme, and it became obvious that they were males—as chromosome tests confirmed. All but two are now living with women. They have male musculature and, although they cannot sire children, they can have sexual intercourse. They have assumed masculine roles in their society. "To the world," says Imperato-McGinley, "they looked like girls when they were younger. But their bodies were actually flooded with testosterone." She concludes that they were able to adjust easily because hidden in the girl's body was a male brain, virilized by testosterone before birth and activated by another rush of testosterone during adolescence.

Although Imperato-McGinley suggests that brain structure determines behavior, another scientist thinks that the reverse may also be true: Anne Petersen, director of the Adolescent Laboratory at the Michael Reese Hospital and Medical Center in Chicago, says that cultural experiences can masculinize or feminize the brain. In a recent study, Petersen found that boys who excel in athletics also excel in spatial reasoning—a skill controlled by the right hemisphere of the cerebral cortex, and defined as the ability to understand maps and mazes or objects rotating in space. Says Petersen, "An athlete must be constantly aware of his own body and a whole constellation of other bodies in space." A daily game of basketball might, through some still mysterious mechanism, stimulate the secretion of hormones that prime a player's brain for success in basketball. The same brain structures would be used to deal with spatial problems. "Women are far less athletic than men," says Petersen, "and also less adept at spatial reasoning. Part of the problem may be their lack of involvement in sports. Perhaps some women just never develop the area of the brain specialized for spatial control."

Like Petersen, endocrinologist Anke Ehrhardt thinks that society plays an important part in shaping gender behavior. Nevertheless, she says, "certain types of sexual behavior are influenced by the sex hormones." Leafing through the clutter of papers and books that cover her desk at New York City's Columbia Presbyterian Medical Center, Ehrhardt cites cases of girls whose adrenal glands, because of an enzyme defect, produced abnormally large amounts of androgens while they were still in the womb. "We find that they are extremely tomboyish," she says. "They are career oriented, and spend little time with dolls. And we've just learned that boys exposed before birth to drugs that contain high doses of feminizing hormones engage in less roughhousing than other boys."

## Animal Behavior

Ehrhardt admits that labeling the pursuit of a career masculine and playing with dolls feminine seems like stereotyping. To substantiate her evidence, she has compared her results with those obtained from studies of animals, whose gender behavior is rigid and easily defined.

Animal physiologists first made the connection between hormones and behavior in 1849, when the German scientist Arnold

Berthold castrated roosters and found that they stopped fighting with other roosters and lost interest in attracting hens. When he transplanted the testicles into the abdominal cavities of the castrated birds, the roosters became aggressive again. Observing that the transplanted testicles did not develop connections with the rooster's nervous system but did develop connections with its circulatory system, he speculated that their influence on behavior came from a blood-borne substance, which was later identified as a hormone.

In 1916, Frank Lillie, a Canadian physiologist, noticed that the freemartin, a genetically female (X-X) cow that looks and acts like a male, always had a male twin. He speculated that the freemartin's gonads were masculinized in the womb by hormones secreted by the testicles of the twin.

Fascinated by this finding, scientists began using testosterone to make "freemartin" guinea pigs, rats, monkeys, and dogs. This set the stage for the landmark experiment conducted at the University of Kansas in 1959 by physiologists William Young and Robert Goy.

"We injected pregnant guinea pigs with huge amounts of testosterone," explains Goy. "This produced a brood of offspring in which those that were genetically female had male genitalia as well as ovaries." When the females were 90 days old, the researchers removed their ovaries and injected some of them with still more testosterone. The injected females began to act like males, mounting other females and trying to dominate the group. Says Goy, "We realized that we had changed the sex of the guinea pig's brain."

The researchers concluded that hormones affect behavior in two ways. Before birth, hormones imprint a code on the brain, "just as light can stamp an image on film," Goy says. "Later, throughout life, other hormones activate the code, much as a developer brings out an image on film. Whether the animal behaves like a male or a female depends on the code."

Goy has spent the past two decades proving that theory for a whole range of species, including the rhesus monkey. Now at the Primate Research Center at the University of Wisconsin in Madison, he has found that masculinized monkeys display sexual behavior that ranges from female to male in direct proportion to the amount of testosterone they are given while in the womb and throughout life. "It doesn't much matter whether it's rough-and-tumble play, mounting peers, or attempting to dominate the group," he says. "It's all related to the duration of treatment."

Perhaps more important, Goy has found that by varying the

treatment he can produce monkeys that are physically female but behave like males. This is proof, he says, "that these animals behave like boys because of masculinizing hormones, not because of a male appearance that causes the other animals to treat them like boys."

Like the human brain, the brain of the rhesus monkey has a highly elaborate and convoluted cortex. But Goy believes that monkeys can be compared with people only up to a point. For while primitive drives may be similar, he says, human beings are guided by their culture to a greater degree than monkeys. "Nevertheless," he adds, "there are instances when people seem to be less bound by culture. Then they begin to look very much like our monkeys."

## Biochemistry

Other scientists have substantiated this evidence with hard biochemical data. To learn where sex hormones operate, neurobiologist Donald Pfaff of New York City's Rockefeller University injected various animals with radioactive hormones and removed their brains. He cut each brain into paper-thin sections, then placed each section on film sensitive to radioactivity. He thus made maps showing that the hormones collected at specific places, now called receptor sites, are similarly located in the brains of species ranging from fish to rats to the rhesus monkey.

The primary site for hormone action, Pfaff saw, was the hypothalamus, a primitive structure at the base of the brain stem. That made sense, because the hypothalamus is the center for sex drive and copulatory behavior. "But the most intriguing thing," says Pfaff, "may be the receptors found in the amygdala [a part of the brain above each ear]. During the 1960s, surgeons found that when they destroyed the amygdala, patients with fits of aggression became completely passive. So we now suspect that sex hormones may control aggression, even fear." Neurologist Bruce McEwen, also of Rockefeller, recently found estrogen receptors in the cerebral cortex of the rat—receptors that disappear three weeks after birth. The cortex controls thought and cognition, but McEwen does not know the significance of these receptors.

The receptors are located at the same sites in both sexes, but because each sex has its own characteristic mix of hormones, male and female brains function differently. To unravel the secret of hormone operation, McEwen has been analyzing the chemistry of the rat brain. He has discovered that receptor sites are hormone-specific; a testosterone site, for example, is insensitive to estrogen. Perhaps more important, he has learned that once hormones pair up with receptors, they mold the structure of the brain by directing nerve cells to manufacture proteins. Early in life, the proteins build nerve cells, creating permanent structures that may exist in the brain of one sex but not the other. Later in life, the proteins produce the chemicals that enable one nerve cell to communicate with another, and precipitate various kinds of sexual behavior.

McEwen and Pfaff have not dissected human brains, but they feel justified in applying some of their findings to people. For, as Pfaff explains, evolution is a conservationist. "As new species evolved, nature didn't throw away old parts of the brain," he says. "Rather, new systems were added. Everyone has a fish brain deep inside. Outside the fish brain there is a reptilian brain, depressingly similar to the way it would look in a lizard. Wrapped around the reptilian brain there is a mammalian brain, and then, finally, the cerebral cortex in such animals as monkeys and human beings." McEwen thinks that the receptors in the hypothalamus probably have similar effects in people and rats. "The difference," he says, "is that human beings can override their primitive drives with nerve impulses from the powerful cerebral cortex."

## Anatomy

Anatomical evidence that sex hormones change the structure of the brain came recently from Roger Gorski, a neuroendocrinologist at the University of California at Los Angeles. Examining the hypothalamus in rats, he found a large cluster of nerve cells in the males and a small cluster in females. By giving a female testosterone shortly after birth, he created a large cluster of cells in her hypothalamus that resembled that in the male. If he castrated a male after birth, its cell cluster shrank. Gorski has no idea what the cell structure signifies, but he does know that it varies with changes in sexual behavior.

The anatomical differences do not stop there. Fernando Nottebohm, of Rockefeller, has discovered a large brain-cell cluster in the male canary and a small one in the female. These cells are not in the spinal cord or the hypothalamus but in the forebrain—the songbird equivalent of the cerebral cortex, the part that controls thought and cognition.

The function that Nottebohm studied was song. Only the male songbird can sing, and the more intricate the song the more females he attracts. That takes brainwork, says Nottebohm. "The canary puts songs together just as the artist creates. A large collection of syllables can be combined in infinite ways to form a repertoire in which each song is unique."

Until Nottebohm discovered the large cluster of male brain

cells that control the muscles of the syrinx, the singing organ, he had assumed that male and female brains were anatomically identical. He found that if he gave female canaries testosterone before they hatched and again during adulthood, they could learn to sing. When he studied the brains of the singing females, he found that their cell clusters had grown. Says Nottebohm, "The intriguing thing is that the size of the repertoire was more or less proportional to the size of the cell clusters."

Scientists studying mammals have also discovered anatomical differences between the sexes in the thinking part of the brain—in this case, the cerebral cortex of the rat. Marian Diamond, of the University of California at Berkeley, discovered that in the male rat the right hemisphere of the cortex was thicker than the left—and that in the female the left was thicker than the right. But if she castrated the male rat at birth or removed the ovaries from the female, she could alter the pattern. Administering female hormones to males and male hormones to females also affected the width of the cortex. Says Diamond, "Hormones present during pregnancy, hormones present in the birth-control pill, all affect the dimensions of the cortex."

Jerre Levy, a neuropsychologist at the University of Chicago, is encouraged by Diamond's findings because they provide strong anatomical evidence for her theory: the cortex is different in men and women, largely because of hormones that early in life alter the organization of the two hemispheres.

Levy is responsible for much of what is known about the human brain's laterality—the separation of the roles performed by the right and left hemispheres. Levy began her work in this field in the 1960s, when she was studying "split brain" patients, epileptics whose hemispheres had been surgically separated as a means of controlling violent seizures. The researchers found that the hemispheres could operate independently of each other, somewhat like two minds in a single head. The right hemisphere specialized in the perception of spatial relationships, like those in mazes and solid geometry, and the left controlled language and rote memory.

Levy has found that these abilities vary with gender. In test after test, men excelled in spatial reasoning and women did better with language. Fascinated by the discrepancy, she decided to test laterality in normal people and based her experiments on a well known fact: light and sound perceived by the eye and ear on one side of the head travel to the hemisphere on the other side for processing.

She discovered that the right ear and eye are more sensitive in women, the left in men. She concluded that the right hemisphere dominates the masculine brain, and the left the feminine.

Levy points to the work of neuropsychologist Deborah Waber, of Harvard Medical School, who found that children reaching puberty earlier than normal have brains that are less lateralized—that is, their left and right hemispheres seem to share more tasks. Because girls generally reach puberty two years before boys, these findings have caused speculation that the bundle of nerve connections, the corpus callosum, between the two hemispheres of the female brain have less time to lateralize, or draw apart, during puberty. If that is true, says Levy, it could help to explain female intuition, as well as male superiority in mechanics and math. The two intimately connected hemispheres of the female brain would communicate more rapidly—an advantage in integrating all the detail and nuance in an intricate situation, but according to Levy a disadvantage "when it comes to homing in on just a few relevant details." With less interference from the left hemisphere, Levy says, a man could "use his right hemisphere more precisely in deciphering a map or finding a three-dimensional object in a two-dimensional representation."

All this brings Levy back to hormones. She thinks that the estrogen that changes the size of the cortex in Marian Diamond's rats may also change the size and organization of the human cortex. Her new tests are designed to study the organization of the cerebral cortex in people with hormonal abnormalities—girls who produce an excess of androgen and boys who are exposed to large amounts of estrogen before birth.

Levy has ambitious plans for future research, including scans of living brains and tests of babies whose mothers have undergone stress during pregnancy. Much remains to be done, for though the existence of physical differences between male and female brains now seems beyond dispute, the consequences are unclear. Talent in math, for example, is obviously not confined to men, nor talent in languages to women; the subtleties seem infinite. Already the new findings promise to color the modern view of the world. But the implications can easily be misconstrued.

Gunther Dörner, an East German hormone researcher, has claimed that he can put an end to male homosexuality by injecting pregnant women with testosterone. Dörner bases his theory on studies done by two American researchers, who subjected pregnant rats to stress by confining them in small cages under bright lights. They found that the rats' male offspring had low levels of testosterone during certain critical periods, and exhibited homosexual behavior. Dörner concluded that stress on pregnant females alters sexual preference patterns in the brains of their male offspring, and that this finding applies to human beings as well. His suggested antidote: testosterone.

His conclusions appall the American researchers, who agree that mothers under stress produce male offspring with abnormal behavior, but argue that Dörner has gone too far. Dörner's work is supported by the East German government, which is notorious in its aversion to homosexuality, and American scientists fear that he may get a chance to put his ideas into practice on human beings.

Another example of misinterpretation is the article that appeared in *Commentary* magazine in December [1980], citing the "latest" in brain research as an argument against equal rights for women. This angers Anne Petersen. "A lot of people have been making a lot of political hoopla about our work," she says. "They've used it to say that the women's movement will fail, that women are inherently unequal. Our research shows nothing of this sort, of course. There are things that men do better, and things that women do better. It's very important to differentiate between the inferences and the scientific findings."

These findings could influence fields ranging from philosophy, psychiatry, and the arts to education, law, and medicine. If women are indeed at a disadvantage in mastering math, there could be different methods of teaching, or acceptance of the fact that math is not important for certain jobs. For example, tests of mathematical competence have been used as criteria for admission to law school, where math is barely used; tests of spatial ability have been used to screen people for all types of nontechnical pursuits. If scientists can prove that such tests discriminate unnecessarily against women, hiring policies could be changed. Eventually, psychiatrists and lawyers may have to assess their male and female clients in a new light. And brain surgeons may have to consider the sex of a patient before operating. For if the two hemispheres of the brain are more intimately connected in women than in men, then women may be able to control a function like speech with either hemisphere. Surgeons could feel confident that a woman would recover the ability to talk, even if her normal speech center were destroyed; they might proceed with an operation that they would hesitate to perform on a man.

Investigators have made amazing progress in their work on the sexes and the brain, but they have really just begun. They will have to link hundreds of findings from widely diverse areas of brain science before they can provide a complete explanation for the shared, but different, humanity of men and women.

## REFLECTING ON MEANING

1. Weintraub summarizes studies from a number of disciplines to support her assertion that male and female brains differ. Does this research establish proof that human brains are masculinized or feminized? What empirical evidence exists for this hypothesis? Can the various theories Weintraub summarizes be considered scientific evidence? Which of these theories are based on proven data? Which seem most reasonable to you? Why?
2. Anne Petersen's research reverses the cause-effect pattern of the majority of the studies Weintraub summarizes. Whereas these studies hypothesize that the brain produces gender-specific behaviors, Petersen conversely suggests that "cultural experiences can masculinize or feminize the brain." What evidence does she offer to support this interpretation of her data? Do you find her claim convincing? Why or why not?
3. Jerre Levy's research focuses on the human brain's "laterality." What is this physical phenomenon? What does it suggest about men's and women's reasoning processes? To what might Petersen attribute the differences that Levy observes in the brains of men and women? What else might cause these differences?

## EXPLORING RHETORICAL STRATEGIES

1. Weintraub's introduction reveals that she is concerned with the way her audience will respond to her essay. In fact, she seems to be addressing at least two different audiences with possibly conflicting interests. Who are these audiences? What evidence can you find of their interests?
2. What in Weintraub's introduction tells you that she is aware that her topic is controversial and that her discussion may further fuel the controversy? Which public group does she clearly wish to disassociate herself from? Why does she want to do this? How does she accomplish her goal?
3. Why does Weintraub make extensive use of animal studies in an essay about humans? Do these studies advance her viewpoint in a constructive way? Is it reasonable to use these studies to theorize about the biological origins of gender-specific thinking patterns and behaviors in humans?

# Masculine/Feminine

## PRUDENCE MACKINTOSH

*As a mother, Prudence Mackintosh planned to raise her sons in a nonsexist way: free of cultural stereotypes about the behavior and aspirations of males and females. Despite her well-intentioned efforts, however, the plan did not succeed. In this essay, she describes her experiences as an "enlightened" mother, and she accounts for her failure to achieve her goal.*

I had every intention to raise liberated, nonviolent sons whose aggressive tendencies would be mollified by a sensitivity and compassion that psychologists claim were denied their father's generation.

I did not buy guns or war toys (although Grandmother did). My boys even had a secondhand baby doll until the garage sale last summer. I did buy Marlo Thomas' *Free to Be You and Me* record, a collection of nonsexist songs, stories, and poems, and I told them time and time again that it was okay to cry and be scared sometimes. I overruled their father and insisted that first grade was much too early for organized competitive soccer leagues. They know that moms *and dads* do dishes and diapers. And although they use it primarily for the convenient bathroom between the alley and the sandpile, my boys know that the storeroom is now mother's office. In such an environment, surely they would grow up free of sex-role stereotypes. At the very least wouldn't they pick up their own socks?

My friends with daughters were even more zealous. They named their daughters strong, cool unisex names like Blakeney, Brett, Brook, Lindsay, and Blair, names that lent themselves to corporate letterheads, not Tupperware party invitations. These moms looked on Barbie with disdain and bought trucks and science kits. They shunned frilly dresses for overalls. They subscribed to Feminist Press and read stories called "My Mother the Mail Carrier" instead of "Sleeping Beauty." At the swimming pool one afternoon, I watched a particularly fervent young mother, ironically clad in a string bikini, encourage her daughter. "You're so strong, Blake! Kick hard, so you'll be the strongest kid in this pool." When my boys splashed water in Blakeney's eyes and she ran whimpering to her mother, this mom exhorted, "You go back in that pool and shake your fist like this and say, 'You do that again and I'll bust your lights out.' " A new generation of little girls, assertive and ambitious, taking a backseat to no one?

It's a little early to assess the results of our efforts, but when my seven-year-old son, Jack, comes home singing—to the tune of *"Frère Jacques"*—"Farrah Fawcett, Farrah Fawcett, I love you" and five minutes later asks Drew, his five-year-old brother, if he'd like his nose to be a blood fountain, either we're backsliding or there's more to this sex-role learning than the home environment can handle.

I'm hearing similar laments from mothers of daughters. "She used to tell everyone that she was going to grow up to be a lawyer just like Daddy," said one, "but she's hedging on that ambition ever since she learned that no one wears a blue fairy tutu in the courtroom." Another mother with two sons, a daughter, and a very successful career notes that, with no special encouragement, only her daughter keeps her room neat and loves to set the table and ceremoniously seat her parents. At a Little League game during the summer, fearful that this same young daughter might be absorbing the stereotype "boys play while girls watch," her parents readily assured her that she too could participate when she was eight years old. "Oh," she exclaimed with obvious delight, "I didn't know they had cheerleaders."

How does it happen? I have my own theories, but decided to do a little reading to see if any of the "experts" agreed with me. I was also curious to find out what remedies they recommended. The books I read propose that sex roles are culturally induced. In simplistic terms, rid the schools, their friends, and the television of sexism, and your daughters will dump their dolls and head straight for the boardroom while your sons contemplate nursing careers. *Undoing Sex Stereotypes* by Marcia Guttentag and Helen Bray is an interesting study of efforts to overcome sexism in the classroom. After reading it, I visited my son's very traditional school and found it guilty of unabashedly perpetrating the myths that feminists abhor. Remember separate water fountains? And how, even if the line was shorter, no boy would be caught dead drinking from the girls' fountain and vice versa? That still happens. "You wouldn't want me to get cooties, would you, Mom?" my son says, defending the practice. What did I expect in a school where the principal still addresses his faculty, who range in age from 23 to 75, as "girls"?

Nevertheless, having been a schoolteacher myself, I am skeptical of neatly programmed nonsexist curriculum packets like Guttentag and Bray's. But if you can wade through the jargon ("people of the opposite sex, hereafter referred to as POTOS"), some of the observations and exercises are certainly thought-provoking and revealing. In one exercise fifth-grade students were asked to list adjectives appropriate to describe women. The struggle some of the children had in shifting their attitudes about traditional male roles is illustrated in this paragraph written by a fifth-grade girl who was asked to write a story about a man using the adjectives she had listed to describe women:

> Once there was a boy who all his life was very *gentle.* He never hit anyone or started a fight and when some of his friends were not feeling well, he was *loving* and *kind* to them. When he got older he never changed. People started not liking him because he was *weak, petite,* and he wasn't like any of the other men—not strong or tough. Most of his life he sat alone thinking about why no one liked him. Then one day he went out and tried to act like the other men. He joined a baseball team, but he was no good, he always got out. Then he decided to join the hockey team. He couldn't play good. He kept on breaking all the rules. So he quit the team and joined the soccer team. These men were *understanding* to him. He was really good at soccer, and was the best on the team. That year they won the championship and the rest of his life he was happy.

After reading this paragraph it occurred to me that this little girl's self-esteem and subsequent role in life would be enhanced by a teacher who spent less time on "nonsexist intervention projects" and more time on writing skills. But that, of course, is not what the study was meant to reveal.

The junior high curriculum suggested by *Undoing Sex Stereotypes* has some laudable consciousness-raising goals. For example, in teaching units called "Women's Roles in American History" and "The Socialization of Women and the Image of Women in the Media" teenagers are encouraged to critically examine television commercials, soap operas, and comic books. But am I a traitor to the cause if I object when the authors in another unit use *Romeo and Juliet* as a study of the status of women? Something is rotten in Verona when we have to consider Juliet's career possibilities and her problems with self-actualization. The conclusions of this project were lost on me; I quit reading when the author began to talk about ninth-graders who were "cognitively at a formal operational level." I don't even know what my "external sociopsychological situation" is. However, I think I did understand some of the conclusions reached by the kids:

"Girls are smart."

"If a woman ran a forklift where my father works, there would be a walkout."

"Men cannot be pom-pom girls."

Eminently more readable, considering that both authors are educators of educators, is *How to Raise Independent and Professionally Successful Daughters,* by Drs. Rita and Kenneth Dunn. The underlying and, I think, questionable assumption in this book is that little boys have been reared correctly all along. Without direct parental intervention, according to the Dunns, daughters tend to absorb and reflect society's values. The Dunns paint a dark picture indeed for the parents who fail to channel their daughters toward professional success. The woman who remains at home with children while her husband is involved in the "real world" with an "absorbing and demanding day-to-day commitment that brings him into contact with new ideas, jobs, and people (attractive self-actualized females)" is sure to experience lowered IQ, according to the Dunns. They go on to predict the husband's inevitable affair and the subsequent divorce, which leaves the wife emotionally depressed and probably financially dependent on her parents.

Now I'm all for women developing competency and self-reliance, but the Dunns' glorification of the professional is excessive. Anyone who has worked longer than a year knows that eventually any job loses most of its glamour. And the world is no less "real" at home. For that matter, mothers at home may be more "real" than bankers or lawyers. How is a corporate tax problem more real than my counseling with the maid whose boyfriend shot her in the leg? How can reading a balance sheet compare with comforting a five-year-old who holds his limp cat and wants to know why we have to lose the things we love? And on the contrary, it is my husband, the professional, who complains of lowered IQ. Though we wooed to Faulkner, my former ace English major turned trial lawyer now has time for only an occasional *Falconer* or Peter Benchley thriller. Certainly there is value in raising daughters to be financially self-supporting, but there is not much wisdom in teaching a daughter that she must achieve professional success or her marriage probably won't last.

In a chapter called "What to Do from Birth to Two," the authors instruct parents to introduce dolls only if they represent adult figures or groups of figures. "Try not to give her her own 'baby.' A baby doll is acceptable only for dramatizing the familiar episodes she has actually experienced, like a visit to the doctor." If some unthinking person should give your daughter a baby doll, and she likes it, the Dunns recommend that you permit her to keep it without exhibiting any negative feelings, "but do not lapse into cuddling it or encouraging her to do so. Treat it as any other object and direct attention to other more beneficial toys." I wonder if the Dunns read an article by Anne Roiphe called "Can You Have Everything and Still Want Babies?" which appeared in *Vogue* a couple of years ago. Ms. Roiphe was deploring the extremes to which our liberation has brought us. "It is nice to have beautiful feet, it may be desirable to have small feet, but it is painful and abusive to bind feet. It is also a good thing for women to have independence, freedom and choice, movement, and opportunity; but I'm not so sure that the current push against mothering will not be another kind of binding of the soul. . . . As women we have thought so little of ourselves that when the troops came to liberate us we rushed into the streets leaving our most valuable attributes behind as if they belonged to the enemy."

The Dunns' book is thorough, taking parents step-by-step through the elementary years and on to high school. Had I been raising daughters, however, I think I would have flunked out in the chapter "What to Do from Age Two to Five." In discussing development of vocabulary, the Doctors Dunn prohibit the use of nonsensical words for bodily functions. I'm sorry, Doctors, but I've experimented with this precise terminology and discovered that the child who yells "I have to defecate, Mom" across four grocery aisles is likely to be left in the store. A family without a few poo-poo jokes is no family at all.

These educators don't help me much in my efforts to liberate my sons. And although I think little girls are getting a better deal with better athletic training and broader options, I believe we're kidding ourselves if we think we can raise our sons and daughters alike. Certain inborn traits seem to be immune to parental and cultural tampering. How can I explain why a little girl baby sits on a quilt in the park thoughtfully examining a blade of grass, while my baby William uproots grass by handfuls and eats it? Why does a mother of very bright and active daughters confide that until she went camping with another family of boys, she feared that my sons had a hyperactivity problem? I'm sure there are plenty of rowdy, noisy little girls, but I'm not just talking about rowdiness and noise. I'm talking about some sort of primal physicalness that causes the walls of my house to pulsate on rainy days. I'm talking about something inexplicable that makes my sons fall into a mad, scrambling, pull-your-ears-off-kick-your-teeth-in heap just before bedtime, when they're not even mad at each other. I mean something that causes them to climb the doorjamb with honey and peanut butter on their hands while giving me a synopsis of *Star Wars* that contains only five intelligible words: "And then this guy, he 'pssshhhhhhh.' And then this thing went 'vronggggggg.' But this little guy said, 'Nong-neee-nonh-nee.' " When Jack and Drew are not kicking a soccer ball or each other, they are kicking the chair legs, the cat, the baby's silver rattle, and, inadvertently, Baby William himself, whom they have affectionately dubbed "Tough Eddy." Staying put in a chair for the duration of a one-course meal is torturous for these boys. They compensate by never quite putting both feet under the table. They sit with one leg doubled under them while the other leg extends to one side. The upper half of the body appears committed to the task at hand—eating—but the lower extremities are poised to lunge should a more compelling distraction present itself. From this position, I have observed, one brother can trip a haughty dessert-eating sibling who is flaunting the fact he ate all his "sweaty little peas." Although we have civilized them to the point that they dutifully mumble, "May I be excused, please?" their abrupt departure from the table invariably overturns at least one chair or whatever milk remains. This sort of constant motion just doesn't lend itself to lessons in thoughtfulness and gentleness.

Despite my encouragement, my sons refuse to invite little girls to play anymore. Occasionally friends leave their small daughters with us while they run errands. I am always curious to see what these females will find of interest in my sons' roomful of Tonka trucks and soccer balls. One morning the boys suggested that the girls join them in playing Emergency with the big red fire trucks and ambulance. The girls were delighted and immediately designated the ambulance as theirs. The point of Emergency, as I have seen it played countless times with a gang of little boys, is to make as much noise with the siren as possible and to crash the trucks into each other or into the leg of a living-room chair before you reach your destination.

The girls had other ideas. I realized why they had selected the ambulance. It contained three dolls: a driver, a nurse, and sick man on the stretcher. My boys have used that ambulance many times, but the dolls were always secondary to the death-defying race with the fire trucks; they were usually just thrown in the back of the van as an afterthought. The girls took the dolls out, stripped and re-dressed them tenderly, and made sure that they were seated in their appropriate places for the first rescue. Once the fire truck had been lifted off the man's leg, the girls required a box of Band-Aids and spent the next half hour making a bed for the patient and reassuring him that he was going to be all right. These little girls and my sons had seen the same NBC "Emergency" series, but the girls had apparently picked up on the show's nurturing aspects, while Jack and Drew were interested only in the equipment, the fast driving, and the sirens. . . .

Of course, I want my sons to grow up knowing that what's inside a woman's head is more important than her appearance, but I'm sure they're getting mixed signals when I delay our departure for the swimming pool to put on lipstick. I also wonder what they make of their father, whose favorite aphorism is "beautiful women rule the world." I suppose what we want for these sons and the women they may marry someday is a sensitivity that enables them to be both flexible and at ease with their respective roles, so that marriage contracts are unnecessary. When my sons bring me the heads of two purple irises from the neighbor's yard and ask, "Are you really the most beautiful mama in the whole world like Daddy says, and did everyone want to marry you?" do you blame me if I keep on waffling?

---

## REFLECTING ON MEANING

1. Mackintosh's humorous depiction of her own and others' experiences traces a change in her attitude about why girls and boys behave in different ways. What was her early assumption about the causes of gender-specific behavior? Where did she find support for this assumption? How did she revise this assumption? What caused her to revise it? To what does she finally attribute gender-based behavior? Do you agree with her conclusion? Why or why not?

2. At a Little League game, Mackintosh writes, one mother was afraid that her daughter "might be absorbing the stereotype 'boys play while girls watch.' " Why was she so concerned about stereotypes? What is a stereotype? What is stereotypical behavior? How are gender stereotypes and stereotypical behavior linked to sexism?

3. Mackintosh says that she surveyed the works of several "experts" to gain insight into the social phenomenon of stereotyping. "The books I read," she explains, "propose that sex roles are culturally induced." What social institutions do these experts pinpoint as the primary problems? How might these institutions encourage or perpetuate sexism and gender stereotypes? What specific

examples does Mackintosh give to support this view? Can you provide others?

## EXPLORING RHETORICAL STRATEGIES

1. Is Mackintosh's purpose immediately evident? What is she trying to achieve in this essay? How does she want her readers to feel about her experiences? About their own efforts to raise children? About social "problems" and individual efforts to solve them? About the nature of social problems? Who is her audience? Can you find evidence to support your inferences about Mackintosh's audience?
2. Mackintosh writes from a particular vantage point: the role of mother. How does this role help shape her choice of topic, her thesis, and her tone? How does this role influence her credibility on the subject? Her credibility in relation to the "experts" she cites? Her credibility with you as a reader? How does this role establish certain expectations of the discussion to come?
3. While Mackintosh seems to conclude that stereotypical behavior is to some degree innate, her concluding paragraph is less resolute. What does this paragraph imply about the success of her efforts to create a gender-neutral home environment? What kind of behavior do her own actions depict? Is this behavior innate? Does she convincingly resolve the biology-society debate? Does she have a vested interest in preserving the attitudes she would like to change?

# Are Women Human?

DOROTHY L. SAYERS

*Are women and men of different species? Is* human *a word exclusively reserved for men? Dorothy Sayers claims that women have for too long suffered the indignities of "classification." She argues that the time has come to admit women to the human race—but not as a class or a group. They are individuals, she argues, entitled as such to the same consideration that men receive as individuals in our society.*

It is the mark of all movements, however well-intentioned, that their pioneers tend, by much lashing of themselves into excitement, to lose sight of the obvious. In reaction against the age-old slogan, "woman is the weaker vessel," or the still more offensive, "woman is a divine creature," we have, I think, allowed ourselves to drift into asserting that "a woman is as good as a man," without always pausing to think what exactly we mean by that. What, I feel, we ought to mean is something so obvious that it is apt to escape attention altogether, viz.: not that every woman is, in virtue of her sex, as strong, clever, artistic, levelheaded, industrious and so forth as any man that can be mentioned; but, that a woman is just as much an ordinary human being as a man, with the same individual preferences, and with just as much right to the tastes and preferences of an individual. What is repugnant to every human being is to be reckoned always as a member of a class and not as an individual person. A certain amount of classification is, of course, necessary for practical purposes: there is no harm in saying that women, as a class, have smaller bones than men, wear lighter clothing, have more hair on their heads and less on their faces, go more pertinaciously to church or the cinema, or have more patience with small and noisy babies. In the same way, we may say that stout people of both sexes are commonly better-tempered than thin ones, or that university dons of both sexes are more pedantic in their speech than agricultural labourers, or that Communists of both sexes are more ferocious than Fascists—or the other way round. What is unreasonable and irritating is to assume that *all* one's tastes and preferences have to be conditioned by the class to which one belongs. That has been the very common error into which men have frequently fallen about women—and it is the error into which feminist women are, perhaps, a little inclined to fall into about themselves.

Take, for example, the very usual reproach that women nowadays always want to "copy what men do." In that reproach there is a great deal of truth and a great deal of sheer, unmitigated and indeed quite wicked nonsense. There are a number of jobs and pleasures which men have in times past cornered for themselves. At one time, for instance, men had a monopoly of classical education. When the pioneers of university training for women demanded that women should be admitted to the universities, the cry went up at once: "Why should women want to know about Aristotle?" The answer is NOT that *all* women would be the better for knowing about Aristotle—still less, as Lord Tennyson seemed to think, that they would be more companionable wives for their husbands if they did know about Aristotle—but simply: "What women want as a class is irrelevant. *I* want to know about Aristotle. It is true that most women care nothing about him, and a great many male undergraduates turn pale and faint at the thought of him—but I, eccentric individual that I am, do want to know about Aristotle, and I submit that there is nothing in my shape or bodily functions which need prevent my knowing about him." . . .

So that when we hear that women have once more laid hands upon something which was previously a man's sole privilege, I think we have to ask ourselves: is this trousers or is it braces? Is it something useful, convenient and suitable to a human being as such? Or is it merely something unnecessary to us, ugly, and adopted merely for the sake of collaring the other fellow's property? These jobs and professions, now. It is ridiculous to take on a man's job just in order to be able to say that "a woman has done it—yah!" The only decent reason for tackling any job is that it is *your* job and *you* want to do it.

At this point, somebody is likely to say: "Yes, that is all very well. But it *is* the woman who is always trying to ape the man. She *is* the inferior being. You don't as a rule find the men trying to take the women's jobs away from them. They don't force their way into the household and turn women out of their rightful occupations."

Of course they do not. They have done it already.

Let us accept the idea that women should stick to their own jobs—the jobs they did so well in the good old days before they started talking about votes and women's rights. Let us return to the Middle Ages and ask what we should get then in return for certain political and educational privileges which we should have to abandon.

It is a formidable list of jobs: the whole of the spinning industry, the whole of the dyeing industry, the whole of the weaving industry. The whole catering industry and—which would not please Lady Astor, perhaps—the whole of the nation's brewing and distilling. All the preserving, pickling and bottling industry, all the bacon-curing. And (since in those days a man was often absent from home for months together on war or business) a very large share in the management of landed estates. Here are the women's jobs—and what has become of them? They are all being handled by men. It is all very well to say that woman's place is the home—but modern civilization has taken all these pleasant and profitable activities out of the home, where the women looked after them, and handed them over to big industry, to be directed and organized by men at the head of large factories. Even the dairy-maid in her simple bonnet has gone, to be replaced by a male mechanic in charge of a mechanical milking plant.

Now, it is very likely that men in big industries do these jobs better than the women did them at home. The fact remains that the home contains much less of interesting activity than it used to contain. What is more, the home has so shrunk to the size of a small flat that—even if we restrict woman's job to the bearing and rearing of families—there is no room for her to do even that. It is useless to urge the modern woman to have twelve children, like her grandmother. Where is she to put them when she has got them? And what modern man wants to be bothered with them? It is perfectly idiotic to take away woman's traditional occupations and then complain because she looks for new ones. Every woman is a human being—one cannot repeat that too often—and a human being *must* have occupation, if he or she is not to become a nuisance to the world.

I am not complaining that the brewing and baking were taken over by the men. If they can brew and bake as well as women or better, then by all means let them do it. But they cannot have it both ways. If they are going to adopt the very sound principle that the job should be done by the person who does it best, then that rule must be applied universally. If the women make better office-workers than men, they must have the office work. If any individual woman is able to make a first-class lawyer, doctor, architect or engineer, then she must be allowed to try her hand at it. Once lay down the rule that the job comes first and you throw that job open to every individual, man or woman, fat or thin, tall or short, ugly or beautiful, who is able to do that job better than the rest of the world.

Now, it is frequently asserted that, with women, the job does not come first. What (people cry) are women doing with this liberty of theirs? What woman really prefers a job to a home and family? Very few, I admit. It is unfortunate that they should so often have to make the choice. A man does not, as a rule, have to choose. He gets both. In fact, if he wants the home and family, he usually has to take the job as well, if he can get it. Nevertheless, there have been women, such as Queen Elizabeth and Florence Nightingale, who had the choice, and chose the job and made a success of it. And there have been and are many men who have sacrificed their careers for women—sometimes, like Antony or Parnell, very disastrously. When it comes to a *choice,* then every man or woman has to choose as an individual human being, and, like a human being, take the consequences.

As human beings! I am always entertained—and also irritated—by the newsmongers who inform us, with a bright air of discovery, that they have questioned a number of female workers and been told by one and all that they are "sick of the office and would love to get out of it." In the name of God, what human being is *not,* from time to time, heartily sick of the office and would *not* love to get out of it? The time of female office-workers is daily wasted in sympathizing with disgruntled male colleagues who yearn to get out of the office. No human being likes work—not day in and day out. Work is notoriously a curse—and if women *liked* everlasting work they would not be human beings at all. *Being* human beings, they like work just as much and just as little as anybody else. They dislike perpetual washing and cooking just as much as perpetual typing and standing behind shop counters. Some of them prefer typing to scrubbing—but that does not mean that they are not, as human beings, entitled to damn and blast the typewriter when they feel that way. The number of men who daily damn and blast typewriters is incalculable; but that does not mean that they would be happier doing a little plain sewing. Nor would the women.

I have admitted that there are very few women who would put their job before every earthly consideration. I will go further and assert that there are very few men who would do it either. In fact, there is perhaps only one human being in a thousand who is passionately interested in his job for the job's sake. The difference is that if that one person in a thousand is a man, we say, simply, that he is passionately keen on his job; if she is a woman, we say she is a freak. It is extraordinarily entertaining to watch the historians of the past, for instance, entangling themselves in what they were pleased to call the "problem" of Queen Elizabeth. They invented the most complicated and astonishing reasons both for her success as a sovereign and for her tortuous matrimonial policy. She was the tool of Burleigh, she was the tool of Leicester, she was the fool of Essex; she was diseased, she was deformed, she was a man in disguise. She was a mystery, and must have some extraordinary solution. Only recently has it occurred to a few enlightened people that the solution might be quite simple after all. She might be one of the rare people who were born into the right job and put that job first. Whereupon a whole series of riddles cleared themselves up by magic. She was in love with Leicester—why didn't she marry him? Well, for the very same reason that numberless kings have not married their lovers—because it would have thrown a spanner into the wheels of the State machine. Why was she so bloodthirsty and unfeminine as to sign the death-warrant of Mary Queen of Scots? For much the same reasons that induced King George V to say that if the House of Lords did not pass the Parliament Bill he would create enough new peers to force it through—because she was, in the measure of her time, a constitutional sovereign, and knew that there was a point beyond which a sovereign could not defy Parliament. Being a rare human being with her eye to the job, she did what was necessary; being an ordinary human being, she hesitated a good deal before embarking on unsavory measures—but as to feminine mystery, there is no such thing about it, and nobody, had she been a man, would have thought either her statesmanship or her humanity in any way mysterious. Remarkable they were—but she was a very remarkable person. Among her most remarkable achievements was that of showing that sovereignty was one of the jobs for which the right kind of woman was particularly well fitted.

Which brings us back to this question of what jobs, if any, are women's jobs. Few people would go so far as to say that all women are well fitted for all men's jobs. When people do say this, it is particularly exasperating. It is stupid to insist that there are as many female musicians and mathematicians as male—the facts are otherwise, and the most we can ask is that if a Dame Ethel Smyth or a Mary Somerville turns up, she shall be allowed to do her work without having aspersions cast either on her sex or her ability. What we ask is to be human individuals, however peculiar and unexpected. It is no good saying: "You are a little girl and therefore you ought to like dolls"; if the answer is, "But I don't," there is no more to be said. Few women happen to be natural born mechanics; but if there is one, it is useless to try and argue her into being something different. What we must *not* do is to argue that the occasional appearance of a female mechanical genius proves that all women would be mechanical geniuses if they were educated. They would not.

Where, I think, a great deal of confusion has arisen is in a failure to distinguish between special *knowledge* and special *ability*. There are certain questions on which what is called "the woman's point of view" is valuable, because they involve special *knowledge*. Women should be consulted about such things as housing and domestic architecture because, under present circumstances, they have still to wrestle a good deal with houses and kitchen sinks and can bring special knowledge to the problem. Similarly, some of them (though not all) know more about children than the majority of men, and their opinion, *as women,* is of value. In the same way, the opinion of colliers is of value about coal-mining, and the opinion of doctors is valuable about disease. But there are other questions—as for example, about literature or finance—on which the "woman's point of view" has no value at all. In fact, it does not exist. No special knowledge is involved, and a woman's opinion on literature or finance is valuable only as the judgment of an individual. I am occasionally desired by congenital imbeciles and the editors of magazines to say something about the writing of detective fiction "from the woman's point of view." To such demands, one can only say, "Go away and don't be silly. You might as well ask what is the female angle on an equilateral triangle." . . .

A man once asked me—it is true that it was at the end of a very good dinner, and the compliment conveyed may have been due to that circumstance—how I managed in my books to write such natural conversation between men when they were by themselves. Was I, by any chance, a member of a large, mixed family with a lot of male friends? I replied that, on the contrary, I was an only child and had practically never seen or spoken to any men of my own age till I was about twenty-five. "Well," said the man, "I shouldn't have expected a woman [meaning me] to have been able to make it so convincing." I replied that I had coped with this difficult problem by making my men talk, as far as possible, like ordinary human beings. This aspect of the matter seemed to surprise the other speaker; he said no more, but took it away to chew it over. One of these days it may quite likely occur to him that women, as well as men, when left to themselves, talk very much like human beings also.

Indeed, it is my experience that both men and women are fundamentally human, and that there is very little mystery about either sex, except the exasperating mysteriousness of human beings in general. And though for certain purposes it may still be necessary, as it undoubtedly was in the immediate past, for women to band themselves together, as women, to secure recognition of their requirements as a sex, I am sure that the time has now come to insist more strongly on each woman's—and indeed each man's—requirements as an individual person. It used to be said that women had no *esprit de corps;* we have proved that we have—do not let us run into the opposite error of insisting that there is an aggressively feminist "point of view" about everything. To oppose one class perpetually to another—young against old, manual labor against brain-worker, rich against poor, woman against man—is to split the foundations of the State; and if the cleavage runs too deep, there remains no remedy but force and dictatorship. If you wish to preserve a free democracy, you must base it—not on classes and categories, for this will land you in the totalitarian State, where no one may act or think except as the member of a category. You must base it upon the individual Tom, Dick and Harry, on the individual Jack and Jill—in fact, upon you and me.

---

## REFLECTING ON MEANING

1. In her opening paragraph, Sayers confronts head-on the issue of classification: "What is repugnant to every human being is to be reckoned always as a member of a class and not as an individual person." What is classification? Why does Sayers find it repugnant? Isn't classifying a useful activity for making sense of the world? Does classifying differ from stereotyping? In what ways are they similar? How are they different?

2. With increasing conviction, Sayers repeatedly asserts that a woman is "just as much an ordinary human being as a man." What does she mean? Why does she feel compelled to emphasize this point? Is she stating and restating the obvious? Do you think there's a need to make this point at all? What specific situation or situations do you think she might be reacting to?

3. What point is Sayers making when she states that a man who likes his job is considered "passionately keen" on it while a woman with the same enthusiasm is considered a "freak"? What social phenomenon does she believe causes such a disparity in perception? Do you think her point is valid? What evidence can you offer to support it? What other examples of this phenomenon can you give?

## EXPLORING RHETORICAL STRATEGIES

1. Sayers's essay is shaped in a way that suggests she is responding to an argument about women. If you were to conceive of her piece as one voice in a conversation among many, how might you describe this conversation? What are the topics being debated? What viewpoints are being expressed? What is Sayers's part in this conversation? If you were to enter this conversation, what might you contribute to it?
2. How would you describe the tone of this essay? For example, is Sayers playful, serious, hostile, conciliatory, exasperated, sarcastic, or sincere? How do her many italicized words contribute to her tone? How is the exclamation "As human beings!" typical of her tone? What image of Sayers does her tone suggest? In what ways does her tone contribute to the persona she adopts in this essay?
3. Sayers integrates the opposition viewpoint throughout her essay. Where and how does she do this? How does this strategy contribute to the structure of the essay? How does the way she introduces various factions of the opposition encourage you to see them in a negative light? For example, what is the effect of referring to one such faction as "newsmongers"?

# The Dangers of Femininity

LUCY GILBERT and
PAULA WEBSTER

*The ideas of a "real man" and a "real woman" operate in powerful ways in society. Lucy Gilbert and Paula Webster take issue with these ideas by arguing that gender differences are not "the natural expression of a genetic blueprint" but "a product of human thought and culture." The authors maintain that embodied in socially constructed gender categories is a fundamental inequity: the belief that "femininity" is inferior to "masculinity" and that women are inferior to men. Thus, Gilbert and Webster conclude, the social "program" for femininity poses a serious dilemma for women: it teaches them to participate actively in their own oppression.*

One day, when Sara was barely nine years old, she sneaked into her brother's room and pulled a pair of jockey shorts and a white T-shirt out of his drawer. Clutching the underwear, she slipped into the bathroom to try them on.

Standing by the sink, she pulled her hair back with a rubber band, slicked it into place with water and stared into the mirror, trying to find a face to fit her new clothes. After forcing her eyes out of focus she thought she saw a more masculine face looking back at her. The effect was thrilling and disorienting, but just what she had desired. She looked like a boy.

Proud of her accomplishment, she went into the kitchen to show her mother the results of her experiment. Her mother, however, did not share her excitement and ordered her to remove her brother's underwear. Sara was not sure why her mother was so upset, but it was clear she had done something wrong. She returned to her room and made the undershirt into a bolero, a simple trick she had learned from her best friend. This time she went to get her mother's approval, sure she had remedied the situation, but Mom didn't seem to like it any better. She did not appreciate such imaginative play and was not going to encourage it. Her mother said that girls don't wear boys' underwear because they don't have what boys have, and she didn't see the joke. Sara felt defeated and humiliated. She learned that boys and girls must stay in their own clothes and in their own place.

Like Sara, many of us can remember the first time we experimented with the rules of masculinity or femininity by trying on clothes, attitudes, or behaviors marked "off limits." Usually someone told us that we couldn't change what nature had intended, that we had to remain girls or boys and find pleasure in the gender we were born to. These secret and transitory journeys into the territory of Otherness must have given us a glimpse of what we wanted to know but we had to renounce them if we were to accomplish our primary social task, to replicate the social system as it is constructed. Breaking the rules for appropriate masculine or feminine behavior introduces us to the dangers of testing the power of cultural assumptions and fears of breaking unnamed taboos. Early in our lives we give up the desire to take such imaginative leaps over the boundaries of difference and lose our curiosity about being the Other. We become the men or women we were meant to be.

The division of humanity into the two gender groups, women and men, begins at the time we are born. Each infant is assigned to one or the other category on the basis of the shape and size of its genitals. Once this assignment is made we become what the culture believes each of us to be—feminine or masculine. Although many people think that men and women are the natural expression of a genetic blueprint, gender is a product of human thought and culture, a social construction that creates the "true nature" of all individuals. Human traits, capabilities, thoughts, and feelings are divided between the genders and come to be recognized and expressed in accordance with a complex set of rules and rituals that are learned to affirm this. Biological males and females are thus transformed by culture into men and women who are socially and psychologically conditioned to become masculine and feminine.

The division of infants into gender categories is based on the belief that men and women are different kinds of beings. The emphasis on difference results in boys and girls being raised and evaluated differently. Although each group is thought to be incomplete, it is assumed that they will come together as a heterosexual couple to achieve a fusion of the traits that keep them separate. Since the original separation of the two places them in opposition and the exclusivity of the assignment enforces their difference, only through heterosexual coupling can each come to appreciate the assumed benefits of complementarity.

The imposition of the culture's two-gender system creates an exclusive gender identity, one that feels natural despite the arduous path each child must follow to be recognized as appropriately feminine or masculine. Once imposed, this identity is internalized and experienced as an unalterable and inevitable reality. As children develop socially and psychologically the effects of difference are reinforced and rooted in the conscious and unconscious mind. The consequences of gender appear to be the result of an inborn personality structure and not the product of social conditioning and psychic structuring.

As men and women proceed through life, they are expected to "do" gender according to the culture's assumptions about proper gender relations. Men must be masculine to women's feminine. Separate and unequal, the two halves of humanity confront each other with expectations for difference, and they are rarely surprised. Conformity to the cultural rules is harnessed when children have no choice but to obey. The desire to have the right kind of child, masculine or feminine, is matched by the parents' need to reproduce the gender system as they know it, and the result is the ongoing re-creation of the present two-gender system.

The division of the world's infants into masculine or feminine would cause no dilemma if there were social parity between the genders, if differences were merely interesting but unimportant. However, in a patriarchal society the two-gender system mandates masculine and feminine beings who are unequal, giving one set social power and the other none. Relatively powerless, and considered inferior to men, all female infants enter a world that devalues and mystifies femininity. Society simultaneously denigrates and idealizes feminine characteristics, placing women on the pedestal and under the boot. The cultural system that defines femininity as inferior to masculinity and women as inferior to men creates a complex conflict of interests between the genders.

Boys and girls are raised with the cultural stereotypes for their gender as guides. To become what they are supposed to be, they must be discouraged from all behavior that does not conform to the notion of the basic nature of masculinity or femininity. Feminine traits must be stamped out of boys, masculine out of girls. To reproduce gender classifications and maintain the boundaries that divide boys from girls, each category must become what the other is not. Femininity and masculinity are conceived as opposites; therefore each child must be taught the limits of its human potential. The cultural rules of difference operate successfully when children can demonstrate that they know what they are and act appropriately masculine or feminine.

The model of masculinity that is presented to the little boy is based on an idealized vision of male power. Mothers want their sons to become the most valued type of male—the "Real Man." Although this ideal is not one to which all men actually conform, the concept dictates parents' attitudes for raising their sons, standards against which many men judge their own behavior and that of other men. Even adult men who reject substantial portions of the model worry about how well they are "doing" masculinity.

The Real Man exhibits all the traits of a strong and self-assured person by being rational, competitive, proud, self-protective, physically powerful, and sexually active. Acting like a Real Man means standing up for your beliefs, pushing your opinions with determination and courage, even against seemingly insurmountable odds. Fighting for justice or doing evil, the Real Man approaches his tasks believing in the righteousness of his cause. If necessary the Real Man will protect those weaker than he, because it is his duty to use his strength for others. Even if he is tyrannical in exercising his power, he gains respect for the force of his will. He may not love conflict but enjoys a good fight since he can show his skills at winning—the only acceptable outcome to his struggles.

The struggles that demand a Real Man's strength are self-chosen. He asserts his individuality and independence even in the face of censure, and is often stimulated to bigger and better projects when he meets with adversity. He speaks with assurance and calm, explaining why tasks must be done his way. He never doubts the meaning of his life, is happy to be alive, and has much to accomplish. He is full of initiative and energy and undertakes all projects with full confidence that he will be successful. Sure of himself, he doesn't understand those who procrastinate because of indecision. He is a man of action, masterful and clever.

A Real Man learns his lessons quickly and applies his knowledge. Proud of his skills, he thinks it foolish to be excessively modest and doesn't consider it boastful to speak about his dreams, his plans, and his successes. He makes his way in the world by mapping strategies for what he wants. He knows he has to get ahead on his own and makes sure he is at the right place at the right time. He knows who can help him, is friendly to the right people, and thinks about the connections necessary to advancing his interests. He doesn't fear imposing himself by demanding too much of other people's time, resources, or energies. He likes to get his own way and uses people if he has to. If he doesn't succeed at first, he pauses briefly and sets off again to battle the elements. He never loses faith or confidence and just keeps fighting. The Real Man is not a quitter.

With his peers he is a loyal friend, but his friendships are based on shared activities—hanging out, doing or watching sports, drinking, camping, or arguing politics—rather than shared feelings. When he has trouble with his wife or his work or his mother, he does not expose his distress to other men lest he feel too vulnerable. Men are his competitors and he doesn't want them to have any advantage over him. He fears that an open expression of his feelings will raise questions about his masculinity. He prefers to stay cool with his buddies and thus ensure that his feelings are not misunderstood.

Although he can and must be serious, and bears the burden of power in society, he knows that a well-rounded person also has to have a good time. He likes to be outdoors, to be physically active, play, or at least watch, sports. His commitment to masculine pursuits is avowed and very strong. He likes men and spends time with them talking about masculine subjects, but not for too long. He has to get on with the business of life, and too much play is frivolous.

The world may think of a Real Man as rigid or tyrannical, but this view does not threaten his masculinity. He has to be strong and sure about his objectives. Even if he blusters and rants and raves to get his way, he is forgiven such excesses because his authority speaks louder than his words, leaving even the most stubborn of his audience in awe at the passion of his desires.

A Real Man believes that life is a game in which there are winners and losers. The weak lose and the strong win. It is not a pretty reality, he will assure you, but that is the way society works. In this dog-eat-dog world, the goal is to get power and forget about approval. To win, it is necessary to get your hands dirty, to take risks, to sell out if need be, but never to suffer defeat, never to surrender. There is something feminine about surrender and passivity and a Real Man avoids them at all costs. Even when he can't avoid losing, he is respected if he gives it all he has. If he surrenders aggressively, with style, he still comes out a winner.

A Real Man likes women, but prefers the company of men, even though he shares his culture's terror of homosexuals, who are not "real" men. He lets women know that he finds them appealing but he is very choosy, interested only in the most attractive. He surveys a room, looking for his "type." He doesn't find most women interesting or intelligent, so he experiments in relationships with those who are at least pretty until he finds his ideal. He wants to be attractive to women so his dress conforms to the popular stereotypes of masculine attire. He can confidently be the casual professor, the immaculate businessman, the trendy hippy, or the macho outdoorsman, never believing that his real personality is obscured by his clothes. He isn't obsessed with his image, but he may spend a lot of time thinking about what he should wear in order to present one aspect or another of his masculine personality.

But women are necessary to validate his masculinity and heterosexuality. No Real Man can prove he is sufficiently masculine if he can't have sex with women. In our patriarchal culture celibate men are ridiculed and suspect. To demonstrate his masculinity a man must sexualize his simplest conversations with women. When having sexual relations with a woman, a man knows he is finally, without a doubt, a man.

To succeed at masculinity a Real Man must always anticipate sexual adventure and be able to initiate and lead in seduction, smoothly encouraging women to surrender and entrust what they say is most precious to them—their bodies and their sexuality. An undeniably Real Man does not have to demand access to women's sexuality; women offer themselves to him with grateful sighs and great expectations.

If a young boy manages to achieve masculinity, as defined and determined by the culture, he will find that the outcome of being a man is to feel good about himself and his work, to feel like a winner. In a male-dominated society like our own, in which boys are valued over girls and men over women, boys will grow up to believe they are more important, more valued, and better than girls. If they can meet the demands of masculinity they come to believe that they deserve the best.

The more masculine a man's behavior, the closer he is to realizing the ideal. Yet exaggeration of masculine characteristics can lead to persistent promotion of self-interest, cold-blooded reason, lack of empathy, ruthless competition, and aggressive sexuality. While these are considered negative traits, going too far, taking masculinity too seriously, men are rarely criticized for being too masculine. How could there be too much of a good thing? Only when men abuse the power given to them by virtue of their gender and become Dr. Strangelove or Jack the Ripper does society turn a negative eye toward them. Men who go too far, out of control, are destined to become victimizers, using their privilege and their power for seemingly incomprehensible motives. Yet, masculinity, as determined by culture and reproduced in the family, assures men that if they follow the rules they will never become helpless victims. Hypermasculinity, although not easy to live with, is never denigrated; it is rather accorded awe and cringing respect. Boys who follow the gender rules become winners and inherit the mantle of authority, legitimacy, and power reserved for men.

While power is the reward for doing masculinity well, powerlessness is the reward for doing femininity well. A girl who becomes the woman she is meant to be receives love, but never power. The cultural stereotype for femininity may be as rigid and self-alienating as the one for masculinity, but its outcomes are different. The program for girls must make them into women, and women must be what men are not. Before they even learn the rules, girls are denied the possibility of ever becoming as special as boys.

The culture's message to girls about who they should be is contained in the stereotype for femininity. While masculinity is defined as a single consistent program for success, femininity is constructed as a formula for surrender. To be considered feminine a girl must suppress the positive traits that are labeled masculine. Each girl must reflect the mirror opposite of what is valued for men; she must learn to mute her strengths, her individuality, deny her own needs, and respond to the world in an emotional and noncompetitive manner. She must take every opportunity to demonstrate that she is a Real Woman, unselfish, flexible, cooperative, and altruistic. Her feminine behavior must conform to the cultural ideals for womanhood, the standard against which she will be judged as an appropriate member of her gender group.

When femininity is done well, girls become women whom men want to love, protect, cherish, and ultimately marry. Women who can stir the passions and imaginations of men should be ultrafeminine, magical child-women who can draw men to their place on the pedestal and make their requests for male help in a sweet and convincing voice.

Femininity creates the Princess/Daddy's Girl, the only woman considered exciting enough to deserve men's romantic attention. She should be fragile and not strong, helpless and insecure about her own worth, ineffectual and not masterful, confused and not rational, demanding but not competitive. She should feel like and act like a princess, waiting to be chosen and awakened by her master's touch. A woman who can pull off this version of the feminine ideal is promised the enduring respect of men and the unremitting jealousy of women. The stakes are high for the Princess, but to become the culture's sweetheart she must follow the rules.

The Princess looks to men for her definition and direction. Since she depends on men to make her feel real she attracts their attention by flattering their masculinity. She assures them she is too fragile to stand on her own and cope with the harsh realities of everyday life. If her check book doesn't balance or the toilet backs up, she throws in the towel and waits for her boyfriend or husband to come home to set things in order. She is easily upset when things don't go her own way but isn't sure how she can take charge. Because she is fragile she expects others to do for her and make things just a little easier—easy enough for her to handle and not get dirty.

To get men to take care of her the Princess shows her helplessness and inability to defend herself. With a roll of her eyes and a careless shrug of her shoulders she gasps in frustration, mocking herself for being a silly incompetent, while seeking a man who will tell her what to do. Afraid of appearing too self-sufficient or resourceful, and therefore unfeminine, she gives up easily and lets others have their own way, sulking all the while.

The Princess is also ineffectual. Although she tries to master the new technology at her office, she can't get it right and refuses to read the manual. When friends make luncheon dates with her, she regularly shows up late explaining that she left the oven on, or just had to finish the dishes before they piled too high. She is the Gracie Allen of the neighborhood and can't accomplish what she sets out to do. Bemused and confused, the Princess is unable to get it together and organize her life.

When confronted by the irritation she provokes, she lowers her head and whispers that she is sorry, or she is shocked—Who, me? She shows her fear of those in authority and her willingness to comply with their wishes. If her boss urges her to stay late to finish some work for his pet project, she finds it impossible to refuse but resents him for asking. She wants to please him, but more than that can't bear to have anyone angry at her. Masking her rage, she complies. She believes that politeness and acquiescence to men will ultimately protect her from their disfavor. She is unwilling to rock the boat. She becomes adept at indirection because making demands is unfeminine and therefore makes her uncomfortable.

She replays her delicate and rather demure behavior by dressing in styles that accentuate her softness and fragility. Hoping to attract the right man, she strikes a pose that is cold and unattainable yet approachable. Since she is not supposed to deliver what she obliquely promises by her sexy little-girl pose, she must be careful to present an understated sexuality, one that will not threaten her image. But the Princess is a little spunky, hedging her bets by acting innocent with just a touch of devil-may-care. Although she refuses to admit that she understands that men ultimately want sex from her, she is willing to flirt. In the end, however, her cleverness must not be taken too seriously. While she can tease and taunt, she must remain sexually aloof so men will not mistake her for a Bad Girl.

The Princess, the most desirable woman in patriarchal culture and fantasy, waits for a man to make her life meaningful. Although many try desperately to become the Princess, an arduous, if not impossible task, few are fully successful. It is difficult to stand around looking helpless when femininity requires so much work. Femininity is a schizophrenic condition since at the very same time that women have to act helpless and passive, we must also act helpful, enduring, nurturing, and assertive (but only in the interests of others). Like our mothers, we should be able to give until it hurts. In addition to confirming heterosexual femininity a woman must also become the tireless worker, the all-giving friend, the woman who takes care of others by putting herself last and making lives better for those more deserving than herself. So the Princess must take off her sequins and put on her apron to become the more ubiquitous version of a real woman, the Good Girl.

The Good Girl plays her role with a Saint in mind. She puts up with life's tragedies and stands steadfastly by when anyone needs her help. As a woman, she is not allowed control over the course of human events, but must be prepared to grit her teeth, endure her hardships, and go on. Her patience and good will in the face of adversity warm the hearts of all who hear of her sacrifice. She can take it and come back for more. Infinitely flexible, the Good Girl bears up under the weight of the world and her subordinate condition. She is strong for others yet her strength is worthy of praise only under adversity, when directed away from herself.

The Good Girl is not obsessed about her good looks or desirability the way the Princess is, at least in public. She is more refined, more sedate, and maddeningly practical. Though she isn't a prude, she refuses to wear clothes that are considered sexy. To her way of thinking, looking or acting seductive or sexual is morally distasteful and ultimately dangerous. Instead of looking fragile, she prefers to be "natural," to let her sense of practicality and good taste be reflected in sturdy and sensible attire. With her plain pumps, good haircut, moderate cleaning bill, and subtle makeup, she takes good care of herself but never looks too "fancy."

If her Gracie Allen sister can't get started because she doesn't know where to begin, the Good Girl is up at dawn planning good works. She likes herself best when she is doing for others, volunteering to watch your kids, make the coffee, and take work home, even before being asked. Tireless and self-effacing, she rejects praise for her work and considers modesty a virtue. Nothing is too much for her because she can handle it all.

While the Princess is reserved, emotionally withholding, the

Good Girl experiences her life as an intense spectacle. She goes up and down, fluctuating between depression and boundless joy, feeling her way through the most difficult situations emotionally but never rationally. She fears being thought of as cold or calculating, even intellectual, and when she wants to get the best for herself and refuses to compromise, she feels she is being selfish—which doesn't sit right with her because that means she's acting like a man. So tirelessly she nurtures until she is ready to fall, which she does with a self-satisfied smile on her face. She makes others happy, thank God.

Instead of making her needs known, the Good Girl forgets to put herself in the picture, assertion coming with difficulty and seeming unfeminine. She plays the waiting game, looking for the right time, the precisely correct moment to state her feelings. She never gets angry when her desires are frustrated; she is happy if you are happy. When conflicts arise she finds a way to play the mediator, to stress the futility of yelling or screaming or trying to get your way. She hates dissension and looks for the middle road, the common good. She is adept at compromise and accommodation, which she finesses with a tolerance that leaves others in her debt. She doesn't carp and complain about the silly things that occupy the more sensitive Princess, who is upset when things don't go her way. The Good Girl navigates through conflict and competition by denying her desire to win and burying her terror of losing. She withdraws when the action gets hot, claiming that the sidelines are fine for her.

The final model for femininity is the Bad Girl, the only woman who lives under the threat of excommunication from the feminine sorority because she doesn't follow the rules of self-denial and compliance. While the Good Girl timidly agrees to other people's desires, and the Princess sweetly demands what she wants, the Bad Girl calculates the costs and benefits of her actions, with a tough and unrelenting rationality. By daring to take herself seriously—like a man—she pursues her desires, even at the risk of appearing dangerous and unfeminine. She seeks pleasure and wants to control her own gratification. She strikes fear in the hearts of both men and women because she seems to be an anomaly of femininity, someone who misunderstands the limits of her gender.

A woman who refuses to act like the Princess or the Good Girl will surely be accused of being bad, the worst insult that can be directed at women, who are supposed to be good before all else. Being bad means not acting like a girl, crossing the line into masculinity, and threatening the assumed natural division between the sexes. No mother wants her daughter to be considered bad;

no woman wants to live with that label as a permanent stigma. If a woman acts out of gender, trying on the masculine privileges, mannerisms, attitudes, or feelings that are off limits, society warns her that she will come to a bad end. A Bad Girl gets hurt, ends up in jail, suffers for her transgressions, and ultimately is alone. Had she only been good and acted like girls are supposed to, she would not find herself abandoned by the company of good women who can now feel better about their own sacrifices to femininity, or the real men whose excitement turns to boredom and then pity.

Little girls learn the complex structure of femininity as they grow up in the family and adopt it as a self-chosen identity after a time. They internalize the construct and take it on as a psychological identity, the only way to know the self—feeling secure when following the prescribed rules. Women come to act, think, and feel feminine, viewing the world and all social relations through the lens of the gender assignment. It feels natural to act like a woman and unnatural to deviate from that "authentic" identity. Acting unfeminine, or feeling out of gender, produces anxiety. A woman who is tempted to stand up for herself, act like a man by being competitive, self-directed, or selfish, experiences confusion about herself and worries that she is being bad, unfeminine, possibly a freak or an unnatural woman. This anxiety has to do with the fear of gender loss—the fear of being beyond the boundaries of femininity, without a solid identity. Without a secure sense of who she is, who she is supposed to be, a woman fears stepping out of the "natural" constraints. Understandably she wants to be normal.

Femininity, like masculinity, is enforced by external threats as well. A woman who tests the limits of gender by pushing beyond the definition of femininity is threatened with loss of approval, love, and male attention. By being pushy, aggressive, assertive, or selfish, she can lose her job, her boyfriend, or her mother's concern. Social conformity maintains the gender system, keeping women acting like women and men acting like men. The fears of rejection and loss of love, coupled with the internal threat of being out of control, going too far, not really acting like a woman, keep all women committed to a social and psychological identity that requires the suppression of autonomous and aggressive desires. Doing femininity well receives the praise of society and the rewards of being an acceptable heterosexual woman, one who can get her man and keep him. If she is good and adheres to the models that the culture values for women, she will come to be known and know herself as a Real Woman, ready to live her life as a subordinate to men without questioning the primary mechanism that reproduces her subordination—the acquisition of femininity.

Since girls cannot be boys, or act like them, girls must accept the script for femininity and live with the contradiction of acting both the fragile femme and the enduring Mother Courage, responding to life with the needs of a dependent child and the strength of an enduring martyr. If they can balance assertion that is not too assertive with dependency that is not too dependent, they are promised the respect of men, their love, and their benevolence. The applause for being good and the threats to self-esteem for being bad keep women in their place in the two-gender system. Women renounce what is self-fulfilling in order to become heterosexual successes.

Because women must "do" femininity in a patriarchal society in which men are more valued than women, being a woman means being subordinate. Boys get more power, more privilege, and, when they are adults, more of what society offers in terms of pleasure and control. Girls get less. They have to take what is offered and not ask for more. Eventually femininity is equated with inferiority and acceptance of deprivation. The conclusion that girls draw from observing and participating in a society that values masculine over feminine is that they must be less deserving, less special and important than boys. Repeated experience with deprivation encourages women to agree with the cultural definition that they are less and shouldn't ask for too much. Femininity, which requires women to be passive, quiet, selfless, and subordinate, sets women up to expect to be the losers and not the winners in the world. Conditioned to accept their own deprivation as "natural," women are poorly prepared to defend their own interests, ask for what they need, or fight for what they want.

Women who follow the rules for femininity come to feel like victims, helpless before the demands of other people, and unable to put their needs first. Refusing to let other people have their way feels bad—uncomfortable and threatening. Women who can't say no to the daily demands for their compliance end up feeling taken advantage of—used. But that seems preferable to feeling selfish. Women who say no, draw boundaries to protect what they think is important, court the danger of other people's anger, irritation, or displeasure. If they are not "good," they fear being "bad." But if they are "good girls," they often end up feeling used, abused, and victimized.

Women who are committed to being good, even when it serves others and not themselves, act out their feminine conditioning. Afraid to be thought rude, unable to draw the line that ensures their own comfort and gratification, they are helpless in situations where other people's needs for satisfaction seem to be more urgent than their own. Acting like the Good Girl even when it feels painful and self-defeating is the only strategy that is familiar, the only one that feels acceptable and right. Women come to believe that they are less, deserve less, and shouldn't complain, confront, or struggle to get what they need.

So women complain about being taken advantage of, but fail to understand why it feels so difficult to defend ourselves. Even in the simplest daily experiences we expect less and consequently get less. We watch ourselves giving up our place in line because we are afraid to protest; we submit to a bad haircut, unable to stop the scissors or walk out. Afraid of being thought too narcissistic, we suffer silently. Some of us spend more time than we want to with friends, children, lovers, and husbands, saying that the others' needs come first. We don't want to disappoint or cause any pain. Women stand ready to serve even when exhausted and indifferent. When someone strongly disagrees with our opinions we are mute, pondering the necessity of speaking up at all. Feeling powerless to assert ourselves, and terrified at the potency of our anger, we retreat into silence, speaking obliquely and indirectly about what we want.

We deny our anger when events don't turn out to our satisfaction and deny our disappointment when our desires are not fulfilled. We blame ourselves for the rejections, power trips, and cruelties of friends and lovers, saying we must have done something to deserve it. We find it hard to believe that people aren't as good as we would like them to be and assume responsibility for unpleasant situations in our lives, thinking we are in control when in fact we are not. If a woman doesn't get the job she wants she usually assumes she wasn't good enough, if she has a fight with her boyfriend she assumes it was her fault, that he was right and she was wrong. Never suspicious of other people's motives, never sure she can trust her feelings, women assume that everybody will protect their interests if they don't make trouble.

The program for femininity and the internal sense of security that keep women hooked on being what they are supposed to be leave them unprepared to define or defend their own interests. Ready to deny the dangers of surrendering to the will of others, women cheerfully walk into situations where defeat is inevitable. We come out feeling bad about ourselves, but never angry, never able to take the reins and get what we want.

Like the bottomless well, the truly feminine woman in all of us is a never-ending source of compassion and nurturance for others. She feels real when she is needed; she sees self-directed choice as something that will alienate her from those whom she cares most about—everybody but herself. Being good for others feels better than being good to herself. Women refuse to act like winners for fear of losing love, respect, or the good will of men and women who they think are better than they and more deserving of having their needs met. Wanting to be good, to be well thought of, to be liked, women passively endure impositions on their time, energy, and will in order to hold on to the good opinion of others. Fearing to ask for more or better, anxious about saying no and refusing to serve, the feminine woman walks a path that leads to self-denial and compliance—the only path for which her conditioning to femininity prepares her.

Because adhering to femininity seems natural, and because this "natural" condition strips women of the resources they need to stand up for themselves and fight back, most women believe that their victimization is inevitable. Since women are frightened of being called selfish, bad, or unfeminine, they often choose to be the losers instead of the winners. Winning assumes that one is better than someone else and doesn't fit in with the feminine self-image. A Real Woman says that it isn't important whether you win or lose, it's how you play the game. And she plays according to the rules of femininity, thereby ensuring her own defeat. Each time she loses, her femininity is validated; she is now the woman she was meant to be.

The woman who plays the Good Girl is promised some compensation for her efforts—the love of a man. The man, romanticized and overrated in the culture, will make up for the deprivations she suffers and assure the woman of her normalcy and worth. A man can lift the veil of social inferiority that women are forced to wear and elevate her above the generally denigrated category of Woman. With a man by her side she feels safer and more valuable, better able to deny her lack of social, economic, and political power. Without a man she will be considered a heterosexual failure, a reject, a poor pitiable creature doomed to invisibility and celibacy. Her aloneness is the living proof of her inability to give, her failure to be feminine.

Masculinity and femininity are played out in the social relations between the sexes. Given the distribution of power and privilege, the relationship is always tinged with the residues of inequality; women must conspicuously demonstrate their admiration for the powerful and their willingness to serve; while men must express their respect for the powerless and their desire to protect. The contradictions of loving those who have more power than you are muted by the ideology of heterosexual romance, which assumes that women choose men because they experience an irresistible attraction to them. Yet a woman *must* choose a man if she is to fulfill her feminine destiny. Without a man she cannot be a "real woman," the only kind men are interested in.

To have their femininity validated, women must gain men's attention and approval. Women go about pleasing men with a single-minded energy they can rarely muster for themselves. Hungry for male recognition and fascinated by masculine power, women dedicate themselves to seeing that men get their way. Men's praise, even when grudgingly given, feels like a warm blanket of security. Putting men's interests first may seem to be a burden but the feminine woman smiles; nothing is too much for the man she loves. If she is successful in making him feel important, she can rest easy, knowing she has done her job well. She now feels worthy and finally visible.

But men demand a lot of women's services to make life warm and cozy. Sometimes a man forgets the limits of his social power and asks for too much, yet unreasonable demands on a woman's time, energy, and nurturing capacities are interpreted as his "needing" her, and above all else she wants to be needed. She understands and is grateful that someone of his stature wants so much from someone like her. She explains that men are tyrants but usually underneath they are babies. "Just another kid to take care of," she tells her friends. But in truth she loves him more because he can lean on her, is willing to put up with his "craziness" because he loves her.

And she forgives him because she knows that men go off sometimes, they are under pressure at work, they need to let off steam—men are like that. She is willing to become his emotional punching bag because he isn't really trying to hurt *her,* he just needs to let it out. She doesn't mind being a victim for a little while because women are like that. She keeps on keeping on. In this way she stops blaming him and relieves him of the responsibility to apologize. She says it was her fault, and she will try to stop complaining, acting so unfeminine, and be a better lover, wife, or girlfriend. She promises him and herself that she will be less angry in the future. The panic passes. He isn't leaving. She rededicates herself to being a good girl, hoping he will treat her better.

Femininity strips a woman of her desire to defend her own interests or to get what she wants from men. She is unprepared to act like a man with men. She says that she just couldn't disappoint him, will not ignore him, and can't change him. She makes jokes about the battle of the sexes with bitterness and resignation. Women have been conditioned, both socially and intrapsychically, to accept the ideology of gender relations and believe there is nothing they can do. Men must win. That's what makes them men. Women have no choice. They have to take what they can get and pretend it is enough.

Conditioned to be feminine, not masculine, women are set up to participate in their own deprivation, especially in their relations with men. Ambivalence about self-worth jockeys with fear of rejection, making a powerful social mandate to serve men feel like a compulsion, natural and even gratifying. Challenging men's authority feels dangerous. Disagreeing with their opinions is an act of insubordination creating a palpable anxiety. It is often easier to be good for him than to be "bad," risking his anger. If men are given power over women in culture and society, women can be thanked for promoting male interests. Even in the face of cruelty and cold indifference, women are junkies for male approval and do almost anything to have it delivered to the door.

Women's responses to impositions from men are predictable. Women endure the dissatisfactions of the gender system, sharing the culture's belief that men must never have their masculinity threatened. A woman who dares to challenge this system risks the anxiety of being out of gender—unnatural and therefore unappealing. She clenches her teeth and remains silent even when feeling violated by his demands. The sadness passes and the anger fades. If he is a "real" man, she as his victim is a "real" woman.

---

## REFLECTING ON MEANING

1. Although Gilbert and Webster acknowledge physical differences between men and women, they assert that gender is "a product of human thought and culture." What do they mean? What role might cultural assumptions and social conditioning play in defining gender? How do sociology, biology, and psychology each define gender? Which definition is most plausible to you? Why?

2. What do Gilbert and Webster mean by the term *gender identity?* What kind of identity does their "masculine" model offer? What assumption about masculinity underlies this model? What identity does the model of "femininity" offer? What assumption informs this model? How would you describe the relationship of the two models? Have Gilbert and Webster accurately depicted the gender identities that society validates?

3. Gilbert and Webster argue that "the division of the world's infants into masculine or feminine would cause no dilemma if there

were social parity between the genders. . . ." What is this dilemma? Do you see evidence that it exists today? What is "social parity"? What evidence can you give to support or refute the authors' assumption that it doesn't exist? Do you think that social parity would resolve the problems of the "two-gender system"?

## EXPLORING RHETORICAL STRATEGIES

1. What audience are Gilbert and Webster addressing in their essay? Is there any evidence that they are addressing a specific audience, defined by such characteristics as gender, race, age, occupation, or social class? How might considerations of audience have contributed to the way they shaped this essay?
2. You may have noticed the authors' unusual choice of words in a few places in the essay. For example, they describe men's and women's gender-specific behavior as "doing gender." What does this phrasing suggest to you about the way men and women behave? How does it advance the authors' point about gender as a social product? Does it influence the tone of the essay?
3. A considerable portion of the essay focuses on men and masculinity. Why, then, does the title address only femininity? Also, the conclusion discusses women who challenge the gender system, but not men. Why not? Are the authors arbitrarily omitting men? Why or why not? Is there any plausible reason for these omissions?

# Chapter 2

# MASCULINITY IN TRANSITION

## What Every Woman Should Know About Men

ALAN ALDA

*With tongue in cheek, Alan Alda portrays stereotypical masculine behavior as a disease. He provides a test for self-diagnosis, several remedies, and some suggestions for those who must cope with a "sufferer" of this gender-specific ailment.*

Everyone knows that testosterone, the so-called male hormone, is found in both men and women. What is not so well known is that men have an overdose.

Until now it has been thought that the level of testosterone in men is normal simply because they have it. But if you consider how abnormal their *behavior* is, then you are led to the hypothesis that almost all men are suffering from *testosterone poisoning*.

The symptoms are easy to spot. Sufferers are reported to show an early preference (while still in the crib) for geometric shapes. Later, they become obsessed with machinery and objects to the exclusion of human values. They have an intense need to rank everything, and are obsessed with size. (At some point in his life, nearly every male measures his penis.)

It is well known that men don't look like other people. They have chicken legs. This is symptomatic of the disease, as is the fact that those men with the most aviary underpinnings will rank women according to the shapeliness of *their* legs.

The pathological violence of most men hardly needs to be mentioned. They are responsible for more wars than any other leading sex.

Testosterone poisoning is particularly cruel because its sufferers usually don't know they have it. In fact, when they are most under its sway they believe that they are at their healthiest and most attractive. They even give each other medals for exhibiting the most advanced symptoms of the illness.

But there is hope.

Sufferers can change (even though it is harder than learning to walk again). They must first realize, however, that they are sick. The fact that this condition is inherited in the same way that dimples are does not make it cute.

Eventually, of course, telethons and articles in the *Reader's Digest* will dramatize the tragedy of testosterone poisoning. In the meantime, it is imperative for your friends and loved ones to become familiar with the danger signs.

*Have the men you know take this simple test for—*

## The Seven Warning Signs of Testosterone Poisoning

1. *Do you have an intense need to win?* When having sex, do you take pride in always finishing before your partner? Do you always ask if this time was "the best"—and gnaw on the bedpost if you get an ambiguous answer?
2. *Does violence play a big part in your life?* Before you answer, count up how many hours you watched football, ice hockey, and children's cartoons this year on television. When someone crosses you, do you wish you could stuff his face full of your fist? Do you ever poke people in your fantasies or throw them to and fro at all? When someone cuts you off in traffic, do violent, angry curses come bubbling out of your mouth before you know it? If so, you're in big trouble, fella, and this is only question number two.
3. *Are you "thing" oriented?* Do you value the parts of a woman's body more than the woman herself? Are you turned on by things that even *remind* you of those parts? Have you ever fallen in love with a really great doorknob?
4. *Do you have an intense need to reduce every difficult situation to charts and figures?* If you were present at a riot, would you tend to count the crowd? If your wife is despondent over a deeply felt setback that has left her feeling helpless, do you take her temperature?

5. *Do you tend to measure things that are really qualitative?* Are you more impressed with how high a male ballet dancer can leap than with what he does while he's up there? Are you more concerned with how long you can spend in bed, and with how many orgasms you can have, than you are with how you or your partner feels while you're there?
6. *Are you a little too mechanically minded?* Would you like to watch a sunset with a friend and feel at one with nature and each other, or would you rather take apart a clock?
7. *Are you easily triggered into competition?* When someone tries to pass you on the highway, do you speed up a little? Do you find yourself getting into contests of crushing beer cans—with the beer still in them?

If you've answered yes to three or fewer of the above questions, you may be learning to deal with your condition. A man answering yes to more than three is considered sick and not someone you'd want to have around in a crisis—such as raising children or growing old together. Anyone answering yes to all seven of the questions should seek help immediately before he kills himself in a high-wire act.

### What to Do If You Suffer from Testosterone Poisoning

1. *Don't panic.* Your first reaction may be that you are sicker than anyone else—or that you are the one man in the world able to fight it off—or, knowing that you are a sufferer, that you are the one man ordained to lead others to health (such as by writing articles about it). These are all symptoms of the disease. Just relax. First, sit back and enjoy yourself. Then find out how to enjoy somebody else.
2. *Try to feel something.* (Not with your hands, you oaf.) Look at a baby and see if you can appreciate it. (Not how *big* it's getting, just how nice she or he is.) See if you can get yourself to cry by some means other than getting hit in the eye or losing a lot of money.
3. *See if you can listen while someone is talking.* Were you the one talking? Perhaps you haven't got the idea yet.
4. *Practice this sentence:* "You know, I think you're right and I'm wrong." (Hint: it is useful to know what the other person thinks before you say this.)

### For Women Only: What to Do If You Are Living with a Sufferer

1. Remember that a little sympathy is a dangerous thing. The sufferer will be inclined to interpret any concern for him as appropriate submissiveness.
2. Let him know that you expect him to fight his way back to health and behave like a normal person—for his own sake, not for yours.
3. Only after he begins to get his condition under control and has actually begun to enjoy life should you let him know that there is no such thing as testosterone poisoning.

---

## REFLECTING ON MEANING

1. What are the symptoms of testosterone "poisoning"? Have you encountered any cases of it in your own experience?
2. According to Alda, what is the "cure" for testosterone poisoning? Do his remedies seem effective?
3. Why does Alda end his essay by claiming that "there is no such thing as testosterone poisoning"? Whom is he talking to? Why does he recommend keeping this "fact" a secret?

## EXPLORING RHETORICAL STRATEGIES

1. How would you describe Alda's tone? Why do you think he chose to adopt this tone? How does it help him make his point?
2. Who is Alda's intended audience? How do you know?
3. What kind of popular article format is Alda spoofing? In what kind of magazine do these articles appear? What are the issues these articles tend to address? What persona do the authors of these articles typically adopt? How does Alda satirize these articles? What effect does he create?

# In Harness: The Male Condition

HERB GOLDBERG

*Are women the only victims of gender stereotyping and social oppression? Herb Goldberg offers an emphatic no to this question. It is time, he argues, for men to "remove the disguises of privilege and reveal the male condition for what it really is."*

Most men live in harness. Richard was one of them. Typically he had no awareness of how his male harness was choking him until his personal and professional life and his body had nearly fallen apart.

Up to that time he had experienced only occasional short bouts of depression that a drink would bring him out of. For Richard it all crashed at an early age, when he was thirty-three. He came for psychotherapy with resistance, but at the instruction of his physician. He had a bad ulcer, was losing weight, and, in spite of repeated warnings that it could kill him, he was drinking heavily.

His personal life was also in serious trouble. He had recently lost his job as a disc jockey on a major radio station because he'd been arrested for drunk driving. He had totaled his car against a tree and the newspapers had a picture of it on the front page. Shortly thereafter his wife moved out, taking with her their eight-year-old daughter. She left at the advice of friends who knew that he had become violent twice that year while drunk.

As he began to talk about himself it became clear that he had been securely fitted into his male harness early in his teens. In high school he was already quite tall and stronger than most. He was therefore urged to go out for basketball, which he did, and he got lots of attention for it.

He had a deep, resonant voice that he had carefully cultivated. He was told that he should go into radio announcing and dramatics, so he got into all the high school plays. In college he majored in theater arts.

In his senior year in college he dated one of the most beautiful and sought-after girls in the junior class. His peer group envied him, which reassured Richard that he had a good thing going. So he married Joanna a year after graduating and took a job with a small radio station in Fresno, California. During the next ten years he played out the male role; he fathered a child and fought his way up in a very competitive profession.

It wasn't until things had fallen apart that he even let himself know that he had any feelings of his own, and in therapy he began to see why it had been so necessary to keep his feelings buried. They were confusing and frightening.

More than anything else, there was a hypersensitive concern over what others thought about him as a "man." As other suppressed feelings began to surface they surprised him. He realized how he had hated the pressures of being a college basketball player. The preoccupation with being good and winning had distorted his life in college.

Though he had been to bed with many girls before marriage and even a few afterward, he acknowledged that rarely was it a genuine turn-on for him. He liked the feeling of being able to seduce a girl but the experience itself was rarely satisfying, so he would begin the hunt for another as soon as he succeeded with one. "Some of those girls were a nightmare," he said. "I would have been much happier without them. But I was caught in the bag of proving myself and I couldn't seem to control it."

The obsessive preoccupation in high school and college with cultivating a deep, resonant "masculine" voice he realized was similar to the obsession some women have with their figures. Though he thought he had enjoyed the attention he got being on stage, he acknowledged that he had really disliked being an entertainer, or "court jester," as he put it.

When he thought about how he had gotten married he became particularly uncomfortable. "I was really bored with Joanna after the first month of dating but I couldn't admit it to myself because I thought I had a great thing going. I married her because I figured if I didn't one of the other guys would. I couldn't let that happen."

Richard had to get sick in his harness and nearly be destroyed by role-playing masculinity before he could allow himself to be a person with his own feelings, rather than just a hollow male image. Had it not been for a bleeding ulcer he might have postponed looking at himself for many years more.

Like many men, Richard had been a zombie, a daytime sleepwalker. Worse still, he had been a highly "successful" zombie, which made it so difficult for him to risk change. Our culture is saturated with successful male zombies, businessman zombies, golf zombies, sports car zombies, playboy zombies, etc. They are playing by the rules of the male game plan. They have lost touch with, or are running away from, their feelings and awareness of themselves as people. They have confused their social masks for their essence and they are destroying themselves while fulfilling the traditional definitions of masculine-appropriate behavior. They set their life sails by these role definitions. They are the heroes, the studs, the providers, the warriors, the empire builders, the fearless ones. Their reality is always approached through these veils of gender expectations.

When something goes seriously wrong, they discover that they are shadows to themselves as well as to others. They are unknown because they have been so busy manipulating and masking themselves in order to maintain and garner more status that a genuine encounter with another person would threaten them, causing them to flee or to react with extreme defensiveness.

Men evaluate each other and are evaluated by many women largely by the degree to which they approximate the ideal masculine model. Women have rightfully lashed out against being placed into a mold and being related to as a sex object. Many women have described their roles in marriage as a form of socially approved prostitution. They assert that they are selling themselves out for an unfulfilling portion of supposed security. For psychologically defensive reasons the male has not yet come to see himself as a prostitute, day in and day out, both in and out of the marriage relationship.

The male's inherent survival instincts have been stunted by the seemingly more powerful drive to maintain his masculine image. He would, for example, rather die in the battle than risk living in a different way and being called a "coward" or "not a man." He would rather die at his desk prematurely than free himself from his compulsive patterns and pursuits. As a recently published study concluded, "A surprising number of men approaching senior citizenship say they would rather die than be buried in retirement."

The male in our culture is at a growth impasse. He won't move—not because he is protecting his cherished central place in the sun, but because he *can't* move. He is a cardboard Goliath precariously balanced and on the verge of toppling over if he is pushed even ever so slightly out of his well-worn path. He lacks the fluidity of the female who can readily move between the traditional definitions of male or female behavior and roles. She can be wife and mother or a business executive. She can dress in typically feminine fashion or adopt the male styles. She will be loved for having "feminine" interests such as needlework or cooking, or she will be admired for sharing with the male in his "masculine" interests. That will make her a "man's woman." She can be sexually assertive or sexually passive. Meanwhile, the male is rigidly caught in his masculine pose and, in many subtle and direct ways, he is severely punished when he steps out of it.

Unlike some of the problems of women, the problems of men are not readily changed through legislation. The male has no apparent and clearly defined targets against which he can vent his rage. Yet he is oppressed by the cultural pressures that have denied him his feelings, by the mythology of the woman and the distorted and self-destructive way he sees and relates to her, by the urgency for him to "act like a man" which blocks his ability to respond to his inner promptings both emotionally and physiologically, and by a generalized self-hate that causes him to feel comfortable only when he is functioning well in harness, or when he lives for joy and for personal growth.

The prevalent "enlightened" male's reaction to the women's liberation movement bears testimony to his inability to mobilize himself on his own behalf. He has responded to feminist assertions by donning sack cloth, sprinkling himself with ashes, and flagellating himself—accusing himself of the very things she is accusing him of. An article entitled, "You've Come a Long Way, Buddy," perhaps best illustrates the male self-hating attitude. In it, the writer said,

> The members of the men's liberation movement are . . . a kind of embarrassing vanguard, the first men anywhere on record to take a political stand based on the idea that what the women are saying is right—men are a bunch of lazy, selfish, horny, unhappy oppressors.

Many other undoubtedly well-intentioned writers on the male condition have also taken a basically guilt- and shame-oriented approach to the male, alternately scolding him, warning him, and preaching to him that he better change and not be a male chauvinist pig anymore. During many years of practice as a psychotherapist, I have never seen a person grow or change in a self-constructive, meaningful way when he was motivated by guilt, shame, or self-hate. That manner of approach smacks of old-time religion and degrades the male by ignoring the complexity of the binds and repressions that are his emotional heritage.

Precisely because the tenor and mood of the male liberation efforts so far have been one of self-accusation, self-hate, and a repetition of feminist assertions, I believe it is doomed to failure in its present form. It is buying the myth that the male is culturally favored—a notion that is clung to despite the fact that every critical statistic in the area of longevity, disease, suicide, crime, accidents, childhood emotional disorders, alcoholism, and drug addiction shows a disproportionately higher male rate.

Many men who join male liberation groups do so to please or impress their women or to learn how to deal with and hold on to their recently liberated wives or girlfriends. Once in a male liberation group they intellectualize their feelings and reactions into lifelessness. In addition, the men tend to put each other down for thinking like "typical male chauvinists" or using words like "broad," "chick," "dike," etc. They have introjected the voices of their feminist accusers and the result is an atmosphere that is joyless, self-righteous, cautious, and lacking in a vitalizing energy. A new, more subtle kind of competitiveness pervades the atmosphere: the competition to be the least competitive and most free of the stereotyped version of male chauvinism.

The women's liberation movement did not effect its astounding impact via self-hate, guilt, or the desire to placate the male. Instead it has been energized by anger and outrage. Neither will the male change in any meaningful way until he experiences his underlying rage toward the endless, impossible binds under which he lives, the rigid definitions of his role, the endless pressure to be all things to all people, and the guilt-oriented, self-denying way he has traditionally related to women, to his feelings, and to his needs.

Because it is so heavily repressed, male rage only manifests itself indirectly and in hidden ways. Presently it is taking the form of emotional detachment, interpersonal withdrawal, and passivity in relationship to women. The male has pulled himself inward in order to deny his anger and to protect himself and others from his buried cascade of resentment and fury. Pathetic, intellectualized attempts not to be a male chauvinist pig will *never* do the job.

There is also a commonly expressed notion that men will somehow be freed as a by-product of the feminist movement. This is a comforting fantasy for the male but I see no basis for it becoming a reality. It simply disguises the fear of actively determining his own change. Indeed, by responding inertly and passively, the male will be moved, but not in a meaningful and productive direction. If there is to be a constructive change for the male he will have to chart his own way, develop his own style, and experience his own anxieties, fear, and rage because *this time mommy won't do it!*

Recently, I asked a number of men to write to me about how they see their condition and what liberation would mean to them. A sense of suffocation and confusion was almost always present.

A forty-six-year-old businessman wrote: "From what do I need to be liberated? I'm too old and tired to worry about myself. I know that I'm only a high-grade mediocrity. I've come to accept a life where the dreams are now all revealed as unreality. I don't know how my role or my son's role should change. If I knew I suppose it would be in any way that would make my wife happier and less of a shrew."

A thirty-nine-year-old carpenter discussing the "joys" of working responded: "I contend that the times in which it is fun and rewarding in a healthy way have been fairly limited. Most of the time it has been a question of running in fear of failure." Referring to his relationships, he continued, "There is another aspect of women's and men's lib that I haven't experienced extensively. This is the creation of close friendships outside of the marriage. My past experiences have been stressful to the point where I am very careful to limit any such contact. What's the fear? I didn't like the sense of insecurity developed by my wife and the internal stresses that I felt. It created guilt feelings."

A fifty-seven-year-old college professor expressed it this way: "Yes, there's a need for male lib and hardly anyone writes about it the way it really is, though a few make jokes. My gut reaction, which is what you asked for, is that men—the famous male chauvinist pigs who neglect their wives, underpay their women employees, and rule the world—are literally slaves. They're out there picking that cotton, sweating, swearing, taking lashes from the boss, working fifty hours a week to support themselves and the plantation, only then to come back to the house to do another twenty hours a week rinsing dishes, toting trash bags, writing checks, and acting as butlers at the parties. It's true of young husbands and middle-aged husbands. Young bachelors may have a nice deal for a couple of years after graduating, but I've forgotten, and I'll never again be young! Old men. Some have it sweet, some have it sour.

"Man's role—how has it affected my life? At thirty-five, I chose to emphasize family togetherness and income and neglect my profession if necessary. At fifty-seven, I see no reward for time spent with and for the family, in terms of love or appreciation. I see a thousand punishments for neglecting my profession. I'm just tired and have come close to just walking away from it and starting over; just research, publish, teach, administer, play tennis, and travel. Why haven't I? Guilt. And love. And fear of loneliness.

How should the man's role in my family change? I really don't know how it can, but I'd like a lot more time to do my thing."

The most remarkable and significant aspect of the feminist movement to date has been woman's daring willingness to own up to her resistances and resentment toward her time-honored, sanctified roles of wife and even mother. The male, however, has yet to fully realize, acknowledge, and rebel against the distress and stifling aspects of many of the roles he plays—from good husband, to good daddy, to good provider, to good lover, etc. Because of the inner pressure to constantly affirm his dominance and masculinity, he continues to act as if he can stand up under, fulfill, and even enjoy all the expectations placed on him no matter how contradictory and devitalizing they are.

It's time to remove the disguises of privilege and reveal the male condition for what it really is.

---

## REFLECTING ON MEANING

1. Goldberg emphasizes that men's roles are more constraining than women's are; in fact, he argues that men are "severely punished" for stepping out of their roles, whereas women can adopt "masculine" behavior without penalty. What evidence does he offer to support these points? Is this evidence convincing? Why or why not? Do you agree or disagree that men are more trapped by gender expectations than women are? Can you think of any instances when men are allowed the freedom not to be "men," or when women are not allowed to shift roles? What are they?

2. Goldberg clearly views "enlightened" males with scorn. Why? Aren't these men attempting to move beyond the masculine roles that Goldberg finds so stifling? How does Goldberg depict these men? How can you reconcile his attitudes toward them with his vision of freedom from the male stereotype? Is Goldberg arguing for gender-neutral roles or for something else? Does he want men to be able to move freely between masculine and feminine roles, or does he want men to reassert their masculinity? How do you know?

3. Goldberg's attitude toward the women's movement is perhaps best described as ambivalent. In several instances he appears to

envy it; in others he displays open hostility toward it. What evidence of both attitudes can you identify in the essay? What might account for his envy? At the same time, why might he display hostility? How can you reconcile these disparate reactions to the women's movement? Are his attitudes reasonable or unreasonable? Why?

## EXPLORING RHETORICAL STRATEGIES

1. What metaphor does Goldberg use to describe the oppression of men? What does it suggest to you about the nature of this oppression? How appropriate is the metaphor? What is Goldberg's thesis? In what ways does the metaphor advance his thesis?

2. Goldberg says that Richard had become a "hollow male image," a man almost "destroyed by role-playing masculinity." What do these descriptions suggest about the nature of Richard's "condition"? How does Goldberg's summary of Richard's life help illustrate his point? How effective is this illustration?

3. What rhetorical strategies has Goldberg borrowed from feminist rhetoric? What kind of persona does he adopt? What is the tone of his essay? How do these strategies work in arguing the case for men's liberation?

# Masculinity: Style and Cult

HAROLD ROSENBERG

*The masculine ideal has played a vital role in the cultural mythology of past societies. But according to Harold Rosenberg, the American version of this ideal has lost any usefulness it may have once had, and attempts to revitalize it are doing more harm than good. In this essay, Rosenberg describes the American masculine ideal, explains what has happened to it, and recommends that it be put aside in favor of a yet-to-emerge "maleness."*

Societies of the past have admired different personifications of the manly virtues: the warrior, the patriarch, the sage; the lover, the seducer; Zeus the Thunderer, Jehovah the Lawgiver.

In America, masculinity is associated primarily with the outdoors, and with such outdoor trades as cattledriving, railroading, whaling, and trucking. The outdoor type is presumed to possess masculine character traits: toughness, resourcefulness, love of being alone, fraternity with animals, and attractiveness to women and the urge to abandon them. To the man of the open spaces is also attributed the ultimate mark of manliness, the readiness to die.

From the outdoors America derives the boots, lumber jackets and shirts, sailor's caps, pipes, and guns that are its paraphernalia of masculinity. Oddly enough, in the United States, military and police uniforms do not confer masculinity, as they do among Cossacks and Hussars. One can as readily imagine women in our army uniform as men. To prove that he was all man, General Patton had to augment his battle costume with a pearl-handled revolver. (It is true, however, that he wrote poetry and may have felt the need to overcome this handicap.)

As to hair, masculinity is ambivalent. Long hair belongs to the style of frontier scouts and trappers, the most male of men. Yet "longhairs" is the name applied to intellectuals, a breed always suspected of sexual inauthenticity. Beards used to be a material evidence of maleness; today they are as frequently an appurtenance of masquerade.

In the last century the outdoors represented genuine hazards. It took self-reliance, identifiable with masculinity (though the pioneer mother had it, too), to venture very far from the farm or town.

Today there are still risky occupations—piloting spaceships, handling nuclear substances—but these trades have become increasingly technical and depersonalized. As for the rugged outdoors, it is used chiefly for sports; and a vacation at a ranch or ski lodge, or shooting lions in Kenya, is about as hazardous as a trip to the Riviera.

The outdoors, representing once-hostile nature, has been transformed into a stage set. Masculinity in the American sense has thus lost its locale and, perhaps, its reason for being. On the neon-lighted lonesome prairie, masculinity is a matter of certain traditional costume details: the cowboy hat, jeans, and guitar. It has become clear that the traditional traits of the man's man (and the ladies' man) can be put on, too. One *plays* manliness, with or without dark goggles.

Big-game hunters, mountain climbers, horsemen, and other representative male types are actors in a charade of nostalgia. Old masculine pursuits, like baseball or wrestling, when carried on at night under the glare of fluorescent tubes, come to resemble spectacles on television and wind up in the living room. In the epoch of the picture window, outdoors and indoors have lost their separateness.

In modern mass societies the uniforms of all kinds of cults compete with one another. Masculinity is one of these cults, and to create an impression the practitioner of maleness must stand out in a crowd. Persons with other interests are not disposed to make an issue of their sex. Only psychiatrists and sociologists complain that boys and girls today look alike and are often mistaken for each other. Even tough adolescents, like members of big-city gangs, don't mind if their girls wear the same shirts and jeans as the men. All are more concerned with identifying themselves as outsiders than as males and females.

Masculinity today is a myth that has turned into a comedy. A ten-gallon hat still seems to bestow upon its wearer the old male attributes of taciturnity, resourcefulness, courage, and love of solitude. At the same time, the virility of the cowboy and the truck driver, like that of the iceman of yesterday, is a joke that everyone sees through.

A person uncertain of his sexual identity dresses up in boots, bandanna, and riding breeches not so much to fool the public as to parade his ambiguity. Those who have gone over the line may advertise their desires for male company by wearing a beard in addition to sheepskins. Women can be masculine too, of course, in the degree necessary to make them irresistible to feminine men.

Hemingway, who constantly kept the issue of masculinity alive in his writings, flaunted both the look of the outdoor man and his presumed character qualities of daring, self-detachment, contempt for the overcivilized, and eagerness to court death.

Hemingway's he-man performance was, among other things, a means of combatting the American stereotype of the writer as a sissy. In the United States, the artist and man of ideas have always lived under the threat of having their masculinity impugned. Richard Hofstadter, in his *Anti-Intellectualism in American Life,* lists a dozen instances in which the "stigma of effeminacy" was branded upon intellectuals by political bullies, ranging from Tammany Hall leaders in the nineteenth century, who attacked reformers as "political hermaphrodites," to Communist Party hacks in the 1930s, who denounced independent writers as "scented whores." Evidently, it has always been possible to convince the common man that his intellectual superiors fall short of him in manliness.

To the overhanging charge of being contaminated by a ladylike occupation, Hemingway responded by injecting the romance of masculinity into the making of literature. At least as far as he was concerned, the sexual legitimacy of the male writer was to be put beyond question. Besides lining up with traditional outdoor types, such as bullfighters and deep-sea fishermen, Hemingway's strategy included identification with the new activist male image of the Depression decade: the leather-jacketed revolutionist allied with the peasant and factory worker. One might say that each of his novels originated in a new choice of male makeup.

Unfortunately, demonstrating his manhood was not enough for Hemingway. He found it necessary to challenge the masculinity of other writers. Like Theodore Roosevelt earlier in the century, he became an instance of the intellectual who slanders intellectuals generally, in the hope of putting himself right with the regular guys. During the Spanish Civil War he forgot himself to the extent of sneering publicly at Leon Trotsky for remaining at his typewriter in Mexico, implying that the former chief of the Red Army lacked the manliness to go to Spain and fight. He, himself, of course, went to Spain to write. In *For Whom the Bell Tolls* he identified himself with the dynamiter Jordan who also shook the earth by his love feats in a sleeping bag.

Thirty years ago not all of Hemingway's contemporaries were

convinced that he had established his masculinity through displaying an appetite for violence, sex, and death. In *no thanks,* e. e. cummings translated Hemingway's romance of maleness back into the daydreams of boyhood:

> what does little Ernest croon
> in his death at afternoon?
> (kow dow r 2 bul retoinis
> wus de woids uf lil Oinis)

To cummings, Hemingway's heroics were not only childish ("lil Oinis") but feminine ("kow dow r").

The post-Hemingway he-man has labored under the handicap of a masculinity that is generally recognized to be a masquerade. The adventurer living dangerously has disintegrated into the tongue-in-cheek élan of James Bond. Neither at work nor at home is maleness any longer endowed with glamour or privilege. The cosmonaut is less a birdman than a specialist minding his signals and dials. The father who has entered into a diapering partnership with his wife has nothing in common with the patriarch. To the public of Norman Mailer (more male?) the outdoor rig (Mailer in sea captain's cap on the jacket of *Advertisements for Myself)* and chronicles of supersex are suspect, both psychologically and as playing to the gallery. It is no secret that a Bogartean toughness with women may represent the opposite of male self-confidence.

The mass media exploit the ambiguity of the male role and the sexual sophistication that goes with the increasing awareness of it. In male comedy teams, one of the partners almost invariably plays the "wife," confident that the audience will know when to smirk. Analysts of mass culture speak of the decline of the American male and of the "masculinity crisis" as topics capable of arousing libidinous responses. The public is given the image of luscious females starving in vain for the attention of men, and of men who, egged on and deprived by frigid seductresses, end by falling into each other's arms.

Masculinity-building is urged, a theme which the media are not slow to adapt for their own purposes. Masculinity is the alfalfa peddled in Marlboro Country. It is the essence of worn leather laced with campfire smoke that provides the aroma of the man of distinction. It also comes in powder form, none genuine without the Shaggy Dog on the wrapping.

To those who resent the fact that their pretension to masculinity is not taken seriously, one means is available for gaining respect: violence. The victim of rape is not inclined to question the virility of her assailant.

The relation between masculinity that has been put into doubt and violence reveals itself most clearly in the recent history of the Civil Rights movement. The black has derived from white America the lesson that physical force is the mark of manhood. White society is "the Man," whose insignia of power are the club, the whip, the bloodhounds. The presence of the Man impeaches the masculinity of the young black and demands that he prove himself. He becomes full grown when he resolves to fight the Man. To confront the Man, the black militant has resurrected the figure of the radical activist of the thirties, the model of Hemingway's he-man, honor-bound to risk his life in physical combat.

An article in the *New York Times Magazine* on the Black Panthers is illustrated by photographs of its two leaders. Both wear the traditional leather jackets and berets of the Left fighters of thirty years ago—these could be photographs of two Lincoln Brigade volunteers. A statement by one of the Panthers touches the philosophical essence of the romantic conception of masculinity: to be a man one must dare to die. "The ghetto black," said Bobby Seale, "isn't afraid to stand up to the cops, because he already lives with violence. He expects to die any day."

In our culture all human attributes tend to be over-defined and become a basis of self-consciousness. The behavioral sciences collaborate with the mass media in making a man anxious about his sex status; both then provide him with models of aggressiveness by which to correct his deficiencies. Yet the present uneasiness about masculinity, coupled with theatrical devices for attaining it, may be more harmful than any actual curtailment of manliness discovered by researchers and editorialists. The real damage may lie in the remedy rather than the ailment, since the desire to have one's masculinity acknowledged may lead, as we have seen, to absurd postures and acts of force. It is hard to believe that Americans would be worse off by becoming more gentle. Nor that mildness in manners and social relations would make them less manly. In the real world nothing is altogether what it is. True maleness is never without its vein of femininity. The Greeks understood this and made it the theme of their tales of sexual metamorphosis, the remarkable account of Hercules, of all men, taking on temporarily the character of a woman and wearing women's clothes. Total masculinity is an ideal of the frustrated, not a fact of biology. With the cult of masculinity put aside, maleness might have a better chance to develop in the United States.

## REFLECTING ON MEANING

1. Rosenberg notes the prominent role of the masculine "ideal" in past societies and describes the unique American version of this ideal. This masculine ideal, Rosenberg claims, has "lost its locale and, perhaps, its reason for being." What does he mean? According to Rosenberg, what has happened to masculinity in America? To what extent does the masculine ideal still play a significant role? To whom is it important?

2. What does Rosenberg mean when he describes masculinity as "a myth that has turned into a comedy" and as "a joke that everyone sees through"? Is he suggesting that the "real men" of the past have become the "wimps" of today? Or that real men never existed? Or that the masculine ideal is a fantasy? What exactly, in Rosenberg's view, has changed? How do you know? Why is masculinity a joke? What is comic about it?

3. The solution to the problem of masculine identity, as Rosenberg sees it, is contained in the statement, "Total masculinity is an ideal of the frustrated, not a fact of biology." What does he mean? Why does he urge that "the cult of masculinity be put aside"? What is the difference between masculinity and maleness? Why does Rosenberg prefer maleness to masculinity? Do you agree with his solution? Why or why not?

## EXPLORING RHETORICAL STRATEGIES

1. What is the extended metaphor that Rosenberg uses to depict the current state of masculinity in America? How many instances of this metaphor can you identify in his essay? In what ways does this metaphor help Rosenberg convey his point? How does it help unify the essay?

2. How is the title of the essay significant? Did you grasp its significance before reading the essay? What did it lead you to expect in the ensuing discussion? What does the word *style* suggest to you? What about the word *cult?* How do these words transform the word *masculinity* in the title?

3. This essay originally appeared in *Vogue* in 1967. Knowing what you do of the sixties and of *Vogue,* can you speculate on the characteristics of Rosenberg's audience? How would you describe it? How is this discussion of masculinity appropriate for its audience?

# Friendships Among Men

## MARC FEIGEN FASTEAU

*Are friendships among men stronger than those among women? Do male and female friendships differ in significant ways? In this selection Marc Feigen Fasteau explores such questions by examining the conclusions of empirical studies, the portraits of male friendships in popular fiction, and his own personal interactions with other men. His answers to these questions may surprise you.*

There is a long-standing myth in our society that the great friendships are between men. Forged through shared experience, male friendship is portrayed as the most unselfish, if not the highest form, of human relationship. The more traditionally masculine the shared experience from which it springs, the stronger and more profound the friendship is supposed to be. Going to war, weathering crises together at school or work, playing on the same athletic team, are some of the classic experiences out of which friendships between men are believed to grow.

By and large, men do prefer the company of other men, not only in their structured time but in the time they fill with optional, nonobligatory activity. They prefer to play games, drink, and talk, as well as work and fight together. Yet something is missing. Despite the time men spend together, their contact rarely goes beyond the external, a limitation which tends to make their friendships shallow and unsatisfying.

My own childhood memories are of doing things with my friends—playing games or sports, building walkie-talkies, going camping. Other people and my relationships to them were never legitimate subjects for attention. If someone liked me, it was an opaque, mysterious occurrence that bore no analysis. When I was slighted, I felt hurt. But relationships with people just happened. I certainly had feelings about my friends, but I can't remember a single instance of trying consciously to sort them out until I was well into college.

For most men this kind of shying away from the personal continues into adult life. In conversations with each other, we hardly ever use ourselves as reference points. We talk about almost everything except how we ourselves are affected by people and events. Everything is discussed as though it were taking place out there somewhere, as though we had no more felt response to it than to the weather. Topics that can be treated in this detached, objective way become conversational mainstays. The few subjects which are fundamentally personal are shaped into discussions of abstract general questions. Even in an exchange about their reactions to liberated women—a topic of intensely personal interest—the tendency will be to talk in general, theoretical terms. Work, at least its objective aspects, is always a safe subject. Men also spend an incredible amount of time rehashing the great public issues of the day. Until early 1973, Vietnam was the workhorse topic. Then came Watergate. It doesn't seem to matter that we've all had a hundred similar conversations. We plunge in for another round, trying to come up with a new angle as much to impress the others with what we know as to keep from being bored stiff.

Games play a central role in situations organized by men. I remember a weekend some years ago at the country house of a law-school classmate as a blur of softball, football, croquet, poker, and a dice-and-board game called Combat, with swimming thrown in on the side. As soon as one game ended, another began. Taken one at a time, these "activities" were fun, but the impression was inescapable that the host, and most of his guests, would do anything to stave off a lull in which they would be together without some impersonal focus for their attention. A snapshot of almost any men's club would show the same thing, ninety percent of the men engaged in some activity—ranging from backgammon to watching the tube—other than, or at least as an aid to, conversation.[1]

My composite memory of evenings spent with a friend at college and later when we shared an apartment in Washington is of conversations punctuated by silences during which we would internally pass over any personal or emotional thoughts which had arisen and come back to the permitted track. When I couldn't get my mind off personal matters, I said very little. Talks with my father have always had the same tone. Respect for privacy was the rationale for our diffidence. His questions to me about how things were going at school or at work were asked as discreetly as he would have asked a friend about someone's commitment to a hospital for the criminally insane. Our conversations, when they touched these matters at all, to say nothing of more sensitive matters, would veer quickly back to safe topics of general interest.

In our popular literature, the archetypal male hero embodying this personal muteness is the cowboy. The classic mold for the character was set in 1902 by Owen Wister's novel *The Virginian* where the author spelled out, with an explicitness that was never again necessary, the characteristics of his protagonist. Here's how it goes when two close friends the Virginian hasn't seen in some time take him out for a drink:

> All of them had seen rough days together, and they felt guilty with emotion.
>
> "It's hot weather," said Wiggin.
>
> "Hotter in Box Elder," said McLean. "My kid has started teething."
>
> Words ran dry again. They shifted their positions, looked in their glasses, read the labels on the bottles. They dropped a word now and then to the proprietor about his trade, and his ornaments.[2]

One of the Virginian's duties is to assist at the hanging of an old friend as a horse thief. Afterward, for the first time in the book, he is visibly upset. The narrator puts his arm around the hero's shoulders and describes the Virginian's reaction:

> I had the sense to keep silent, and presently he shook my hand, not looking at me as he did so. He was always very shy of demonstration.[3]

And, for explanation of such reticence, "As all men know, he also knew that many things should be done in this world in silence, and that talking about them is a mistake."[4]

There are exceptions, but they only prove the rule.

One is the drunken confidence: "Bob, ole boy, I gotta tell ya—being divorced isn't so hot. . . . [and see, I'm too drunk to be held responsible for blurting it out]." Here, drink becomes an excuse for exchanging confidences and a device for periodically loosening the restraint against expressing a need for sympathy and support from other men—which may explain its importance as a male ritual.[5] Marijuana fills a similar need.

Another exception is talking to a stranger—who may be either someone the speaker doesn't know or someone who isn't in the same social or business world. (Several black friends told me that they have been on the receiving end of personal confidences from white acquaintances that they were sure had not been shared with white friends.) In either case, men are willing to talk about themselves only to other men with whom they do not have to compete or whom they will not have to confront socially later.

Finally, there is the way men depend on women to facilitate certain conversations. The women in a mixed group are usually the ones who make the first personal reference, about themselves or others present. The men can then join in without having the onus for initiating a discussion of "personalities." Collectively, the men can "blame" the conversation on the women. They can also feel in these conversations that since they are talking "to" the women instead of "to" the men, they can be excused for deviating from the masculine norm. When the women leave, the tone and subject invariably shift away from the personal.

The effect of these constraints is to make it extraordinarily difficult for men to really get to know each other. A psychotherapist who has conducted a lengthy series of encounter groups for men summed it up:

> With saddening regularity [the members of these groups] described how much they wanted to have closer, more satisfying relationships with other men: "I'd settle for having one really close man friend. I supposedly have some close men friends now. We play golf or go for a drink. We complain about our jobs and our wives. I care about them and they care about me. We even have some physical contact—I mean we may even give a hug on a big occasion. But it's not enough."[6]

The sources of this stifling ban on self-disclosure, the reasons why men hide from each other, lie in the taboos and imperatives of the masculine stereotype.

To begin with, men are supposed to be functional, to spend their time working or otherwise solving or thinking about how to solve problems. Personal reaction, how one feels about something, is considered dysfunctional, at best an irrelevant distraction from the expected objectivity. Only weak men, and women, talk about—i.e., "give in," to their feelings. "I group my friends in two ways," said a business executive:

> those who have made it and don't complain and those who haven't made it. And only the latter spend time talking to their wives about their problems and how bad their boss is and all

> that. The ones who concentrate more on communicating . . . are those who have realized that they aren't going to make it and therefore they have changed the focus of attention.[7]

In a world which tells men they have to choose between expressiveness and manly strength, this characterization may be accurate. Most of the men who talk personally to other men *are* those whose problems have gotten the best of them, who simply can't help it. Men not driven to despair don't talk about themselves, so the idea that self-disclosure and expressiveness are associated with problems and weakness becomes a self-fulfilling prophecy.

Obsessive competitiveness also limits the range of communication in male friendships. Competition is the principal mode by which men relate to each other—at one level because they don't know how else to make contact, but more basically because it is the way to demonstrate, to themselves and others, the key masculine qualities of unwavering toughness and the ability to dominate and control. The result is that they inject competition into situations which don't call for it.

In conversations, you must show that you know more about the subject than the other man, or at least as much as he does. For example, I have often engaged in a contest that could be called My Theory Tops Yours, disguised as a serious exchange of ideas. The proof that it wasn't serious was that I was willing to participate even when I was sure that the participants, including myself, had nothing fresh to say. Convincing the other person—victory—is the main objective, with control of the floor an important tactic. Men tend to lecture at each other, insist that the discussion follow their train of thought, and are often unwilling to listen.[8] As one member of a men's rap group said,

> When I was talking I used to feel that I had to be driving to a point, that it had to be rational and organized, that I had to persuade at all times, rather than exchange thoughts and ideas.[9]

Even in casual conversation some men hold back unless they are absolutely sure of what they are saying. They don't want to have to change a position once they have taken it. It's "just like a woman" to change your mind, and, more important, it is inconsistent with the approved masculine posture of total independence.

Competition was at the heart of one of my closest friendships, now defunct. There was a good deal of mutual liking and respect. We went out of our way to spend time with each other and wanted to work together. We both had "prospects" as "bright young men" and the same "liberal but tough" point of view. We recognized this about each other, and this recognition was the basis of our respect and of our sense of equality. That we saw each other as equals was important—our friendship was confirmed by the reflection of one in the other. But our constant and all-encompassing competition made this equality precarious and fragile. One way or another, everything counted in the measuring process. We fought out our tennis matches as though our lives depended on it. At poker, the two of us would often play on for hours after the others had left. These *mano a mano* poker marathons seem in retrospect especially revealing of the competitiveness of the relationship: playing for small stakes, the essence of the game is in outwitting, psychologically beating down the other player—the other skills involved are negligible. Winning is the only pleasure, one that evaporates quickly, a truth that struck me in inchoate form every time our game broke up at four A.M. and I walked out the door with my five-dollar winnings, a headache, and a sense of time wasted. Still, I did the same thing the next time. It was what we did together, and somehow it counted. Losing at tennis could be balanced by winning at poker; at another level, his moving up in the federal government by my getting on the *Harvard Law Review.*

This competitiveness feeds the most basic obstacle to openness between men, the inability to admit to being vulnerable. Real men, we learn early, are not supposed to have doubts, hopes and ambitions which may not be realized, things they don't (or even especially do) like about themselves, fears and disappointments. Such feelings and concerns, of course, are part of everyone's inner life, but a man must keep quiet about them. If others know how you really feel you can be hurt, and that in itself is incompatible with manhood. The inhibiting effect of this imperative is not limited to disclosures of major personal problems. Often men do not share even ordinary uncertainties and half-formulated plans of daily life with their friends. And when they do, they are careful to suggest that they already know how to proceed—that they are not really asking for help or understanding but simply for particular bits of information. Either way, any doubts they have are presented as external, carefully characterized as having to do with the issue as distinct from the speaker. They are especially guarded about expressing concern or asking a question that would invite personal comment. It is almost impossible for men to simply exchange thoughts about matters involving them personally in a comfortable, non-crisis atmosphere. If a friend tells you of his concern that he and a colleague are always disagreeing, for example, he is likely to quickly supply his own explanation—something like "different professional backgrounds." The effect is to rule out observations or suggestions that do not fit within this already reconnoitered protective structure. You don't suggest, even if you believe it is true, that in fact the disagreements arise because he presents his ideas in a way which tends to provoke a hostile reaction. It would catch him off guard; it would be something he hadn't already thought of and accepted about himself and, for that reason, no matter how constructive and well-intentioned you might be, it would put you in control for the moment. He doesn't want that; he is afraid of losing your respect. So, sensing he feels that way, because you would yourself, you say something else. There is no real give-and-take.

It is hard for men to get angry at each other honestly. Anger between friends often means that one has hurt the other. Since the straightforward expression of anger in these situations involves an admission of vulnerability, it is safer to stew silently or find an "objective" excuse for retaliation. Either way, trust is not fully restored.

Men even try not to let it show when they feel good. We may report the reasons for our happiness, if they have to do with concrete accomplishments, but we try to do it with a straight face, as if to say, "Here's what happened, but it hasn't affected my grown-up unemotional equilibrium, and I am not asking for any kind of response." Happiness is a precarious, "childish" feeling, easy to shoot down. Others may find the event that triggers it trivial or incomprehensible, or even threatening to their own self-esteem—in the sense that if one man is up, another man is down. So we tend not to take the risk of expressing it.

What is particularly difficult for men is seeking or accepting help from friends. I, for one, learned early that dependence was unacceptable. When I was eight, I went to a summer camp I disliked. My parents visited me in the middle of the summer and, when it was time for them to leave, I wanted to go with them. They refused, and I yelled and screamed and was miserably unhappy for the rest of the day. That evening an older camper comforted me, sitting by my bed as I cried, patting me on the back soothingly and saying whatever it is that one says at times like that. He was in some way clumsy or funny-looking, and a few days later I joined a group of kids in cruelly making fun of him, an act which upset me, when I thought about it, for years. I can only explain it in terms of my feeling, as early as the age of eight, that by needing and accepting his help and comfort I had compromised myself, and took it out on him.

"You can't express dependence when you feel it," a corporate executive said, "because it's a kind of absolute. If you are loyal 90% of the time and disloyal 10%, would you be considered loyal? Well, the same happens with independence: you are either dependent or independent; you can't be both."[10] "Feelings of dependence," another explained, "are identified with weakness or 'untoughness' and our culture doesn't accept those things in men."[11] The result is that we either go it alone or "act out certain games or rituals to provoke the desired reaction in the other and have our needs satisfied without having to ask for anything."[12]

Somewhat less obviously, the expression of affection also runs into emotional barriers growing out of the masculine stereotype. When I was in college, I was suddenly quite moved while attending a friend's wedding. The surge of feeling made me uncomfortable and self-conscious. There was nothing inherently difficult or, apart from the fact of being moved by a moment of tenderness, "unmasculine" about my reaction. I just did not know how to deal with or communicate what I felt. "I consider myself a sentimentalist," one man said, "and I think I am quite able to express my feelings. But the other day my wife described a friend of mine to some people as my best friend and I felt embarrassed when I heard her say it."[13]

A major source of these inhibitions is the fear of being, or being thought, homosexual. Nothing is more frightening to a heterosexual man in our society. It threatens, at one stroke, to take away every vestige of his claim to a masculine identity—something like knocking out the foundations of a building—and to expose him to the ostracism, ranging from polite tolerance to violent revulsion, of his friends and colleagues. A man can be labeled as homosexual not just because of overt sexual acts but because of almost any sign of behavior which does not fit the masculine stereotype. The touching of another man, other than shaking hands or, under emotional stress, an arm around the shoulder, is taboo. Women may kiss each other when they meet; men are uncomfortable when hugged even by close friends.[14] Onlookers might misinterpret what they saw, and, more important, what would we think of ourselves if we felt a twinge of sensual pleasure from the embrace.

Direct verbal expressions of affection or tenderness are also something that only homosexuals and women engage in. Between "real" men affection has to be disguised in gruff, "you old son-of-a-bitch" style. Paradoxically, in some instances, terms of endearment between men can be used as a ritual badge of manhood, dangerous medicine safe only for the strong. The flirting with homosexuality that characterizes the initiation rites of many fraternities and men's clubs serves this purpose. Claude Brown wrote about black life in New York City in the 1950s:

> The term ["baby"] had a hip ring to it. . . . It was like saying, "Man, look at me. I've got masculinity to spare. . . . I can say 'baby' to another cat and he can say 'baby' to me, and we can say it with strength in our voices." If you could say it, this meant that you really had to be sure of yourself, sure of your masculinity.[15]

Fear of homosexuality does more than inhibit the physical display of affection. One of the major recurring themes in the men's groups led by psychotherapist Don Clark was:

> A large segment of my feelings about other men are unknown or distorted because I am afraid they might have something to do with homosexuality. Now I'm lonely for other men and don't know how to find what I want with them.

As Clark observes, "The spectre of homosexuality seems to be the dragon at the gateway to self-awareness, understanding, and acceptance of male-male needs. If a man tries to pretend the dragon is not there by turning a blind eye to erotic feelings for all other males, he also blinds himself to the rich variety of feelings that are related."[16]

The few situations in which men do acknowledge strong feelings of affection and dependence toward other men are exceptions which prove the rule. With "cop couples," for example, or combat soldier "buddies," intimacy and dependence are forced on the men by their work—they have to ride in the patrol car or be in the same foxhole with somebody—and the jobs themselves have such highly masculine images that the men can get away with behavior that would be suspect under any other conditions.

Furthermore, even these combat-buddy relations, when looked at closely, turn out not to be particularly intimate or personal. Margaret Mead has written:

> During the last war English observers were confused by the apparent contradiction between American soldiers' emphasis on the buddy, so grievously exemplified in the break-downs that followed a buddy's death, and the results of detailed inquiry which showed how transitory these buddy relationships were. It was found that men actually accepted their buddies as derivatives from their outfit, and from accidents of asso-

ciation, rather than because of any special personality characteristics capable of ripening into friendship.[17]

One effect of the fear of appearing to be homosexual is to reinforce the practice that two men rarely get together alone without a reason. I once called a friend to suggest that we have dinner together. "O.K.," he said. "What's up?" I felt uncomfortable telling him that I just wanted to talk, that there was no other reason for the invitation.

Men get together to conduct business, to drink, to play games and sports, to re-establish contact after long absences, to participate in heterosexual social occasions—circumstances in which neither person is responsible for actually wanting to see the other. Men are particularly comfortable seeing each other in groups. The group situation defuses any possible assumptions about the intensity of feeling between particular men and provides the safety of numbers—"All the guys are here." It makes personal communication, which requires a level of trust and mutual understanding not generally shared by all members of a group, more difficult and offers an excuse for avoiding this dangerous territory. And it provides what is most sought after in men's friendships: mutual reassurance of masculinity.

Needless to say, the observations in this chapter did not spring full-blown from my head. The process started when I began to understand that, at least with Brenda, a more open, less self-protective relationship was possible.

## NOTES

1. Women may use games as a reason for getting together—bridge clubs, for example. But the show is more for the rest of the world—to indicate that they are doing *something*—and the games themselves are not the only means of communication.
2. Owen Wister, *The Virginian* ([Macmillan: 1902] Grosset & Dunlap ed.: 1929), pp. 397–98.
3. Ibid., p. 343.
4. Ibid., p. 373.
5. Lionel Tiger, *Men in Groups* (Random House: 1969), p. 185.
6. Don Clark, "Homosexual Encounter in All-Male Groups," in L. Solomon and B. Berzon (eds.), *New Perspectives on Encounter Groups* (Jossey-Bass: 1972), pp. 376–77. See also Alan Booth, "Sex and Social Participation," *American Sociological Review*, Vol. 37 (April 1972), p. 183, an empirical study showing that, contrary to Lionel Tiger's much publicized assertion *(Men in Groups)*, women form stronger and closer friendship bonds with each other than men do.

7. Fernando Bartolomé, "Executives as Human Beings," *Harvard Business Review,* Vol. 50 (November–December 1972), p. 64.
8. The contrast with women on this point is striking. Casual observation will confirm that women's conversations move more quickly, with fewer long speeches and more frequent changes of speaker.
9. *Boston Globe,* March 12, 1972, p. B-1.
10. Bartolomé, op. cit., p. 65.
11. Ibid., p. 64.
12. Ibid., p. 66.
13. Ibid., p. 64.
14. Ibid., p. 65.
15. Claude Brown, *Manchild in the Promised Land* ([Macmillan: 1965] Signet ed.: 1965), p. 171.
16. Clark, op. cit., p. 378.
17. Margaret Mead, *Male and Female* ([William Morrow: 1949] Mentor ed.: 1949), p. 214.

## REFLECTING ON MEANING

1. Fasteau's essay opens with the statement, "There is a long-standing myth in our society that the great friendships are between men." Do you agree or disagree that this is the prevailing social view? Does this view reflect reality, or is it an unexamined assumption? Why might friendships among men be considered stronger than friendships among women? According to Fasteau, what is the foundation of male friendship? Why have women been excluded from the "great friendship" myth?
2. What additional dimension of male friendship does the Virginian's behavior illustrate? What statement sums up the Virginian's philosophy on interacting with other men? Do you think that most men subscribe to this code of conduct? What examples can you give to support this view? Are there any situations in which men might not behave according to this code? What allows them to disregard it in certain situations?
3. Fasteau says that men's interactions with men are restricted by "taboos and imperatives of the masculine stereotype." Do you agree that this stereotype influences their behavior? What does this stereotype suggest that men should be and do? What does it not allow them to be or to do? Why doesn't this stereotype affect men when they interact with women? Doesn't it seem reasonable to assume that a man would be even more concerned about his masculinity when he's talking with a woman? How might this apparent contradiction be explained?

## EXPLORING RHETORICAL STRATEGIES

1. Fasteau gathers many different kinds of evidence to support his thesis. What are some examples of the evidence he uses? Do you find his synthesis of these different kinds of evidence effective? Why or why not? What are the categories into which you can sort this evidence? How are the various kinds equally or not equally valid? Do you find one kind more effective than another? Why or why not? What purpose does each kind of evidence serve?

2. This essay is a chapter from Fasteau's *The Male Machine,* a book published in 1974. What does the title of the book suggest about Fasteau's views on men's roles in society? Knowing the title and having read the chapter that appears here, what can you infer about the rest of the book? What might it be about? What would you expect Fasteau's larger thesis to be?

3. If men really are worried about being thought homosexual, as Fasteau claims, do you think Fasteau had to be careful about the persona he presents in this essay? How would the nature of his topic—friendships among men—predispose his audience to feel about his discussion and him? How might it have presented a difficult rhetorical situation for Fasteau? Does anything in the essay suggest that he was at all concerned about this situation?

# The Androgynous Male

NOEL PERRIN

*Are all men 100 percent "masculine" and all women 100 percent "feminine"? Does the masculine/feminine classification system account for the majority of people? Noel Perrin doesn't think so. In this essay, Perrin identifies yet another group of people, those who can't be squeezed into either gender category: androgynes. Androgynes, he maintains, enjoy the best of both worlds because they are freer to be themselves than either of the two gender models permits.*

The summer I was 16, I took a train from New York to Steamboat Springs, Colo., where I was going to be assistant horse wrangler at a camp. The trip took three days, and since I was much too shy to talk to strangers, I had quite a lot of time for reading. I read all of *Gone with the Wind.* I read all the interesting articles in a couple of magazines I had, and then I went back and read all the dull stuff. I also took all the quizzes, a thing of which magazines were even fuller then than now.

The one that held my undivided attention was called "How Masculine/Feminine Are You?" It consisted of a large number of inkblots. The reader was supposed to decide which of four objects each blot most resembled. The choices might be a cloud, a steam engine, a caterpillar and a sofa.

When I finished the test, I was shocked to find that I was barely masculine at all. On a scale of 1 to 10, I was about 1.2. Me, the horse wrangler? (And not just wrangler, either. That summer, I had to skin a couple of horses that died—the camp owner wanted the hides.)

The results of that test were so terrifying to me that for the first time in my life I did a piece of original analysis. Having unlimited time on the train, I looked at the "masculine" answers over and over, trying to find what it was that distinguished real men from people like me—and eventually I discovered two very simple patterns. It was "masculine" to think the blots looked like man-made objects, and "feminine" to think they looked like natural objects. It was masculine to think they looked like things capable of causing harm, and feminine to think of innocent things.

Even at 16, I had the sense to see that the compilers of the test were using rather limited criteria—maleness and femaleness are both more complicated than *that*—and I breathed a huge sigh of relief. I wasn't necessarily a wimp, after all.

That the test did reveal something other than the superficiality of its makers I realized only many years later. What it revealed was that there is a large class of men and women both, to which I belong, who are essentially androgynous. That doesn't mean we're gay, or low in the appropriate hormones, or uncomfortable performing the jobs traditionally assigned our sexes. (A few years after that summer, I was leading troops in combat and, unfashionable as it now is to admit this, having a very good time. War is exciting. What a pity the 20th century went and spoiled it with high-tech weapons.)

What it does mean to be spiritually androgynous is a kind of freedom. Men who are all-male, or he-man, or 100 percent red-blooded Americans, have a little biological set that causes them to be attracted to physical power, and probably also to dominance. Maybe even to watching football. I don't say this to criticize them. Completely masculine men are quite often wonderful people: good husbands, good (though sometimes overwhelming) fathers, good members of society. Furthermore, they are often so unselfconsciously at ease in the world that other men seek to imitate them. They just aren't as free as us androgynes. They pretty nearly have to be what they are; we have a range of choices open.

The sad part is that many of us never discover that. Men who are not 100 percent red-blooded Americans—say, those who are only 75 percent red-blooded—often fail to notice their freedom. They are too busy trying to copy the he-men ever to realize that men, like women, come in a wide variety of acceptable types. Why this frantic imitation? My answer is mere speculation, but not casual. I have speculated on this for a long time.

Partly they're just envious of the he-man's unconscious ease. Mostly they're terrified of finding that there may be something wrong with them deep down, some weakness at the heart. To avoid discovering that, they spend their lives acting out the role that the he-man naturally lives. Sad.

One thing that men owe to the women's movement is that this kind of failure is less common than it used to be. In releasing themselves from the single ideal of the dependent woman, women have more or less incidentally released a lot of men from the single ideal of the dominant male. The one mistake the feminists have made, I think, is in supposing that *all* men need this release, or that the world would be a better place if all men achieved it. It wouldn't. It would just be duller.

So far I have been pretty vague about just what the freedom of the androgynous man is. Obviously it varies with the case. In the case I know best, my own, I can be quite specific. It has freed me most as a parent. I am, among other things, a fairly good natural mother. I like the nurturing role. It makes me feel good to see a child eat—and it turns me to mush to see a 4-year-old holding a glass with both small hands, in order to drink. I even enjoyed sewing patches on the knees of my daughter Amy's Dr. Dentons when she was at the crawling stage. All that pleasure I would have lost if I had made myself stick to the notion of the paternal role that I started with.

Or take a smaller and rather ridiculous example. I feel free to kiss cats. Until recently it never occurred to me that I would want to, though my daughters have been doing it all their lives. But my elder daughter is now 22, and in London. Of course, I get to look after her cat while she is gone. He's a big, handsome farm cat named Petrushka, very unsentimental, though used from kittenhood to being kissed on the top of the head by Elizabeth. I've gotten very fond of him (he's the adventurous kind of cat who likes to climb hills with you), and one night I simply felt like kissing him on the top of the head, and did. Why did no one tell me sooner how silky cat fur is?

Then there's my relation to cars. I am completely unembarrassed by my inability to diagnose even minor problems in whatever object I happen to be driving, and don't have to make some insider's remark to mechanics to try to establish that I, too, am a "Man with His Machine."

The same ease extends to household maintenance. I do it, of course. Service people are expensive. But for the last decade my house has functioned better than it used to because I've had the aid of a volume called "Home Repairs Any Woman Can Do," which is pitched just right for people at my technical level. As a youth, I'd as soon have touched such a book as I would have become a transvestite. Even though common sense says there is really nothing sexual whatsoever about fixing sinks.

Or take public emotion. All my life I have easily been moved by certain kinds of voices. The actress Siobhan McKenna's, to take a notable case. Give her an emotional scene in a play, and within 10 words my eyes are full of tears. In boyhood, my great dread was that someone might notice. I struggled manfully, you might say, to suppress this weakness. Now, of course, I don't see it as a weakness at all, but as a kind of fulfillment. I even suspect that the true he-men feel the same way, or one kind of them does, at least, and it's only the poor imitators who have to struggle to repress themselves.

Let me come back to the inkblots, with their assumption that masculine equates with machinery and science, and feminine with art and nature. I have no idea whether the right pronoun for God is He, She or It. But this I'm pretty sure of. If God could somehow be induced to take that test, God would not come out macho, and not feminismo, either, but right in the middle. Fellow androgynes, it's a nice thought.

---

## REFLECTING ON MEANING

1. Why is Perrin able to discredit so easily the gender quiz he took? What do the criteria the quiz makers used to define masculinity and femininity tell you about the ways gender identities are often delimited? What do they tell you about the validity of tests?
2. What does it mean to be androgynous? Is the androgyny Perrin describes a biological phenomenon? What kind of freedom does he claim androgynes possess? What might an androgynous woman be like? Is androgyny an unachievable ideal, or do you know people you would consider androgynous? What makes them androgynous?
3. What does Perrin seem thankful to feminists for? What have they accomplished for women *and* men? Why does Perrin view their accomplishment for men as "incidental"? Is the goal of feminism to liberate only women or all people from gender stereotypes? Why do you think so?

## EXPLORING RHETORICAL STRATEGIES

1. Perrin uses several interesting words in his essay: *macho, feminismo, androgyne.* What do these words mean? What do they suggest? How does the word *androgyne* itself convey the ideas of masculinity and femininity?
2. What is Perrin's purpose in this essay? How do you think he wanted his audience to respond to his topic? In speculating on these questions, consider the effect of his final paragraph on the

essay as a whole and on his audience as well. How did it affect you?

3. This essay originally appeared in 1984 in a feature column of the *New York Times* called "On Men." Who do you think might read such a column? Both men and women? Why or why not? Is there any evidence within the essay itself to indicate that Perrin is speaking to both men and women? Who are his "fellow androgynes"? Women and men or men exclusively?

# Sexual Culture

## EDMUND WHITE

*In this essay, writer Edmund White challenges social assumptions about gay society. White attempts to define what it means to be gay, and he argues that sexuality alone cannot adequately define either "gays" or "straights." His observations on both gay and straight culture are thought-provoking and controversial.*

Do gay men have friends—I mean," she said, "are they friends with each other?" Since the woman asking was a New Yorker, the owner of one of the city's simplest and priciest restaurants, someone who's known gays all her life, I found the question honest, shocking, and revealing of a narrow but bottomless abyss between us.

Of course New York is a city of total, even absolute strangers rubbing shoulders: the Hasidim in their yellow school bus being conveyed back to Brooklyn from the jewelry district, beards and black hats glimpsed through mud-splattered windows in a sun-dimmed daguerreotype; the junkie pushing the baby carriage and telling his wife, the prostitute, as he points to his tattooed biceps, "I haven't partied in this vein for years"; Moonies doing calisthenics at midnight in their Eighth Avenue center high above empty Thirty-fourth Street. . . . But this alienation wasn't religious or ethnic. The woman and I spoke the same language, knew the same people; we both considered Marcella Hazan fun but no substitute for Simone Beck. How odd that she, as lower-upper-middle-class as I, shouldn't know whether gay men befriended one another.

It was then that I saw how mysterious gay culture is—not homosexuality, which is merely an erotic tropism, but modern American gay culture, which is a special way of laughing, spending money, ordering priorities, encoding everything from song lyrics to mirror-shiny military shoes. None of the usual modes for a subculture will do, for gay men are brought up by heterosexuals to be straight, they seek other men through what feels very much like a compulsion though they enter the ghetto by choice, yet once they make that choice it reshapes their lives, even their bodies, certainly their wardrobes. Many gay men live among straights as Marranos, those Spanish Jews who pretended during the Inquisition to convert to Christianity but continued to observe the old rites in cellars, when alone, in the greatest secrecy. Gays aren't *like* blacks or Jews since they often *are* black or Jewish, and their affectional preference isn't a color or a religion though it has spawned a culture not unlike an ethnic minority's. Few Jews have Christian siblings, but most gays have straight brothers and sisters or at least straight parents. Many American Jews have been raised to feel they belong to the Chosen People, at once superior and inferior to gentiles, but every gay discovers his sexual nature with a combination of pain and relief, regret at being excluded from the tribe but elation at discovering the solution to the puzzle.

Gays aren't a nationality. They aren't Chicanos or Italo-Americans or Irish-Americans, but they do constitute one of the most potent political forces in big cities such as New York, Philadelphia, Washington (where gays and blacks elected Marion Barry mayor), Houston, Los Angeles, and San Francisco (where gays are so numerous they've splintered into countless factions, including the lesbian S/M group Samois and the Sisters of Perpetual Indulgence, a group of drag nuns, one of whose members ran in a cowl and wimple as a candidate in the last citywide election). Not ethnic but a minority, not a polis but political, not a nationality but possessed of a costume, customs, and a patois, not a class but an economic force (not only as a market for records, films, vacations, and clothes but also as an army of worker ants who, for better or worse, have gentrified the center cities, thereby creating a better tomorrow for single young white heterosexual professionals).

Imagine a religion one enters against one's parents' will—and against one's own. Imagine a race one joins at sixteen or sixty without changing one's hue or hair texture (unless at the tanning or beauty salon). Imagine a sterile nation without descendants but with a long, misty regress of ancestors, without an articulated self-definition but with a venerable history. Imagine an exclusive club that includes a P.R. (Puerto Rican) boy of sixteen wearing ankle-high black-and-white Converse basketball shoes and a petrol green shirt sawed off to reveal a Praxitelean stomach—and also includes a P.R. (Public Relations) WASP executive of forty in his Prince of Wales plaids and Cole-Haan tasseled loafers.

If one is gay, one is always in a crucial relationship to gayness as such, a defining category that is so full it is nearly empty (Renaud Camus writes: "Homosexuality is always elsewhere because it is everywhere"). No straight man stands in rapt contemplation of his straightness unless he's an ass. To be sure, heterosexuals may wonder over the significance of their homosexual fantasies, though even that morbid exercise is less popular now than formerly; as Barbara Ehrenreich acutely observes in her new study of the heterosexual male revolt, *The Hearts of Men,* the emergence of gay liberation ended the period in which everyone suspected everyone else of being "latently" homosexual. Now there are open homosexuals, and heterosexual men are exempt from the automatic suspicion of deviance.

No homosexual can take his homosexuality for granted. He must sound it, palpate it, auscultate it as though it were the dead limb of a tree or the living but tricky limb of a body; for that reason all homosexuals are "gay philosophers" in that they must invent themselves. At a certain point one undergoes a violent conversion into a new state, the unknown, which one then sets about knowing as one will. Surely everyone experiences his or her life as an artifact, as molten glass being twirled and pinched into a shape to cool, or as a novel at once capacious and suspenseful, but no one is more a *Homo faber* (in the sense of both "fabricator" and "fabulist") than a homo. It would be vain, of course, to suggest that this creativity is praiseworthy, an ambition rather than a response.

Sometimes I try to imagine how straights—not fundamentalist know-nothings, not rural innocents, not Freudian bigots, but educated urban heterosexuals—look at gay men (do they even see lesbians?). When they see gay men, what do they see? A mustache, a pumped-up body in black jeans and a tank top, an eye-catching tattoo (braided rope around the biceps)? And what do they think ("they," in this case, *hypocrite lecteur,* being *you*)? Do you see something at once ludicrous and mildly enviable in the still youthful but overexercised body of this forty-year-old clone with the aggressive stare and soft voice? If you're a woman, do you find so much preening over appearance in a grown man . . . well, if not offensive, at least unappetizing; energy better spent on a career, on a family—on you? If you're a man, does it incense you that this jerk is out of harness, too loose, too free, has so lightly made a mockery of manhood? Once, on a radio call-in show a cop called in to tell me he had to admire the old-style queens back when it was rough being queer but that now, jeez, these guys swapping spit wit' a goil one week, wit' a guy the next, they're too lazy, they just don't know the fine art of being a man, it's all just too easy.

Your sentiments, perhaps?

Do you see gays as menacing satyrs, sex fiends around whom it's dangerous to drop your soap, *and* as feeble sissies, frail wood nymphs locked within massive trunks and limbs? Or, more positively if just as narrowly, are you a sybaritic het who greets the sight of gays with cries of glee, convinced you've stumbled on liberty hall, where sexual license of every sort—including your sort—is bound to reign? In fact, such sybarites often do regard gay men as comrades in arms, fellow libertines, and fellow victims in a country phobic to pleasure.

Or do gays just irk you? Do you regard them as a tinselly distraction in your peripheral vision? As errant, obstinate atoms that can't be drawn into any of the usual social molecules, men who if they insist on their gayness won't really do at any of the solemnities, from dinner parties to debutante balls, all of which depend on strict gender dimorphism for a rational seating plan? Since any proper gathering requires the threat of adultery for excitement and the prospect of marriage as a justification, of what earthly use are gays? Even the few fearless straight guys who've invaded my gay gym drift toward one another, not out of soap-dropping panic but because otherwise their dirty jokes fall on deaf or prettily blushing ears and their taunting, butt-slapping mix of rivalry and camaraderie provokes a weird hostility or a still weirder thrill.

And how do gays look at straights? In Andrew Holleran's superb new novel, *Nights in Aruba,* the narrator wonders "what it would be like to be the head of a family, as if with that all my problems would drop away, when in fact they would have merely been replaced by another set. I would not have worried about the size of my penis, the restrictions of age, the difficulty of finding love; I would have worried about mortgages, tuition, my youngest daughter's asthma, my competition at Shearson Loeb Rhoades." What makes this speculation so characteristically gay is that it is so focused on the family man, for if the nineteenth-century tart required, even invented the convent-bred virgin to contemplate, in the same way the homosexual man today must insult and revere, mock and envy this purely imaginary bourgeois paterfamilias, a creature extinct except in gay fantasies. Meanwhile, of course, the family man devotes his time to scream therapy and tai chi, ticking off Personals in the *Village Voice* and wriggling out of visits from his kids, two punked-out teens who live in a feminist compound with his divorced wife, now a lesbian potter of great sensitivity and verve if low energy.

So much for how the two sexes (straight and gay) regard each other. If the camera were to pull back and frame both worlds in the lens, how would the two systems compare?

The most obvious difference is that whereas heterosexuality does include two sexes, since homosexuality does not it must improvise a new polarity moment by moment. Such a polarity seems necessary to sexual desire, at least as it is constructed in our culture. No wonder that some gay men search out the most extreme opposites (someone of a distant race, a remote language, another class or age); no wonder that even that convinced heterosexual Flaubert was finally able to unbend with a boy prostitute in Egypt, an exotic who provided him with all the difference desire might demand. Other gay men seek out their twins—so that the beloved, I suppose, can stand in for oneself as one bows down to this false god and plays in turn his father, teacher, son, godfather, or god. Still others institutionalize the polarity in that next-best thing to heterosexuality: sadomasochism, the only vice that anthologizes all family and romantic relationships.

Because every gay man loves men, he comes to learn at first hand how to soothe the savage breast of the male ego. No matter how passive or girlish or shy the new beau might be in the boudoir, he will become the autocrat of the dinner table. Women's magazines are always planning articles on gay men and straight women; I'd say what they have most in common, aside from a few shared sexual techniques, is a body of folk wisdom about that hardhead, that bully, that maddeningly self-involved creature, the human male. As studies have surprisingly shown, men talk more than women, interrupt them more often, and determine the topics of conversation and object to women's assertions with more authority and frequency. When two gay men get together, especially after the first romantic urge to oblige the other wanes, a struggle for conversational dominance ensues, a conflict only symptomatic of larger arguments over every issue from where to live to how and whom to entertain.

To be sure, in this way the gay couple resembles the straight duo that includes an assertive, liberated woman. But while most of the young straight liberated women I know, at least, may protect their real long-range interests (career, mode of life, emotional needs) with vigilance, they're still willing to accommodate *him* in little social ways essential to harmony.

One benign side of straight life is that women conceive of men as "characters," as full-bodied, multifaceted beings who are first social, second familial, third amorous or amicable, and only finally physical. I'm trying politely to say that women are lousy judges of male beauty; they're easily taken in by such superficial traits as loyalty, dependability, charm, a sense of humor. Women don't, or at least didn't, judge men as so much beefcake. But men, both straight and gay, start with looks, the most obvious currency of value, worth, price. Let's say that women see men as characters in a long family novel in which the men are introduced complete with phrenology, genealogy, and one annoying and two endearing traits, whereas men see their partners (whether male or female) as cars, makes to be instantly spotted, appraised, envied, made. A woman wants to be envied for her husband's goodness, his character, whereas a man wants to be envied for his wife's beauty, rarity, status—her drivability. Straight life combines the warmth and *Gemütlichkeit* of the nineteenth-century bourgeois (the woman) with the steely corporate ethos of the twentieth-century functionary (the man). If gay male life, freed of this dialectic, has become supremely efficient (the trapdoor beside the bed) and only momentarily intimate (a whole life cycle compressed into the one-night stand), then the gain is dubious, albeit an extreme expression of one trend in our cultural economy.

But of course most morality, that is, popular morality—not real morals, which are unaffected by consensus, but mores, which are a form of fashion—is nothing but a species of nostalgia, a cover-up for pleasurable and profitable but not yet admissible innovations. If so many people condemn promiscuity, they do so at least partly because there is no available rhetoric that could condone, much less glamorize, impermanence in love. Nevertheless, it strikes me that homosexuals, masters of improvisation fully at home with the arbitrary and equipped with an internal compass that orients them instantly to any social novelty, are perhaps the most sensitive indicators of the future.

The birthrate declines, the divorce rate climbs, and popular culture (movies, television, song lyrics, advertising, fashions, journalism) is so completely and irrevocably secularized that the so-called religious revival is of no more lasting importance than the fad for Kabuki in a transistorized Japan—a temporary throwback, a slight brake on the wheel. In such a world the rate of change is so rapid that children, once they are in school, can learn little from their parents but must assimilate new forms of behavior from their peers and new information from specialized instructors. As a result, parental authority declines, and the demarcations between the generations become ever more formidable. Nor do the parents regret their loss of control, since they're devoting all their energy to cultivating the inner self in the wholesale transition of our society from an ethic of self-sacrifice to one of self-indulgence, the so-called aristocraticization of middle-class life that has dominated the peaceful parts of this century in the industrialized West.

In the contemporary world the nineteenth-century experiment of companionate marriage, never very workable, has collapsed utterly. The exact nature of the collapse isn't very clear yet because of our distracting, probably irrelevant habit of psychologizing every crisis (thus the endless speculations in the lowbrow press on the Irresponsible Male and the Defeminized Female or the paradoxical and cruelly impracticable advice to women readers to "go for it all—family, career, marriage, romance, *and* the reveries of solitude"). We treat the failure of marriage as though it were the failure of individuals to achieve it—a decline in grit or maturity or commitment or stamina rather than the unraveling of a poorly tied knot. Bourgeois marriage was meant to concentrate friendship, romance, and sex into an institution at once familial and economic. Only the most intense surveillance could keep such a bulky, ill-assorted load from bursting at the seams. Once the hedonism of the '60s relaxed that tension, people began to admit that friendship tranquilizes sexual desires (when mates become siblings, the incest taboo sets in) and that romance is by its very nature evanescent though indefinitely renewable given an endless supply of fresh partners. Neither sexual nor romantic attraction, so capricious, so passionate, so unstable, could ever serve as the basis for an enduring relationship, which can be balanced only on the plinth of esteem, that easy, undramatic, intimate kind of love one would say resembled family love if families were more loving.

It is this love that so many gay couples know about, aim for, and sometimes even express. If all goes well, two gay men will meet through sex, become lovers, weather the storms of jealousy and the diminution of lust, develop shared interests (a hobby, a business, a house, a circle), and end up with a long-term, probably sexless camaraderie that is not as disinterested as friendship or as seismic as passion or as charged with contradiction as fraternity. Younger gay couples feel that this sort of relationship, when it happens to them, is incomplete, a compromise, and they break up in order to find total fulfillment (i.e., tireless passion) elsewhere. But older gay couples stay together, cultivate their mild, reasonable love, and defend it against the ever-present danger of the sexual allure exercised by a newcomer. For the weak point of such marriages is the eternally recurring fantasy, first in one partner and then the other, of "total fulfillment." Needless to say, such couples can wreak havoc on the newcomer who fails to grasp that Bob and Fred are not just roommates. They may have separate bedrooms and regular extracurricular sex partners or even beaux, but Bob monitors Fred's infatuations with an eye attuned to nuance, and at a certain point will intervene to banish a potential rival.

I think most straight people would find these arrangements more scandalous than the infamous sexual high jinks of gays. Because these arrangements have no name, no mythology, no public or private acknowledgment, they're almost invisible even to the participants. Thus if you asked Bob in a survey what he wanted, he might say he wanted a "real" lover. He might also say Fred was "just a roommate, my best friend, we used to be lovers." So much for explicit analysis, but over the years Bob has cannily steered his affair with Fred between the Scylla of excessive fidelity (which is finally so dull no two imaginative gay men could endure it) and the Charybdis of excessive tolerance (which could leave both men feeling so neglected they'd seek love elsewhere for sure).

There are, of course, countless variants to this pattern. The men live together or they don't. If they don't, they can maintain the civilized fiction of romance for years. They plan dates, honeymoons, take turns sleeping over at each other's house, and avoid conflicts about domestic details. They keep their extracurricular sex lives separate, they agree not to snoop—or they have three-ways. Or one of the pair has an active sex life and the other has abandoned the erotic arena.

Are gay men friends with each other? the woman asked me.

The question may assume that gays are only sexual, and that a man eternally on the prowl can never pause for mere affection—that a gay Don Juan is lonely. Or perhaps the question reveals a confusion about a society of one gender. Since a straight woman has other women for friends and men for lovers, my questioner might have wondered how the same sex could serve in both capacities.

The first supposition—that gay men are only sexual—is an ancient prejudice, and like all prejudices mostly untrue but in one sense occasionally accurate. If politically conscious homosexuals prefer the word *gay* to *homosexual,* they do so because they want to make the world regard attraction to members of the same gender as an affectional preference as well as a sexual orientation.

For instance, there are some gay men who prefer the feel of women's bodies to men's, who are even more comfortable sexually with women, but whose emotions crave contact with other men. Gay men have unfinished emotional business with other men—scary, promising, troubling, absorbing business—whereas their sentiments toward women (at least women not in their family) are much simpler, more stable, less fraught. Affection, passionate affection, is never simple; it is built out of equal parts of yearning, fear, and appetite. For that reason the friendship of one gay man fiercely drawn to another is as tense as any heterosexual passion, whereas a sexless, more disinterested gay friendship is as relaxed, as good-tempered as a friendship, say, between two straight men.

Gay men, then, do divide other gays into two camps—those who are potential partners (lovers) and those who are not (friends). But where gay life is more ambiguous than the world at large (and possibly for that reason more baffling to outsiders) is that the members of the two camps, lovers and friends, are always switching places or hovering somewhere in the margin between. It is these unconfessed feelings that have always intrigued me the most as a novelist—the unspoken love between two gay men, say, who pretend they are just friends, cruising buddies, merely filling in until Mr. Right comes along (mercifully, he never does).

In one sense, the public's prejudice about a gay obsession with sex is valid. The right to have sex, even to look for it, has been so stringently denied to gays for so many centuries that the drive toward sexual freedom remains a bright, throbbing banner in the fierce winds whipping over the ghetto. Laws against sex have always created the biggest problems for homosexuals; they helped to define the very category of homosexuality. For that reason, the gay community, despite its invention of a culture no more eroticized than any other, still cannot give up its origin in sexual desire and its suppression.

But what about the "excessive" promiscuity of gay men, the infamous quickies, a phenomenon only temporarily held in check by the AIDS crisis? Don't the quickies prove that gay men are essentially bizarre, fundamentally lacking in judgment—*oversexed?* Of course, gay men behave as all men would were they free of the strictures of female tastes, needs, prohibitions, and expectations. There is nothing in gay male life that cannot be attributed either to its minority status or to its all-male population. All men want quick, uncomplicated sexual adventure (as well as sustained romantic passion); in a world of all men, that desire is granted.

The very universality of sexual opportunity within the modern gay ghetto has, paradoxically, increased the importance of friendship. In a society not based on the measured denial or canalization of sexual desire, there is more energy left over for friendship. Relationships are less loaded in gay life (hence the celebrated gay irony, a levity equivalent to seeing through conventions). In so many ways gays are still prisoners of the dominant society, but in this one regard gays are freer than their jailers: because gay relationships are not disciplined by religious, legal, economic, and political ceremonies but only by the dictates of conscience and the impulses of the heart, they don't stand for anything larger. They aren't symbols but realities, not laws but entities sufficient unto themselves, not consequential but ecstatic.

---

## REFLECTING ON MEANING

1. The question "Are gay men friends with each other?" illuminates a certain assumption about the accepted definition of gayness. What is this assumption? How does society define gayness? Why does White make a distinction between *gay* and *homosexual?* What is gay culture? By implication, what is White suggesting about the labels *straight* and *heterosexual?* About straight culture? Do you agree that culture, rather than sexuality, provides a firmer foundation for defining both gays and straights? Why or why not?
2. White argues that the most obvious difference between homosexual and heterosexual relationships is that homosexuals "must improvise a new polarity moment by moment." How do gays achieve "polarity" in their relationships? What polarity is inherent in straight relationships? According to White, why is polarity an essential component of all sexual relationships? Do you agree that "polarity seems necessary to sexual desire"? Why or why not?
3. Consider White's observation on the similarities between gay men and straight women: "I'd say what they have most in common, aside from a few shared sexual techniques, is a body of folk wisdom about that hardhead, that bully, that maddeningly self-involved creature, the human male." What is White suggesting about the way both gays and women perceive their male partners? What is he suggesting about the ways they interact with male partners? Do you think that White's observation is valid or reasonable? Why or why not?

## EXPLORING RHETORICAL STRATEGIES

1. Well into the essay, why does the "they" of White's discussion shift to a "you"? Who is the "you" that White addresses? Is this "you" gay or straight? What effect does this shift in address create? As you were reading, how did it make you feel? Why do you think White makes this shift? What is his strategy here? In what ways does it help him make his point?
2. Another of White's strategies is to highlight the role of perception in determining our realities. At one point in his essay, White clues us in to one of his strategies for making this point: "If the camera were to pull back and frame both worlds in the lens, how would the two systems compare?" What is this strategy? What was his camera focused on prior to this statement? What kind of "picture" was he presenting? How does the perspective he offers change in the discussion that follows this statement? In what ways does this strategy help him make his point about the ways perception influences reality?
3. How might you characterize the tone of White's essay? If you could hear him speaking, what tone of voice would he be using? How has White used tone to convey a certain picture of himself to his audience? How would you describe the persona he adopts in this essay?

# Chapter 3

# FEMININITY AND SISTERHOOD

## Woman as Other

SIMONE DE BEAUVOIR

*In this selection, philosopher Simone de Beauvoir explores the historical oppression of women. She examines the concepts of* woman *and* man *in relation to the larger concept of* humanity *and concludes that women's status is not simply a matter of definition but a fundamental way of thinking that has political consequences.*

What is a woman?

To state the question is, to me, to suggest, at once, a preliminary answer. The fact that I ask it is in itself significant. A man would never get the notion of writing a book on the peculiar situation of the human male. But if I wish to define myself, I must first of all say: "I am a woman"; on this truth must be based all further discussion. A man never begins by presenting himself as an individual of a certain sex; it goes without saying that he is a man. The terms *masculine* and *feminine* are used symmetrically only as a matter of form, as on legal papers. In actuality the relation of the two sexes is not quite like that of two electrical poles, for man represents both the positive and the neutral, as is indicated by the common use of *man* to designate human beings in general; whereas woman represents only the negative, defined by limiting criteria, without reciprocity. In the midst of an abstract discussion it is vexing to hear a man say: "You think thus and so because you are a woman"; but I know that my only defense is to reply: "I think thus and so because it is true," thereby removing my subjective self from the argument. It would be out of the question to reply: "And you think the contrary because you are a man," for it is understood that the fact of being a man is no peculiarity. A man is in the right in being a man; it is the woman who is in the wrong. It amounts to this: just as for the ancients there was an absolute vertical with reference to which the oblique was defined, so there is an absolute human type, the masculine. Woman has ovaries, a uterus; these peculiarities imprison her in her subjectivity, circumscribe her within the limits of her own nature. It is often said that she thinks with her glands. Man superbly ignores the fact that his anatomy also includes glands, such as the testicles, and that they secrete hormones. He thinks of his body as a direct and normal connection with the world, which he believes he apprehends objectively, whereas he regards the body of woman as a hindrance, a prison, weighed down by everything peculiar to it. "The female is a female by virtue of a certain *lack* of qualities," said Aristotle; "we should regard the female nature as afflicted with a natural defectiveness." And St. Thomas for his part pronounced woman to be an "imperfect man," an "incidental" being. This is symbolized in Genesis where Eve is depicted as made from what Bossuet called "a supernumerary bone" of Adam.

Thus humanity is male and man defines woman not in herself but as relative to him; she is not regarded as an autonomous being. Michelet writes: "Woman, the relative being. . . ." And Benda is most positive in his *Rapport d'Uriel:* "The body of man makes sense in itself quite apart from that of woman, whereas the latter seems wanting in significance by itself. . . . Man can think of himself without woman. She cannot think of herself without man." And she is simply what man decrees; thus she is called "the sex," by which is meant that she appears essentially to the male as a sexual being. For him she is sex—absolute sex, no less. She is defined and differentiated with reference to man and not he with reference to her; she is the incidental, the inessential as opposed to the essential. He is the Subject, he is the Absolute—she is the Other.

The category of the *Other* is as primordial as consciousness itself. In the most primitive societies, in the most ancient mythologies, one finds the expression of a duality—that of the Self and the Other. This duality was not originally attached to the division of the sexes; it was not dependent upon any empirical facts. It is revealed in such works as that of Granet on Chinese thought and those of Dumézil on the East Indies and Rome. The feminine element was at first no more involved in such pairs as Varuna-

Mitra, Uranus-Zeus, Sun-Moon, and Day-Night than it was in the contrasts between Good and Evil, lucky and unlucky auspices, right and left, God and Lucifer. Otherness is a fundamental category of human thought.

Thus it is that no group ever sets itself up as the One without at once setting up the Other over against itself. If three travelers chance to occupy the same compartment, that is enough to make vaguely hostile "others" out of all the rest of the passengers on the train. In small-town eyes all persons not belonging to the village are "strangers" and suspect; to the native of a country all who inhabit other countries are "foreigners"; Jews are "different" for the anti-Semite, Negroes are "inferior" for American racists, aborigines are "natives" for colonists, proletarians are the "lower class" for the privileged.

Lévi-Strauss, at the end of a profound work on the various forms of primitive societies, reaches the following conclusion: "Passage from the state of Nature to the state of Culture is marked by man's ability to view biological relations as a series of contrasts; duality, alternation, opposition, and symmetry, whether under definite or vague forms, constitute not so much phenomena to be explained as fundamental and immediately given data of social reality." These phenomena would be incomprehensible if in fact human society were simply a *Mitsein* or fellowship based on solidarity and friendliness. Things become clear, on the contrary, if, following Hegel, we find in consciousness itself a fundamental hostility toward every other consciousness; the subject can be posed only in being opposed—he sets himself up as the essential, as opposed to the other, the inessential, the object.

But the other consciousness, the other ego, sets up a reciprocal claim. The native traveling abroad is shocked to find himself in turn regarded as a "stranger" by the natives of neighboring countries. As a matter of fact, wars, festivals, trading, treaties, and contests among tribes, nations, and classes tend to deprive the concept *Other* of its absolute sense and to make manifest its relativity; willy-nilly, individuals and groups are forced to realize the reciprocity of their relations. How is it, then, that this reciprocity has not been recognized between the sexes, that one of the contrasting terms is set up as the sole essential, denying any relativity in regard to its correlative and defining the latter as pure otherness? Why is it that women do not dispute male sovereignty? No subject will readily volunteer to become the object, the inessential; it is not the Other who, in defining himself as the Other, establishes the One. The Other is posed as such by the One in defining himself as the One. But if the Other is not to regain the status of being the One, he must be submissive enough to accept this alien point of view. Whence comes this submission in the case of woman?

There are, to be sure, other cases in which a certain category has been able to dominate another completely for a time. Very often this privilege depends upon inequality of numbers—the majority imposes its rule upon the minority or persecutes it. But women are not a minority, like the American Negroes or the Jews; there are as many women as men on earth. Again, the two groups concerned have often been originally independent; they may have been formerly unaware of each other's existence, or perhaps they recognized each other's autonomy. But a historical event has resulted in the subjugation of the weaker by the stronger. The scattering of the Jews, the introduction of slavery into America, the conquests of imperialism are examples in point. In these cases the oppressed retained at least the memory of former days; they possessed in common a past, a tradition, sometimes a religion or a culture.

The parallel drawn by Bebel between women and the proletariat is valid in that neither ever formed a minority nor a separate collective unit of mankind. And instead of a single historical event it is in both cases a historical development that explains their status as a class and accounts for the membership of *particular individuals* in that class. But proletarians have not always existed, whereas there have always been women. They are women in virtue of their anatomy and physiology. Throughout history they have always been subordinated to men, and hence their dependency is not the result of a historical event or a social change—it was not something that *occurred.* The reason why otherness in this case seems to be an absolute is in part that it lacks the contingent or incidental nature of historical facts. A condition brought about at a certain time can be abolished at some other time, as the Negroes of Haiti and others have proved; but it might seem that a natural condition is beyond the possibility of change. In truth, however, the nature of things is no more immutably given, once for all, than is historical reality. If woman seems to be the inessential which never becomes the essential, it is because she herself fails to bring about this change. Proletarians say "We"; Negroes also. Regarding themselves as subjects, they transform the bourgeois, the whites, into "others." But women do not say "We," except at some congress of feminists of similar formal demonstration; men say "women," and women use the same word in referring to themselves. They do not authentically assume a subjective attitude. The proletarians have accomplished the revolution in Russia, the Negroes in Haiti, the Indochinese are battling for it in Indochina; but the women's effort has never been anything more than a symbolic agitation. They have gained only what men have been willing to grant; they have taken nothing, they have only received.

The reason for this is that women lack concrete means for organizing themselves into a unit which can stand face to face with the correlative unit. They have no past, no history, no religion of their own; and they have no such solidarity of work and interest as that of the proletariat. They are not even promiscuously herded together in the way that creates community feeling among the American Negroes, the ghetto Jews, the workers of Saint-Denis, or the factory hands of Renault. They live dispersed among the males, attached through residence, housework, economic condition, and social standing to certain men—fathers or husbands—more firmly than they are to other women. If they belong to the bourgeoisie, they feel solidarity with men of that class, not with proletarian women; if they are white, their allegiance is to white men, not to Negro women. The proletariat can propose to massacre the ruling class, and a sufficiently fanatical Jew or Negro might dream of getting sole possession of the atomic bomb and making humanity wholly Jewish or black; but woman cannot even dream of exterminating the males. The bond that unites her to her oppressors is not comparable to any other. The division of the sexes is a biological fact, not an event in human history. Male and female stand opposed within a primordial *Mitsein,* and woman has not broken it. The couple is a fundamental unity with its two halves riveted together, and the cleavage of society along the line of sex is impossible. Here is to be found the basic trait of woman: she is the Other in a totality of which the two components are necessary to one another.

One could suppose that this reciprocity might have facilitated the liberation of woman. When Hercules sat at the feet of Omphale and helped with her spinning, his desire for her held him captive; but why did she fail to gain a lasting power? To revenge herself on Jason, Medea killed their children; and this grim legend would seem to suggest that she might have obtained a formidable influence over him through his love for his offspring. In *Lysistrata* Aristophanes gaily depicts a band of women who joined forces to gain social ends through the sexual needs of their men; but this is only a play. In the legend of the Sabine women, the latter soon abandoned their plan of remaining sterile to punish their ravishers. In truth woman has not been socially emancipated through man's need—sexual desire and the desire for offspring—which makes the male dependent for satisfaction upon the female.

Master and slave, also, are united by a reciprocal need, in this case economic, which does not liberate the slave. In the relation of master to slave the master does not make a point of the need that he has for the other; he has in his grasp the power of satisfying this need through his own action; whereas the slave, in his dependent condition, his hope and fear, is quite conscious of the need he has for his master. Even if the need is at bottom equally urgent for both, it always works in favor of the oppressor and against the oppressed. That is why the liberation of the working class, for example, has been slow.

Now, woman has always been man's dependent, if not his slave; the two sexes have never shared the world in equality. And even today woman is heavily handicapped, though her situation is beginning to change. Almost nowhere is her legal status the same as man's, and frequently it is much to her disadvantage. Even when her rights are legally recognized in the abstract, long-standing custom prevents their full expression in the mores. In the economic sphere men and women can almost be said to make up two castes; other things being equal, the former hold the better jobs, get higher wages, and have more opportunity for success than their new competitors. In industry and politics men have a great many more positions and they monopolize the most important posts. In addition to all this, they enjoy a traditional prestige that the education of children tends in every way to support, for the present enshrines the past—and in the past all history has been made by men. At the present time, when women are beginning to take part in the affairs of the world, it is still a world that belongs to men—they have no doubt of it at all and women have scarcely any. To decline to be the Other, to refuse to be a party to the deal—this would be for women to renounce all the advantages conferred upon them by their alliance with the superior caste. Man-the-sovereign will provide woman-the-liege with material protection and will undertake the moral justification of her existence; thus she can evade at once both economic risk and the metaphysical risk of a liberty in which ends and aims must be contrived without assistance. Indeed, along with the ethical urge of each individual to affirm his subjective existence, there is also the temptation to forgo liberty and become a thing. This is an inauspicious road, for he who takes it—passive, lost, ruined—becomes henceforth the creature of another's will, frustrated in his transcendence and deprived of every value. But it is an easy road; on it one avoids the strain involved in undertaking an authentic existence. When man makes of woman the *Other,* he may, then, expect her to manifest deep-seated tendencies toward complicity. Thus, woman may fail to lay claim to the status of subject because she lacks definite resources, because she feels the necessary bond that ties her to man regardless of reciprocity, and because she is often very well pleased with her role as the *Other*.

---

## REFLECTING ON MEANING

1. De Beauvoir argues that the act of defining oneself is different for women and men. What is the difference? Where must a woman's definition start? Why? Why doesn't a man have to begin defining himself in this way?
2. What does it mean to define man as the "subject" and woman as the "other"? What is de Beauvoir suggesting about the relationship of men and women to each other and to humanity in general? What is the definition of *human* and *humanity* according to this system?
3. As a social group defined as "other," what do women have in common with ethnic minorities and the working class? What are the differences? What has caused the oppression of each of these groups? What allows some of them to unite to resist oppression? What makes women's oppression a "natural condition" rather than the result of a historical event? Does this suggest that women cannot hope or seek to overcome their oppression? Why or why not?

## EXPLORING RHETORICAL STRATEGIES

1. "Woman As Other" was published in 1949 as a chapter in de Beauvoir's *The Second Sex.* What does the title of the book suggest about the status of women? How does the chapter reprinted here connect to this idea? What other topics might you expect de Beauvoir to discuss in the remaining chapters of her book? Why?
2. Who is de Beauvoir's intended audience? How do you know? Do you think she expected her audience to resist or to accept her observations on women's status? How do you know? Would readers today respond in the same way? Why or why not?
3. What kind of persona does de Beauvoir adopt? What does the type of evidence she uses tell you about her persona? Why doesn't

she use personal experiences, anecdotes, and interviews to make her case? How is her persona appropriate for her intended audience?

---

# Psychology Constructs the Female

## NAOMI WEISSTEIN

---

*Although scientific research may seem to offer irrefutable proof of natural differences in men's and women's behavior, Naomi Weisstein suggests otherwise. In a carefully crafted refutation of the "evidence," Weisstein argues that the most basic assumptions of psychological research are misinformed. Furthermore, she contends, research in biology and anthropology has been selectively applied in order to support misleading conceptions of the behavior considered natural to women and men.*

It is an implicit assumption that the area of psychology which concerns itself with personality has the onerous but necessary task of describing the limits of human possibility. Thus when we are about to consider the liberation of women, we naturally look to psychology to tell us what "true" liberation would mean: what would give women the freedom to fulfill their own intrinsic natures. Psychologists have set about describing the true natures of women with a certainty and a sense of their own infallibility rarely found in the secular world. Bruno Bettelheim, of the University of Chicago, tells us that

> We must start with the realization that, as much as women want to be good scientists or engineers, they want first and foremost to be womanly companions of men and to be mothers.

Erik Erikson of Harvard University, upon noting that young women often ask whether they can "have an identity before they know whom they will marry, and for whom they will make a home," explains somewhat elegiacally that

> Much of a young woman's identity is already defined in her kind of attractiveness and in the selectivity of her search for the man (or men) by whom she wishes to be sought. . . .

Mature womanly fulfillment, for Erikson, rests on the fact that a woman's

> . . . somatic design harbors an "inner space" destined to bear the offspring of chosen men, and with it, a biological, psychological, and ethical commitment to take care of human infancy.

Some psychiatrists even see the acceptance of woman's role by women as a solution to social problems. "Woman is nurturance . . . ," writes Joseph Rheingold (1964), a psychiatrist at the Harvard Medical School, " . . . anatomy decrees the life of a woman . . . when women grow up without dread of their biological functions and without subversion by feminist doctrine, and therefore enter upon motherhood with a sense of fulfillment and altruistic sentiment, we shall attain the goal of a good life and a secure world in which to live it."

These views from men who are assumed to be experts reflect, in a surprisingly transparent way, the cultural consensus. They not only assert that a woman is defined by her ability to attract men, they see no alternative definitions. They think that the definition of a woman in terms of a man is the way it should be; and they back it up with psychosexual incantation and biological ritual curses. A woman has an identity if she is attractive enough to obtain a man, and thus, a home; for this will allow her to set about her life's task of "joyful altruism and nurturance."

Business certainly does not disagree. If views such as Bettelheim's and Erikson's do indeed have something to do with real liberation for women, then seldom in human history has so much money and effort been spent on helping a group of people realize their true potential. Clothing, cosmetics, home furnishings, are multi-million dollar businesses: if you don't like investing in firms that make weaponry and flaming gasoline, then there's a lot of hard cash in "inner space." Sheet and pillowcase manufacturers are concerned to fill this inner space:

> Mother, for a while this morning, I thought I wasn't cut out for married life. Hank was late for work and forgot his apricot

> juice and walked out without kissing me, and when I was all alone I started crying. But then the postman came with the sheets and towels you sent, that look like big bandana handkerchiefs, and you know what I thought? That those big red and blue handkerchiefs are for girls like me to dry their tears on so they can get busy and do what a housewife has to do. Throw open the windows and start getting the house ready, and the dinner, maybe clean the silver and put new geraniums in the box. *Everything to be ready for him when he walks through that door.*[1]

Of course, it is not only the sheet and pillowcase manufacturers, the cosmetics industry, the home furnishings salesmen who profit from and make use of the cultural definitions of man and woman. The example above is blatantly and overtly pitched to a particular kind of sexist stereotype: the child nymph. But almost all aspects of the media are normative, that is, they have to do with the ways in which beautiful people, or just folks, or ordinary Americans, should live their lives. They define the possible; and the possibilities are usually in terms of what is male and what is female. Men and women alike are waiting for Hank, the Silva Thins man, to walk back through that door.

It is an interesting but limited exercise to show that psychologists and psychiatrists embrace these sexist norms of our culture, that they do not see beyond the most superficial and stultifying media conceptions of female nature, and that their ideas of female nature serve industry and commerce so well. Just because it's good for business doesn't mean it's wrong. What I will show is that it *is wrong;* that there isn't the tiniest shred of evidence that these fantasies of servitude and childish dependence have anything to do with women's true potential; that the idea of the nature of human possibility which rests on the accidents of individual development of genitalia, on what is possible today because of what happened yesterday, on the fundamentalist myth of sex organ causality, has strangled and deflected psychology so that it is relatively useless in describing, explaining, or predicting humans and their behavior.

It then goes without saying that present psychology is less than worthless in contributing to a vision which could truly liberate—men as well as women.

The central argument of my paper, then, is this. Psychology has nothing to say about what women are really like, what they need and what they want, essentially because psychology does not know. I want to stress that this failure is not limited to women; rather, the kind of psychology which has addressed itself to how people act and who they are has failed to understand, in the first place, why people act the way they do, and certainly failed to understand what might make them act differently.

The kind of psychology which has addressed itself to these questions divides into two professional areas: academic personality research, and clinical psychology and psychiatry. The basic reason for failure is the same in both these areas: the central assumption for most psychologists of human personality has been that human behavior rests on an individual and inner dynamic, perhaps fixed in infancy, perhaps fixed by genitalia, perhaps simply arranged in a rather immovable cognitive network. But this assumption is rapidly losing ground as personality psychologists fail again and again to get consistency in the assumed personalities of their subjects. Meanwhile, the evidence is collecting that what a person does and who she believes herself to be, will in general be a function of what people around her expect her to be, and what the overall situation in which she is acting implies that she is. Compared to the influence of the social context within which a person lives, his or her history and "traits," as well as biological makeup, may simply be random variations, "noise" superimposed on the true signal which can predict behavior.

Some academic personality psychologists are at least looking at the counter evidence and questioning their theories; no such corrective is occurring in clinical psychology and psychiatry: Freudians and neo-Freudians, nudie-marathonists and touchy-feelies, classicists and swingers, clinicians and psychiatrists, simply refuse to look at the evidence against their theory and practice. And they support their theory and practice with stuff so transparently biased as to have absolutely no standing as empirical evidence.

To summarize: the first reason for psychology's failure to understand what people are and how they act is that psychology has looked for inner traits when it should have been looking for social context; the second reason for psychology's failure is that the theoreticians of personality have generally been clinicians and psychiatrists, and they have never considered it necessary to have evidence in support of their theories.

## Theory Without Evidence

Let us turn to this latter cause of failure first: the acceptance by psychiatrists and clinical psychologists of theory without evidence. If we inspect the literature of personality, it is immediately obvious that the bulk of it is written by clinicians and psychiatrists, and that the major support for their theories is "years of intensive clinical experience." This is a tradition started by Freud. His "insights" occurred during the course of his work with his patients. Now there is nothing wrong with such an approach to theory *formulation;* a person is free to make up theories with any inspiration that works: divine revelation, intensive clinical practice, a random numbers table. But he/she is not free to claim any validity for his/her theory until it has been tested and confirmed. But theories are treated in no such tentative way in ordinary clinical practice. Consider Freud. What he thought constituted evidence violated the most minimal conditions of scientific rigor. In *The Sexual Enlightenment of Children,* the classic document which is supposed to demonstrate empirically the existence of a castration complex and its connection to a phobia, Freud based his analysis on the reports of the father of the little boy, himself in therapy, and a devotee of Freudian theory. I really don't have to comment further on the contamination in this kind of evidence. It is remarkable that only recently has Freud's classic theory on the sexuality of women—the notion of the double orgasm—been actually tested physiologically and found just plain wrong. Now those who claim that fifty years of psychoanalytic experience constitute evidence enough of the essential truths of Freud's theory should ponder the robust health of the double orgasm. Did women, until Masters and Johnson,[2] believe they were having two different kinds of orgasm? Did their psychiatrists badger them into reporting something that was not true? If so, were there other things they reported that were also not true? Did psychiatrists ever learn anything different than their theories had led them to believe? If clinical experience means anything at all, surely we should have been done with the double orgasm myth long before the Masters and Johnson studies.

But certainly, you may object, "years of intensive clinical experience" is the only reliable measure in a discipline which relies for its findings on insight, sensitivity, and intuition. The problem with insight, sensitivity, and intuition, is that they can confirm for all time the biases that one started with. People used to be absolutely convinced of their ability to tell which of their number were engaging in witchcraft. All it required was some sensitivity to the workings of the devil.

Years of intensive clinical experience is not the same thing as empirical evidence. The first thing an experimenter learns in any kind of experiment which involves humans is the concept of the "double blind." The term is taken from medical experiments, where one group is given a drug which is presumably supposed to change behavior in a certain way, and a control group is given a placebo.

If the observers or the subjects know which group took which drug, the result invariably comes out on the positive side for the new drug. Only when it is not known which subject took which pill is validity remotely approximated. In addition, with judgments of human behavior, it is so difficult to precisely tie down just what behavior is going on, let alone what behavior should be expected, that one must test again and again the reliability of judgments. How many judges, blind, will agree in their observations? Can they replicate their own judgments at some later time? When, in actual practice, these judgment criteria are tested for clinical judgments, then we find that the judges cannot judge reliably, nor can they judge consistently: they do no better than chance in identifying which of a certain set of stories were written by men and which by women; which of a whole battery of clinical test results are the products of homosexuals and which are the products of heterosexuals, and which, of a battery of clinical test results *and* interviews (where questions are asked such as "Do you have delusions?") are products of psychotics, neurotics, psychosomatics, or normals. Lest this summary escape your notice, let me stress the implications of these findings. The ability of judges, chosen for their clinical expertise, to distinguish male heterosexuals from male homosexuals on the basis of three widely used clinical projective tests—the Rorschach, the TAT, and the MAP—was *no better than chance.* The reason this is such devastating news, of course, is that sexuality is supposed to be of fundamental importance in the deep dynamic of personality; if what is considered gross sexual deviance cannot be caught, then what are psychologists talking about when they, for example, claim that at the basis of paranoid psychosis is "latent homosexual panic"? They can't even identify what homosexual anything is, let alone "latent homosexual panic."[3] More frightening, expert clinicians cannot be consistent on what diagnostic category to assign to a person, again on the basis of both tests and interviews; a number of normals in the Little and Schneidman study were described as psychotic, in such categories as "schizophrenic with homosexual tendencies" or "schizoid character with depressive trends." But most disheartening, when the judges were asked to rejudge the test protocols some weeks later, their diagnoses of the same subjects on the basis of the same protocol differed markedly from their initial judgments. It is obvious that even simple descriptive conventions in clinical psychology cannot be consistently applied; if clinicians were as faulty in recognizing food from non-food, they'd poison themselves and starve to death. That their descriptive conventions have any explanatory significance is therefore, of course, out of the question.

As a graduate student at Harvard some years ago, I was a member of a seminar which was asked to identify which of two piles of a clinical test, the TAT, had been written by males and which by females. Only four students out of twenty identified the piles correctly, and this was after one and a half months of intensively studying the differences between men and women. Since this result is below chance—that is, the result would occur by chance about four out of a thousand times—we may conclude that there *is* finally a consistency here; students are judging knowledgeably within the context of psychological teaching about the differences between men and women; the teachings themselves are simply erroneous.

You may argue that the theory may be scientifically "unsound" but at least it cures people. There is no evidence that it does. In 1952, Eysenck reported the results of what is called an "outcome of therapy" study of neurotics which showed that, of the patients who received psychoanalysis the improvement rate was 44 percent; of the patients who received psychotherapy the improvement rate was 64 percent; and of the patients who received no treatment at all the improvement rate was 72 percent. These findings have never been refuted; subsequently, later studies have confirmed the negative results of the Eysenck study. How can clinicians and psychiatrists, then, in all good conscience, continue to practice? Largely by ignoring these results and being careful not to do outcome-of-therapy studies. The attitude is nicely summarized by Rotter: "Research studies in psychotherapy tend to be concerned more with psychotherapeutic procedure and less with outcome. . . . To some extent, it reflects an interest in the psychotherapy situation as a kind of personality laboratory." Some laboratory.

## The Social Context

Thus, since we can conclude that because clinical experience and tools can be shown to be worse than useless when tested for consistency, efficacy, agreement, and reliability, we can safely conclude that theories of a clinical nature advanced about women are also worse than useless. I want to turn now to the second major point in my paper, which is that, even when psychological theory is constructed so that it may be tested, and rigorous standards of evidence are used, it has become increasingly clear that in order to understand why people do what they do, and certainly in order to change what people do, psychologists must turn away from the theory of the causal nature of the inner dynamic and look to the social context within which individuals live.

Before examining the relevance of this approach to the question of women, let me first sketch the groundwork for this assertion.

In the first place, it is clear that personality tests never yield consistent predictions; a rigid authoritarian on one measure will be an unauthoritarian on the next. But the reason for this inconsistency is only now becoming clear, and it seems overwhelmingly to have much more to do with the social situation in which the subject finds him/herself than with the subject him/herself.

In a series of brilliant experiments, Rosenthal and his coworkers have shown that if one group of experimenters has one hypothesis about what they expect to find, and another group of experimenters has the opposite hypothesis, both groups will obtain results in accord with their hypotheses. The results obtained are not due to mishandling of data by biased experimenters; rather, somehow, the bias of the experimenter creates a changed environment in which subjects actually act differently. For instance, in one experiment, subjects were to assign numbers to pictures of men's faces, with high numbers representing the subject's judgment that the man in the picture was a successful person, and low numbers representing the subject's judgment that the man in the picture was an unsuccessful person. Prior to running the subjects, one group of experimenters was told that the subjects tended to rate the faces high; another group of experimenters was told that the subjects tended to rate the faces low. Each group of experimenters was instructed to follow precisely the same procedure: they were required to read to subjects a set of instructions, and to say *nothing else.* For the 375 subjects run, the results showed clearly that those subjects who performed the task with experimenters who expected high ratings gave high ratings, and those subjects who performed the task with experimenters who expected low ratings gave low ratings. How did this happen? The experimenters all used the same words; it was something in their conduct which made one group of subjects do one thing, and another group of subjects do another thing.[4]

The concreteness of the changed conditions produced by expectation is a fact, a reality: even with animal subjects, in two separate studies, those experimenters who were told that rats learning mazes had been especially bred for brightness obtained better learning from their rats than did experimenters believing their rats to have been bred for dullness. In a very recent study, Rosenthal and Jacobson (1968) extended their analysis to the natural classroom situation. Here, they tested a group of students and reported to the teachers that some among the students tested "showed great promise." Actually, the students so named had been selected on a random basis. Some time later, the experimenters retested the group of students: those students whose teachers had been told that they were "promising" showed real and dramatic increments in their IQs as compared to the rest of the students. Something in the conduct of the teachers towards those who the teachers believed to be the "bright" students, made those students brighter.

Thus, even in carefully controlled experiments, and with no outward or conscious difference in behavior, the hypotheses we start with will influence enormously the behavior of another organism. These studies are extremely important when assessing the validity of psychological studies of women. Since it is beyond doubt that most of us start with notions as to the nature of men and women, the validity of a number of observations of sex differences is questionable, even when these observations have been made under carefully controlled conditions. Second, and more important, the Rosenthal experiments point quite clearly to the influence of social expectation. In some extremely important ways, people are what you expect them to be, or at least they behave as you expect them to behave. Thus, if women, according to Bettelheim, want first and foremost to be good wives and mothers, it is extremely likely that this is what Bruno Bettelheim, and the rest of society, want them to be.

There is another series of brilliant social psychological experiments which point to the overwhelming effect of social context. These are the obedience experiments of Stanley Milgram in which subjects are asked to obey the orders of unknown experimenters, orders which carry with them the distinct possibility that the subject is killing somebody.

In Milgram's experiments, a subject is told that he/she is administering a learning experiment, and that he/she is to deal out shocks each time the other "subject" (in reality, a confederate of the experimenter) answers incorrectly. The equipment appears to provide graduated shocks ranging upwards from 15 volts through 450 volts; for each of four consecutive voltages there are verbal descriptions such as "mild shock," "danger, severe shock," and, finally, for the 435- and 450-volt switches, a red XXX marked over the switches. Each time the stooge answers incorrectly, the subject is supposed to increase the voltage. As the voltage increases, the stooge begins to cry in pain; he/she demands that the experiment stop; finally, he/she refuses to answer at all. When he/she stops responding, the experimenter instructs the subject to continue increasing the voltage; for each shock administered the stooge shrieks in agony. Under these conditions, about $62\frac{1}{2}$ percent of the subjects administered shocks that they believed to be possibly lethal.

No tested individual differences between subjects predicted how many would continue to obey, and which would break off the experiment. When forty psychiatrists predicted how many of a group of 100 subjects would go on to give the lethal shock, their predictions were orders of magnitude below the actual percentages; most expected only one-tenth of one percent of the subjects to obey to the end.

But even though *psychiatrists* have no idea how people will behave in this situation, and even though individual differences do not predict which subjects will obey and which will not, it is easy to predict when subjects will be obedient and when they will be defiant. All the experimenter has to do is change the social situation. In a variant of Milgram's experiment, two stooges were present in addition to the "victim"; these worked along with the subject in administering electric shocks. When these two stooges refused to go on with the experiment, only 10 percent of the subjects continued to the maximum voltage. This is critical for personality theory. It says that behavior is predicted from the social situation, not from the individual history.

Finally, an ingenious experiment by Schachter and Singer showed that subjects injected with adrenalin, which produces a state of physiological arousal in all but minor respects identical to that which occurs when subjects are extremely afraid, became euphoric when they were in a room with a stooge who was acting euphoric, and became extremely angry when they were placed in a room with a stooge who was acting extremely angry.

To summarize: If subjects under quite innocuous and noncoercive social conditions can be made to kill other subjects and under other types of social conditions will positively refuse to do so; if subjects can react to a state of physiological fear by becoming euphoric because there is somebody else around who is euphoric, or angry because there is somebody else around who is angry; if students become intelligent because teachers expect them to be intelligent, and rats run mazes better because experimenters are told the rats are bright, then it is obvious that a study of human behavior requires, first and foremost, a study of the social contexts within which people move, the expectations as to how they will behave, and the authority which tells them who they are and what they are supposed to do.

## Biologically Based Theories

Biologists also have at times assumed they could describe the limits of human potential from their observations not of human, but of animal behavior. Here, as in psychology, there has been no end of theorizing about the sexes, again with a sense of absolute certainty surprising in "science." These theories fall into two major categories.

One category of theory argues that since females and males differ in their sex hormones, and sex hormones enter the brain, there must be innate behavioral differences. But the only thing this argument tells us is that there are differences in physiological state. The problem is whether these differences are at all relevant to behavior.

Consider, for example, differences in levels of the sex hormone testosterone. A man who calls himself Tiger[5] has recently argued that the greater quantities of testosterone found in human males as compared with human females (of a certain age group) determine innate differences in aggressiveness, competitiveness, dominance, ability to hunt, ability to hold public office, and so forth. But Tiger demonstrates in this argument the same manly and courageous refusal to be intimidated by evidence which we have already seen in our consideration of the clinical and psychiatric tradition. The evidence does not support his argument, and in most cases, directly contradicts it. Testosterone level does not seem to be related to hunting ability, dominance, or aggression, or competitiveness. As Storch has pointed out, all normal *male mammals* in the reproductive age group produce much greater quantities of testosterone than females; yet many of these males are neither hunters nor are they aggressive (e.g. rabbits). And, among some hunting mammals, such as the large cats, it turns out that more hunting is done by the female than the male. And there exist primate species where the female is clearly more aggressive, competitive, and dominant than the male. Thus, for some species, being female, and therefore, having less testosterone than the male of that species means hunting more, or being more aggressive, or being more dominant. Nor does having *more* testosterone preclude behavior commonly thought of as "female"; there exist primate species where females do not touch infants except to feed them; the males care for the infants at all times. So it is not clear what testosterone or any other sex-hormonal difference means for differences in nature, or sex-role behavior.

In other words, one can observe identical types of behavior which have been associated with sex (e.g. "mothering") in males and females, despite known differences in physiological state, i.e. sex hormones, genitalia, etc. What about the converse to this? That is, can one obtain differences in behavior given a single physiological state? The answer is overwhelmingly yes, not only as regards non-sex-specific hormones (as in the Schachter and Singer experiment cited above), but also as regards gender itself. Studies of hermaphrodites with the same diagnosis (the genetic, gonadal, hormonal sex, the internal reproductive organs, and the ambiguous appearances of the external genitalia were identical) have shown that one will consider oneself male or female depending simply on whether one was defined and raised as male or female:

> There is no more convincing evidence of the power of social interaction on gender-identity differentiation than in the case of congenital hermaphrodites who are of the same diagnosis and similar degree of hermaphroditism but are differently assigned and with a different postnatal medical and life history. (Money, 1970, p. 743)

Thus, for example, if out of two individuals diagnosed as having the adrenogenital syndrome of female hermaphroditism, one is raised as a girl and one as a boy, each will act and identify her/himself accordingly. The one raised as a girl will consider herself a girl; the one raised as a boy will consider himself a boy; and each will conduct her/himself successfully in accord with that self-definition.

So, identical behavior occurs given different physiological states; and different behavior occurs given an identical physiological starting point. So it is not clear that differences in sex hormones are at all relevant to behavior.

The other category of theory based on biology, a reductionist theory, goes like this. Sex-role behavior in some primate species is described, and it is concluded that this is the "natural" behavior for humans. Putting aside the not insignificant problem of observer bias (for instance, Harlow, of the University of Wisconsin, after observing differences between male and female rhesus monkeys, quotes Laurence Sterne to the effect that women are silly and trivial, and concludes that "men and women have differed in the past and they will differ in the future"), there are a number of problems with this approach.

The most general and serious problem is that there are no grounds to assume that anything primates do is necessarily natural, or desirable in humans, for the simple reason that humans are not non-humans. For instance, it is found that male chimpanzees placed alone with infants will not "mother" them. Jumping from hard data to ideological speculation, researchers conclude from this information that *human* females are necessary for the safe growth of human infants. It would be reasonable to conclude, following this logic, that it is quite useless to teach human infants to speak, since it has been tried with chimpanzees and it does not work.

One strategy that has been used is to extrapolate from primate behavior to "innate" human preference by noticing certain trends in primate behavior as one moves phylogenetically closer to humans. But there are great difficulties with this approach. When behaviors from lower primates are directly opposite to those of higher primates, or to those one expects of humans, they can be dismissed on evolutionary grounds—higher primates and/or humans grew out of that kid stuff. On the other hand, if the behavior of higher primates is counter to the behavior considered natural for humans, while the behavior of some lower primate is considered the natural one for humans, the higher primate behavior can be dismissed also, on the grounds that it has diverged from an older, prototypical pattern. So either way, one can select those behaviors one wants to prove innate for humans. In addition, one does not know whether the sex-role behavior exhibited is dependent on the phylogenetic rank, or on the environmental conditions (both physical and social) under which different species live.

Is there then any value at all in primate observations as they relate to human females and males? There is a value but it is limited: its function can be no more than to show some extant examples of diverse sex-role behavior. It must be stressed, however, that this is an extremely limited function. The extant behavior does not begin to suggest all the possibilities, either for non-human primates or for humans. Bearing these caveats in mind, it is nonetheless interesting that if one inspects the limited set of observations of existing non-human primate sex-role behaviors, one finds, in fact, a much larger range of sex-role behavior than is commonly believed to exist. "Biology" appears to limit very little; the fact that a female gives birth does not mean, even in non-humans, that she necessarily cares for the infant (in marmosets, for instance, the male carries the infant at all times except when the infant is feeding); "natural" female and male behavior varies all the way from females who are much more aggressive and competitive than males (e.g. Tamarins) and male "mothers" (e.g. Titi monkeys, night monkeys, and marmosets[6]) to submissive and passive females and male antagonists (e.g. rhesus monkeys).

But even for the limited function that primate arguments serve, the evidence has been misused. Invariably, those primates have been cited which exhibit exactly the kind of behavior that the proponents of the biological fixedness of human female behavior wish were true for humans. Thus, baboons and rhesus monkeys are generally cited: males in these groups exhibit some of the most irritable and aggressive behavior found in primates, and if one wishes to argue that females are naturally passive and submissive, these groups provide vivid examples. There are abundant counter examples, such as those mentioned above; in fact, in general, a counter example can be found for every sex-role behavior cited, including, as mentioned in the case of marmosets, male "mothers."

But the presence of counter examples has not stopped florid and overarching theories of the natural or biological basis of male privilege from proliferating. For instance, there have been a number of theories dealing with the innate incapacity in human males for monogamy. Here, as in most of this type of theorizing, baboons are a favorite example, probably because of their fantasy value: the family unit of the hamadryas baboon, for instance, consists of a highly constant pattern of one male and a number of females and their young. And again, the counter examples, such as the invariably monogamous gibbon, are ignored.

An extreme example of this maiming and selective truncation of the evidence in the service of a plea for the maintenance of male privilege is a recent book, *Men in Groups* by Tiger. The central claim of this book is that females are incapable of "bonding" as in "male bonding." What is "male bonding"? Its surface definition is simple: " . . . a particular relationship between two or more males such that they react differently to members of their bonding units as compared to individuals outside of it." If one deletes the word male, the definition, on its face, would seem to include all organisms that have any kind of social organization. But this is not what Tiger means. For instance, Tiger asserts that females are incapable of bonding; and this alleged incapacity indicates to Tiger that females should be restricted from public life. Why is bonding an exclusively male behavior? Because, says Tiger, it is seen in male primates. All male primates? No, very few male primates. Tiger cites two examples where male bonding is seen: rhesus monkeys and baboons. Surprise, surprise. But not even all baboons: as mentioned above, the hamadryas social organization consists of one-male units; so does that of the gelada baboon. And the great apes do not go in for male bonding much either. The "male bond" is hardly a serious contribution to scholarship; one reviewer for *Science* has observed that the book " . . . shows basically more resemblance to a partisan political tract than to a work of objective social science," with male bonding being " . . . some kind of behavioral phlogiston."

In short, primate arguments have generally misused the evidence; primate studies themselves have, in any case, only the very limited function of describing some possible sex-role behavior; and at present, primate observations have been sufficiently limited so that even the range of possible sex-role behavior for non-human primates is not known. This range is not known since there is only minimal observation of what happens to behavior if the physical or social environment is changed. In one study, different troops of Japanese macaques were observed. Here, there appeared to be cultural differences: males in 3 out of the 18 troops observed differed in the amount of their aggressiveness and infant-caring behavior. There could be no possibility of differential evolution here; the differences seemed largely transmitted by infant socialization. Thus, the very limited evidence points to some plasticity in the sex-role behavior of non-human primates; if we can figure out experiments which massively change the social organization of primate groups, it is possible that we might observe great changes in behavior. At present, however, we must conclude that given a constant physical environment, non-human primates do not change their social conditions by themselves very much and thus the "innateness" and fixedness of their behavior is simply not known. Thus, even if there were some way, which there isn't, to settle on the behavior of a particular primate species as being the "natural" way for humans, we would not know whether or not this were simply some function of the present social organization of that species. And finally, once again it must be stressed that even if non-human primate behavior turned out to be relatively fixed, this would say little about our behavior. More immediate and relevant evidence, e.g. the evidence from social psychology, points to the enormous plasticity in human behavior, not only from one culture to the next, but from one experimental group to the next. One of the most salient features of human social organization is its variety; there are a number of cultures where there is at least a rough equality between men and women. In summary, primate arguments can tell us very little about our "innate" sex-role behavior; if they tell us anything at all, they tell us that there is no one biologically "natural" female or male behavior, and that sex-role behavior in non-human primates is much more varied than has previously been thought.

## Conclusion

In brief, the uselessness of present psychology (and biology) with regard to women is simply a special case of the general conclusion: one must understand the social conditions under which humans live if one is going to attempt to explain their behavior. And, to understand the social conditions under which women live, one must understand the social expectations about women.

How are women characterized in our culture, and in psychology? They are inconsistent, emotionally unstable, lacking in a strong conscience or superego, weaker, "nurturant" rather than productive, "intuitive" rather than intelligent, and, if they are at all "normal," suited to the home and the family. In short, the list adds up to a typical minority group stereotype of inferiority: if they know their place, which is in the home, they are really quite lovable, happy, childlike, loving creatures. In a review of the intellectual differences between little boys and little girls, Eleanor Maccoby has shown that there are no intellectual differences until about high school, or, if there are, girls are slightly ahead of boys. At high school, girls begin to do worse on a few intellectual tasks, such as arithmetic reasoning, and beyond high school, the achievement of women now measured in terms of productivity and accomplishment drops off even more rapidly. There are a number of other, non-intellectual tests which show sex differences; I choose the intellectual differences since it is seen clearly that women start becoming inferior. It is no use to talk about women being different but equal; all of the tests I can think of have a "good" outcome and a "bad" outcome. Women usually end up at the "bad" outcome. In light of social expectations about women, what is surprising is that little girls don't get the message that they are supposed to be stupid until high school; and what is even more remarkable is that some women resist this message even after high school, college, and graduate school.

My paper began with remarks on the task of the discovery of the limits of human potential. Psychologists must realize that it is they who are limiting discovery of human potential. They refuse to accept evidence, if they are clinical psychologists, or, if they are rigorous, they assume that people move in a context-free ether, with only their innate dispositions and their individual traits determining what they will do. Until psychologists begin to respect evidence, and until they begin looking at the social context within which people move, psychology will have nothing of substance to offer in this task of discovery. I don't know what immutable differences exist between men and women apart from differences in their genitals; perhaps there are some other unchangeable differences; probably there are a number of irrelevant differences. But it is clear that until social expectations for men and women are equal, until we provide equal respect for both men and women, our answers to this question will simply reflect our prejudices.

## NOTES

1. Fieldcrest advertisement in the *New Yorker,* 1965. My italics.
2. W. H. Masters and V. E. Johnson, *Human Sexual Response* (Boston: Little, Brown, 1966).
3. It should be noted that psychologists have been as quick to assert absolute truths about the nature of homosexuality as they have about the nature of women. The arguments presented in this paper apply equally to the nature of homosexuality: psychologists know nothing about it; there is no more evidence for the "naturalness" of heterosexuality. Psychology has functioned as a pseudoscientific buttress for patriarchal ideology and patriarchal social organization: women's liberation and gay liberation fight against a common victimization.
4. I am indebted to Jesse Lemisch for his valuable suggestions in the interpretation of these studies.
5. H. N. G. Schwarz-Belkin claims that the name was originally Mouse, but this may be a reference to an earlier L. Tiger (putative).
6. All these are lower-order primates, which makes their behavior with reference to humans unnatural, or more natural; take your choice.

---

## REFLECTING ON MEANING

1. According to Weisstein, what is the mission of the field of psychology? What issues do psychologists address in their practice and research? What is their "central assumption" about why human beings behave as they do? Why does Weisstein find this assumption erroneous? To what extent do you find this assumption valid or invalid?
2. Weisstein argues that psychologists' views are merely reflections of a "cultural consensus" on human behavior. What does she mean by cultural consensus? What is the cultural consensus on the behavior of women and men? What role do business and the media play in establishing and reinforcing a consensus on gender-typed behavior? How does business "make use of the cultural definitions of man and woman"? According to Weisstein, how does psychology both draw on and reinforce these cultural definitions? To what extent do you agree that this poses a problem in society?
3. Weisstein claims that theorists in psychology do not have evidence for their theories about women, and therefore their theories are "worse than useless." Do they offer any evidence at all? What kind? Why doesn't Weisstein consider this "evidence"? What do you think Weisstein's definition of evidence is? To what extent do you agree that these theories require the kind of evidence

Weisstein demands? For Weisstein, why does lack of such evidence make these theories potentially harmful?

## EXPLORING RHETORICAL STRATEGIES

1. Weisstein is particularly careful in constructing her argument, outlining assertions in advance, providing detailed evidence, and presenting summaries at appropriate intervals. Why is her argument constructed in this way? What might this pattern have to do with her purpose? What does the pattern illuminate about the arguments she criticizes? How does the essay's pattern contribute to her point?

2. Weisstein's tone might be described as skeptical or, perhaps, wry. To conclude her discussion of the failure of psychological theory to "cure" people, for example, she cites Rotter's commentary on the preoccupation of research studies with "the psychotherapy situation as a kind of personality laboratory" and responds with a simple two-word observation: "Some laboratory." What is the effect of this statement? How does it encourage you to view psychological research? In what ways is this an appropriate conclusion to the first part of her argument? What are some other examples of Weisstein's wry tone?

3. The full title of Weisstein's essay is "Psychology Constructs the Female, or, The Fantasy Life of the Male Psychologist (with Some Attention to the Fantasies of His Friends, the Male Biologist and the Male Anthropologist)." What does this title lead readers to expect in the essay? What does the word *construct* suggest about the nature and origins of women's gender identity? What does Weisstein imply by attributing a gender to researchers and theorists working in psychology, biology, and anthropology? What do *fantasy life* and *fantasy* suggest about the vested interest these male professionals may have in theories about women? To what extent does the title forecast and summarize Weisstein's main point?

# Emotion

## SUSAN BROWNMILLER

*Do men and women differ in temperament? Susan Brownmiller explores answers to this question by examining emotions considered "appropriate" for each gender, as well as the way society perceives and evaluates these emotions. Women, she concludes, are caught in a double bind: they are not only forced to express their emotions in "feminine" ways, but society itself defines these ways in negative terms.*

A 1970 landmark study, known in the field as Broverman and Broverman, reported that "Cries very easily" was rated by a group of professional psychologists as a highly feminine trait. "Very emotional," "Very excitable in a minor crisis" and "Feelings easily hurt" were additional characteristics on the femininity scale. So were "Very easily influenced," "Very subjective," "Unable to separate feelings from ideas," "Very illogical" and "Very sneaky." As might be expected, masculinity was defined by opposing, sturdier values: "Very direct," "Very logical," "Can make decisions easily," "Never cries." The importance of Broverman and Broverman was not in nailing down a set of popular assumptions and conventional perceptions—masculine-feminine scales were well established in the literature of psychology as a means of ascertaining normality and social adjustment—but in the authors' observation that stereotypic femininity was a grossly negative assessment of the female sex and, furthermore, that many so-called feminine traits ran counter to clinical descriptions of maturity and mental health.

Emotional femininity is a tough nut to crack, impossible to quantify yet hard to ignore. As the task of conforming to a specified physical design is a gender mission that few women care to resist, conforming to a prepackaged emotional design is another imperative task of gender. To satisfy a societal need for sexual clarification, and to justify second-class status, an emblematic constellation of inner traits, as well as their outward manifestations, has been put forward historically by some of the world's great thinkers as proof of the "different" feminine nature.

"Woman," wrote Aristotle, "is more compassionate than man,

more easily moved to tears. At the same time, she is more jealous, more querulous, more apt to scold and to strike. She is, furthermore, more prone to despondency and less hopeful than man, more void of shame or self-respect, more false of speech, more deceptive and of more retentive memory. She is also more wakeful, more shrinking, more difficult to rouse to action, and she requires a smaller amount of nutriment."

Addressing a suffrage convention in 1855, Ralph Waldo Emerson had kindlier words on the nature of woman, explicating the nineteenth-century view that her difference was one of superior virtue. "Women," he extolled, "are the civilizers of mankind. What is civilization? I answer, the power of good women. . . . The starry crown of woman is in the power of her affection and sentiment, and the infinite enlargements to which they lead." (In less elevated language, the Emersonian view was perhaps what President Reagan had in mind when he cheerfully stated, "Why, if it wasn't for women, we men would still be walking around in skin suits carrying clubs.")

A clarification is in order. Are women believed to possess a wider or deeper emotional range, a greater sensitivity, say, to the beauties of nature or to the infinite complexities of feeling? Any male poet, artist, actor, marine biologist or backpacker would strenuously object. Rather, it is commonly agreed that women are tossed and buffeted on the high seas of emotion, while men have the tough mental fiber, the intellectual muscle, to stay in control. As for the civilizing influence, surely something more is meant than sophistication, culture and taste, using the correct fork or not belching after dinner. The idealization of emotional femininity, as women prefer to see themselves affirmed, is more exquisitely romantic: a finer temperament in a more fragile vessel, a gentler nature ruled by a twin need to love and to be protected: one who appreciates—without urgency to create—good art, music, literature and other public expressions of the private soul; a flamebearer of spiritual values by whose shining example the men of the world are inspired to redemption and to accomplish great things.

Two thousands years ago *Dominus flevit,* Jesus wept as he beheld Jerusalem. "Men ceased weeping," proposed Simone de Beauvoir, "when it became unfashionable." Now it is Mary, *Mater Dolorosa,* who weeps with compassion for mankind. In mystical visions, in the reliquaries of obscure churches and miraculous shrines, the figure of the Virgin, the world's most feminine woman, has been seen to shed tears. There are still extant cultures in which men are positively lachrymose (and kissy-kissy) with no seeming detriment to their masculine image, but the Anglo-Saxon tradition, in particular, requires keeping a stiff upper lip. Weeping, keening women shrouded in black are an established fixture in mourning rites in many nations. Inconsolable grief is a feminine role, at least in its unquiet representations. In what has become a stock photograph in the national news magazines, women weep for the multitudes when national tragedy (a terrorist bombing, an air crash, an assassination) strikes.

The catharsis of tears is encouraged in women—"There, there, now, let it all out"—while a man may be told to get a grip on himself, or to gulp down a double Scotch. Having "a good cry" in order to feel better afterward is not usually recommended as a means of raising the spirits of men, for the cathartic relief of succumbing to tears would be tempered by the uncomfortable knowledge that the loss of control was hardly manly. In the 1972 New Hampshire Presidential primary, Senator Edmund Muskie, then the Democratic front-runner, committed political suicide when he publicly cried during a campaign speech. Muskie had been talking about some harsh press comments directed at his wife when the tears filled his eyes. In retrospect it was his watershed moment: Could a man who became tearful when the going got rough in a political campaign be expected to face the Russians? To a nation that had delighted in the hatless, overcoatless macho posturing of John F. Kennedy, the military successes of General Ike and the irascible outbursts of "Give 'em hell" Harry Truman, the answer was No. Media accounts of Muskie's all-too-human tears were merciless. In the summer of 1983 the obvious and unshakable grief displayed by Israeli prime minister Menachem Begin after the death of his wife was seized upon by the Israeli and American press as evidence that a tough old warrior had lost his grip. Sharing this perception of his own emotional state, perhaps, Begin shortly afterward resigned.

Expressions of anger and rage are not a disqualifying factor in the masculine disposition. Anger in men is often understood, or excused, as reasonable or just. Anger in men may even be cast in a heroic mold—a righteous response to an insult against honor that will preclude a manly, aggressive act. Because competitive acts of personal assertion, not to mention acts of outright physical aggression, are known to flow from angry feelings, anger becomes the most unfeminine emotion a woman can show.

Anger in a woman isn't "nice." A woman who seethes with anger is "unattractive." An angry woman is hard, mean and nasty; she is unreliably, unprettily out of control. Her face contorts into unpleasant lines: the jaw juts, the eyes are narrowed, the teeth are bared. Anger is a violent snarl and a hostile threat, a declaration of war. The endless forbearance demanded of women, described as the feminine virtue of patience, prohibits an angry response. Picture a charming old-fashioned scene: The mistress of the house bends low over her needlework, cross-stitching her sampler: "Patience is a virtue, possess it if you can / Seldom seen in women, never seen in man." Does the needle jab through the cloth in uncommon fury? Does she prick her thumb in frustration?

Festering without a permissible release, women's undissolved anger has been known to seep out in petty, mean-spirited ways—fits of jealousy, fantasies of retaliation, unholy plots of revenge. Perhaps, after all, it is safer to cry. "Woman's aptitude for facile tears," wrote Beauvoir, "comes largely from the fact that her life is built upon a foundation of impotent revolt."[1]

Beauvoir hedged her bet, for her next words were these: "It is also doubtless true that physiologically she has less nervous control than a man." Is this "doubtless true," or is it more to the point, as Beauvoir continues, that "her education has taught her to let herself go more readily"?

Infants and children cry out of fear, frustration, discomfort, hunger, anxiety at separation from a parent, and rage. Surveying all available studies of crying newborns and little children, psychologists Eleanor Maccoby and Carol Jacklin found no appreciable sexual difference. If teenage girls and adult women are known to cry more than men—and there is no reason to question the popular wisdom in this regard—should the endocrine changes of adolescence be held to account? What of those weepy "blue days" of premenstrual tension that genuinely afflict so many women? What about mid-life depression, known in some circles as "the feminine malady"? Are these conditions, as some men propose, a sign of "raging hormonal imbalance" that incapacitates the cool, logical functioning of the human brain? Or does feminine depression result, as psychiatrist Willard Gaylin suggests, when confidence in one's coping mechanism is lost?

Belief in a biological basis for the instability of female emotions has a notorious history in the development of medical science. Hippocrates the physician held that hysteria was caused by a wandering uterus that remained unfulfilled. Discovery in the seventeenth century that the thyroid gland was larger in women inspired the proposition that the thyroid's function was to give added grace to the feminine neck, but other beliefs maintained that the gland served to flush impurities from the blood before it reached the brain. A larger thyroid "was necessary to guard the female system from the influence of the more numerous causes of irritation and vexation" to which the sex was unfortunately disposed. Nineteenth-century doctors averred that womb-related disorders were the cause of such female complaints as "nervous prostration." For those without money to seek out a physician's care, Lydia E. Pinkham's Vegetable Compound and other patent medicines were available to give relief. In the 1940s and '50s, prefrontal lobotomy was briefly and tragically in vogue for a variety of psychiatric disorders, particularly among women, since the surgical procedure had a flattening effect on raging emotions. Nowadays Valium appears to suffice.

Beginning in earnest in the 1960s, one line of research has attempted to isolate premenstrual tension as a contributing cause of accidents, suicide, admittance to mental hospitals and the commission of violent crimes. Mood swings, irritability and minor emotional upsets probably do lead to more "acting out" by females at a cyclical time in the month, but what does this prove beyond the increasingly accepted fact that the endocrine system has a critical influence on the human emotional threshold? Suicide, violent crime and dangerous psychiatric disorders are statistically four to nine times more prevalent in men. Should we theorize, then, that "raging hormonal imbalance" is a chronic, year-round condition in males? A disqualifying factor? By any method of calculation and for whatever reason—hormonal effects, the social inhibitions of femininity, the social pleasure of the masculine role, or all of these—the female gender is indisputably less prone to irrational, antisocial behavior. The price of inhibited anger and a nonviolent temperament may well be a bucketful of tears.

Like the emotion of anger, exulting in personal victory is a harshly unfeminine response. Of course, good winners of either sex are supposed to display some degree of sportsmanlike humility, but the merest hint of gloating triumph—"Me, me, me, I did it!"—is completely at odds with the modesty and deference expected of women and girls. Arm raised in a winner's salute, the ritualized climax of a prizefight, wrestling match or tennis championship, is unladylike, to say the least. The powerful feeling that victory engenders, the satisfaction of climbing to the top of the heap or clinching a deal, remains an inappropriate emotion. More appropriate to femininity are the predictable tears of the new Miss America as she accepts her crown and scepter. Trembling lip and brimming eyes suggest a Cinderella who has stumbled upon good fortune through unbelievable, undeserved luck. At her moment of victory the winner of America's favorite pageant appears overcome, rather than superior in any way. A Miss America who raised her scepter high like a trophy would not be in keeping with the feminine ideal.

The maidenly blush, that staple of the nineteenth-century lady's novel, was an excellent indicator of innocent virginal shyness in contrast to the worldliness and sophistication of men. In an age when a variety of remarks, largely sexual, were considered uncouth and not for the ears of virtuous women, the feminine blush was an expected response. On the other side of the ballroom, men never blushed, at least not in romantic fiction, since presumably they were knowledgeable and sexually practiced. Lowered eyes, heightened color, breathlessness and occasional swooning were further proofs of a fragile and innocent feminine nature that required protection in the rough, indelicate masculine world. (In the best-selling Harlequin and Silhouette books devoured by romance addicts who need the quick fix, the maidenly blush is alive and well.)

In a new age of relative sexual freedom, or permissiveness, at any rate, squeals and moans replace the blush and the downcast eye. Screaming bobbysoxers who fainted in the aisle at the Paramount Theater when a skinny young Frank Sinatra crooned his love ballads during the 1940s (reportedly, the first wave of fainting girls was staged by promoters) presaged the whimpering orgasmic ecstasy at rock concerts in huge arenas today. By contrast, young men in the audience automatically rise to their feet and whistle and shout when the band starts to play, but they seldom appear overcome.

Most emphatically, feminine emotion has gotten louder. The ribald squeal of the stereotypic serving wench in Elizabethan times, a supposed indicator of loose, easy ways, seems to have lost its lower-class stigma. One byproduct of our media-obsessed society, in which privacy is considered a quaint and rather old-fashioned human need, has been the reproduction of the unmistakable sounds of female orgasm on a record (Donna Summer's "Love to Love You Baby," among other hits). More than commercialization of sex is operative here. Would the sounds of male orgasm suffice for a recording, and would they be unmistakable? Although I have seen no studies on this interesting sex difference, I believe it can be said that most women do vocalize more loudly and uncontrollably than men in the throes of sexual passion. Is this response physiological, compensatory or merely symptomatic of the feminine mission to display one's feelings (and the corresponding masculine mission to keep their feelings under control)?

Feminine emotion specializes in sentimentality, empathy and

admissions of vulnerability—three characteristics that most men try to avoid. Linking these traits to female anatomy became an article of faith in the Freudian school. Erik Erikson, for one, spoke of an "inner space" (he meant the womb) that yearns for fulfillment through maternal love. Helene Deutsch, the grande dame of Freudian feminine psychology, spoke of psychic acceptance of hurt and pain; menstrual cramps, defloration and the agonies of childbirth called for a masochistic nature she believed was innate.

Love of babies, any baby and all babies, not only one's own, is a celebrated and anticipated feminine emotion, and a woman who fails to ooh and ahh at the snapshot of a baby or cuddle a proffered infant in her arms is instantly suspect. Evidence of a maternal nature, of a certain innate competence when handling a baby or at least some indication of maternal longing, becomes a requirement of gender. Women with no particular feeling for babies are extremely reluctant to admit their private truth, for the entire weight of woman's place in the biological division of labor, not to mention the glorification of motherhood as woman's greatest and only truly satisfactory role, has kept alive the belief that all women yearn to fulfill their biological destiny out of a deep emotional need. That a sizable number of mothers have no genuine aptitude for the job is verified by the records of hospitals, family courts and social agencies where cases of battery and neglect are duly entered—and perhaps also by the characteristic upper-class custom of leaving the little ones to the care of the nanny. But despite this evidence that day-to-day motherhood is not a suitable or a stimulating occupation for all, the myth persists that a woman who prefers to remain childless must be heartless or selfish or less than complete.

Books have been written on maternal guilt and its exploitation, on the endemic feeling that whatever a mother does, her loving care may be inadequate or wrong, with consequences that can damage a child for life. Trends in child care (bottle feeding, demand feeding, not picking up the crying baby, delaying the toilet training or giving up an outside job to devote one's entire time to the family) illuminate the fear of maternal inadequacy as well as the variability or "expert" opinion in each generation. Advertising copywriters successfully manipulate this feminine fear when they pitch their clients' products. A certain cereal, one particular brand of packaged white bread, must be bought for the breakfast table or else you have failed to love your child sufficiently and denied him the chance to "build a strong body twelve ways." Until the gay liberation movement began to speak for itself, it was a commonplace of psychiatric wisdom that a mother had it within her power to destroy her son's heterosexual adjustment by failing to cut his baby curls, keep him away from dance class or encourage his interest in sports.

A requirement of femininity is that a woman devote her life to love—to mother love, to romantic love, to religious love, to amorphous, undifferentiated caring. The territory of the heart is admittedly a province that is open to all, but women alone are expected to make an obsessional career of its exploration, to find whatever adventure, power, fulfillment or tragedy that life has to offer within its bounds. There is no question that a woman is apt to feel most feminine, most confident of her interior gender makeup, when she is reliably within some stage of love—even the girlish crush or the stage of unrequited love or a broken heart. Men have suffered for love, and men have accomplished great feats in the name of love, but what man has ever felt at the top of his masculine form when he is lovesick or suffering from heartache?

Gloria Steinem once observed that the heart is a sex-distinctive symbol of feminine vulnerability in the marketing of fashion. Heart-shaped rings and heart-shaped gold pendants and heart-shaped frames on red plastic sunglasses announce an addiction to love that is beyond the pale of appropriate design for masculine ornamentation. (A man does not wear his heart on his sleeve.) The same observation applies a little less stringently to flowers.

Rare is the famous girl singer, whatever her age, of popular music (blues, country, Top Forty, disco or rock) who is not chiefly identified with some expression of love, usually its downside. Torchy bittersweet ballads and sad, suffering laments mixed with vows of eternal fidelity to the rotten bastard who done her wrong communicate the feminine message of love at any cost. Almost unique to the female singer, I think, is the poignant anthem of battered survival, from Fanny Brice's "My Man" to Gloria Gaynor's "I Will Survive," that does not quite shut the door on further emotional abuse if her man should return.

But the point is not emotional abuse (except in extreme, aberrant cases); the point is feeling. Women are instructed from childhood to be keepers of the heart, keepers of the sentimental memory. In diaries, packets of old love letters and family albums, in slender books of poetry in which a flower is pressed, a woman's emotional history is preserved. Remembrance of things past—the birthday, the anniversary, the death—is a feminine province. In the social division of labor, the wife is charged with maintaining the emotional connection, even with the husband's side of the family. Her thoughtful task is to make the long-distance call, select the present and write the thank-you note (chores that secretaries are asked to do by their bosses). Men are busy; they move forward. A woman looks back. It is significant that in the Biblical parable it was Lot's wife who looked back for one last precious glimpse of their city, their home, their past (and was turned into a pillar of salt).

Love confirms the feminine psyche. A celebrated difference between men and women (either women's weakness or women's strength, depending on one's values) is the obstinate reluctance, the emotional inability of women to separate sex from love. Understandably. Love makes the world go round, and women are supposed to get dizzy—to rise, to fall, to feel alive in every pore, to be undone. In place of a suitable attachment, an unlikely or inaccessible one may have to do. But more important, sex for a woman, even in an age of accessible contraception, has reproductive consequences that render the act a serious affair. Casual sex can have a most uncasual resolution. If a young girl thinks of love and marriage while a boy thinks of getting laid, her emotional commitment is rooted not only in her different upbringing but in her reproductive biology as well. Love, then, can become an alibi for thoughtless behavior, as it may also become an identity, or a distraction, à la Emma Bovary or Anna Karenina, from the frustrations of a limited life.[2]

Christian houses of worship, especially in poor neighborhoods, are filled disproportionately by women. This phenomenon may not be entirely attributable to the historic role of the Catholic and Protestant religions in encouraging the public devotions of women (which Judaism and Islam did not), or because women have more time for prayer, or because in the Western world they are believed to be more religious by nature. Another contributing factor may be that the central article of Christian faith, "Jesus loves you," has particular appeal for the gender that defines itself through loving emotions.

Women's special interest in the field of compassion is catered to and promoted. Hollywood "weepies," otherwise known as four-handkerchief movies, were big-studio productions that were tailored to bring in female box-office receipts. Columns of advice to the lovelorn, such as the redoubtable "Dear Dorothy Dix" and the current "Dear Abby," were by tradition a woman's slot on daily newspapers, along with the coverage of society births and weddings, in the days when females were as rare in a newsroom as they were in a coal mine. In the heyday of the competitive tabloids, sob-sister journalism, that newsroom term for a human-interest story told with heart-wrenching pathos (usually by a tough male reporter who had the formula down pat), was held in contempt by those on the paper who covered the "hard stuff" of politics, crime and war. (Nathanael West's famous antihero labored under the byline of Miss Lonelyhearts.) Despite its obvious audience appeal, "soft stuff" was, and is, on the lower rungs of journalism—trivial, weak and unmanly.

In Government circles during the Vietnam war, it was considered a sign of emotional softness, of lily-livered liberals and nervous nellies, to suggest that Napalmed babies, fire-bombed villages and defoliated crops were reason enough to pull out American forces. The peace movement, went the charge, was composed of cowards and fuzzy thinkers. Suspicion of an unmanly lack of hard practical logic always haunts those men who espouse peace and nonviolence, but women, the weaker sex, are permitted a certain amount of emotional leeway. Feminine logic, after all, is reputedly governed by the heartstrings. Compassion and sentiment are the basis for its notorious "subjectivity" compared to the "objectivity" of men who use themselves as the objective standard.

As long as the social division of labor ordains that women should bear the chief emotional burden of caring for human life from the cradle to the grave while men may demonstrate their dimorphic difference through competitive acts of physical aggression, emblematic compassion and fear of violence are compelling reasons for an aversion to war and other environmental hazards. When law and custom deny the full range of public expression and economic opportunity that men claim for themselves, a woman must place much of her hopes, her dreams, her feminine identity and her social importance in the private sphere of personal relations, in the connective tissue of marriage, family, friendship and love. In a world out of balance, where men are taught to value toughness and linear vision as masculine traits that enable them to think strategically from conquest to conquest, from campaign to campaign without looking back, without getting sidetracked by vulnerable feelings, there is, and will be, an emotional difference between the sexes, a gender gap that may even appear on a Gallup poll.

If a true shape could emerge from the shadows of historic oppression, would the gender-specific experience of being female still suggest a range of perceptions and values that differ appreciably from those of men? It would be premature to offer an answer. Does a particular emotion ultimately resist separation from its historic deployment in the sexual balance of power? In the way of observation, this much can be said: The entwining of anatomy, history and culture presents such a persuasive emotional argument for a "different nature" that even the best aspects of femininity collaborate in its perpetuation.

## NOTES

1. "Facile" is the English translator's match for the French *facile*, more correctly rendered as "easy." Beauvoir did not mean to ascribe a stereotype superficiality to women in her remark.
2. The overwhelming influence of feminine love is frequently offered as a mitigating explanation by women who do unfeminine things. Elizabeth Bentley, the "Red Spy Queen" of the cold war Fifties, attributed her illegal activities to her passion for the Russian master spy Jacob Golos. Judith Coplon's defense for stealing Government documents was love for another Russian, Valentin Gubichev. More recently, Jean Harris haplessly failed to convince a jury that her love for "Scarsdale diet" Doctor Herman Tarnower was so great that she could not possibly have intended to kill him.

---

# REFLECTING ON MEANING

1. Brownmiller says that the significance of the study by Broverman and Broverman is *not* its confirmation of gender stereotyping in society. Rather, she claims, the study is important because it showed (a) that "stereotypic femininity was a grossly negative assessment of the female sex," and (b) that "many so-called feminine traits ran counter to clinical descriptions of mental health." What distinction is Brownmiller making? Is it important? Why or why not? Does the study suggest that women are emotionally unhealthy, or does it imply something else? How do you know?

2. Brownmiller asserts that "a requirement of femininity is that a woman devote her life to love"; in fact, she says, women are required to make an "obsessional career" of love. What is her evidence for this assertion? Do you agree with it? What are some of your own experiences and observations that support or refute her point? Why aren't men expected to devote their lives to love? Or are they?

3. Consider the essay's concluding statement: "The entwining of anatomy, history and culture presents such a persuasive emotional argument for a 'different nature' that even the best aspects of femininity collaborate in its perpetuation." What are the "best aspects" of femininity? In what ways and for what reasons might femininity cooperate in maintaining the idea that women and men have different temperaments? What is Brownmiller ultimately suggesting about the origins of this idea? To what extent do you agree or disagree with her? Why?

## EXPLORING RHETORICAL STRATEGIES

1. Brownmiller hints at her thesis early in the essay by stating that femininity is a socially constructed myth. She doesn't explicitly state her thesis, however, until she reaches her next-to-last paragraph. What is her thesis? Why do you think she delayed stating it until the end of the essay? What are the advantages she gained in doing this?

2. Throughout the essay, Brownmiller employs an interesting device, a kind of reverse image: Miss America raising "her scepter high like a trophy"; a man overcome with tears, or "lovesick or suffering from heartache"; a woman sewing in "fury" and "frustration"; the sounds of male orgasm on a top-forty recording. What is your reaction to these images? What is the effect of this device? How do these reversals help Brownmiller make her point?

3. The nature of Brownmiller's voice in this essay is, as she says of feminine emotions, "a tough nut to crack." Her diction ranges from the formal to the colloquial; she even uses clichés. What overall tone does her varied use of language create? What kind of persona has it helped her create? What is your image of Brownmiller? What are your reactions to this image?

# Sisterhood

## GLORIA STEINEM

*In this essay, Gloria Steinem describes the changes that "sisterhood" brought about in her own life and the lives of other women. She describes sisterhood as a process that brings together women of different ages, races, and economic standing through discovery of their shared experiences as women.*

A very, very long time ago (about three or four years), I took a certain secure and righteous pleasure in saying the things that women are supposed to say. I remember with pain—

"My work won't interfere with marriage. After all, I can always keep my typewriter at home." Or:

"I don't want to write about women's stuff. I want to write about foreign policy." Or:

"Black families were forced into matriarchy, so I see why black women have to step back and let their men get ahead." Or:

"I know we're helping Chicano groups that are tough on women, but *that's their culture*." Or:

"Who would want to join a women's group? I've never been a joiner, have you?" Or (when bragging):

"He says I write like a man."

I suppose it's obvious from the kinds of statements I chose that I was secretly nonconforming. I wasn't married. I was earning a living at a profession I cared about. I had basically—if quietly—opted out of the "feminine" role. But that made it all the more necessary to repeat the conventional wisdom, even to look as conventional as I could manage, if I was to avoid some of the punishments reserved by society for women who don't do as society says. I therefore learned to Uncle Tom with subtlety, logic, and humor. Sometimes, I even believed it myself.

If it weren't for the women's movement, I might still be dissembling away. But the ideas of this great sea-change in women's view of ourselves are contagious and irresistible. They hit women like a revelation, as if we had left a dark room and walked into the sun.

At first my discoveries seemed personal. In fact, they were the same ones so many millions of women have made and are continuing to make. Greatly simplified, they go like this: Women are human beings first, with minor differences from men that apply largely to the single act of reproduction. We share the dreams, capabilities, and weaknesses of all human beings, but our occasional pregnancies and other visible differences have been used—even more pervasively, if less brutally, than racial differences have been used—to create an "inferior" group and an elaborate division of labor. The division is continued for a clear if often unconscious reason: the economic and social profit of males as a group.

Once this feminist realization dawned, I reacted in what turned out to be predictable ways. First, I was amazed at the simplicity and obviousness of a realization that made sense, at last, of my life experience. I couldn't figure out why I hadn't seen it before. Second, I realized how far that new vision of life was from the system around us, and how tough it would be to explain this feminist realization at all, much less to get people (especially, though not only, men) to accept so drastic a change.

But I tried to explain. God knows (*she* knows) that women try. We make analogies with other groups that have been marked for subservient roles in order to assist blocked imaginations. We supply endless facts and statistics of injustice, reeling them off until we feel like human information-retrieval machines. We lean heavily on the device of reversal. (If there is a male reader to whom all my *pre*realization statements seem perfectly logical, for instance, let him read each sentence with "men" substituted for "women"—or himself for me—and see how he feels: "My work won't interfere with marriage. . . ."; ". . . Chicano groups that are tough on men. . . ." You get the idea.)

We even use logic. If a woman spends a year bearing and nursing a child, for instance, she is supposed to have the primary responsibility for raising that child to adulthood. That's logic by the male definition, but it often makes women feel children are their only function, keeps them from doing any other kind of work, or discourages them from being mothers at all. Wouldn't it be just as logical to say that the child has two parents, therefore both are equally responsible for child rearing, and the father should compensate for that extra year by spending *more* than half the time caring for the child? Logic is in the eye of the logician.

Occasionally, these efforts at explaining actually succeed. More often, I get the feeling that most women are speaking Urdu and most men are speaking Pali.

Whether joyful or painful, both kinds of reaction to our discovery have a great reward. They give birth to sisterhood.

First, we share the exhilaration of growth and self-discovery, the sensation of having the scales fall from our eyes. Whether we are giving other women this new knowledge or receiving it from them, the pleasure for all concerned is enormous. And very moving.

In the second stage, when we're exhausted from dredging up facts and arguments for the men whom we had previously thought advanced and intelligent, we make another simple discovery: women understand. We may share experiences, make jokes, paint pictures, and describe humiliations that mean little to men, but *women understand.*

The odd thing about these deep and personal connections among women is that they often leap barriers of age, economics, worldly experience, race, culture—all the barriers that, in male or mixed society, seem so impossible to cross.

I remember meeting with a group of women in Missouri who, because they had come in equal numbers from the small town and from its nearby campus, seemed to be split between wives with white gloves welded to their wrists and students with boots who used words like "imperialism" and "oppression." Planning for a child-care center had brought them together, but the meeting seemed hopeless until three of the booted young women began to argue among themselves about a young male professor. The leader of the radicals on campus, he accused all women unwilling to run Mimeograph machines of not being sufficiently devoted to the cause. As for child-care centers, he felt their effect of allowing women to compete with men for jobs was part of a dreaded "feminization" of the American male and American culture.

"He sounds just like my husband," said one of the white-gloved women. "He wants me to have bake sales and collect door-to-door for his Republican party."

The young women had sense enough to take it from there. What difference did boots or white gloves make if they were all getting treated like servants and children? Before they broke up, they were discussing some subjects that affected them all (like the myth of the vaginal orgasm) and planning to meet every week. "Men think we're whatever it is we do for men," explained one of the housewives. "It's only by getting together with other women that we'll ever find out who we are."

Even racial barriers become a little less formidable once we discover this mutuality of our life experiences as women. At a meeting run by black women domestics who had formed a job cooperative in Alabama, a white housewife asked me about the consciousness-raising sessions or "rap groups" that are often an organic path to feminism. I explained that while men, even minority men, usually had someplace—a neighborhood, a bar, a street corner, something—where they could get together and be themselves, women were isolated in their houses and families; isolated from other females. We had no street corners, no bars, no offices, no territory that was recognized as ours. Rap groups were an effort to create something of our own, a free place—an occasional chance for total honesty and support from our sisters.

As I talked about isolation, about the feeling that there must be something wrong with us if we aren't content to be housekeepers and mothers, tears began to stream down the cheeks of this dignified woman—clearly as much of a surprise to her as to us. For the black women, some distance was bridged by seeing this white woman cry.

"He does it to us both, honey," said the black woman next to her, putting an arm around her shoulders. "If it's your own kitchen or somebody else's, you still don't get treated like people. Women's work just doesn't count."

The meeting ended with the housewife organizing a support group of white women who would extract from their husbands a living wage for domestic workers and help them fight the local authorities who opposed any pay raises; a support group without which the domestic workers felt their small and brave cooperative could not survive.

As for the "matriarchal" argument that I swallowed in prefeminist days, I now understand why many black women resent it and feel that it's the white sociologists' way of encouraging the black community to imitate a white suburban life-style. "If I end up cooking grits for revolutionaries," explained a black woman poet from Chicago, "it isn't my revolution. Black men and women need to work together: you can't have liberation for half a race." In fact, some black women wonder if criticism of the strength they were forced to develop isn't a way to keep half the black community working at lowered capacity and lowered pay, as well as to attribute some of black men's sufferings to black women, instead of to their real source—white racism. I wonder with them.

Looking back at all those male-approved things I used to say, the basic hang-up seems clear—a lack of esteem for women, whatever our race, and for myself.

This is the most tragic punishment that society inflicts on any second-class group. Ultimately the brainwashing works, and we ourselves come to believe our group is inferior. Even if we achieve a little success in the world and think of ourselves as "different," we don't want to associate with our group. We want to identify up, not down (clearly my problem in not wanting to join women's groups). We want to be the only woman in the office, or the only black family on the block, or the only Jew in the club.

The pain of looking back at wasted, imitative years is enormous. Trying to write like men. Valuing myself and other women according to the degree of our acceptance by men—socially, in politics, and in our professions. It's as painful as it is now to hear two grown-up female human beings competing with each other on the basis of their husband's status, like servants whose identity rests on the wealth or accomplishments of their employers.

And this lack of esteem that makes us put each other down is still the major enemy of sisterhood. Women who are conforming to society's expectations view the nonconformists with justifiable alarm. *Those noisy, unfeminine women,* they say to themselves. *They will only make trouble for us all.* Women who are quietly nonconforming, hoping nobody will notice, are even more alarmed because they have more to lose. And that makes sense, too.

The status quo protects itself by punishing all challengers, especially women whose rebellion strikes at the most fundamental social organization: the sex roles that convince half the population that its identity depends on being first in work or in war, and the other half that it must serve as docile, unpaid, or underpaid labor.

In fact, there seems to be no punishment inside the white male club that quite equals the ridicule and personal viciousness reserved for women who rebel. Attractive or young women who act forcefully are assumed to be either unnatural or male-controlled. If they succeed, it could only have been sexually, through men. Old women or women considered unattractive by male standards are accused of acting out of bitterness, because they could not get a man. Any woman who chooses to behave like a full human being should be warned that the armies of the status quo will treat her as something of a dirty joke. That's their natural and first weapon. She will *need* sisterhood.

All of that is meant to be a warning but not a discouragement. There are more rewards than punishments.

For myself, I can now admit anger and use it constructively, where once I would have submerged it and let it fester into guilt or collect for some destructive explosion.

I have met brave women who are exploring the outer edge of human possibility, with no history to guide them, and with a courage to make themselves vulnerable that I find moving beyond the words to express it.

I no longer think that I do not exist, which was my version of that lack of self-esteem afflicting many women. (If male standards weren't natural to me, and they were the only standards, how could I exist?) This means that I am less likely to need male values and approval and am less vulnerable to classic arguments. ("If you don't like me, you're not a real woman"—said by a man who is coming on. "If you don't like me, you can't relate to other people, you're not a real person"—said by anyone who understands blackmail as an art.)

I can sometimes deal with men as equals and therefore can afford to like them for the first time.

I have discovered politics that are not intellectual or superimposed. They are organic. I finally understand why for years I inexplicably identified with "out" groups: I belong to one, too. And I know it will take a coalition of such groups to achieve a society in which, at a minimum, no one is born into a second-class role because of visible difference, because of race or of sex.

I no longer feel strange by myself or with a group of women in public. I feel just fine.

I am continually moved to discover I have sisters.

I am beginning, just beginning, to find out who I am.

---

## REFLECTING ON MEANING

1. Steinem describes a stage in her life when she was "secretly nonconforming." What conventions wasn't she conforming to? Given her nonconformity, why did she nevertheless find it "necessary to repeat the conventional wisdom" and to look "conventional"? What does *conventional* mean in this context? Why was she so concerned about being seen as conventional? Why does she say that she had "learned to Uncle Tom"?

2. According to Steinem, what is sisterhood? What are its origins? How, in Steinem's view, is it more a process than a state of being? What does it achieve? What kinds of people does it bring together? How? What kind of bond does it create?

3. What does Steinem mean when she says that "outsiders" such as women "want to identify up, not down"? Why do they want

to do this? In what ways might "identifying up" be a positive move for an individual? In what ways might it be negative? Why?

## EXPLORING RHETORICAL STRATEGIES

1. "Sisterhood" was first published in *Ms.* magazine in 1972. For what audience was Steinem writing? What evidence in the essay, if any, suggests that she expected resistance from her audience? What assumptions do you think she expected her intended audience to share with her? How might "Sisterhood" have been different if Steinem had been writing for a magazine such as *Family Circle* or *GQ*?

2. Analogies, facts and statistics, logic, and the "device of reversal"—these are some of the strategies feminists use to support their beliefs, according to Steinem. To what extent does Steinem herself use these kinds of evidence to support her thesis? Which of these ways of supporting a point do you find especially effective? What other kinds of support does Steinem provide? To what extent does she rely on personal experience, anecdotes, and concrete examples? How do these sources of support influence the tone of her essay?

3. To illustrate how sisterhood emphasizes connections among women in disparate situations, Steinem tells the stories of three women: a young student whose male professor expected her "to run Mimeograph machines" for "the cause"; a "white-gloved" woman whose husband wanted her to hold "bake sales and collect door-to-door for his Republican party"; and a black woman who announced, "If I end up cooking grits for revolutionaries, it isn't my revolution." How does the concrete detail of each situation make these examples effective? How does the common theme running through the examples reinforce Steinem's point?

# TAKING A STAND
## QUESTIONS FOR CONSIDERATION

1. In this part, several authors describe differences between women and men. Pick an area of difference that interests you (for example, verbal ability, conversational style, personality, values), summarize the observations of the appropriate authors on the nature of this difference, and draw your own conclusions about its significance. How pervasive is the difference? To what extent and in what ways does it influence the lives of women and men? What "rules" does it suggest for "feminine" and "masculine" codes of conduct? In what ways does it fit into a larger system of gender differences? How does it contribute to socially accepted definitions of masculinity and femininity? In thinking about this topic, you may wish to consider the essays by Gilbert and Webster, Adams, Goldberg, Rosenberg, and Brownmiller; you may also find helpful the essays by Steinem and Lakoff that appear in Part III.

2. Adams and Weintraub both review research that confirms biological origins for some of the differences between women and men. Weisstein, however, refutes such conclusions. Do Adams's and Weintraub's essays hold up under Weisstein's scrutiny of scientific research? Are their arguments still as convincing as they were when you first read them? How does Weisstein's discussion help put Adams's and Weintraub's beliefs into context?

3. Gilbert and Webster explore the social consequences of raising and evaluating girls and boys by differing criteria, whereas Mackintosh suggests that such differences are not directly responsible for gender-specific behavior. Define the issue these authors explore and describe their viewpoints before shaping your own position. Are girls and boys raised differently? In what ways? Does society—especially parents and teachers—have differing expectations of them? To what extent do these differences shape the personalities and temperaments of the women and men these children become? To what extent does it shape their desires, ambitions, and options in life?

4. Brownmiller argues that the rules of "femininity" are very much alive, despite advances in achieving women's rights. Conversely, Rosenberg argues that the idea of "masculinity" is dying. What do you think? Are models of masculinity and femininity still operative? Do they still influence men's and women's ways of thinking and acting? Is one model perhaps changing more than

the other? Are these ideas dying out, or have they simply been modified?

5. The cluster of essays on men and masculinity suggests that women aren't the only ones "trapped" by social models of gender behavior. According to Alda, Goldberg, Rosenberg, and Fasteau, how are men, too, expected to behave in ways appropriate to their sex? According to these authors, to what extent are men's personalities, temperaments, and life options influenced by social expectations? Do you agree that men suffer social oppression as a consequence of gender roles? What is the nature of this oppression? How is it different from that of women? To what extent, if any, do masculine roles translate into social power and feminine roles into powerlessness? Why? How might exploring the nature of these roles help explain gender inequities in society? What insights does Brownmiller provide to help you explore these questions?

6. The relationship between gender difference and social inequality is itself a controversial issue. De Beauvoir's discussion of women suggests that the very idea of difference is at the root of women's oppression. Conversely, Gilbert and Webster argue that hierarchical value systems, rather than difference, cause women to be oppressed. And Weintraub goes so far as to suggest that the more we know about gender differences, the greater the chance that women can achieve real social equality. What is the central issue in this debate? On what point, if any, do these authors agree? Where do their viewpoints diverge? To what extent does their disagreement derive from differing assumptions about the origins of gender differences? To what extent do you find social inequity a consequence of the idea of difference? To what extent do you find it an unrelated issue?

7. Perrin celebrates an androgynous freedom that allows him to adopt "feminine" behavior at will, whereas Goldberg argues that women can shift roles if they choose, but men are not permitted the luxury of acting "out of role" at all. Gilbert and Webster suggest that both men and women are severely punished for behaving in ways considered inappropriate for their gender. What do you think? Are children punished for such "inappropriate" behavior? Are adults also punished? Do both genders have the option of acting out of role? Do either men or women have more freedom to do so? In shaping your response, you might want to draw on the essays of several other authors, especially Rosenberg, Fasteau, and Brownmiller.

8. Aren't women considered human? Sayers and de Beauvoir examine this issue at length, and Gilbert and Webster also suggest

that society perceives men and women as "different kinds of beings." Why is this a recurring issue in discussions of women? What does it suggest about the nature of women's oppression? How do both White's and de Beauvoir's explorations of identity and self-definition illuminate this issue? According to these authors, what problems do women and gay men share in defining themselves? Why do they encounter these difficulties? What does this issue suggest about homosexuals and women as oppressed groups in society? What other similarities exist between the two groups? What is the significance of such similarities?

9. Several of the authors represented hold assumptions about the goals and achievements of feminism. What are their assumptions? In what ways do they agree or disagree? What might account for their differing perspectives on feminism? What do you think the goals of feminism are? In establishing your own position, you may want to explore the essays by Adams, Weintraub, Goldberg, and Steinem.

# Part II

# Women's Role: Historical Perspectives

Although there has been intense interest in gender relations over the last three decades, the subject certainly is not new. The role and status of women have been topics of discussion since the earliest writings of the Greek philosophers. Not surprisingly, many of the same themes addressed by feminist scholars in the 1990s were also discussed by writers in the nineteenth century and even as far back as Plato. Part II contributes a historical perspective to our exploration of women's role in society.

The first section includes four essays that reveal attitudes about women in past eras. Plato discusses the differences between men and women and the role women should play in an ideal society. Mary Daly interprets biblical history from a feminist perspective, connecting sexist assumptions in the Bible to the historical oppression of women. Pope Pius XI reaffirms the views on marriage and the role of women held for centuries by the Catholic church. And Dorothy Gies McGuigan documents historical discrimination against women and the obstacles they faced in obtaining an education.

The second section continues our historical perspective with a look at some of the earliest truly "feminist" writings. Mary Wollstonecraft, a courageous, pioneering feminist of the late eighteenth century, writes articulately about the bitter oppression of women by an unfeeling patriarchal society. John Stuart Mill argues forcefully that our social and legal institutions have conspired to make men tyrants over their wives, and that such tyranny is out of place in a democratic society. Charlotte Perkins Gilman, who like Mill also wrote in the nineteenth century, examines the economic status of women, claiming that what little economic power they do enjoy they derive solely from marriage. In two separate selections written in the first few decades of this century, Margaret Sanger champions women's right to control their bodies. Finally, Virginia Woolf describes the obstacles, psychological and social, that she—and, by extension, other women in the early part of our century—encountered in pursuing a career.

From Plato's *Republic* to the early feminists' writings decrying the economic oppression of women, questions of gender have remained crucial issues throughout the ages. Part II illustrates that women of the late twentieth century share many of the same struggles with their historical counterparts.

# Chapter 4

## VOICES FROM AND ABOUT THE PAST

### The Role of Women in the Ideal Society

PLATO

*In this excerpt from Plato's* Republic, *Socrates and Glaucon discuss how women should fit into the ideal society. The crux of their debate remains relevant even today: if men and women are indeed different, to what extent should their differences influence their position, status, and function in society?*

It may be right after the men have played their part that the women should come on in their turn, especially when you demand it in this way. For men who are, by nature and education, such as we have described, there is, in my opinion, no right possession or use of children and women except along the lines on which we originally started them. We tried in our argument, if you remember, to make our men like guardians of a flock."

"Yes."

"Then let us follow this up and give corresponding rules for birth and nurture, and see whether we approve the result or not."

"How?" he asked.

"In this way. Do we think that the females of watchdogs ought to watch as well as the males, ought to hunt with them, and generally share their occupations, or should they be kept indoors in the kennels, on the ground that breeding and rearing the puppies disables them for anything else, while the hard work and all the care of the flocks is reserved for the males?"

"They should share in everything," he said. "Only we treat the females as the weaker and the males as the stronger."

"Can you," I said, "use any living creature for the same work as another unless you rear and train it in the same way?"

"No," he said.

"Then if we employ women at the same tasks as men, we must give them the same instruction?"

"Yes."

"The men were given music and gymnastic."

"Yes."

"Then we must assign to the women also these two arts, and the art of war in addition, and treat them in the same way."

"That follows from what you say," he said. . . .

"But must we not first come to an agreement as to whether these proposals are practical or not, and allow any one, whether he is a jester or a serious person, to raise the question whether female human nature is capable of sharing with the male in all his occupations, or in none of them, or whether it is capable of some and not of others, and to ask in the last case to which of these classes warfare belongs? Would not this naturally be the best beginning, and lead to the best conclusion?"

"Much the best," he said.

"Then," I said, "shall we on behalf of these other people put the question to ourselves, that the other side may not be besieged without having defenders?"

"There is nothing to hinder us," he said.

"Then shall we say on their behalf: 'Socrates and Glaucon, there is no need for others to raise an objection against you. For in the beginning of your settlement of the city, you yourselves admitted that each should, as nature provides, do his own work, one person one work.' "

"I think we did. How could we do otherwise?"

" 'But is not a woman by nature very different from a man?' "

"Certainly she is different."

" 'And ought not different tasks be assigned to different individuals in accordance with the nature of each?' "

"Yes."

" 'Then are you not mistaken and inconsistent now in maintaining, as you do, that men and women should do the same things, seeing that they have widely different natures?' Will you be able to offer any defence to that, my wonderful friend?"

"It is certainly not easy just at the moment," he said. "But I shall have to ask you, as I do now, to interpret our argument also, whatever it is."

"This, Glaucon," I said, "with many other similar difficulties, is what I have foreseen all this time. For that was why I was afraid, and hesitated to touch on the law concerning the possession and nurture of women and children."

"I don't wonder," he said. "By Zeus, no, it is not an easy task."

"It is not," I said. "But the truth is, whether a man falls into a small swimming-bath or into the middle of the mighty ocean, he has to swim all the same."

"Certainly."

"Well, then, we must strike out and try to get safe out of the argument, in the hope of a dolphin taking us up, or of some other impossible means of salvation."

"It looks like it," he said.

"Come, then," I said, "let us see whether we can possibly find a way out. We admit that different natures ought to do different things, and that the natures of a man and of a woman are different, but now we say that these different natures should do the same things. Is that the accusation against us?"

"It is."

"A noble thing, Glaucon," I said, "is the power of the art of controversy."

"Why do you say so?"

"Because," I said, "many people seem to me to fall into it quite against their will, and to think that discussion which is really contention, because they cannot examine the subject of their argument by analysing its various forms, but will urge their contradiction of what has been said in reliance on the mere sound of the word, dealing with one another by contention, and not by scientific argument."

"Yes," he said, "that happens with very many people. But does it touch us at this moment?"

"Most certainly it does," I said, "for we seem, quite against our will, to be dealing with controversial arguments."

"In what way?"

"When we insist that what are not the same natures ought not to have the same pursuits, we cling to the verbal point most bravely and contentiously, but we have never inquired at all of what kind were the sameness and the difference and with reference to what we were then distinguishing them, when we proposed to give different pursuits to different natures, and the same pursuits to the same natures."

"No," he said, "we did not inquire."

"In the same way," I said, "we might evidently ask ourselves whether bald and hairy men had the same or opposite natures; and, agreeing that they have opposite natures, might forbid hairy men to be shoemakers if bald men are, or forbid bald men if hairy men are."

"Well, that would be ridiculous," he said.

"But would it not be ridiculous," I said, "simply because, in that proposition, we did not mean same and different in general? Our rule was only directed against that particular form of likeness and difference which concerns those particular pursuits. We meant, for example, that the soul possessed of medical capacity and a doctor have the same nature. Do you agree with me?"

"I do."

"But a doctor and a carpenter have different natures."

"Of course."

"Then," I said, "if we find either the male or the female sex excelling the other in any art or other pursuit, then we shall say that this particular pursuit must be assigned to one and not to the other; but if we find that the difference simply consists in this, that the female conceives and the male begets, we shall not allow that that goes any way to prove that a woman differs from a man with reference to the subject of which we are speaking, and we shall still consider that our guardians and their wives ought to follow the same pursuits."

"And quite rightly," he said.

"Is not our next step to invite the supporters of the contrary opinion to show us in reference to what art or what pursuit among all those required for the service of the city, the nature of men and women is not the same, but different?"

"That is certainly just."

"Perhaps others might make the same reply as was made by you a little while ago, that it is not easy to give a satisfactory answer at the moment, but that it would not be difficult after consideration."

"They might."

"Then shall we request our objector to follow us, in the hope that we may prove to him that there is no occupation in the organization of the city which is peculiar to women?"

"Certainly."

" 'Come, then,' we shall say to him, 'answer this. When you say that one man has a natural talent for anything, and another is naturally unfitted for it, do you mean that the first learns it easily, while the second learns it with difficulty? that the first, after a little study, would find out much for himself in the subject which he has studied; but the second, in spite of much study and practice, would not even keep what he had learned? that in the one the mind would be well served by the bodily powers, in the other it would be thwarted? Are not these the only signs by which you meant to determine in any case natural talent or the want of it?' "

"No one," he said, "will name any others."

"Then, do you know any human occupation in which the male sex does not in all these particulars surpass the female? Need I bore you by referring to weaving and the making of pastry and preserves, in which, indeed, the female sex is considered to excel, and where their discomfiture is most laughed at?"

"What you say is true," he said. "Speaking generally, the one sex is easily beaten by the other all round. There are indeed many cases of women being better than men in many different employments, but, as a general rule, it is as you say."

"Then, my friend, there is not one of those pursuits by which the city is ordered which belongs to women as women, or to men as men; but natural aptitudes are equally distributed in both kinds of creatures. Women naturally participate in all occupations, and so do men; but in all women are weaker than men."

"Certainly."

"Shall we, then, assign all occupations to men and none to women?"

"Of course not."

"But we shall say, I fancy, that one woman is by nature fit for medicine, and another not; one musical, and another unmusical?"

"Surely."

"And is not one woman a lover of gymnastic and of war, and another unwarlike and no lover of gymnastic?"

"I should think so."

"And one a lover and another a hater of wisdom; one spirited, another spiritless?"

"Yes."

"Then one woman will be capable of being a guardian and another not. For did we not select just this nature for our men guardians?"

"We did."

"Then for the purposes of guarding the city the nature of men and women is the same, except that women are naturally weaker, men naturally stronger?"

"Apparently."

"Then we must select women of the necessary character to share the life of men of like character and guard the city along with them, inasmuch as they are capable and of a kindred nature?"

"Certainly."

"Then must we not assign the same occupations to the same natures?"

"Yes."

"So we are come round to what we said before, and allow that there is nothing unnatural in assigning music and gymnastic to the wives of the guardians?"

"Most certainly."

"Then our legislation has not been an impracticable dream, seeing that we have made our law in accordance with nature? Present conditions which depart from this are evidently much more a departure from nature."

"Evidently."

"Now were we not inquiring whether our proposals are practicable and desirable?"

"We were."

"And we are agreed that they are practicable?"

"Yes."

"Then we must next come to an agreement on their desirability?"

"Obviously."

"Then surely if women are to become fit to be guardians, we shall not have one education to make guardians of the men and another for the women, especially when education will have the same nature to work upon?"

"No."

"What is your opinion in a question like this?"

"Like what?"

"How do you conceive to yourself one man as better and another as worse? or do you think that all are alike?"

"Certainly not."

"Then, in this city which we were founding, do you think that our guardians, who have received the education we have described, will be better men than the shoemakers who have been trained in shoemaking?"

"The question is ridiculous," he said.

"I understand," I said. "Then are not these the best of all the citizens?"

"Much the best."

"Further, will not these women be the best of the women?"

"Yes, much the best also."

"Then is anything better for a city than that it should contain the best possible men and women?"

"Nothing."

## REFLECTING ON MEANING

1. One of the questions Socrates and Glaucon attempt to answer is the extent to which women's and men's differences are the result of nature or learning. What does Socrates mean by "natural talent" and "natural aptitudes"? Is he implying that the differences are innate or socially constructed?
2. Socrates suggests that perhaps the nature of women's and men's differences, rather than the fact of difference itself, is the key. This difference, he says, is that "the female conceives and the male begets." To what extent does this difference influence the accepted division of labor in society? Should reproductive functions determine one's fitness in other avenues of life? What seems to be Socrates' answer to this question? Do you agree or disagree? Why?
3. During their discussion, Socrates and Glaucon explore the question of differences in men's and women's education and the fitness of women for combat. What are the implications of their discussion for these questions? What are your views?

## EXPLORING RHETORICAL STRATEGIES

1. Socrates compares men and women to male and female watchdogs. In what ways does this analogy help him advance the discussion? How does framing the issue of difference in another context illuminate assumptions about the social roles of men and women? Is the analogy appropriate? Why or why not?
2. The Socratic dialogue differs significantly from the traditional thesis-driven argumentative essay. In what ways does it differ? What are the advantages of dialogue as a genre? What are its limitations?
3. Socrates makes a distinction between "discussion" and "contention." What is this distinction? Do you consider this dialogue a form of discussion or contention? Why?

# I Thank Thee, Lord, That Thou Has Not Created Me a Woman

MARY DALY

*A contemporary theologian and philosopher, Mary Daly reinterprets the Bible and Christian history to show how they "have served as powerful instruments for the reinforcement of the subjection of women in Western society."*

The situation of women in Western society has always been fraught with ambiguity. The writings of innumerable authors in a variety of fields attest to the existence of the problem, although there is by no means agreement concerning the nature of the problem. Adherents of the "eternal feminine" mystique accept as normative the feminine stereotypes of our culture, according to which a "true woman" does not achieve self-actualization through intellectual creativity and participation in political, economic, and social life on a level equal to that of men. Rather, according to this view, her destiny lies in generic fulfillment through motherhood, physical or spiritual, and in being a helpmate to her husband. Opposition to this position is strong. Radically opposed to the idea that the feminine stereotype is "natural" are the findings of anthropology, which suggest that "many, if not all, of the personality traits that we have called masculine or feminine are as lightly linked to sex, as are the clothing, the manners, and the form of head-dress that a society at a given period assigns to sex." Recent research in experimental psychology also tends to refute the idea that the cluster of qualities expressed by the "eternal feminine" stereotype are innate and peculiar to women. A growing number of authors argue that the characteristics of the "eternal feminine" are opposed to those of a developing, authentic person, who must be unique, self-critical, active, and searching. Modern feminists argue that the biological burdens associated with maternity and the restrictions imposed by cultural conditioning have held women back from the attainment of full human stature. They note with irony that the compensation offered by society to women for acceptance of the restrictions which it has imposed upon them in the political, economic, social, educational, and moral spheres has been imprisonment upon a pedestal.

The oppressive situation of women in ancient times is reflected in the Bible. The authors of both the Old and the New Testaments were men of their times, and it would be naive to think that they were free of the prejudices of their epochs. Indeed, the Bible contains much to jolt the modern woman, who is accustomed to think of herself, at least to some extent, as an autonomous person. In the writings of the Old Testament, women emerge as subjugated and inferior beings. Although the wife of an Israelite was not on the level of a slave, and however much better off she was than wives in other Near-Eastern nations, it is indicative of her inferior condition that the wife addressed her husband as a slave addressed his master, or a subject his king. In the Decalogue a man's wife is listed among his possessions, along with such items as his ox and his ass (Exodus 20:17; Deuteronomy 5:21). While her husband could repudiate her, she could not claim a divorce. Misconduct on the part of the wife was severely punished among the ancient Hebrews, whereas infidelity on the part of the man was punished only if he violated the rights of another man by taking a married woman as his accomplice. A man could sell his daughter as well as his slaves. If a couple did not have children, it was assumed to be the fault of the wife. In summary, although Hebrew women were honored as parents and often treated with kindness, their social and legal status was that of subordinate beings. Hebrew males prayed: "I thank thee, Lord, that thou has not created me a woman."

Throughout the centuries, Christian authors have placed great importance upon the account of the creation of Eve in the second chapter of Genesis. Combined with the story of the Fall, this seemed to present irrefutable evidence of woman's essentially inferior intellectual and moral stature. Indeed, through the ages the antifeminine tradition in Christian culture has justified itself to a large extent on the story of the origin and activities of the "first mother," which until recently was not understood to be androcentric myth but rather was taken as straight historical fact. A psychoanalyst who is also a student of biblical literature has summarized the situation succinctly: "The biblical story of Eve's birth is the hoax of the millennia."

Androcentric tendencies in Western culture, rooted also in the profound misogynism of the Greeks, are reflected in the New Testament as well, which in turn has served as a basis for their perpetuation throughout Christendom. The most strikingly antifeminine passages are in the Pauline texts. Paul was greatly concerned with order in society and in Christian assemblies in particular. It seemed important to him that women should not have a predominant place in Christian assemblies, that they should not "speak" in public or unveil their heads. This could have caused scandal and ridicule of the new sect, which already had to face charges of immorality and effeminacy. Thus he repeatedly insisted upon "correct" sexual behavior, including the subjection of wives at meetings. Paul went further and looked for theological justification for the prevailing customs. Thus, for example: "For a man ought not to cover his head, since he is the image and glory of God; but woman is the glory of man. For man was not made from woman, but woman from man. Neither was man created for woman, but woman for man" (I Corinthians 11:7ff.). Paul was basing his theological assertion here upon the then commonly held interpretation of Genesis. The extent of the effect is inestimable. For nearly two thousand years sermons and pious literature have been based upon the "glory of man" theme, and this has been accepted as God's inspired word.

Another frequently quoted Pauline text (probably not written by Paul but traditionally attributed to him) based on the then current interpretation of Genesis and used ever since as authority for the subordination of women is the following:

> Let a woman learn in silence with all submissiveness. I permit no woman to teach or to have authority over men; she is to keep silent. For Adam was formed first, then Eve; and Adam was not deceived, but the woman was deceived and became a transgressor. Yet woman will be saved through bearing children, if she continues in faith and love and holiness, with modesty (I Timothy 2:11–15).

As for women's place in domestic society, the Pauline teaching was most explicit: "As the Church is subject to Christ, so let wives be subject in everything to their husbands" (Ephesians 5:24).

Such texts, understood as divinely inspired and without reference to the cultural context in which they were written, have served as powerful instruments for the reinforcement of the subjection of women in Western society. They have been used by religious authorities down through the centuries as a guarantee of divine approval for the transformation of woman's subordinate status from a contingent fact into an immutable norm of the feminine condition. They have been instrumental in withholding from women equal education, legal and economic equality, and access to the professions.

The low esteem for women in Western society during the early centuries of Christianity is reflected in the writings of the Church Fathers. The characteristics they considered to be typically feminine include fickleness and shallowness, garrulousness and weakness, slowness of understanding, and instability of mind. There were some violent tirades, such as that of Tertullian: "Do you not know that you are Eve? . . . You are the devil's gateway. . . . How easily you destroyed man, the image of God. Because of the death which you brought upon us, even the Son of God had to die" (*De cultu feminarum,* libri duo I, 1). On the whole, the attitude was one of puzzlement over the seemingly incongruous fact of woman's existence. Augustine summed up the general idea in saying that he did not see in what way it could be said that woman was made to be a help for man, if the work of child-bearing be excluded.

The Fathers found in Genesis an "explanation" of woman's inferiority which served as a guarantee of divine approval for perpetuating the situation which made her inferior. There was uncritical acceptance of the androcentric myth of Eve's creation and refusal, in varying degrees of inflexibility, to grant that woman is the image of God—an attitude in large measure inspired by Paul's first epistle to the Corinthians. Thus Augustine wrote that only man is the image and glory of God. According to him, since the believing woman cannot lay aside her sex, she is restored to the image of God only where there is no sex, that is, in the spirit (*De Trinitate,* XII, 7).

Together with the biblical account and the teachings of Church Fathers, those living in the early centuries of the Christian era were confronted with an image of women produced by oppressive conditions which were universal. A girlhood of strict seclusion and of minimal education prepared them for the life of mindless subordinates. This was followed by an early marriage which effectively cut them off from the possibility of autonomous action for the rest of their lives. Their inferiority was a fact; it appeared to be "natural." Thus experience apparently supported the rib story just as the myth itself helped "explain" the common experience of women as incomplete and lesser humans. The vicious circle was complete.

## REFLECTING ON MEANING

1. Daly implicates the story of Eve's creation and the story of the Fall in the historical oppression of women. What are these stories? Why does Daly call them examples of "androcentric myth" as opposed to "straight historical fact"? How have these biblical accounts helped shape the position of women in Western society?
2. Daly maintains that the Pauline texts include the "most strikingly anti-feminine passages" in the New Testament. What do these passages say about women? Why does Daly discuss Paul's values when she presents his writings? According to Daly, why is it naive to think that the authors of the biblical accounts and the Church Fathers were "free of the prejudices of their epochs"? Why is it important to consider the cultural context in which the books of the Bible and the texts of the Church Fathers were produced?
3. What is the "vicious circle" that Daly alludes to? What does she mean when she states that women's "inferiority was a fact"? To what extent, if any, does Christianity still perpetuate this circle? To what extent, if any, does it still perpetuate the "myth" of women's inferiority?

## EXPLORING RHETORICAL STRATEGIES

1. What kinds of evidence does Daly provide to support her assertions? On what foundation is her argument based? Do you find her reinterpretation of history reasonable albeit controversial? Why or why not?
2. What is the tone of Daly's essay? How does it contribute to the persona she creates? What is your reaction to this persona? How do you think she expected readers to respond to her views? Why?
3. In her last paragraph, Daly places the words *natural* and *explain* in quotation marks. Why? How does this emphasis change the meaning of these words? How does it help Daly convey her point of view? Why, also, does she refer to the biblical account of the creation of Eve as the "rib story"? What is the effect of this strategy?

# On Christian Marriage

## POPE PIUS XI

*Pope Pius XI issued the encyclical, or official papal letter,* Casti Connubii *on the subject of marriage and the family in 1930. Defining marriage as a holy sacrament, Pope Pius reaffirms traditional Christian views on the relationship of spouses within the family.*

How great is the dignity of chaste wedlock, Venerable Brethren, may be judged best from this that Christ Our Lord, Son of the Eternal Father, having assumed the nature of fallen man, not only, with His loving desire of compassing the redemption of our race, ordained it in an especial manner as the principle and foundation of domestic society and therefore of all human intercourse, but also raised it to the rank of a truly and "great sacrament" of the New Law, restored it to the original purity of its divine institution, and accordingly entrusted all its discipline and care to His spouse the Church.

In order, however, that amongst men of every nation and every age the desired fruits may be obtained from this renewal of matrimony, it is necessary, first of all, that men's minds be illuminated with the true doctrine of Christ regarding it; and secondly, that Christian spouses, the weakness of their wills strengthened by the internal grace of God, shape all their ways of thinking and of acting in conformity with that pure law of Christ so as to obtain true peace and happiness for themselves and for their families.

Yet not only do We, looking with paternal eye on the universal world from this Apostolic See as from a watchtower, but you also, Venerable Brethren, see, and seeing deeply grieve with Us that a great number of men, forgetful of that divine work of renewal, either entirely ignore or shamelessly deny the great sanctity of Christian wedlock, or relying on the false principles of a new and utterly perverse morality, too often trample it underfoot. And since these most pernicious errors and depraved morals have begun to spread even amongst the faithful and are gradually gaining ground, in Our office as Christ's Vicar upon earth and Supreme Shepherd and Teacher We consider it Our duty to raise Our voice to keep the flock committed to Our care from poisoned pastures and, as far as in Us lies, to preserve it from harm.

We have decided therefore to speak to you, Venerable Brethren, and through you to the whole Church of Christ and indeed to the whole human race, on the nature and dignity of Christian marriage, on the advantages and benefits which accrue from it to the family and to human society itself, on the errors contrary to this most important point of the Gospel teaching, on the vices opposed to conjugal union, and lastly on the principal remedies to be applied. In so doing We follow the footsteps of Our predecessor, Leo XIII, of happy memory, whose encyclical *Arcanum,* published fifty years ago, We hereby confirm and make Our own, and while We wish to expound more fully certain points called for by the conditions and needs of our times, nevertheless We declare that, far from being obsolete, it retains its full force at the present day.

And to begin with that same encyclical, which is almost wholly concerned in vindicating the divine institution of matrimony, its sacramental dignity, and its perpetual stability, let it be repeated as an immutable and inviolable fundamental doctrine that matrimony was not instituted or restored by man but by God; not by man were the laws made to strengthen and confirm and elevate it, but by God, the Author of nature, and by Christ Our Lord by Whom nature was restored, and hence these laws cannot be subject to any human decrees or to any contrary pact even of the spouses themselves. This is the doctrine of Holy Scripture, this is the constant tradition of the Universal Church, this is the solemn definition of the sacred Council of Trent, which declares and establishes from the words of Holy Writ itself that God is the Author of the perpetual stability of the marriage bond, its unity and its firmness. . . .

[The] mutual inward moulding of husband and wife, this determined effort to perfect each other, can in a very real sense, as the Roman Catechism teaches, be said to be the chief reason and purpose of matrimony, provided matrimony be looked at not in the restricted sense as instituted for the proper conception and education of the child, but more widely as the blending of life as a whole and the mutual interchange and sharing thereof.

By this same love it is necessary that all the other rights and duties of the marriage state be regulated as the words of the Apostle: "Let the husband render the debt to the wife, and the wife also in like manner to the husband, not only a law of justice, but of charity."

Domestic society being confirmed, therefore, by this bond of love, there should flourish in it that "order of love," as St. Augustine calls it. This order includes both the primacy of the husband with regard to the wife and children, the ready subjection of the wife and her willing obedience, which the Apostle commends in these words: "Let women be subject to their husbands as to the Lord, because the husband is the head of the wife, as Christ is the head of the church."

This subjection, however, does not deny or take away the liberty which fully belongs to the woman both in view of her dignity as a human person, and in view of her most noble office as wife and mother and companion; nor does it bid her obey her husband's every request if not in harmony with right reason or with the dignity due to a wife; nor, in fine, does it imply that the wife should be put on a level with those persons who in law are called minors, to whom it is not customary to allow free exercise of their rights on account of their lack of mature judgment, or of their ignorance of human affairs. But it forbids that exaggerated liberty which cares not for the good of the family; it forbids that in this body which is the family, the heart be separated from the head to the great detriment of the whole body and the proximate danger of ruin. For if the man is the head, the woman is the heart, and as he occupies the chief place in ruling, so she may and ought to claim for herself the chief place in love.

Again, this subjection of wife to husband in its degree and manner may vary according to the different conditions of persons, place and time. In fact, if the husband neglect his duty, it falls to the wife to take his place in directing the family. But the structure of the family and its fundamental law, established and confirmed by God, must always and everywhere be maintained intact.

With great wisdom Our predecessor Leo XIII, of happy memory, in the encyclical on *Christian Marriage* which We have already mentioned, speaking of this order to be maintained between man and wife, teaches: "The man is the ruler of the family, and the head of the woman; but because she is flesh of his flesh and bone of his bone, let her be subject and obedient to the man, not as a servant but as a companion, so that nothing be lacking of honor or of dignity in the obedience which she pays. Let divine charity be the constant guide of their mutual relations, both in him who rules and in her who obeys, since each bears the image, the one of Christ, the other of the Church." . . .

The same false teachers who try to dim the luster of conjugal faith and purity do not scruple to do away with the honorable and trusting obedience which the woman owes to the man. Many of them even go further and assert that such a subjection of one party to the other is unworthy of human dignity, that the rights of husband and wife are equal; wherefore, they boldly proclaim, the emancipation of women has been or ought to be effected. This emancipation, in their opinion, must be threefold, in the ruling of the domestic society, in the administration of family affairs and in the rearing of the children. It must be social, economic, physiological; physiological, that is to say, the woman is to be freed at her own good pleasure from the burdensome duties properly belonging to a wife as companion and mother (We have already said that this is not an emancipation but a crime); social inasmuch as the wife being freed from the care of children and family, should, to the neglect of these, be able to follow her own bent and devote herself to business and even public affairs; finally economic, whereby the woman even without the knowledge and against the will of her husband may be at liberty to conduct and administer her own affairs, giving her attention chiefly to these rather than to children, husband and family.

This, however, is not the true emancipation of woman, nor that rational and exalted liberty which belongs to the noble office of a Christian woman and wife; it is rather the debasing of the womanly character and the dignity of motherhood, and indeed of the whole family, as a result of which the husband suffers the loss of his wife, the children of their mother and the home and the whole family of an ever watchful guardian. More than this, this false liberty and unnatural equality with the husband is to the detriment of the woman herself, for if the woman descends from her truly regal throne to which she has been raised within the walls of the home by means of the Gospel, she will soon be reduced to the old state of slavery (if not in appearance, certainly in reality) and become, as amongst the pagans, the mere instrument of man.

This equality of rights, which is so much exaggerated and distorted, must indeed be recognized in those rights which belong to the dignity of the human soul and which are proper to the marriage contract and inseparably bound up with wedlock. In such things undoubtedly both parties enjoy the same rights and are bound by the same obligations; in other things there must be a certain inequality and due accommodation, which is demanded by the good of the family and the right ordering and unity and stability of home life.

As, however, the social and economic conditions of the married woman must in some way be altered on account of the changes in social intercourse, it is part of the office of the public authority to adapt the civil rights of the wife to modern needs and requirements, keeping in view what the natural disposition and temperament of the female sex, good morality, and the welfare of the family demand, and provided always that the essential order of the domestic society remain intact, founded as it is on something higher than human authority and wisdom, namely on the authority and wisdom of God, and so not changeable by public laws or at the pleasure of private individuals.

---

## REFLECTING ON MEANING

1. According to Pope Pius, marriage is designed and authorized by whom? What significance does this authorization hold for the views on marriage and family that he outlines?
2. What is the "order of love" in marriage that Pope Pius affirms? What is its "structure" and "fundamental law"? What earlier sources does he draw on to outline the implications of this order?
3. Pope Pius claims that the "subjection" he describes "does not deny or take away the liberty which fully belongs to the woman." Moreover, he asserts that the equality some have called for is not "emancipation but a crime," a "debasing of the womanly character and the dignity of motherhood." How does Pope Pius justify his assertions? Do you find his reasoning acceptable or not? Why?

## EXPLORING RHETORICAL STRATEGIES

1. Definition is an important element of Pope Pius's argument in this letter. How does he define such concepts as marriage, subjection, obedience, and emancipation? In what ways are these definitions crucial to his reasoning?
2. Pope Pius outlines and refutes opposing viewpoints in his letter. What strategies does he use to disarm opponents? Do you find his arguments effective? Why or why not?
3. Analogy plays a key role in the argument Pope Pius presents. What instances of analogy can you find? How do they help advance his conception of gender roles in marriage?

# To Be a Woman and a Scholar

DOROTHY GIES McGUIGAN

---

*Throughout the centuries, education and the professions were closed to women. Despite seemingly insurmountable barriers, however, some women became scholars in their own right. As Dorothy Gies McGuigan suggests in this survey, the efforts of these women to educate themselves illuminate the historical plight that all women faced.*

On a Saturday morning in June exactly three hundred years ago this year [1978], the first woman in the world to receive a doctoral degree mounted a pulpit in the cathedral of Padua to be examined in Aristotelian dialectics.

Her name was Elena Lucrezia Cornaro Piscopia. She was thirty-two years old, single, daughter of one of the wealthiest families in Venice. Precociously brilliant, she had begun to study Aristotle at the age of seven. Her father had backed her studies and supplied the best of tutors; by the time she enrolled in the University of Padua, she knew not only Latin and Greek, French, English, and Spanish, but also Hebrew, Arabic, and Chaldaic.

News of the unique phenomenon of a woman scholar had drawn such throngs to witness her doctoral trial that it had to be moved from the hall of the University of Padua into the cathedral. Elena had first applied to take her doctorate in theology, but the Chancellor of the university's Theological Faculty, Cardinal Gregorio Barbarigo, Bishop of Padua, had refused indignantly. "Never," he replied. "Woman is made for motherhood, not for learning." He wrote later of the incident, "I talked with a French cardinal about it and he broke out in laughter." Reluctantly Barbarigo agreed that she be allowed to take the doctoral examination in philosophy. A modest, deeply religious young woman, Elena Cornaro had quailed before the prospect of the public examination; it was her proud, ambitious father who had insisted. A half hour before the solemn program began, Elena expressed such anguish and reluctance that her confessor had to speak very sternly to persuade her to go through with it. Her examiners were not lenient because of her sex, for the prestige of the university was at stake. But Elena's replies—in Latin, of course—were so brilliant that the judges declared the doctorate in philosophy was "hardly an honor for so towering an intellect." The doctoral ring was placed on Elena's finger, the ermine cape of teacher laid about her shoulders, and the laurel crown of poet placed on her dark curly head. The entire assembly rose and chanted a Te Deum.

What was it like to be a gifted woman, an Elena Cornaro, three hundred years ago? What happened to a bright woman in the past who wanted to study another culture, examine the roots of a language, master the intricacies of higher mathematics, write a book—or prevent or cure a terrible disease?

To begin with, for a woman to acquire anything that amounted to real learning, she needed four basics.

She needed to survive. In the seventeenth century women's life expectancy had risen only to thirty-two; not until 1750 did it begin to rise appreciably and reach, in the mid-nineteenth century, age forty-two. A woman ambitious for learning would do well to choose a life of celibacy, not only to avoid the hazards of childbirth but because there was no room for a scholar's life within the confines of marriage and childbearing. Elena Cornaro had taken a vow of chastity at the age of eleven, turned down proposals of marriage to become an oblate of the Benedictine Order.

Secondly, to aspire to learning a woman needed basic literacy; she had to be one of the fortunate few who learned at least to read and write. Although literacy studies in earlier centuries are still very incomplete and comparative data on men's and women's literacy are meager, it appears that before 1650 a bare 10 percent of women in the city of London could sign their names. What is most striking about this particular study is that when men are divided by occupation—with clergy and the professions at the top, 100 percent literate, and male laborers at the bottom of the scale, about 15 percent literate—women as a group fell below even unskilled male laborers in their rate of literacy. By about 1700 half the women in London could sign their names; in the provinces women's literacy remained much lower.

The third fundamental a woman needed if she aspired to learning was, of course, an economic base. It was best to be born, like Elena Cornaro, to a family of wealth who owned a well-stocked library and could afford private tutors. For girls of poor families the chance of learning the bare minimum of reading and writing was small. Even such endowed charity schools as Christ's Hospital in London were attended mostly by boys; poor girls in charity schools were apt to have their literacy skills slighted in favor of catechism, needlework, knitting, and lace-making in preparation for a life in domestic service.

The fourth fundamental a woman scholar needed was simply a very tough skin, for she was a deviant in a society where the learned woman, far from being valued, was likely to hear herself preached against in the pulpit and made fun of on the public stage. Elena Cornaro was fortunate to have been born in Italy, where an array of learned women had flourished during the Renaissance and where the woman scholar seems to have found a more hospitable ambiance than in the northern countries.

In eighteenth-century England the gifted writer Lady Mary Wortley Montagu, writing in 1753 about proposed plans for a little granddaughter's education, admonished her daughter with some bitterness "to conceal whatever Learning [the child] attains, with as much solicitude as she would hide crookedness or lameness."

In post-Renaissance Europe two overriding fears dominated thinking on women's education: the fear that learning would unfit women for their social role, defined as service to husband and children and obedience to the church; and, a corollary of the first, that open access to education would endanger women's sexual purity. For while humanist philosophy taught that education led to virtue, writers on education were at once conflicted when they applied the premise to women. Nearly all, beginning with the influential sixteenth-century Juan Luis Vives, opted for restricting women's learning. Only a few radical thinkers—some men, such as Richard Mulcaster in Tudor England and the extraordinary Poullain de la Barre in seventeenth-century France, some women, like the feisty Bathsua Makin and revolutionary Mary Wollstonecraft—spoke out for the full development of women's intellectual potential.

In any case, since institutions of higher learning were designed for young men entering the professions—the church, the law, government service—from which women were excluded, they were excluded too from the universities that prepared for them. And, just as importantly, they were excluded from the grammar or preparatory schools, whose curriculum was based on Latin, the code language of the male intellectual elite. Since most scholarly texts were written in Latin, ignorance of that language prevented women from reading scholarly literature in most fields—which only gradually and belatedly became available in translation.

Richard Hyrde, a tutor in the household of Sir Thomas More and himself a defender of learning in women, cited the common opinion:

> . . . that the frail kind of women, being inclined of their own courage unto vice, and mutable at every newelty [*sic*], if they should have skill in many things that must be written in the Latin and Greek tongue . . . it would of likelihood both inflame their stomachs a great deal the more to that vice, that men say they be too much given unto of their own nature already and instruct them also with more subtility and conveyance, to set forward and accomplish their froward intent and purpose.

And yet, despite all the hurdles, some bright women did manage to make a mark as scholars and writers. Sometimes girls listened in on their brothers' tutored lessons. A fortunate few, like Elena Cornaro, had parents willing and able to educate daughters equally with sons. The daughters of Sir Thomas More, of the Earl of Arundel, and of Sir Anthony Cooke in Tudor England were given excellent educations. Arundel's daughter, Lady Joanna Lumley, produced the earliest known English translation of a Greek drama.

But by far the largest number of women scholars in the past were almost totally self-educated. Through sheer intellectual curiosity, self-discipline, often grinding hard work, they taught themselves what they wanted to know. Such self-teaching may well be the only truly joyous form of learning. Yet it has its drawbacks: it may also be haphazard and superficial. Without access to laboratory, lecture, and dissecting table, it was all but impossible for women to train themselves in higher mathematics, for instance, in science, in anatomy.

Mary Wollstonecraft wrote in 1792 that most women who have acted like rational creatures or shown any vigor of intellect have accidentally been allowed "to run wild," and running wild in the family library was the usual way intellectually ambitious women educated themselves. Such a self-taught scholar was Elizabeth Tanfield, Viscountess Cary, who as a girl in Elizabethan England taught herself French, Spanish, Italian, Latin, and added Hebrew "with very little teaching." Her unsympathetic mother refused to allow her candles to read at night, so Elizabeth bribed the servants, and by her wedding day—she was married at fifteen—she had run up a candle debt of a hundred pounds. She wrote numerous translations, poetry—most of which she destroyed—and at least one play, *Mariam, the Faire Queen of Jewry.*

Very often the critical phase of women's intellectual development took place at a different period in their lives from the normal time of men's greatest development. Gifted women often came to a period of intellectual crisis and of intense self-teaching during adulthood.

When Christine de Pisane, daughter of the Italian astrologer and physician at the court of Charles V of France, found herself widowed at twenty-five with three children to support, she turned to writing—certainly one of the first, if not the first, woman in Europe to support herself through a literary career. But Christine found her education wholly inadequate, and at the age of thirty-four she laid down a complete course of study for herself, teaching herself Latin, history, philosophy, literature. She used her pen later on to urge better educational opportunities for women, to defend her sex from the charges of such misogynistic writers as Jean de Meung. In her book, *The City of Ladies,* Christine imagined talented women building a town for themselves where they could lead peaceful and creative lives—an existence impossible, she considered, in fifteenth century France.

Like Christine de Pisane, the Dutch scholar Anna van Schurman of Utrecht, a contemporary of Elena Cornaro, found her early education superficial and unsatisfying. Like most upper middle class girls of the seventeenth century, Anna, precocious though she was, had been taught chiefly to sing nicely, to play musical instruments, to carve portraits in boxwood and wax, to do needlework and tapestry and cut paperwork. At the age of twenty-eight, frustrated by the lack of intellectual stimulation in her life, Anna turned her brilliant mind to serious studies, became one of the finest Latinists of her day, learned Hebrew, Syriac, Chaldaic, wrote an Ethiopian grammar that was the marvel of Dutch scholars, carried on an international correspondence—in Latin, of course—with all the leading scholars of continental Europe. When a professor of theology at Leyden wrote that women were barred from equality with men "by the sacred laws of nature," Anna wrote a Latin treatise in reply in 1641, defending the intellectual capacity of women and urging, as Christine de Pisane had, much greater educational opportunities. Her work was widely translated and made Anna van Schurman a model for women scholars all over Europe.

In France, during the lifetime of Anna van Schurman, a group of bright, intellectually malnourished women—most of them convent-educated—developed one of the most ingenious devices for women's lifelong learning. Bored with the dearth of cultivated conversation at the French court, the Marquise de Rambouillet Mlle de Scudéry, Mme de Lafayette, and a host of others opened their town houses in Paris, invited men and women of talent and taste to hone their wits and talk of science and philosophy, literature and language, love and friendship. The salon has been described as "an informal university for women." Not only did it contribute to adult women's education, but it shaped standards of speaking and writing for generations in France and profoundly influenced French culture as a whole.

An offshoot of the salons were the special lecture courses offered by eminent scholars in chemistry, etymology, and other subjects—lectures largely attended by women. Fontenelle wrote his popular book on astronomy, *The Plurality of Worlds,* specifically for a female readership, and Descartes declared he had written his *Discourse on Method* in French rather than Latin so that women too would be able to read it.

There was, rather quickly, a backlash. Molière's satires on learned women did much to discredit the ladies who presided at salons—and who might at times be given to a bit of overelegance in speech and manner. When Abbé Fénélon wrote his influential treatise, *On the Education of Girls,* in 1686—just eight years after Elena Cornaro had won her doctorate—he mentioned neither Elena Cornaro nor Anna van Schurman nor Christine de Pisane. He inveighed against the pernicious effect of the salons. Declaring that "A woman's intellect is normally more feeble and her curiosity greater than those of men, it is undesirable to set her to studies which may turn her head. A girl," admonished that worthy French cleric, "must learn to obey without respite, to hold her peace and allow others to do the talking. Everything is lost if she obstinately tries to be clever and to get a distaste for domestic duties. The virtuous woman spins, confines herself to her home, keeps quiet, believes and obeys."

So much for the encouragement of women scholars in late seventeenth century France.

Across the Channel in England in the second half of the seventeenth century, bright ambitious women were studying not only the classics and languages but learning to use the newly perfected telescope and microscope, and to write on scientific subjects. Margaret Cavendish, Duchess of Newcastle, a remarkable woman with a wide-ranging mind and imagination, wrote not only biography, autobiography, and romance, but also popular science—she called it "natural philosophy"—directed especially to women readers. The versatile and talented writer Aphra Behn—the first woman in England to make her living by her pen—translated Fontenelle's *Plurality of Worlds* into English in 1688. In the preface she declared she would have preferred to write an original work on astronomy but had "neither health nor leisure" for such a project; it was, in fact, the year before her death and she was already ailing. But she defended the Copernican system vigorously against the recent attack by a Jesuit priest, did not hesitate to criticize the author, Fontenelle, and to correct an error in the text on the height of the earth's atmosphere.

But the learned lady in England as in France found herself criticized from the pulpit and satirized on the stage. Margaret Cavendish was dubbed "Mad Madge of Newcastle." Jonathan Swift poked fun at Mary Astell for her proposal to found a women's college. Thomas Wright in *The Female Virtuosos,* the anonymous authors of *The Humours of Oxford* and *Female Wits,* Shadwell, Congreve, and others lampooned the would-be woman scholar. The shy poet, Anne, Countess of Winchilsea, who had only reluctantly identified herself as author of a published volume of verse, was cruelly pilloried by Pope and Gay in their play *Three Hours After Marriage.* And Aphra Behn, author of a phenomenal array of plays, poems, novels, and translations, could read this published verse about herself and her work at about the same time she was translating Fontenelle:

> Yet hackney writers, when their verse did fail
> To get 'em brandy, bread and cheese, and ale,
> Their wants by prostitution were supplied;
> Show but a tester [sixpence] you might up and ride;
> For punk and poetess agree so pat
> You cannot well be this, and not be that.

So if one asks what it was like to be a gifted woman, to aspire to learning at the time of Elena Cornaro, the answer might be that it was a difficult and demanding choice, requiring not merely intellectual gifts but extraordinary physical and mental stamina, and only a rare few women succeeded in becoming contributing scholars and writers. All the usual scholarly careers were closed to women, so that even for women who succeeded in educating themselves to the level of their male colleagues, the opportunities to support themselves were meager.

In a day when it was considered impermissible for a woman to speak in public, it was also considered inappropriate and unfeminine to draw attention to herself by publishing a work under her own name. Many—perhaps most—women scholars and writers—from Anne, Countess of Winchilsea, Lady Mary Wortley Montagu down to Fanny Burney and Jane Austen—published their works at first either anonymously or pseudonymously. Nor was Elizabeth Tanfield the only woman scholar who destroyed her own writings before they were published.

And what of Elena Cornaro's life after she won her doctorate in 1678? During the six years she lived after that event, she divided her time between scholarly pursuits and service to the poor, sick, and needy. Baroque Italy paid honor to its unique woman scholar. Certainly Elena Cornaro aroused no antagonisms, but rather filled with discretion the approved nunlike role designated for the woman in Catholic countries who chose not to marry. Scholars and statesmen from several countries made a point of visiting her in Padua, and she was invited to join fellow scholars in the Academy of Ricovrati in Padua. When she died of tuberculosis in 1684 at the age of thirty-eight—a disease that was in a measure responsible for her eminence, for she had been sent to Padua partly to escape the damp air of Venice—her funeral attracted a greater throng than her doctoral examination. A delegation of distinguished university faculty accompanied the procession through the streets of Padua, and on her coffin were heaped books in the languages she had mastered and the sciences she had studied. She was buried in the Chapel of St. Luke among the Benedictine monks, having carefully instructed her maid to sew her robe together at the hem so that even in death her modesty would be preserved.

Of her writings very little has survived. She had arranged to have her correspondence and many of her manuscripts destroyed before she died, and the remainder of her writings were disseminated as souvenirs among family and friends.

After Elena Cornaro's death a half century passed before a second woman, again Italian, Laura Maria Catherina Bassi, was awarded a doctorate at the University of Bologna. Not until 150 years later did American universities admit women for degrees, and two centuries passed before Oxford and Cambridge conferred degrees on women. Only in our own decade, in 1970, did the Catholic Church finally award the degree of Doctor of Theology that had been denied Elena Cornaro to two women: one to the sixteenth century Spanish saint, Teresa of Avila, the other to fourteenth century St. Catherine of Siena, who had in fact never learned to read and write. One hopes that in some academic elysium those two saintly ladies are proudly showing off their belated scholarly credentials.

## REFLECTING ON MEANING

1. In the past, what obstacles to education have women faced? What four basics, according to McGuigan, did they need in order to overcome these obstacles? Why were these considerations so important? What were the odds that a woman would be able to meet these needs? Why didn't men encounter the same obstacles? Does McGuigan imply that all men had access to education? What limitations might some men have confronted? In what ways were these limitations compounded for women?
2. What social prejudices was a learned woman likely to encounter? Why would others have considered her deviant? Why did Lady Montagu counsel her daughter to conceal her own daughter's learning? For what reasons was education considered superfluous and even negative for women?
3. McGuigan suggests that women who did become educated had to take special care to fulfill "feminine" roles in other aspects of their lives. What specific behaviors did they adopt? In what ways did this make their scholarly pursuits more socially acceptable?

## EXPLORING RHETORICAL STRATEGIES

1. McGuigan frames her survey of learned women with the story of Elena Cornaro. Why does she do this? In what ways does this story establish a foundation for the rest of the essay?
2. How does McGuigan's encapsulated history of learned women advance the main point she makes? How does it help answer the questions that she initiates the essay with?
3. The essay concludes with an ironic twist that brings her survey into the seventies. What is the irony of the Catholic church's honoring two women with the title Doctor of Theology? What point do you think McGuigan is making by ending on this note?

# Chapter 5

## EQUALITY AND FEMINISM

# *From* A Vindication of the Rights of Woman

MARY WOLLSTONECRAFT

*In 1792 Mary Wollstonecraft published* A Vindication of the Rights of Woman, *a treatise arguing that women and men must share true equality before either can be free. In the following excerpt she indicts the "false system of education" that perpetuates women's inequality, and she proposes a new system that will allow women to become independent, calling for nothing less than a "revolution in female manners."*

### Introduction

. . . I have turned over various books written on the subject of education, and patiently observed the conduct of parents and the management of schools; but what has been the result?—a profound conviction that the neglected education of my fellow-creatures is the grand source of the misery I deplore; and that women, in particular, are rendered weak and wretched by a variety of concurring causes, originating from one hasty conclusion. The conduct and manners of women, in fact, evidently prove that their minds are not in a healthy state; for, like the flowers which are planted in too rich a soil, strength and usefulness are sacrificed to beauty; and the flaunting leaves, after having pleased a fastidious eye, fade, disregarded on the stalk, long before the season when they ought to have arrived at maturity. One cause of this barren blooming I attribute to a false system of education, gathered from the books written on this subject by men who, considering females rather as women than human creatures, have been more anxious to make them alluring mistresses than affectionate wives and rational mothers; and the understanding of the sex has been so bubbled by this specious homage, that the civilized women of the present century, with a few exceptions, are only anxious to inspire love, when they ought to cherish a nobler ambition, and by their abilities and virtues exact respect.

In a treatise, therefore, on female rights and manners, the works which have been particularly written for their improvement must not be overlooked; especially when it is asserted, in direct terms, that the minds of women are enfeebled by false refinement; that the books of instruction, written by men of genius, have had the same tendency as more frivolous productions; and that, in the true style of Mahometanism, they are treated as a kind of subordinate beings, and not as a part of the human species, when improveable reason is allowed to be the dignified distinction which raises men above the brute creation, and puts a natural sceptre in a feeble hand.

Yet, because I am a woman, I would not lead my readers to suppose that I mean violently to agitate the contested question respecting the quality or inferiority of the sex; but as the subject lies in my way, and I cannot pass it over without subjecting the main tendency of my reasoning to misconstruction, I shall stop a moment to deliver, in a few words, my opinion. In the government of the physical world it is observable that the female in point of strength is, in general, inferior to the male. This is the law of nature; and it does not appear to be suspended or abrogated in favour of woman. A degree of physical superiority cannot, therefore, be denied—and it is a noble prerogative! But not content with this natural pre-eminence, men endeavour to sink us still lower, merely to render us alluring objects for a moment; and women, intoxicated by the adoration which men, under the influence of their senses, pay them, do not seek to obtain a durable interest in their hearts, or to become the friends of the fellow creatures who find amusement in their society. . . .

My own sex, I hope, will excuse me, if I treat them like rational creatures, instead of flattering their *fascinating* graces, and viewing them as if they were in a state of perpetual childhood, unable to stand alone. I earnestly wish to point out in what true dignity and human happiness consists—I wish to persuade women to endeavour to acquire strength, both of mind and body, and to convince them that the soft phrases, susceptibility of heart, delicacy of sentiment, and refinement of taste, are almost synonymous with epithets of weakness, and that those beings who are only the objects of pity and that kind of love, which has been termed its sister, will soon become objects of contempt.

Dismissing, then, those pretty feminine phrases, which the men condescendingly use to soften our slavish dependence, and despising that weak elegancy of mind, exquisite sensibility, and sweet docility of manners, supposed to be the sexual characteristics of the weaker vessel, I wish to show that elegance is inferior to virtue, that the first object of laudable ambition is to obtain a character as a human being, regardless of the distinction of sex; and that secondary views should be brought to this simple touchstone. . . .

The education of women has, of late, been more attended to than formerly; yet they are still reckoned a frivolous sex, and ridiculed or pitied by the writers who endeavour by satire or instruction to improve them. It is acknowledged that they spend many of the first years of their lives in acquiring a smattering of accomplishments; meanwhile strength of body and mind are sacrificed to libertine notions of beauty, to the desire of establishing themselves,—the only way women can rise in the world,—by marriage. And this desire making mere animals of them, when they marry they act as such children may be expected to act:—they dress; they paint, and nickname God's creatures. Surely these weak beings are only fit for a seraglio!—Can they be expected to govern a family with judgment, or take care of the poor babes whom they bring into the world? . . .

Woman are, in fact, so much degraded by mistaken notions of female excellence, that I do not mean to add a paradox when I assert, that this artificial weakness produces a propensity to tyrannize, and gives birth to cunning, the natural opponent of strength, which leads them to play off those contemptible infantine airs that undermine esteem even whilst they excite desire. Let men become more chaste and modest, and if women do not grow wiser in the same ratio, it will be clear that they have weaker understandings. It seems scarcely necessary to say, that I now speak of the sex in general. Many individuals have more sense than their male relatives; and, as nothing preponderates where there is a constant struggle for an equilibrium, without it has naturally more gravity, some women govern their husbands without degrading themselves, because intellect will always govern.

## The Prevailing Opinion of a Sexual Character Discussed

To account for, and excuse the tyranny of man, many ingenious arguments have been brought forward to prove, that the two sexes, in the acquirement of virtue, ought to aim at attaining a very different character: or, to speak explicitly, women are not allowed to have sufficient strength of mind to acquire what really deserves the name of virtue. Yet it should seem, allowing them to have souls, that there is but one way appointed by Providence to lead *mankind* to either virtue or happiness.

If then women are not a swarm of ephemeron triflers, why should they be kept in ignorance under the specious name of innocence? Men complain, and with reason, of the follies and caprices of our sex, when they do not keenly satirize our headstrong passions and grovelling vices.—Behold, I should answer, the natural effect of ignorance! The mind will ever be unstable that has only prejudices to rest on, and the current will run with destructive fury when there are no barriers to break its force. Women are told from their infancy, and taught by the example of their mothers, that a little knowledge of human weakness, justly termed cunning, softness of temper, *outward* obedience, and a scrupulous attention to a puerile kind of propriety, will obtain for them the protection of man; and should they be beautiful, everything else is needless, for, at least, twenty years of their lives. . . .

By individual education, I mean, for the sense of the word is not precisely defined, such an attention to a child as will slowly sharpen the senses, form the temper, regulate the passions as they begin to ferment, and set the understanding to work before the body arrives at maturity; so that the man may only have to proceed, not to begin, the important task of learning to think and reason.

To prevent any misconstruction, I must add, that I do not believe that a private education can work the wonders which some sanguine writers have attributed to it. Men and women must be educated, in a great degree, by the opinions and manners of the society they live in. In every age there has been a stream of popular opinion that has carried all before it, and given a family character, as it were, to the century. It may then fairly be inferred, that, till society be differently constituted, much cannot be expected from education. It is, however, sufficient for my present purpose to assert, that, whatever effect circumstances have on the abilities, every being may become virtuous by the exercise of its own reason; for if but one being was created with vicious inclinations, that is positively bad, what can save us from atheism? or if we worship a God, is not that God a devil?

Consequently, the most perfect education, in my opinion, is such an exercise of the understanding as is best calculated to strengthen the body and form the heart. Or, in other words, to enable the individual to attain such habits of virtue as will render it independent. In fact, it is a farce to call any being virtuous whose virtues do not result from the exercise of its own reason. This was Rousseau's opinion respecting men: I extend it to women, and confidently assert that they have been drawn out of their sphere by false refinement, and not by an endeavour to acquire masculine qualities. Still the regal homage which they receive is so intoxicating, that till the manners of the times are changed, and formed on more reasonable principles, it may be impossible to convince them that the illegitimate power, which they obtain, by degrading themselves, is a curse, and that they must return to nature and equality, if they wish to secure the placid satisfaction that unsophisticated affections impart. . . .

Many are the causes that, in the present corrupt state of society, contribute to enslave women by cramping their understandings and sharpening their senses. One, perhaps, that silently does more mischief than all the rest, is their disregard of order.

To do everything in an orderly manner, is a most important precept, which women, who, generally speaking, receive only a disorderly kind of education, seldom attend to with that degree of exactness that men, who from their infancy are broken into method, observe. This negligent kind of guess-work, for what other epithet can be used to point out the random exertions of a sort of instinctive common sense, never brought to the test of reason? prevents their generalizing matters of fact—so they do to-day, what they did yesterday, merely because they did it yesterday.

This contempt of the understanding in early life has more baneful consequences than is commonly supposed; for the little knowledge which women of strong minds attain, is, from various circumstances, of a more desultory kind than the knowledge of men, and it is acquired more by sheer observations on real life, than from comparing what has been individually observed with the results of experience generalized by speculation. Led by their dependent situation and domestic employments more into society, what they learn is rather by snatches; and as learning is with them, in general, only a secondary thing, they do not pursue any one branch with that persevering ardour necessary to give vigour to the faculties, and clearness to the judgment. In the present state of society, a little learning is required to support the character of a gentleman; and boys are obliged to submit to a few years of discipline. But in the education of women, the cultivation of the understanding is always subordinate to the acquirement of some corporeal accomplishment; even while enervated by confinement and false notions of modesty, the body is prevented from attaining that grace and beauty which relaxed half-formed limbs never exhibit. Besides, in youth their faculties are not brought forward by emulation; and having no serious scientific study, if they have natural sagacity it is turned too soon on life and manners. They dwell on effects, and modifications, without tracing them back to causes; and complicated rules to adjust behaviour are a weak substitute for simple principles.

As a proof that education gives this appearance of weakness to females, we may instance the example of military men, who are, like them, sent into the world before their minds have been stored with knowledge or fortified by principles. The consequences are similar; soldiers acquire a little superficial knowledge, snatched from the muddy current of conversation, and, from continually mixing with society, they gain, what is termed a knowledge of the world; and this acquaintance with manners and customs has frequently been confounded with a knowledge of the human heart. But can the crude fruit of casual observation, never brought to the test of judgment, formed by comparing speculation and experience, deserve such a distinction? Soldiers, as well as women, practise the minor virtues with punctilious politeness. Where is then the sexual difference, when the education has been the same? All the difference that I can discern, arises from the superior advantage of liberty, which enables the former to see more of life. . . .

Standing armies can never consist of resolute, robust men; they may be well disciplined machines, but they will seldom contain men under the influence of strong passions, or with very vigorous faculties. And as for any depth of understanding, I will venture to affirm, that it is as rarely to be found in the army as amongst women; and the cause, I maintain, is the same. It may be further observed, that officers are also particularly attentive to their persons, fond of dancing, crowded rooms, adventures, and ridicule. Like the *fair* sex, the business of their lives is gallantry.—They were taught to please, and they only live to please. Yet they do not lose their rank in the distinction of sexes, for they are still reckoned superior to women, though in what their superiority consists, beyond what I have mentioned, it is difficult to discover.

The great misfortune is this, that they both acquire manners before morals, and a knowledge of life before they have, from reflection, any acquaintance with the grand ideal outline of human nature. The consequence is natural; satisfied with common nature, they become a prey to prejudices, and taking all their opinions on credit, they blindly submit to authority. So that, if they have any sense, it is a kind of instinctive glance, that catches proportions, and decides with respect to manners; but fails when arguments are to be pursued below the surface, or opinions analyzed.

May not the same remark be applied to women? Nay, the argument may be carried still further, for they are both thrown out of a useful station by the unnatural distinctions established in civilized life. Riches and hereditary honours have made cyphers of women to give consequence to the numerical figure; and idleness has produced a mixture of gallantry and despotism into society, which leads the very men who are the slaves of their mistresses to tyrannize over their sisters, wives, and daughters. This is only keeping them in rank and file, it is true. Strengthen the female mind by enlarging it, and there will be an end to blind obedience; but, as blind obedience is ever sought for by power, tyrants and sensualists are in the right when they endeavour to keep women in the dark, because the former only want slaves, and the latter a play-thing. The sensualist, indeed, has been the most dangerous of tyrants, and women have been duped by their lovers as princes by their ministers, whilst dreaming that they reigned over them. . . .

Women are, therefore, to be considered either as moral beings, or so weak that they must be entirely subjected to the superior faculties of men.

Let us examine this question. Rousseau declares that a woman should never, for a moment, feel herself independent, that she should be governed by fear to exercise her natural cunning, and made a coquetish slave in order to render her a more alluring object of desire, a *sweeter* companion to man, whenever he chooses to relax himself. He carries the arguments, which he pretends to draw from the indications of nature, still further, and insinuates that truth and fortitude, the corner stones of all human virtue, should be cultivated with certain restrictions, because, with respect to the female character, obedience is the grand lesson which ought to be impressed with unrelenting rigour.

What nonsense! When will a great man arise with sufficient

strength of mind to puff away the fumes which pride and sensuality have thus spread over the subject! If women are by nature inferior to men, their virtues must be the same in quality, if not in degree, or virtue is a relative idea; consequently, their conduct should be founded on the same principles, and have the same aim. . . .

Youth is the season for love in both sexes; but in those days of thoughtless enjoyment provision should be made for the more important years of life, when reflection takes place of sensation. But Rousseau, and most of the male writers who have followed his steps, have warmly inculcated that the whole tendency of female education ought to be directed to one point:—to render them pleasing.

Let me reason with the supporters of this opinion who have any knowledge of human nature, do they imagine that marriage can eradicate the habitude of life? The woman who has only been taught to please will soon find that her charms are oblique sunbeams, and that they cannot have much effect on her husband's heart when they are seen every day, when the summer is passed and gone. Will she then have sufficient native energy to look into herself for comfort, and cultivate her dormant faculties? or, is it not more rational to expect that she will try to please other men; and, in the emotions raised by the expectation of new conquests, endeavour to forget the mortification her love or pride has received? When the husband ceases to be a lover—and the time will inevitably come, her desire of pleasing will then grow languid, or become a spring of bitterness; and love, perhaps, the most evanescent of all passions, gives place to jealousy or vanity.

I now speak of women who are restrained by principle or prejudice; such women, though they would shrink from an intrigue with real abhorrence, yet, nevertheless, wish to be convinced by the homage of gallantry that they are cruelly neglected by their husbands; or, days and weeks are spent in dreaming of the happiness enjoyed by congenial souls till their health is undermined and their spirits broken by discontent. How then can the great art of pleasing be such a necessary study? it is only useful to a mistress; the chaste wife, and serious mother, should only consider her power to please as the polish of her virtues, and the affection of her husband as one of the comforts that render her task less difficult and her life happier.—But, whether she be loved or neglected, her first wish should be to make herself respectable, and not to rely for all her happiness on a being subject to like infirmities with herself. . . .

Women ought to endeavour to purify their heart; but can they do so when their uncultivated understandings make them entirely dependent on their senses for employment and amusement, when no noble pursuit sets them above the little vanities of the day, or enables them to curb the wild emotions that agitate a reed over which every passing breeze has power? To gain the affections of a virtuous man, is affectation necessary? Nature has given woman a weaker frame than man; but, to ensure her husband's affections, must a wife, who by the exercise of her mind and body whilst she was discharging the duties of a daughter, wife, and mother, has allowed her constitution to retain its natural strength, and her nerves a healthy tone, is she, I say, to condescend to use art and feign a sickly delicacy in order to secure her husband's affection? Weakness may excite tenderness, and gratify the arrogant pride of man; but the lordly caresses of a protector will not gratify a noble mind that pants for, and deserves to be respected. Fondness is a poor substitute for friendship!

In a seraglio, I grant, that all these arts are necessary; the epicure must have his palate tickled, or he will sink into apathy; but have women so little ambition as to be satisfied with such a condition? Can they supinely dream life away in the lap of pleasure, or the languor of weariness, rather than assert their claim to pursue reasonable pleasures and render themselves conspicuous by practising the virtues which dignify mankind? Surely she has not an immortal soul who can loiter life away merely employed to adorn her person, that she may amuse the languid hours, and soften the cares of a fellow-creature who is willing to be enlivened by her smiles and tricks, when the serious business of life is over.

Besides, the woman who strengthens her body and exercises her mind will, by managing her family and practising various virtues, become the friend, and not the humble dependent of her husband; and if she, by possessing such substantial qualities, merit his regard, she will not find it necessary to conceal her affection, nor to pretend to an unnatural coldness of constitution to excite her husband's passions. In fact, if we revert to history, we shall find that the women who have distinguished themselves have neither been the most beautiful nor the most gentle of their sex. . . .

## The Same Subject Continued

. . . Women are every where in this deplorable state; for, in order to preserve their innocence, as ignorance is courteously termed, truth is hidden from them, and they are made to assume an artificial character before their faculties have acquired any strength. Taught from their infancy that beauty is woman's sceptre, the mind shapes itself to the body, and, roaming round its gilt cage, only seeks to adorn its prison. Men have various employments and pursuits which engage their attention, and give a character to the opening mind; but women, confined to one, and having their thoughts constantly directed to the most insignificant part of themselves, seldom extend their views beyond the triumph of the hour. But were their understanding once emancipated from the slavery to which the pride and sensuality of man and their short-sighted desire, like that of dominion in tyrants, of present sway, has subjected them, we should probably read of their weaknesses with surprise. . . .

Let not men then in the pride of power, use the same arguments that tyrannic kings and venal ministers have used, and fallaciously assert that woman ought to be subjected because she has always been so. But, when man, governed by reasonable laws, enjoys his natural freedom, let him despise woman, if she do not share it with him; and, till that glorious period arrives, in descanting on the folly of the sex, let him not overlook his own.

Women, it is true, obtaining power by unjust means, by practising or fostering vice, evidently lose the rank which reason would assign them, and they become either abject slaves or capricious tyrants. They lose all simplicity, all dignity of mind, in acquiring power, and act as men are observed to act when they have been exalted by the same means.

It is time to effect a revolution in female manners—time to restore to them their lost dignity—and make them, as a part of the human species, labour by reforming themselves to reform the world. It is time to separate unchangeable morals from local manners. If men be demi-gods—why let us serve them! And if the dignity of the female soul be as disputable as that of animals—if their reason does not afford sufficient light to direct their conduct whilst unerring instinct is denied—they are surely of all creatures the most miserable! and, bent beneath the iron hand of destiny, must submit to be a *fair defect* in Creation. But to justify the ways of Providence respecting them, by pointing out some irrefragable reason for thus making such a large portion of mankind accountable and not accountable, would puzzle the subtilest casuist. . . .

Why do men halt between two opinions, and expect impossibilities? Why do they expect virtue from a slave, from a being whom the constitution of civil society has rendered weak, if not vicious?

Still I know that it will require a considerable length of time to eradicate the firmly rooted prejudices which sensualists have planted; it will also require some time to convince women that they act contrary to their real interest on an enlarged scale, when they cherish or affect weakness under the name of delicacy, and to convince the world that the poisoned source of female vices and follies, if it be necessary, in compliance with custom, to use synonymous terms in a lax sense, has been the sensual homage paid to beauty. . . .

Besides, if women be educated for dependence; that is, to act according to the will of another fallible being, and submit, right or wrong, to power, where are we to stop? Are they to be considered as viceregents allowed to reign over a small domain, and answerable for their conduct to a higher tribunal, liable to error?

It will not be difficult to prove that such delegates will act like men subjected by fear, and make their children and servants endure their tyrannical oppression. As they submit without reason, they will, having no fixed rules to square their conduct by, be kind, or cruel, just as the whim of the moment directs; and we ought not to wonder if sometimes, galled by their heavy yoke, they take a malignant pleasure in resting it on weaker shoulders. . . .

With respect to religion, she never presumed to judge for herself; but conformed, as a dependent creature should, to the ceremonies of the church which she was brought up in, piously believing that wiser heads than her own have settled that business:—and not to doubt is her point of perfection. She therefore pays her tythe of mint and cummin—and thanks her God that she is not as other women are. These are the blessed effects of a good education! These the virtues of man's help-mate! . . .

I wish to sum up what I have said in a few words, for I here throw down my gauntlet, and deny the existence of sexual virtues, not excepting modesty. For man and woman, truth, if I understand the meaning of the word, must be the same; yet to the fanciful female character, so prettily drawn by poets and novelists, demanding the sacrifice of truth and sincerity, virtue becomes a relative idea, having no other foundation than utility, and of that utility men pretend arbitrarily to judge, shaping it to their own convenience.

Women, I allow, may have different duties to fulfil; but they are *human* duties, and the principles that should regulate the discharge of them, I sturdily maintain, must be the same.

To become respectable, the exercise of their understanding is necessary, there is no other foundation for independence of character; I mean explicitly to say that they must only bow to the authority of reason, instead of being the *modest* slaves of opinion.

In the superior ranks of life how seldom do we meet with a man of superior abilities, or even common acquirements? The reason appears to me clear, the state they are born in was an unnatural one. The human character has ever been formed by the employments the individual, or class, pursues; and if the faculties are not sharpened by necessity, they must remain obtuse. The argument may fairly be extended to women; for, seldom occupied by serious business, the pursuit of pleasure gives that insignificancy to their character which renders the society of the *great* so insipid. The same want of firmness, produced by a similar cause, forces them both to fly from themselves to noisy pleasures, and artificial passions, till vanity takes place of every social affection, and the characteristics of humanity can scarcely be discerned. Such are the blessings of civil governments, as they are at present organized, that wealth and female softness equally tend to debase mankind, and are produced by the same cause; but allowing women to be rational creatures, they should be incited to acquire virtues which they may call their own, for how can a rational being be ennobled by anything that is not obtained by its *own* exertions? . . .

## Of the Pernicious Effects Which Arise from the Unnatural Distinctions Established in Society

. . . though I consider that women in the common walks of life are called to fulfil the duties of wives and mothers, by religion and reason, I cannot help lamenting that women of a superior cast have not a road open by which they can pursue more extensive plans of usefulness and independence. I may excite laughter, by dropping a hint, which I mean to pursue, some future time, for I really think that women ought to have representatives, instead of being arbitrarily governed without having any direct share allowed them in the deliberations of government.

But, as the whole system of representation is now, in this country, only a convenient handle for despotism, they need not complain, for they are as well represented as a numerous class of hard working mechanics, who pay for the support of royalty when they can scarcely stop their children's mouths with bread. How are they represented whose very sweat supports the splendid stud of an heir apparent, or varnishes the chariot of some female favourite who looks down on shame? Taxes on the very necessaries of life, enable an endless tribe of idle princes and princesses to pass with stupid pomp before a gaping crowd, who almost worship the very parade which costs them so dear. This is mere gothic grandeur, something like the barbarous useless parade of having sentinels on horseback at Whitehall, which I could never view without a mixture of contempt and indignation. . . .

But what have women to do in society? I may be asked, but to loiter with easy grace; surely you would not condemn them all to suckle fools and chronicle small beer! No. Women might certainly study the art of healing, and be physicians as well as nurses. And midwifery, decency seems to allot to them, though I am afraid the word midwife, in our dictionaries, will soon give place to *accoucheur,* and one proof of the former delicacy of the sex be effaced from the language.

They might, also, study politics, and settle their benevolence on the broadest basis; for the reading of history will scarcely be more useful than the perusal of romances, if read as mere biography; if the character of the times, the political improvements, arts, &c. be not observed. In short, if it be not considered as the history of man; and not of particular men, who filled a niche in the temple of fame, and dropped into the black rolling stream of time, that silently sweeps all before it, into the shapeless void called—eternity. For shape, can it be called, "that shape hath none"?

Business of various kinds, they might likewise pursue, if they were educated in a more orderly manner, which might save many from common and legal prostitution. Women would not then marry for a support, as men accept of places under government, and neglect the implied duties; nor would an attempt to earn their own subsistence, a most laudable one! sink them almost to the level of those poor abandoned creatures who live by prostitution. For are not milliners and mantua-makers reckoned the next class? The few employments open to women, so far from being liberal, are menial; and when a superior education enables them to take charge of the education of children as governesses, they are not treated like the tutors of sons, though even clerical tutors are not always treated in a manner calculated to render them respectable in the eyes of their pupils, to say nothing of the private comfort of the individual. But as women educated like gentlewomen, are never designed for the humiliating situation which necessity sometimes forces them to fill, these situations are considered in the light of a degradation; and they know little of the human heart, who need to be told, that nothing so painfully sharpens sensibility as such a fall in life.

Some of these women might be restrained from marrying by a proper spirit or delicacy, and others may not have had it in their power to escape in this pitiful way from servitude; is not that government then very defective, and very unmindful of the happiness of one half of its members, that does not provide for honest, independent women, by encouraging them to fill respectable stations? But in order to render their private virtue a public benefit, they must have a civil existence in the state, married or single; else we shall continually see some worthy woman, whose sensibility has been rendered painfully acute by undeserved contempt, droop like "the lily broken down by a plow-share."

It is a melancholy truth; yet such is the blessed effect of civilization! the most respectable women are the most oppressed; and, unless they have understandings far superiour to the common run of understandings, taking in both sexes, they must, from being treated like contemptible beings, become contemptible. How many women thus waste life away the prey of discontent, who might have practised as physicians, regulated a farm, managed a shop, and stood erect, supported by their own industry, instead of hanging their heads surcharged with the dew of sensibility, that consumes the beauty to which it at first gave lustre; nay, I doubt whether pity and love are so near akin as poets feign, for I have seldom seen much comparison excited by the helplessness of females, unless they were fair; then, perhaps, pity was the soft handmaid of love, or the harbinger of lust. . . .

. . . I then would fain convince reasonable men of the importance of some of my remarks, and prevail on them to weigh dispassionately the whole tenor of my observations.—I appeal to their understandings; and, as a fellow-creature, claim, in the name of my sex, some interest in their hearts. I entreat them to assist to emancipate their companion, to make her a *help meet* for them!

Would men but generously snap our chains, and be content with rational fellowship instead of slavish obedience, they would find us more observant daughters, more affectionate sisters, more faithful wives, more reasonable mothers—in a word, better citizens. We should then love them with true affection, because we should learn to respect ourselves; and the peace of mind of a worthy man would not be interrupted by the idle vanity of his wife, nor the babes sent to nestle in a strange bosom, having never found a home in their mother's. . . .

## On National Education

. . . True taste is ever the work of the understanding employed in observing natural effects; and till women have more understanding, it is vain to expect them to possess domestic taste. Their lively senses will ever be at work to harden their hearts, and the emotions struck out of them will continue to be vivid and transitory, unless a proper education store their mind with knowledge.

It is the want of domestic taste, and not the acquirement of knowledge, that takes women out of their families, and tears the smiling babe from the breast that ought to afford it nourishment. Women have been allowed to remain in ignorance, and slavish dependence, many, very many years, and still we hear of nothing but their fondness of pleasure and sway, their preference of rakes and soldiers, their childish attachment to toys, and the vanity that makes them value accomplishments more than virtues. . . .

Let an enlightened nation then try what effect reason would have to bring them back to nature, and their duty; and allowing them to share the advantages of education and government with man, see whether they will become better, as they grow wiser and become free. They cannot be injured by the experiment; for it is not in the power of man to render them more insignificant than they are at present.

To render this practicable, day schools, for particular ages, should be established by government, in which boys and girls might be educated together. The school for the younger children, from five to nine years of age, ought to be absolutely free and open to all classes. A sufficient number of masters should also be chosen by a select committee, in each parish, to whom any complaint of negligence, &c. might be made, if signed by six of the children's parents. . . .

. . . to prevent any of the distinctions of vanity, they should be dressed alike, and all obliged to submit to the same discipline, or leave the school. The school-room ought to be surrounded by a large piece of ground, in which the children might be usefully exercised, for at this age they should not be confined to any sedentary employment for more than an hour at a time. But these relaxations might all be rendered a part of elementary education, for many things improve and amuse the senses, when introduced as a kind of show, to the principles of which, dryly laid down, children would turn a deaf ear. For instance, botany, mechanics, and astronomy. Reading, writing, arithmetic, natural history, and some simple experiments in natural philosophy, might fill up the day; but these pursuits should never encroach on gymnastic plays in the open air. The elements of religion, history, the history of man, and politics, might also be taught by conversations, in the socratic form.

After the age of nine, girls and boys, intended for domestic employments, or mechanical trades, ought to be removed to other schools, and receive instruction, in some measure appropriated to the destination of each individual, the two sexes being still together in the morning; but in the afternoon, the girls should attend a school where plain-work, mantua-making, millinery, &c. would be their employment.

The young people of superior abilities, or fortune, might now be taught, in another school, the dead and living languages, the elements of science, and continue the study of history and politics, on a more extensive scale, which would not exclude polite literature.

Girls and boys still together? I hear some readers ask: yes. And I should not fear any other consequence than that some early attachment might take place; which, whilst it had the best effect on the moral character of the young people, might not perfectly agree with the views of the parents, for it will be a long time, I fear, before the world will be so far enlightened that parents, only anxious to render their children virtuous, shall allow them to choose companions for life themselves. . . .

In this plan of education the constitution of boys would not be ruined by the early debaucheries, which now make men so selfish, or girls rendered weak and vain, by indolence, and frivolous pursuits. But, I presuppose, that such a degree of equality should be established between the sexes as would shut out gallantry and coquetry, yet allow friendship and love to temper the heart for the discharge of higher duties.

These would be schools of morality—and the happiness of man, allowed to flow from the pure springs of duty and affection, what advances might not the human mind make? Society can only be happy and free in proportion as it is virtuous; but the present distinctions, established in society, corrode all private, and blast all public virtue.

I have already inveighed against the custom of confining girls to their needle, and shutting them out from all political and civil employments; for by thus narrowing their minds they are rendered unfit to fulfil the peculiar duties which nature has assigned them.

Only employed about the little incidents of the day, they necessarily grow up cunning. My very soul has often sickened at observing the sly tricks practised by women to gain some foolish thing on which their silly hearts were set. Not allowed to dispose of money, or call any thing their own, they learn to turn the market penny; or, should a husband offend, by staying from home, or give rise to some emotions of jealousy—a new gown, or any pretty bawble, smooths Juno's angry brow.

But these *littlenesses* would not degrade their character, if women were led to respect themselves, if political and moral subjects were opened to them; and I will venture to affirm that this is the only way to make them properly attentive to their domestic duties.—An active mind embraces the whole circle of its duties, and finds time enough for all. It is not, I assert, a bold attempt to emulate masculine virtues; it is not the enchantment of literary pursuits, or the steady investigation of scientific subjects, that leads women astray from duty. No, it is indolence and vanity—the love of pleasure and the love of sway, that will reign paramount in an empty mind. I say empty emphatically, because the education which women now receive scarcely deserves the name. For the little knowledge that they are led to acquire, during the important years of youth, is merely relative to accomplishments; and accomplishments without a bottom, for unless the understanding be cultivated, superficial and monotonous is every grace. Like the charms of a made up face, they only strike the senses in a crowd; but at home, wanting mind, they want variety. The consequence is obvious; in gay scenes of dissipation we meet the artificial mind and face, for those who fly from solitude dread, next to solitude, the domestic circle; not having it in their power to amuse or interest, they feel their own insignificance, or find nothing to amuse or interest themselves.

Besides, what can be more indelicate than a girl's *coming out* in the fashionable world? Which, in other words, is to bring to market a marriageable miss, whose person is taken from one public place to another, richly caparisoned. Yet, mixing in the giddy circle under restraint, these butterflies long to flutter at large, for the first affection of their souls is their own persons, to which their attention has been called with the most sedulous care whilst they were preparing for the period that decides their fate for life. Instead of pursuing this idle routine, sighing for tasteless shew, and heartless state, with what dignity would the youths of both sexes form attachments in the schools that I have cursorily pointed out; in which, as life advanced, dancing, music, and drawing, might be admitted as relaxations, for at these schools young people of fortune ought to remain, more or less, till they were of age. Those, who were designed for particular professions, might attend, three or four mornings in the week, the schools appropriated for their immediate instruction. . . .

I know that libertines will also exclaim, that woman would be unsexed by acquiring strength of body and mind, and that beauty, soft bewitching beauty! would no longer adorn the daughters of men. I am of a very different opinion, for I think that, on the contrary, we should then see dignified beauty, and true grace; to produce which, many powerful physical and moral causes would concur.—Not relaxed beauty, it is true, or the graces of helplessness; but such as appears to make us respect the human body as a majestic pile fit to receive a noble inhabitant, in the relics of antiquity. . . .

Besides, understanding is necessary to give variety and interest to sensual enjoyments, for low, indeed, in the intellectual scale, is the mind that can continue to love when neither virtue nor sense give a human appearance to an animal appetite. But sense will always preponderate; and if women be not, in general, brought more on a level with men, some superiour women, like the Greek courtezans, will assemble the men of abilities around them, and draw from their families many citizens, who would have stayed at home had their wives had more sense, or the graces which result from the exercise of understanding and fancy, the legitimate parents of taste. A woman of talents, if she be not absolutely ugly, will always obtain great power, raised by the weakness of her sex; and in proportion as men acquire virtue and delicacy, by the exertion of reason, they will look for both in women, but they can only acquire them in the same way that men do. . . .

I speak of the improvement and emancipation of the whole sex, for I know that the behaviour of a few women, who, by accident, or following a strong bent of nature, have acquired a portion of knowledge superiour to that of the rest of their sex, has often been overbearing; but there have been instances of women who, attaining knowledge, have not discarded modesty, nor have they always pedantically appeared to despise the ignorance which they laboured to disperse in their own minds. The exclamations then which any advice respecting female learning, commonly produces, especially from pretty women, often arise from envy. When they chance to see that even the lustre of their eyes, and the flippant sportiveness of refined coquetry will not always secure them attention, during a whole evening, should a woman of a more cultivated understanding endeavour to give a rational turn to the conversation, the common source of consolation is, that such women seldom get husbands. What arts have I not seen silly women use to interrupt by *flirtation,* a very significant word to describe such a manoeuvre, a rational conversation which made the men forget that they were pretty women.

But, allowing what is very natural to man, that the possession of rare abilities is really calculated to excite over-weening pride, disgusting in both men and women—in what a state of inferiority must the female faculties have rusted when such a small portion of knowledge as those women attained, who have sneeringly been termed learned women, could be singular?—Sufficiently so to puff up the possessor, and excite envy in her contemporaries, and some of the other sex. Nay, has not a little rationality exposed many women to the severest censure? I advert to well known facts, for I have frequently heard women ridiculed, and every little weakness exposed, only because they adopted the advice of some medical men, and deviated from the beaten track in their mode of treating their infants. I have actually heard this barbarous aversion to innovation carried still further, and a sensible woman stigmatized as an unnatural mother, who has thus been wisely solicitous to preserve the health of her children, when in the midst of her care she has lost one by some of the casualties of infancy, which no prudence can ward off. Her acquaintance have observed, that this was the consequence of new-fangled notions—the new-fangled notions of ease and cleanliness. And those who pretending to experience, though they have long adhered to prejudices that have, according to the opinion of the most sagacious physicians, thinned the human race, almost rejoiced at the disaster that gave a kind of sanction to prescription.

Indeed, if it were only on this account, the national education of women is of the utmost consequence, for what a number of human sacrifices are made to that moloch prejudice! and in how many ways are children destroyed by the lasciviousness of man? The want of natural affection, in many women, who are drawn from their duty by the admiration of men, and the ignorance of others, render the infancy of man a much more perilous state than that of brutes; yet men are unwilling to place women in situations proper to enable them to acquire sufficient understanding to know how even to nurse their babes.

So forcibly does this truth strike me, that I would rest the whole tendency of my reasoning upon it, for whatever tends to incapacitate the maternal character, takes woman out of her sphere. . . .

In public schools women, to guard against the errors of ignorance, should be taught the elements of anatomy and medicine, not only to enable them to take proper care of their own health, but to make them rational nurses of their infants, parents, and husbands; for the bills of mortality are swelled by the blunders of self-willed old women, who give nostrums of their own without knowing any thing of the human frame. It is likewise proper only in a domestic view, to make women acquainted with the anatomy of the mind, by allowing the sexes to associate together in every pursuit; and by leading them to observe the progress of the human understanding in the improvement of the sciences and arts; never forgetting the science of morality, or the study of the political history of mankind. . . .

. . . The conclusion which I wish to draw, is obvious; make

women rational creatures, and free citizens, and they will quickly become good wives, and mothers; that is—if men do not neglect the duties of husbands and fathers.

Discussing the advantages which a public and private education combined, as I have sketched, might rationally be expected to produce, I have dwelt most on such as are particularly relative to the female world, because I think the female world oppressed; yet the gangrene, which the vices engendered by oppression have produced, is not confined to the morbid part, but pervades society at large: so that when I wish to see my sex become more like moral agents, my heart bounds with the anticipation of the general diffusion of that sublime contentment which only morality can diffuse. . . .

---

## REFLECTING ON MEANING

1. What is the "false system of education" that Wollstonecraft describes? What kind of training does it offer to women? What does it lead women to value and to desire? In what ways does it result in either slavishness or tyranny? According to Wollstonecraft, what would be the "most perfect education"? How would it differ from the system she indicts?
2. A large section of Wollstonecraft's treatise is a reasoned response to Rousseau's views on women. From Wollstonecraft's rebuttal, what can you deduce about Rousseau's views? According to Rousseau, what larger purpose do women serve in society? What does he think the goal of their education should be?
3. Wollstonecraft argues that true equality will make women better wives and mothers. Why does she repeatedly make this point? Do you think she is reinforcing sexist views on the role of women? Why or why not?

## EXPLORING RHETORICAL STRATEGIES

1. Wollstonecraft states that her purpose is "to persuade women." To what extent do you agree that she addresses her argument to women exclusively? What evidence suggests that she also addresses men?
2. A crux of Wollstonecraft's argument is the comparison between women and "military men." What is the purpose of this extended

analogy? What point does it allow Wollstonecraft to make about differences between women and men? How effective is this device?

3. Wollstonecraft speaks to us across a time span of nearly two centuries. Do you find her argument still relevant? Why or why not? How do you think modern readers would react to her essay if they assumed that its author was contemporary?

---

# *From* The Subjection of Women

## JOHN STUART MILL

*A nineteenth-century British thinker and parliamentarian, John Stuart Mill was a powerful speaker for women's rights. In the following selection, an excerpt from* The Subjection of Women *(1869), Mill argues that "the legal subordination of one sex to the other . . . is wrong in itself" and should be "replaced by a principle of perfect equality."*

### 1

The object of this Essay is to explain as clearly as I am able, the grounds of an opinion which I have held from the very earliest period when I had formed any opinions at all on social or political matters, and which, instead of being weakened or modified, has been constantly growing stronger by the progress of reflection and the experience of life: That the principle which regulates the existing social relations between the two sexes—the legal subordination of one sex to the other—is wrong in itself, and now one of the chief hindrances to human improvement; and that it ought to be replaced by a principle of perfect equality, admitting no power or privilege on the one side, nor disability on the other. . . .

The generality of a practice is in some cases a strong presumption that it is, or at all events once was, conducive to laudable ends. This is the case, when the practice was first adopted, or afterwards kept up, as a means to such ends, and was grounded on experience of the mode in which they could be most effectually attained. If the authority of men over women, when first established, had been the result of a conscientious comparison between different modes of constituting the government of society; if, after trying various other modes of social organization—the government of women over men, equality between the two, and such mixed and divided modes of government as might be invented—it had been decided, on the testimony of experience, that the mode in which women are wholly under the rule of men, having no share at all in public concerns, and each in private being under the legal obligation of obedience to the man with whom she has associated her destiny, was the arrangement most conducive to the happiness and well being of both; its general adoption might then be fairly thought to be some evidence that, at the time when it was adopted, it was the best: though even then the considerations which recommended it may, like so many other primeval social facts of the greatest importance, have subsequently, in the course of ages, ceased to exist. But the state of the case is in every respect the reverse of this. In the first place, the opinion in favour of the present system, which entirely subordinates the weaker sex to the stronger, rests upon theory only; for there never has been trial made of any other: so that experience, in the sense in which it is vulgarly opposed to theory, cannot be pretended to have pronounced any verdict. And in the second place, the adoption of this system of inequality never was the result of deliberation, or forethought, or any social ideas, or any notion whatever of what conduced to the benefit of humanity or the good order of society. It arose simply from the fact that from the very earliest twilight of human society, every woman (owing to the value attached to her by men, combined with her inferiority in muscular strength) was found in a state of bondage to some man. Laws and systems of polity always begin by recognising the relations they find already existing between individuals. They convert what was a mere physical fact into a legal right, give it the sanction of society, and principally aim at the substitution of public and organized means of asserting and protecting these rights, instead of the irregular and lawless conflict of physical strength. . . .

. . . We now live—that is to say, one or two of the most advanced nations of the world now live—in a state in which the law of the strongest seems to be entirely abandoned as the regulating principle of the world's affairs: nobody professes it, and, as regards most of the relations between human beings, nobody is permitted to practise it. When any one succeeds in doing so, it is under cover of some pretext which gives him the semblance of having some general social interest on his side. This being the ostensible state of things, people flatter themselves that the rule of mere force is ended; that the law of the strongest cannot be the reason of existence of anything which has remained in full operation down to the present time. However any of our present institutions may have begun, it can only, they think, have been preserved to this period of advanced civilization by a well-grounded feeling of its adaptation to human nature, and conduciveness to the general good. They do not understand the great vitality and durability of institutions which place right on the side of might; how intensely they are clung to; how the good as well as the bad propensities and sentiments of those who have power in their hands, become identified with retaining it; how slowly these bad institutions give way, one at a time, the weakest first, beginning with those which are least interwoven with the daily habits of life; and how very rarely those who have obtained legal power because they first had physical, have ever lost their hold of it until the physical power had passed over to the other side. Such shifting of the physical force not having taken place in the case of women; this fact, combined with all the peculiar and characteristic features of the particular case, made it certain from the first that this branch of the system of right founded on might, though softened in its most atrocious features at an earlier period than several of the others, would be the very last to disappear. It was inevitable that this one case of a social relation grounded on force, would survive through generations of institutions grounded on equal justice, an almost solitary exception to the general character of their laws and customs; but which, so long as it does not proclaim its own origin, and as discussion has not brought out its true character, is not felt to jar with modern civilization, any more than domestic slavery among the Greeks jarred with their notion of themselves as a free people. . . .

. . . Whatever gratification of pride there is in the possession of power, and whatever personal interest in its exercise, is in this case not confined to a limited class, but common to the whole male sex. Instead of being, to most of its supporters, a thing desirable chiefly in the abstract, or, like the political ends usually contended for by factions, of little private importance to any but the leaders; it comes home to the person and hearth of every male head of a family, and of every one who looks forward to being so. The clodhopper exercises, or is to exercise, his share of the power equally with the highest nobleman. And the case is that in which the desire of power is the strongest: for every one who desires power, desires it most over those who are nearest to him, with whom his life is passed, with whom he has most concerns in common, and in whom any independence of his authority is oftenest likely to interfere with his individual preferences. If, in the other cases specified, powers manifestly grounded only on force, and having so much less to support them, are so slowly and with so much difficulty got rid of, much more must it be so with this, even if it rests on no better foundation than those. We must consider, too, that the possessors of the power have facilities in this case, greater than in any other, to prevent any uprising against it. Every one of the subjects lives under the very eye, and almost, it may be said, in the hands, of one of the masters—in closer intimacy with him than with any of her fellow-subjects; with no means of combining against him, no power of even locally overmastering him, and, on the other hand, with the strongest motives for seeking his favour and avoiding to give him offence. In struggles for political emancipation, everybody knows how often its champions are bought off by bribes, or daunted by terrors. In the case of women, each individual of the subject-class is in a chronic state of bribery and intimidation combined. In setting up the standard of resistance, a large number of the leaders, and still more of the followers, must make an almost complete sacrifice of the pleasures or the alleviations of their own individual lot. If ever any system of privilege and enforced subjection had its yoke tightly riveted on the necks of those who are kept down by it, this has. . . .

Some will object, that a comparison cannot fairly be made between the government of the male sex and the forms of unjust power which I have adduced in illustration of it, since these are arbitrary, and the effect of mere usurpation, while it on the contrary is natural. But was there ever any domination which did not appear natural to those who possessed it? There was a time when the division of mankind into two classes, a small one of masters and a numerous one of slaves, appeared, even to the most cultivated minds, to be a natural, and the only natural, condition of the human race. . . . The subjection of women to men being a universal custom, any departure from it quite naturally appears unnatural. But how entirely, even in this case, the feeling is dependent on custom, appears by ample experience. Nothing so much astonishes the people of distant parts of the world, when they first learn anything about England, as to be told that it is under a queen; the thing seems to them so unnatural as to be almost incredible. To Englishmen this does not seem in the least degree unnatural, because they are used to it; but they do feel it unnatural that women should be soldiers or Members of Parliament. In the feudal ages, on the contrary, war and politics were not thought unnatural to women, because not unusual; it seemed natural that women of the privileged classes should be of manly character, inferior in nothing but bodily strength to their husbands and fathers. . . .

But, it will be said, the rule of men over women differs from all these others in not being a rule of force: it is accepted voluntarily; women make no complaint, and are consenting parties to it. In the first place, a great number of women do not accept it. Ever since there have been women able to make their sentiments known by their writings (the only mode of publicity which society permits to them), an increasing number of them have recorded protests against their present social condition: and recently many thousands of them, headed by the most eminent women known to the public, have petitioned Parliament for their admission to the Parliamentary Suffrage. The claim of women to be educated as solidly, and in the same branches of knowledge, as men, is urged with growing intensity, and with a great prospect of success; while the demand for their admission into professions and occupations hitherto closed against them, becomes every year more urgent. Though there are not in this country, as there are in the United States, periodical Conventions and an organised party to agitate for the Rights of Women, there is a numerous and active Society organized and managed by women, for the more limited object of obtaining the political franchise. Nor is it only in our own country and in America that women are beginning to protest, more or less collectively, against the disabilities under which they labour. . . . It is a political law of nature that those who are under any power of ancient origin, never begin by complaining of the power itself, but only of its oppressive exercise. There is never any want of women who complain of ill usage by their husbands. There would be infinitely more, if complaint were not the greatest of all provocatives to a repetition and increase of the ill usage. It is this which frustrates all attempts to maintain the power but protect the woman against its abuses. In no other case (except that of a child) is the person who has been proved judicially to have suffered an injury, replaced under the physical power of the culprit who inflicted it. Accordingly wives, even in the most extreme and protracted cases of bodily ill usage, hardly ever dare avail themselves of the laws made for their protection: and if, in a moment of irrepressible indignation, or by the interference of neighbours, they are induced to do so, their whole effort afterwards is to disclose as little as they can, and to beg off their tyrant from his merited chastisement.

All causes, social and natural, combine to make it unlikely that women should be collectively rebellious to the power of men. They are so far in a position different from all other subject classes, that their masters require something more from them than actual service. Men do not want solely the obedience of women, they want their sentiments. All men, except the most brutish, desire to have, in the woman most nearly connected with them, not a forced slave but a willing one, not a slave merely, but a favourite. They have therefore put everything in practice to enslave their minds. The masters of all other slaves rely, for maintaining obedience, on fear; either fear of themselves, or religious fears. The masters of women wanted more than simple obedience, and they turned the whole force of education to effect their purpose. All women are brought up from the very earliest years in the belief that their ideal of character is the very opposite to that of men; not self-will, and government by self-control, but submission, and yielding to the control of others. All the moralities tell them that it is the duty of women, and all the current sentimentalities that it is their nature, to live for others; to make complete abnegation of themselves, and to have no life but in their affections. And by their affections are meant the only ones they are allowed to have—those to the men with whom they are connected, or to the children who constitute an additional and indefeasible tie between them and a man. When we put together three things—first, the natural attraction between opposite sexes; secondly, the wife's entire dependence on the husband, every privilege or pleasure she has being either his gift, or depending entirely on his will; and lastly, that the principal object of human pursuit, consideration, and all objects of social ambition, can in general be sought or obtained by her only through him, it would be a miracle if the object of being attractive to men had not become the polar star of feminine education and formation of character. And, this great means of influence over the minds of women having been acquired, an instinct of selfishness made men avail themselves of it to the utmost as a means of holding women in subjection, by representing to them meekness, submissiveness, and resignation of all individual will into the hands of a man, as an essential part of sexual attractiveness. Can it be doubted that any of the other yokes which mankind have succeeded in breaking, would have subsisted till now if the same means had existed, and had been as sedulously used, to bow down their minds to it? . . .

The preceding considerations are amply sufficient to show

that custom, however universal it may be, affords in this case no presumption, and ought not to create any prejudice, in favour of the arrangements which place women in social and political subjection to men. But I may go farther, and maintain that the course of history, and the tendencies of progressive human society, afford not only no presumption in favour of this system of inequality of rights, but a strong one against it; and that, so far as the whole course of human improvement up to this time, the whole stream of modern tendencies, warrants any inference on the subject, it is, that this relic of the past is discordant with the future, and must necessarily disappear. . . .

## 2

. . . I am far from pretending that wives are in general no better treated than slaves; but no slave is a slave to the same lengths, and in so full a sense of the word, as a wife is. Hardly any slave, except one immediately attached to the master's person, is a slave at all hours and all minutes; in general he has, like a soldier, his fixed task, and when it is done, or when he is off duty, he disposes, within certain limits, of his own time, and has a family life into which the master rarely intrudes. "Uncle Tom" under his first master had his own life in his "cabin," almost as much as any man whose work takes him away from home, is able to have in his own family. But it cannot be so with the wife. Above all, a female slave has (in Christian countries) an admitted right, and is considered under a moral obligation, to refuse to her master the last familiarity. Not so the wife: however brutal a tyrant she may unfortunately be chained to—though she may know that he hates her, though it may be his daily pleasure to torture her, and though she may feel it impossible not to loathe him—he can claim from her and enforce the lowest degradation of a human being, that of being made the instrument of an animal function contrary to her inclinations. While she is held in this worst description of slavery as to her own person, what is her position in regard to the children in whom she and her master have a joint interest? They are by law *his* children. He alone has any legal rights over them. Not one act can she do towards or in relation to them, except by delegation from him. Even after he is dead she is not their legal guardian, unless he by will has made her so. He could even send them away from her, and deprive her of the means of seeing or corresponding with them, until this power was in some degree restricted by Serjeant Talfourd's Act. This is her legal state. And from this state she has no means of withdrawing herself. If she leaves her husband, she can take nothing with her, neither her children nor anything which is rightfully her own. If he chooses, he can compel her to return, by law, or by physical force; or he may content himself with seizing for his own use anything which she may earn, or which may be given to her by her relations. It is only legal separation by a decree of a court of justice, which entitles her to live apart, without being forced back into the custody of an exasperated jailer—or which empowers her to apply any earnings to her own use, without fear that a man whom perhaps she has not seen for twenty years will pounce upon her some day and carry all off. This legal separation, until lately, the courts of justice would only give at an expense which made it inaccessible to any one out of the higher ranks. Even now it is only given in cases of desertion, or of the extreme of cruelty; and yet complaints are made every day that it is granted too easily. Surely, if a woman is denied any lot in life but that of being the personal body-servant of a despot, and is dependent for everything upon the chance of finding one who may be disposed to make a favourite of her instead of merely a drudge, it is a very cruel aggravation of her fate that she should be allowed to try this chance only once. The natural sequel and corollary from this state of things would be, that since her all in life depends upon obtaining a good master, she should be allowed to change again and again until she finds one. I am not saying that she ought to be allowed this privilege. That is a totally different consideration. The question of divorce, in the sense involving liberty of remarriage, is one into which it is foreign to my purpose to enter. All I now say is, that to those to whom nothing but servitude is allowed, the free choice of servitude is the only, though a most insufficient, alleviation. Its refusal completes the assimilation of the wife to the slave—and the slave under not the mildest form of slavery: for in some slave codes the slave could, under certain circumstances of ill usage, legally compel the master to sell him. But no amount of ill usage, without adultery superadded, will in England free a wife from her tormentor.

I have no desire to exaggerate, nor does the case stand in any need of exaggeration. I have described the wife's legal position, not her actual treatment. The laws of most countries are far worse than the people who execute them, and many of them are only able to remain laws by being seldom or never carried into effect. If married life were all that it might be expected to be, looking to the laws alone, society would be a hell upon earth. Happily there are both feelings and interests which in many men exclude, and in most, greatly temper, the impulses and propensities which lead to tyranny: and of those feelings, the tie which connects a man with his wife affords, in a normal state of things, incomparably the strongest example. The only tie which at all approaches to it, that between him and his children, tends, in all save exceptional cases, to strengthen, instead of conflicting with, the first. Because this is true; because men in general do not inflict, nor women suffer, all the misery which could be inflicted and suffered if the full power of tyranny with which the man is legally invested were acted on; the defenders of the existing form of the institution think that all its iniquity is justified, and that any complaint is merely quarrelling with the evil which is the price paid for every great good. But the mitigations in practice, which are compatible with maintaining in full legal force this or any other kind of tyranny, instead of being any apology for despotism, only serve to prove what power human nature possesses of reacting against the vilest institutions, and with what vitality the seeds of good as well as those of evil in human character diffuse and propagate themselves. Not a word can be said for despotism in the family which cannot be said for political despotism. . . .

## 3

On the other point which is involved in the just equality of women, their admissibility to all the functions and occupations hitherto retained as the monopoly of the stronger sex, I should anticipate no difficulty in convincing any one who has gone with me on the subject of the equality of women in the family. I believe that their disabilities elsewhere are only clung to in order to maintain their subordination in domestic life; because the generality of the male sex cannot yet tolerate the idea of living with an equal. Were it not for that, I think that almost every one, in the existing state of opinion in politics and political economy, would admit the injustice of excluding half the human race from the greater number of lucrative occupations, and from almost all high social functions; ordaining from their birth either that they are not, and cannot by any possibility become, fit for employments which are legally open to the stupidest and basest of the other sex, or else that however fit they may be, those employments shall be interdicted to them, in order to be preserved for the exclusive benefit of males. In the last two centuries, when (which was seldom the case) any reason beyond the mere existence of the fact was thought to be required to justify the disabilities of women, people seldom assigned as a reason their inferior mental capacity; which, in times when there was a real trial of personal faculties (from which all women were not excluded) in the struggles of public life, no one really believed in. The reason given in those days was not women's unfitness, but the interest of society, by which was meant the interest of men: just as the *raison d'état,* meaning the convenience of the government, and the support of existing authority, was deemed a sufficient explanation and excuse for the most flagitious crimes. In the present day, power holds a smoother language, and whomsoever it oppresses, always pretends to do so for their own good: accordingly, when anything is forbidden to women, it is thought necessary to say, and desirable to believe, that they are incapable of doing it, and that they depart from their real path of success and happiness when they aspire to it. But to make this reason plausible (I do not say valid), those by whom it is urged must be prepared to carry it to a much greater length than any one ventures to do in the face of present experience. It is not sufficient to maintain that women on the average are less gifted than men on the average, with certain of the higher mental faculties, or that a smaller number of women than of men are fit for occupations and functions of the highest intellectual character. It is necessary to maintain that no women at all are fit for them, and that the most eminent women are inferior in mental faculties to the most mediocre of the men on whom those functions at present devolve. For if the performance of the function is decided either by competition, or by any mode of choice which secures regard to the public interest, there needs to be no apprehension that any important employments will fall into the hands of women inferior to average men, or to the average of their male competitors. The only result would be that there would be fewer women than men in such employments; a result certain to happen in any case, if only from the preference always likely to be felt by the majority of women for the one vocation in which there is nobody to compete with them. Now, the most determined depreciator of women will not venture to deny, that when we add the experience of recent times to that of ages past, women, and not a few merely, but many women, have proved themselves capable of everything, perhaps without a single exception, which is done by men, and of doing it successfully and creditably. The utmost that can be said is, that there are many things which none of them have succeeded in doing as well as they have been done by some men—many in which they have not reached the very highest rank. But there are extremely few, dependent only on mental faculties, in which they have not attained the rank next to the highest. Is not this enough, and much more than enough, to make it a tyranny to them, and a detriment to society, that they should not be allowed to compete with men for the exercise of these functions? Is it not a mere truism to say, that such functions are often filled by men far less fit for them than numbers of women, and who would be beaten by women in any fair field of competition? What difference does it make that there may be men somewhere, fully employed about other things, who may be still better qualified for the things in question than these women? Does not this take place in all competitions? Is there so great a superfluity of men fit for high duties, that society can afford to reject the service of any competent person? Are we so certain of always finding a man made to our hands for any duty or function of social importance which falls vacant, that we lose nothing by putting a ban upon one-half of mankind, and refusing beforehand to make their faculties available, however distinguished they may be? And even if we could do without them, would it be consistent with justice to refuse to them their fair share of honour and distinction, or to deny to them the equal moral right of all human beings to choose their occupation (short of injury to others) according to their own preferences, at their own risk? Nor is the injustice confined to them: it is shared by those who are in a position to benefit by their services. To ordain that any kind of persons shall not be physicians, or shall not be advocates, or shall not be Members of Parliament, is to injure not them only, but all who employ physicians or advocates, or elect Members of Parliament, and who are deprived of the stimulating effect of greater competition on the exertions of the competitors, as well as restricted to a narrower range of individual choice. . . .

**4**

. . . Think what it is to a boy, to grow up to manhood in the belief that without any merit or any exertion of his own, though he may be the most frivolous and empty or the most ignorant and stolid of mankind, by the mere fact of being born a male he is by right the superior of all and every one of an entire half of the human race: including probably some whose real superiority to himself he has daily or hourly occasion to feel; but even if in his whole conduct he habitually follows a woman's guidance, still, if he is a fool, she thinks that of course she is not, and cannot be, equal in ability and judgment to himself; and if he is not a fool, he does worse—he sees that she is superior to him, and believes that, notwithstanding her superiority, he is entitled to command and she is bound to obey. What must be the effect on his character, of this lesson? And men of the cultivated classes are often not aware how deeply it sinks into the immense majority of male minds. For, among right-feeling and well-bred people, the inequality is kept as much as possible out of sight; above all, out of sight of the children. As much obedience is required from boys to their mother as to their father: they are not permitted to domineer over their sisters, nor are they accustomed to see these postponed to them, but the contrary; the compensations of the chivalrous feeling being made prominent, while the servitude which requires them is kept in the background. Well brought-up youths in the higher classes thus often escape the bad influences of the situation in their early years, and only experience them when, arrived at manhood, they fall under the dominion of facts as they really exist. Such people are little aware, when a boy is differently brought up, how early the notion of his inherent superiority to a girl arises in his mind; how it grows with his growth and strengthens with his strength; how it is inoculated by one schoolboy upon another; how early the youth thinks himself superior to his mother, owing her perhaps forbearance, but no real respect; and how sublime and sultan-like a sense of superiority he feels, above all, over the woman whom he honours by admitting her to a partnership of his life. Is it imagined that all this does not pervert the whole manner of existence of the man, both as an individual and as a social being? . . .

. . . If no authority, not in its nature temporary, were allowed to one human being over another, society would not be employed in building up propensities with one hand which it has to curb with the other. The child would really, for the first time in man's existence on earth, be trained in the way he should go, and when he was old there would be a chance that he would not depart from it. But so long as the right of the strong to power over the weak rules in the very heart of society, the attempt to make the equal right of the weak the principle of its outward actions will always be an uphill struggle; for the law of justice, which is also that of Christianity, will never get possession of men's inmost sentiments; they will be working against it, even when bending to it.

The second benefit to be expected from giving to women the free use of their faculties, by leaving them the free choice of their employments, and opening to them the same field of occupation and the same prizes and encouragements as to other human beings, would be that of doubling the mass of mental faculties available for the higher service of humanity. Where there is now one person qualified to benefit mankind and promote the general improvement, as a public teacher, or an administrator of some branch of public or social affairs, there would then be a chance of two. . . .

. . . The association of men with women in daily life is much closer and more complete than it ever was before. Men's life is more domestic. Formerly, their pleasures and chosen occupations were among men, and in men's company: their wives had but a fragment of their lives. At the present time, the progress of civilisation, and the turn of opinion against the rough amusements and convivial excesses which formerly occupied most men in their hours of relaxation—together with (it must be said) the improved tone of modern feeling as to the reciprocity of duty which binds the husband towards the wife—have thrown the man very much more upon home and its inmates, for his personal and social pleasures: while the kind and degree of improvement which has been made in women's education, has made them in some degree capable of being his companions in ideas and mental tastes, while leaving them, in most cases, still hopelessly inferior to him. His desire of mental communion is thus in general satisfied by a communion from which he learns nothing. An unimproving and unstimulating companionship is substituted for (what he might otherwise have been obliged to seek) the society of his equals in powers and his fellows in the higher pursuits. We see, accordingly, that young men of the greatest promise generally cease to improve as soon as they marry, and, not improving, inevitably degenerate. If the wife does not push the husband forward, she always holds him back. He ceases to care for what she does not care for; he no longer desires, and ends by disliking and shunning, society congenial to his former aspirations, and which would now shame his falling-off from them; his higher faculties both of mind and heart cease to be called into activity. And this change coinciding with the new and selfish interests which are created by the family, after a few years he differs in no material respect from those who have never had wishes for anything but the common vanities and the common pecuniary objects.

What marriage may be in the case of two persons of cultivated faculties, identical in opinions and purposes, between whom there exists that best kind of equality, similarity of powers and capacities with reciprocal superiority in them—so that each can enjoy the luxury of looking up to the other, and can have alternately the pleasure of leading and of being led in the path of development—I will not attempt to describe. To those who can conceive it, there is no need; to those who cannot, it would appear the dream of an enthusiast. But I maintain, with the profoundest conviction, that this, and this only, is the ideal of marriage; and that all opinions, customs, and institutions which favour any other notion of it, or turn the conceptions and aspirations connected with it into any other direction, by whatever pretences they may be coloured, are relics of primitive barbarism. The moral regeneration of mankind will only really commence, when the most fundamental of the social relations is placed under the rule of equal justice, and when human beings learn to cultivate their strongest sympathy with an equal in rights and in cultivation.

Thus far, the benefits which it has appeared that the world would gain by ceasing to make sex a disqualification for privileges and a badge of subjection, are social rather than individual; consisting in an increase of the general fund of thinking and acting power, and an improvement in the general conditions of the association of men with women. But it would be a grievous understatement of the case to omit the most direct benefit of all, the unspeakable gain in private happiness to the liberated half of the species; the difference to them between a life of subjection to the will of others, and a life of rational freedom. After the primary necessities of food and raiment, freedom is the first and strongest want of human nature. . . .

When we consider the positive evil caused to the disqualified half of the human race by their disqualification—first in the loss of the most inspiriting and elevating kind of personal enjoyment, and next in the weariness, disappointment, and profound dissatisfaction with life, which are so often the substitute for it; one feels that among all the lessons which men require for carrying on the struggle against the inevitable imperfections of their lot on earth, there is no lesson which they more need, than not to add to the evils which nature inflicts, by their jealous and prejudiced restrictions on one another. Their vain fears only substitute other and worse evils for those which they are idly apprehensive of: while every restraint on the freedom of conduct of any of their human fellow-creatures (otherwise than by making them responsible for any evil actually caused by it), dries up *pro tanto* the principal fountain of human happiness, and leaves the species less rich, to an inappreciable degree, in all that makes life valuable to the individual human being.

---

## REFLECTING ON MEANING

1. According to Mill, what is the nature of women's subjection? In what ways are they oppressed? Why don't they rise up against their oppressors? Why don't they resist? How does their subjection represent a "branch of the system of right founded on might," as Mill puts it?

2. What distinction does Mill make between nature and custom? What definitions does he provide for natural and unnatural? How do these conceptions relate to the difficulty of recognizing women's oppression? How did their subjection come to seem so natural?

3. From a nineteenth-century perspective, Mill describes how women's subjection affects home and marriage. What observations does he make? To what extent are these observations valid today? How, if at all, does women's status influence family interactions in this decade?

## EXPLORING RHETORICAL STRATEGIES

1. What is Mill's main idea? Is he successful in making a convincing argument for it? Why or why not?

2. Mill effectively integrates opposing viewpoints in his essay. What are some of the opposing views he discusses? In what ways does he refute them? How does this strategy help him advance his own viewpoint?

3. What is the primary analogy Mill uses to illustrate the nature of women's subjection? In what ways does he extend this analogy? How does it help him make women's subjection seem less "natural"?

# *From* Women and Economics

## CHARLOTTE PERKINS GILMAN

*The nineteenth-century American feminist Charlotte Perkins Gilman examines the economic status of women in the following excerpt from her book* Women and Economics, *published in 1898. She maintains that society places women in a situation in which their only "personal profit" derives directly from "their power to win and hold the other sex." Gilman outlines a system of child care that would release women from this bondage and transform the mother from "home servant" to "social servant."*

The economic status of the human race in any nation, at any time, is governed mainly by the activities of the male: the female obtains her share in the racial advance only through him.

Studied individually, the facts are even more plainly visible, more open and familiar. From the day laborer to the millionaire, the wife's worn dress or flashing jewels, her low roof or her lordly one, her weary feet or her rich equipage,—these speak of the economic ability of the husband. The comfort, the luxury, the necessities of life itself, which the woman receives, are obtained by the husband, and given her by him. And, when the woman, left alone with no man to "support" her, tries to meet her own economic necessities, the difficulties which confront her prove conclusively what the general economic status of the woman is. . . . But we are instantly confronted by the commonly received opinion that, although it must be admitted that men make and distribute the wealth of the world, yet women earn their share of it as wives. This assumes either that the husband is in the position of employer and the wife as employee, or that marriage is a "partnership," and the wife an equal factor with the husband in producing wealth. . . .

Women consume economic goods. What economic product do they give in exchange for what they consume? The claim that marriage is a partnership, in which the two persons married produce wealth which neither of them, separately, could produce, will not bear examination. A man happy and comfortable can produce more than one unhappy and uncomfortable, but this is as true of a father or son as of a husband. To take from a man any of the conditions which make him happy and strong is to cripple his industry, generally speaking. But those relatives who make him happy are not therefore his business partners, and entitled to share his income.

Grateful return for happiness conferred is not the method of exchange in a partnership. The comfort a man takes with his wife is not in the nature of a business partnership, nor are her frugality and industry. A housekeeper, in her place, might be as frugal, as industrious, but would not therefore be a partner. Man and wife are partners truly in their mutual obligation to their children,—their common love, duty, and service. But a manufacturer who marries, or a doctor, or a lawyer, does not take a partner in his business, when he takes a partner in parenthood, unless his wife is also a manufacturer, a doctor, or a lawyer. . . .

If the wife is not, then, truly a business partner, in what way does she earn from her husband the food, clothing, and shelter she receives at his hands? By house service, it will be instantly replied. This is the general misty idea upon the subject,—that women earn all they get, and more, by house service. Here we come to a very practical and definite economic ground. Although not producers of wealth, women serve in the final processes of preparation and distribution. Their labor in the household has a genuine economic value.

For a certain percentage of persons to serve other persons, in order that the ones so served may produce more, is a contribution not to be overlooked. The labor of women in the house, certainly, enables men to produce more wealth than they otherwise could; and in this way women are economic factors in society. But so are horses. The labor of horses enables men to produce more wealth than they otherwise could. The horse is an economic factor in society. But the horse is not economically independent, nor is the woman. . . .

The labor which the wife performs in the household is given as part of her functional duty, not as employment. The wife of the poor man, who works hard in a small house, doing all the work for the family, or the wife of the rich man, who wisely and gracefully manages a large house and administers its functions, each is entitled to fair pay for services rendered.

To take this ground and hold it honestly, wives, as earners through domestic service, are entitled to the wages of cooks, housemaids, nursemaids, seamstresses, or housekeepers, and to no more.

This would of course reduce the spending money of the wives of the rich, and put it out of the power of the poor man to "support" a wife at all, unless, indeed, the poor man faced the situation fully, paid his wife her wages as house servant, and then she and he combined their funds in the support of their children. He would be keeping a servant: she would be helping keep the family. But nowhere on earth would there be "a rich woman" by these means. Even the highest class of private housekeeper, useful as her services are, does not accumulate a fortune. . . .

But the salient fact in this discussion is that, whatever the economic value of the domestic industry of women is, they do not get it. The women who do the most work get the least money, and the women who have the most money do the least work. Their labor is neither given nor taken as a factor in economic exchange. It is held to be their duty as women to do this work; and their economic status bears no relation to their domestic labors, unless an inverse one. Moreover, if they were thus fairly paid,—given what they earned, and no more,—all women working in this way would be reduced to the economic status of the house servant. Few women—or men either—care to face this condition. The ground that women earn their living by domestic labor is instantly forsaken, and we are told that they obtain their livelihood as mothers. This is a peculiar position. We speak of it commonly enough, and often with deep feeling, but without due analysis. . . .

If this is so, if motherhood is an exchangeable commodity given by women in payment for clothes and food, then we must of course find some relation between the quantity or quality of the motherhood and the quantity and quality of the pay. This being true, then the women who are not mothers have no economic status at all; and the economic status of those who are must be shown to be relative to their motherhood. This is obviously absurd. The childless wife has as much money as the mother of many,—more; for the children of the latter consume what would otherwise be hers; and the inefficient mother is no less provided for than the efficient one. Visibly, and upon the face of it, women are not maintained in economic prosperity proportioned to their motherhood. Motherhood bears no relation to their economic status. . . . The claim of motherhood as a factor in economic exchange is false to-day. But suppose it were true. Are we willing to hold this ground, even in theory? Are we willing to consider motherhood as a business, a form of commercial exchange? Are the cares and duties of the mother, her travail and her love, commodities to be exchanged for bread?

It is revolting so to consider them; and, if we dare face our own thoughts, and force them to their logical conclusion, we shall see that nothing could be more repugnant to human feeling, or more socially and individually injurious, than to make motherhood a trade. Driven off these alleged grounds of women's economic independence; shown that women, as a class, neither produce nor distribute wealth; that women, as individuals, labor mainly as house servants, are not paid as such, and would not be satisfied with such an economic status if they were so paid; that wives are not business partners or co-producers of wealth with their husbands, unless they actually practise the same profession; that they are not salaried as mothers, and that it would be unspeakably degrading if they were,—what remains to those who deny that women are supported by men? This . . . —that the function of maternity unfits a woman for economic production, and, therefore, it is right that she should be supported by her husband. . . .

. . . Because of her maternal duties, the human female is said to be unable to get her own living. As the maternal duties of other females do not unfit them for getting their own living and also the livings of their young, it would seem that the human maternal duties require the segregation of the entire energies of the mother to the service of the child during her entire adult life, or so large a proportion of them that not enough remains to devote to the individual interests of the mother. . . .

Is this the condition of human motherhood? Does the human mother, by her motherhood, thereby lose control of brain and body, lose power and skill and desire for any other work? Do we see before us the human race, with all its females segregated entirely to the uses of motherhood, consecrated, set apart, specially developed, spending every power of their nature on the service of their children?

We do not. We see the human mother worked far harder than a mare, laboring her life long in the service, not of her children only, but of men; husbands, brothers, fathers, whatever male relatives she has; for mother and sister also; for the church a little, if she is allowed; for society, if she is able; for charity and education and reform,—working in many ways that are not the ways of motherhood.

It is not motherhood that keeps the housewife on her feet from dawn till dark; it is house service, not child service. Women work longer and harder than most men, and not solely in maternal duties. . . . Many mothers, even now, are wage-earners for the family, as well as bearers and rearers of it. And the women who are not so occupied, the women who belong to rich men,—here perhaps is the exhaustive devotion to maternity which is supposed to justify an admitted economic dependence. But we do not find it even among these. Women of ease and wealth provide for their children better care than the poor woman can; but they do not spend more time upon it themselves, nor more care and effort. They have other occupation.

In spite of her supposed segregation to maternal duties, the human female, the world over, works at extra-maternal duties for hours enough to provide her with an independent living, and then is denied independence on the ground that motherhood prevents her working! . . .

With the growth of civilization, we have gradually crystallized into law the visible necessity for feeding the helpless female; and even old women are maintained by their male relatives with a comfortable assurance. But to this day—save, indeed, for the increasing army of women wage-earners, who are changing the face of the world by their steady advance toward economic independence—the personal profit of women bears but too close a relation to their power to win and hold the other sex. From the odalisque with the most bracelets to the débutante with the most bouquets, the relation still holds good,—woman's economic profit comes through the power of sex-attraction.

When we confront this fact boldly and plainly in the open market of vice, we are sick with horror. When we see the same economic relation made permanent, established by law, sanctioned and sanctified by religion, covered with flowers and incense and all accumulated sentiment, we think it innocent, lovely, and right. The transient trade we think evil. The bargain for life we think good. But the biological effect remains the same. In both cases the female gets her food from the male by virtue of her sex-relationship to him. In both cases, perhaps even more in marriage because of its perfect acceptance of the situation, the female of genus homo, still living under natural law, is inexorably modified to sex in an increasing degree. . . .

Another instance of so grossly unjust, so palpable, so general an evil that it has occasionally aroused some protest even from our dull consciousness is this: the enforced attitude of the woman toward marriage. To the young girl, as has been previously stated, marriage is the one road to fortune, to life. She is born highly specialized as a female: she is carefully educated and trained to realize in all ways her sex-limitations and her sex-advantages. What she has to gain even as a child is largely gained by feminine tricks and charms. Her reading, both in history and fiction, treats of the same position for women; and romance and poetry give it absolute predominance. Pictorial art, music, the drama, society, everything, tells her that she is *she,* and that all depends on whom she marries. Where young boys plan for what they will achieve and attain, young girls plan for whom they will achieve and attain. . . .

With such a prospect as this before her; with an organization specially developed to this end; with an education adding every weight of precept and example, of wisdom and virtue, to the natural instincts; with a social environment the whole machinery of which is planned to give the girl a chance to see and to be seen, to provide her with "opportunities"; and with all the pressure of personal advantage and self-interest added to the sex-instinct,—what one would logically expect is a society full of desperate and eager husband-hunters, regarded with popular approval.

Not at all! Marriage is the woman's proper sphere, her divinely ordered place, her natural end. It is what she is born for, what she is trained for, what she is exhibited for. It is, moreover, her means of honorable livelihood and advancement. *But*—she must not even look as if she wanted it! She must not turn her hand over to get it. She must sit passive as the seasons go by, and her "chances" lessen with each year. Think of the strain on a highly sensitive nervous organism to have so much hang on one thing, to see the possibility of attaining it grow less and less yearly, and to be forbidden to take any step toward securing it! This she must bear with dignity and grace to the end. . . .

The cruel and absurd injustice of blaming the girl for not getting what she is allowed no effort to obtain seems unaccountable; but it becomes clear when viewed in connection with the sexuo-economic relation. Although marriage is a means of livelihood, it is not honest employment where one can offer one's labor without shame, but a relation where the support is given outright, and enforcement by law in return for the functional service of the woman, the "duties of wife and mother." Therefore no honorable woman can ask for it. . . .

. . . Half the human race is denied free productive expression, is forced to confine its productive human energies to the same channels as its reproductive sex-energies. Its creative skill is confined to the level of immediate personal bodily service, to the making of clothes and preparing of food for individuals. No social service is possible. While its power of production is checked, its power of consumption is inordinately increased by the showering upon it of the "unearned increment" of masculine gifts. For the woman there is, first, no free production allowed; and, second, no relation maintained between what she does produce and what she consumes. She is forbidden to make, but encouraged to take. Her industry is not the natural output of creative energy, not the work she does because she has the inner power and strength to do it; nor is her industry even the measure of her gain. She has, of course, the natural desire to consume; and to that is set no bar save the capacity or the will of her husband.

Thus we have painfully and laboriously evolved and carefully maintain among us an enormous class of non-productive consumers,—a class which is half the world, and mother of the other half. We have built into the constitution of the human race the habit and desire of taking, as divorced from its natural precursor and concomitant of making. . . . To consume food, to consume clothes, to consume houses and furniture and decorations and ornaments and amusements, to take and take and take forever,—from one man if they are virtuous, from many if they are vicious, but always to take and never to think of giving anything in return except their womanhood,—this is the enforced condition of the mothers of the race. What wonder that their sons go into business "for what there is in it"! What wonder that the world is full of the desire to get as much as possible and to give as little as possible! . . .

. . .[T]he consuming female, debarred from any free production, unable to estimate the labor involved in the making of what she so lightly destroys, and her consumption limited mainly to those things which minister to physical pleasure, creates a market for sensuous decoration and personal ornament, for all that is luxurious and enervating, and for a false and capricious variety in such supplies, which operates as a most deadly check to true industry and true art. As the priestess of the temple of consumption, as the limitless demander of things to use up, her economic influence is reactionary and injurious. Much, very much, of the current of useless production in which our economic energies run waste—man's strength poured out like water on the sand—depends on the creation and careful maintenance of this false market, this sink into which human labor vanishes with no return. Woman, in her false economic position, reacts injuriously upon industry, upon art, upon science, discovery, and progress. The sexuo-economic relation in its effect on the constitution of the individual keeps alive in us the instincts of savage individualism which we should otherwise have well outgrown. It sexualizes our industrial relation and commercializes our sex-relation. And, in the external effect upon the market, the over-sexed woman, in her unintelligent and ceaseless demands, hinders and perverts the economic development of the world. . . .

Economic independence for women necessarily involves a change in the home and family relation. But, if that change is for the advantage of individual and race, we need not fear it. It does not involve a change in the marriage relation except in withdrawing the element of economic dependence, nor in the relation of mother to child save to improve it. But it does involve the exercise of human faculty in women, in social service and exchange rather than in domestic service solely. This will of course require the introduction of some other form of living than that which now obtains. It will render impossible the present method of feeding the world by means of millions of private servants, and bringing up children by the same hand. . . .

Perhaps it is worth while to examine the nature of our feeling toward that social institution called "the family," and the probable effect upon it of the change in woman's economic status.

Marriage and "the family" are two institutions, not one, as is commonly supposed. We confuse the natural result of marriage in children, common to all forms of sex-union, with the family,—a purely social phenomenon. Marriage is a form of sex-union recognized and sanctioned by society. It is a relation between two or more persons, according to the custom of the country, and involves mutual obligations. Although made by us an economic relation, it is not essentially so, and will exist in much higher fulfilment after the economic phase is outgrown. . . .

The family is a decreasing survival of the earliest grouping known to man. Marriage is an increasing development of high social life, not fully evolved. So far from being identical with the family, it improves and strengthens in inverse ratio to the family. . . . There was no conception of marriage as a personal union for life of two well-matched individuals during the patriarchal era. Wives were valued merely for child-bearing. The family needed numbers of its own blood, especially males; and the man-child was the price of favor to women then. . . . Its bonds of union were of the loosest,—merely common paternity, with a miscellaneous maternity of inimical interests. Such a basis forever forbade any high individualization, and high individualization with its demands for a higher marriage forbids any numerical importance to the family. Marriage has risen and developed in social importance as the family has sunk and decreased. . . .

If there should be built and opened in any of our large cities to-day a commodious and well-served apartment house for professional women with families, it would be filled at once. The apartments would be without kitchens; but there would be a kitchen belonging to the house from which meals could be served to the families in their rooms or in a common dining-room, as preferred. It would be a home where the cleaning was done by efficient workers, not hired separately by the families, but engaged by the manager of the establishment; and a roof-garden, day nursery, and kindergarten, under well-trained professional nurses and teachers, would insure proper care of the children. The demand for such provision is increasing daily, and must soon be met, not by a boarding-house or a lodging-house, a hotel, a restaurant, or any makeshift patching together of these; but by a permanent provision for the needs of women and children, of family privacy with collective advantage. This must be offered on a business basis to prove a substantial business success; and it will so prove, for it is a growing social need. . . .

. . . Many would so desire, keeping their own rooms, their personal inner chambers, inviolate from other presence than that of their nearest and dearest. . . . Of all popular paradoxes, none is more nakedly absurd than to hear us prate of privacy in a place where we cheerfully admit to our table-talk and to our door service—yes, and to the making of our beds and to the handling of our clothing—a complete stranger. . . .

This stranger all of us who can afford it summon to our homes, . . . —with this observing and repeating army lodged in the very bosom of the family, may we not smile a little bitterly at our fond ideal of "the privacy of the home"? The swift progress of professional sweepers, dusters, and scrubbers, through rooms where they were wanted, and when they were wanted, would be at least no more injurious to privacy than the present method. Indeed, the exclusion of the domestic servant, and the entrance of woman on a plane of interest at once more social and more personal, would bring into the world a new conception of the sacredness of privacy, a feeling for the rights of the individual as yet unknown.

In reconstructing in our minds the position of woman under conditions of economic independence, it is most difficult to think of her as a mother.

We are so unbrokenly accustomed to the old methods of motherhood, so convinced that all its processes are interrelative and indispensable, and that to alter one of them is to endanger the whole relation, that we cannot conceive of any desirable change.

When definite plans for such change are suggested,—ways in which babies might be better cared for than at present,—we either deny the advantages of the change proposed or insist that these advantages can be reached under our present system. Just as in cooking we seek to train the private cook and to exalt and purify the private taste, so in baby-culture we seek to train the individual mother, and to call for better conditions in the private home; in both cases ignoring the relation between our general system and its particular phenomena. Though it may be shown, with clearness, that in physical conditions the private house, as a place in which to raise children, may be improved upon, yet all the more stoutly do we protest that the mental life, the emotional life, of the home is the best possible environment for the young.

There was a time in human history when this was true. While progress derived its main impetus from the sex-passion, and the highest emotions were those that held us together in the family relation, such education and such surroundings as fostered and intensified these emotions were naturally the best. But in the stage into which we are now growing, when the family relation is only a part of life, and our highest duties lie between individuals in social relation, the child has new needs. . . .

. . . [W]e have reached a stage where individual and racial progress is best served by the higher specialization of individuals and by a far wider sense of love and duty. This change renders the psychic condition of home life increasingly disadvantageous. We constantly hear of the inferior manners of the children of to-day, of the restlessness of the young, of the flat treason of deserting parents. It is visibly not so easy to live at home as it used to be. Our children are not more perversely constituted than the children of earlier ages, but the conditions in which they are reared are not suited to develop the qualities now needed in human beings.

This increasing friction between members of families should not be viewed with condemnation from a moral point of view, but studied with scientific interest. If our families are so relatively uncomfortable under present conditions, are there not conditions wherein the same families could be far more comfortable? . . . It is in the training of children . . . that the private home has ceased to be sufficient, or the isolated, primitive, dependent woman capable. Not that the mother does not have an intense and overpowering sense of loyalty and of duty; but it is duty to individuals, just as it was in the year one. What she is unable to follow, in her enforced industrial restriction, is the higher specialization of labor, and the honorable devotion of human lives to the development of their work. . . .

She cannot teach what she does not know. She cannot in any sincerity uphold as a duty what she does not practise. The child learns more of the virtues needed in modern life—of fairness, of justice, of comradeship, of collective interest and action—in a common school than can be taught in the most perfect family circle. We may preach to our children as we will of the great duty of loving and serving one's neighbor; but what the baby is born into, what the child grows up to see and feel, is the concentration of one entire life—his mother's—upon the personal aggrandizement of one family, and the human service of another entire life—his father's—so warped and strained by the necessity of "supporting his family" that treason to society is the common price of comfort in the home. . . .

And this is the atmosphere in which the wholly home-bred, mother-taught child grows up. Why should not food and clothes and the comforts of his own people stand first in his young mind? Does he not see his mother, the all-loved, all-perfect one, peacefully spending her days in the arrangement of these things which his father's ceaseless labor has procured? Why should he not grow up to care for his own, to the neglect and willing injury of all the rest, when his earliest, deepest impressions are formed under such exclusive devotion?

It is not the home as a place of family life and love that injures the child, but as the centre of a tangled heap of industries, low in their ungraded condition, and lower still because they are wholly personal. Work the object of which is merely to serve one's self is the lowest. Work the object of which is merely to serve one's family is the next lowest. Work the object of which is to serve more and more people, in widening range . . . is social service in the fullest sense, and the highest form of service that we can reach. . . .

We suffer also, our lives long, from an intense self-consciousness, from a sensitiveness beyond all need; we demand measureless personal attention and devotion, because we have been born and reared in a very hot-bed of these qualities. A baby who spent certain hours of every day among other babies, being cared for because he was a baby, and not because he was "my baby," would grow to have a very different opinion of himself from that which is forced upon each new soul that comes among us by the ceaseless adoration of his own immediate family. What he needs to learn at once and for all, to learn softly and easily, but inexorably, is that he is one of many. We all dimly recognize this in our praise of large families, and in our saying that "an only child is apt to be selfish." So is an only family. The earlier and more easily a child can learn that human life means many people, and their behavior to one another, the happier and stronger and more useful his life will be.

This could be taught him with no difficulty whatever, under certain conditions, just as he is taught his present sensitiveness and egotism by the present conditions. It is not only temperature and diet and rest and exercise which affect the baby. "He does love to be noticed," we say. "He is never so happy as when he has a dozen worshippers around him." But what is the young soul learning all the while? What does he gather, as he sees and hears and slowly absorbs impressions? With the inflexible inferences of a clear, young brain, unsupplied with any counter-evidence until later in life, he learns that women are meant to wait on people, to get dinner, and sweep and pick up things; that men are made to bring home things, and are to be begged of according to circumstances; that babies are the object of concentrated admiration; that their hair, hands, feet, are specially attractive; that they are the heated focus of attention, to be passed from hand to hand, swung and danced and amused most violently, and also be laid aside and have nothing done to them, with no regard to their preference in either case. . . .

. . . [W]hile we flatter ourselves that things remain the same, they are changing under our very eyes from year to year, from day to day. Education, hiding itself behind a wall of books, but consisting more and more fully in the grouping of children and in the training of faculties never mentioned in the curriculum,—education, which is our human motherhood, has crept nearer and nearer to its true place, its best work,—the care and training of the little child. Some women there are, and some men, whose highest service to humanity is the care of children. Such should not concentrate their powers upon their own children alone,—a most questionable advantage,—but should be so placed that their talent and skill, their knowledge and experience, would benefit the largest number of children. . . .

As we now arrange life, our children must take their chances while babies, and live or die, improve or deteriorate, according to the mother to whom they chance to be born. An inefficient mother does not prevent a child from having a good college education; but the education of babyhood, the most important of all, is wholly in her hands. It is futile to say that mothers should be taught how to fulfil their duties. You cannot teach every mother to be a good school educator or a good college educator. Why should you expect every mother to be a good nursery educator? . . .

The growth and change in home and family life goes steadily on under and over and through our prejudices and convictions; and the education of the child has changed and become a social function, while we still imagine the mother to be doing it all. . . .

We think no harm of motherhood because our darlings go out each day to spend long hours in school. The mother is not held neglectful, nor the child bereft. It is not called a "separation of mother and child." There would be no further harm or risk or loss in a babyhood passed among such changed surroundings and skilled service as should meet its needs more perfectly than it is possible for the mother to meet them alone at home.

Better surroundings and care for babies, better education, do not mean, as some mothers may imagine, that the tiny monthling is to be taught to read, or even that it is to be exposed to cabalistical arrangements of color and form and sound which shall mysteriously force the young intelligence to flower. It would mean, mainly, a far quieter and more peaceful life than is possible for the heavily loved and violently cared for baby in the busy household; and the impressions which it did meet would be planned and maintained with an intelligent appreciation of its mental powers. The mother would not be excluded, but supplemented, as she is now, by the teacher and the school. . . .

. . . The mother as a social servant instead of a home servant will not lack in true mother duty. She will love her child as well, perhaps better, when she is not in hourly contact with it, when she goes from its life to her own life, and back from her own life to its life, with ever new delight and power. She can keep the deep, thrilling joy of motherhood far fresher in her heart, far more vivid and open in voice and eyes and tender hands, when the hours of individual work give her mind another channel for her own part of the day. From her work, loved and honored though it is, she will return to the home life, the child life, with an eager, ceaseless pleasure, cleansed of all the fret and fraction and weariness that so mar it now.

---

## REFLECTING ON MEANING

1. According to Gilman, why is it wrong to assume that women's economic power derives from their role in marriage partnerships, from their work in the household, or from their maternal duties? What is the actual source of their economic worth? Why does Gilman suggest that this situation should make us "sick with horror"? What is the role of marriage and family in this economic arrangement? What makes marriage a "means of livelihood" but "not honest employment"?
2. What point does Gilman make about the influence of women on general economic development? What does calling woman the "priestess of the temple of consumption" suggest about women's economic influence? Why does Gilman frame their influence in negative terms? Do you agree with her assessment? Why or why not?
3. Gilman asserts that "economic independence for women necessarily involves a change in the home and family relation." Why

is this the case, according to Gilman? What kinds of changes does she suggest? What effect does she believe these changes will have on child-raising methods? What will they accomplish for women in the long run?

## EXPLORING RHETORICAL STRATEGIES

1. What is the main idea that Gilman expresses in this selection? How do her discussions of child care and of women as consumers relate to this larger idea?
2. Rather than beginning her discussion by stating what the basis of women's economic status is, Gilman presents and refutes views that run counter to her own. In other words, she works toward her thesis by a process of elimination. What is the effect of this strategy? Is it successful?
3. Gilman makes extensive use of rhetorical questions. What instances of this device can you identify? How do these questions help shape the development of her discussion? What do they suggest about her awareness of audience?

---

# Awakening and Revolt

## MARGARET SANGER

*Margaret Sanger was a leader in the American birth control movement in the second decade of this century. She served as a catalyst for bringing the issue of contraception to the forefront, organizing international conferences and establishing many clinics. In "Awakening and Revolt," an excerpt from* My Fight for Birth Control, *published in 1931, Sanger relates how her eyes were initially opened to the plight of women who had no way to prevent pregnancy.*

Early in the year 1912 I came to a sudden realization that my work as a nurse and my activities in social service were entirely palliative and consequently futile and useless to relieve the misery I saw all about me. . . .

Were it possible for me to depict the revolting conditions existing in the homes of some of the women I attended in that one year, one would find it hard to believe. There was at that time, and doubtless is still today, a sub-stratum of men and women whose lives are absolutely untouched by social agencies.

The way they live is almost beyond belief. They hate and fear any prying into their homes or into their lives. They resent being talked to. The women slink in and out of their homes on their way to market like rats from their holes. The men beat their wives sometimes black and blue, but no one interferes. The children are cuffed, kicked and chased about, but woe to the child who dares to tell tales out of the home! Crime or drink is often the source of this secret aloofness, usually there is something to hide, a skeleton in the closet somewhere. The men are sullen, unskilled workers, picking up odd jobs now and then, unemployed usually, sauntering in and out of the house at all hours of the day and night.

The women keep apart from other women in the neighborhood. Often they are suspected of picking a pocket or "lifting" an article when occasion arises. Pregnancy is an almost chronic condition amongst them. I knew one woman who had given birth to eight children with no professional care whatever. The last one was born in the kitchen, witnessed by a son of ten years who, under his mother's direction, cleaned the bed, wrapped the placenta and soiled articles in paper, and threw them out of the window into the court below. . . .

In this atmosphere abortions and birth become the main theme of conversation. On Saturday nights I have seen groups of fifty to one hundred women going into questionable offices well known in the community for cheap abortions. I asked several women what took place there, and they all gave the same reply: a quick examination, a probe inserted into the uterus and turned a few times to disturb the fertilized ovum, and then the woman was sent home. Usually the flow began the next day and often continued four or five weeks. Sometimes an ambulance carried the victim to the hospital for a curetage, and if she returned home at all she was looked upon as a lucky woman.

This state of things became a nightmare with me. There seemed no sense to it all, no reason for such waste of mother life, no right to exhaust women's vitality and to throw them on the scrap-heap before the age of thirty-five.

Everywhere I looked, misery and fear stalked—men fearful of losing their jobs, women fearful that even worse conditions might come upon them. The menace of another pregnancy hung like a sword over the head of every poor woman I came in contact with that year. The question which met me was always the same: What can I do to keep from it? or, What can I do to get out of this? Sometimes they talked among themselves bitterly.

"It's the rich that know the tricks," they'd say, "while we have all the kids." Then, if the women were Roman Catholics, they talked about "Yankee tricks," and asked me if I knew what the Protestants did to keep their families down. When I said that I didn't believe that the rich knew much more than they did I was laughed at and suspected of holding back information for money. They would nudge each other and say something about paying me before I left the case if I would reveal the "secret." . . .

Finally the thing began to shape itself, to become accumulative during the three weeks I spent in the home of a desperately sick woman living on Grand Street, a lower section of New York's East Side.

Mrs. Sacks was only twenty-eight years old; her husband, an unskilled worker, thirty-two. Three children, aged five, three and one, were none too strong nor sturdy, and it took all the earnings of the father and the ingenuity of the mother to keep them clean, provide them with air and proper food, and give them a chance to grow into decent manhood and womanhood.

Both parents were devoted to these children and to each other. The woman had become pregnant and had taken various drugs and purgatives, as advised by her neighbors. Then, in desperation, she had used some instrument lent to her by a friend. She was found prostrate on the floor amidst the crying children when her husband returned from work. Neighbors advised against the ambulance, and a friendly doctor was called. The husband would not hear of her going to a hospital, and as a little money had been saved in the bank a nurse was called and the battle for that precious life began.

It was in the middle of July. The three-room apartment was turned into a hospital for the dying patient. Never had I worked so fast, never so concentratedly as I did to keep alive that little mother. Neighbor women came and went during the day doing the odds and ends necessary for our comfort. The children were sent to friends and relatives and the doctor and I settled ourselves to outdo the force and power of an outraged nature.

Never had I known such conditions could exist. July's sultry days and nights were melted into a torpid inferno. Day after day, night after night, I slept only in brief snatches, ever too anxious about the condition of that feeble heart bravely carrying on, to stay long from the bedside of the patient. . . .

At the end of two weeks recovery was in sight, and at the end of three weeks I was preparing to leave the fragile patient to take up the ordinary duties of her life, including those of wifehood and motherhood. Everyone was congratulating her on her recovery. All the kindness of sympathetic and understanding neighbors poured in upon her in the shape of convalescent dishes, soups, custards, and drinks. Still she appeared to be despondent and worried. She seemed to sit apart in her thoughts as if she had no part in these congratulatory messages and endearing welcomes. I thought at first that she still retained some of her unconscious memories and dwelt upon them in her silences.

But as the hour for my departure came nearer, her anxiety increased, and finally with trembling voice she said: "Another baby will finish me, I suppose."

"It's too early to talk about that," I said, and resolved that I would turn the question over to the doctor for his advice. When he came I said: "Mrs. Sacks is worried about having another baby."

"She well might be," replied the doctor, and then he stood before her and said: "Any more such capers, young woman, and there will be no need to call me."

"Yes, yes—I know, Doctor," said the patient with trembling voice, "but," and she hesitated as if it took all of her courage to say it, "*what* can I do to prevent getting that way again?"

"Oh ho!" laughed the doctor good naturedly, "You want your cake while you eat it too, do you? Well, it can't be done." Then, familiarly slapping her on the back and picking up his hat and bag to depart, he said: "I'll tell you the only sure thing to do. Tell Jake to sleep on the roof!"

With those words he closed the door and went down the stairs, leaving us both petrified and stunned.

Tears sprang to my eyes, and a lump came in my throat as I looked at that face before me. It was stamped with sheer horror. I thought for a moment she might have gone insane, but she conquered her feelings, whatever they may have been, and turning to me in desperation said: "He can't understand, can he?—he's a man after all—but you do, don't you? You're a woman and you'll tell me the secret and I'll never tell it to a soul."

She clasped her hands as if in prayer, she leaned over and looked straight into my eyes and beseechingly implored me to tell her something—something *I really did not know.* It was like being on a rack and tortured for a crime one had not committed. To plead guilty would stop the agony; otherwise the rack kept turning.

I had to turn away from that imploring face. I could not answer her then. I quieted her as best I could. She saw that I was moved by the tears in my eyes. I promised that I would come back in a few days and tell her what she wanted to know. The few simple means of limiting the family like *coitus interruptus* or the condom were laughed at by the neighboring women when told these were the means used by men in the well-to-do families. That was not believed, and I knew such an answer would be swept aside as useless were I to tell her this at such a time.

A little later when she slept I left the house, and made up my mind that I'd keep away from those cases in the future. I felt helpless to do anything at all. I seemed chained hand and foot, and longed for an earthquake or a volcano to shake the world out of its lethargy into facing these monstrous atrocities.

The intelligent reasoning of the young mother—how to *prevent* getting that way again—how sensible, how just she had been—yes, I promised myself I'd go back and have a long talk with her and tell her more, and perhaps she would not laugh but would believe that those methods were all that were really known.

But time flew past, and weeks rolled into months. That wistful, appealing face haunted me day and night. I could not banish from my mind memories of that trembling voice begging so humbly for knowledge she had a right to have. I was about to retire one night three months later when the telephone rang and an agitated man's voice begged me to come at once to help his wife who was sick again. It was the husband of Mrs. Sacks, and I intuitively knew before I left the telephone that it was almost useless to go.

I dreaded to face that woman. I was tempted to send someone else in my place. I longed for an accident on the subway, or on the street—anything to prevent my going into that home. But on I went just the same. I arrived a few minutes after the doctor, the same one who had given her such noble advice. The woman was dying. She was unconscious. She died within ten minutes after my arrival. It was the same result, the same story told a thousand times before—death from abortion. She had become pregnant, had used drugs, had then consulted a five-dollar professional abortionist, and death followed.

The doctor shook his head as he rose from listening for the heart beat. I knew she had already passed on; without a groan, a sigh or recognition of our belated presence she had gone into the Great Beyond as thousands of mothers go every year. I looked at that drawn face now stilled in death. I placed her thin hands across her breast and recalled how hard they had pleaded with me on that last memorable occasion of parting. The gentle woman, the devoted mother, the loving wife had passed on leaving behind her a frantic husband, helpless in his loneliness, bewildered in his helplessness as he paced up and down the room, hands clenching his head, moaning "My God! My God! My God!"

The Revolution came—but not as it has been pictured nor as history relates that revolutions have come. It came in my own life. It began in my very being as I walked home that night after I had closed the eyes and covered with a sheet the body of that little helpless mother whose life had been sacrificed to ignorance.

After I left that desolate house I walked and walked and walked; for hours and hours I kept on, bag in hand, thinking, regretting, dreading to stop; fearful of my conscience, dreading to face my own accusing soul. At three in the morning I arrived home still clutching a heavy load the weight of which I was quite unconscious.

I entered the house quietly, as was my custom, and looked out of the window down upon the dimly lighted, sleeping city. As I stood at the window and looked out, the miseries and problems of that sleeping city arose before me in a clear vision like a panorama: crowded homes, too many children; babies dying in infancy; mothers overworked; baby nurseries; children neglected and hungry—mothers so nervously wrought they could not give the little things the comfort nor care they needed; mothers half sick most of their lives—"always ailing, never failing"; women made into drudges; children working in cellars; children aged six and seven pushed into the labor market to help earn a living; another baby on the way; still another; yet another; a baby born dead—great relief; an older child dies—sorrow, but nevertheless relief—insurance helps; a mother's death—children scattered into institutions; the father, desperate, drunken; he slinks away to become an outcast in a society which has trapped him. . . .

. . . For hours I stood, motionless and tense, expecting something to happen. I watched the lights go out, I saw the darkness gradually give way to the first shimmer of dawn, and then a colorful sky heralded the rise of the sun. I knew a new day had come for me and a new world as well.

It was like an illumination. I could now see clearly the various social strata of our life; all its mass problems seemed to be centered around uncontrolled breeding. There was only one thing to be done: call out, start the alarm, set the heather on fire! Awaken the womanhood of America to free the motherhood of the world! I released from my almost paralyzed hand the nursing bag which unconsciously I had clutched, threw it across the room, tore the uniform from my body, flung it into a corner, and renounced all palliative work forever.

I would never go back again to nurse women's ailing bodies while their miseries were as vast as the stars. I was now finished with superficial cures, with doctors and nurses and social workers who were brought face to face with this overwhelming truth of women's needs and yet turned to pass on the other side. They must be made to see these facts. I resolved that women should have knowledge of contraception. They have every right to know about their own bodies. I would strike out—I would scream from the housetops. I would tell the world what was going on in the lives of these poor women. I *would* be heard. No matter what it should cost. *I would be heard.*

---

## REFLECTING ON MEANING

1. What reasons does Sanger give to explain why she became dissatisfied with her work as a nurse? Why does she call this work "palliative"? How did the work she was later to do differ from her earlier work?

2. Sanger did not return to Mrs. Sacks in a few days, as she had promised she would. Why do you think she chose not to?

3. What does Sanger mean when she says that "the Revolution came"? In what ways was this revolution a personal one? What larger revolution is she also alluding to?

## EXPLORING RHETORICAL STRATEGIES

1. What is the significance of the title of this selection? In what ways was Sanger's experience an awakening? In what ways was it also a revolt?

2. Sanger does a good job of showing what she saw as well as describing what she experienced. Where does she help her audience see for themselves what she saw? What does she accomplish in doing this?

3. What is the effect of the repetition in Sanger's concluding paragraph? In what ways does she use italics to lend an oral quality

to her sentences? In what ways does she effectively express the depth of her commitment to the cause of birth control?

# Birth Control—A Parent's Problem or Woman's?

## MARGARET SANGER

*In this excerpt from* Woman and the New Race, *published in 1920, Margaret Sanger shifts away from the personal perspective of the preceding selection to argue that women must take responsibility for birth control.*

The problem of birth control has arisen directly from the effort of the feminine spirit to free itself from bondage. Woman herself has wrought that bondage through her reproductive powers and while enslaving herself has enslaved the world. The physical suffering to be relieved is chiefly woman's. Hers, too, is the love life that dies first under the blight of too prolific breeding. Within her is wrapped up the future of the race—it is hers to make or mar. All of these considerations point unmistakably to one fact—it is woman's duty as well as her privilege to lay hold of the means of freedom. Whatever men may do, she cannot escape the responsibility. For ages she has been deprived of the opportunity to meet this obligation. She is now emerging from her helplessness. Even as no one can share the suffering of the overburdened mother, so no one can do this work for her. Others may help, but she and she alone can free herself.

The basic freedom of the world is woman's freedom. A free race cannot be born of slave mothers. A woman enchained cannot choose but give a measure of that bondage to her sons and daughters. No woman can call herself free who does not own and control her body. No woman can call herself free until she can choose consciously whether she will or will not be a mother.

It does not greatly alter the case that some women call themselves free because they earn their own livings, while others profess freedom because they defy the conventions of sex relationship. She who earns her own living gains a sort of freedom that is not to be undervalued, but in quality and in quantity it is of little account beside the untrammeled choice of mating or not mating, of being a mother or not being a mother. She gains food and clothing and shelter, at least, without submitting to the charity of her companion, but the earning of her own living does not give her the development of her inner sex urge, far deeper and more powerful in its outworkings than any of these externals. In order to have that development, she must still meet and solve the problem of motherhood.

With the so-called "free" woman, who chooses a mate in defiance of convention, freedom is largely a question of character and audacity. If she does attain to an unrestricted choice of a mate, she is still in a position to be enslaved through her reproductive powers. Indeed, the pressure of law and custom upon the woman not legally married is likely to make her more of a slave than the woman fortunate enough to marry the man of her choice.

Look at it from any standpoint you will, suggest any solution you will, conventional or unconventional, sanctioned by law or in defiance of law, woman is in the same position, fundamentally, until she is able to determine for herself whether she will be a mother and to fix the number of her offspring. This unavoidable situation is alone enough to make birth control, first of all, a woman's problem. On the very face of the matter, voluntary motherhood is chiefly the concern of the woman.

It is persistently urged, however, that since sex expression is the act of two, the responsibility of controlling the results should not be placed upon woman alone. Is it fair, it is asked, to give her, instead of the man, the task of protecting herself when she is, perhaps, less rugged in physique than her mate, and has, at all events, the normal, periodic inconveniences of her sex?

We must examine this phase of her problem in two lights—that of the ideal, and of the conditions working toward the ideal. In an ideal society, no doubt, birth control would become the concern of the man as well as the woman. The hard, inescapable fact which we encounter to-day is that man has not only refused any such responsibility, but has individually and collectively sought to prevent woman from obtaining knowledge by which she could assume this responsibility for herself. She is still in the position of a dependent to-day because her mate has refused to consider her as an individual apart from his needs. She is still bound because she has in the past left the solution of the problem to him. Having left it to him, she finds that instead of rights, she has only such privileges as she has gained by petitioning, coaxing and cozening. Having left it to him, she is exploited, driven and enslaved to his desires.

While it is true that he suffers many evils as the consequence of this situation, she suffers vastly more. While it is true that he should be awakened to the cause of these evils, we know that they come home to her with crushing force every day. It is she who has the long burden of carrying, bearing and rearing the unwanted children. . . . It is her heart that the sight of the deformed, the subnormal, the undernourished, the overworked child smites first and oftenest and hardest. It is *her* love life that dies first in the fear of undesired pregnancy. It is her opportunity for self expression that perishes first and most hopelessly because of it.

Conditions, rather than theories, facts, rather than dreams, govern the problem. They place it squarely upon the shoulders of woman. She has learned that whatever the moral responsibility of the man in this direction may be, he does not discharge it. She has learned that, lovable and considerate as the individual husband may be, she has nothing to expect from men in the mass, when they make laws and decree customs. She knows that regardless of what ought to be, the brutal, unavoidable fact is that she will never receive her freedom until she takes it for herself.

Having learned this much, she has yet something more to learn. Women are too much inclined to follow in the footsteps of men, to try to think as men think, to try to solve the general problems of life as men solve them. If after attaining their freedom, women accept conditions in the spheres of government, industry, art, morals and religion as they find them, they will be but taking a leaf out of man's book. The woman is not needed to do man's work. She is not needed to think man's thoughts. She need not fear that the masculine mind, almost universally dominant, will fail to take care of its own. Her mission is not to enhance the masculine spirit, but to express the feminine; hers is not to preserve a man-made world, but to create a human world by the infusion of the feminine element into all of its activities.

Woman must not accept; she must challenge. She must not be awed by that which has been built up around her; she must reverence that within her which struggles for expression. Her eyes must be less upon what is and more clearly upon what should be. She must listen only with a frankly questioning attitude to the dogmatized opinions of man-made society. When she chooses her new, free course of action, it must be in the light of her own opinion—of her own intuition. Only so can she give play to the feminine spirit. Only thus can she free her mate from the bondage which he wrought for himself when he wrought hers. Only thus can she restore to him that of which he robbed himself in restricting her. Only thus can she remake the world. . . .

Woman must have her freedom—the fundamental freedom of choosing whether or not she shall be a mother and how many children she will have. Regardless of what man's attitude may be, that problem is hers—and before it can be his, it is hers alone.

She goes through the vale of death alone, each time a babe is born. As it is the right neither of man nor the state to coerce her into this ordeal, so it is her right to decide whether she will endure it. That right to decide imposes upon her the duty of clearing the way to knowledge by which she may make and carry out the decision.

Birth control is woman's problem. The quicker she accepts it as hers and hers alone, the quicker will society respect motherhood. The quicker, too, will the world be made a fit place for her children to live.

---

## REFLECTING ON MEANING

1. According to Sanger, why is birth control necessarily a concern of women but not of men? Do you agree that women should take complete responsibility for contraception? Should it be a joint responsibility shared by a man and a woman? Why or why not?
2. Sanger asserts that "no woman can call herself free who does not own and control her body." What does she mean? To what extent does contraception provide such control? To what extent do you agree or disagree with Sanger's assertion? Why?
3. Attaining freedom, Sanger maintains, is not enough; rather, women must "challenge" the masculine world. What does she mean? According to Sanger, how would such an endeavor also free men?

## EXPLORING RHETORICAL STRATEGIES

1. Sanger uses the language of slavery to describe mandatory pregnancy. Is her analogy appropriate? What rhetorical strength does she derive from it?

2. What is Sanger's tone in this excerpt? How does her tone reinforce her purpose? In what ways does the tone of this selection differ from that of "Awakening and Revolt"? What similarities do you see?

3. Part of the rhetorical strength of this selection derives from Sanger's effective use of repetition in sentence structure. How many instances of repetition can you find? What effect does it create?

# Professions for Women

## VIRGINIA WOOLF

*Virginia Woolf explores an important women's issue from the perspective of her experiences as a writer. In relating her own struggles to pursue her chosen profession, Woolf describes the "phantoms and obstacles" that everywhere confront career women. Woolf originally presented this essay as a talk at a meeting of the Women's Service League in 1931.*

When your secretary invited me to come here, she told me that your Society is concerned with the employment of women and she suggested that I might tell you something about my own professional experiences. It is true I am a woman; it is true I am employed; but what professional experiences have I had? It is difficult to say. My profession is literature; and in that profession there are fewer experiences for women than in any other, with the exception of the stage—fewer, I mean, that are peculiar to women. For the road was cut many years ago—by Fanny Burney, by Aphra Behn, by Harriet Martineau, by Jane Austen, by George Eliot—many famous women, and many more unknown and forgotten, have been before me, making the path smooth, and regulating my steps. Thus, when I came to write, there were very few material obstacles in my way. Writing was a reputable and harmless occupation. The family peace was not broken by the scratching of a pen. No demand was made upon the family purse. For ten and sixpence one can buy paper enough to write all the plays of Shakespeare—if one has a mind that way. Pianos and models, Paris, Vienna and Berlin, masters and mistresses, are not needed by a writer. The cheapness of writing paper is, of course, the reason why women have succeeded as writers before they have succeeded in the other professions.

But to tell you my story—it is a simple one. You have only got to figure to yourselves a girl in a bedroom with a pen in her hand. She had only to move that pen from left to right—from ten o'clock to one. Then it occurred to her to do what is simple and cheap enough after all—to slip a few of those pages into an envelope, fix a penny stamp in the corner, and drop the envelope into the red box at the corner. It was thus that I became a journalist; and my effort was rewarded on the first day of the following month—a very glorious day it was for me—by a letter from an editor containing a cheque for one pound ten shillings and sixpence. But to show you how little I deserve to be called a professional woman, how little I know of the struggles and difficulties of such lives, I have to admit that instead of spending that sum upon bread and butter, rent, shoes and stockings, or butcher's bills, I went out and bought a cat—a beautiful cat, a Persian cat, which very soon involved me in bitter disputes with my neighbours.

What could be easier than to write articles and to buy Persian cats with the profits? But wait a moment. Articles have to be about something. Mine, I seem to remember, was about a novel by a famous man. And while I was writing this review, I discovered that if I were going to review books I should need to do battle with a certain phantom. And the phantom was a woman, and when I came to know her better I called her after the heroine of a famous poem, The Angel in the House. It was she who used to come between me and my paper when I was writing reviews. It was she who bothered me and wasted my time and so tormented me that at last I killed her. You who come of a younger and happier generation may not have heard of her—you may not know what I mean by the Angel in the House. I will describe her as shortly as I can. She was intensely sympathetic. She was immensely charming. She was utterly unselfish. She excelled in the difficult arts of family life. She sacrificed herself daily. If there was chicken, she took the leg; if there was a draught she sat in it—in short she was so constituted that she never had a mind or a wish of her own, but preferred to sympathize always with the minds and wishes of others. Above all—I need not say it—she was pure. Her purity was supposed to be her chief beauty—her blushes, her great grace. In those days—the last of Queen Victoria—every house had its Angel. And when I came to write I encountered her with the very first words. The shadow of her wings fell on my page; I heard the rustling of her skirts in the room. Directly, that is to say, I took my pen in hand to review that novel by a famous man, she slipped behind me and whispered: "My dear, you are a young woman. You are writing about a book that has been written by a man. Be sympathetic; be tender; flatter; deceive; use all the arts and wiles of our sex. Never let anybody guess that you have a mind of your own. Above all, be pure." And she made as if to guide my pen. I now record the one act for which I take some credit to myself, though the credit rightly belongs to some excellent ancestors of mine who left me a certain sum of money—shall we say five hundred pounds a year?—so that it was not necessary for me to depend solely on charm for my living. I turned upon her and caught her by the throat. I did my best to kill her. My excuse, if I were to be had up in a court of law, would be that I acted in self-defence. Had I not killed her she would have killed me. She would have plucked the heart out of my writing. For, as I found, directly I put pen to paper, you cannot review even a novel without having a mind of your own, without expressing what you think to be the truth about human relations, morality, sex. And all these questions, according to the Angel in the House, cannot be dealt with freely and openly by women; they must charm, they must conciliate, they must—to put it bluntly—tell lies if they are to succeed. Thus, whenever I felt the shadow of her wing or the radiance of her halo upon my page, I took up the inkpot and flung it at her. She died hard. Her fictitious nature was of great assistance to her. It is far harder to kill a phantom than a reality. She was always creeping back when I thought I had despatched her. Though I flatter myself that I killed her in the end, the struggle was severe; it took much time that had better have been spent upon learning Greek grammar; or in roaming the world in search of adventures. But it was a real experience; it was an experience that was bound to befall all women writers at that time. Killing the Angel in the House was part of the occupation of a woman writer.

But to continue my story. The Angel was dead; what then remained? You may say that what remained was a simple and common object—a young woman in a bedroom with an inkpot. In other words, now that she had rid herself of falsehood, that young woman had only to be herself. Ah, but what is "herself"? I mean, what is a woman? I assure you, I do not know. I do not believe that you know. I do not believe that anybody can know until she has expressed herself in all the arts and professions open to human skill. That indeed is one of the reasons why I have come here—out of respect for you, who are in process of showing us by your experiments what a woman is, who are in process of providing us, by your failures and successes, with that extremely important piece of information.

But to continue the story of my professional experiences. I made one pound ten and six by my first review; and I bought a Persian cat with the proceeds. Then I grew ambitious. A Persian cat is all very well, I said; but a Persian cat is not enough. I must have a motor car. And it was thus that I became a novelist—for it is a very strange thing that people will give you a motor car if you will tell them a story. It is a still stranger thing that there is nothing so delightful in the world as telling stories. It is far pleasanter than writing reviews of famous novels. And yet, if I am to obey your secretary and tell you my professional experiences as a novelist, I must tell you about a very strange experience that befell me as a novelist. And to understand it you must try first to imagine a novelist's state of mind. I hope I am not giving away professional secrets if I say that a novelist's chief desire is to be as unconscious as possible. He has to induce in himself a state of perpetual lethargy. He wants life to proceed with the utmost quiet and regularity. He wants to see the same faces, to read the same books, to do the same things day after day, month after month, while he is writing, so that nothing may break the illusion in which he is living—so that nothing may disturb or disquiet the mysterious nosings about, feelings round, darts, dashes and sudden discoveries of that very shy and illusive spirit, the imagination. I suspect that this state is the same both for men and women. Be that as it may, I want you to imagine me writing a novel in a state of trance. I want you to figure to yourself a girl sitting with a pen in her hand, which for minutes, and indeed for hours, she never dips into the inkpot. The image that comes to my mind when I think of this girl is the image of a fisherman lying sunk in dreams on the verge of a deep lake with a rod held out over the water. She was letting her imagination sweep unchecked round every rock and cranny of the world that lies submerged in the depths of our unconscious being. Now came the experience, the experience that I believe to be far commoner with women writers than with men. The line raced through the girl's fingers. Her imagination had rushed away. It had sought the pools, the depths, the dark places where the largest fish slumber. And then there was a smash. There was an explosion. There was foam and confusion. The imagination had dashed itself against something hard. The girl was roused from her dream. She was indeed in a state of the most acute and difficult distress. To speak without figure she had thought of something, something about the body, about the passions which it was unfitting for her as a woman to say. Men, her reason told her, would be shocked. The consciousness of what men will say of a woman who speaks the truth about her passions had roused her from her artist's state of unconsciousness. She could write no more. The trance was over. Her imagination could work no longer. This I believe to be a very common experience with women writers—they are impeded by the extreme conventionality of the other sex. For though men sensibly allow themselves great freedom in these respects, I doubt that they realize or can control the extreme severity with which they condemn such freedom in women.

These then were two very genuine experiences of my own. These were two of the adventures of my professional life. The first—killing the Angel in the House—I think I solved. She died. But the second, telling the truth about my own experiences as a body, I do not think I solved. I doubt that any woman has solved it yet. The obstacles against her are still immensely powerful—and yet they are very difficult to define. Outwardly, what is simpler than to write books? Outwardly, what obstacles are there for a woman rather than for a man? Inwardly, I think, the case is very different: she has still many ghosts to fight, many prejudices to overcome. Indeed it will be a long time still, I think, before a woman can sit down to write a book without finding a phantom to be slain, a rock to be dashed against. And if this is so in literature, the freest of all professions for women, how is it in the new professions which you are now for the first time entering?

Those are the questions that I should like, had I time, to ask you. And indeed, if I have laid stress upon these professional experiences of mine, it is because I believe that they are, though in different forms, yours also. Even when the path is nominally open—when there is nothing to prevent a woman from being a doctor, a lawyer, a civil servant—there are many phantoms and obstacles, as I believe, looming in her way. To discuss and define them is I think of great value and importance; for thus only can the labour be shared, the difficulties be solved. But besides this, it is necessary also to discuss the ends and the aims for which we are fighting, for which we are doing battle with these formidable obstacles. Those aims cannot be taken for granted; they must be perpetually questioned and examined. The whole position, as I see it—here in this hall surrounded by women practising for the first time in history I know not how many different professions—is one of extraordinary interest and importance. You have won rooms of your own in the house hitherto exclusively owned by men. You are able, though not without great labour and effort, to pay the rent. You are earning your five hundred pounds a year. But this freedom is only a beginning; the room is your own, but it is still bare. It has to be furnished; it has to be decorated; it has to be shared. How are you going to furnish it, how are you going to decorate it? With whom are you going to share it, and upon what terms? These, I think, are questions of the utmost importance and interest. For the first time in history you are able to ask them; for the first time you are able to decide for yourselves what the answers should be. Willingly would I stay and discuss those questions and answers—but not tonight. My time is up; and I must cease.

---

## REFLECTING ON MEANING

1. Why does Woolf attribute her own and other women's success as writers to the "cheapness of writing paper"? What is she implying about the reasons women have often not been able to enter other professions? What does she later suggest about her own socioeconomic status and her ability to become a writer?
2. Who is the "Angel in the House"? In what ways did she torment Woolf? How did Woolf "kill" her? What does the Angel represent? Do you agree that this experience was "bound to befall all women writers at that time"? Why doesn't Woolf extend this experience to men writers? To what extent do all women who pursue careers find themselves battling the Angel?
3. What were the "smash" and the "explosion" that ended Woolf's imaginative flight as she wrote? In what ways does this experience illustrate the difficulties she faced in trying to tell "the truth" about her "own experiences as a body"? What does Woolf mean, exactly? To what extent is this a problem for all women?

## EXPLORING RHETORICAL STRATEGIES

1. Woolf clearly intends her experience to illustrate the professional dilemma faced by all women. How is she able to relate her personal experience to the experience of other women? How does she generalize her own experience to explain the difficulties career women face?

2. How would you describe the tone of Woolf's essay? How do her digressions—for example, her discussion of the Persian cat—contribute to her tone? How do these digressions also advance her main idea?

3. In her conclusion, Woolf speaks of a room in a house. What is the function of this metaphor? How does it relate to her main idea?

# TAKING A STAND
## QUESTIONS FOR CONSIDERATION

1. In describing historical conditions for women and making proposals for change, several authors in this part define what full freedom for women would entail. Survey the essays of at least four authors and deduce their definitions of freedom for women. What do their definitions have in common? How do they differ? Which definition do you consider most fundamental to the issue of women's freedom? Why? You may wish to review essays by McGuigan, Wollstonecraft, Mill, Gilman, and Sanger.

2. Has the status of women changed over the centuries? Drawing on the historical insights offered by at least three authors, argue that significant headway toward equality for women has or has not been made in the twentieth century. Amply describe past conditions, and explain in detail how women's status has or has not changed. In exploring this issue, be sure to consider the extent to which the questions raised in the selection from Plato's *Republic* are still relevant today.

3. Mill, Woolf, and McGuigan suggest that women's intellectual achievements have been limited by social and economic oppression. How does each of these authors explain why women have not been more successful in intellectual endeavors? Do you agree or disagree that women's achievements in these areas have been handicapped by circumstance? To what extent are current conditions perhaps more conducive to such achievements?

4. Daly traces the origin of women's oppression to the Bible and the Church Fathers, whereas Pope Pius XI's encyclical summarizes the views of the Catholic church as they stood as recently as 1930. Drawing on Daly's survey and the papal encyclical, determine the extent to which the church's views changed over the centuries. Do you agree or disagree that the Christian religion has reinforced and continues to reinforce women's oppression? Why?

5. Wollstonecraft, McGuigan, and Mill examine women's education. What are their conclusions? What do they suggest? Has women's access to a real education changed over the centuries? In shaping your response, you may want to consider the essays in Part IV by Rich and Thomas.

# Part III

# Language and Sexism

Many language experts contend that language shapes reality, that how we talk (or write) about a subject dictates what we think about it. These experts also argue that what a society "thinks" about a subject changes as its language about that subject changes. These notions are central concerns of feminist scholars who have demonstrated that the English language is especially sexist—that is, that it tends to acknowledge male experience and values while trivializing female experience and values. The essays in Part III examine the role of language in reinforcing sexist assumptions, but they also imply that such attitudes can change if we alter our language.

The authors of the first group of essays, under the heading "Sexist Language," analyze the kinds of linguistic discrimination inherent in English. Casey Miller and Kate Swift enumerate instances of linguistic sexism and conclude that such language ignores women as persons. Alleen Pace Nilsen examines dictionary definitions to show how language influences culture. Miller and Swift, in another essay, point out that in our society women's names are less important than men's. Whereas these authors suggest that changing our language will help change sexist assumptions, Cyra McFadden disagrees, finding such attempts at linguistic reform naive and silly.

In the second group of essays, several authors examine the role of conversation. Robin Lakoff notes differences between how women and men talk and shows that such differences reveal a "linguistic double standard." Gloria Steinem summarizes research on the "politics of conversation" and the effects of masculine and feminine "styles" of conversation.

Although it remains to be seen whether sexist attitudes will diminish as the English language becomes less gender-biased, what is certain is that authors such as those represented in Part III have made great inroads in raising consciousness about just how male-dominant English really is.

# Chapter 6

## SEXIST LANGUAGE

### One Small Step for Genkind

CASEY MILLER and KATE SWIFT

*In this essay Casey Miller and Kate Swift contend that the English language "operates to keep women invisible." They survey instances of sexism in English and call for linguistic reform that will acknowledge women as "real people."*

A riddle is making the rounds that goes like this: A man and his young son were in an automobile accident. The father was killed and the son, who was critically injured, was rushed to a hospital. As attendants wheeled the unconscious boy into the emergency room, the doctor on duty looked down at him and said, "My God, it's my son!" What was the relationship of the doctor to the injured boy?

If the answer doesn't jump to your mind, another riddle that has been around a lot longer might help: The blind beggar had a brother. The blind beggar's brother died. The brother who died had no brother. What relation was the blind beggar to the blind beggar's brother?

As with all riddles, the answers are obvious once you see them: The doctor was the boy's mother and the beggar was her brother's sister. Then why doesn't everyone solve them immediately? Mainly because our language, like the culture it reflects, is male oriented. To say that a woman in medicine is an exception is simply to confirm that statement. Thousands of doctors are women, but in order to be seen in the mind's eye, they must be called women doctors.

Except for words that refer to females by definition (mother, actress, Congresswoman), and words for occupations traditionally held by females (nurse, secretary, prostitute), the English language defines everyone as male. The hypothetical person ("If a man can walk 10 miles in two hours . . ."), the average person ("the man in the street") and the active person ("the man on the move") are male. The assumption is that unless otherwise identified, people in general—including doctors and beggars—are men. It is a semantic mechanism that operates to keep women invisible: *man* and *mankind* represent everyone; *he* in generalized use refers to either sex; the "land where our fathers died" is also the land of our mothers—although they go unsung. As the beetle-browed and mustachioed man in a Steig cartoon says to his two male drinking companions, "When I speak of mankind, one thing I *don't* mean is womankind."

Semantically speaking, woman is not one with the species of man, but a distinct subspecies. "Man," says the 1971 edition of the Britannica Junior Encyclopedia, "is the highest form of life on earth. His superior intelligence, combined with certain physical characteristics, have enabled man to achieve things that are impossible for other animals." (The prose style has something in common with the report of a research team describing its studies on "the development of the uterus in rats, guinea pigs and men.") As though quoting the Steig character, still speaking to his friends in McSorley's, the Junior Encyclopedia continues: "Man must invent most of his behavior, because he lacks the instincts of lower animals. . . . Most of the things he learns have been handed down from his ancestors by language and symbols rather than by biological inheritance."

Considering that for the last 5,000 years society has been partriarchal, that statement explains a lot. It explains why Eve was made from Adam's rib instead of the other way around, and who invented all those Adam-rib words like *fe*male and *wo*man in the first place. It also explains why, when it is necessary to mention woman, the language makes her a lower caste, a class separate from the rest of man; why it works to "keep her in her place."

This inheritance through language and other symbols begins in the home (also called a man's castle) where man and wife (not husband and wife, or man and woman) live for a while with their children. It is reinforced by religious training, the educational system, the press, government, commerce and the law. As Andrew

Greeley wrote not long ago in his magazine, "man is a symbol-creating animal. He orders and interprets his reality by his symbols, and he uses the symbols to reconstruct that reality."

Consider some of the reconstructed realities of American history. When school children learn from their textbooks that the early colonists gained valuable experience in governing themselves, they are not told that the early colonists who were women were denied the privilege of self-government; when they learn that in the 18th century the average man had to manufacture many of the things he and his family needed, they are not told that this "average man" was often a woman who manufactured much of what she and her family needed. Young people learn that intrepid pioneers crossed the country in covered wagons with their wives, children and cattle; they do not learn that women themselves were intrepid pioneers rather than part of the baggage.

In a paper published this year in Los Angeles as a guide for authors and editors of social-studies textbooks, Elizabeth Burr, Susan Dunn and Norma Farquhar document unintentional skewings of this kind that occur either because women are not specifically mentioned as affecting or being affected by historical events, or because they are discussed in terms of outdated assumptions. "One never sees a picture of women captioned simply 'farmers' or 'pioneers,' " they point out. The subspecies nomenclature that requires a caption to read "women farmers" or "women pioneers" is extended to impose certain jobs on women by definition. The textbook guide gives as an example the word *housewife,* which it says not only "suggests that domestic chores are the exclusive burden of females," but gives "female students the idea that they were born to keep house and teaches male students that they are automatically entitled to laundry, cooking and housecleaning services from the women in their families."

Sexist language is any language that expresses such stereotyped attitudes and expectations, or that assumes the inherent superiority of one sex over the other. When a woman says of her husband, who has drawn up plans for a new bedroom wing and left out closets, "Just like a man," her language is as sexist as the man's who says, after his wife has changed her mind about needing the new wing after all, "Just like a woman."

Male and female are not sexist words, but masculine and feminine almost always are. Male and female can be applied objectively to individual people and animals and, by extension, to things. When electricians and plumbers talk about male and female couplings, everyone knows or can figure out what they mean. The terms are graphic and culture free.

Masculine and feminine, however, are as sexist as any words can be, since it is almost impossible to use them without invoking cultural stereotypes. When people construct lists of "masculine" and "feminine" traits they almost always end up making assumptions that have nothing to do with innate differences between the sexes. We have a friend who happens to be going through the process of pinning down this very phenomenon. He is 7 years old and his question concerns why his coats and shirts button left over right while his sister's button the other way. He assumes it must have something to do with the differences between boys and girls, but he can't see how.

What our friend has yet to grasp is that the way you button your coat, like most sex-differentiated customs, has nothing to do with real differences but much to do with what society wants you to feel about yourself as a male or female person. Society decrees that it is appropriate for girls to dress differently from boys, to act differently, and to think differently. Boys must be masculine, whatever that means, and girls must be feminine.

Unabridged dictionaries are a good source for finding out what society decrees to be appropriate, though less by definition than by their choice of associations and illustrations. Words associated with males—*manly, virile* and *masculine,* for example—are defined through a broad range of positive attributes like strength, courage, directness and independence, and they are illustrated through such examples of contemporary usage as "a manly determination to face what comes," "a virile literary style," "a masculine love of sports." Corresponding words associated with females are defined with fewer attributes (though weakness is often one of them) and the examples given are generally negative if not clearly pejorative: "feminine wiles," "womanish tears," "a womanlike lack of promptness," "convinced that drawing was a waste of time, if not downright womanly."

Male-associated words are frequently applied to females to describe something that is either incongruous ("a mannish voice") or presumably commendable ("a masculine mind," "she took it like a man"), but female-associated words are unreservedly derogatory when applied to males, and are sometimes abusive to females as well. The opposite of "masculine" is "effeminate," although the opposite of "feminine" is simply "unfeminine."

One dictionary, after defining the word *womanish* as "suitable to or resembling a woman," further defines it as "unsuitable to a man or to a strong character of either sex." Words derived from "sister" and "brother" provide another apt example, for whereas "sissy," applied either to a male or female, conveys the message that sisters are expected to be timid and cowardly, "buddy" makes clear that brothers are friends.

The subtle disparagement of females and corresponding approbation of males wrapped up in many English words is painfully illustrated by "tomboy." Here is an instance where a girl who likes sports and the out-of-doors, who is curious about how things work, who is adventurous and bold instead of passive, is defined in terms of something she is not—a boy. By denying that she can be the person she is and still be a girl, the word surreptitiously undermines her sense of identity: it says she is unnatural. A "tomboy," as defined by one dictionary, is a "girl, especially a young girl, who behaves like a spirited boy." But who makes the judgment that she is acting like a spirited boy, not a spirited girl? Can it be a coincidence that in the case of the dictionary just quoted the editor, executive editor, managing editor, general manager, all six members of the Board of Linguists, the usage editor, science editor, all six general editors of definitions, and 94 out of the 104 distinguished experts consulted on usage—are men?

It isn't enough to say that any invidious comparisons and stereotypes lexicographers perpetuate are already present in the culture. There are ways to define words like womanly and tomboy that don't put women down, though the tradition has been otherwise. Samuel Johnson, the lexicographer, was the same Dr. Johnson who said, "A woman preaching is like a dog's walking on his hind legs. It is not done well; but you are surprised to find it done at all."

Possibly because of the negative images associated with womanish and womanlike, and with expressions like "woman driver" and "woman of the street," the word woman dropped out of fashion for a time. The women at the office and the women on the assembly line and the women one first knew in school all became ladies or girls or gals. Now a countermovement, supported by the very term women's liberation, is putting back into words like woman and sister and sisterhood the meaning they were losing by default. It is as though, in the nick of time, women had seen that the language itself could destroy them.

Some long-standing conventions of the news media add insult to injury. When a woman or girl makes news, her sex is identified at the beginning of a story, if possible in the headline or its equivalent. The assumption, apparently, is that whatever event or action is being reported, a woman's involvement is less common and therefore more newsworthy than a man's. If the story is about achievement, the implication is: "pretty good for a woman." And because people are assumed to be male unless otherwise identified, the media have developed a special and extensive vocabulary to avoid the constant repetition of "woman." The results, "Grandmother Wins Nobel Prize," "Blonde Hijacks Airliner," "Housewife to Run for Congress," convey the kind of information that would be ludicrous in comparable headlines if the subjects were men. Why, if "Unsalaried Husband to Run for Congress" is unacceptable to editors, do women have to keep explaining that to describe them through external or superficial concerns reflects a sexist view of women as decorative objects, breeding machines and extensions of men, not real people?

Members of the Chicago chapter of the National Organization for Women recently studied the newspapers in their area and drew up a set of guidelines for the press. These include cutting out descriptions of the "clothes, physical features, dating life and marital status of women where such references would be considered inappropriate if about men"; using language in such a way as to include women in copy that refers to homeowners, scientists and business people where "newspaper descriptions often convey the idea that all such persons are male"; and displaying the same discretion in printing generalizations about women as would be shown toward racial, religious and ethnic groups. "Our concern with what we are called may seem trivial to some people," the women said, "but we regard the old usages as symbolic of women's position within this society."

The assumption that an adult woman is flattered by being called a girl is matched by the notion that a woman in a menial or poorly paid job finds compensation in being called a lady. Ethel Strainchamps has pointed out that since lady is used as an adjective with nouns designating both high and low occupations (lady wrestler, lady barber, lady doctor, lady judge), some writers assume they can use the noun form without betraying value judgments. Not so, Strainchamps says, rolling the issue into a spitball: "You may write, 'He addressed the Republican ladies,' or 'The Democratic ladies convened' . . . but I have never seen 'the Communist ladies' or 'the Black Panther ladies' in print."

Thoughtful writers and editors have begun to repudiate some of the old usages. "Divorcée," "grandmother" and "blonde," along with "vivacious," "pert," "dimpled" and "cute," were dumped by the Washington Post in the spring of 1970 by the executive editor, Benjamin Bradlee. In a memo to his staff, Bradlee wrote, "The meaningful equality and dignity of women is properly under scrutiny today . . . because this equality has been less than meaningful and the dignity not always free of stereotype and condescension."

What women have been called in the press—or at least the

part that operates above ground—is only a fraction of the infinite variety of alternatives to "women" used in the subcultures of the English-speaking world. Beyond "chicks," "dolls," "dames," "babes," "skirts" and "broads" are the words and phrases in which women are reduced to their sexuality and nothing more. It would be hard to think of another area of language in which the human mind has been so fertile in devising and borrowing abusive terms. In "The Female Eunuch," Germaine Greer devotes four pages to anatomical terms and words for animals, vegetables, fruits, baked goods, implements and receptacles, all of which are used to dehumanize the female person. Jean Faust, in an article aptly called "Words That Oppress," suggests that the effort to diminish women through language is rooted in a male fear of sexual inadequacy. "Woman is made to feel guilty for and akin to natural disasters," she writes; "hurricanes and typhoons are named after her. Any negative or threatening force is given a feminine name. If a man runs into bad luck climbing up the ladder of success (a male-invented game), he refers to the 'bitch goddess' success."

The sexual overtones in the ancient and no doubt honorable custom of calling ships "she" have become more explicit and less honorable in an age of air travel: "I'm Karen. Fly me." Attitudes of ridicule, contempt and disgust toward female sexuality have spawned a rich glossary of insults and epithets not found in dictionaries. And the usage in which four-letter words meaning copulate are interchangeable with cheat, attack and destroy can scarcely be unrelated to the savagery of rape.

In her updating of Ibsen's "A Doll's House," Clare Boothe Luce has Nora tell her husband she is pregnant—"In the way only men are supposed to get pregnant." "Men, pregnant?" he says, and she nods; "With ideas. Pregnancies there [*she taps his head*] are masculine. And a very superior form of labor. Pregnancies here [*taps her tummy*] are feminine—a very inferior form of labor."

Public outcry followed a revised translation of the New Testament describing Mary as "pregnant" instead of "great with child." The objections were made in part on esthetic grounds: there is no attractive adjective in modern English for a woman who is about to give birth. A less obvious reason was that replacing the euphemism with a biological term undermined religious teaching. The initiative and generative power in the conception of Jesus are understood to be God's; Mary, the mother, was a vessel only.

Whether influenced by this teaching or not, the language of human reproduction lags several centuries behind scientific understanding. The male's contribution to procreation is still described as though it were the entire seed from which a new life grows: the initiative and generative power involved in the process are thought of as masculine, receptivity and nurturance as feminine. "Seminal" remains a synonym for "highly original," and there is no comparable word to describe the female's equivalent contribution.

An entire mythology has grown from this biological misunderstanding and its semantic legacy; its embodiment in laws that for centuries made women nonpersons was a key target of the 19th-century feminist movement. Today, more than 50 years after women finally won the basic democratic right to vote, the word "liberation" itself, when applied to women, means something less than when used of other groups of people. An advertisement for the N.B.C. news department listed Women's Liberation along with crime in the streets and the Vietnam war as "bad news." Asked for his views on Women's Liberation, a highly placed politician was quoted as saying, "Let me make one thing perfectly clear. I wouldn't want to wake up next to a lady pipe-fitter."

One of the most surprising challenges to our male-dominated culture is coming from within organized religion, where the issues are being stated, in part, by confronting the implications of traditional language. What a growing number of theologians and scholars are saying is that the myths of the Judeo-Christian tradition, being the products of patriarchy, must be reexamined, and that the concept of an exclusively male ministry and the image of a male god have become idolatrous.

Women are naturally in the forefront of this movement, both in their efforts to gain ordination and full equality and through their contributions to theological reform, although both these efforts are often subtly diminished. When the Rev. Barbara Anderson was ordained by the American Lutheran Church, one newspaper printed her picture over a caption headed "Happy Girl." Newsweek's report of a protest staged last December [1971] by women divinity students at Harvard was jocular ("another tilt at the windmill") and sarcastic: "Every time anyone in the room lapsed into what [the students] regarded as male chauvinism—such as using the word 'mankind' to describe the human race in general—the outraged women . . . drowned out the offender with earpiercing blasts from party-favor kazoos. . . . What annoyed the women most was the universal custom of referring to God as 'He.' "

The tone of the report was not merely unfunny; it missed the connection between increasingly outmoded theological language and the accelerating number of women (and men) who are dropping out of organized religion, both Jewish and Christian. For language, including pronouns, can be used to construct a reality that simply mirrors society's assumptions. To women who are committed to the reality of religious faith, the effect is doubly painful. Professor Harvey Cox, in whose classroom the protest took place, stated the issue directly: The women, he said, were raising the "basic theological question of whether God is more adequately thought of in personal or suprapersonal terms."

Toward the end of Don McLean's remarkable ballad "American Pie," a song filled with the imagery of abandonment and disillusion, there is a stanza that must strike many women to the quick. The church bells are broken, the music has died; then:

> And the three men I admire most,
> The Father, Son and the Holy Ghost,
> They caught the last train for the Coast—
> The day the music died.

Three men I admired most. There they go, briefcases in hand and topcoats buttoned left over right, walking down the long cold platform under the city, past the baggage wagons and the hissing steam onto the Pullman. Bye, bye God—all three of you—made in the image of male supremacy. Maybe out there in L.A. where the weather is warmer, someone can believe in you again.

The Roman Catholic theologian Elizabeth Farians says "the bad theology of an overmasculinized church continues to be one of the root causes of women's oppression." The definition of oppression is "to crush or burden by abuse of power or authority; burden spiritually or mentally as if by pressure."

When language oppresses, it does so by any means that disparage and belittle. Until well into the 20th century, one of the ways English was manipulated to disparage women was through the addition of feminine endings to nonsexual words. Thus a woman who aspired to be a poet was excluded from the company of real poets by the label poetess, and a women who piloted an airplane was denied full status as an aviator by being called an aviatrix. At about the time poetess, aviatrix, and similar Adam-ribbisms were dropping out of use, H. W. Fowler was urging that they be revived. "With the coming expansion of women's vocations," he wrote in the first edition (1926) of "Modern English Usage," "feminines for vocation-words are a special need of the future." There can be no doubt he subsconsciously recognized the relative status implied in the *-ess* designations. His criticism of a woman who wished to be known as an author rather than an authoress was that she had no need "to raise herself to the level of the male author by asserting her right to his name."

Who has the prior right to a name? The question has an interesting bearing on words that were once applied to men alone, or to both men and women, but now, having acquired abusive associations, are assigned to women exclusively. Spinster is a gentle case in point. Prostitute and many of its synonyms illustrate the phenomenon better. If Fowler had chosen to record the changing usage of harlot from hired man (in Chaucer's time) through rascal and entertainer to its present definition, would he have maintained that the female harlot is trying to raise herself to the level of the male harlot by asserting her right to his name? Or would he have plugged for harlotress?

The demise of most *-ess* endings came about before the start of the new feminist movement. In the second edition of "Modern English Usage," published in 1965, Sir Ernest Gowers frankly admitted what his predecessors had been up to. "Feminine designations," he wrote, "seem now to be falling into disuse. Perhaps the explanation of this paradox is that it symbolizes the victory of women in their struggle for equal rights; it reflects the abandonment by men of those ideas about women in the professions that moved Dr. Johnson to his rude remark about women preachers."

If Sir Ernest's optimism can be justified, why is there a movement back to feminine endings in such words as chairwoman, councilwoman and congresswoman? Betty Hudson, of Madison, Conn., is campaigning for the adoption of "selectwoman" as the legal title for a female member of that town's executive body. To have to address a woman as "Selectman," she maintains, "is not only bad grammar and bad biology, but it implies that politics is still, or should be, a man's business." A valid argument, and one that was, predictably, countered by ridicule, the surefire weapon for undercutting achievement. When the head of the Federal Maritime Commission, Helen D. Bentley, was named "Man of the Year" by an association of shipping interests, she wisely refused to be drawn into light-hearted debate with interviewers who wanted to make the award's name a humorous issue. Some women, of course, have yet to learn they are invisible. An 8-year-old who visited the American Museum of Natural History with her Brownie Scout troop went through the impressive exhibit on pollution and overpopulation called "Can Man Survive?" Asked afterward, "Well, can he?" she answered, "I don't know about him, but we're working on it in Brownies."

Nowhere are women rendered more invisible by language than in politics. The United States Constitution, in describing the qualifications for Representative, Senator and President, refers to each as *he*. No wonder Shirley Chisholm, the first woman since 1888 to make a try for the Presidential nomination of a major party, has found it difficult to be taken seriously.

The observation by Andrew Greeley already quoted—that "man" uses "his symbols" to reconstruct "his reality"—was not made in reference to the symbols of language but to the symbolic impact the "nomination of a black man for Vice-Presidency" would have on race relations in the United States. Did the author assume the generic term "man" would of course be construed to include "woman"? Or did he deliberately use a semantic device to exclude Shirley Chisholm without having to be explicit?

Either way, his words construct a reality in which women are ignored. As much as any other factor in our language, the ambiguous meaning of *man* serves to deny women recognition as people. In a recent magazine article, we discussed the similar effect on women of the generic pronoun *he*, which we proposed to replace by a new common gender pronoun *tey*. We were immediately told, by a number of authorities, that we were dabbling in the serious business of linguistics, and the message that reached us from these scholars was loud and clear: It - is - absolutely - impossible - for - anyone - to - introduce - a - new - word - into - the - language - just - because - there - is - a - need - for - it, so - stop - wasting - your - time.

When words are suggested like "herstory" (for history), "sportsoneship" (for sportsmanship) and "mistresspiece" (for the work of a Virginia Woolf) one suspects a not-too-subtle attempt to make the whole language problem look silly. But unless Alexander Pope, when he wrote "The proper study of mankind is man," meant that women should be relegated to the footnotes (or, as George Orwell might have put it, "All men are equal, but men are more equal than women"), viable new words will surely someday supersede the old.

Without apologies to Freud, the great majority of women do not wish in their hearts that they were men. If having grown up with a language that tells them they are at the same time men and not men raises psychic doubts for women, the doubts are not of their sexual identity but of their human identity. Perhaps the present unrest surfacing in the Women's Movement is part of an evolutionary change in our particular form of life—the one form of all in the animal and plant kingdoms that orders and interprets its reality by symbols. The achievements of the species called man have brought us to the brink of self-destruction. If the species survives into the next century with the expectation of going on, it may only be because we have become part of what Harlow Shapley calls the psychozoic kingdom, where brain overshadows brawn and rationality has replaced superstition.

Searching the roots of Western civilization for a word to call this new species of man and woman, someone might come up with *gen,* as in genesis and generic. With such a word, *man* could be used exclusively for males as *woman* is used for females, for gen would include both sexes. Like the words deer and bison, gen would be both plural and singular. Like progenitor, progeny, and generation, it would convey continuity. Gen would express the warmth and generalized sexuality of generous, gentle, and genuine; the specific sexuality of genital and genetic. In the new family of gen, girls and boys would grow to genhood, and to speak of genkind would be to include all the people of the earth.

---

## REFLECTING ON MEANING

1. Miller and Swift argue that the English language is sexist in several ways: (a) it assumes that "unless otherwise identified, people in general . . . are men"; (b) it represents women as a kind of "subspecies"; (c) it depicts women in negative terms; and (d) it reduces women "to their sexuality and nothing more." What examples do the authors provide to support each assertion? Do you find their assertions convincing? Why or why not?

2. What are some examples of sexist language that men use? That women use? Do men and women use sexist language in reference to persons of the same gender? According to Miller and Swift, why doesn't a speaker's gender determine whether an utterance is sexist?

3. What do you think of Miller and Swift's solution to the problem of sexism in language? How viable is their solution? Is it possible to change the English language? Would doing so change cultural attitudes and assumptions about gender?

## EXPLORING RHETORICAL STRATEGIES

1. What is the effect of the riddles with which Miller and Swift begin their essay? Were you able to solve them? How do these riddles both illuminate the problem of sexism in English and implicate the reader in it?

2. What famous words does the title "One Small Step for Genkind" echo? What is the connection between this historic event and the essay's thesis? How does the title provide an ironic commentary on the idea of human progress?

3. This essay originally appeared in 1972 in the *New York Times Magazine*. Are the ideas it presents still controversial? Are they still relevant? Has the English language changed to the extent that Miller and Swift's argument no longer seems necessary?

---

# Sexism in English: A 1990s Update

## ALLEEN PACE NILSEN

*What can language reveal about society? According to Alleen Pace Nilsen, language is "like an X-ray" that provides "visible evidence of invisible thoughts." In this essay, Nilsen reports on the results of her two-decade-long investigation of American English usage, a study that illuminates many of the "invisible" sexist assumptions operating in society at large.*

Twenty years ago I embarked on a study of the sexism inherent in American English. I had just returned to Ann Arbor, Michigan, after living for two years (1967–69) in Kabul, Afghanistan, where I had begun to look critically at the role society assigned to women. The Afghan version of the *chaderi* prescribed for Moslem women was particularly confining. Afghan jokes and folklore were blatantly sexist, such as this proverb: "If you see an old man, sit down and take a lesson; if you see an old woman, throw a stone."

But it wasn't only the native culture that made me question women's roles, it was also the American community.

Most of the American women were like myself—wives and

mothers whose husbands were either career diplomats, employees of USAID, or college professors who had been recruited to work on various contract teams. We were suddenly bereft of our traditional roles: some of us became alcoholics, others got very good at bridge, while still others searched desperately for ways to contribute either to our families or to the Afghans. The local economy provided few jobs for women and certainly none for foreigners; we were isolated from former friends and the social goals we had grown up with.

When I returned in the fall of 1969 to the University of Michigan in Ann Arbor, I was surprised to find that many other women were also questioning the expectations they had grown up with. In the spring of 1970, a women's conference was announced. I hired a babysitter and attended, but I returned home more troubled than ever. The militancy of these women frightened me. Since I wasn't ready for a revolution, I decided I would have my own feminist movement. I would study the English language and see what it could tell me about sexism. I started reading a desk dictionary and making notecards on every entry that seemed to tell something about male and female. I soon had a dog-eared dictionary, along with a collection of note cards filling two shoe boxes.

Ironically, I started reading the dictionary because I wanted to avoid getting involved in social issues, but what happened was that my notecards brought me right back to looking at society. Language and society are as intertwined as a chicken and an egg. The language a culture uses is telltale evidence of the values and beliefs of that culture. And because there is a lag in how fast a language changes—new words can easily be introduced, but it takes a long time for old words and usages to disappear—a careful look at English will reveal the attitudes that our ancestors held and that we as a culture are therefore predisposed to hold. My notecards revealed three main points. Friends have offered the opinion that I didn't need to read the dictionary to learn such obvious facts. Nevertheless, it was interesting to have linguistic evidence of sociological observations.

## Women Are Sexy; Men Are Successful

First, in American culture a woman is valued for the attractiveness and sexiness of her body, while a man is valued for his physical strength and accomplishments. A woman is sexy. A man is successful.

A persuasive piece of evidence supporting this view are the eponyms—words that have come from someone's name—found in English. I had a two-and-a-half-inch stack of cards taken from men's names but less than a half-inch stack from women's names, and most of those came from Greek mythology. In the words that came into American English since we separated from Britain, there are many eponyms based on the names of famous American men: *Bartlett pear, boysenberry, diesel engine, Franklin stove, Ferris wheel, Gatling gun, mason jar, sideburns, sousaphone, Schick test,* and *Winchester rifle.* The only common eponyms taken from American women's names are *Alice blue* (after Alice Roosevelt Longworth), *bloomers* (after Amelia Jenks Bloomer), and *Mae West jacket* (after the buxom actress). Two out of the three feminine eponyms relate closely to a woman's physical anatomy, while the masculine eponyms (except for *sideburns* after General Burnsides) have nothing to do with the namesake's body but, instead, honor the man for an accomplishment of some kind.

Although in Greek mythology women played a bigger role than they did in the biblical stories of the Judeo-Christian cultures and so the names of goddesses are accepted parts of the language in such place names as Pomona from the goddess of fruit and Athens from Athena and in such common words as *cereal* from Ceres, *psychology* from Psyche, and *arachnoid* from Arachne, the same tendency to think of women in relation to sexuality is seen in the eponyms *aphrodisiac* from Aphrodite, the Greek name for the goddess of love and beauty, and *venereal disease* from Venus, the Roman name for Aphrodite.

Another interesting word from Greek mythology is *Amazon.* According to Greek folk etymology, the *a* means "without" as in *atypical* or *amoral,* while *mazon* comes from *mazos* meaning "breast" as still seen in *mastectomy.* In the Greek legend, Amazon women cut off their right breasts so that they could better shoot their bows. Apparently, the storytellers had a feeling that for women to play the active, "masculine" role the Amazons adopted for themselves, they had to trade in part of their femininity.

This preoccupation with women's breasts is not limited to ancient stories. As a volunteer for the University of Wisconsin's *Dictionary of American Regional English* (*DARE*), I read a western trapper's diary from the 1930s. I was to make notes of any unusual usages or language patterns. My most interesting finding was that the trapper referred to a range of mountains as *The Teats,* a metaphor based on the similarity between the shapes of the mountains and women's breasts. Because today we use the French wording, *The Grand Tetons,* the metaphor isn't as obvious, but I wrote to mapmakers and found the following listings: *Nippletop* and *Little Nipple Top* near Mount Marcy in the Adirondacks; *Nipple Mountain* in Archuleta County, Colorado; *Nipple Peak* in Coke County, Texas;

*Nipple Butte* in Pennington, South Dakota; *Squaw Peak* in Placer County, California (and many other locations); *Maiden's Peak* and *Squaw Tit* (they're the same mountain) in the Cascade Range in Oregon; *Mary's Nipple* near Salt Lake City, Utah; and *Jane Russell Peaks* near Stark, New Hampshire.

Except for the movie star Jane Russell, the women being referred to are anonymous—it's only a sexual part of their body that is mentioned. When topographical features are named after men, it's probably not going to be to draw attention to a sexual part of their bodies but instead to honor individuals for an accomplishment. For example, no one thinks of a part of the male body when hearing a reference to Pike's Peak, Colorado, or Jackson Hole, Wyoming.

Going back to what I learned from my dictionary cards, I was surprised to realize how many pairs of words we have in which the feminine word has acquired sexual connotations while the masculine word retains a serious businesslike aura. For example, a *callboy* is the person who calls actors when it is time for them to go on stage, but a *call girl* is a prostitute. Compare *sir* and *madam. Sir* is a term of respect, while *madam* has acquired the specialized meaning of a brothel manager. Something similar has happened to *master* and *mistress.* Would you rather have a painting by an *old master* or an *old mistress?*

It's because the word *woman* had sexual connotations, as in "She's his woman," that people began avoiding its use, hence such terminology as *ladies' room, lady of the house,* and *girls' school* or *school for young ladies.* Feminists, who ask that people use the term *woman* rather than *girl* or *lady,* are rejecting the idea that *woman* is primarily a sexual term. They have been at least partially successful in that today *woman* is commonly used to communicate gender without intending implications about sexuality.

I found two hundred pairs of words with masculine and feminine forms, e.g., *heir-heiress, hero-heroine, steward-stewardess, usher-usherette.* In nearly all such pairs, the masculine word is considered the base, with some kind of a feminine suffix being added. The masculine form is the one from which compounds are made, e.g., from *king-queen* comes *kingdom* but not *queendom,* from *sportsman-sportslady* comes *sportsmanship* but not *sportsladyship.* There is one—and only one—semantic area in which the masculine word is not the base or more powerful word. This is in the area dealing with sex and marriage. When someone refers to a *virgin,* a listener will probably think of a female, unless the speaker specifies *male* or uses a masculine pronoun. The same is true for *prostitute.*

In relation to marriage, there is much linguistic evidence

showing that weddings are more important to women than to men. A woman cherishes the wedding and is considered a bride for a whole year, but a man is referred to as a groom only on the day of the wedding. The word *bride* appears in *bridal attendant, bridal gown, bridesmaid, bridal shower,* and even *bridegroom. Groom* comes from the Middle English *grom,* meaning "man," and in the sense is seldom used outside of the wedding. With most pairs of male/female words, people habitually put the masculine word first, *Mr. and Mrs., his and hers, boys and girls, men and women, kings and queens, brothers and sisters, guys and dolls,* and *host and hostess,* but it is the *bride and groom* who are talked about, not the *groom and bride.*

The importance of marriage to a woman is also shown by the fact that when a marriage ends in death, the woman gets the title of *widow.* A man gets the derived title of *widower.* This term is not used in other phrases or contexts, but *widow* is seen in *widowhood, widow's peak,* and *widow's walk.* A *widow* in a card game is an extra hand of cards, while in typesetting it is an extra line of type.

How changing cultural ideas bring changes to language is clearly visible in this semantic area. The feminist movement has caused the differences between the sexes to be downplayed, and since I did my dictionary study two decades ago, the word *singles* has largely replaced such sex specific and value-laden terms as *bachelor, old maid, spinster, divorcée, widow,* and *widower.* And in 1970 I wrote that when a man is called *a professional* he is thought to be a doctor or a lawyer, but when people hear a woman referred to as *a professional* they are likely to think of a prostitute. That's not as true today because so many women have become doctors and lawyers that it's no longer incongruous to think of women in those professional roles.

Another change that has taken place is in wedding announcements. They used to be sent out from the bride's parents and did not even give the name of the groom's parents. Today, most couples choose to list either all or none of the parents' names. Also it is now much more likely that both the bride and groom's picture will be in the newspaper, while a decade ago only the bride's picture was published on the "Women's" or the "Society" page. Even the traditional wording of the wedding ceremony is being changed. Many officials now pronounce the couple "husband and wife" instead of the old "man and wife," and they ask the bride if she promises "to love, honor, and cherish," instead of "to love, honor, and obey."

## Women Are Passive; Men Are Active

The wording of the wedding ceremony also relates to the second point that my cards showed, which is that women are expected to play a passive or weak role while men play an active or strong role. In the traditional ceremony, the official asks, "Who gives the bride away?" and the father answers, "I do." Some fathers answer, "Her mother and I do," but that doesn't solve the problem inherent in the question. The idea that a bride is something to be handed over from one man to another bothers people because it goes back to the days when a man's servants, his children, and his wife were all considered to be his property. They were known by his name because they belonged to him, and he was responsible for their actions and their debts.

The grammar used in talking or writing about weddings as well as other sexual relationships shows the expectation of men playing the active role. Men *wed* women while women *become* brides of men. A man *possesses* a woman; he *deflowers* her; he *performs;* he *scores;* he *takes away* her virginity. Although a woman can *seduce* a man, she cannot offer him her virginity. When talking about virginity, the only way to make the woman the actor in the sentence is to say that "She lost her virginity," but people lose things by accident rather than by purposeful actions, and so she's only the grammatical, not the real-life, actor.

The reason that women tried to bring the term *Ms.* into the language to replace *Miss* and *Mrs.* relates to this point. Married women resent being identified only under their husband's names. For example, when Susan Glascoe did something newsworthy, she would be identified in the newspaper only as Mrs. John Glascoe. The dictionary cards showed what appeared to be an attitude on the part of the editors that it was almost indecent to let a respectable woman's name march unaccompanied across the pages of a dictionary. Women were listed with male names whether or not the male contributed to the woman's reason for being in the dictionary or in his own right was as famous as the woman. For example, Charlotte Brontë was identified as Mrs. Arthur B. Nicholls, Amelia Earhart as Mrs. George Palmer Putnam, Helen Hayes as Mrs. Charles MacArthur, Jenny Lind as Mme. Otto Goldschmit, Cornelia Otis Skinner as the daughter of Otis, Harriet Beecher Stowe as the sister of Henry Ward Beecher, and Edith Sitwell as the sister of Osbert and Sacheverell. A very small number of women got into the dictionary without the benefit of a masculine escort. They were rebels and crusaders: temperance leaders Frances Elizabeth Caroline Willard and Carry Nation, women's rights leaders Carrie Chapman Catt and Elizabeth Cady Stanton, birth control educator Margaret Sanger, religious leader Mary Baker Eddy, and slaves Harriet Tubman and Phillis Wheatley.

Etiquette books used to teach that if a woman had *Mrs.* in front of her name, then the husband's name should follow because *Mrs.* is an abbreviated form of *Mistress* and a woman couldn't be a mistress of herself. As with many arguments about "correct" language usage, this isn't very logical because *Miss* is also an abbreviation of *Mistress.* Feminists hoped to simplify matters by introducing *Ms.* as an alternative to both *Mrs.* and *Miss,* but what happened is that *Ms.* largely replaced *Miss,* to become a catch-all business title for women. Many married women still prefer the title *Mrs.,* and some resent being addressed with the term *Ms.* As one frustrated newspaper reporter complained, "Before I can write about a woman, I have to know not only her marital status but also her political philosophy." The result of such complications may contribute to the demise of titles, which are already being ignored by many computer programmers who find it more efficient to simply use names, for example in a business letter: "Dear Joan Garcia," instead of "Dear Mrs. Joan Garcia," "Dear Ms. Garcia," or "Dear Mrs. Louis Garcia."

The titles given to royalty provide an example of how males can be disadvantaged by the assumption that they are always to play the more powerful role. In British royalty, when a male holds a title, his wife is automatically given the feminine equivalent. But the reverse is not true. For example, a *count* is a high political officer with a *countess* being his wife. The same is true for a *duke* and a *duchess* and a *king* and a *queen.* But when a female holds the royal title, the man she marries does not automatically acquire the matching title. For example, Queen Elizabeth's husband has the title of *prince* rather than *king,* but if Prince Charles should become king while he is still married to Lady or Princess Diana, she will be known as the queen. The reasoning appears to be that since masculine words are stronger, they are reserved for true heirs and withheld from males coming into the royal family by marriage. If Prince Philip were called *King Philip,* it would be much easier for British subjects to forget where the true power lies.

The names that people give their children show the hopes and dreams they have for them, and when we look at the differences between male and female names in a culture, we can see the cumulative expectations of that culture. In our culture girls often have names taken from small, aesthetically pleasing items, e.g., *Ruby, Jewel,* and *Pearl. Esther* and *Stella* mean "star," *Ada* means "ornament," and *Vanessa* means "butterfly." Boys are more likely to be given names with meanings of power and strength, e.g., *Neil* means "champion," *Martin* is from Mars, the God of War, *Raymond* means "wise protection," *Harold* means "chief of the army," *Ira* means "vigilant," *Rex* means "king," and *Richard* means "strong king."

We see similar differences in food metaphors. Food is a passive substance just sitting there waiting to be eaten. Many people have recognized this and so no longer feel comfortable describing women as "delectable morsels." However, when I was a teenager, it was considered a compliment to refer to a girl (we didn't call anyone a *woman* until she was middle-aged) as a *cute tomato,* a *peach,* a *dish,* a *cookie, honey, sugar,* or *sweetie-pie.* When being affectionate, women will occasionally call a man *honey* or *sweetie,* but in general, food metaphors are used much less often with men than with women. If a man is called *a fruit,* his masculinity is being questioned. But it's perfectly acceptable to use a food metaphor if the food is heavier and more substantive than that used for women. For example pin-up pictures of women have long been known as *cheesecake,* but when Burt Reynolds posed for a nude centerfold the picture was immediately dubbed *beefcake,* cf. *a hunk of meat.* That such sexual references to men have come into the language is another reflection of how society is beginning to lessen the differences between their attitudes toward men and women.

Something similar to the *fruit* metaphor happens with references to plants. We insult a man by calling him a *pansy,* but it wasn't considered particularly insulting to talk about a girl being a *wallflower,* a *clinging vine,* or a *shrinking violet,* or to give girls such names as *Ivy, Rose, Lily, Iris, Daisy, Camellia, Heather,* and *Flora.* A plant metaphor can be used with a man if the plant is big and strong, for example, Andrew Jackson's nickname of *Old Hickory.* Also, the phrases *blooming idiots* and *budding geniuses* can be used with either sex, but notice how they are based on the most active thing a plant can do which is to bloom or bud.

Animal metaphors also illustrate the different expectations for males and females. Men are referred to as *studs, bucks,* and *wolves* while women are referred to with such metaphors as *kitten, bunny, beaver, bird, chick,* and *lamb.* In the 1950s we said that boys went *tomcatting,* but today it's just *catting around* and both boys and girls do it. When the term *foxy,* meaning that someone was sexy, first became popular it was used only for girls, but now someone of either sex can be described as *a fox.* Some animal metaphors that are used predominantly with men have negative connotations based on the size and/or strength of the animals, e.g., *beast, bull-headed, jackass, rat, loanshark,* and *vulture.* Negative metaphors used with women are based on smaller animals, e.g., *social butterfly, mousy, catty,* and *vixen.* The feminine terms connote action, but not the same kind of large scale action as with the masculine terms.

## Women Are Connected with Negative Connotations; Men with Positive Connotations

The final point that my notecards illustrated was how many positive connotations are associated with the concept of masculine, while there are either trivial or negative connotations connected with the corresponding feminine concept. An example from the animal metaphors makes a good illustration. The word *shrew* taken from the name of a small but especially vicious animal was defined in my dictionary as "an ill-tempered scolding woman," but the word *shrewd* taken from the same root was defined as "marked by clever, discerning awareness" and was illustrated with the phrase "a shrewd businessman."

Early in life, children are conditioned to the superiority of the masculine role. As child psychologists point out, little girls have much more freedom to experiment with sex roles than do little boys. If a little girl acts like a *tomboy,* most parents have mixed feelings, being at least partially proud. But if their little boy acts like a *sissy* (derived from *sister*), they call a psychologist. It's perfectly acceptable for a little girl to sleep in the crib that was purchased for her brother, to wear his hand-me-down jeans and shirts, and to ride the bicycle that he has outgrown. But few parents would put a boy baby in a white and gold crib decorated with frills and lace, and virtually no parents would have their little boys wear his sister's hand-me-down dresses, nor would they have their son ride a girl's pink bicycle with a flower-bedecked basket. The proper names given to girls and boys show this same attitude. Girls can have "boy" names—*Chris, Craig, Jo, Kelly, Shawn, Teri, Toni,* and *Sam*—but it doesn't work the other way around. A couple of generations ago, *Beverly, Francis, Hazel, Marion,* and *Shirley* were common boys' names. As parents gave these names to more and more girls, they fell into disuse for males, and some older men who have these names prefer to go by their initials or by such abbreviated forms as *Haze* or *Shirl.*

When a little girl is told to *be a lady,* she is being told to sit with her knees together and to be quiet and dainty. But when a little boy is told to *be a man* he is being told to be noble, strong, and virtuous—to have all the qualities that the speaker looks on as desirable. The concept of manliness has such positive connotations that it used to be a compliment to call someone a *he-man,* to say that he was doubly a man. Today many people are more ambivalent about this term and respond to it much as they do to the word *macho.* But calling someone a *manly man* or a *virile man* is nearly always meant as a compliment. *Virile* comes from the Indo-

European *vir* meaning "man," which is also the basis of *virtuous.* Contrast the positive connotations of both *virile* and *virtuous* with the negative connotations of *hysterical.* The Greeks took this latter word from their name for *uterus* (as still seen in *hysterectomy*). They thought that women were the only ones who experienced uncontrolled emotional outbursts, and so the condition must have something to do with a part of the body that only women have.

Differences in the connotations between positive male and negative female connotations can be seen in several pairs of words that differ denotatively only in the matter of sex. *Bachelor* as compared to *spinster* or *old maid* has such positive connotations that women try to adopt them by using the term *bachelor-girl* or *bachelorette. Old maid* is so negative that it's the basis for metaphors: pretentious and fussy old men are called *old maids,* as are the leftover kernels of unpopped popcorn, and the last card in a popular children's game.

*Patron* and *matron* (Middle English for *father* and *mother*) have such different levels of prestige that women try to borrow the more positive masculine connotations with the word *patroness,* literally "female father." Such a peculiar term came about because of the high prestige attached to *patron* in such phrases as *a patron of the arts* or *a patron saint. Matron* is more apt to be used in talking about a woman in charge of a jail or a public restroom.

When men are doing jobs that women often do, we apparently try to pay the men extra by giving them fancy titles, for example, a male cook is more likely to be called a *chef* while a male steamstress will get the title of *tailor.* The armed forces have a special problem in that they recruit under such slogans as "The Marine Corps builds men!" and "Join the Army! Become a Man." Once the recruits are enlisted, they find themselves doing much of the work that has been traditionally thought of as "women's work." The solution to getting the work done and not insulting anyone's masculinity was to change the titles as shown below:

| | |
|---|---|
| waitress | orderly |
| nurse | medic or corpsman |
| secretary | clerk-typist |
| assistant | adjutant |
| dishwasher or kitchen helper | KP (kitchen police) |

Compare *brave* and *squaw.* Early settlers in America truly admired Indian men and hence named them with a word that carried connotations of youth, vigor, courage. But they used the Algonquin's name for "woman" and over the years it developed almost opposite connotations to those of *brave. Wizard* and *witch* contrast almost as much. The masculine *wizard* implies skill and wisdom combined with magic, while the feminine *witch* implies evil intentions combined with magic. Part of the unattractiveness of both *witch* and *squaw* is that they have been used so often to refer to old women, something with which our culture is particularly uncomfortable, just as the Afghans were. Imagine my surprise when I ran across the phrases *grandfatherly advice* and *old wives' tales* and realized that the underlying implication is the same as the Afghan proverb about old men being worth listening to while old women talk only foolishness.

Other terms that show how negatively we view old women as compared to young women are *old nag* as compared to *filly, old crow* or *old bat* as compared to *bird,* and of being *catty* as compared to being *kittenish.* There is no matching set of metaphors for men. The chicken metaphor tells the whole story of a woman's life. In her youth she is a *chick.* Then she marries and begins *feathering her nest.* Soon she begins feeling *cooped up,* so she goes to *hen parties* where she *cackles* with her friends. Then she has her *brood,* begins to *henpeck* her husband, and finally turns into an *old biddy.*

I embarked on my study of the dictionary not with the intention of prescribing language change but simply to see what the language would tell me about sexism. Nevertheless I have been both surprised and pleased as I've watched the changes that have occurred over the past two decades. I'm one of those linguists who believes that new language customs will cause a new generation of speakers to grow up with different expectations. This is why I'm happy about people's efforts to use inclusive language, to say *he or she* or *they* when speaking about individuals whose names they do not know. I'm glad that leading publishers have developed guidelines to help writers use language that is fair to both sexes, and I'm glad that most newspapers and magazines list women by their own names instead of only by their husbands' names and that educated and thoughtful people no longer begin their business letters with "Dear Sir" or "Gentlemen," but instead use a memo form or begin with such salutations as "Dear Colleagues," "Dear Reader," or "Dear Committee Members." I'm also glad that such words as *poetess, authoress, conductress,* and *aviatrix* now sound quaint and old-fashioned and that *chairman* is giving way to *chair* or *head, mailman* to *mail carrier, clergyman* to *clergy,* and *stewardess* to *flight attendant.* I was also pleased when the National Oceanic and Atmospheric Administration bowed to feminist complaints and in the late 1970s began to alternate men's and women's names for hurricanes. However, I wasn't so pleased to discover that the change did not immediately erase sexist thoughts from everyone's mind, as shown by a headline about Hurricane David in a 1979 New York tabloid, "David Rapes Virgin Islands." More recently a similar metaphor appeared in a headline in the *Arizona Republic* about Hurricane Charlie, "Charlie Quits Carolinas, Flirts with Virginia."

What these incidents show is that sexism is not something existing independently in American English or in the particular dictionary that I happened to read. Rather, it exists in people's minds. Language is like an X ray in providing visible evidence of invisible thoughts. The best thing about people being interested in and discussing sexist language is that as they make conscious decisions about what pronouns they will use, what jokes they will tell or laugh at, how they will write their names, or how they will begin their letters, they are forced to think about the underlying issue of sexism. This is good because as a problem that begins in people's assumptions and expectations, it's a problem that will be solved only when a great many people have given it a great deal of thought.

---

## REFLECTING ON MEANING

1. Through analyzing language usage, Nilsen identifies three cultural assumptions about women and men:

   - "In American culture a woman is valued for the attractiveness and sexiness of her body, while a man is valued for his physical strengths and accomplishments. A woman is sexy. A man is successful."
   - "Women are expected to play a passive or weak role while men play an active or strong role."
   - "Many positive connotations are associated with the concept of masculine, while there are either trivial or negative connotations connected with the corresponding feminine concept."

   What evidence does she provide to support these assertions? Do you think that her inferences about language are reasonable? Why or why not?

2. Nilsen lists several word pairs whose feminine elements carry sexual connotations, whereas their masculine counterparts con-

vey a "serious businesslike aura." What are some of these word pairs? Do you agree or disagree with Nilsen's conclusions about these words? According to Nilsen, how are such word pairs beginning to reflect social change?

3. Nilsen explores the relationship between society and language, asserting that they are "as intertwined as a chicken and an egg." What does she mean? Do you agree with her viewpoint? Why or why not? How might sexist language not only reflect but reinforce sexism in society? How do the connections between language and society help explain why Nilsen's note cards brought her "right back to looking at society"?

## EXPLORING RHETORICAL STRATEGIES

1. Nilsen begins her essay by describing the personal and political events that spurred her interest in sexist language. Why does she preface her observations on the English language with this kind of introduction? What do the events she describes have to do with her topic? How does this information advance her thesis about language and society?
2. What principle does Nilsen use to structure the body of her essay? In what format does she present her main points, secondary points, and evidence? How does this structure facilitate a reader's understanding of and response to her argument?
3. Nilsen provides numerous pieces of evidence from a dictionary to support her assertions; in fact, the essay nearly becomes a catalogue of specific examples. Why does she include so many examples? What considerations about her topic and audience may have persuaded her to provide this much evidence to illustrate her assertions?

# Women and Names

## CASEY MILLER and KATE SWIFT

*Names are powerful symbols of identity in society. Yet, as Casey Miller and Kate Swift point out, "women's names are less important than men's"—so much so that women routinely surrender them when they marry. This custom, as well as others, they argue, "reinforces the powerful myth that pervades the rest of our language—the myth that the human race is essentially male."*

The photograph of the three bright, good-looking young people in the Army recruitment ad catches the eye. All three have a certain flair, and one knows just by looking at the picture that they are enjoying life and glad they joined up. They are typical Americans, symbols of the kind of people the modern Army is looking for. The one closest to the camera is a white male. His name, as can be seen from the neat identification tag pinned to the right pocket of his regulation blouse, is Spurgeon. Behind him and slightly to the left is a young black man. He is wearing a decoration of some kind, and his name is Sort—. Perhaps it is Sorter or Sortman—only the first four letters show. A young woman, who is also white, stands behind Spurgeon on the other side. She is smiling and her eyes shine; she looks capable. She is probably wearing a name tag too, but because Spurgeon is standing between her and the camera, her name is hidden. She is completely anonymous.

The picture is not a candid shot; it was carefully posed. The three models were chosen from thousands of possible recruits. They are the same height; they all have dark hair and are smiling into the camera. They look like students, and the copy says the Army will pay 75 per cent of their tuition if they work for a college degree. It is no accident that two are white, one black, or that two are male, one female. Nor is it an accident that Spurgeon stands in front of the others at the apex of a triangle, or that, since someone had to be anonymous, the woman was chosen.[1]

In our society women's names are less important than men's. The reasons why are not hard to identify, but the consequences for both men and women are more far-reaching than members of either sex, with a few notable exceptions, have been prepared to admit or even, until recently, to examine. Like other words, names are symbols; unlike other words, what they symbolize is unique. A thousand John Does and Jane Roes may live and die, but no bearer of those names has the same inheritance, the same history, or the same fears and expectations as any other. It therefore seems legitimate to ask what effect our naming customs have on girls and boys and on the women and men they grow into. Are the symbol-words that become our names more powerful than other words?

Few people can remember learning to talk. The mystery of language is rarely revealed in a single moment of electrifying insight like Helen Keller's, when suddenly, at the age of seven, the deaf and blind child realized for the first time the connection between the finger signals for w-a-t-e-r her teacher was tapping into her palm and "the wonderful cool something" that flowed from the pump spout onto her other hand.[2]

From what scholars report about the way children normally acquire speech, it seems probable that "learning to talk" is actually the measured release, in conjunction with experience, of an innate capacity for language that is common to all human beings.[3] We are no more likely to remember the process than we are to remember growing taller. What one may remember is a particular moment—seeing the yardstick exactly even with the latest pencil line marking one's height on the door jamb or learning a word for some particular something one had been aware of but could not name: tapioca, perhaps, or charisma, or a cotter pin. Anyone who has ever said, "so *that's* what those things are called," knows the experience.

When children are first learning to talk they go through a series of similar experiences. The very act of learning what a person or thing is called brings the object into the child's ken in a new way. It has been made specific. Later, the specific will also become general, as when the child calls any small, furry animal a "kitty." Words are symbols; their meanings can be extended.

Amanda, who is twenty months old, has spurts of learning names. "Mum," she says to her mother while pointing to the box. "Mum," she says again, pointing to the doorknob. "What is it?" she is asking without using words. "Tell me its name." When she calls her mother by a name, she knows her mother will respond to it. She knows that she, Amanda, has a name. It is important to her, for she has already become aware of herself as a thing different from everything else. As a psychologist might put it, her ego is emerging. Hearing her name, being called by it, is part of the process.

Amanda makes certain sounds, naming food or her bottle, that tell her parents she is hungry or thirsty. Before long she will speak of herself in the third person: " 'Manda want apple." " 'Manda come too." She may repeat her name over and over, perhaps mixing it with nonsense syllables. It is like a charm. It may be the first word she learns to spell. She will delight in seeing the letters of her name, this extension of herself, on her toothbrush or drinking mug. They belong to her, not to her brother or to her mother or father.

When children begin to play with other children and when they finally go to school, their names take on a public dimension. The child with a "funny" name is usually in for trouble, but most kids are proud of their names and want to write them on their books and pads and homework. There was a time when older children carved their names or initials on trees. Now that there are so many people and so few trees, the spray can has taken over from the jackknife, but the impulse to put one's identifying mark where all the world can see it is as strong as ever. The popularity of commercially produced name-on objects of every kind, from tee-shirts to miniature license plates, also attests to the importance youngsters (and a lot of grown-ups too) place on claiming and proclaiming their names.

Given names are much older than surnames, of course, probably as old as language itself. One can imagine that as soon as our ancient forebears started using sounds to represent actions or objects, they also began to distinguish each other in the same way. One might even speculate that the people who most often assigned sounds to others were those who produced and cared for the group's new members. Commenting on the assumption of philologists that the exchange of meaningful vocal sounds began among males as they worked and hunted together—hence the so-called "yo-heave-ho" and "bow-wow" theories of language origin—Ethel Strainchamps, a psycholinguist, notes that most philologists have in the past been men. Considering the importance to human survival of communication between mother and child when open fires, venomous reptiles, and other hazards were everywhere, "it might have occurred to a woman that a 'no-no' theory was more likely," Strainchamps says.[4] Perhaps her suggestion should be taken a step further: who knows that it was not the creative effort of women, striving to communicate with each new baby, calling it by a separate and distinguishing sound, that freed the primordial human mind from the prison of animal grunts and led in time to the development of language?

Inevitably, some people dislike the names they have been given, and many children go through a phase of wanting to be called something else. For no apparent reason Anne announces that her name is really Koko and she will not answer to any other. For months nothing will change her resolve. She is Koko—and then one day she is Anne again. But if Cecil decides he wants to be called Jim, or Fanny elects to be known as Jill, the reasons may be less obscure: names do seem to give off vibrations of a sort, and other people's response to your name becomes a part of their response to you. Some psychologists think that given names are signals of parental expectations: children get the message and act on it either positively or negatively. One study claims to show, for example, that names can be "active" or "passive." If you call your son Mac or Bart he will become a more active person than if you call him Winthrop or Egbert. Your daughter is more likely to be outgoing and confident, according to this theory, if you call her Jody rather than Letitia. It follows, though, that if Jody prefers to be called Letitia, she is letting it be known that she sees herself in a more passive and dependent way than you anticipated.[5]

Last names, too, can be positive or negative. Some carry a mystique of greatness or honor: Randolph, Diaz, Morgenthau, Saltonstall. Others are cumbersome, or they invite cruel or tasteless jokes. Many people decide, for one reason or another, to change their last names, but a great many more take pride today in being identified as a Klein or a Mackenzie, a Giordano or a Westervelt. The first-and-last-name mix which a person grows up with—that combination of particular and general, of personal and traditional—is not lightly exchanged for another.

Whether a name is self-chosen or bestowed at birth, making it one's own is an act of self-definition. When a former Cabinet member who had been involved in the Watergate scandal asked the Senate investigating committee to give back his good name, he was speaking metaphorically, for no one had taken his name away. What he had lost, justly or unjustly, was his public image as a person of integrity and a servant of the people. One's name also represents one's sense of power and self-direction. "I'm so tired I don't know my own name" is a statement of confusion and fatigue. *Your* name, the beginning of your answer to "Who am I?" is the outermost of the many layers of identity reaching inward to the real you. It is one of the significant differences between you and, let's say, a rose, which is named but does not know it. Yet it is one of the things a little girl grows up knowing she will be expected to lose if she marries.

The loss of women's last names may seem compensated for by a custom in first-naming that allows girls to be called by a version of their fathers' names, so that—after a fashion, at least—continuity is restored. In this post-Freudian age it would be bad form to give a boy a version of his mother's first name. Nevertheless, if a couple named Henrietta and Frank should decide to call their son Henry, chances are an earlier Henry, after whom Henrietta was named, provides the necessary male for him to identify with. In any case, the name has come back into its own: it stands foursquare and solid, which is seldom true of the derivative names given to girls. The strength of John is preserved in Joan and Jean, but these are exceptions. Names like Georgette and Georgina, Josephine, Paulette and Pauline, beautiful as they may sound, are diminutives. They are copies, not originals, and like so many other words applied to women, they can be diminishing.

A man in most Western societies can not only keep his name for his lifetime but he can pass it on intact to his son, who in turn can pass it on to *his* son. The use of a surname as a given name is also usually reserved for males, presumably on the grounds that such names do not have a sufficiently "feminine" sound for the "weaker sex." When tradition permits the giving of a family surname to daughters, as in the American South, a woman can at least retain her identification with that branch of her family. Once a surname has gained popularity as a girl's name, however, it is likely to face extinction as a boy's name. Shirley, for example, an old Yorkshire family name meaning "shire meadow," was once given as a first name only to boys. Not until Charlotte Brontë wrote *Shirley*—a novel published in 1849, whose central character, Shirley Keeldar, was modeled on Charlotte's sister Emily—was it used for a girl.[6] Since then, Shirley has become popular as a girl's name but has dropped out of use as a boy's. Names like Leslie, Beverly, Evelyn, and Sidney may be traveling the same route. Once they have become popular as women's names, their histories as surnames are forgotten, and before long they may be given to girls exclusively.

In English, names like Charity, Constance, Patience, Faith, Hope, Prudence, and Honor no longer have popular equivalents for males, as they often do in other languages. The qualities described are not limited to females, of course, and yet to name a son Honor or Charity, even if doing so breaks no objective rule, would somehow run counter to social expectations. This may be true in part because such names are subjective, expressing more intimately than would seem appropriate for a boy the parents' expectations for their offspring. Or the principle that applied in the case of Shirley may apply here, for once a name or a word becomes associated with women, it is rarely again considered suitable for men.

One of the most useful functions of a given name is to serve as a quick identifier of sex. Nearly everyone, whether they admit it or not, is interested in knowing what sex an unknown person is. You get a postcard from a friend saying he will be stopping by to see you next week with someone named Lee, and chances are the first question that pops into your mind is not whether Lee is young or old, black or white, clever or dull, but whether Lee will turn out to be female or male. Still, natural curiosity does not entirely explain the annoyance or embarrassment some people seem to feel when women have names that are not specifically female by tradition or why names that become associated with women are thenceforth out of bounds for men.

If quick sex identification were the only consideration, the long male tradition of using initials in place of first names would not have come about. People with names like J. P. Morgan, P. T. Barnum, and L. L. Bean were always male—or were they? No one could stop women from sneaking under the flap of *that* tent, and in fact so many did that the practice had to be disallowed. In the early years of this century Columbia University, which in its academic bulletins identified male faculty members only by their surnames and initials, wrote out the names of women faculty members in full—lest anyone unintentionally enroll in a course taught by a woman.[7]

Perhaps it is because of the transience of women's last names that their first names seem often to be considered the logical, appropriate, or even polite counterpart of men's surnames, and the news media frequently reflect this feeling. When Secretary of State Henry Kissinger and Nancy Maginnis were married, many news stories called them "Kissinger and Nancy" after the first paragraph. The usage is so accepted, and its belittling implications so subliminal, that it often persists in defiance of changes taking place all about it. In a magazine story on the atypical career choices of six graduate students, the subhead read "Stereotypes fade as men and women students . . . prepare to enter fields previously dominated almost exclusively by the opposite sex." Three women going into dentistry, business administration, and law were introduced by their full names, as were three men whose fields of study were nursing, library science, and primary education. The men were then referred to as Groves, White, and Fondow, while the women became Fran, Carol, and Pam.[8]

Children, servants, and other presumed inferiors are apt to be first-named by adults and employers and by anyone else who is older, richer, or otherwise assumed to be superior. In turn, those in the first category are expected to address those in the second by their last names prefixed with an appropriate social or professional title. People on a fairly equal footing, however, either first-name each other or by mutual if unspoken agreement use a more formal mode of address.

As it happens, even though the average full-time working woman in the United States is slightly older than the average man who is employed full-time, she makes only slightly more than half the salary he makes.[9] This may explain why a great many more women than men are called by their first names on the job and why, in offices where most of the senior and junior executives are men and most of the secretaries and clerks are women, the first-naming of all women—including executives, if any—easily becomes habitual. Or it could be that women are at least slightly less impressed by the thought of their own importance, slightly more inclined to meet their colleagues and employees on equal terms. When a reporter asked newly elected Governor Ella Grasso of Connecticut what she wanted to be called and she answered, "People usually call me Ella," a new benchmark for informality must have been set in the other forty-nine state capitals. Unless men respond in the same spirit, however, without taking advantage of what is essentially an act of generosity, women like Governor Grasso will have made a useless sacrifice, jeopardizing both their identity and their prestige.

In the whole name game, it is society's sanction of patronymy that most diminishes the importance of women's names—and that sanction is social only, not legal. In the United States no state except Hawaii legally requires a woman to take her husband's name when she marries, although social pressures in the other states are almost as compelling.[10] The very fact that until recently few women giving up their names realized they were not required to do so shows how universal the expectation is. Any married couple who agree that the wife will keep her own name are in for harassment, no matter how legal their stand: family, friends, the Internal Revenue Service, state and local agencies like motor vehicle departments and voter registrars, hotels, credit agencies, insurance companies are all apt to exert pressure on them to conform. One judge is quoted as saying to a married woman who wanted to revert to her birth name, "If you didn't want his name, why did you get married?

Why didn't you live with him instead?"[11] To thus equate marriage with the desire of some women to be called "Mrs." and the desire of some men to have "a Mrs." is insulting to both sexes; yet the equation is so widely accepted that few young people growing up in Western societies think in any different terms.

The judge just quoted was, in effect, defining what a family is in a patronymical society like ours where only males are assured permanent surnames they can pass on to their children. Women are said to "marry into" families, and families are said to "die out" if an all-female generation occurs. The word family, which comes from the Latin *famulus,* meaning a servant or slave, is itself a reminder that wives and children, along with servants, were historically part of man's property. When black Americans discard the names of the slaveholders who owned their forebears, they are consciously disassociating their sense of identity from the property status in which their ancestors were held. To adopt an African name is one way of identifying with freedom and eradicating a link to bondage. The lot of married women in Western society today can hardly be called bondage, but to the degree that people's names are a part of themselves, giving them up, no matter how willingly, is tantamount to giving up some part of personal, legal, and social autonomy.

Since a surname defines a family and identifies its members, a man who marries and has children extends his family, but a woman in marrying gives up her "own" family and joins in extending another's. She may be fully aware that she brings to her new family—to her children and grandchildren—the genetic and cultural heritage of her parents and grandparents, but the lineages she can trace are ultimately paternal. Anyone who decides to look up their ancestors through marriage and birth records in town halls and genealogical societies may find paternal lines going back ten or fifteen generations or more, whereas with few exceptions maternal ones end after two or three. The exceptions are interesting for they emphasize how important the lost information from maternal lines really is. Stephen Birmingham, writing about America's blue-blooded families, notes that " 'Who is she?' as a question may mean, 'What was her maiden name?' It may also mean what was her mother's maiden name, and what was her grandmother's maiden name, and so on."[12] Blue bloods, in other words, care a lot about "maiden names," and rightly so, considering that the inputs of maternal genes and culture have as great an effect on offspring as paternal inputs.

Obviously we all have as many female ancestors as male ancestors, but maternal lineages, marked with name changes in every generation, are far more difficult to trace. To most of us the identity of our mother's mother's mother's mother, and that of *her* mother, and on back, are lost forever. How is one affected by this fading out of female ancestors whose names have disappeared from memory and the genealogical records? Research on the subject is not readily available, if it exists at all, but it seems likely that daughters are affected somewhat differently from sons. If it is emotionally healthy, as psychologists believe, for a child to identify with the parent of the same sex, would it not also be healthy for a child to identify with ancestors of the same sex?

A boy, knowing he comes from a long line of males bearing the name Wheelwright, for example, can identify with his forefathers: Johnny Wheelwright in the 1970s, if he wants to, can imagine some medieval John in whose workshop the finest wheels in the land were fashioned, a John who had a son, who had a son, who had a son, until at last Johnny Wheelwright himself was born. No line of identifiable foremothers stretches back into the past to which his sister Mary can lay claim. Like Johnny, she is a Wheelwright, assigned by patronymy to descent from males. What neither boy nor girl will ever be able to trace is their equally direct descent from, let's say, a woman known as the Healer, a woman whose daughter's daughter's daughter, through the generations, passed on the skilled hands which both John and Mary may have inherited.

Imagine, in contrast to Johnny Wheelwright, a hypothetical woman of today whose name is Elizabeth Jones. If you were to ask, in the manner of a blue blood, "Who is she?" you might be told, "She was a Fliegendorf. Her people were Pennsylvania Dutch farmers who came over from Schleswig-Holstein in the seventeenth century." Actually, that tells a fraction of the story. This hypothetical Elizabeth Jones's mother—who met her father at an Army post during the Second World War—was a Woslewski whose father emigrated from Poland as a boy, lived in Chicago, and there married a Quinn whose mother came from Canada and was a Vallière. The mother of that Vallière was the great-great-granddaughter of a woman whose given name was the equivalent of "Deep Water" and who belonged to a group of native North Americans called the Têtes de Boule by French explorers.

Elizabeth Jones's father's mother, in Pennsylvania, had been a Bruhofer, whose mother had been a Gruber, whose mother, a Powell, was born in Georgia and was the great-great-granddaughter of a woman brought to this country from Africa in the hold of a slave ship.

Thus, although Elizabeth Jones is said to have been a Fliegendorf whose people came from Schleswig-Holstein in the sixteen hundreds, fewer than 5 per cent of her two thousand or so direct ancestors who were alive in that century had any connection with Schleswig-Holstein, and only one of those who made the passage to America was born with the name Fliegendorf. The same may be said, of course, of Elizabeth Jones's brother, Ed Fliegendorf's relationship to the Fliegendorf family or Johnny Wheelwright's relationship to the bearers of his name. Yet so strong is our identification with the name we inherit at birth that we tend to forget both the rich ethnic mix most of us carry in our genes and the arbitrary definition of "family" that ultimately links us only to the male line of descent.

This concept of family is one of the reasons why most societies through most of history have placed greater value on the birth of a male child than of a female child. Ours is no exception. A recent survey reported in *Psychology Today* showed that a higher percentage of prospective parents in the United States would prefer to have a son than a daughter as a first or only child. The percentage who feel this way, however, has dropped from what it was only twenty years ago.[13] Responding to the report, a reader expressed his opinion that the change could be attributed to "a breakdown in the home-and-family ideal" among young parents today. "The son," he wrote in a letter to the editor, "and in particular the eldest son, is strongly tied to the archetypal family; first as its prime agent of continuation, and also as the future guardian and master of the home."[14] Here, then, family and name are seen as synonymous, the male is the prime if not only progenitor, and even the order of birth among male children affects the model of an ideal family.

One could not ask for a better example of how patronymy reinforces the powerful myth that pervades the rest of our language—the myth that the human race is essentially male. The obvious first reaction to such a statement may be to say, "But that's absurd. No one thinks of the race as essentially male." And yet we do. As the social critic Elizabeth Janeway has pointed out, a myth does not really describe a situation; rather, it tries to bring about what it declares to exist.[15]

A childless couple adopted a baby girl. When asked why they chose a girl rather than a boy, they explained that if she did not live up to their expectations because of her genetic heritage, "at least she won't carry on the family." Journalist Mike McGrady states the myth of racial maleness even more tellingly in an article about sperm banking: "One customer . . . gave a reason for depositing sperm that may foreshadow the future: it was to carry on the family line should his male offspring prove sterile. What we are talking about here," McGrady said, "is not fertility insurance but immortality insurance."[16] This customer, then, believes he cannot be linked to future generations through his female offspring, should they prove fertile. His immortality, one must conclude, is not in his sperm or his genes but in his name.

"One's name and strong devotion to it," wrote an Austrian philosopher, Otto Weininger, around the turn of the century, "are even more dependent on personality than is the sense of property. . . . Women are not bound to their names with any strong bond. When they marry they give up their own name and assume that of their husband without any sense of loss. . . . The fundamental namelessness of the woman is simply a sign of her undifferentiated personality."[17] Weininger, whose book *Sex and Character* had a brief but powerful influence on popular psychology, is of historical interest because he articulated the myth of humanity's maleness at a time when the first wave of feminism was beginning to be taken seriously by governments, trade unions, and other institutions in England and the United States as well as in Europe. In describing the "fundamental namelessness" of woman as "a sign of her undifferentiated personality," Weininger was building support for his premise that "women have no existence and no essence . . . no share in ontological reality, no relation to the thing-in-itself, which, in the deepest interpretation, is the absolute, is God."[18]

Otto Weininger was aware of the movement for women's rights and was deeply disturbed by it. He may well have heard of the noted American feminist Lucy Stone, whose decision to keep her birth name when she married Henry Blackwell in 1855 had created consternation on both sides of the Atlantic. An eloquent speaker with a free and fearless spirit, Stone was widely known as an antislavery crusader. After the Civil War her organizing efforts helped secure passage of the Fourteenth Amendment, which extended the vote to freed slaves who were men. She devoted the rest of her long, productive life to the cause of suffrage for women and founded and edited the *Woman's Journal,* for forty-seven years the major weekly newspaper of the women's movement.

It is especially relevant that among Lucy Stone's many important contributions to history she is best known today for her refusal to give up her name. Her explanation, "My name is the symbol of my identity and must not be lost," was a real shocker to anyone who had not considered the possibility that a married woman could have an individual identity—and in the nineteenth century that meant almost everyone. The law did not recognize such a possibility, as the famous English jurist William Blackstone made clear when he summarized the rule of "coverture," influencing both British and American law for well over a hundred years. "By marriage," he wrote, "the husband and wife are one person in the law—that is, the very being or legal existence of the woman is suspended during the marriage. . . ."[19]

The suspended existence of the married woman came to be well symbolized in the total submersion of a wife's identity in her husband's name—preceded by "Mrs." The use of designations like "Mrs. John Jones" does not go back much before 1800. Martha Washington would have been mystified to receive a letter addressed to "Mrs. George Washington," for at that time the written abbreviation *Mrs.,* a social title applied to any adult woman, was used interchangeably with its spelled-out form *mistress* and was probably pronounced the same way. "Mistress George" would have made little sense.

Lucy Stone's example was followed in the late nineteenth and early twentieth centuries by small but increasing numbers of women, mostly professional writers, artists, and scientists. The Lucy Stone League, founded in New York in 1921, was the first organization to help women with the legal and bureaucratic difficulties involved in keeping their names after marriage. Its early leaders included Jane Grant, co-founder with her first husband, Harold Ross, of the *New Yorker* magazine, and journalist Ruth Hale who in 1926 asked rhetorically how men would respond to the suggestion that they give up *their* names. The suggestion does not often arise, but a psychologist recently described the reaction of one husband and father when someone in his family raised the possibility of changing the family name because they didn't like it:

"He suddenly realized that it was a traumatic thing for him to consider giving up his last name," according to Dr. Jack Sawyer of Northwestern University. "He said he'd never realized before that 'only men have real names in our society, women don't.' And it bothered him also that his name should be a matter of such consequence for him. He worried about his professional standing, colleagues trying to contact him—all kinds of things that women face as a matter of course when they get married. Men have accepted the permanency of their names as one of the rights of being male, and it was the first time he realized how much his name was part of his masculine self-image."[20]

Lucy Stone, whose self-image was comfortably female but not feminine, agreed to be known as Mrs. Stone after her marriage.

Through this compromise with custom she avoided the somewhat schizophrenic situation many well-known women face when they use their birth names professionally and their husbands' names socially, thus becoming both Miss Somebody and Mrs. Somebody Else. The Pulitzer prize–winning novelist Jean Stafford wants to be "saluted as *Miss* Stafford if the subject at hand has to do with me and my business or as *Mrs.* Liebling if inquiries are being made about my late husband."[21] Miss Stafford objects to being addressed as "Ms.," a title that Lucy Stone would probably have welcomed had it existed in her time.

During the nearly two centuries in which the use of the distinguishing marital labels Miss or Mrs. for women was rigidly enforced by custom, the labels tended to become parts of women's names, in effect replacing their given names. A boarding school founded by Sarah Porter in Farmington, Connecticut, soon became known as Miss Porter's School. After the actress Minnie Maddern married Harrison Grey Fiske, she became famous as Mrs. Fiske. In the following classroom dialogue, the columnist Ellen Cohn provides a classic example of how the custom works:

> *Question:* Who is credited with discovering radium?
> *Answer* (all together): Madam Curie.
> *Teacher:* Well, class, the woman (who was indeed married to a man named Pierre Curie) had a first name all her own. From now on let's call her Marie Curie.
> *Question:* Can Madam Curie ever be appropriately used?
> *Answer:* Of course. Whenever the inventor of the telephone is called Mr. Bell.[22]

Through the transience and fragmentation that have traditionally characterized women's names, some part of the human female self-image has been sacrificed. It is hardly surprising, therefore, that the second wave of feminist consciousness brought a serious challenge to patronymy and to the assignment of distinguishing marital labels to women. To be named and defined by someone else is to accept an imposed identity—to agree that the way others see us is the way we really are. Naming conventions, like the rest of language, have been shaped to meet the interests of society, and in patriarchal societies the shapers have been men. What is happening now in language seems simply to reflect the fact that, in the words of Dr. Pauli Murray, "women are seeking their own image of themselves nurtured from within rather than imposed from without."[23]

## NOTES


1. The recruitment ad appeared in the September 30, 1974, issue of *Time* magazine, pp. 84–85. By the following year, similar ads were posed in such a way that the name of each recruit was visible.
2. Helen Keller, *The Story of My Life,* Garden City, N.Y., Doubleday & Company, 1955, p. 36. (First published in 1902.)
3. Eric H. Lenneberg, "On Explaining Language," *Science,* May 9, 1969, pp. 635–43.
4. Ethel Strainchamps, "Our Sexist Language," in Vivian Gornick and Barbara K. Moran, eds., *Woman in Sexist Society,* New York, Basic Books, 1971, p. 247.
5. The study by James Bruning and William Albott, reported in the March 1974 issue of *Human Behavior,* was described by Melvin Maddocks, the Christian Science Monitor News Service, and reprinted in the *Middletown* (Conn.) *Press,* June 26, 1974.
6. Linwood Sleigh and Charles Johnson, *Apollo Book of Girls' Names,* New York, Thomas Y. Crowell Company, 1962, p. 194.
7. Alice H. Bonnell, "Women at Columbia: The Long March to Equal Opportunities," *Columbia Reports,* May 1972.
8. University of North Carolina News Bureau press release reprinted in the university's *Alumni Review,* November 1971.
9. Based on figures reported in *The World Almanac & Book of Facts 1975,* New York, Newspaper Enterprise Association, 1974.
10. "Booklet for Women Who Wish to Determine Their Own Names After Marriage," Barrington, Ill., Center for a Woman's Own Name, 1974, p. 7.
11. Quoted by Carmen Rubio in "Staying Single—In Name Only," *Sunday, The Hartford Courant Magazine,* February 2, 1975.
12. Stephen Birmingham, *The Right People: A Portrait of the American Social Establishment,* Boston, Little, Brown and Company, 1968, p. 9.
13. "Newsline," *Psychology Today,* August 1974, p. 29.
14. Robert T. Means, Jr., Letter to the Editor, *Psychology Today,* November 1974, p. 14.
15. Elizabeth Janeway, *Man's World, Woman's Place: A Study in Social Mythology,* New York, A Delta Book, Dell Publishing Company, 1971, p. 337.
16. Mike McGrady, "Family Banking," *New York* magazine, June 12, 1972, p. 42.
17. Otto Weininger, *Sex and Character,* New York, G. P. Putnam's Sons, 1906, p. 206. This is the "authorized translation from the sixth German edition"; also published in London by William Heinemann.
18. Ibid., p. 286.
19. Quoted by Lucy Komisar, *The New Feminism,* New York, Warner Paperback Library, 1971, p. 81. Blackstone's *Commentaries* was first published in 1765–69.
20. Arline Brecher, "Male Lib: The Men Who Want Human Liberation:

An Interview with Psychologist Jack Sawyer," *New Woman,* February 1972, p. 73.

21. Jean Stafford, "Don't Use Ms. with Miss Stafford, Unless You Mean ms.," *New York Times,* September 21, 1973, p. 36.
22. Ellen Cohn, "The Liberated Woman," *New York Sunday News* magazine, June 17, 1973, p. 4.
23. Pauli Murray, testimony before Rep. Edith Green's Special Subcommittee on Education in Support of Section 805 of H.R. 16098, June 19, 1970, U. S. Government Printing Office, 1970.

---

## REFLECTING ON MEANING

1. "In our society women's names are less important than men's. The reasons why are not hard to identify, but the consequences for both men and women are more far-reaching than members of either sex . . . have been prepared to admit or even, until recently, to examine." What are some of these consequences, according to Miller and Swift?

2. What are some of the naming customs that Miller and Swift discuss? What does a person's name represent to him or her? What does it represent in society? What connections between name and identity do Miller and Swift make?

3. According to Miller and Swift, "first-naming" often reflects a power inequity between women and men. What is first-naming? In what situations does it occur? Do you agree that it trivializes women and their accomplishments? Why or why not?

4. Miller and Swift trace a link between our conception of family and male surnames. What is this link? How does it influence the way we think about "family"? Why do Miller and Swift implicate it in the "suspended existence of the married woman"? What do they mean?

## EXPLORING RHETORICAL STRATEGIES

1. Miller and Swift begin their essay by describing a recruitment ad. In what ways does the ad relate to their thesis? How does it provide a springboard for the rest of the essay? Why do they say that the ad's format did not occur by accident?

2. Although Miller and Swift's essay focuses on women and names, they make a larger point about the English language. What is this point? How do their assertions about names support this point?
3. What different kinds of evidence do Miller and Swift offer to support their assertions?

# In Defense of Gender

## CYRA McFADDEN

*Although Cyra McFadden acknowledges that the English language is sexist, she finds attempts to reform it "ludicrous." In this brief commentary on our linguistic state of affairs, she satirizes such efforts and argues that they are counterproductive.*

So pervasive is the neutering of the English language on the progressive West Coast, we no longer have people here, only persons: male persons and female persons, chairpersons and doorpersons, waitpersons, mailpersons—who may be either male or female mailpersons—and refuse-collection persons. In the classified ads, working mothers seek childcare persons, though one wonders how many men (archaic for "male person") take care of child persons as a full-time occupation. One such ad, fusing non-sexist language and the most popular word in the California growth movement, solicits a "nurtureperson."

Dear gents and ladies, as I might have addressed you in less troubled times, this female person knows firsthand the reasons for scourging sexist bias from the language. God knows what damage was done me, at fifteen, when I worked in my first job—as what is now known as a newspaper copyperson—and came running to the voices of men barking, "Boy!"

No aspirant to the job of refuse-collection person myself, I nonetheless take off my hat (a little feathered number, with a veil) to those of my own sex who may want both the job and a genderless title with it. I argue only that there must be a better way, and I wish person or persons unknown would come up with one.

Defend it on any grounds you choose; the neutering of spoken and written English, with its attendant self-consciousness, remains ludicrous. In print, those "person" suffixes and "he/she's" jump out from the page, as distracting as a cloud of gnats, demanding that the reader note the writer's virtue. "Look what a nonsexist writer person I am, voiding the use of masculine forms for the generic."

Spoken, they leave conversation fit only for the Coneheads on "Saturday Night Live." "They have a daily special," a woman at the next table told her male companion in Perry's, a San Francisco restaurant. "Ask your waitperson." In a Steig cartoon, the words would have marched from her mouth in the form of a computer printout.

In Berkeley, Calif., the church to which a friend belongs is busy stripping its liturgy of sexist references. "They've gone berserk," she writes, citing a reading from the pulpit of a verse from 1 Corinthians. Neutered, the once glorious passage becomes "Though I speak with the tongues of persons and of angels . . ." So much for sounding brass and tinkling cymbals.

The parson person of the same church is now referring to God as "He/She" and changing all references accordingly—no easy undertaking if he intends to be consistent. In the following, the first pronoun would remain because at this primitive stage of human evolution, male persons do not give birth to babies: "And she brought forth her first-born son/daughter, and wrapped him/her in swaddling clothes, and laid him/her in a manger; because there was no room for them in the inn. . . ."

As the after-dinner speaker at a recent professional conference, I heard a text replete with "he/she's" and "his/her's" read aloud for the first time. The hapless program female chairperson stuck with the job chose to render these orally as "he-slash-she" and "his-slash-her," turning the following day's schedule for conference participants into what sounded like a replay of the Manson killings.

Redress may be due those of us who, though female, have answered to masculine referents all these years, but slashing is not the answer; violence never is. Perhaps we could right matters by using feminine forms as the generic for a few centuries, or simply agree on a per-woman lump-sum payment.

Still, we would be left with the problem of referring, without bias, to transpersons. These are not bus drivers or Amtrak conductors but persons in transit from one gender to the other—or so I interpret a fund-driven appeal asking me to defend their civil rights, along with those of female and male homosexuals.

Without wishing to step on anyone's civil rights, I hope transpersons are not the next politically significant pressure group. If they are, count on it, they will soon want their own pronouns.

In the tradition of the West, meanwhile, feminists out here wrestle the language to the ground, plant a foot on its neck and remove its masculine appendages. Take the local art critic Beverly Terwoman.

She is married to a man surnamed Terman. She writes under "Terwoman," presumably in the spirit of *vive la différence.* As a letter to the editor of the paper for which she writes noted, however, "Terwoman" is not ideologically pure. It still contains "man," a syllable reeking of all that is piggy and hairy-chested.

Why not Beverly Terperson? Or better, since "Terperson" contains "son," "Terdaughter"? Or a final refinement, Beverly Ter?

Beverly Terwoman did not dignify this sexist assault with a reply. The writer of the letter was a male person, after all, probably the kind who leaves his smelly sweat socks scattered around the bedroom floor.

No one wins these battles anyway. In another letter to the same local weekly, J. Seibert, female, lets fire at the printing of an interview with Phyllis Schlafly. Not only was the piece "an offense to everything that Marin County stands for," but "it is even more amusing that your interview was conducted by a male.

"This indicates your obvious assumption that men understand women's issues better than women since men are obviously more intelligent (as no doubt Phyllis would agree)."

A sigh suffuses the editor's note that follows: "The author of the article, Sydney Weisman, is a female."

So the war of the pronouns and suffixes rages, taking no prisoners except writers. Neuter your prose with all those clanking "he/she's," and no one will read you except Alan Alda. Use masculine forms as the generic, and you have joined the ranks of the oppressor. None of this does much to encourage friendly relations between persons, transpersons or—if there are any left—people.

I also have little patience with the hyphenated names more and more California female persons adopt when they marry, in the interests of retaining their own personhood. These accomplish their intention of declaring the husband separate but equal. They are hell on those of us who have trouble remembering one name, much less two. They defeat answering machines, which can't handle "Please call Gwendolyn Grunt-Messerschmidt." And in this culture, they retain overtones of false gentility.

Two surnames, to me, still bring to mind the female writers of bad romances and Julia Ward Howe.

It's a mug's game, friends, this neutering of a language already fat, bland and lethargic, and it's time we decide not to play it. This female person is currently writing a book about rodeo. I'll be dragged behind a saddle bronc before I will neuter the text with "cowpersons."

---

## REFLECTING ON MEANING

1. McFadden's essay provides a glimpse into the various ways speakers and writers have confronted the masculine bias inherent in the English language. How have people attempted to surmount this bias? What specific strategies have they employed?
2. Although McFadden agrees with feminist critics that the English language is sexist, she ridicules past and current attempts to reform it. According to McFadden, what is the problem with nonsexist pronoun usage and *-person* suffixes? Why does she find them silly? What examples does she give to illustrate her point that these attempts are absurd? Do you agree? Why or why not?
3. Almost as an afterthought, McFadden turns her attention to hyphenated surnames as well as pronouns and suffixes. Why does she do this? What is her objection to hyphenated surnames? Do you agree or disagree that such names are, like many new gender-neutral coinages, unwieldy?

## EXPLORING RHETORICAL STRATEGIES

1. How would you describe McFadden's tone in this essay? Consider how such comments as these contribute to her tone:

> Dear gents and ladies, as I might have addressed you in less troubled times, this female person knows firsthand the reasons for scourging sexist bias from the language.
>
> No aspirant to the job of refuse-collection person myself, I nonetheless take off my hat (a little feathered number, with a veil) to those of my own sex who may want both the job and a genderless title with it.

> This female person is currently writing a book about rodeo. I'll be dragged behind a saddle bronc before I will neuter the text with "cowpersons."

2. McFadden's word play provides a sophisticated and amusing dimension to her essay. In what ways is her use of the word *neuter* particularly appropriate for her discussion? What point does she make by her pun on the meaning of *slash* in discussing such constructions as *he/she?* Through such word play, how does she develop an analogy between her subject and the ideas of violence and war?
3. Much of the strength of McFadden's argument derives from the concrete images she constructs to convey her perspective on the abstract topic of language and sexism. What are some of these images? How do they help her convey her point of view? What makes this strategy effective?

# Chapter 7

## CONVERSATION AND GENDER

### You Are What You Say

ROBIN LAKOFF

*In this essay the noted linguist Robin Lakoff turns her attention to differences in the ways women and men talk. She claims that "cultural bias" influences the way women are taught to talk, in effect placing them in a no-win position in conversational dynamics.*

"Women's language" is that pleasant (dainty?), euphemistic, never-aggressive way of talking we learned as little girls. Cultural bias was built into the language we were allowed to speak, the subjects we were allowed to speak about, and the ways we were spoken of. Having learned our linguistic lesson well, we go out in the world, only to discover that we are communicative cripples—damned if we do, and damned if we don't.

If we refuse to talk "like a lady," we are ridiculed and criticized for being unfeminine. ("She thinks like a man" is, at best, a left-handed compliment.) If we do learn all the fuzzy-headed, unassertive language of our sex, we are ridiculed for being unable to think clearly, unable to take part in a serious discussion, and therefore unfit to hold a position of power.

It doesn't take much of this for a woman to begin feeling she deserves such treatment because of inadequacies in her own intelligence and education.

"Women's language" shows up in all levels of English. For example, women are encouraged and allowed to make far more precise discriminations in naming colors than men do. Words like *mauve, beige, ecru, aquamarine, lavender,* and so on, are unremarkable in a woman's active vocabulary, but largely absent from that of most men. I know of no evidence suggesting that women actually *see* a wider range of colors than men do. It is simply that fine discriminations of this sort are relevant to women's vocabularies, but not to men's; to men, who control most of the interesting affairs of the world, such distinctions are trivial—irrelevant.

In the area of syntax, we find similar gender-related peculiarities of speech. There is one construction, in particular, that women use conversationally far more than men: the tag question. A tag is midway between an outright statement and a yes-no question; it is less assertive than the former, but more confident than the latter.

A *flat statement* indicates confidence in the speaker's knowledge and is fairly certain to be believed; a *question* indicates a lack of knowledge on some point and implies that the gap in the speaker's knowledge can and will be remedied by an answer. For example, if, at a Little League game, I have had my glasses off, I can legitimately ask someone else: "Was the player out at third?" A *tag question,* being intermediate between statement and question, is used when the speaker is stating a claim, but lacks full confidence in the truth of that claim. So if I say, "Is Joan here?" I will probably not be surprised if my respondent answers "no"; but if I say, "Joan is here, isn't she?" instead, chances are I am already biased in favor of a positive answer, wanting only confirmation. I still want a response, but I have enough knowledge (or think I have) to predict that response. A tag question, then, might be thought of as a statement that doesn't demand to be believed by anyone but the speaker, a way of giving leeway, of not forcing the addressee to go along with the views of the speaker.

Another common use of the tag question is in small talk when the speaker is trying to elicit conversation: "Sure is hot here, isn't it?"

But in discussing personal feelings or opinions, only the speaker normally has any way of knowing the correct answer. Sentences such as "I have a headache, don't I?" are clearly ridiculous. But there are other examples where it is the speaker's opinions, rather than perceptions, for which corroboration is sought, as in "The situation in Southeast Asia is terrible, isn't it?"

While there are, of course, other possible interpretations of a sentence like this, one possibility is that the speaker has a particular answer in mind—"yes" or "no"—but is reluctant to state it baldly. This sort of tag question is much more apt to be used by women than by men in conversation. Why is this the case?

The tag question allows a speaker to avoid commitment, and thereby avoid conflict with the addressee. The problem is that, by so doing, speakers may also give the impression of not really being sure of themselves, or looking to the addressee for confirmation of their views. This uncertainty is reinforced in more subliminal ways, too. There is a peculiar sentence intonation-pattern, used almost exclusively by women, as far as I know, which changes a declarative answer into a question. The effect of using the rising inflection typical of a yes-no question is to imply that the speaker is seeking confirmation, even though the speaker is clearly the only one who has the requisite information, which is why the question was put to her in the first place:

> (Q) When will dinner be ready?
> (A) Oh . . . around six o'clock . . . ?

It is as though the second speaker were saying, "Six o'clock—if that's okay with you, if you agree." The person being addressed is put in the position of having to provide confirmation. One likely consequence of this sort of speech-pattern in a woman is that, often unbeknownst to herself, the speaker builds a reputation of tentativeness, and others will refrain from taking her seriously or trusting her with any real responsibilities, since she "can't make up her mind," and "isn't sure of herself."

Such idiosyncrasies may explain why women's language sounds much more "polite" than men's. It is polite to leave a decision open, not impose your mind, or views, or claims, on anyone else. So a tag question is a kind of polite statement, in that it does not force agreement or belief on the addressee. In the same way a request is a polite command, in that it does not force obedience on the addressee, but rather suggests something be done as a favor to the speaker. A clearly stated order implies a threat of certain consequences if it is not followed, and—even more impolite—implies that the speaker is in a superior position and able to enforce the order. By couching wishes in the form of a request, on the other hand, a speaker implies that if the request is not carried out, only the speaker will suffer; noncompliance cannot harm the addressee. So the decision is really left up to the addressee. The distinction becomes clear in these examples:

> Close the door.
> Please close the door.
> Will you close the door?
> Will you please close the door?
> Won't you close the door?

In the same ways as words and speech patterns used *by* women undermine her image, those used *to describe* women make matters even worse. Often a word may be used of both men and women (and perhaps of things as well); but when it is applied to women, it assumes a special meaning that, by implication rather than outright assertion, is derogatory to women as a group.

The use of euphemisms has this effect. A euphemism is a substitute for a word that has acquired a bad connotation by association with something unpleasant or embarrassing. But almost as soon as the new word comes into common usage, it takes on the same old bad connotations, since feelings about the things or people referred to are not altered by a change of name; thus new euphemisms must be constantly found.

There is one euphemism for *woman* still very much alive. The word, of course, is *lady*. *Lady* has a masculine counterpart, namely *gentleman,* occasionally shortened to *gent.* But for some reason *lady* is very much commoner than *gent(leman).*

The decision to use *lady* rather than *woman,* or vice versa, may considerably alter the sense of a sentence, as the following examples show:

(a) A woman (lady) I know is a dean at Berkeley.
(b) A woman (lady) I know makes amazing things out of shoelaces and old boxes.

The use of *lady* in (a) imparts a frivolous, or nonserious, tone to the sentence: the matter under discussion is not one of great moment. Similarly, in (b), using *lady* here would suggest that the speaker considered the "amazing things" not to be serious art, but merely a hobby or an aberration. If *woman* is used, she might be a serious sculptor. To say *lady doctor* is very condescending, since no one ever says *gentleman doctor* or even *man doctor.* For example, mention in the San Francisco *Chronicle* of January 31, 1972, of Madalyn Murray O'Hair as the *lady atheist* reduces her position to that of scatterbrained eccentric. Even *woman atheist* is scarcely defensible: sex is irrelevant to her philosophical position.

Many women argue that, on the other hand, *lady* carries with it overtones recalling the age of chivalry: conferring exalted stature on the person so referred to. This makes the term seem polite at first, but we must also remember that these implications are perilous: they suggest that a "lady" is helpless, and cannot do things by herself.

*Lady* can also be used to infer frivolousness, as in titles of organizations. Those that have a serious purpose (not merely that of enabling "the ladies" to spend time with one another) cannot use the word *lady* in their titles, but less serious ones may. Compare the *Ladies' Auxiliary* of a men's group, or the *Thursday Evening Ladies' Browning and Garden Society* with *Ladies' Liberation* or *Ladies' Strike for Peace.*

What is curious about this split is that *lady* is in origin a euphemism—a substitute that puts a better face on something people find uncomfortable—for *woman.* What kind of euphemism is it that subtly denigrates the people to whom it refers? Perhaps *lady* functions as a euphemism for *woman* because it does not contain the sexual implications present in *woman*: it is not "embarrassing" in that way. If this is so, we may expect that, in the future, *lady* will replace woman as the primary word for the human female, since *woman* will have become too blatantly sexual. That this distinction is already made in some contexts at least is shown in the following examples, where you can try replacing *woman* with *lady*:

(a) She's only twelve, but she's already a woman.
(b) After ten years in jail, Harry wanted to find a woman.
(c) She's my woman, see, so don't mess around with her.

Another common substitute for *woman* is *girl.* One seldom hears a man past the age of adolescence referred to as a boy, save in expressions like "going out with the boys," which are meant to suggest an air of adolescent frivolity and irresponsibility. But women of all ages are "girls": one can have a man—not a boy—Friday, but only a girl—never a woman or even a lady—Friday; women have girlfriends, but men do not—in a nonsexual sense—have boyfriends. It may be that this use of *girl* is euphemistic in the same way the use of *lady* is: in stressing the idea of immaturity, it removes the sexual connotations lurking in *woman. Girl* brings to mind irresponsibility: you don't send a girl to do a woman's errand (or even, for that matter, a boy's errand). She is a person who is both too immature and too far from real life to be entrusted with responsibilities or with decisions of any serious or important nature.

Now let's take a pair of words which, in terms of the possible relationships in an earlier society, were simple male-female equivalents, analogous to *bull* : *cow.* Suppose we find that, for independent reasons, society has changed in such a way that the original meanings now are irrelevant. Yet the words have not been discarded, but have acquired new meanings, metaphorically related to their original senses. But suppose these new metaphorical uses are no longer parallel to each other. By seeing where the parallelism breaks down, we discover something about the different roles played by men and women in this culture. One good example of such a divergence through time is found in the pair, *master* : *mistress*. Once used with reference to one's power over servants, these words have become unusable today in their original master-servant sense as the relationship has become less prevalent in our society. But the words are still common.

Unless used with reference to animals, *master* now generally refers to a man who has acquired consummate ability in some field, normally nonsexual. But its feminine counterpart cannot be used this way. It is practically restricted to its sexual sense of "paramour." We start out with two terms, both roughly paraphrasable as "one who has power over another." But the masculine form, once one person is no longer able to have absolute power over another, becomes usable metaphorically in the sense of "having power over *something*." *Master* requires as its object only the name of some activity, something inanimate and abstract. But *mistress* requires a masculine noun in the possessive to precede it. One cannot say: "Rhonda is a mistress." One must be *someone's* mistress. A man is defined by what he does, a woman by her sexuality, that is, in terms of one particular aspect of her relationship to men. It is one thing to be an *old master* like Hans Holbein, and another to be an *old mistress*.

The same is true of the words *spinster* and *bachelor*—gender words for "one who is not married." The resemblance ends with the definition. While *bachelor* is a neutral term, often used as a compliment, *spinster* normally is used pejoratively, with connotations of prissiness, fussiness, and so on. To be a bachelor implies that one has the choice of marrying or not, and this is what makes the idea of a bachelor existence attractive, in the popular literature. He has been pursued and has successfully eluded his pursuers. But a spinster is one who has not been pursued, or at least not seriously. She is old, unwanted goods. The metaphorical connotations of *bachelor* generally suggest sexual freedom; of *spinster*, puritanism or celibacy.

These examples could be multiplied. It is generally considered a *faux pas*, in society, to congratulate a woman on her engagement, while it is correct to congratulate her fiancé. Why is this? The reason seems to be that it is impolite to remind people of things that may be uncomfortable to them. To congratulate a woman on her engagement is really to say, "Thank goodness! You had a close call!" For the man, on the other hand, there was no such danger. His choosing to marry is viewed as a good thing, but not something essential.

The linguistic double standard holds throughout the life of the relationship. After marriage, bachelor and spinster become man and wife, not man and woman. The woman whose husband dies remains "John's widow"; John, however, is never "Mary's widower."

Finally, why is it that salesclerks and others are so quick to call women customers "dear," "honey," and other terms of endearment they really have no business using? A male customer would never put up with it. But women, like children, are supposed to enjoy these endearments, rather than being offended by them.

In more ways than one, it's time to speak up.

---

## REFLECTING ON MEANING

1. According to Lakoff, what is "women's language"? What characteristics does it have? What are some specific examples? What are its origins? What effect does such language have on others' perceptions of women and on women's perceptions of themselves?

2. Lakoff identifies a "linguistic double standard" at work in the connotations of such words as *woman, lady,* and *girl,* and she traces the history of paired words such as *master* and *mistress* to show "something about the different roles played by men and women in this culture." What is the point she is making? What difference in the social status of men and women does her survey suggest?

3. Lakoff claims that salesclerks and other people feel free to address a woman customer in ways that "a male customer would never put up with." What does she mean? Do you agree that men and women are addressed differently by such people? Why aren't men subject to the same forms of address?

## EXPLORING RHETORICAL STRATEGIES

1. Well into her essay, Lakoff's focus shifts from the "words and speech patterns used by women" to words "used to *describe*

women." What is the difference between these two topics? How do they complement each other? How do they both work to advance her main idea?

2. What evidence can you find to show that Lakoff was thinking about her readers as she wrote this essay? What is the significance of the "we" in her opening paragraphs? How does this "we" differ from the "we" that appears as the essay develops? What was Lakoff trying to achieve with these two distinct uses of "we"?

3. In what ways is Lakoff's concluding statement appropriate to her topic? What does it reveal about her purpose for writing this essay? What is she trying to accomplish by ending in this way?

# Men and Women Talking

## GLORIA STEINEM

*In this selection Gloria Steinem takes a controversial look at the "politics of conversation"—the dynamics of communication between women and men. Her essay debunks several common myths about women and outlines strategies for subverting the hierarchy of gender that influences everyday conversation.*

Once upon a time (that is, just a few years ago), psychologists believed that the way we chose to communicate was largely a function of personality. If certain conversational styles turned out to be more common to one sex than the other (more abstract and aggressive talk for men, for instance, more personal and equivocal talk for women), then this was just another tribute to the influence of biology on personality.

Consciously or otherwise, feminists have challenged this assumption from the beginning. Many of us learned a big lesson in the sixties when our generation spoke out on the injustices of war, as well as of race and class; yet women who used exactly the same words and style as our male counterparts were less likely to be listened to or to be taken seriously. When we tried to talk about this and other frustrations, the lack of listening got worse, with opposition and even ridicule just around every corner. Only women's own meetings and truth telling began to confirm what we had thought each of us was alone in experiencing. It was also those early consciousness-raising groups that began to develop a more cooperative, less combative way of talking, an alternative style that many women have maintained and been strengthened by ever since.

The problem is that this culturally different form has remained an almost totally female event. True, it has helped many, many women arrive at understanding each other and working out strategies for action. But as an influence on the culturally male style of public talking, it has remained almost as removed as its more domestic versions of the past.

One reason for our decade or so of delay in challenging existing styles of talking makes good tactical sense. Our first task was to change the words themselves. We did not feel included (and usage studies showed that, factually, we were not) in hundreds of such supposedly generic terms as *mankind* and *he, the brotherhood of man* and *statesman.* Nor could we fail to see the racial parallels to being identified as "girls" at advanced ages, or with first names only, or by our personal connection (or lack of one) to a member of the dominant group.

Hard as it was (and still is), this radical act of seizing the power to name ourselves and our experience was easier than taking on the politics of conversation. Documenting society-wide patterns of talking required expensive research and surveys. Documenting the sexism in words, and even conjuring up alternatives, took only one courageous woman scholar and a dictionary (for instance, *Guidelines for Equal Treatment of the Sexes,* the pioneering work of Alma Graham for McGraw-Hill). That was one good economic reason why such works were among the first and best by feminist scholars.

In retrospect, the second cause for delay makes less feminist sense—the long popularity of assertiveness training. Though most women needed to be more assertive (or even more aggressive, though that word was considered too controversial), many of these courses taught women how to play the existing game, not how to change the rules. Unlike the feminist assault on sexist language, which demanded new behavior from men, too, assertiveness training was more reformist than revolutionary. It pushed one-way change for women only, thus seeming to confirm masculine-style communication as the only adult model or the most effective one.

Certainly, many individual women were helped, and many men were confronted with the educational experience of an assertive woman, but the larger impact was usually to flatter the existing masculine game of talk-politics by imitating it.

Since then, however, a few feminist scholars have had the time and resources to document conversational patterns of mixed- and single-sex groups, both here and in Europe. Traditional scholarship, influenced by feminism, has also begun to look at conversational styles as functions of power and environment. For instance, employees pursue topics raised by their employers more than the reverse, older people feel free to interrupt younger ones, and subordinates are more polite than bosses. Since women share all those conversational habits of the less powerful, even across the many lines of class and status that divide us, how accidental can that be?

Even the new feminist-influenced research has a long way to go in neutralizing the masculine bias of existing studies. For instance, *talking* is assumed to be the important and positive act, while *listening,* certainly a productive function, is the subject of almost no studies at all.

Nonetheless, there is enough new scholarship to document different styles, to point out some deficiencies in the masculine model of communicating, and to give us some ideas on how to create a synthesis of both that could provide a much wider range of alternatives for women *and* for men.

## I

*Have you assumed that women talk more than men—and thus may dominate in discussion if nowhere else?* If so, you're not alone. Researchers of sex differences in language started out with that assumption. So did many feminists, who often explained women's supposedly greater penchant for talking as compensation for a lack of power to act.

In fact, however, when Dale Spender, an English feminist and scholar, surveyed studies of talkativeness for her recent book, *Man Made Language,* she concluded that "perhaps in more than any other research area, findings were in complete contradiction with the stereotype. . . . There has not been one study which provides evidence that women talk more than men, and there have been numerous studies which indicate that men talk more than women."

Her conclusion held true regardless of whether the study in question asked individuals to talk into a tape recorder with no group interaction; or compared men and women talking on television; or measured amounts of talk in mixed groups (even among male and female state legislators); or involved group discussions of a subject on which women might be expected to have more expertise. (At a London workshop on sexism and education, for instance, the five men present managed to talk more than their thirty-two female colleagues combined.)

Some studies of male silence in heterosexual couples might seem to counter these results, but Spender's research supports their conclusion that a major portion of female talk in such one-to-one situations is devoted to drawing the man out, asking questions, introducing multiple subjects until one is accepted by him, or demonstrating interest in the subjects he introduces. Clearly, male silence (or silence from a member of any dominant group) is not necessarily the same as listening. It might mean a rejection of the speaker, a refusal to become vulnerable through self-revelation, or a decision that this conversation is not worthwhile. Similarly, talking by the subordinate group is not necessarily an evidence of power. Its motive may be a Scheherazade-like need to intrigue and thus survive, or simply to explain and justify one's actions.

In addition to a generally greater volume of talk, however, men interrupt women more often than vice versa. This is true both in groups and in couples. Male interruptions of women also bring less social punishment than female interruptions of men. Men also interrupt women more often than women interrupt each other.

Moreover, males are more likely to police the subject matter of conversation in mixed-sex groups. One study of working-class families showed that women might venture into such "masculine" topics as politics or sports, and men might join "feminine" discussions of domestic events, but in both cases, it was the men who ridiculed or otherwise straightened out nonconformers who went too far. Even in that London workshop on sexism, for instance, the concrete experiences of the female participants were suppressed in favor of the abstract, general conclusions on sexism that were preferred by the men. The few males present set the style for all the females.

How did the myth of female talkativeness and conversational dominance get started? Why has this supposed female ability been so accepted that many sociologists, and a few battered women themselves, have even accepted it as a justification for some men's violence against their wives?

The uncomfortable truth seems to be that the amount of talk by women has been measured less against the amount of men's talk than against the expectation of female silence.

Indeed, women who accept and set out to disprove the myth of the talkative woman may pay the highest price of all. In attempting to be the exceptions, we silence ourselves. If that is so, measuring our personal behavior against real situations and real studies should come as a relief, a confirmation of unspoken feelings.

We are not crazy, for instance, if we feel that, when we finally do take the conversational floor in a group, we are out there in exposed verbal flight, like fearful soloists plucked from the chorus. We are not crazy to feel that years of unspoken thoughts are bottled up inside our heads, and come rushing out in a way that may make it hard to speak calmly, even when we finally have the chance.

Once we give up searching for approval for stifling our thoughts, or by imitating the male norm of abstract, assertive communicating, we often find it easier to simply say what needs to be said, and thus to earn respect and approval. Losing self-consciousness and fear allows us to focus on the content of what we are saying instead of on ourselves.

Women's well-developed skill as listeners, perhaps the real source of our much-vaunted "intuition," should not be left behind. We must retain it for ourselves and teach it to men by bringing it with us into our work and daily lives, but that will only happen if we affirm its value. Female culture does have a great deal to contribute to the dominant one. Furthermore, women might feel better about talking equally, selecting subjects, and even interrupting occasionally if we took the reasonable attitude that we are helping men to become attentive and retentive listeners, too. We are paying them the honor of communicating as honestly as we can and treating them as we would want to be treated. After all, if more men gained sensitive listening skills, they would have "intuition," too.

*These are practical exercises for achieving a change in the balance of talk.* Try tape-recording a dinner-table conversation or meeting (in the guise of recording facts, so participants don't become self-conscious about their talk politics), then play the tape back to the same group, and ask them to add up the number of minutes talked, interruptions, and subject introductions for each gender. Or give a dozen poker chips to each participant in a discussion, and require that one chip be given up each time a person speaks. Or break the silence barrier for those who rarely talk by going around the room once at the beginning of each meeting, consciousness-raising-style, with a question that each participant must answer personally, even if it's only a self-introduction. (It is said that the British Labour party was born only after representatives of its warring factions spent an hour moving their conference table into a larger room.

That one communal act broke down individual isolation, just as one round of communal speaking helps break the ice.)

If such methods require more advance planning or influence on the group than you can muster, or if you're trying to sensitize just one person, try some individual acts. Discussing the results of studies on who talks more can produce some very healthy self-consciousness in both women and men. If one group member speaks rarely, try addressing more of your own remarks to her (or him) directly. On the other hand, if one man (or woman) is a domineering interrupter, try objecting directly, interrupting in return, timing the minutes of his or her talk, or just being inattentive. If someone cuts you off, say with humor, "That's one," then promise some conspicuous act when the interruptions get to three. Keep score on "successful" topic introductions, add them up by gender, and announce them at the discussion's end.

If questions and comments following a lecture come mostly from men, stand up and say so. It may be a learning moment for everyone. The prevalence of male speakers in mixed audiences has caused some feminist lecturers to reserve equal time for questions from women only.

To demonstrate the importance of listening as a positive act, try giving a quiz on the content of female and male speakers. Hopefully you *won't* discover the usual: that men often remember what male speakers say better than they remember female speakers' content; that women often remember male content better, too, but that women listen and retain the words of *both* sexes somewhat better than men do.

Check the talk politics concealed in your own behavior. Does your anxiety level go up (and your hostess instincts quiver) when women are talking and men are listening, but not the reverse? For instance, men often seem to feel okay about "talking shop" for hours while women listen, but women seem able to talk in men's presence for only a short time before feeling anxious, apologizing, and encouraging the men to speak. If you start to feel wrongly uncomfortable about making males listen, try this exercise: *keep on talking,* and encourage your sisters to do the same. Honor men by treating them as honestly as you treat women. You will be allowing them to learn.

## II

*Here are three popular assumptions: (1) Women talk about themselves, personalize, and gossip more than men do. (2) Men would rather talk to groups of men than to mixed groups, and women prefer mixed groups to all-female ones. (3) Women speakers and women's issues are hampered by the feminine style of their presentation.* As you've probably guessed by now, most evidence is to the contrary of all three beliefs.

After recording the conversational themes of single-sex and mixed-sex groups, for instance, social psychologist Elizabeth Aries found that men in all-male groups were more likely to talk about themselves than were women in all-female ones. Men were also more likely to use self-mentions to demonstrate superiority or aggressiveness, while women used them to share an emotional reaction to what was being said by others.

Phil Donahue, one of the country's most experienced interviewers, capsulizes the cultural difference between men and women this way: "If you're in a social situation, and women are talking to each other, and one woman says, 'I was hit by a car today,' all the other women will say, 'You're kidding! What happened? Where? Are you all right?' In the same situation with males, one male says, 'I was hit by a car today.' I guarantee you that there will be another male in the group who will say, 'Wait till I tell you what happened to *me*.' "

If quantity of talking about oneself is a measure of "personalizing," and self-aggrandizement through invoking the weakness of others is one characteristic of gossip, then men may be far more "gossipy" than women—especially when one includes sexual bragging.

In addition, subjects introduced by males in mixed groups are far more likely to "succeed" than subjects introduced by women, and, as Aries concluded, women in mixed groups are more likely to interact with men than with other women. Thus, it's not unreasonable to conclude that mixed groups spend more time discussing the lives and interests of male participants than of female ones.

On the other hand, research by Aries and others shows that women are more likely to discuss human relationships. Since "relationships" often fall under "gossip" in men's view, this may account for the frequent male observation that women "personalize" everything. Lecturers often comment, for instance, that women in an audience ask practical questions about their own lives, while men ask abstract questions about groups or policies. When the subject is feminism, women tend to ask about practical problems. Men are more likely to say something like, "But how will feminism impact the American family?"

To quote Donahue, who deals with mostly female audiences: "I've always felt a little anxious about the possibility of a program at night with a male audience. The problem as I perceive it—and this is a generalization—is that men tend to give you a speech, whereas women will ask a question and then listen for the answer and make another contribution to the dialogue. In countless situations I have a male in my audience stand up and say in effect, 'I don't know what you're arguing about; here's the answer to this thing.' And then proceed to give a mini-speech."

Aries also documented the more cooperative, rotating style of talk and leadership in women-only groups: the conscious or unconscious habit of "taking turns." As a result, women actually prefer talking in their own single-sex groups for the concrete advantages of both having a conversational turn and being listened to. On the other hand, she confirmed research that shows male-only groups to have more stable hierarchies, with the same one or several talkers dominating most of the time.

As Aries points out, no wonder men prefer the variation and opportunity of mixed-sex audiences. They combine the seriousness of a male presence with more choice of styles—and, as Spender adds caustically, the assurance of at least some noncompetitive listeners.

Women's more gentle delivery, "feminine" choice of adjectives, and greater attention to grammar and politeness have been heavily criticized. Linguist Robin Lakoff pioneered the exposure of "ladylike" speech as a double bind that is both required of little girls, and used as a reason why, as adults, they may not be seen as forceful or serious. (Even Lakoff seems to assume, however, that female speech is to be criticized as the deficient form, while male speech is the norm and thus escapes equal comment.) Sociologist Arlie Hochschild also cites some survival techniques of racial minorities that women of all races seem to share: playing dumb and dissembling, for instance, or expressing frequent approval of others.

But whether this criticism of female speech patterns is justified or not, there is also evidence that a rejection of the way a woman speaks is often a way of blaming or dismissing her without dealing with the content of what she is saying.

For instance, women speakers are more likely to hear some version of "You have a good point, but you're not making it effectively," or "Your style is too aggressive/weak/loud/quiet." It is with such paternalistic criticisms that male politicians often dismiss the serious message of a female colleague, or that husbands turn aside the content of arguments made by their wives.

It is also such criticisms that allow women candidates to be rejected without dealing with the substance of the issues they raise.

When Bella Abzug of New York and Gloria Schaeffer of Connecticut both ran for political office in one recent year, each was said to have a personal style that would prevent her from being an effective senator: Abzug because she was "too abrasive and aggressive," and Schaeffer because she was "too ladylike and quiet." Style was made the central issue by the press, and thus became one in the public-opinion polls. Both were defeated.

There are three anomalies that give away this supposedly "helpful" criticism. First, it is rarely used when a woman's message is not challenging to male power. (How often are women criticized for being too fierce in defense of their families? How often was Phyllis Schlafly criticized for being too aggressive in her opposition to the Equal Rights Amendment?) Second, the criticism is rarely accompanied by real support, even when the critic presents himself (or herself) as sympathetic. (Women political candidates say they often get critiques of their fund-raising techniques instead of cash, even from people who agree with them on issues.) Finally, almost everyone, regardless of status, feels a right to criticize. (Women professors report criticism of their teaching style from young students, as do women bosses from their employees.)

Just as there is a conversational topic that men in a group often find more compelling than any introduced by a woman (even when it's exactly the same topic, but *re*introduced by a man), or a political issue that is "more important" than any of concern to women, so there is usually a better, more effective style than the one a woman happens to be using.

Men *would* support us, we are told, if only we learned how to ask for their support in the right way. It's a subtle and effective way of blaming the victim.

*What can we do to break through these stereotypes?* Keeping notes for one meeting or one week on the male/female ratio of gossip or self-mentions could be educational. Declaring a day's moratorium on all words that end in "-tion" and all generalities might encourage men to state their personal beliefs *without* disguising them as general conclusions.

As a personal exercise, try countering slippery abstractions with tangible examples. When David Susskind and Germaine Greer were guests on the same television talk show, for instance, Susskind used general, pseudoscientific statements about women's monthly emotional changes as a way of excusing the injustices cited by this very intelligent woman. Finally, Greer turned politely to Susskind and said, "Tell me, David. Can you tell if I'm menstruating right now—or not?" She not only eliminated any doubts raised by Susskind's statements, but subdued his pugnacious style for the rest of the show.

Men themselves are working to break down the generalities and competitiveness that a male-dominant culture has imposed on them. Some are meeting in all-male consciousness-raising groups, learning how to communicate more openly and personally among themselves.

Many women are also trying to break down the barriers we ourselves maintain. For instance, women's preference for talking to one another has a great deal to do with the shorthand that shared experience provides. Furthermore, the less powerful group usually knows the powerful one much better than vice versa—blacks have had to understand whites in order to survive, women have had to know men—yet the powerful group can afford to regard the less powerful one as a mystery. Indeed, the idea of differentness and the Mysterious Other may be necessary justifications for the power imbalance and the lack of empathy it requires.

One result is that, even when the powerful group *wants* to listen, the other may despair of talking: it's just too much trouble to explain. Recognizing this unequal knowledge encourages women to talk about themselves to men, at least to match the time they spend talking about themselves. After all, they cannot read our minds.

On issues of style, role reversals are enlightening. For instance, ask a man who is critical of "aggressive" women to try to argue a serious political point while speaking "like a lady." A woman candidate might also ask critics to write a speech in the style they think she should use. Responding in kind can create a quick reversal. There's a certain satisfaction to saying, in the middle of a man's impassioned speech: "I suppose you have a point to make, but you're not expressing it well. Now, if you just used more personal examples. If you changed your language, your timing, and perhaps your suit. . . ."

Finally, if all talk fails, try putting the same message in writing. The point is to get your message across, whether or not the man in question can separate it from the medium.

## III

*Women's higher-pitched voices and men's lower ones are the result of physiology. Because deep voices are more pleasant and authoritative, women speakers will always have a problem. Besides, female facial expressions and gestures aren't as forceful . . . and so on.* It's true that tone of voice is partly created by throat construction and the resonance of bones. Though there is a big area of male-female overlap in voice tone, as well as in size, strength, and other physical attributes, we assume that all men will have a much deeper pitch than all women.

In fact, however, no one knows exactly how much of our speaking voices are imitative and culturally produced. Studies of young boys before puberty show that their vocal tones may deepen *even before physiological changes can account for it.* They are imitating the way the males around them speak. Dale Spender cites a study of males who were not mute, but who were born deaf and thus unable to imitate sound. Some of them never went through an adolescent voice change at all.

Whatever the mix of physiological and cultural factors, however, the important point is that the *acceptance* of vocal tone is definitely cultural and therefore subject to change.

In Japan, for instance, a woman's traditionally high-pitched, soft speaking voice is considered a very important sexual attribute. (When asked in a public-opinion poll what attribute they found most attractive in women, the majority of Japanese men said "voice.") Though trained to speak in upper registers, Japanese women, like many of their sisters around the world, often speak in lower tones when men are not present. They may even change their language as well. (A reporter's tapes of Japanese schoolgirls talking among themselves caused a scandal. They were using masculine word endings and verbs in a country where the language is divided into formally masculine and feminine forms.) Thus, Japanese men may find a high voice attractive not for itself but for its tribute to a traditional subservience.

Some American women also cultivate a high, childish, or whispery voice à la Marilyn Monroe. We may sense that a women is talking to a man on the other end of the phone, or a man to a woman, because she lightens her normal tone and he deepens his.

A childlike or "feminine" vocal style becomes a drawback, however, when women try for any adult or powerful role. Female reporters were kept out of television and radio for years by the argument that their voices were too high, grating, or nonauthoritative to speak the news credibly. Even now, women's voices may be thought more suitable for human interest and "soft news," while men still announce "hard news." In the early days of television, women were allowed to do the weather reports—very sexily. When meteorology and weather maps became the vogue, however, most stations switched to men. Even now, 85 percent of all voice-overs on television ads, including those for women's products, are done by men. Even on floor wax and detergents, men are likely to be the voices of expertise and authority.

In the long run, however, men may suffer more from cultural restrictions on tone of voice than women do. Linguist Ruth Brend's study of male and female intonation patterns in the United States, for instance, disclosed four contrasting levels used by women in normal speech, but only three levels used by men. This isn't a result of physiology: men also have at least four levels available to them, but they rarely use the highest one. Thus, women may speak publicly in both high and low tones with some degree of social acceptability, but men must use their lower tones only. It's okay to flatter the ruling class with imitation, just as it's okay for women to wear pants or for blacks to speak and dress like Establishment whites, but it's less okay for men to wear feminine clothes, for whites to adopt black speech and street style, or for men to imitate or sound like women. (Such upper-class exceptions as the female-impersonating shows put on by the Hasty Pudding Club at Harvard or by the very rich men of the Bohemian Grove in California seem to indicate that even ridicule of women requires security. It's much less likely to happen at the working-class level of bowling clubs and bars.)

As the price of "masculinity," men as a group are losing variety in their speech and an ability to express a full range of emotions. The higher proportion of masculine monotones is also a penalty to the public ear.

In the same way, physical expressiveness may be viewed as "feminine." Women can be vivacious. We are allowed more varieties of facial expression and gestures. Men must be rocklike. Certainly, some emotive and expressive men are being imprisoned by that belief.

The down side is that women's greater range of expression is also used to ridicule females as emotionally unstable. That sad point is made by Nancy Henley in *Body Politics: Power, Sex, and Nonverbal Communication.* "Women's facial expressivity," she explains, "has been allowed a wider range than men's, encompassing within the sex stereotype not only pleasant expressions, but negative ones like crying." Since males are encouraged to leave crying and other emotional expression in their childhoods, females who retain this human ability are often compared to children.

Nonetheless, women's wider range also allows us to recognize more physical expression when we see it. Henley refers to a study showing that women of all races and black men usually do better than white men at identifying nonverbal emotional clues. We're both less imprisoned by the rocklike mask of being in control, and more needful of the survival skill of paying attention.

In short, women need to affirm and expand expressiveness, but men are also missing some major ways of signalling the world and getting signals back.

*You can't change vocal cords (theirs or ours), but you can make sure they're being well used.* Tape-record women talking together, then record the same people talking to men. It's a good way to find out whether we're sending out geishalike tonal clues. Some women are neglecting our lower range. Others, especially when trying to be taken seriously, are overcompensating for supposed emotionalism by narrowing to a "reasonable" monotone. Men may also change under pressure of taped evidence: for instance, the contrast between their dullness when talking with men and their expressiveness when talking to children. Many actors, female and male, are living testimonials to how much and how quickly—with effort, exercise, and freedom—a vocal range can change.

Most important, remember that there is nothing *wrong* with women's voices, and no subject or emotion they cannot convey. This is especially important for women who are lonely tokens. The first women in law and business schools, the board room, or the assembly line, often report that the sound of their own voices comes as a shock—a major barrier to reciting in class, speaking up on policy, or arguing in union meetings. It may take a while for words said in a female voice to be taken seriously, but a head-turning response to the unusual sound is also a tribute to its owner as a courageous pioneer.

The advent of video recorders is a major breakthrough in understanding and changing our nonverbal expressions. Watching the incontrovertible evidence of how we come across to others can be more useful than years of psychiatry. Many men and boys could also benefit from such expressiveness exercises as a game of charades, or communicating with children. Women and girls can free body movements through sports, a conscious effort to take up more space when sitting or standing, and using body language we may not use only when relaxed with other women. Many of us could benefit from watching female impersonators and learning the many ways in which we have been trained to be female impersonators, too.

The point is not that one gender's cultural style is superior to the other's. The current "feminine" style of communicating may be better suited to, say, the performing arts, medical diagnosis, and conflict resolution. It has perfected emotional expressiveness, careful listening, and a way of leaving an adversary with dignity intact. The current "masculine" style may be better suited to, say, procedural instruction, surgical teams and other situations requiring hierarchical command, and job interviews. It has perfected linear and abstract thinking, quick commands, and a willingness to speak well of oneself or present views with assertiveness. But we will never achieve this full human circle of expression if women imitate the male "adult" style. We have to teach as well as learn.

A feminist assault on the politics of talking, and listening, is a radical act. It's a way of transforming the cultural vessel in which both instant communication and long-term anthropological change are carried. Unlike the written word, or visual imagery, or any form of communication divorced from our presence, talking and listening won't allow us to hide. There is no neutral page, image, sound, or even a genderless name to protect us. We are demanding to be accepted and understood by all the senses and for our whole selves.

That's precisely what makes the change so difficult. And so crucial.

---

## REFLECTING ON MEANING

1. Steinem presents several prevalent social myths about women and conversation. What are these myths? Are they still prevalent today?

2. Steinem's summary of research into the "politics of conversation" addresses several important topics: the roles women and men play in mixed-gender conversation, the different ways men and women are perceived in mixed-gender conversation, and the physiology of speech in relation to social values. According to Steinem, what does research suggest about these issues?

3. Steinem also cites research that suggests men and women have very different conversational styles. What differences does she point out? What is the "masculine" style? What is the "feminine" style?

## EXPLORING RHETORICAL STRATEGIES

1. Steinem begins her essay with the words "Once upon a time (that is, just a few years ago) . . ." What is the significance of this opening? What does this allusion suggest about her perspective on her topic?
2. The essay seems to have multiple purposes. What evidence can you find to delineate these various purposes? Does Steinem successfully fulfill all of them? In what ways?
3. What evidence of Steinem's intended audience can you find? How might women and men respond differently to her essay? How might Steinem need to change her discussion to address an audience of the opposite gender?

## TAKING A STAND
### QUESTIONS FOR CONSIDERATION

1. The authors represented in this part explore the nature and effect of sexism in the English language. Do you agree that English is inherently sexist? Why or why not? Summarize the views of at least two authors on the nature of sexism in the English language, and explain why you agree or disagree.

2. Although Miller and Swift, Nilsen, and Lakoff suggest that sexism in the English language has profound consequences for society, McFadden seems less convinced of the seriousness of this issue. What effect does linguistic sexism have on society? What problems does it create for women? In what ways, if any, does it contribute to their oppression? Survey the viewpoints of at least two authors, including McFadden, and argue that sexism in the English language is or is not a serious problem.

3. A key point on which the debate about sexism in language turns is whether language simply reflects cultural assumptions about gender or whether it actually creates and perpetuates sexist attitudes. Drawing on the essays by Miller and Swift, Nilsen, McFadden, and Lakoff, determine your stand on this issue. Does sexism in English mirror or create sexist attitudes in society? What implications for change does your position suggest? Why?

4. To support their contention that English is indeed a sexist language, Miller and Swift, Nilsen, and Lakoff explore words, their origins, and their changing definitions. How does vocabulary reveal such cultural assumptions? Isn't a dictionary supposed to be unbiased, even objective? What do these authors' analyses of vocabulary suggest about the nature of reality?

5. What are some of the ways in which women and men have attempted to neutralize sexist bias in the English language? Summarize and evaluate the efforts and proposals described by at least two authors in this part, and present your own plan for change. In what ways is your plan similar to theirs? How does your plan differ? What makes your plan more effective?

6. Miller and Swift argue that naming customs reflect and reinforce sexist attitudes; McFadden, however, mocks the hyphenated surname, one way in which women have attempted to overcome bias. Is the hyphenated surname a trivial solution to this problem? What would you do to change naming customs to make them less biased? Consider the undermining of women's identity

that Miller and Swift describe, and propose a solution that would make naming customs gender-neutral.

7. Both Steinem and Lakoff are less concerned with the English language than with the ways in which women talk with others. What do you think about their conclusions on the ways women interact with others? Do you agree with Lakoff's observation that women are more hesitant in speaking than men? Do you agree with Steinem's statement that men interrupt women in conversation more often than the reverse? To what extent is conversation influenced by social attitudes about gender? In shaping your response, consider your own personal experiences and observations, and closely observe men and women talking. What patterns do you notice?

# Part IV

## Gender and Social Institutions

As people become increasingly sensitive to the powerful role gender plays in almost every aspect of life, more and more attention is being focused on its effect on such cherished social institutions as the educational system, the home, and the family. In fact, these institutions serve as barometers of how much influence changing gender roles have had in society. The essays in Part IV address each of these institutions.

The authors of the first group of essays examine the influence of sexism on the educational experiences of women. Matina Horner's research demonstrates that women confront a "psychological barrier" to achievement in that they often fear both failure *and* success. Adrienne Rich suggests that women will not receive a true education until substantive changes are made in the educational system. And M. Carey Thomas provides a historical perspective in describing how female students at the turn of the century sometimes experienced debilitating anxiety, insecurity, and diffidence.

In "The Home," the second group of essays, several writers give us a glimpse of gender and home life. Judy Syfers defines the traditional role of wife as that of a servant whose main responsibility is to support her husband. Simone de Beauvoir analyzes the nature of housework and argues that it serves to reinforce women's subordinate status. Attempting to reverse these discriminatory gender roles, Rich Greenberg traded his job for "house fatherhood" and recounts both the pleasures and the frustrations of his new role.

The subject of the final group of essays is how changing gender roles are transforming the structure of the family and creating new dilemmas, especially for women. Deborah Fallows probes the complexity of a major life choice that many women must make: whether to pursue a career or to become a "full-time mother." Whereas Fallows herself opted for motherhood, Nancy Friday challenges the very notion of "mother love," arguing that it is a socially constructed illusion. Betty Rollin elaborates on this viewpoint, asserting that mothering (just like fathering) is not a biologically predestined instinct; rather, it is an impulse created by social conditioning. Finally, Lindsy Van Gelder describes how the social and legal institution of marriage discriminates against gay couples, leading often to great emotional frustration and bitterness.

Together, these essays suggest some of the ways in which gender operates within social institutions, and they illustrate that as our conceptions of gender change, so too do those institutions. Although the changes have been largely positive, the essays in this section demonstrate that major, substantive change is needed in our basic attitudes toward gender before institutions such as the family and the educational system will provide women and men with equally beneficial experiences.

# Chapter 8

# THE EDUCATIONAL SYSTEM

## Fail: Bright Woman

MATINA HORNER

*Achievement motivation is an area that researchers have explored extensively, but as Matina Horner points out, these studies have been largely based on men. Setting out to rectify this omission, Horner conducted a study to "explore the basis for sex differences in achievement motivation." The results of her research are startling: afraid of failure* and *success, women face a "psychological barrier" to achievement.*

Consider Phil, a bright young college sophomore. He has always done well in school, he is in the honors program, he has wanted to be a doctor as long as he can remember. We ask him to tell us a story based on one clue: *"After first-term finals, John finds himself at the top of his medical school class."* Phil writes:

> John is a conscientious young man who worked hard. He is pleased with himself. John has always wanted to go into medicine and is very dedicated. . . . John continues working hard and eventually graduates at the top of his class.

Now consider Monica, another honors student. She too has always done well and she too has visions of a flourishing career. We give her the same clue, but with "Anne" as the successful student—*after first-term finals, Anne finds herself at the top of her medical school class.* Instead of identifying with Anne's triumph, Monica tells a bizarre tale:

> Anne starts proclaiming her surprise and joy. Her fellow classmates are so disgusted with her behavior that they jump on her in a body and beat her. She is maimed for life.

Next we ask Monica and Phil to work on a series of achievement tests by themselves. Monica scores higher than Phil. Finally we get them together, competing against each other on the same kind of tests. Phil performs magnificently, but Monica dissolves into a bundle of nerves.

The glaring contrast between the two stories and the dramatic changes in performance in competitive situations illustrate important differences between men and women in reacting to achievement.

In 1953, David McClelland, John Atkinson and colleagues published the first major work on the "achievement motive." Through the use of the Thematic Apperception Test (TAT), they were able to isolate the psychological characteristic of a *need to achieve.* This seemed to be an internalized standard of excellence, motivating the individual to do well in any achievement-oriented situation involving intelligence and leadership ability. Subsequent investigators studied innumerable facets of achievement motivation: how it is instilled in children, how it is expressed, how it relates to social class, even how it is connected to the rise and fall of civilizations. The result of all this research is an impressive and a theoretically consistent body of data about the achievement motive—in men.

Women, however, are conspicuously absent from almost all of the studies. In the few cases where the ladies were included, the results were contradictory or confusing. So women were eventually left out altogether. The predominantly male researchers apparently decided, as Freud had before them, that the only way to understand woman was to turn to the poets. Atkinson's 1958 book, *Motives in Fantasy, Action and Society,* is an 800-page compilation of all of the theories and facts on achievement motivation in men. Women got a footnote, reflecting the state of the science.

To help remedy this lopsided state of affairs, I undertook to explore the basis for sex differences in achievement motivation. But where to begin?

My first clue came from the one consistent finding on the women: they get higher test-anxiety scores than do the men. Eleanor Maccoby has suggested that the girl who is motivated to achieve is defying conventions of what girls "should" do. As a result, the intellectual woman pays a price in anxiety. Margaret Mead concurs, noting that intense intellectual striving can be viewed as "competitively aggressive behavior." And of course Freud thought that the whole essence of femininity lay in repressing aggressiveness (and hence intellectuality).

Thus consciously or unconsciously the girl equates intellectual achievement with loss of femininity. A bright woman is caught in a double bind. In testing and other achievement-oriented situations she worries not only about failure, but also about success. If she fails, she is not living up to her own standards of performance; if she succeeds, she is not living up to societal expectations about the female role. Men in our society do not experience this kind of ambivalence, because they are not only permitted but actively encouraged to do well.

For women, then, the desire to achieve is often contaminated by what I call the *motive to avoid success.* I define it as the fear that success in competitive achievement situations will lead to negative consequences, such as unpopularity and loss of femininity. This motive, like the achievement motive itself, is a stable disposition within the person, acquired early in life along with other sex-role standards. When fear of success conflicts with a desire to be successful, the result is an inhibition of achievement motivation.

I began my study with several hypotheses about the motive to avoid success:

1. Of course, it would be far more characteristic of women than of men.
2. It would be more characteristic of women who are capable of success and who are career-oriented than of women not so motivated. Women who are not seeking success should not, after all, be threatened by it.
3. I anticipated that the anxiety over success would be greater in competitive situations (when one's intellectual performance is evaluated against someone else's) than in noncompetitive ones (when one works alone). The aggressive, masculine aspects of achievement striving are certainly more pronounced in competitive settings, particularly when the opponent is male. Women's anxiety should therefore be greatest when they compete with men.

I administered the standard TAT achievement motivation measures to a sample of 90 girls and 88 boys, all undergraduates at the University of Michigan. In addition, I asked each to tell a story based on the clue described before: *After first-term finals, John (Anne) finds himself (herself) at the top of his (her) medical school class.* The girls wrote about Anne, the boys about John.

Their stories were scored for "motive to avoid success" if they expressed any negative imagery that reflected concern about doing well. Generally, such imagery fell into three categories:

1. The most frequent Anne story reflected strong fears of social rejection as a result of success. The girls in this group showed anxiety about becoming unpopular, unmarriageable and lonely.

> Anne is an acne-faced bookworm. She runs to the bulletin board and finds she's at the top. As usual she smarts off. A chorus of groans is the rest of the class's reply. . . . She studies 12 hours a day, and lives at home to save money. "Well it certainly paid off. All the Friday and Saturday nights without dates, fun—I'll be the best woman doctor alive." And yet a twinge of sadness comes thru—she wonders what she really has. . . .
>
> Although Anne is happy with her success she fears what will happen to her social life. The male med. students don't seem to think very highly of a female who has beaten them in their field. . . . She will be a proud and successful but alas a very *lonely* doctor.
>
> Anne doesn't want to be number one in her class . . . she feels she shouldn't rank so high because of social reasons. She drops down to ninth in the class and then marries the boy who graduates number one.
>
> Anne is pretty darn proud of herself, but everyone hates and envies her.

2. Girls in the second category were less concerned with issues of social approval or disapproval; they were more worried about definitions of womanhood. Their stories expressed guilt and despair over success, and doubts about their femininity or normality.

> Unfortunately Anne no longer feels so certain that she really wants to be a doctor. She is worried about herself and wonders if perhaps she isn't normal. . . . Anne decides not to continue with her medical work but to take courses that have a deeper personal meaning for her.
>
> Anne feels guilty. . . . She will finally have a nervous breakdown and quit medical school and marry a successful young doctor.

> Anne is pleased. She had worked extraordinarily hard and her grades showed it. "It is not enough," Anne thinks. "I am not happy." She didn't even want to be a doctor. She is not sure what she wants. Anne says to hell with the whole business and goes into social work—not hardly as glamorous, prestigious or lucrative; but she is happy.

3. The third group of stories did not even try to confront the ambivalence about doing well. Girls in this category simply denied the possibility that any mere woman could be so successful. Some of them completely changed the content of the clue, or distorted it, or refused to believe it, or absolved Anne of responsibility for her success. These stories were remarkable for their psychological ingenuity:

> Anne is a *code name* for a nonexistent person created by a group of med. students. They take turns writing exams for Anne.
>
> Anne is really happy she's on top, though *Tom is higher than she*—though that's as it should be. . . . Anne doesn't mind Tom winning.
>
> Anne is talking to her counselor. Counselor says she will make a fine *nurse.*
>
> It was *luck* that Anne came out on top because she didn't want to go to medical school anyway.

Fifty-nine girls—over 65 percent—told stories that fell into one or another of the above categories. But only eight boys, fewer than 10 percent, showed evidence of the motive to avoid success. (These differences are significant at better than the .0005 level.) In fact, sometimes I think that most of the young men in the sample were incipient Horatio Algers. They expressed unequivocal delight at John's success (clearly John had worked hard for it), and projected a grand and glorious future for him. There was none of the hostility, bitterness and ambivalence that the girls felt for Anne. In short, the differences between male and female stories based on essentially the same clue were enormous.

Two of the stories are particularly revealing examples of this male-female contrast. The girls insisted that Anne give up her career for marriage:

> Anne has a boyfriend, Carl, in the same class and they are quite serious. . . . She wants him to be scholastically higher

> than she is. Anne will deliberately lower her academic standing the next term, while she does all she subtly can to help Carl. His grades come up and Anne soon drops out of medical school. They marry and he goes on in school while she raises their family.

But of course the boys would ask John to do no such thing:

> John has worked very hard and his long hours of study have paid off. . . . He is thinking about his girl, Cheri, whom he will marry at the end of med. school. He realizes he can give her all the things she desires after he becomes established. He will go on in med. school and be successful in the long run.

Success inhibits social life for the girls; it enhances social life for the boys.

Earlier I suggested that the motive to avoid success is especially aroused in competitive situations. In the second part of this study I wanted to see whether the aggressive overtones of competition against men scared the girls away. Would competition raise their anxiety about success and thus lower their performance?

First I put all of the students together in a large competitive group, and gave them a series of achievement tests (verbal and arithmetic). I then assigned them randomly to one of three other experimental conditions. One-third worked on a similar set of tests, each in competition with a member of the same sex. One-third competed against a member of the opposite sex. The last third worked by themselves, a non-competitive condition.

Ability is an important factor in achievement motivation research. If you want to compare two persons on the strength of their *motivation* to succeed, how do you know that any differences in performance are not due to initial differences in *ability* to succeed? One way of avoiding this problem is to use each subject as his own control; that is, the performance of an individual working alone can be compared with his score in competition. Ability thus remains constant; any change in score must be due to motivational factors. This control over ability was, of course, possible only for the last third of my subjects: the 30 girls and 30 boys who had worked alone *and* in the large group competition. I decided to look at their scores first.

Performance changed dramatically over the two situations. A large number of men did far better when they were in competition than when they worked alone. For the women the reverse was true. Fewer than one-third of the women, but more than two-thirds of the men, got significantly higher scores in competition.

When we looked at just the girls in terms of the motive to avoid success, the comparisons were even more striking. As predicted, the students who felt ambivalent or anxious about doing well turned in their best scores when they worked by themselves. Seventy-seven percent of the girls who feared success did better alone than in competition. Women who were low on the motive, however, behaved more like the men: 93 percent of them got higher scores in competition. (Results significant at the .005.)

**Female Fear of Success and Performance**

| | *Perform Better Working Alone* | *Perform Better in Competition* |
|---|---|---|
| High fear of success | 13 | 4 |
| Low fear of success | 1 | 12 |

As a final test of motivational differences, I asked the students to indicate on a scale from 1 to 100 "How important was it for you to do well in this situation?" The high-fear-of-success girls said that it was much more important for them to do well when they worked alone than when they worked in either kind of competition. For the low-fear girls, such differences were not statistically significant. Their test scores were higher in competition, as we saw, and they thought that it was important to succeed no matter what the setting. And in all experimental conditions—working alone, or in competition against males or females—high-fear women consistently lagged behind their fearless comrades on the importance of doing well.

The findings suggest that most women will fully explore their intellectual potential only when they do not need to compete—and least of all when they are competing with men. This was most true of women with a strong anxiety about success. Unfortunately, these are often the same women who could be very successful if they were free from that anxiety. The girls in my sample who feared success also tended to have high intellectual ability and histories of academic success. (It is interesting to note that all but two of these girls were majoring in the humanities and in spite of very high grade points aspired to traditional female careers: housewife, mother, nurse, schoolteacher. Girls who did not fear success, however, were aspiring to graduate degrees and careers in such scientific areas as math, physics and chemistry.)

We can see from this small study that achievement motivation in women is much more complex than the same drive in men. Most men do not find many inhibiting forces in their path if they are able and motivated to succeed. As a result, they are not threatened by competition; in fact, surpassing an opponent is a source of pride and enhanced masculinity.

If a woman sets out to do well, however, she bumps into a number of obstacles. She learns that it really isn't ladylike to be too intellectual. She is warned that men will treat her with distrustful tolerance at best, and outright prejudice at worst, if she pursues a career. She learns the truth of Samuel Johnson's comment, "A man is in general better pleased when he has a good dinner upon his table, than when his wife talks Greek." So she doesn't learn Greek, and the motive to avoid success is born.

In recent years many legal and educational barriers to female achievement have been removed; but it is clear that a psychological barrier remains. The motive to avoid success has an all-too-important influence on the intellectual and professional lives of women in our society. But perhaps there is cause for optimism. Monica may have had Anne maimed for life, but a few of the girls forecast a happier future for our medical student. Said one:

> Anne is quite a lady—not only is she tops academically, but she is liked and admired by her fellow students—quite a trick in a man-dominated field. She is brilliant—but she is also a woman. She will continue to be at or near the top. And . . . always a lady.

---

## REFLECTING ON MEANING

1. Horner's study consisted of several distinct tests, each designed to answer a specific question. What questions was she trying to answer? How did she go about answering each one? What did she discover about achievement motivation in women and men?

2. "The findings suggest that most women will fully explore their intellectual potential only when they do not need to compete—and least of all when they are competing with men." What does this statement suggest to you about women and professional success? What does it suggest about education? How might the educational system be made more advantageous for women?

3. "In recent years many legal and educational barriers to female achievement have been removed; but it is clear that a psychological barrier remains." What barrier does Horner refer to? Why does she consider it a psychological barrier? What does this

statement suggest about the nature of gender-based behavior? What does it suggest about the nature of sexism? Why haven't legal and educational advances in the last twenty years resolved the problem of sexism?

## EXPLORING RHETORICAL STRATEGIES

1. Horner begins and ends her essay by citing responses from her experimental study. Why does she open and close in this way? What effect did the disparity between the responses quoted at the beginning of the selection have on you? What effect did the concluding response have on you?
2. Horner's essay originally appeared in 1969 in *Psychology Today*. Based on her essay, what can you surmise about the readers of that magazine? What expectations might they have about reporting on experimental studies? Why do you think Horner described her methodology so extensively?
3. Horner explains why she conducted her study, but why—beyond reporting her conclusions—did she write this essay? What was her purpose? Was she trying to pass on information about her work or to advance a viewpoint? What does her tone reveal about her likely intentions?

# Taking Women Students Seriously

ADRIENNE RICH

*In this essay, originally presented as an address at a meeting on women's education, Adrienne Rich describes the influence that sexism has on the educational experiences of women at the postsecondary level. The essay is an impassioned plea to begin the process of change that must take place before women can truly become educated as women.*

I see my function here today as one of trying to create a context, delineate a background, against which we might talk about women as students and students as women. I would like to speak for a while about this background, and then I hope that we can have, not so much a question period, as a raising of concerns, a sharing of questions for which we as yet may have no answers, an opening of conversations which will go on and on.

When I went to teach at Douglass, a women's college, it was with a particular background which I would like briefly to describe to you. I had graduated from an all-girls' school in the 1940s, where the head and the majority of the faculty were independent, unmarried women. One or two held doctorates, but had been forced by the Depression (and by the fact that they were women) to take secondary school teaching jobs. These women cared a great deal about the life of the mind, and they gave a great deal of time and energy—beyond any limit of teaching hours—to those of us who showed special intellectual interest or ability. We were taken to libraries, art museums, lectures at neighboring colleges, set to work on extra research projects, given extra French or Latin reading. Although we sometimes felt "pushed" by them, we held those women in a kind of respect which even then we dimly perceived was not generally accorded to women in the world at large. They were vital individuals, defined not by their relationships but by their personalities; and although under the pressure of the culture we were all certain we wanted to get married, their lives did not appear empty or dreary to us. In a kind of cognitive dissonance, we knew they were "old maids" and therefore supposed to be bitter and lonely; yet we saw them vigorously involved with life. But despite their existence as alternate models of women, the *content* of the education they gave us in no way prepared us to survive as women in a world organized by and for men.

From that school, I went on to Radcliffe, congratulating myself that now I would have great men as my teachers. From 1947 to 1951, when I graduated, I never saw a single woman on a lecture platform, or in front of a class, except when a woman graduate student gave a paper on a special topic. The "great men" talked of other "great men," of the nature of Man, the history of Mankind, the future of Man; and never again was I to experience, from a teacher, the kind of prodding, the insistence that my best could be even better, that I had known in high school. Women students were simply not taken very seriously. Harvard's message to women was an elite mystification: we were, of course, part of Mankind; we were special, achieving women, or we would not have been there; but of course our real goal was to marry—if possible, a Harvard graduate.

In the late sixties, I began teaching at the City College of New York—a crowded, public, urban, multiracial institution as far removed from Harvard as possible. I went there to teach writing in the SEEK [Search for Education, Elevation, and Knowledge] Program, which predated Open Admissions and which was then a kind of model for programs designed to open up higher education to poor, black, and Third World students. Although during the next few years we were to see the original concept of SEEK diluted, then violently attacked and betrayed, it was for a short time an extraordinary and intense teaching and learning environment. The characteristics of this environment were a deep commitment on the part of teachers to the minds of their students; a constant, active effort to create or discover the conditions for learning, and to educate ourselves to meet the needs of the new college population; a philosophical attitude based on open discussion of racism, oppression, and the politics of literature and language; and a belief that learning in the classroom could not be isolated from the student's experience as a member of an urban minority group in white America. Here are some of the kinds of questions we, as teachers of writing, found ourselves asking:

1. What has been the student's experience of education in the inadequate, often abusively racist public school system, which rewards passivity and treats a questioning attitude or independent mind as a behavior problem? What has been her or his experience in a society that consistently undermines the selfhood of

the poor and the nonwhite? How can such a student gain that sense of self which is necessary for active participation in education? What does all this mean for us as teachers?
2. How do we go about teaching a canon of literature which has consistently excluded or depreciated nonwhite experience?
3. How can we connect the process of learning to write well with the student's own reality, and not simply teach her/him how to write acceptable lies in standard English?

When I went to teach at Douglass College in 1976, and in teaching women's writing workshops elsewhere, I came to perceive stunning parallels to the questions I had first encountered in teaching the so-called disadvantaged students at City. But in this instance, and against the specific background of the women's movement, the questions framed themselves like this:

1. What has been the student's experience of education in schools which reward female passivity, indoctrinate girls and boys in stereotypic sex roles, and do not take the female mind seriously? How does a woman gain a sense of her *self* in a system—in this case, patriarchal capitalism—which devalues work done by women, denies the importance and uniqueness of female experience, and is physically violent toward women? What does this mean for a woman teacher?
2. How do we, as women, teach women students a canon of literature which has consistently excluded or depreciated female experience, and which often expresses hostility to women and validates violence against us?
3. How can we teach women to move beyond the desire for male approval and getting "good grades" and seek and write their own truths that the culture has distorted or made taboo? (For women, of course, language itself is exclusive: I want to say more about this further on.)

In teaching women, we have two choices: to lend our weight to the forces that indoctrinate women to passivity, self-depreciation, and a sense of powerlessness, in which case the issue of "taking women students seriously" is a moot one; or to consider what we have to work against, as well as with, in ourselves, in our students, in the content of the curriculum, in the structure of the institution, in the society at large. And this means, first of all, taking ourselves seriously: Recognizing that central responsibility of a woman to herself, without which we remain always the Other, the defined, the object, the victim; believing that there is a unique quality of validation, affirmation, challenge, support, that one woman can offer another. Believing in the value and significance of women's experience, traditions, perceptions. Thinking of ourselves seriously, not as one of the boys, not as neuters, or androgynes, but *as women.*

Suppose we were to ask ourselves, simply: What does a woman need to know? Does she not, as a self-conscious, self-defining human being, need a knowledge of her own history, her much-politicized biology, an awareness of the creative work of women of the past, the skills and crafts and techniques and powers exercised by women in different times and cultures, a knowledge of women's rebellions and organized movements against our oppression and how they have been routed or diminished? Without such knowledge women live and have lived without context, vulnerable to the projections of male fantasy, male prescriptions for us, estranged from our own experience because our education has not reflected or echoed it. I would suggest that not biology, but ignorance of our selves, has been the key to our powerlessness.

But the university curriculum, the high-school curriculum, do not provide this kind of knowledge for women, the knowledge of Womankind, whose experience has been so profoundly different from that of Mankind. Only in the precariously budgeted, much-condescended-to area of women's studies is such knowledge available to women students. Only there can they learn about the lives and work of women other than the few select women who are included in the "mainstream" texts, usually misrepresented even when they do appear. Some students, at some institutions, manage to take a majority of courses in women's studies, but the message from on high is that this is self-indulgence, soft-core education: the "real" learning is the study of Mankind.

If there is any misleading concept, it is that of "coeducation": that because women and men are sitting in the same classrooms, hearing the same lectures, reading the same books, performing the same laboratory experiments, they are receiving an equal education. They are not, first because the content of education itself validates men even as it invalidates women. Its very message is that men have been the shapers and thinkers of the world, and that this is only natural. The bias of higher education, including the so-called sciences, is white and male, racist and sexist; and this bias is expressed in both subtle and blatant ways. I have mentioned already the exclusiveness of grammar itself: "The student should test himself on the above questions"; "The poet is representative. He stands among partial men for the complete man." Despite a few halfhearted departures from custom, what the linguist Wendy Martyna has named "He-Man" grammar prevails throughout the culture. The efforts of feminists to reveal the profound ontological implications of sexist grammar are routinely ridiculed by academicians and journalists, including the professedly liberal *Times* columnist Tom Wicker and the professed humanist Jacques Barzun. Sexist grammar burns into the brains of little girls and young women a message that the male is the norm, the standard, the central figure beside which we are the deviants, the marginal, the dependent variables. It lays the foundation for androcentric thinking, and leaves men safe in their solipsistic tunnel-vision.

Women and men do not receive an equal education because outside the classroom women are perceived not as sovereign beings but as prey. The growing incidence of rape on and off the campus may or may not be fed by the proliferations of pornographic magazines and X-rated films available to young males in fraternities and student unions; but it is certainly occurring in a context of widespread images of sexual violence against women, on billboards and in so-called high art. More subtle, more daily than rape is the verbal abuse experienced by the woman student on many campuses—Rutgers for example—where, traversing a street lined with fraternity houses, she must run a gauntlet of male commentary and verbal assault. The undermining of self, of a woman's sense of her right to occupy space and walk freely in the world, is deeply relevant to education. The capacity to think independently, to take intellectual risks, to assert ourselves mentally, is inseparable from our physical way of being in the world, our feelings of personal integrity. If it is dangerous for me to walk home late of an evening from the library, *because I am a woman and can be raped,* how self-possessed, how exuberant can I feel as I sit working in that library? How much of my working energy is drained by the subliminal knowledge that, as a woman, I test my physical right to exist each time I go out alone? Of this knowledge, Susan Griffin has written:

> . . . more than rape itself, the fear of rape permeates our lives. And what does one do from day to day, with *this* experience, which says, without words and directly to the heart, *your existence, your experience, may end at any moment.* Your experience may end, and the best defense against this is not to be, to deny being in the body, as a self, to . . . avert your gaze, make yourself, as a presence in the world, less felt.

Finally, rape of the mind. Women students are more and more often now reporting sexual overtures by male professors—one part of our overall growing consciousness of sexual harassment in the workplace. At Yale a legal suit has been brought against the university by a group of women demanding an explicit policy against sexual advances toward female students by male professors. Most young women experience a profound mixture of humiliation and intellectual self-doubt over seductive gestures by men who have the power to award grades, open doors to grants and graduate school, or extend special knowledge and training. Even if turned aside, such gestures constitute mental rape, destructive to a woman's ego. They are acts of domination, as despicable as the molestation of the daughter by the father.

But long before entering college the woman student has experienced her alien identity in a world which misnames her, turns her to its own uses, denying her the resources she needs to become self-affirming, self-defined. The nuclear family teaches her that relationships are more important than selfhood or work; that "whether the phone rings for you, and how often," having the right clothes, doing the dishes, take precedence over study or solitude; that too much intelligence or intensity may make her unmarriageable; that marriage and children—service to others—are, finally, the points on which her life will be judged a success or a failure. In high school, the polarization between feminine attractiveness and independent intelligence comes to an absolute. Meanwhile, the culture resounds with messages. During Solar Energy Week in New York I saw young women wearing "ecology" T-shirts with the legend: CLEAN, CHEAP, AND AVAILABLE; a reminder of the 1960s antiwar button which read: CHICKS SAY YES TO MEN WHO SAY NO. Department store windows feature female mannequins in chains, pinned to the wall with legs spread, smiling in positions of torture. Feminists are depicted in the media as "shrill," "strident," "puritanical," or "humorless," and the lesbian choice—the choice of the woman-identified woman—as pathological or sinister. The young woman sitting in the philosophy classroom, the political science lecture, is already gripped by tensions between her nascent sense of self-worth, and the battering force of messages like these.

Look at a classroom: look at the many kinds of women's faces, postures, expressions. Listen to the women's voices. Listen to the silences, the unasked questions, the blanks. Listen to the small, soft voices, often courageously trying to speak up, voices of women taught early that tones of confidence, challenge, anger, or assertiveness, are strident and unfeminine. Listen to the voices of the women and the voices of the men; observe the space men allow themselves, physically and verbally, the male assumption that people will listen, even when the majority of the group is female. Look at the faces of the silent, and of those who speak. Listen to a woman groping for language in which to express what is on her mind, sensing that the terms of academic discourse are not her language, trying to cut down her thought to the dimensions of a discourse not intended for her *(for it is not fitting that a woman speak in public)*; or reading her paper aloud at breakneck speed, throwing her words away, deprecating her own work by a reflex prejudgment: *I do not deserve to take up time and space.*

As women teachers, we can either deny the importance of this context in which women students think, write, read, study, project their own futures; or try to work with it. We can either teach passively, accepting these conditions, or actively, helping our students identify and resist them.

One important thing we can do is *discuss* the context. And this need not happen only in a women's studies course; it can happen anywhere. We can refuse to accept passive, obedient learning and insist upon critical thinking. We can become harder on our women students, giving them the kinds of "cultural prodding" that men receive, but on different terms and in a different style. Most young women need to have their intellectual lives, their work, legitimized against the claims of family, relationships, the old message that a woman is always available for service to others. We need to keep our standards very high, not to accept a woman's preconceived sense of her limitations; we need to be hard to please, while supportive of risk-taking, because self-respect often comes only when exacting standards have been met. At a time when adult literacy is generally low, we need to demand more, not less, of women, both for the sake of their futures as thinking beings, and because historically women have always had to be better than men to do half as well. A romantic sloppiness, an inspired lack of rigor, a self-indulgent incoherence, are symptoms of female self-deprecation. We should help our women students to look very critically at such symptoms, and to understand where they are rooted.

Nor does this mean we should be training women students to "think like men." Men in general think badly: in disjuncture from their personal lives, claiming objectivity where the most irrational passions seethe, losing, as Virginia Woolf observed, their senses in the pursuit of professionalism. It is not easy to think like a woman in a man's world, in the world of the professions; yet the capacity to do that is a strength which we can try to help our students develop. To think like a woman in a man's world means thinking critically, refusing to accept the givens, making connections between facts and ideas which men have left unconnected. It means remembering that every mind resides in a body; remaining accountable to the female bodies in which we live; constantly retesting given hypotheses against lived experience. It means a constant critique of language, for as Wittgenstein (no feminist) observed, "The limits of my language are the limits of my world." And it means that most difficult thing of all: listening and watching in art and literature, in the social sciences, in all the descriptions we are given of the world, for the silences, the absences, the nameless, the unspoken, the encoded—for there we will find the true knowledge of women. And in breaking those silences, naming our selves, uncovering the hidden, making ourselves present, we begin to define a reality which resonates to *us*, which affirms *our* being, which allows the woman teacher and the woman student alike to take ourselves, and each other, seriously: meaning, to begin taking charge of our lives.

---

## REFLECTING ON MEANING

1. According to Rich, what is the message the educational system conveys to women? How do university curricula, the composition of university faculties, and the interaction between faculty members and women students contribute to this message? Do you agree or disagree with Rich's observations? Why? What has been your experience in higher education so far?
2. Why does Rich find "coeducation" such a misleading concept? What does the term imply about the nature of education for women and men? What does it reveal about what matters where men and women are concerned? In what ways does it reinforce the gender-based hierarchy in society?
3. Rich states that "outside the classroom women are perceived not as sovereign beings but as prey." What does she mean? What connection is she making between the fear of rape and women students and their educational pursuits at the university? What does she mean by "rape of the mind"?
4. Why does Rich caution against teaching women to "think like men"? What does she mean when she says women must learn to "think like a woman in a man's world"? What kind of educational goals is she urging? What kinds of changes would her goals bring about in university curricula and classrooms?

## EXPLORING RHETORICAL STRATEGIES

1. Rich's essay contains much evidence of its original form as a public address to a specific audience. What contributes to the "oral" quality of the essay? What evidence can you find of the composition of the original audience? Who are the people Rich addressed at the meeting where she originally delivered this talk?
2. Rich begins her critique of postsecondary education by outlining her own career as a student and a professor. Why does she do this? How does her recounting her background establish her credibility? What does it help her achieve in relation to her audience?
3. Near the end of her essay, Rich asks her audience to visualize a classroom and to listen to the voices there. What is the effect of her repeated injunctions to her audience to "listen"? How do these injunctions provide a foundation for the plea with which she concludes her essay: that her audience begin to "discuss" the problem and work toward "breaking those silences" that place women at a disadvantage in education?

# Educated Woman

## M. CAREY THOMAS

*A former president of Bryn Mawr College, M. Carey Thomas lived from 1857 to 1935. In this excerpt from* The Educated Woman in America, *Thomas depicts the insecurity and anxiety women who wished to go to college once experienced and the conditions that reinforced their negative self-images. From her perspective in the past, she looks forward to a brighter future for women in postsecondary education and the great "social changes which are preparing the way for the coming economic independence of women."*

The passionate desire of women of my generation for higher education was accompanied thruout its course by the awful doubt, felt by women themselves as well as by men, as to whether women as a sex were physically and mentally fit for it. I think I can best make this clear to you if I refer briefly to my own experience. I cannot remember the time when I was not sure that studying and going to college were the things above all others which I wished to do. I was always wondering whether it could be really true, as every one thought, that boys were cleverer than girls. Indeed, I cared so much that I never dared to ask any grown-up person the direct question, not even my father or mother, because I feared to hear the reply. I remember often praying about it, and begging God that if it were true that because I was a girl I could not successfully master Greek and go to college and understand things to kill me at once, as I could not bear to live in such an unjust world. When I was a little older I read the Bible entirely thru with passionate eagerness because I had heard it said that it proved that women were inferior to men. Those were not the days of the higher criticism. I can remember weeping over the account of Adam and Eve because it seemed to me that the curse pronounced on Eve might imperil girls' going to college; and to this day I can never read many parts of the Pauline epistles without feeling again the sinking of the heart with which I used to hurry over the verses referring to women's keeping silence in the churches and asking their husbands at home. I searched not only the Bible, but all other books I could get for light on the woman question.

I read Milton with rage and indignation. Even as a child I knew him for the woman hater he was. The splendor of Shakespeare was obscured to me then by the lack of intellectual power in his greatest women characters. Even now it seems to me that only Isabella in *Measure for Measure* thinks greatly, and weighs her actions greatly, like a Hamlet or a Brutus.

I can well remember one endless scorching summer's day when sitting in a hammock under the trees with a French dictionary, blinded by tears more burning than the July sun, I translated the most indecent book I have ever read, Michelet's famous—were it not now forgotten, I should be able to say infamous—book on woman, *La femme.* I was beside myself with terror lest it might prove true that I myself was so vile and pathological a thing. Between that summer's day in 1874 and a certain day in the autumn in 1904, thirty years had elapsed. Altho during these thirty years I had read in every language every book on women that I could obtain, I had never chanced again upon a book that seemed to me so to degrade me in my womanhood as the seventh and seventeenth chapters on women and women's education, of President Stanley Hall's *Adolescence.* Michelet's sickening sentimentality and horrible over-sexuality seemed to me to breathe again from every psuedo-scientific page. But how vast the difference between then and now in my feelings, and in the feelings of every woman who has had to do with the education of girls! Then I was terror-struck lest I, and every other woman with me, were doomed to live as pathological invalids in a universe merciless to women as a sex. Now we know that it is not we, but the man who believes such things about us, who is himself pathological, blinded by neurotic mists of sex, unable to see that women form one-half of the kindly race of normal, healthy human creatures in the world; that women, like men, are quickened and inspired by the same study of the great traditions of their race, by the same love of learning, the same love of science, the same love of abstract truth; that women, like men, are immeasurably benefited, physically, mentally and morally, and are made vastly better mothers, as men are made vastly better fathers, by subordinating the distracting instincts of sex to the simple human fellowship of similar education and similar intellectual and social ideals.

It was not to be wondered at that we were uncertain in those old days as to the ultimate result of women's education. Before I myself went to college I had never seen but one college woman. I had heard that such a woman was staying at the house of an acquaintance. I went to see her with fear. Even if she had appeared in hoofs and horns I was determined to go to college all the same.

But it was a relief to find this Vassar graduate tall and handsome and dressed like other women. When, five years later, I went to Leipzig to study after I had been graduated from Cornell, my mother used to write me that my name was never mentioned to her by the women of her acquaintance. I was thought by them to be as much of a disgrace to my family as if I had eloped with the coachman. Now, women who have been to college are as plentiful as blackberries on summer hedges. Even my native city of Baltimore is full of them, and women who have in addition studied in Germany are regarded with becoming deference by the very Baltimore women who disapproved of me.

During the quarter of the century of the existence of the Association of Collegiate Alumnae two generations of college women have reached mature life, and the older generation is now just passing off the stage. We are therefore better prepared than ever before to give an account of what has been definitely accomplished, and to predict what will be the tendencies of women's college and university education in the future.

The curriculum of our women's colleges has steadily stiffened. Women, both in separate, and in coeducational colleges, seem to prefer the old-fashioned, so-called disciplinary studies. They disregard the so-called accomplishments. I believe that today more women than men are receiving a thoro college education, even altho in most cases they are receiving it sitting side by side with men in the same college lecture rooms.

We are now living in the midst of great and, I believe on the whole beneficent, social changes which are preparing the way for the coming economic independence of women.

In order to prepare for this economic independence, we should expect to see what is now taking place. Colleges for women and college departments of coeducational universities are attended by ever-increasing numbers of women students. In seven of the largest western universities women already outnumber men in the college departments. . . .

Just because women have shown such an aptitude for a true college education and such delight in it, we must be careful to maintain it for them in its integrity. We must see to it that its disciplinary quality is not lowered by the insertion of so-called practical courses which are falsely supposed to prepare for life. Women are rapidly coming to control women's college education. It rests with us to decide whether we shall barter for a mess of pottage the inheritance of the girls of this generation which the girls of my generation agonized to obtain for themselves and for other girls.

## REFLECTING ON MEANING

1. According to Thomas, why did women of her generation suffer such "awful doubt," such insecurity and anxiety about whether they were "physically and mentally fit" for higher education? What was the nature of her own self-doubt? Why wasn't she able to dismiss without a second thought the notion that being a woman made her unfit for such an endeavor?
2. Thomas recalls the "rage and indignation" with which she read the poet Milton, "weeping" over the biblical story of Adam and Eve, and missing the greatness of Shakespeare. She also expresses the terror that various books on women caused her. What exactly did she find so distressing about these works? What caused her to react to them in this way? Why would these works affect the way she perceived herself?
3. How would you describe the optimism Thomas expresses about conditions at the time this selection was written? What is she optimistic about? In what ways is her optimism justified? What does she seem to have reservations about? From the perspective of today, how would you evaluate her forecast for the future of women in higher education?

## EXPLORING RHETORICAL STRATEGIES

1. What is Thomas's purpose in this short excerpt from her book? What is the idea she is trying to express?
2. Thomas's description of her generation's anxiety about higher education is framed in largely subjective terms: her own experiences, feelings, and reactions to very private events. Do you think this strategy strengthens or weakens the picture she paints? Why? Does such subjective experience support her observations about women in general? Why or why not?
3. In these few paragraphs, Thomas manages to look back to the past, to observe the present, and to look forward to the future. How does she integrate all of these perspectives into her essay? How does each perspective provide a foundation for the other?

# Chapter 9

## THE HOME

# I Want a Wife

## JUDY SYFERS

*Judy Syfers examines the family role of the wife in this satirical essay. Both humorous and thought-provoking, her treatment of the subject pivots on a comparison between wives and servants. Syfers concludes that it would be unreasonable for anyone, including women,* not *to want a wife.*

I belong to that classification of people known as wives. I am A Wife. And, not altogether incidentally, I am a mother.

Not too long ago a male friend of mine appeared on the scene fresh from a recent divorce. He had one child, who is, of course, with his ex-wife. He is looking for another wife. As I thought about him while I was ironing one evening, it suddenly occurred to me that I, too, would like to have a wife. Why do I want a wife?

I would like to go back to school so that I can become economically independent, support myself, and, if need be, support those dependent upon me. I want a wife who will work and send me to school. And while I am going to school I want a wife to take care of my children. I want a wife to keep track of the children's doctor and dentist appointments. And to keep track of mine, too. I want a wife to make sure my children eat properly and are kept clean. I want a wife who will wash the children's clothes and keep them mended. I want a wife who is a good nurturant attendant to my children, who arranges for their schooling, makes sure that they have an adequate social life with their peers, takes them to the park, the zoo, etc. I want a wife who takes care of the children when they are sick, a wife who arranges to be around when the children need special care, because, of course, I cannot miss classes at school. My wife must arrange to lose time at work and not lose the job. It may mean a small cut in my wife's income from time to time, but I guess I can tolerate that. Needless to say, my wife will arrange and pay for the care of the children while my wife is working.

I want a wife who will take care of *my* physical needs. I want a wife who will keep my house clean. A wife who will pick up after my children, a wife who will pick up after me. I want a wife who will keep my clothes clean, ironed, mended, replaced when need be, and who will see to it that my personal things are kept in their proper place so that I can find what I need the minute I need it. I want a wife who cooks the meals, a wife who is a *good* cook. I want a wife who will plan the menus, do the necessary grocery shopping, prepare the meals, serve them pleasantly, and then do the cleaning up while I do my studying. I want a wife who will care for me when I am sick and sympathize with my pain and loss of time from school. I want a wife to go along when our family takes a vacation so that someone can continue to care for me and my children when I need a rest and change of scene.

I want a wife who will not bother me with rambling complaints about a wife's duties. But I want a wife who will listen to me when I feel the need to explain a rather difficult point I have come across in my course of studies. And I want a wife who will type my papers for me when I have written them.

I want a wife who will take care of the details of my social life. When my wife and I are invited out by my friends, I want a wife who will take care of the babysitting arrangements. When I meet people at school that I like and want to entertain, I want a wife who will have the house clean, will prepare a special meal, serve it to me and my friends and not interrupt when I talk about things that interest me and my friends. I want a wife who will have arranged that the children are fed and ready for bed before my guests arrive so that the children do not bother us. I want a wife who takes care of the needs of my guests so that they feel comfortable, who makes sure that they have an ashtray, that they are passed the hors d'oeuvres, that they are offered a second helping of the food, that their wine glasses are replenished when necessary, that their coffee is served to them as they like it. And I want a wife who knows that sometimes I need a night out by myself.

I want a wife who is sensitive to my sexual needs, a wife who makes love passionately and eagerly when I feel like it, a wife who makes sure that I am satisfied. And, of course, I want a wife who will not demand sexual attention when I am not in the mood for it. I want a wife who assumes the complete responsibility for birth control, because I do not want more children. I want a wife who will remain sexually faithful to me so that I do not have to clutter up my intellectual life with jealousies. And I want a wife who understands that *my* sexual needs may entail more than strict adherence to monogamy. I must, after all, be able to relate to people as fully as possible.

If, by chance, I find another person more suitable as a wife than the wife I already have, I want the liberty to replace my present wife with another one. Naturally, I will expect a fresh, new life; my wife will take the children and be solely responsible for them so that I am left free.

When I am through with school and have a job, I want my wife to quit working and remain at home so that my wife can more fully and completely take care of a wife's duties.

My God, who *wouldn't* want a wife?

---

## REFLECTING ON MEANING

1. In her first sentence, Syfers establishes wives as a separate class of people who are expected to fulfill certain obligations within the family unit. Are women indeed a separate class of people? To what extent do you find Syfers's delineation of wives reasonable?

2. Syfers is clearly satirizing a male attitude. What is this attitude? How prevalent is it? In what ways, if any, has she depicted it accurately?

3. According to Syfers, what specific jobs do women perform for their husbands? How does she categorize these jobs? Do you agree that women are expected to perform these many tasks? Why or why not?

## EXPLORING RHETORICAL STRATEGIES

1. How would you describe the tone of Syfers's essay? What strategies does she use to achieve her tone? How does her tone contribute to the persona that she constructs? How would you describe this persona?

2. The list of responsibilities that Syfers compiles sounds rather like a job description. What is the cumulative effect of her inventory of responsibilities? In what ways does this listing strategy help her make her point about wives?
3. Syfers makes effective use of rhetorical questions in two places in her essay: near the beginning, when she asks "Why do I want a wife?" and at the end, when she closes the essay with a one-sentence paragraph asking "My God, who *wouldn't* want a wife?" How do these two questions contribute to the overall essay? How do they "frame" the essay?

---

# The Married Woman

## SIMONE DE BEAUVOIR

---

*In this selection the philosopher Simone de Beauvoir examines the role that the home and housework play in the suppression of women. She concludes that for woman, they reinforce a subordinate status and remove from her control the "very meaning of her life."*

Few tasks are more like the torture of Sisyphus than housework, with its endless repetition: the clean becomes soiled, the soiled is made clean, over and over, day after day. The housewife wears herself out marking time, she makes nothing, simply perpetuates the present. She never senses conquest of a positive Good, but rather indefinite struggle against negative Evil. A young pupil writes in her essay: "I shall never have housecleaning day"; she thinks of the future as constant progress toward some unknown summit; but one day, as her mother washes the dishes, it comes over her that both of them will be bound to such rites until death. Eating, sleeping, cleaning—the years no longer rise up toward heaven, they lie spread out ahead, gray and identical. The battle against dust and dirt is never won.

Washing, ironing, sweeping, ferreting out rolls of lint from under wardrobes—all this halting of decay is also the denial of life; for time simultaneously creates and destroys, and only its negative aspect concerns the housekeeper. Hers is the position of the Manichaeist, regarded philosophically. The essence of Manichaeism is not solely to recognize two principles, the one good, the other evil; it is also to hold that the good is attained through the abolition of evil and not by positive action. In this sense Christianity is hardly Manichaeist in spite of the existence of the devil, for one fights the demon best by devoting oneself to God and not by endeavoring to conquer the evil one directly. Any doctrine of transcendence and liberty subordinates the defeat of evil to progress toward the good. But woman is not called upon to build a better world: her domain is fixed and she has only to keep up the never ending struggle against the evil principles that creep into it; in her war against dust, stains, mud, and dirt she is fighting sin, wrestling with Satan.

But it is a sad fate to be required without respite to repel an enemy instead of working toward positive ends, and very often the housekeeper submits to it in a kind of madness that may verge on perversion, a kind of sado-masochism. The maniac housekeeper wages her furious war against dirt, blaming life itself for the rubbish all living growth entails. When any living being enters her house, her eye gleams with a wicked light: "Wipe your feet, don't tear the place apart, leave that alone!" She wishes those of her household would hardly breathe; everything means more thankless work for her. Severe, preoccupied, always on the watch, she loses *joie de vivre,* she becomes overprudent and avaricious. She shuts out the sunlight, for along with that come insects, germs, and dust, and besides, the sun ruins silk hangings and fades upholstery; she scatters naphthalene, which scents the air. She becomes bitter and disagreeable and hostile to all that lives: the end is sometimes murder.

The healthy young woman will hardly be attracted by so gloomy a vice. Such nervousness and spitefulness are more suited to frigid and frustrated women, old maids, deceived wives, and those whom surly and dictatorial husbands condemn to a solitary and empty existence. I knew an old beldame, once gay and coquettish, who got up at five each morning to go over her closets; married to a man who neglected her, and isolated on a lonely estate, with but one child, she took to orderly housekeeping as others take to drink. In this insanity the house becomes so neat and clean that one hardly dares live in it; the woman is so busy she forgets her own existence. A household, in fact, with its meticulous and limitless tasks, permits to woman a sado-masochistic flight from herself as she contends madly with the things around her and with herself in a state of distraction and mental vacancy. And this flight may often have a sexual tinge. It is noteworthy that the rage for cleanliness is highest in Holland, where the women are cold, and in puritanical civilizations, which oppose an ideal of neatness and purity to the joys of the flesh. If the Mediterranean Midi lives in a state of joyous filth, it is not only because water is scarce there: love of the flesh and its animality is conducive to toleration of human odor, dirt, and even vermin.

The preparation of food, getting meals, is work more positive in nature and often more agreeable than cleaning. First of all it means marketing, often the bright spot of the day. And gossip on doorsteps, while peeling vegetables, is a gay relief for solitude; to go for water is a great adventure for half-cloistered Mohammedan women; women in markets and stores talk about domestic affairs, with a common interest, feeling themselves members of a group that—for an instant—is opposed to the group of men as the essential to the inessential. Buying is a profound pleasure, a discovery, almost an invention. As Gide says in his *Journal,* the Mohammedans, not knowing gambling, have in its place the discovery of hidden treasure; that is the poetry and the adventure of mercantile civilizations. The housewife knows little of winning in games, but a solid cabbage, a ripe Camembert, are treasures that must be cleverly won from the unwilling storekeeper; the game is to get the best for the least money; economy means not so much helping the budget as winning the game. She is pleased with her passing triumph as she contemplates her well-filled larder.

Gas and electricity have killed the magic of fire, but in the country many women still know the joy of kindling live flames from inert wood. With her fire going, woman becomes a sorceress; by a simple movement, as in beating eggs, or through the magic of fire, she effects the transmutation of substances: matter becomes food. There is enchantment in these alchemies, there is poetry in making preserves; the housewife has caught duration in the snare of sugar, she has enclosed life in jars. Cooking is revolution and creation; and a woman can find special satisfaction in a successful cake or a flaky pastry, for not everyone can do it: one must have the gift.

Here again the little girl is naturally fond of imitating her elders, making mud pies and the like, and helping roll real dough in the kitchen. But as with other housework, repetition soon spoils these pleasures. The magic of the oven can hardly appeal to Mexican Indian women who spend half their lives preparing tortillas, identical from day to day, from century to century. And it is impossible to go on day after day making a treasure-hunt of the marketing or ecstatically viewing one's highly polished faucets. The male and female writers who lyrically exalt such triumphs are persons who are seldom or never engaged in actual housework. It is tiresome, empty, monotonous, as a career. If, however, the individual who does such work is also a producer, a creative worker, it is as naturally integrated in life as are the organic functions; for this reason housework done by men seems much less dismal; it represents for them merely a negative and inconsequential moment from which they quickly escape. What makes the lot of the wife-servant ungrateful is the division of labor which dooms her completely to the general and the inessential. Dwelling-place and food are useful for life but give it no significance: the immediate goals of the housekeeper are only means, not true ends. She endeavors, naturally, to give some individuality to her work and to make it seem essential. No one else, she thinks, could do her work as well; she has her rites, superstitions, and ways of doing things. But too often her "personal note" is but a vague and meaningless rearrangement of disorder.

Woman wastes a great deal of time and effort in such striving for originality and unique perfection; this gives her task its meticulous, disorganized, and endless character and makes it difficult to estimate the true load of domestic work. Recent studies show that for married women housework averages about thirty hours per week, or three fourths of a working week in employment. This is enormous if done in addition to a paid occupation, little if the woman has nothing else to do. The care of several children will naturally add a good deal to woman's work: a poor mother is often working all the time. Middle-class women who employ help, on the other hand, are almost idle; and they pay for their leisure with ennui. If they lack outside interests, they often multiply and complicate their domestic duties to excess, just to have something to do.

The worst of it all is that this labor does not even tend toward the creation of anything durable. Woman is tempted—and the more so the greater pains she takes—to regard her work as an end in itself. She sighs as she contemplates the perfect cake just out of the oven: "it's a shame to eat it!" It is really too bad to have husband and children tramping with their muddy feet all over her waxed hardwood floors! When things are used they are soiled or destroyed—we have seen how she is tempted to save them from being used; she keeps preserves until they get moldy; she locks up the parlor. But time passes inexorably; provisions attract rats; they become wormy; moths attack blankets and clothing. The world is not a dream carved in stone, it is made of dubious stuff subject to rot; edible material is as equivocal as Dali's fleshy watches: it seems inert, inorganic, but hidden larvae may have changed it into a cadaver. The housewife who loses herself in things becomes dependent, like the things, upon the whole world: linen is scorched, the roast burns, chinaware gets broken; these are absolute disasters, for when things are destroyed, they are gone forever. Permanence and security cannot possibly be obtained through them. The pillage and bombs of war threaten one's wardrobes, one's house.

The products of domestic work, then, must necessarily be consumed; a continual renunciation is required of the woman whose operations are completed only in their destruction. For her to acquiesce without regret, these minor holocausts must at least be reflected in someone's joy or pleasure. But since the housekeeper's labor is expended to maintain the *status quo,* the husband, coming into the house, may notice disorder or negligence, but it seems to him that order and neatness come of their own accord. He has a more positive interest in a good meal. The cook's moment of triumph arrives when she puts a successful dish on the table: husband and children receive it with warm approval, not only in words, but by consuming it gleefully. The culinary alchemy then pursues its course, food becomes chyle and blood.

Thus, to maintain living bodies is of more concrete, vital interest than to keep a fine floor in proper condition; the cook's effort is evidently transcended toward the future. If, however, it is better to share in another's free transcendence than to lose oneself in things, it is not less dangerous. The validity of the cook's work is to be found only in the mouths of those around her table; she needs their approbation, demands that they appreciate her dishes and call for second helpings; she is upset if they are not hungry, to the point that one wonders whether the fried potatoes are for her husband or her husband for the fried potatoes. This ambiguity is evident in the general attitude of the housekeeping wife: she takes care of the house for her husband; but she also wants him to spend all he earns for furnishings and an electric refrigerator. She desires to make him happy; but she approves of his activities only in so far as they fall within the frame of happiness she has set up.

There have been times when these claims have in general found satisfaction: times when such felicity was also man's ideal, when he was attached above all to his home, to his family, and when even the children chose to be characterized by their parents, their traditions, and their past. At such times she who ruled the home, who presided at the dinner table, was recognized as supreme; and she still plays this resplendent role among certain landed proprietors and wealthy peasants who here and there perpetuate the patriarchal civilization.

But on the whole marriage is today a surviving relic of dead ways of life, and the situation of the wife is more ungrateful than formerly, because she still has the same duties but they no longer confer the same rights, privileges, and honors. Man marries today to obtain an anchorage in immanence, but not to be himself confined therein; he wants to have hearth and home while being free to escape therefrom; he settles down but often remains a vagabond at heart; he is not contemptuous of domestic felicity, but he does not make of it an end in itself; repetition bores him; he seeks after novelty, risk, opposition to overcome, companions and friends who take him away from solitude *à deux*. The children, even more than their father, want to escape beyond family limits: life for them lies elsewhere, it is before them; the child always seeks what is different. Woman tries to set up a universe of permanence and continuity; husband and children wish to transcend the situation she creates, which for them is only a given environment. This is why, even if she is loath to admit the precarious nature of the activities to which her whole life is devoted, she is nevertheless led to impose her services by force: she changes from mother and housewife into harsh stepmother and shrew.

Thus woman's work within the home gives her no autonomy; it is not directly useful to society, it does not open out on the future, it produces nothing. It takes on meaning and dignity only as it is linked with existent beings who reach out beyond themselves, transcend themselves, toward society in production and action. That is, far from freeing the matron, her occupation makes her dependent upon husband and children; she is justified through them; but in their lives she is only an inessential intermediary. That "obedience" is legally no longer one of her duties in no way changes her situation; for this depends not on the will of the couple but on the very structure of the conjugal group. Woman is not allowed to *do* something positive in her work and in consequence win recognition as a complete person. However respected she may be, she is subordinate, secondary, parasitic. The heavy curse that weighs upon her consists in this: the very meaning of her life is not in her hands. That is why the successes and the failures of her conjugal life are much more gravely important for her than for her husband; he is first a citizen, a producer, secondly a husband; she is before all, and often exclusively, a wife; her work does not take her out of her situation; it is from the latter, on the contrary, that her work takes its value, high or low. Loving, generously devoted, she will perform her tasks joyously; but they will seem to her mere dull drudgery if she performs them with resentment. In her destiny they will never play more than an inessential role; they will not be a help in the ups and downs of conjugal life. We must go on to see, then, how woman's condition is concretely experienced in life—this condition which is characterized essentially by the "service" of the bed and the "service" of the housekeeping and in which woman finds her place of dignity only in accepting her vassalage.

---

## REFLECTING ON MEANING

1. According to de Beauvoir, what is the nature of housework? What distinguishes it from other tasks? In what ways is it an activity that simply "perpetuates the present"? How does it represent a "denial of life"? To what extent do you agree or disagree with these views?

2. What are the implications of housework for women? How does it shape their relationships with others, their perceptions of themselves, and the quality of their lives? Why doesn't housework have the same implications for men?

3. De Beauvoir asserts that in former times housework did not pose such a serious dilemma for women: "But on the whole marriage is today a surviving relic of dead ways of life, and the situation of the wife is more ungrateful than formerly, because she still has the same duties but they no longer confer the same rights, privileges, and honors." What has changed over the centuries? What "rights, privileges, and honors" in the past mitigated the endless drudgery of household chores?

## EXPLORING RHETORICAL STRATEGIES

1. De Beauvoir makes effective use of analogy to illustrate several of her points. What is appropriate about her comparison of housework to the "torture of Sisyphus"? What point is she making when she compares housekeeping to "service" and the woman's condition to "vassalage"?

2. How would you characterize the tone of de Beauvoir's essay? What kind of persona has she constructed in this piece? How would you describe her relationship to her audience?
3. This selection originally appeared in 1952 in de Beauvoir's book *The Second Sex.* Does her depiction of women and housework still seem valid to you? Why or why not?

# Escaping the Daily Grind for Life as a House Father

## RICK GREENBERG

*Rick Greenberg tells of leaving his job—"escaping the treadmill"—and taking on the duties and responsibilities of "house fatherhood." His account of his experience illuminates the difficulties and also the joys of reversing traditional gender roles with his wife, certainly a radical step in today's society.*

"You on vacation?" my neighbor asked.

My 15-month-old son and I were passing her yard on our daily hike through the neighborhood. It was a weekday afternoon and I was the only working-age male in sight.

"I'm uh . . . working out of my house now," I told her.

Thus was born my favorite euphemism for house fatherhood, one of those new life-style occupations that is never merely mentioned. Explained, yes. Defended. Even rhapsodized about. I was tongue-tied then, but no longer. People are curious and I've learned to oblige.

I joined up earlier this year when I quit my job—a dead-end, ulcer-producing affair that had dragged on interminably. I left to be with my son until something better came along. And if nothing did, I'd be with him indefinitely.

This was no simple transition. I had never known a house

father, never met one. I'd only read about them. They were another news magazine trend. Being a traditionalist, I never dreamed I'd take the plunge.

But as the job got worse, I gave it serious thought. And more thought. And in the end, I still felt ambivalent. This was a radical change that seemed to carry as many drawbacks as benefits. My dislike for work finally pushed me over the edge. That, and the fact that we had enough money to get by.

Escaping the treadmill was a bold stroke. I had shattered my lethargy and stopped whining, and for that I was proud.

Some friends said they were envious. Of course they weren't quitting one job without one waiting—the ultimate in middle-class taboos. That ran through my mind as I triumphantly, and without notice, tossed the letter of resignation on my boss' desk. Then I walked away wobbly-kneed.

The initial trauma of quitting, however, was mitigated by my eagerness to raise our son. Mine was the classic father's lament. I felt excluded. I had become "the man who got home after dark," that other person besides Mama. It hurt when I couldn't quiet his crying.

I sensed that staying home would be therapeutic. The chronic competitiveness and aggressiveness that had served me well as a daily journalist would subside. Something better would emerge, something less obnoxious. My ulcer would heal. Instead of beating deadlines, I'd be doing something important for a change. This was heresy coming from a newspaper gypsy, but it rang true.

There was unease, too. I'd be adrift, stripped of the home-office-home routine that had defined my existence for more than a decade. No more earning a living. No benchmarks. Time would be seamless. Would Friday afternoons feel the same?

The newness of it was scary.

Until my resignation, my wife and I typified today's baby-boomer couples, the want-it-all generation. We had two salaries, a full-time nanny and guilt pangs over practicing parenthood by proxy.

Now, my wife brings home the paychecks, the office problems and thanks for good work on the domestic front. With me at home, her work hours are more flexible. Nanny-less, I change diapers, prepare meals and do all the rest. And I wonder what comes next.

What if I don't find another job? My field is tight. At 34, I'm not getting any more marketable and being out of work doesn't help.

As my father asked incredulously: "Is this going to be what you do?"

Perhaps. I don't know. I wonder myself. It's even more baffling to my father, the veteran of a long and traditional 9-to-5 career. For most of it, my mother stayed home. My father doesn't believe in trends. All he knows is that his only son—with whom he shares so many traits—has violated the natural order of men providing and women raising children. In his view, I've shown weakness and immaturity by succumbing to a bad job.

But he's trying to understand, and I think he will.

I'm trying to understand it myself. House fatherhood has been humbling, rewarding and unnerving.

"It's different," I tell friends. "Different."

Imagine never having to leave home for the office in the morning. That's how different. No dress-up, no commute. Just tumble out of bed and you're there. House fathering is not for claustrophobics.

I find myself enjoying early morning shopping. My son and I arrive right after the supermarket opens. The place is almost empty. For the next hour we glide dreamily, cruising the aisles to a Muzak accompaniment. This is my idyll. My son likes it, too; he's fascinated by the spectacle.

Housekeeping still doesn't seem like work, and that's by design. I've mastered the art of doing just enough chores to get by. This leaves me enough free time. Time to read and write and daydream. Time with my son. Time to think about the structure.

So much time, and so little traditional structure, that the days sometimes blur together. I remember on Sunday nights literally dreading the approaching work week, the grind. Today, the close of the weekend still triggers a shiver of apprehension; I now face the prospect of a week without tangible accomplishments, a void.

On our hikes to the playground, I can feel my old identity fading. All around are people with a mission, a sense of purpose. Workers. And then there's the rest of us—the stroller and backpack contingent. The moms, the nannies, and me. I wonder if I've crossed over a line never to return.

Still, the ulcer seems to be healing. I take pride in laying out a good dinner for the family and in pampering my wife after a tough day at the office. I love reading to my son. Running errands isn't even so bad. A lot of what had been drudgery or trivia is taking on new meaning; maybe I'm mellowing.

Which is ironic. To be a truly committed and effective at-home parent, there must be this change—a softening, a contentment with small pleasures, the outwardly mundane. This is a time of reduced demands and lowered expectations. Progress is gradual, often agonizingly so. Patience is essential. Ambition and competitiveness are anathema. Yet eliminating these last two qualities—losing the edge—could ruin my chances of resurrecting my career. I can't have it both ways.

The conflict has yet to be resolved. And it won't be unless I make a firm commitment and choose one life style over the other. I'm not yet ready for that decision.

In the meantime, a wonderful change is taking place in our home. Amid all the uncertainties, my son and I have gotten to know each other. He can't put a phrase together, but he confides in me. It can be nothing more than a grin or a devilish look. He tries new words on me, new shtick. We roll around a lot; we crack each other up. I'm no longer the third wheel, the man who gets home after dark. Now, I'm as much a part of his life as his mother is. I, too, can stop his crying. So far, that has made the experiment worthwhile.

---

## REFLECTING ON MEANING

1. What does Greenberg's initial defensiveness about his new role in the family suggest about the way others perceived him? Why did his neighbor assume he was on vacation? Why did his father react so negatively to his new status? How do you think most women and men would react? What is your reaction?
2. Greenberg clearly sees himself as apart from the mainstream of society, the "people with a mission, a sense of purpose," the people who would consider it unspeakable not to work. How does the family unit relate to these values? What roles are outlined for women and men in the family? In what ways is a person occupied with child rearing a person without a mission or a sense of purpose?
3. "I can't have it both ways," Greenberg laments, echoing the dilemma that most women face: choosing between a career and a family. Is it possible to have both? What obstacles confront a person who tries to have it both ways? How do men in most cases manage to juggle both?

## EXPLORING RHETORICAL STRATEGIES

1. Greenberg begins his essay with an anecdote about a neighbor. Is this an effective way to begin? Why or why not? How does the anecdote help him illustrate his thesis?

2. The essay contains the occasional "sentence fragment"—a group of words punctuated as a sentence but lacking an element considered necessary to a sentence, such as a subject or a finite verb. In addition, Greenberg uses one-sentence paragraphs. Both devices are often regarded as incorrect. How many instances of each device can you identify? In what ways does Greenberg use these devices to his benefit?

3. Greenberg's essay is organized so that the present conflict he faces isn't addressed until the conclusion. Why do you think he delays telling about this conflict until the end of the essay? What effect does he achieve in doing so?

# Chapter 10

## THE FAMILY

## Why Mothers Should Stay Home

### DEBORAH FALLOWS

*At a time when many women are rejectinig traditional roles in the home and pursuing careers, Deborah Fallows decided to leave a successful career to stay home with her young children. In this excerpt from her book* A Mother's Work, *Fallows tells about some of the difficulties that have resulted from her decision, and she argues that motherhood has a poor image in our society. Her essay effectively illuminates the complexity of sorting out the "comparative importance of career and motherhood."*

About 18 months ago, when our first son was three years old and our second was about to be born, I decided to stop working and stay at home with our children. At the time, I wrote an article about the myth of the superwoman, saying that contrary to the prevailing notion of the day, it was not possible to be both a full-time career woman and a full-fledged mother. I said that while everyone recognizes the costs a stay-at-home mother pays in terms of power, prestige, money, and advancement in traditional careers, we are not always aware of or do not so readily admit what a full-time working woman loses and gives up in terms of mothering.

I've been at home with our children for almost a year and a

half now, and I've learned a number of things about my choice. My convictions about the importance of mothering, which were based more on intuition than experience at the time, run even deeper and stronger. Nothing means more to me now than the hours I spend with my children, but I find myself coping with a problem I hadn't fully foreseen. It is the task of regearing my life, of learning to live as a full-time mother without a professional career but still with many of the interests and ambitions that I had before I had children. And this is the hard part. It means unraveling those long-held life plans for a certain kind of career and deciding which elements are possible to keep and which I must discard. Perhaps even more important, it means changing the way I've been taught to think about myself and value the progress of my life.

My mother became a mother in 1946; she had gone to college, studied music, and worked for a year at her father's office. Then she married and had my sister by the time she was 22. She wasn't expected to have a career outside the home, and she didn't. When I was growing up, the only mothers who worked were those who, as we whispered, "had to." Even the high school teachers, who we recognized probably weren't doing it just for the money, were slightly suspect.

But between my mother's time and our own, the climate of opportunity and expectations for women started to change. Betty Friedan and *The Feminine Mystique* came between all of those mothers and all of us daughters. The small town in northern Ohio where I grew up was not exactly a hotbed of feminist activity, but even there the signals for young women were changing in the mid-sixties. We were raised with a curious mixture of hope of becoming homecoming queen and pressure to run for student council president. When I was 11, the mothers in our neighborhood bundled off their awkward, preadolescent daughters to Saturday morning charm classes, where we learned how to walk on a straight line, one foot directly in front of the other, and the proper way to don a coat. We all felt a little funny and humiliated, but we didn't say anything. By the time we were 17, we were May Queens, princesses, head drum majorettes, and cheerleaders, but we were also class valedictorians, editors of the school paper and yearbook, student directors of the school band, and candidates for six-year medical programs, Seven Sisters colleges, and honors programs at the Big Ten universities. I admit with some embarrassment that my two most thrilling moments in high school were being chosen for the homecoming court and being named first-chair trumpet in the concert band.

*This* was the way we were supposed to achieve—to be both beautiful and brilliant, charming and accomplished. It was one step beyond what our mothers did: we were aiming to be class presidents, not class secretaries; for medical school, not nursing school; we were building careers, not just jobs to tide us over before we landed husbands and started raising babies.

When I made my decision to stop working and stay home with our children, it was with a mixture of feelings. Part was defiance of the background I've just described—how could feminism dare tell me that I couldn't choose, with *pride*, motherhood alone? Part was anxiety—how could I keep some grasp on my extra-mothering self, on the things I had really enjoyed doing before I had children? I didn't want to become what the world kept telling me housewives are—ladies whose interests are confined to soap operas and the laundry. Certainly I knew from my own mother and from other women who had spent their middle years as full-time mothers that it was possible to be a thoughtful and sensitive person and still be a mother. But I didn't know how, and I didn't know where to turn to ask. Even my mother didn't have the answers. She was surprised when I told her I wanted to stop working and stay home with my kids. "You young women seem to handle everything so easily, so smoothly," she told me. "I never knew you were so torn between being a mother and being a professional."

The arrival of children in a woman's late twenties or early thirties can be handy, of course, because it means you can finish your education and start a career before taking "time out" to start your family. But it's also awkward.

At my tenth college reunion last June, I found that many of my friends had just become partner or vice-president of one thing or another, doctor-in-charge of some ward, tenured professor, editor-in-chief, and so forth. In these moments, I feel as if everyone is growing up around me. My reactions, though human, are not altogether pretty. I feel sorry for myself—there but for two small children go I. I feel frustrated in being passed over for things I know I could handle as well as or better than the next person. I feel anxious, wondering if I am going to "lose my touch," get rusty, boring, old, trivial too quickly. And I am afraid that in putting aside my professional ambitions just now, I may be putting aside forever the chance to attain the levels I once set for myself.

All of us, I think, spend time once in a while pondering the "what ifs" of our lives, and we all experience momentary pangs of self-pity over the course we've taken. I know I'm not an exception to this, but I also know that when I add up the pluses and minuses my choice was right for me, and it might be right for other women.

## The Importance of "Quantity" Time

The first adjustment on that first morning that I dressed for motherhood rather than for success was to believe intellectually in what I felt emotionally: that it was as important, as worthy for me to spend my time with my small children as to study, do research, try cases, or invest a bank's money. Furthermore, I had to believe it was worth it to the children to have me—not someone else—there most of the time. There are a thousand small instances I have witnessed over the past year and a half that illustrate this feeling. One that stays in my mind happened last summer.

I had just dropped off our older son at the morning play camp at the neighborhood school. I was about to drive off when a little boy about eight years old burst out of the school and ran down the front steps in tears. His mother was on her way down the walk and of course she saw him. She led him over to the steps, took his hands in hers, looked him directly in the eyes, and talked with him softly but deliberately for a few minutes, calming him down so he could go back inside happily and she could go on her way. What I recognized in that instant was something I'd been trying to put my finger on for months. I'd witnessed dozens of similar events, when a child was simply overwhelmed by something, and I knew there was a difference—a distinct difference in the way parents respond at such moments from the way I had seen babysitters or maids act, however loving and competent they may have been. Parents seem to have some combination of self-assurance, completeness, deliberateness, and consistency. If that boy had been my son, I would have wanted to be with him, too.

Perhaps this one episode was no more important than the many reprimands or comforts I give my children during the day. But the more I'm around my children, the more such instances I happen to see and deal with. Perhaps a thousand of these episodes add up to the values and security I want to give my children.

I spend a lot of time with my children at playgrounds. We often go out on nice afternoons when our older son gets home from school, sampling new ones or returning to old favorites. I particularly like playgrounds because of the balance they afford: they encourage the kids to strike out on their own but let me be there as a fallback. I've watched my older son in his share of small fistfights and scuffles, and I have been able to let him fight without intervening. He knows I'm there and runs back as often for protection as for nice things like a "Mom, see what I can do." Or our younger son toddles toward the big slide and needs me to follow him up and hold him as we slide down together. After so many hours, we've developed a style of play. I think my children know what to expect of me and I have learned their limits. I've watched the styles of many mothers and children, and you often can see, after a time, a microcosm of their lives together. I've also seen plenty of children there with full-time maids. The maids have their own styles, which usually are different from the mothers'. I've never seen a maid slide down a slide with her small charge, but I have seen plenty scold children for climbing too high on the jungle gym, and I've seen plenty step in to stop the sandfights before anyone gets dirty or hurt. There's a reason for this, of course: a maid has a lot to explain if a youngster arrives home with a bloody nose, but a mother doesn't. Sometimes, I think, the nose is worth the lesson learned from it, yet that is something only a parent—not a maid or babysitter—can take the responsibility to decide.

It has taken me a few years to realize I have very high standards for my role as a mother. I don't have to be a supermom who makes my children's clothes (I really can't sew), who does all the volunteer work at school (I do my share), or who cooks gourmet meals (we eat a lot of hamburgers). But I have to be around my children—a lot. I have to know them as well as I possibly can and see them in as many different environments and moods as possible in order to know best how to help them grow up—by comforting them, letting them alone, disciplining and enjoying them, being dependable but not stifling. What I need with them is time—in quantity, not quality.

I'm not talking about being with my children every minute of the day. From the time they were several months old, we sent them out for short periods to the favorite neighborhood babysitter's. By the time he was two and a half, our older son was in a co-op nursery school (my husband and I would take turns doing parent duty for the 17 kids); now he's in pre-kindergarten for a full school day. These periods away from me are clearly important for my sanity, as well as for my children's socialization, their development of trust in people, and their ability to experience other ways of living. But there is a big difference between using childcare from 8 to 6, Monday through Friday, and using a babysitter or a nursery school three mornings a week.

I realize that not everyone enjoys the luxury of choice. Some of my female friends work because it's the only way to make ends meet. But I think a lot of people pretend they have less room for choice than they really do. For some women, the reason may be the feeling—which is widespread among men—that their dignity and success are related to how much money they earn. For others, there is a sense of independence that comes with earning money that is hard to give up. (I know that I felt freer to buy things, especially for myself, or spend money on babysitters when I was contributing to the family income.) And still others define "necessities" in an expensive way: I've heard more than one woman say she "has to work" to keep up payments on the second house. Such a woman is the parallel to the government appointee who "has to resign" from his post to return to his former profession because he "can no longer afford government service."

Even though some women do have a choice, I am not suggesting that all the responsibility for home and children should lie with the mother. While my husband and I are an example of a more traditional family, with a breadwinning father, a full-time mother, and two children, he shares with me many of the family responsibilities: night-tending, diapering, bathing, cooking, and playtime. A woman's decision to stay home or work is, at worst, a decision made by herself and, at best, a decision made with her spouse.

But with all these qualifications noted, I still know that my own choice is to stay with my children. Why does this seem to be at odds with the climate of the times, especially among certain feminists? I think it is because of a confused sense of ambition—based, in turn, on a mistaken understanding of what being a housewife or mother actually means.

While the world's idea of the comparative importance of career and motherhood may have changed a good deal since my mother's time, the general understanding of what motherhood means for those who choose it has not changed or advanced. And that may be the real problem for many women of my generation: who can blame them for shying away from a commitment to full-time motherhood if they're told, despite raising children, that motherhood is a vapid life of chores, routines, and TV? I couldn't stand motherhood myself if that were true. One of my many discoveries as a mother is that motherhood requires not the renunciation of my former ambitions but rather their refinement.

Even for those who intend to rush straight back to work, motherhood involves some interruption in the normal career plan. Separating people, even temporarily, from their professional identities, can help them see the difference between the ambition to *be*—to have an impressive job title to drop at cocktail parties—and the ambition to *do* specific things that seem satisfying and rewarding. The ambition to be is often a casualty of motherhood; the ambition to do need not be.

I see many of my friends intensely driven to keep doing things, to keep involved in their former interests, or to develop entirely new ones that they can learn from and grow with. In the free time they manage to set aside—thanks to babysitters, co-op babycare, naptimes, grandmothers' help, and husbands like mine who spend a lot of time with the children—they are thinking and doing.

Women I have talked to have described how, after some months or years of settling into motherhood, their sense of what work is worth, and what they're looking for in work, has greatly changed. They are less tolerant, more selective, more demanding in what they do. One woman said that before she had children she would focus on a "cause," and was willing to do just about anything as her job toward that cause. Now she's still interested in advancing the cause, but she has no patience for busywork. In the limited time she can spare from her family, she wants to do things that really count, work in areas where her efforts make a difference. I'm not suggesting narcissism here but a clearer focus on a search for some long-range goal, some tangible accomplishment, a feeling so necessary during the season of child-raising when survival from one end of the day to the other is often the only achievement.

Each one's search is different, depending on factors like her husband's job (if she has a husband) and the extent of his role as a caretaker, her children's needs, her family's financial situation, and her personal lifestyle.

One of my friends had taught English in public high schools for the last ten years. She was the kind of teacher you remember fondly from your own childhood and hope your kids are lucky enough to have because she's dedicated, demanding, and creative. She expanded her subject to include other humanities, keeping herself several steps ahead of her students by reading and studying on her own, traveling to see museums and exhibits firsthand, collecting slides and books as she goes. She has a new baby daughter now and has stopped working to stay home with her child. She's decided to go back to school next fall, taking one or two courses at a time, to pursue a master's in fine arts—a chance to study formally what she's mostly taught herself and to return to her job someday with an even better background and more ideas for her teaching.

Going to school can be perfect for new mothers, as many in my own mother's generation found. It requires very little time away from home, which means cutting down on time away from the children as well as on child-care costs. It can be cheap, as with my friend, who can attend a virtually tuition-free state university. You can pace your work to suit demands at home by carefully choosing the number of courses you take and the type of work required. And it's physically easy but intellectually challenging—the complement to the other demands of the early years of mothering.

Other mothers I know do different things with their time. One friend, formerly a practicing lawyer and now a full-time mother, volunteers some of her time to advising the League of Women Voters on legal matters. Another, formerly a producer at a big radio station, now produces her own shows, albeit at a slower pace. A third quit her job to raise her daughter but spends a lot of time on artistic projects, which she sells.

But if there's no real blueprint for what a modern mother should be, you wouldn't know it from what comes through in the media. On the *Today Show* last summer, for instance, Jane Pauley interviewed Felice Schwartz, the president of Catalyst, an organization that promotes career development for women. They were discussing women's changing lifestyles. Ms. Schwartz said that now women are going back to work full-time four months after having children, while 15 years ago they were taking 20 years off to have them. "Isn't that fantastic progress?" she said. Fantastic it certainly is; progress it is not, except toward the narrowest and least generous notion of what achievement means for women or for humanity. Progress such as this is a step not toward "liberation" but toward the enslavement to career that has been the least attractive aspect of masculine success.

What it is really like to be a mother today seems to be a secret that's kept from even my contemporaries who may be considering motherhood themselves. At a dinner recently, I sat near a young woman about my age, a New York television producer and recently anointed White House fellow. She and my husband and I were having a conversation about bureaucracy and what she found new or interesting or surprising about it in her new position. After several minutes, she turned away from my husband to me directly and said, "And how old are your children, Debbie?" It wasn't the question—not at all—but the tone that was revealing, the unattractive, condescending tone I've heard many older people use with youngsters, or doctors with patients. If I'd had her pegged as a fast-track super-achiever, she had me pegged as little mother and lady of the house.

Hurt and anger were the wrong feelings at a moment like that, although I felt them. Instead, I should have felt sorry for her, not because of her own choice but because she had no sense that a choice exists—waiting to be made by women like her and like me. The choice is *not* to be either a career woman or a dumb housewife. The issue is one that she, a woman at the age when careers take off and childbearing ability nears its eleventh hour, should be sensitive to and think about.

---

## REFLECTING ON MEANING

1. Fallows asserts that there is "a distinct difference in the way parents respond" to their children—that a maid, for example, cannot provide the same care that a mother can. What is the difference she sees? Do you agree that children need the kind of interaction that only a mother can provide? Do you agree that mothers do, in fact, provide such responses? Why or why not?
2. The problem, Fallows suggests, rests in the way society depicts motherhood and career. She argues that we have "a mistaken understanding of what being a housewife or mother actually means," on the one hand, and that, on the other, we are too ready to see careers for women as "fantastic progress" when they may simply be a step toward the "enslavement to career that has been the least attractive aspect of masculine success." How is motherhood viewed in our society? How are careers for women regarded? Which does society seem to value more? Why?
3. Fallows claims that "motherhood requires not the renunciation of my former ambitions but rather their refinement." According to Fallows, what ambitions does motherhood allow women to pursue? Are you convinced that she herself is convinced of her claim? How does this statement relate to the dilemma that she describes at the beginning of her essay?
4. Fallows acknowledges that not all women have the "luxury of choice," and she describes some of the circumstances of her own life that made staying at home possible. She does not, however, elaborate on who such women might be, opting instead to discuss women she feels "pretend they have less room for choice than they really do." Who are the women who are not able to choose to stay at home? What circumstances are necessary for this "luxury"? Why doesn't Fallows tell more about these women and their circumstances? Why does she elaborate on those who, in her view, only think they don't have the option of choice?

## EXPLORING RHETORICAL STRATEGIES

1. Fallows relates that her decision to become a full-time mother was premised on a feeling—an assumption—that "it was worth

it to the children to have me—not someone else—there most of the time." What evidence does she give to validate this assumption? Do you find it convincing? Why or why not?

2. On the surface, Fallows seems to be arguing for *choice,* a stand her conclusion highlights. Nevertheless, her argument does not really derive from the middle ground; in fact, she subtly advances a particular point of view. What is this point of view? In what ways does she convey it? How does her discussion of women who "pretend" not to have the option of choice belie her avowed thesis? How does her concluding anecdote about the New York television producer reveal her actual viewpoint? What, does she assume, has this woman not considered? Is this the case?

3. What picture of feminism emerges from Fallows's essay? Is it accurate to suggest that some feminists denigrate motherhood? Is it accurate to suggest that feminists are preoccupied with such male values as success in a career? Why or why not?

# Mother Love

## NANCY FRIDAY

*In this essay Nancy Friday examines the concept of "mother love." She argues that it is an illusion reinforced by "constant emotional denial," a lie that inhibits women's self-development and their relationships with their daughters.*

We are raised to believe that mother love is different from other kinds of love. It is not open to error, doubt, or the ambivalence of ordinary affections. This is an illusion.

Mothers may love their children, but they sometimes do not like them. The same woman who may be willing to put her body between her child and a runaway truck will often resent the day-by-day sacrifice the child unknowingly demands of her time, sexuality, and self-development.

A woman without a daughter may try to explore life's infinite possibilities. Her own mother left out so much. But when a daughter is born, fears she thought she had conquered long ago are re-aroused. Now there is another person, not simply dependent on her, but *like* her, and therefore subject to all the dangers she has fought all her life. The mother's progress into a larger sexuality is halted. Ground gained that she could have held alone is abandoned. She retreats and entrenches herself in the cramped female stance of security and defense. The position is fondly hailed as mother protector. It is the position of fear. She may be only half alive but she is safe, and so is her daughter. She now defines herself not as a woman but primarily as a mother. Sex is left out, hidden from the girl who must never think of her mother in danger: in sex. It is only with the greatest effort that the girl will be able to think of herself that way.

When women's lives were more predictable, we could more easily afford this enigmatic picture of womanhood. When we had no alternative but to repeat our mother's life, our mistakes and disappointments were pretty much confined to her space, her margin of error and unhappiness. I do believe our grandmothers, even our mothers, were happier; not knowing as much as we do and not having our options, there was less to be unhappy about. A woman might give up her sexuality, hate being a housewife, not like children, but if every woman was doing it, how could she articulate her frustration? She could feel it certainly, but you can't want what you don't know about. Television, for instance, gave them no sense of thwarted expectations. Today women's lives are changing at a rate and by a necessity we couldn't control if we wanted to; we need all the energy that suppression consumes. If we are going to fill more than women's traditional role, we can't afford the exhaustion that goes with constant emotional denial. There are pressures on women other than the "maternal instinct." They are the new economic and social demands. Even if we decide to lead our mothers' lives, the fact is that our daughters may not. We may continue, through denial and repression, to keep alive the idealization of motherhood for another generation, but where will that leave her?

If women are going to be lawyers as well as mothers, they must differentiate between the two, and then differentiate once again about their sexuality. That is the third—and *not* mutually exclusive—option. As the world changes, and women's place in it, mothers must consciously present this choice to their daughters. A woman may incorporate all three choices within herself—and even more—but at any given moment she must be able to say to herself and her daughter, "I chose to have you because I wanted to be a mother. I chose to work—to have a career, to be in politics, to play the piano—because that gives me a different feeling of value about myself, a value that is not greater nor lesser than motherhood, only different. Whether you choose to work or not, to be a mother or not, it will have nothing to do with your sexuality. Sexuality is the third option—as meaningful as either of the other two."

The truth is that the woman and the mother are often at war with one another—in the same body. Like so many women since the world began, my mother could not believe in this opposition of the two desires. Tradition, society, her parents, religion itself told her that there was no conflict; that motherhood was the logical and natural end product of sex. Instead of believing what every woman's body tells every woman's mind, that sexuality and eroticism are a fundamentally different and opposite drive to motherhood, my mother accepted the lie. She took as her act of faith the proposition that if she were a real woman, she would be a good mother and I would grow up the same. If I repeated her path and pattern of motherhood, it would justify and place the final stamp of value on what she had done. It would say her attitude, behavior, and deepest feelings were not split, but were in fact in harmony, a woman in unison with nature.

Some women do make this choice gladly. They may be the majority, but my mother was not one of them. As I am not—her daughter in this too. Even in a good marriage, many women resent the matronly, nonsexual role their children force them to play. My mother didn't even have a good marriage; she was a young widow.

Frightened as she was, as much in need of my father as my sister and I were of her, mother had no choice but to pretend that my sister and I were the most important part of her life; that neither fear, youth and inexperience, loss, loneliness or her own needs could shake the unqualified and invincible love she felt for us. My mother had no body of woman-to-woman honesty and shared experience to use in her fight against the folk wisdom that said just being a woman carried all the inherent wisdom needed to be a mother—that it was either "natural" to her, or she was a failure as a woman.

In all the years we lived together, it is a shame we never talked honestly about our feelings. What neither of us knew then was that I could have stood honesty, no matter how frightening. Her angers, disillusionments, fears of failure, rage—emotions I seldom saw—I could have come to terms with them if she had been able to speak to me. I would have grown used to the idea that while mother loved me, at times other emotions impaired that love, and developed trust that in time her love for me would always return. Instead, I was left trying to believe in some perfect love she said she had for me, but in which I could not believe. I did not understand why I couldn't feel it no matter what her words said. I grew to believe that love itself, from her or anybody else, was a will-o'-the-wisp, coming or going for reasons I could not control. Never knowing when or why I was loved, I grew afraid to depend on it.

The older I get, the more of my mother I see in myself. The more opposite my life and my thinking grow from hers, the more of her I hear in my voice, see in my facial expression, feel in the emotional reactions I have come to recognize as my own. It is almost as if in extending myself, the circle closes in to completion. She was my first and most lasting model. To say her image is not still a touchstone in my life—and mine in hers—would be another lie. I am tired of lies. They have stood in the way of my understanding myself all my life. I have always known that what my husband loves most in me is that I have my own life. I have always felt that I had partially deceived him in this; I am very clever at pretense. My work, my marriage, and my new relationships with other women are beginning to make his assumptions about me true—that I am an independent, separate individual. They have allowed me to respect myself, and admire my own sex. What still stands between me and the person I would like to be is this illusion of perfect love between my mother and me. It is a lie I can no longer afford.

---

## REFLECTING ON MEANING

1. According to Friday, what is the social conception of "mother love"? How does society distinguish a mother's love from other kinds of love? What about this conception does Friday find difficult to accept? Do you agree that society defines a mother's love in this way? Do you agree that this definition presents problems for women? Why or why not?

2. Most people would agree that women are faced with choosing between children and a career, but Friday adds a third choice to the traditional dilemma. What is this option? What implications does having children raise for it? In what ways is it a "fun-

damentally different and opposite drive to motherhood"? What implications does having a career raise for it?

3. A prevailing motif in Friday's essay is her stress on illusion and lies. What point is Friday making? Why does she feel this lie has had such a profound effect on her life? Is her response to it reasonable? Why or why not?

## EXPLORING RHETORICAL STRATEGIES

1. Friday's viewpoint seems to derive primarily from her relationship with her own mother. Is she thus justified in generalizing her observations to all women? Why or why not? Do her points seem reasonable despite their foundation in a single, personal relationship? Why or why not?
2. Does Friday clearly define the options she outlines for women? Does she show how they relate to one another? In what ways, if any, do you find her efforts to define her terms effective?
3. Both the first two paragraphs and the concluding sentence hit with a punch. How did you react to them when you read Friday's essay? Using them as clues, what kind of audience do you think Friday was thinking about when she wrote this essay? How might such an audience respond to her opening and closing strategies?

# Motherhood: Who Needs It?

BETTY ROLLIN

*As Betty Rollin points out in this essay, society has long subscribed to the notion that "having babies is something that all normal women instinctively want and need and will enjoy doing." She argues that this myth of motherhood survives today, despite women's advances in the professions, despite their legal and economic achievements, and despite the "overwhelming maternal unhappiness and incompetence" that it engenders. The time has come, she asserts, for the myth to be exposed.*

Motherhood is in trouble, and it ought to be. A rude question is long overdue: Who needs it? The answer used to be (1) society and (2) women. But now, with the impending horrors of overpopulation, society desperately *doesn't* need it. And women don't need it either. Thanks to the Motherhood Myth—the idea that having babies is something that all normal women instinctively want and need and will enjoy doing—they just *think* they do.

The notion that the maternal wish and the activity of mothering are instinctive or biologically predestined is baloney. Try asking most sociologists, psychologists, psychoanalysts, biologists—many of whom are mothers—about motherhood being instinctive: it's like asking department store presidents if their Santa Clauses are real. "Motherhood—instinctive?" shouts distinguished sociologist/author Dr. Jessie Bernard. "Biological destiny? Forget biology! If it were biology, people would die from not doing it."

"Women don't need to be mothers any more than they need spaghetti," says Dr. Richard Rabkin, a New York psychiatrist. "But if you're in a world where everyone is eating spaghetti, thinking they need it and want it, you will think so too. Romance has really contaminated science. So-called instincts have to do with stimulation. They are not things that well up inside of you."

"When a woman says with feeling that she craved her baby from within, she is putting into biological language what is psychological," says University of Michigan psychoanalyst and motherhood-researcher Dr. Frederick Wyatt. "There are no instincts," says Dr. William Goode, president-elect of the American Sociological Association. "There are reflexes, like eye-blinking, and drives, like sex. There is no innate drive for children. Otherwise, the enormous cultural pressures that there are to reproduce wouldn't exist. There are no cultural pressures to sell you on getting your hand out of the fire."

There are, to be sure, biologists and others who go on about biological destiny, that is, the innate or instinctive goal of motherhood. (At the turn of the century, even good old capitalism was explained by a theorist as "the *instinct* of acquisitiveness.") And many psychoanalysts will hold the Freudian view that women feel so rotten about not having a penis that they are necessarily propelled into the child-wish to replace the missing organ. Psychoanalysts also make much of the psychological need to repeat what one's parent of the same sex has done. Since every woman has a mother, it is considered normal to wish to imitate one's mother by being a mother.

There is, surely, a wish to pass on love if one has received it, but to insist women must pass it on in the same way is like insisting that every man whose father is a gardener has to be a gardener. One dissenting psychoanalyst says, simply, "There is a wish to comply with one's biology, yes, but we needn't and sometimes we shouldn't." (Interestingly, the woman who has been the greatest contributor to child therapy and who has probably given more to children than anyone alive is Dr. Anna Freud, Freud's magnificent daughter, who is not a mother.)

Anyway, what an expert cast of hundreds is telling us is, simply, that biological *possibility* and desire are not the same as biological *need.* Women have childbearing equipment. To choose not to use the equipment is no more blocking what is instinctive than it is for a man who, muscles or no, chooses not to be a weight lifter.

So much for the wish. What about the "instinctive" *activity* of mothering? One animal study shows that when a young member of a species is put in a cage, say, with an older member of the same species, the latter will act in a protective, "maternal" way. But that goes for both males and females who have been "mothered" themselves. And studies indicate that a human baby will also respond to whoever is around playing mother—even if it's father. Margaret Mead and many others frequently point out that mothering can be a fine occupation, if you want it, for either sex. Another experiment with monkeys who were brought up without mothers found them lacking in maternal behavior toward their own offspring. A similar study showed that monkeys brought up without other monkeys of the opposite sex had no interest in mating—all of which suggests that both mothering and mating behavior are learned, not instinctual. And, to turn the cart (or the baby carriage) around, baby ducks who lovingly follow their mothers seemed, in the mother's absence, to just as lovingly follow wooden ducks or even vacuum cleaners.

If motherhood isn't instinctive, when and why, then, was the Motherhood Myth born? Until recently, the entire question of maternal motivation was academic. Sex, like it or not, meant babies. Not that there haven't always been a lot of interesting contraceptive tries. But until the creation of the diaphragm in the 1880's, the birth of babies was largely unavoidable. And, generally speaking, nobody really seemed to mind. For one thing, people tend to be sort of good sports about what seems to be inevitable. For another, in the past, the population needed beefing up. Mortality rates were high, and agricultural cultures, particularly, have always needed children to help out. So because it "just happened" and because it was needed, motherhood was assumed to be innate.

Originally, it was the word of God that got the ball rolling with "Be fruitful and multiply," a practical suggestion, since the only people around then were Adam and Eve. But in no time, supermoralists like St. Augustine changed the tone of the message: "Intercourse, even with one's legitimate wife, is unlawful and wicked where the conception of the offspring is prevented," he, we assume, thundered. And the Roman Catholic position was thus cemented. So then and now, procreation took on a curious value among people who viewed (and view) the pleasures of sex as sinful. One could partake in the sinful pleasure, but feel vindicated by the ensuing birth. Motherhood cleaned up sex. Also, it cleaned up women, who have always been considered somewhat evil, because of Eve's transgression (". . . but the woman was deceived and became a transgressor. Yet woman will be saved through bearing children . . . ," I Timothy, 2:14–15), and somewhat dirty because of menstruation.

And so, based on need, inevitability, and pragmatic fantasy—the Myth *worked,* from society's point of view—the Myth grew like corn in Kansas. And society reinforced it with both laws and propaganda—laws that made woman a chattel, denied her education and personal mobility, and madonna propaganda that she was beautiful and wonderful doing it and it was all beautiful and wonderful to do. (One rarely sees a madonna washing dishes.)

In fact, the Myth persisted—breaking some kind of record

for long-lasting fallacies—until something like yesterday. For as the truth about the Myth trickled in—as women's rights increased, as women gradually got the message that it was certainly possible for them to do most things that men did, that they live longer, that their brains were not tinier—then, finally, when the really big news rolled in, that they could *choose* whether or not to be mothers—what happened? The Motherhood Myth soared higher than ever. As Betty Friedan made oh-so-clear in *The Feminine Mystique,* the '40's and '50's produced a group of ladies who not only had babies as if they were going out of style (maybe they were) but, as never before, they turned motherhood into a cult. First, they wallowed in the aesthetics of it all—natural childbirth and nursing became maternal musts. Like heavy-bellied ostriches, they grounded their heads in the sands of motherhood, only coming up for air to say how utterly happy and fulfilled they were. But, as Mrs. Friedan says only too plainly, they weren't. The Myth galloped on, moreover, long after making babies had turned from practical asset to liability for both individual parents *and* society. With the average cost of a middle-class child figured conservatively at $30,000 (not including college), any parent knows that the only people who benefit economically from children are manufacturers of consumer goods. Hence all those gooey motherhood commercials. And the Myth gathered momentum long after sheer numbers, while not yet extinguishing us, have made us intensely uncomfortable. Almost all of our societal problems, from minor discomforts like traffic to major ones like hunger, the population people keep reminding us, have to do with there being too many people. And who suffers most? The kids who have been so mindlessly brought into the world, that's who. They are the ones who have to cope with all of the difficult and dehumanizing conditions brought on by overpopulation. They are the ones who have to cope with the psychological nausea of feeling unneeded by society. That's not the only reason for drugs, but, surely, it's a leading contender.

Unfortunately, the population curbers are tripped up by a romantic, stubborn, ideological hurdle. How can birth-control programs really be effective as long as the concept of glorious motherhood remains unchanged? (Even poor old Planned Parenthood has to euphemize—why not Planned Unparenthood?) Particularly among the poor, motherhood is one of the few inherently positive institutions that are accessible. As Berkeley demographer Judith Blake points out, "Poverty-oriented birth control programs do not make sense as a welfare measure . . . as long as existing pronatalist policies . . . encourage mating, pregnancy, and the care, support, and rearing of children." Or, she might have added, as long as the less-than-idyllic child-rearing part of motherhood remains "in small print."

Sure, motherhood gets dumped on sometimes: Philip Wylie's Momism got going in the '40's and Philip Roth's *Portnoy's Complaint* did its best to turn rancid the chicken-soup concept of Jewish motherhood. But these are viewed as the sour cries of a black humorist here, a malcontent there. Everyone shudders, laughs, but it's like the mouse and the elephant joke. Still, the Myth persists. Last April, a Brooklyn woman was indicted on charges of manslaughter and negligent homicide—eleven children died in a fire in a building she owned and criminally neglected—"But," sputtered her lawyer, "my client, Mrs. Breslow, is a mother, a grandmother, and a great-grandmother!"

Most remarkably, the Motherhood Myth persists in the face of the most overwhelming maternal unhappiness and incompetence. If reproduction were merely superfluous and expensive, if the experience were as rich and rewarding as the cliché would have us believe, if it were a predominantly joyous trip for everyone riding—mother, father, child—then the going everybody-should-have-two-children plan would suffice. Certainly, there are a lot of joyous mothers, and their children and (sometimes, not necessarily) their husbands reflect their joy. But a lot of evidence suggests that for more women than anyone wants to admit, motherhood can be miserable. ("If it weren't," says one psychiatrist wryly, "the world wouldn't be in the mess it's in.")

There is a remarkable statistical finding from a recent study of Dr. Bernard's, comparing the mental illness and unhappiness of married mothers and single women. The latter group, it turned out, was both markedly less sick and overtly more happy. Of course, it's not easy to measure slippery attitudes like happiness. "Many women have achieved a kind of reconciliation—a conformity," says Dr. Bernard,

> that they interpret as happiness. Since feminine happiness is supposed to lie in devoting one's life to one's husband and children, they do that; so *ipso facto,* they assume they are happy. And for many women, untrained for independence and "processed" for motherhood, they find their state far preferable to the alternatives, which don't really exist.

Also, unhappy mothers are often loath to admit it. For one thing, if in society's view not to be a mother is to be a freak, not to be a *blissful* mother is to be a witch. Besides, unlike a disappointing marriage, disappointing motherhood cannot be terminated by divorce. Of course, none of that stops such a woman from expressing her dissatisfaction in a variety of ways. Again, it is not only she who suffers but her husband and children as well. Enter the harridan housewife, the carping shrew. The realities of motherhood can turn women into terrible people. And, judging from the 50,000 cases of child abuse in the U.S. each year, some are worse than terrible.

In some cases, the unpleasing realities of motherhood begin even before the beginning. In *Her Infinite Variety,* Morton Hunt describes young married women pregnant for the first time as "very likely to be frightened and depressed, masking these feelings in order not to be considered contemptible. The arrival of pregnancy interrupts a pleasant dream of motherhood and awakens them to the realization that they have too little money, or not enough space, or unresolved marital problems. . . ."

The following are random quotes from interviews with some mothers in Ann Arbor, Mich., who described themselves as reasonably happy. They all had positive things to say about their children, although when asked about the best moment of their day, they *all* confessed it was when the children were in bed. Here is the rest:

> Suddenly I had to devote myself to the child totally. I was under the illusion that the baby was going to fit into my life, and I found that I had to switch my life and my schedule to fit *him.* You think, "I'm in love, I'll get married, and we'll have a baby." First there's two, then three, it's simple and romantic. You don't even think about the work. . . .
>
> You never get away from the responsibility. Even when you leave the children with a sitter, you are not out from under the pressure of the responsibility. . . .
>
> I hate ironing their pants and doing their underwear, and they never put their clothes in the laundry basket. . . . As they get older, they make less demands on our time because they're in school, but the demands are greater in forming their values. . . . Best moment of the day is when all the children are in bed. . . . The worst time of the day is 4 P.M., when you have to get dinner started, the kids are tired, hungry and crabby—everybody wants to talk to you about *their* day . . . your day is only half over.
>
> Once a mother, the responsibility and concern for my children became so encompassing. . . . It took a great deal of will to keep up other parts of my personality. . . . To me, mother-

> hood gets harder as they get older because you have less control. . . . In an abstract sense, I'd have several. . . . In the non-abstract, I would not have any. . . .
>
> I had anticipated that the baby would sleep and eat, sleep and eat. Instead, the experience was overwhelming. I really had not thought particularly about what motherhood would mean in a realistic sense. I want to do *other* things, like to become involved in things that are worthwhile—I don't mean women's clubs—but I don't have the physical energy to go out in the evenings. I feel like I'm missing something . . . the experience of being somewhere with people and having them talking about something—something that's going on in the world.

Every grownup person expects to pay a price for his pleasures, but seldom is the price as vast as the one endured "however happily" by most mothers. We have mentioned the literal cost factor. But what does that mean? For middle-class American women, it means a life style with severe and usually unimagined limitations; i.e., life in the suburbs, because who can afford three bedrooms in the city? And what do suburbs mean? For women, suburbs mean other women and children and leftover peanut-butter sandwiches and car pools and seldom-seen husbands. Even the Feminine Mystiqueniks—the housewives who finally admitted that their lives behind brooms (OK, electric brooms) were driving them crazy—were loath to trace their predicament to their children. But it is simply a fact that a childless married women has no child-work and little housework. She can live in a city, or, if she still chooses the suburbs or the country, she can leave on the commuter train with her husband if she wants to. Even the most ardent job-seeking mother will find little in the way of great opportunities in Scarsdale. Besides, by the time she wakes up, she usually lacks both the preparation for the outside world and the self-confidence to get it. You will say there are plenty of city-dwelling working mothers. But most of those women do additional-funds-for-the-family kind of work, not the interesting career kind that takes plugging during childbearing years.

Nor is it a bed of petunias for the mother who does make it professionally. Says writer critic Marya Mannes:

> If the creative woman has children, she must pay for this indulgence with a long burden of guilt, for her life will be split three ways between them and her husband and her work. . . . No woman with any heart can compose a paragraph when her child is in trouble. . . . The creative woman has no wife to protect her from intrusion. A man at his desk in a room with

> closed door is a man at work. A woman at a desk in any room is available.

Speaking of jobs, do remember that mothering, salary or not, is a job. Even those who can afford nurses to handle the nitty-gritty still need to put out emotionally. "Well-cared-for" neurotic rich kids are not exactly unknown in our society. One of the more absurd aspects of the Myth is the underlying assumption that, since most women are biologically equipped to bear children, they are psychologically, mentally, emotionally, and technically equipped (or interested) to rear them. Never mind happiness. To assume that such an exacting, consuming, and important task is something almost all women are equipped to do is far more dangerous and ridiculous than assuming that everyone with vocal chords should seek a career in the opera.

A major expectation of the Myth is that children make a not-so-hot marriage hotter, or a hot marriage, hotter still. Yet almost every available study indicates that childless marriages are far happier. One of the biggest, of 850 couples, was conducted by Dr. Harold Feldman of Cornell University, who states his finding in no uncertain terms: "Those couples with children had a significantly lower level of marital satisfaction than did those without children." Some of the reasons are obvious. Even the most adorable children make for additional demands, complications, and hardships in the lives of even the most loving parents. If a woman feels disappointed and trapped in her mother role, it is bound to affect her marriage in any number of ways: she may take out her frustrations directly on her husband, or she may count on him too heavily for what she feels she is missing in her daily life.

". . . You begin to grow away from your husband," says one of the Michigan ladies. "He's working on his career and you're working on your family. But you both must gear your lives to the children. You do things the children enjoy, more than things you might enjoy." More subtle and possibly more serious is what motherhood may do to a woman's sexuality. Often when the stork flies in, sexuality flies out. Both in the emotional minds of some women *and* in the minds of their husbands, when a woman becomes a mother, she stops being a woman. It's not only that motherhood may destroy her physical attractiveness, but its madonna concept may destroy her *feelings* of sexuality.

And what of the payoff? Usually, even the most self-sacrificing of maternal self-sacrificers expects a little something back. Gratified parents are not unknown to the Western world, but there are probably at least just as many who feel, to put it crudely, short-changed. The experiment mentioned earlier—where the baby ducks followed vacuum cleaners instead of their mothers—indicates that what passes for love from baby to mother is merely a rudimentary kind of object attachment. Without necessarily feeling like a Hoover, a lot of women become disheartened because babies and children are not only not interesting to talk to (not everyone thrills at the wonders of da-da-ma-ma talk) but they are generally not empathetic, considerate people. Even the nicest children are not capable of empathy, surely a major ingredient of love, until they are much older. Sometimes they're never capable of it. Dr. Wyatt says that often, in later years particularly, when most of the "returns" are in, it is the "good mother" who suffers most of all. It is then she must face a reality: The child—the appendage with her genes—is not an appendage, but a separate person. What's more, he or she may be a separate person who doesn't even like her—or whom she doesn't really like.

So if the music is lousy, how come everyone's dancing? Because the motherhood minuet is taught freely from birth, and whether or not she has rhythm or likes the music, every woman is expected to do it. Indeed, she *wants* to do it. Little girls start learning what to want—and what to be—when they are still in their cribs. Dr. Miriam Keiffer, a young social psychologist at Bensalem, the Experimental College of Fordham University, points to studies showing that

> at six months of age, mothers are already treating their baby girls and boys quite differently. For instance, mothers have been found to touch, comfort, and talk to their females more. If these differences can be found at such an early stage, it's not surprising that the end product is as different as it is. What is surprising is that men and women are, in so many ways, similar.

Some people point to the way little girls play with dolls as proof of their innate motherliness. But remember, little girls are *given* dolls. When Margaret Mead presented some dolls to New Guinea children, it was the boys, not the girls, who wanted to play with them, which they did by crooning lullabies and rocking them in the most maternal fashion.

By the time they reach adolescence, most girls, unconsciously or not, have learned enough about role definition to qualify for a master's degree. In general, the lesson has been that no matter what kind of career thoughts one may entertain, one must, first and foremost, be a wife and mother. A girl's mother is usually her first teacher. As Dr. Goode says, "A woman is not only taught by society to have a child; she is taught to have a child who will have a child." A woman who has hung her life on the Motherhood Myth will almost always reinforce her young married daughter's early training by pushing for grandchildren. Prospective grandmothers are not the only ones. Husbands, too, can be effective sellers. After all, they have the Fatherhood Myth to cope with. A married man is *supposed* to have children. Often, particularly among Latins, children are a sign of potency. They help him assure the world—and himself—that he is the big man he is supposed to be. Plus, children give him both immortality (whatever that means) and possibly the chance to become more in his lifetime through the accomplishments of his children, particularly his son. (Sometimes it's important, however, for the son to do better, but not *too* much better.)

Friends, too, can be counted on as myth-pushers. Naturally one wants to do what one's friends do. One study, by the way, found a correlation between a woman's fertility and that of her three closest friends. The negative sell comes into play here, too. We have seen what the concept of non-mother means (cold, selfish, unwomanly, abnormal). In practice, particularly in the suburbs, it can mean, simply, exclusion—both from child-centered activities (that is, most activities) and child-centered conversations (that is, most conversations). It can also mean being the butt of a lot of unfunny jokes. ("Whaddya waiting for? An immaculate conception? Ha ha.") Worst of all, it can mean being an object of pity.

In case she's escaped all those pressures (that is, if she was brought up in a cave), a young married woman often wants a baby just so that she'll (1) have something to do (motherhood is better than clerk/typist, which is often the only kind of job she can get, since little more has been expected of her and, besides, her boss also expects her to leave and be a mother); (2) have something to hug and possess, to be needed by and have power over; and (3) have something to *be*—e.g., a baby's mother. Motherhood affords an instant identity. First, through wifehood, you are somebody's wife; then you are somebody's mother. Both give not only identity and activity, but status and stardom of a kind. During pregnancy, a woman can look forward to the kind of attention and pampering she may not ever have gotten or may never otherwise get. Some women consider birth the biggest accomplishment of their lives, which may be interpreted as saying not much for the rest of their lives. As Dr. Goode says, "It's like the gambler who may know the roulette wheel is crooked, but it's the only game in town." Also, with motherhood, the feeling of accomplishment is immediate. It is really much faster and easier to make a baby than paint a painting, or write a book, or get to the point of accomplishment in a job. It is also easier in a way to shift focus from self-development to child development—particularly since, for women, self-development is considered selfish. Even unwed mothers may achieve a feeling of this kind. (As we have seen, little thought is given to the aftermath.) And, again, since so many women are underdeveloped as people, they feel that, besides children, they have little else to give—to themselves, their husbands, to their world.

You may ask why then, when the realities do start pouring in, does a woman want to have a second, third, even fourth child? OK, (1) just because reality is pouring in doesn't mean she wants to *face* it. A new baby can help bring back some of the old illusions. Says psychoanalyst Dr. Natalie Shainess, "She may view each successive child as a knight in armor that will rescue her from being a 'bad unhappy mother.' " (2) Next on the horror list of having no children, is having one. It suffices to say that only children are not only OK, they even have a high rate of exceptionality. (3) Both parents usually want at least one child of each sex. The husband, for reasons discussed earlier, probably wants a son. (4) The more children one has, the more of an excuse one has not to develop in any other way.

What's the point? A world without children? Of course not. Nothing could be worse or more unlikely. No matter what anyone says in *Look* or anywhere else, motherhood isn't about to go out like a blown bulb, and who says it should? Only the Myth must go out, and now it seems to be dimming.

The younger-generation females who have been reared on the Myth have not rejected it totally, but at least they recognize it can be more loving to children not to have them. And at least they speak of adopting children instead of bearing them. Moreover, since the new nonbreeders are "less hung-up" on ownership, they seem to recognize that if you dig loving children, you don't necessarily have to own one. The end of the Motherhood Myth might make available more loving women (and men!) for those children who already exist.

When motherhood is no longer culturally compulsory, there will, certainly, be less of it. Women are now beginning to think and do more about development of self, of their individual resources. Far from being selfish, such development is probably our only hope. That means more alternatives for women. And more alternatives mean more selective, better, happier, motherhood—and childhood and husbandhood (or manhood) and peoplehood. It is not a question of whether or not children are sweet and marvelous to have and rear; the question is, even if that's so, whether or not one wants to pay the price for it. It doesn't make sense any more to pretend that women need babies, when what they really need is themselves. If God were still speaking to us in a voice we could hear, even He would probably say, "Be fruitful. Don't multiply."

---

## REFLECTING ON MEANING

1. According to Rollin, what is the Motherhood Myth? How does the myth shape women's needs and desires? What are its political, economic, and personal implications for women? What effect does it have on the interaction between wives and husbands? On women's self-concepts and their sexuality? On the children that it encourages them to have? Even today, why do women become trapped in the myth?

2. What is the Fatherhood Myth that Rollin describes? In what ways does it differ from the myth of motherhood? In what ways does it complement the motherhood myth? How are men, too, indoctrinated with the belief that they must have children? Why doesn't the myth have the same implications for men as it has for women?

3. "The notion that the maternal wish and the activity of mothering are instinctive or biologically predestined is baloney," asserts Rollin. To what extent do you agree or disagree with this statement? Have your own desires and needs been shaped by the myths of motherhood or fatherhood? In what ways?

## EXPLORING RHETORICAL STRATEGIES

1. How would you describe the tone that Rollin establishes in this essay? How does her tone contribute to the persona that she presents? What is your reaction to this persona?

2. Rollin relies a great deal on analogy to make her points. What examples of analogy can you identify in her essay? What is the effect that these analogies create? How do they contribute to her tone and persona?

3. Rollin relies in many cases on colloquial diction to express her viewpoints. What examples of colloquial diction can you find in

the essay? What effect does, for example, saying that God "got the ball rolling" have on you as a reader? How does such language further her thesis?

# Marriage as a Restricted Club

## LINDSY VAN GELDER

*The right to marry is something that many people take for granted, but as Lindsy Van Gelder points out, gay couples do not have this right. In this essay, which originally appeared in* Ms., *Van Gelder describes the emotional and social frustrations that confront gay couples and argues that they should indeed have the legal right to marry.*

Several years ago, I stopped going to weddings. In fact, I no longer celebrate the wedding anniversaries or engagements of friends, relatives, or anyone else, although I might wish them lifelong joy in their relationships. My explanation is that the next wedding I attend will be my own—to the woman I've loved and lived with for nearly six years.

Although I've been legally married to a man myself (and come close to marrying two others), I've come, in these last six years with Pamela, to see heterosexual marriage as very much a restricted club. (Nor is this likely to change in the near future, if one can judge by the recent clobbering of what was actually a rather tame proposal to recognize "domestic partnerships" in San Francisco.) Regardless of the *reason* people marry—whether to save on real estate taxes or qualify for married students housing or simply to express love—lesbians and gay men can't obtain the same results should they desire to do so. It seems apparent to me that few friends of Pamela's and mine would even join a club that excluded blacks, Jews, or women, much less assume that they could expect their black, Jewish, or female friends to toast their new status with champagne. But probably no other stand of principle we've ever made in our lives has been so misunderstood, or caused so much bad feeling on both sides.

Several people have reacted with surprise to our views, it never having occurred to them that gay people *can't* legally marry. (Why on earth did they think that none of us had bothered?) The most common reaction, however, is acute embarrassment, followed by a denial of our main point—that the about-to-be-wed person is embarking on a privileged status. (One friend of Pamela's insisted that lesbians are "lucky" not to have to agonize over whether or not to get married.) So wrapped in gauze is the institution of marriage, so ingrained the expectation that brides and grooms can enjoy the world's delighted approval, that it's hard for me not to feel put on the defensive for being so mean-spirited, eccentric, and/or politically rigid as to boycott such a happy event.

Another question we've fielded more than once (usually from our most radical friends, both gay and straight) is why we'd want to get married in the first place. In fact, I have mixed feelings about registering my personal life with the state, but—and this seems to me to be the essence of radical politics—I'd prefer to be the one making the choice. And while feminists in recent years have rightly focused on puncturing the Schlaflyite myth of the legally protected homemaker, it's also true that marriage does confer some very real dollars-and-cents benefits. One example of inequity is our inability to file joint tax returns, although many couples, both gay and straight, go through periods when one partner in the relationship is unemployed or makes considerably less money than the other. At one time in our relationship, Pamela—who is a musician—was between bands and earning next to nothing. I was making a little over $37,000 a year as a newspaper reporter, a salary that put me in the 42 percent tax bracket—about $300 a week taken out of my paycheck. If we had been married, we could have filed a joint tax return and each paid taxes on half my salary, in the 25 or 30 percent bracket. The difference would have been nearly $100-a-week in our pockets.

Around the same time, Pamela suffered a months'-long illness which would have been covered by my health insurance if she were my spouse. We were luckier than many; we could afford it. But on top of the worry and expense involved (and despite the fact that intellectually we believe in the ideal of free medical care for everyone), we found it almost impossible to avoid internalizing a sense of personal failure—the knowledge that *because of who we are, we can't take care of each other.* I've heard of other gay people whose lovers were deported because they couldn't marry them and enable them to become citizens; still others who were barred from intensive-care units where their lovers lay stricken because they weren't "immediate family."

I would never begrudge a straight friend who got married to save a lover from deportation or staggering medical bills, but the truth is that I no longer sympathize with most of the less tangible justifications. This includes the oft-heard "for the sake of the children" argument, since (like many gay people, especially women) I *have* children, and I resent the implication that some families are more "legitimate" than others. (It's important to safeguard one's children's rights to their father's property, but a legal contract will do the same thing as marriage.)

But the single most painful and infuriating rationale for marriage, as far as I'm concerned, is the one that goes: "We wanted to stand up and show the world that we've made a *genuine* commitment." When one is gay, such sentiments are labeled "flaunting." My lover and I almost never find ourselves in public settings outside the gay ghetto where we are (a) perceived to be a couple at all (people constantly ask us if we're sisters, although we look nothing like each other), and (b) valued as such. Usually we're forced to choose between being invisible and being despised. "Making a genuine commitment" in this milieu is like walking a highwire without a net—with most of the audience not even watching and a fair segment rooting for you to fall. A disproportionate number of gay couples do.

I think it's difficult for even my closest, most feminist straight women friends to empathize with the intensity of my desire to be recognized as Pamela's partner. (In fact, it may be harder for feminists to understand than for others; I know that when I was straight, I often resented being viewed as one half of a couple. My struggle was for an independent identity, not the cojoined one I now crave.) But we are simply not considered *authentic,* and the reminders are constant. Recently at a party, a man I'd known for years spied me across the room and came over to me, arms outstretched, big happy-to-see-you grin on his face. Pamela had a gig that night and wasn't at the party; my friend's wife was there but in another room, and I hadn't seen her yet. "How's M——?" I asked the man. "Oh, she's fine," he replied, continuing to smile pleasantly. "Are you and Pam still together?"

Our sex life itself is against the law in many states, of course, and like all lesbians and gay men, we are without many other rights, both large and small. (In Virginia, for instance, it's technically against the law for us to buy liquor.) But as a gay couple, we are also most likely to be labeled and discriminated against in those very settings that, for most heterosexual Americans, constitute the most relaxed and personal parts of life. Virtually every tiny public act of togetherness—from holding hands on the street to renting a hotel room to dancing—requires us constantly to risk humiliation (I think, for example, of the two California women who were recently thrown out of a restaurant that had special romantic tables for couples), sexual harassment (it's astonishing how many men can't resist coming on to a lesbian couple), and even physical assault. A great deal of energy goes into just expecting possible trouble. It's a process which, after six years, has become second nature for me—but occasionally, when I'm in Provincetown or someplace else with a large lesbian population, I experience the *absence* of it as a feeling of virtual weightlessness.

What does all this have to do with my friends' weddings? Obviously, I can't expect my friends to live my life. But I do think that lines are being drawn in this "pro-family" Reagan era, and I have no choice about what side I'm placed on. My straight friends do, and at the very least, I expect them to acknowledge that. I certainly expect them to understand why I don't want to be among the rice-throwers and well-wishers at their weddings; beyond that, I would hope that they would commit themselves to fighting for my rights—preferably in personally visible ways, like marching in gay pride parades. But I also wish they wouldn't get married, period. And if that sounds hard-nosed, I hope I'm only proving my point—that not being able to marry isn't a minor issue.

Not that my life would likely be changed as the result of any individual straight person's symbolic refusal to marry. (Nor, for that matter, do all gay couples want to be wed.) But it's a political reality that heterosexual live-together couples are among our best tactical allies. The movement to repeal state sodomy laws has profited from the desire of straight people to keep the government out of *their* bedrooms. Similarly, it was a heterosexual New York woman who went to court several years ago to fight her landlord's demand that she either marry her live-in boyfriend or face eviction for violating a lease clause prohibiting "unrelated" tenants—and whose struggle led to the recent passage of a state rent law that had ramifications for thousands of gay couples, including Pamela and me.

The right wing has seized on "homosexual marriage" as its bottom-line scare phrase in much the same way that "Would you want your sister to marry one?" was brandished 25 years ago. *They* see marriage as their turf. And so when I see feminists crossing into that territory of respectability and "sinlessness," I feel my buffer zone slipping away. I feel as though my friends are taking off their armbands, leaving me exposed.

---

## REFLECTING ON MEANING

1. What reasons does Van Gelder offer to justify her refusal to attend weddings or to celebrate the wedding anniversaries and engagements of her heterosexual friends and relatives? Why does she "no longer sympathize with most of the less tangible justifications" for marriage? Why does she want her heterosexual friends to refuse to marry? Why does she feel threatened, vulnerable, and alone when she sees her feminist friends marry?

2. Speaking of straight couples who say they married to "show the world that we've made a *genuine* commitment," Van Gelder says, "When one is gay, such sentiments are labeled 'flaunting.' " What kind of double standard is she describing? To what extent do you agree with this observation? Why would gay couples be judged differently from straight couples?

3. What various reactions to her views does Van Gelder describe? When you read the essay, did your own reaction fall into one of these categories? What accounts for your reaction and for the reaction of the people Van Gelder tells about?

4. Van Gelder says that "it may be harder for feminists to understand" her desire to marry. Why would it be more difficult for feminists to sympathize with Van Gelder's desires?

## EXPLORING RHETORICAL STRATEGIES

1. Van Gelder's essay pivots on an analogy between marriage and a "restricted club." In what ways is this analogy effective? How does Van Gelder extend the analogy? How does it help you understand the point she makes?

2. Who do you think Van Gelder's original audience for this essay was? What evidence can you find to help you identify this audience? Do you think she was successful in helping her audience understand her perspective? Why or why not?

3. In explaining her decision not to attend weddings, Van Gelder says that it's hard for her not to feel "defensive for being so mean-spirited, eccentric, and/or politically rigid as to boycott such a happy event." Do you find any evidence of defensiveness in the language of this essay? To what extent was she successful in creating a persona that could transcend her defensiveness?

# TAKING A STAND
## QUESTIONS FOR CONSIDERATION

1. In this part, several essays suggest that social institutions—namely, the educational system, the home, the family, and marriage—reinforce gender-based social stereotypes and women's oppression. Pick one of these institutions, summarize the observations of the appropriate authors, and draw your own conclusions. To what extent does the institution reinforce these roles? In what ways? To what extent does it, perhaps, simply reflect rather than shape them? What exactly is the nature of the cause-effect relationship at work in this case? In what ways, if any, does the institution create similar problems for men? In shaping your response, also consider the essays by Charlotte Perkins Gilman and Mary Wollstonecraft (both in Part II) and John Kenneth Galbraith (in Part VI).

2. Is the educational system in the United States sexist? Rich, Thomas, and Horner all suggest that it is. Write an essay in which you summarize the views of these authors, and either refute or confirm their viewpoints. In exploring this issue, draw on your own observations and experiences as a student, and survey both male and female students to determine if women and men do, in fact, have different experiences in educational institutions. What patterns, if any, emerge from your data?

3. Rich identifies a problem in the educational system and outlines changes that would make it more responsive to women's needs. To what extent does she accurately pinpoint the problem? To what extent does her solution resolve the problem? Beginning with a summary of Rich's viewpoint, identify what you see as the central problem in women's education and design an educational system that would resolve it. In outlining the problem that you identify, consider Horner's conclusions about women and competition and Thomas's insights into women's negative self-images.

4. To pursue a career or to have a family—this is a choice that many women face, as Fallows suggests. But Greenberg claims that he, too, struggles with the professional consequences of his decision to remain home to care for his family. As he puts it, "I can't have it both ways." What are the differences, if any, in Fallows's and Greenberg's situations? To what extent is the career-or-family dilemma limited to women? To what extent is it a choice that men must make as well? In shaping your response, consider the ways in which this dilemma has affected or might affect your own life plans.

5. Friday, Rollins, and Fallows all explore motherhood as a social institution. Fallows argues that motherhood isn't valued as much as it should be because it has acquired a poor image in our culture. Friday and Rollins assert opposing views—Friday, that society paints too rosy a picture of motherhood, and Rollins, that it is a "myth" actively creating damage in society. What are the images of motherhood promoted in our society? To what extent are they illusion or reality? What are the images of fatherhood? To what extent are they, too, illusion or reality? What is the social significance of motherhood and fatherhood? How do our concepts of these institutions shape our lives?

6. Although de Beauvoir sees marriage as a "relic of dead ways of life," Van Gelder laments that she isn't allowed to participate in this social and legal ritual. Why? What is the nature of de Beauvoir's and Van Gelder's seeming disagreement? To what extent might Van Gelder agree with de Beauvoir's assessment of marriage? In what ways? Do you agree that marriage is an empty institution? To what extent is marriage a symbolic act? What is its value? What is the future of marriage in our society? In exploring this issue, you may also wish to consider Edmund White's perspectives on marriage (Part I).

7. Syfers, de Beauvoir, and Greenberg present contradictory views of housework. According to Syfers, it symbolizes women's servitude, a viewpoint de Beauvoir extends when she calls it the "torture of Sisyphus" and argues that it places women in "vassalage." Greenberg, however, doesn't have any problem with housework; in fact, he claims that "housekeeping still doesn't seem like work." What accounts for the differing perspectives of these authors? Why do Syfers and de Beauvoir find housework empty and degrading, whereas Greenberg actually seems to enjoy it? Summarize the attitudes of these authors, and take a stand on this issue.

# Part V

# Gender and Public Policy

Sexual equality and other issues related to gender and public policy have always led, it seems, to fierce debate. This has been the case especially since the sixties as more people became conscious of the sometimes devastating effects of sexism. The three public policy issues that have captured the most attention during the last few decades are comparable worth, pornography, and abortion. The selections in Part V indicate just how controversial these three issues are.

Feminists have long pointed out that female-oriented jobs—nursing, for example—usually do not pay as well as male-dominated jobs that require the same level of training and expertise. Many believe that the state can rectify this problem by passing legislation to ensure that all workers receive comparable pay for comparable worth. The authors of the two essays in the first section express opposing viewpoints on this question. Teresa Amott and Julie Matthaei suggest that comparable worth legislation could lead to radical social changes beneficial to everyone. Charles Krauthammer, however, warns that such legislation would create "sheer social chaos."

Pornography, too, is a controversial public issue. Susan Brownmiller complains that pornography is "anti-female propaganda" because it dehumanizes women, making them into things, objects of desire. Edward Donnerstein, Daniel Linz, and Steven Penrod contend that the real danger of pornography is not sexual explicitness but the linking of violence with sex. Regardless of the harmfulness of pornography, says Susan Jacoby, we must not whittle away at the First Amendment guarantee of free speech by censoring material deemed obscene.

More than any other public issue related to gender, the question of whether abortion should be legal has created deep divisions in American society. From the passionate pro-choice writings of the early part of this century to feminists' political rally cries of the nineties, abortion remains an issue central to the women's movement. Judith Jarvis Thomson, on the one hand, constructs an elaborate analytical rationale for allowing women freedom of choice. Former president Ronald Reagan, on the other hand, argues that the state must "protect the sanctity of all human life." Ellen Willis disagrees, asserting that abortion is not a human life issue but a feminist issue—a matter of forcing a woman to bear a child against her will. Finally, Linda Bird Francke reveals in a personal account how difficult the abortion issue is and how someone can harbor a plethora of conflicting emotions about it.

Clearly, the essays in Part V do not exhaust the range of perspectives on these troubling subjects, but they do suggest how complex, heated, and seemingly unresolvable they are. The debates will undoubtedly continue, and future legislation on these issues may well help shape the future of the women's movement and of gender relations in the United States well into the twenty-first century.

# Chapter 11

# COMPARABLE WORTH

## Comparable Worth, Incomparable Pay

TERESA AMOTT and
JULIE MATTHAEI

*Unequal pay for women and men has long been a topic of concern in the United States. Teresa Amott and Julie Matthaei, both professors of economics, examine the idea of comparable worth as a means of bridging the gender gap in income. They briefly trace its history and identify ways of implementing it. Finally, they place comparable worth in a larger context, looking at its potential for "radical" change in society.*

### The Emergence of the Comparable-Worth Strategy

When the Equal Pay Act of 1963 prohibited unequal pay for equal work and the broader Civil Rights Act of 1964 set affirmative action into motion, many assumed that the gap between men and women's wages would close. Instead, the average salary for a woman working full-time year-round remained roughly 60 percent of the salary earned by a man. The constancy of the wage gap in the face of anti-discrimination legislation drew attention to the fact that women and men rarely hold the same jobs. Traditional sex roles and outright sex discrimination by employers and workers have had the result of excluding women from most occupations other than homemaking and its labor market extensions. Those paid occupations open to women shared low pay, few opportunities for advancement, and often centered around nurturing and serving others. Throughout the decade of the 1970s, over 40 percent of all women workers were concentrated in 10 occupations, most of which were over 70 percent female—for example, nursing, secretarial and clerical work, teaching, and food service. In contrast, men, especially white men, had more job options and more opportunity for high pay and promotion. For instance, stock clerks, predominantly male, earn more than bank tellers, who are predominantly female, and registered nurses earn less than mail carriers. As a result of this occupational segregation, legislation prohibiting unequal pay for equal jobs failed to address the heart of pay inequity between the sexes: men and women earning unequal pay for different jobs.

The idea of comparable worth was devised to raise women's wages in female-dominated occupations up to the level paid in male occupations of "comparable worth." Also known as pay equity, comparable worth means that jobs deemed to be of "equal value to the employer" should pay the same, regardless of their sex or race-typing. The first wage comparability case before the courts was based on race.[1] However, subsequent attempts to apply the Civil Rights Act to non-identical jobs have focused on wage differences origins from gender-based job segregation.

Some of the first attempts to broaden the concept of equal pay emerged during World War II, when unions such as the UAW and the IUE fought differential pay for men and women workers in order to prevent an overall reduction in pay scales and to generate greater unity between men and women workers.[2] Since then, the ranks of pay equity advocates have grown and a more feminist construction has been placed on the concept. Women's rights groups, working women's organizations and unions representing women workers are currently pursuing three strategies for achieving comparable worth corrections to pay inequities based on sex or color: litigation, collective bargaining, and legislation. Often a combination of these strategies is utilized by pay equity advocates.

## LITIGATION

Prior to a 1981 Supreme Court decision, the courts were uniformly unfriendly to charges of sex discrimination in pay across different jobs. In Denver, where nurses charged discrimination because the city paid them less than tree trimmers and sign painters, the judge ruled against the nurses, arguing that the doctrine of comparable worth was "pregnant with the possibility of disrupting the entire economic system."[3] In 1981, however, the Supreme Court ruled that Title VII of the 1964 Civil Rights Act could be applied to prohibit wage differences in similar, but not identical, jobs.[4] Since then, there have been lower court decisions, such as one in the state of Washington, which have awarded back pay to women whose jobs have been systematically undervalued.

### COLLECTIVE BARGAINING

A variety of unions, including AFSCME, CWA, IUE, SEIU, UAW, UE and others, have adopted pay equity as a goal in bargaining, as well as in membership education and lobbying. Most efforts have focused on public employees, largely because information on pay scales is more accessible, and state agencies may be more vulnerable to public pressure brought through community-labor alliances. Local 101 of AFSCME in San Jose, California is one of the public sector success stories. These city employees struck to win a substantial pay increase and "special adjustments" to upgrade jobs held predominantly by women.[5] Unions often combine litigation with bargaining, as in the case of an IUE local which won pay equity raises for women workers employed at a Massachusetts General Electric plant.

### LEGISLATION

Many states have adopted legislation calling for a pay equity study of state employment, and others, including California, Minnesota and Washington, have passed statutes which require public sector wages to be set on the basis of comparable worth.[6] In Idaho, a law which assigns pay in state positions on the basis of skill and responsibility has produced a 16 percent increase in pay for female clerical workers. Other states have begun to raise wages in predominantly women's jobs without explicit recourse to comparable worth. In New Mexico, for instance, over $3 million was appropriated in 1983 to raise the wages of the lowest paid state employees, over 80 percent of them women, even though a job evaluation study has not yet been completed.

## Implementing Comparable Worth

The primary mechanism for implementing comparable worth in wage structures is the job-analysis/job-evaluation study, and efforts for pay equity usually involve ridding an existing study of inherent sex bias and/or demanding a formal job evaluation study where one does not exist.

Job evaluation studies were in use long before pay equity advocates recognized their potential in comparable-worth struggles. Generally speaking, most large, bureaucratic firms and state agencies do not negotiate a wage directly with each employee, but rather assign an employee to a particular rung of a job ladder. The worker's position on the job ladder determines his or her wages. Workers in the same job would thus receive the same salary, while workers in different jobs would be paid differently. To determine pay scales, large firms use fairly systematic job analysis/evaluation schemes, often prepared by outside consultants. The first step of the study analyzes jobs through examination of job descriptions and, sometimes, discussions with workers. In the most common type of evaluation, known as a point-factor system, points are assigned to each job on the basis of criteria (factors) such as skills, effort, responsibility, and working conditions. In the final stage of the process, dollar values are assigned to the points in each category. The same procedures, and often the same consultants, are used for job evaluations in pay equity cases. In smaller firms, the process is much more informal, but rankings of jobs are still undertaken.

Despite the aura of objectivity surrounding these studies, there is no objective way to determine the relative productivity of jobs. Due to the division of labor, a myriad of different workers contribute to the output of any product, and it is impossible to distinguish their different contributions. How can one technically measure the relative importance of dieticians, nurses, or pharmacological staff to a hospital? Normally, hospital administrators pay market wages—the amount needed to attract workers—and infer the relative worth of these different workers from their wage rates. Job evaluation studies, on the other hand, attempt to determine relative productivity of jobs apart from the market. To do this, they must subjectively choose a set of factors and weights. There are many ways in which sex, race, and class bias can enter into the calculations.

One critical area is the selection and definition of factors to be evaluated. For example, it is common to define responsibility as supervisory responsibility over other workers, machines, or money. In this case, child care workers would receive low points for "responsibility" even though their jobs entail enormous responsibility for children under their care. Similarly, skilled activities such as nurturing and guidance are rarely counted, causing traditional women's jobs to receive lower points than men's jobs. Boredom from routinized work is not commonly considered worthy of points as an adverse working condition, although outdoor work and heavy lifting are.

Another critical area is the weighting of different factors, accomplished either through the number of points allocated to each factor or by the method which assigns dollars to points. This has the effect of determining the relative worth of different factors, and generally involves sophisticated statistical techniques such as multiple regression analysis. In effect, consulting firms specializing in job evaluations rely on previous correlations between existing pay scales and measured factor points to predict for new clients what a job's salary should be. From the perspective of the employer, the best point rankings are those which duplicate the existing pay hierarchy as closely as possible, since this seemingly "objective" technique can then be used to legitimize pay differentials. This means that job evaluation schemes usually embody existing pay practices, complete with sex, race, or gender bias. For example, the maximum number of points assigned for responsibility may be 2000, while adverse working conditions are awarded only a maximum of 200 points; this would ensure that managerial jobs pay more than service or operative jobs.

Despite these biased methods, current methods of evaluating jobs can still be used to win pay raises for those in "undervalued" work. For example, most studies have found that male and female jobs with equal point evaluations are paid differently because of the weighing of different factors mentioned above or because firms use different ranking schemes for different types of jobs. In these cases, legislation or bargaining agreements mandating equal pay for jobs of equal point value (under the same ranking scheme) can achieve somewhere between 5 and 25 percent pay increases.[7]

Much more can be won by eliminating bias from the technique. This requires wide access to information about existing or contemplated job evaluation studies. We need to disseminate information on how consulting firms such as Hay Associates, which serves approximately 40 per cent of the Fortune 500 companies,[8] conduct their studies, and we need to bargain for input at all stages of the evaluation process. The more we involve ourselves in the technique, taking power from the technocrats, the more success we will have. Progress has already been achieved in this area. Most unions have staff members who are experts on the technique and feminist proponents of comparable worth are currently at work expanding the definitions of factors so as to recognize the value of women's traditional work skills. (One of the most important redefinitions has been the inclusion of responsibility for children as a compensable factor.) More work needs to be done to rid the method of race and class bias.

## How Radical Is Comparable Worth?

While comparable worth directly challenges sexual inequality in the labor market, it may also have the potential for other radical change.

Comparable worth promises to undermine male supremacy outside the labor market as well. Feminists have long noted the way in which the lower wages of women have reinforced the traditional nuclear family and women's responsibility for unpaid work in the home.

As long as women are denied access to men's jobs, and few women's jobs pay a living wage, women are under strong economic pressure to marry. Married women's financial dependence upon their husbands contributes to sexual inequality within marriage. The economic costs of leaving or being left by one's husband are illustrated by the high percentage of women heading families on their own who live in poverty. The risk of poverty is highest for women of color; in 1982, 56.2 percent of black and 55.4 percent of Latino families headed by women were poor.

In addition, comparable worth subjects the pay structure to scrutiny it rarely receives. Conventional economic wisdom argues that in the "perfectly competitive market economy," workers are paid according to their "marginal product," that is, according to their contributions to the production process. (In graduate school, one of our teachers built models which assumed that women were 60 percent as productive as men, justifying this with the fact that full-time women workers earned on average, 60 percent as much as men!) Comparable worth debunks such convenient rationalizations of the pay structure, and the sexist assumptions they both reflect and create, by showing that the force behind pay differences has not been productivity differences but rather power and discrimination. Thus, it presents a radical critique of our system of income distribution through the "free market," and presents an alternative way of achieving what the market had promised: the distribution of income to workers according to their contributions in a manner which is fair and incentive-creating at the same time.

Finally, while comparable worth does not directly attack occupational segregation by sex, it may do so indirectly. On the one hand, by making traditionally feminine jobs palatable to women, comparable worth may reduce the incentives for women to seek entrance into male-dominated, more privileged jobs. On the other hand, as traditionally feminine jobs begin to offer wages comparable to those of masculine jobs, more men will find them attractive. Also, as women begin to fight for and expect working conditions comparable to those of men, they may find men's jobs more desirable, and be more willing to fight to get them.

## Broadening the Comparable-Worth Agenda

Comparable worth gains effectiveness and constituency when combined with other progressive demands.

Conservative economists have warned that raising wages for women's work would create uncontrollable inflation. While firms will try to increase their prices (and state agencies, their tax revenues), the inflationary impact would depend upon the magnitude and speed of the pay equity adjustment, as well as the ability of firms and governments to pass on the costs. (This, in turn, depends upon the degree of monopoly power and citizen resistance to tax increases.) Finally, inflation is not the worst of all evils, and can be limited by the use of wage-price controls, long a demand of progressives.

What is more worrisome are the other possible reactions of firms and state agencies to an increase in the price of women's labor: automation, elimination of state programs, and runaway shops to countries in which women still provide a super-exploitable labor force. Already, computerization is threatening clerical workers and job flight has created massive structural unemployment in the U.S. In order for comparable worth struggles not to exacerbate these problems, they must be pursued in conjunction with demands for job security, retraining, and plant-closing legislation.

So as to aid all undervalued workers, pay equity must also be extended to include comparisons between comparable but racially segregated jobs. Even this extension will not solve all workers' problems. Workers without jobs will not benefit, nor will workers in those jobs calculated to have the least worth. Since these are the main job problems faced by men of color, comparable worth offers little to them. Raising pay for women in certain jobs reduces inequality between women and men on the same level of the job hierarchy, but increases the relative poverty of those at the bottom of the hierarchy. Their problems can only be solved by a more comprehensive restructuring of work and by a deeper and more radical discussion of the worth of work.

As currently practiced, the doctrine of comparable worth accepts the idea of a hierarchy of workers, more or less "worthy" on the basis of some objective criteria. However, as radicals become involved in decisions about what factors should merit higher pay, we may well begin to question the rationale for the hierarchy itself. If the discussion of what makes work worthy is extended to the grass roots, we may well determine that all jobs are equally worthy. We may decide that workers in unskilled, routinized jobs may be doing the hardest work of all, for such work saps and denies their very humanity. Why should those whose jobs give them the most opportunity to develop and use their abilities also be paid the most? The traditional argument—that higher pay must be offered as an incentive for workers to gain skills and training—is contradicted by the fact that our highly paid jobs attract many more workers than employers demand. And given unequal access to education and training, a hierarchical pay scheme becomes a mechanism for the intergenerational transmission of wealth privilege, with its historically linked racism, sexism, and classism.

We see comparable worth as one of the most innovative and promising approaches to redressing sexual inequality. In fact, given the present reactionary climate, it is one of the few struggles in which tangible progress against injustice is being achieved. Furthermore, as we have pointed out, it raises larger questions about the fairness of the "free market" system, questions which may even undermine the rationale for income inequality.

## NOTES

1. The case was *Quarles* v. *Phillip Morris.* For more information, see Judy Scales-Trent, "Comparable Worth: Is This a Theory for Black Workers?" Unpublished paper, State University of New York at Buffalo Law School, 1984.
2. Ruth Milkman, "The Reproduction of Job Segregation by Sex: A Study of the Sexual Division in the Auto and Electrical Manufacturing Industries in the 1960s." Ph.D. Dissertation, University of California at Berkeley, 1981.
3. League of Women Voters Education Fund, "Women and Work: Pay Equity," Publication No. 110, 1982.
4. Ibid. The decision was *County of Washington, Oregon* v. *Gunther,* and involved female jail matrons who were paid 70 per cent of the salary for male guards.
5. Ibid.
6. A good source of information on state and local government pay equity initiatives is "Who's Working for Working Women," published by the Comparable Worth Project, the National Committee on Pay Equity and the National Women's Political Caucus in 1984. The pamphlet contains an excellent bibliography and a list of resource groups in each state. To order, write the National Committee on Pay Equity, 1201 16th Street, N.W., Suite 422, Washington, D.C., 20036.
7. For more information on the uses and limitations of job evaluation schemes, see Helen Remick, ed., *Comparable Worth and Wage Discrimination: Technical Possibilities and Political Realities,* Temple University Press,

1984, and Donald Treiman and Heidi Hartman, *Women Work and Wages: Equal Pay for Jobs of Equal Value,* National Academy of Sciences, 1981.

8. Ronnie Steinberg, "A Want of Harmony: Perspectives on Wage Discrimination," in Remick, op. cit.

---

## REFLECTING ON MEANING

1. What do Amott and Matthaei mean by "occupational segregation"? What kinds of jobs do women typically hold? According to Amott and Matthaei, why have these jobs usually been underpaid? What reasons have others given to account for the low pay of workers in these jobs?

2. What is the difficulty in determining the importance of a job, its relative productivity, or the level of skill it requires? What methods have traditionally been used to assign pay scales for specific jobs? What is the problem with these methods? In what ways can they be influenced by gender, race, and class bias? What changes in these methods do Amott and Matthaei suggest?

3. What would some of the political and social consequences of achieving comparable worth be? In what ways might it influence, for example, the traditional nuclear family unit, women's role as housekeepers, and the economic pressure many women feel to marry? What current problems could comparable worth exacerbate?

4. According to Amott and Matthaei, comparable worth shows that "the force behind pay differences has not been productivity differences but rather power and discrimination." Do you agree with this conclusion? Why or why not?

## EXPLORING RHETORICAL STRATEGIES

1. What is the main point that Amott and Matthaei make? What evidence do they provide to support their assertions? Do you find this evidence convincing? Why or why not?

2. How would you describe the tone of this essay? In what ways does its tone add to or detract from the authors' credibility? How does the tone contribute to the persona that the authors present in this piece? What is your reaction to this persona? Can you account for your reaction?

3. This essay originally appeared in 1984 in the magazine *Radical America*. Based on evidence from the essay, what can you surmise about the readers of this publication?

---

# The Just Wage: From Bad to Worth

## CHARLES KRAUTHAMMER

---

*A writer for* The New Republic *and a former political speechwriter, Charles Krauthammer takes issue with the concept of comparable worth. He argues that it is a ludicrous notion that, if implemented, will create social and economic mayhem.*

The latest entry on the list of sacred democratic causes is comparable worth. According to that doctrine, it is demonstrable that low-paying female-dominated jobs, like nursing, are worth as much (to employers or society) as "comparable" male-dominated jobs, like plumbing, and that therefore by right and by law they should be paid the same. Comparable worth has become not only *the* women's issue of the 1980s, but also the most prominent civil rights issue not specifically directed at blacks. The Democratic Party has warmly embraced it. Every one of its presidential candidates has endorsed it. In the 1984 platform, that sea of well-intended ambiguity and evasion, there are few islands of certainty. Comparable worth is one of them.

Comparable worth is advancing in the courts, too. In 1981 the Supreme Court opened the door a crack by ruling that female prison guards could sue for violation of the equal-pay provisions of the 1964 Civil Rights Act, even though they did not do precisely the same work as the better-paid male prison guards. That narrow ruling was broken open in December 1983 in a sweeping victory for comparable worth in Washington State. A federal district judge found the state guilty of massive discrimination because its female-dominated jobs were paying less than "comparable" male-dominated jobs. He ordered an immediate increase in the women's wages and restitution for past injury. The back pay alone will run into the hundreds of millions of dollars.

Comparable worth may indeed be an idea whose time has come. Where does it come from? When the plumber makes a house call and charges forty dollars an hour to fix a leak, the instinct of most people is to suspect that the plumber is overpaid—the beneficiary of some combination of scarce skills, powerful unions, and dumb luck. The instinct of comparable worth advocates is to see the plumber's wage as a standard of fairness, to conclude that the rest of us (meaning: women) are underpaid, and to identify discrimination as the source of that underpayment. But since overt discrimination on the basis of sex has been legally forbidden for twenty years, to make that charge stick nowadays requires a bit of subtlety.

One claim is that women's wages are depressed today because of a legacy of past discrimination: namely, the "crowding" of women into certain fields (like nursing, teaching, secretarial work), thus artifically depressing their wages. Did sexual stereotyping really "crowd" women into their jobs? Sexual stereotyping worked both ways: it kept women in, but it also kept men out, thus artificially excluding potential wage competition from half the population, and, more important, from about two-thirds to three-quarters of the labor force (because of the higher participation-rate of men). Sex-segregation is obviously unfair, but it is hard to see how it caused downward pressure on women's wages when, at the same time, through the socially enforced exclusion of men, it sheltered "women's work" from a vast pool of competitors. Moreover, as the social barriers that kept men and women from entering each other's traditional fields have fallen during the last twenty years, there has been much more movement of women into men's fields than vice versa. "Women's work" is less crowded than ever.

If the crowding argument is weak, then one is forced to resort to the "grand conspiracy" theory. "The system of wages was set up by a grand conspiracy, so to speak, that has held down the wages of women to minimize labor costs," explained the business agent of the union that in 1981 struck for and won a famous comparable-worth settlement in San Jose. But since to minimize labor costs employers try to hold down the wages of everyone, the thrust of the argument must be that there is a particular desire to do so additionally in the case of women. In other words, the market is inherently discriminatory. Women nurses are paid less than they deserve, simply because they are women. How to prove it? Comparing their wages to that of male nurses won't do, since their pay is, by law, equal. So one must compare nurses' wages to that of, say, plumbers, show that nurses make less, and claim that nurses are discriminated against because they deserve—they are worth—the same.

What is the basis of that claim? In San Jose, Washington State, and other comparable-worth cases, the basis is a "study." A consultant is called in to set up a committee to rank every job according to certain criteria. In Washington State, the Willis scale gives marks for "knowledge and skills," "mental demands," "accountability," and "working conditions." The committee then awards points in each category to every job, tallies them up, and declares those with equal totals to have—*voilà!*—comparable worth.

There is no need to belabor the absurdity of this system, so I'll stick to the high points. It is, above all, a mandate for arbitrariness: every subjective determination, no matter how whimsically arrived at, is first enshrined in a number to give it an entirely specious solidity, then added to another number no less insubstantial, to yield a total entirely meaningless. (An exercise: compare, with numbers, the "mental demands" on a truck driver and a secretary.) Everything is arbitrary: the categories, the rankings, even the choice of judges. And even if none of this were true, even if every category were ontologically self-evident, every ranking mathematically precise, every judge Solomonic, there remains one factor wholly unaccounted for which permits the system to be skewed in any direction one wishes: the *weight* assigned to each category. In the Willis scale, points for "knowledge and skills" are worth as much as points for "working conditions." But does ten points in knowledge and skills make up for ten points in hazardous working conditions? Who is to say that a secretary's two years of college are equal in worth to—and not half or double the worth of—the trucker's risk of getting killed on the highways? Mr. Willis, that's who.

Conclusions based on such "studies" are not a whit less capricious than the simple assertion, "secretaries are worth as much as truck drivers." Trotting out Willis, of course, allows you to dress up a feeling in scientific trappings. It allows H.R. 4599, Representative Mary Rose Oakar's bill legislating comparable worth in federal employment, to dispose of the arbitrariness problem in the *definitions.* "Job evaluation technique" is defined as "an objective method of determining the comparable value of different jobs." Next problem.

Some advocates of comparable worth, aware of this objectivity conundrum and perhaps less confident that it can be defined out of existence, propose an alternate solution. Instead of ranking the intrinsic worth of the job (by admittedly arbitrary criteria), they propose ranking the worth of the worker. Barbara Bergmann, an economist at the University of Maryland, believes that people with similar qualifications, training and experience should be receiving the same return on their "human capital." Breaking new ground in discrimination theory, she claims that "in a nondiscriminatory setup, identical people should be paid identically." And what makes people identical? Their credentials: qualifications, training, experience. This is not just credentialism gone wild, and highly disadvantageous to non-yuppy workers with poor résumés, who need the help of the women's movement the most; it leads to the logical absurdity that people should be paid not for the actual work they do, but for the work they *could* do. We've gone from equal pay for equal work to equal pay for comparable work, to equal pay for potential work. Summarizing the Bergmann position, the Center for Philosophy in Public Policy at the University of Maryland explains helpfully that "if a nursing supervisor could do the work of a higher-paid hospital purchasing agent, then her wages should be the same as his." But why stop there? What if her credentials are the same as those of the hospital administrator, or her city councillor, or her U.S. Senator? And what about the starving actress, waiting on tables for a living? If she can act as well as Bo Derek (to set a standard anyone can meet), shouldn't she be getting a million dollars a year—that is, if the "setup" is to deserve the adjective "nondiscriminatory"?

Now, even if there were a shred of merit in any of these systems for determining comparable worth, we should be wary of implementing them if only because of the sheer social chaos they would create. The only sure consequence of comparable worth one can foresee was described by the winning attorney in the Washington State case: "This decision . . . should stimulate an avalanche of private litigation on behalf of the victims of discrimination." The judicial and bureaucratic monster comparable worth will call into being—a whole new layer of judges, court-appointed "masters" (there already is one in the Washington State suit), lawyers, and consultants—will not just sit once to fix wages and then retire. The process will be endless. Fairness will require constant readjustment. There will still exist such a thing as supply and demand. Even if comparable worth advocates succeed in abolishing it for women's work (remember, Washington State was found to have broken the law for paying women market wages rather than comparable worth wages), it will still operate for men's wages, the standard by which women's (comparable-worth) wages will be set. Now, what if nurses are awarded plumbers' pay, and there develops a housing slowdown and a plumber surplus, and plumbers' wages fall? Will nurses' salaries have to be ratcheted down? And if not, what is to prevent the plumbers from suing, alleging they are underpaid relative to comparably equal nurses?

Which brings us to the equity problem. Almost everyone feels he or she is underpaid. Moreover, even a plumber can point to at least one person or group of persons who are getting more than they are "worth." Why can't he claim that class of people as the equitable standard, and march to court demanding restitution? If comparable worth is simple justice, as its advocates claim, why should only women be entitled to it? Why not comparable worth for everyone?

The whole search for the "just wage," which is what comparable worth is all about, is, like the search for the "just price," inherently elusive in a capitalist system. It is not that justice has nothing to say about wages and prices in a market economy, but that what it does say it says negatively. For example, it declares that whatever the wage, it must be the same for people regardless of sex, race or other characteristics; but it doesn't say what the wage should be. Even the minimum-wage law says merely that a wage may not be below a certain floor. (Even capitalism has a notion of exploitative labor.) Beyond that, the law is silent. The reason it is silent, the reason we decide to let the market decide, is no great mystery. It was first elaborated by Adam Smith, and amplified by the experience of the Soviet Union and other command economies. Market economies are agnostic on the question of a just wage or a just price not simply because of a philosophical belief that the question, if it is a question, is unanswerable, but also because of the belief, and the experience, that attempts to answer it have a habit of leaving everyone worse off than before.

Finally, even granting that women in traditionally female jobs are underpaid, it is not as if we live in a fixed economy which blocks off all avenues of redress. If secretaries are indeed paid less than they are "worth," they have several options. One is suggested by Coleman Young, the mayor of Detroit, a former labor leader and no conservative: "If a painter makes more than a secretary, then let more women be painters. Equal opportunity and affirmative action is how you do that." A woman entering the labor force today has no claim that she has been crowded into low-paying professions because of discrimination. She has choices.

Older women, of course, who have already invested much in their professions, are more constrained. But they have the same avenues open to them—such as organizing—as other similarly constrained (predominantly male) workers who struggle for higher wages in other settings. In Denver, for example, nurses sought comparable-worth wage gains in court and lost; they then went on strike and won. True, in some occupations, even strong unions can't raise wages very much. But as the president of the International Ladies Garment Workers Union (85 percent female) explained in objecting to a highfalutin AFL-CIO endorsement of comparable worth, the problem is not discrimination but the market. His workers have low wages because they compete with workers overseas who are paid thirty cents an hour. Comparable-worth doctrine may declare that garment workers ought to be making as much as truck drivers. But if the theory ever became practice, garment workers would be free of more than discrimination. They would be free of their jobs.

Why is the obvious about comparable worth so rarely heard? Why is it for Democrats the ultimate motherhood issue? Because here again the party of the big heart identifies a class of people who feel they aren't getting their just due, blames that condition on a single cause (discrimination), then offers a "rational" solution, on whose messy details it prefers not to dwell. But those details add up to a swamp of mindless arbitrariness and bureaucratic inefficiency, shrouded in a fine mist of pseudo-scientific objectivity. And the surest results will be unending litigation and an entirely new generation of inequities. These inequities, moreover, will be frozen in place by force of law, and thus that much more difficult to dislodge.

Comparable worth asks the question: How many nurses would it take to screw in a lightbulb? The joke is that, having not the faintest idea, it demands that a committee invent an answer, that the answer become law and that the law supplant the market. Even Karl Marx, who also had legitimate complaints about the equity of wages set by the market, had a more plausible alternative.

---

## REFLECTING ON MEANING

1. Krauthammer refutes two arguments made by advocates of comparable worth: the "crowding argument" and the "grand conspiracy theory." What are these arguments? What is the essence of Krauthammer's counterargument for each position? Do you agree or disagree with his reasoning? Consider, for example, why " 'women's work' is less crowded than ever," and whether

the author is justified in mocking the notion that "the market is inherently discriminatory."

2. Krauthammer is concerned that comparable worth will result in "sheer social chaos." What form does he believe this chaos will take? Are his fears justified? Do you find his qualm that everyone will want comparable worth reasonable? Will such a policy affect only women's salaries, or will it by definition extend pay equity to all?

3. What is the significance of Krauthammer's allusion to Karl Marx in the final paragraph of this essay? What is the "more plausible alternative" that Marx offers? Is Krauthammer suggesting that Marx's approach is actually more plausible, or is he implying something else?

## EXPLORING RHETORICAL STRATEGIES

1. Consider the point of view conveyed in the opening sentence of this essay: "The latest entry on the list of sacred democratic causes is comparable worth." What point of view does Krauthammer communicate through word choice? How does this statement immediately tell you the author's opinion of comparable worth?

2. What is the significance of the joke that appears in the essay's conclusion? In what ways does it provide an appropriate summary for Krauthammer's argument?

3. What is the tone of this essay? In what ways does Krauthammer achieve this tone? What kind of persona does it help him create? Is this persona appropriate—that is, does it add to his credibility?

# Chapter 12

## PORNOGRAPHY

## Pornography: Anti-Female Propaganda

SUSAN BROWNMILLER

*In this excerpt from* Against Our Will: Men, Women, and Rape, *Susan Brownmiller argues that the pornography debate has been clouded by the notion that it is a First Amendment issue. She reframes the debate, showing that it is the "undiluted essence of anti-female propaganda," designed to dehumanize woman by making her body the "private property" of man.*

Pornography has been so thickly glossed over with the patina of chic these days in the name of verbal freedom and sophistication that important distinctions between freedom of political expression (a democratic necessity), honest sex education for children (a social good) and ugly smut (the deliberate devaluation of the role of women through obscene, distorted depictions) have been hopelessly confused. Part of the problem is that those who traditionally have been the most vigorous opponents of porn are often those same people who shudder at the explicit mention of any sexual subject. Under their watchful, vigilante eyes, frank and free dissemination of educational materials relating to abortion, contraception, the act of birth, and female biology in general is also dangerous, subversive, and dirty. (I am not unmindful that a frank and free discussion of rape, "the unspeakable crime," might well give these righteous vigilantes further cause to shudder.) Because the battle lines were falsely drawn a long time ago, before there was a vocal women's movement, the anti-pornography forces appear to be, for the most part, religious, Southern, conservative, and right-wing, while the pro-porn forces are identified as Eastern, atheistic, and liberal.

But a woman's perspective demands a totally new alignment, or at least a fresh appraisal. The majority report of the President's Commission on Obscenity and Pornography (1970), a report that argued strongly for the removal of all legal restrictions on pornography, soft and hard, made plain that 90 percent of all pornographic material is geared to the male heterosexual market (the other 10 percent is geared to the male homosexual taste), that buyers of porn are "predominantly white, middle-class, middle-aged married males," and that the graphic depictions, the meat and potatoes of porn, are of the naked female body and of the multiplicity of acts done to that body.

Discussing the content of stag films, "a familiar and firmly established part of the American scene," the commission report dutifully, if foggily, explained, "Because pornography historically has been thought to be primarily a masculine interest, the emphasis in stag films seems to represent the preferences of the middle-class American male. Thus male homosexuality and bestiality are relatively rare while lesbianism is rather common."

The commissioners in this instance had merely verified what purveyors of porn have always known: hard-core pornography is not a celebration of sexual freedom; it is a cynical exploitation of female sexual activity through the device of making all such activity, and consequently all females, "dirty." Heterosexual male consumers of pornography are frankly turned on by watching lesbians in action (although never in the final scenes, but always as a curtain raiser); they are turned off with the sudden swiftness of a water faucet by watching naked men act upon each other. One study quoted in the commission report came to the unastounding conclusion that "seeing a stag film in the presence of male peers bolsters masculine esteem." Indeed. The men in groups who watch the films, it is important to note, are *not* naked.

When male response to pornography is compared to female response, a pronounced difference in attitude emerges. According to the commission, "Males report being more highly aroused by depictions of nude females, and show more interest in depictions of nude females than [do] females." Quoting the figures of Alfred Kinsey, the commission noted that a majority of males (77 percent) were "aroused" by visual depictions of explicit sex while a majority of females (68 percent) were not aroused. Further, "females more often than males reported 'disgust' and 'offense.' "

From whence comes this female disgust and offense? Are females sexually backward or more conservative by nature? The gut distaste that a majority of women feel when we look at pornography, a distaste that, incredibly, it is no longer fashionable to admit, comes, I think, from the gut knowledge that we and our bodies are being stripped, exposed, and contorted for the purpose of ridicule to bolster that "masculine esteem" which gets its kick and sense of power from viewing females as anonymous, panting playthings, adult toys, dehumanized objects to be used, abused, broken, and discarded.

This, of course, is also the philosophy of rape. It is no accident (for what else could be its purpose?) that females in the pornography genre are depicted in two cleanly delineated roles: as virgins who are caught and "banged" or as nymphomaniacs who are never sated. The most popular and prevalent pornographic fantasy combines the two: an innocent, untutored female is raped and "subjected to unnatural practices" that turn her into a raving, slobbering nymphomaniac, a dependent sexual slave who can never get enough of the big, male cock.

There can be no "equality" in porn, no female equivalent, no turning of the tables in the name of bawdy fun. Pornography, like rape, is a male invention, designed to dehumanize women, to reduce the female to an object of sexual access, not to free sensuality from moralistic or parental inhibition. The staple of porn will always be the naked female body, breasts and genitals exposed, because as man devised it, her naked body is the female's "shame," her private parts the private property of man, while his are the ancient, holy, universal, patriarchal instrument of his power, his rule by force over *her*.

Pornography is the undiluted essence of anti-female propaganda. Yet the very same liberals who were so quick to understand the method and purpose behind the mighty propaganda machine of Hitler's Third Reich, the consciously spewed-out anti-Semitic caricatures and obscenities that gave an ideological base to the Holocaust and the Final Solution, the very same liberals who, enlightened by blacks, searched their own conscience and came to understand that their tolerance of "nigger" jokes and portrayals of shuffling, rolling-eyed servants in movies perpetuated the degrading myths of black inferiority and gave an ideological base to the continuation of black oppression—these very same liberals now fervidly maintain that the hatred and contempt for women that find expression in four-letter words used as expletives and in what are quaintly called "adult" or "erotic" books and movies are a valid extension of freedom of speech that must be preserved as a Constitutional right.

To defend the right of a lone, crazed American Nazi to grind out propaganda calling for the extermination of all Jews, as the ACLU has done in the name of free speech, is, after all, a self-righteous and not particularly courageous stand, for American Jewry is not currently threatened by storm troopers, concentration camps and imminent extermination, but I wonder if the ACLU's position might change if, come tomorrow morning, the bookstores and movie theatres lining Forty-second Street in New York City were devoted not to the humiliation of women by rape and torture, as they currently are, but to a systematized, commercially successful propaganda machine depicting the sadistic pleasures of gassing Jews or lynching blacks?

Is this analogy extreme? Not if you are a woman who is conscious of the ever-present threat of rape and the proliferation of a cultural ideology that makes it sound like "liberated" fun. The majority report of the President's Commission on Obscenity and Pornography tried to pooh-pooh the opinion of law enforcement agencies around the country that claimed their own concrete experience with offenders who were caught with the stuff led them to conclude that pornographic material is a causative factor in crimes of sexual violence. The commission maintained that it was not possible at this time to scientifically prove or disprove such a connection.

But does one need scientific methodology in order to conclude that the anti-female propaganda that permeates our nation's cultural output promotes a climate in which the acts of sexual hostility directed against women are not only tolerated but ideologically encouraged? A similar debate has raged for many years over whether or not the extensive glorification of violence (the gangster as hero; the loving treatment accorded bloody shoot-'em-ups in movies, books, and on TV) has a causal effect, a direct relationship to the rising rate of crime, particularly among youth. Interestingly enough, in this area—nonsexual and not specifically related to abuses against women—public opinion seems to be swinging to the position that explicit violence in the entertainment media does have a deleterious effect; it makes violence commonplace, numbingly routine, and no longer morally shocking.

More to the point, those who call for a curtailment of scenes of violence in movies and on television in the name of sensitivity, good taste, and what's best for our children are not accused of being pro-censorship or against freedom of speech. Similarly, minority group organizations, black, Hispanic, Japanese, Italian, Jewish, or American Indian, that campaign against ethnic slurs and demeaning portrayals in movies, on television shows, and in commercials are perceived as waging a just political fight, for if a minority group claims to be offended by a specific portrayal, be it Little Black Sambo or the Frito Bandito, and relates it to a history of ridicule and oppression, few liberals would dare to trot out a Constitutional argument in theoretical opposition, not if they wish to maintain their liberal credentials. Yet when it comes to the treatment of women, the liberal consciousness remains fiercely obdurate, refusing to be budged, for the sin of appearing square or prissy in the age of so-called sexual revolution has become the worst offense of all.

---

## REFLECTING ON MEANING

1. Brownmiller maintains that for the issue of pornography "the battle lines were falsely drawn a long time ago." What does she mean? Whom does she place on each side, and what are their stances on pornography? Why does she feel that "a woman's perspective demands a totally new alignment, or at least a fresh appraisal"? In what ways does a feminist perspective redraw the battle lines? How is pornography a gender issue?

2. "Hard-core pornography is not a celebration of sexual freedom; it is a cynical exploitation of female sexual activity through the device of making all such activity, and consequently all females, 'dirty.' " Do you agree with this statement? Why or why not? What would a "celebration of sexual freedom" be? How would it differ from pornography as Brownmiller defines it?

3. According to Brownmiller, how does pornography reinforce the gender hierarchy? Why can there be "no 'equality' in porn, no female equivalent, no turning of the tables in the name of bawdy fun"? What makes it a "male invention"? What "philosophy" do pornography and rape share?

4. How are women depicted in pornography? Is Brownmiller concerned with nudity, or is she concerned with something else? What does she see as the social consequences of the propagation of pornography for women?

## EXPLORING RHETORICAL STRATEGIES

1. Brownmiller's argument pivots on several crucial analogies. What are these analogies? In what ways are they appropriate or inappropriate? How do they help Brownmiller advance her viewpoint? How do they help her approach the issue from a fresh perspective?
2. How would you describe the voice that speaks in this essay? What kind of persona does Brownmiller create? How is she able to ensure that she isn't mistaken for one of the many opponents of pornography who "shudder at the explicit mention of any sexual subject" and who see all sexual matters as "dangerous, subversive, and dirty"?
3. To what extent does Brownmiller explicitly define pornography? Can you derive her definition from her argument?

---

# The Question of Pornography

EDWARD I. DONNERSTEIN,
DANIEL G. LINZ, and STEVEN PENROD

---

*In the following essay, which originally appeared in 1986 in* Psychology Today, *Edward Donnerstein, Daniel Linz, and Steven Penrod examine the link between violent pornography and aggression toward women. Scrutinizing a government report on pornography released in 1986, they criticize it for not acknowledging that it is violent—and not sexually explicit—material that presents the "most clear and present danger" for society.*

In July 1986, the United States Attorney General's Commission on Pornography issued its final report on a subject that is as complex as the human condition. While many people have commented upon the report, few have actually read it and fewer still understand its implications.

As social scientists and two of the researchers whose work was cited throughout the two-volume work, we feel it necessary to point out that the report fell short of our expectations in several important respects. First, there are factual problems with the report, representing serious errors of commission. Several of the contentions made in its pages cannot be supported by empirical evidence. Some commission members apparently did not understand or chose not to heed some of the fundamental assumptions in the social science research on pornography. Second, and perhaps more importantly, the commission members have committed a serious error of omission. The single most important problem in the media today, as clearly indicated by social science research, is not pornography but violence.

The report begins with some history about previous attempts to examine the question of pornography. One of the most important of these was the President's Commission on Obscenity and Pornography, which issued its final report in 1970. "More than in 1957, when the law of obscenity became inextricably a part of constitutional law, more than in 1970 when the President's Commission on Obscenity and Pornography issued its report . . . we live in a society unquestionably pervaded by sexual explicitness," the current report states. It goes on to point out, quite rightly, that the most dangerous form of pornography is that which includes specifically violent themes. But then the report adds: "Increasingly, the most prevalent forms of pornography . . . fit this description. . . . It is with respect to material of this variety that the scientific findings and ultimate conclusions of the 1970 Commission are least reliable for today, precisely because material of this variety was largely absent from that Commission's inquiries."

It is popularly assumed—and the members of the commission appear to share this assumption—that images of violence have become more prevalent in pornography in recent years. Interestingly, there has never been a systematic content analysis of X-rated books, films, and magazines that would be needed to support such a conclusion. But there are a handful of studies, concentrating on specific media, that at least call this notion into question.

One of the most recent of these was undertaken by sociologist Joseph E. Scott of Ohio State University. He examined the content of cartoons in *Playboy* magazine from 1954 to 1983 and found that there was indeed a period—around 1977—when the violent content peaked. But just as there had been an increase in violence in the years before 1977, there has been a like decrease since. Further, he notes that sexually violent material seems to occur on an average of about 1 page every 3,000 and in fewer than 4 pictures out of 1,000—a level that would have to be considered barely noticeable.

In addition, there is evidence indicating a different sort of trend in sexually oriented videocassettes. Psychologist Ted Palys of Simon Fraser University analyzed the content of 150 randomly selected home videos, most of which were produced between 1979 and 1983. He divided these films into "Triple X," in which sexual activity is explicit and graphic, and "Adult," in which no explicit sex is shown but nudity and "implied" sexual behavior is allowed.

Palys found that the Adult films actually portrayed a higher percentage of aggressive scenes and more severe and graphic forms of aggression than did the Triple X videos. More important, there was no increase in aggressive images between 1979 and 1983 for either type of video. In fact, as Palys notes, the difference between these two types of videos may be widening over time, primarily because of decreases in sexual violence in the Triple X category.

At least for now we cannot legitimately conclude that pornography has become more violent since the time of the 1970 Pornography Commission. The results of the few studies that have been done are inconclusive and inconsistent, but at least a few of them point in the opposite direction. Perhaps it is because all forms of pornography are more prevalent now than they once were that we are more aware of the sexually violent forms of pornography.

What is so particularly evil about violent pornography? Here, the commission does not mince words: "In both clinical and experimental settings, exposure to sexually violent materials has indicated an increase in the likelihood of aggression." The commission goes on to state that "finding a link between aggressive behavior toward women and sexual violence . . . requires assumptions not found exclusively in the experimental evidence. We see no reason, however, not to make these assumptions." The assumptions include the idea (in the commission's words) that "increased aggressive behavior towards women is causally related, for an aggregate population, to increased sexual violence."

One persuasive reason to be careful about an intuitive leap like this, however, is a closer examination of the empirical evidence—what it says and what it does not say. We have no argument with the commission on its first point. Experiments by psychologist Neil Malamuth at the University of California, Los Angeles, suggest that, especially when the experimenter appears to condone aggression against women, men act more aggressively toward women in a laboratory after having been exposed to sexually violent stories. But a question that the prudent reader might raise is: "How long do these effects last?" In the vast majority of studies, aggressive behavior is measured almost immediately after exposure to the violent pornographic films. But is the effect cumulative or does it disappear over time?

In one study by Malamuth and psychologist Joseph Ceniti, college-aged men were exposed to violent and nonviolent sexual material over a four-week period. They watched two feature-length films each week and read similar materials. About seven days later, they were (according to the researchers' plan) angered by a woman working with the researchers and then given an opportunity to act aggressively against her. Contrary to expectations, the men who had been exposed to pornography were no more aggressive against her than were those not exposed to pornography. For the moment, then, we do not know if repeated exposure has a cumulative effect or if such effects are only temporary. But the evidence, such as it is, points toward the latter conclusion. This fact seems not to have been given sufficient consideration by the commission.

In addition, there is evidence that particular themes in pornography might be especially harmful. Recent research indicates that it is specifically the message that women find force or aggression pleasurable that seems to be important in influencing men's perceptions and attitudes about rape. For example, in a study Donnerstein conducted with psychologist Leonard Berkowitz, men were shown one of two films, both aggressively violent and sexually explicit. In both, a young woman arrives at the home of two young men to study. She is shoved around, tied up, stripped, slapped, and ultimately raped by both men. In one version of the film ("positive ending"), the woman is shown smiling at the end and in no way resisting. A narrative added to the film indicates that she eventually becomes a willing participant. In the version with a "negative ending," the reaction of the woman is not clear, but the voice-over indicates that she found the experience humiliating and disgusting.

Men who saw the positive-ending film interpreted the film itself as less aggressive and said that the woman suffered less, enjoyed herself more, and was more responsible for what happened than did the men who saw the negative ending. This seems fairly clear evidence that the different messages in the two films affected the men's attitudes in different ways.

But this literature can be tricky to interpret. In one study by Malamuth, researcher Scott Haber and psychologist Seymour Feshbach, for example, men read several stories, some of which were about a woman being raped. When the men were asked how likely they would be to behave as the rapist did if they knew they would not be caught, more than half indicated some likelihood of behaving that way. Many assume that this surprisingly high percentage was due to the effects of men being exposed to violent pornography. As the commission report concludes, "substantial exposure to sexually violent materials . . . bears a causal relationship to anti-social acts of sexual violence and, for some subgroups, possibly to unlawful acts of sexual violence."

Yet nothing could be further from the truth. In none of the studies by Malamuth has a measure of motivation such as "likelihood to rape" ever changed as a result of exposure to pornography. If the men reported feeling this way, it might be because they were generally callous about rape to begin with. As Malamuth has noted, men who indicate some likelihood that they might commit rape (if not caught) are more sexually aroused by and more attracted to violent materials, but there is no reason to think that exposure to violent pornography is the cause of these predispositions.

Malamuth and psychologist James Check again asked men to read two stories. Some first read a story with a "positive ending," in which the woman becomes sexually aroused; others read a story with a negative ending; then all of the men read a realistic depiction of a rape. But first, the researchers classified the men as "more likely to rape" or "less likely to rape" based upon their answer to the question, "Would you rape if you knew you would not be caught?"

While both groups were more likely to view the woman in the second story as enjoying rape if they had read the positive-ending story first, the "more likely to rape" men seemed much more affected by exposure to this sort of pornography. They agreed much more frequently with statements suggesting that women enjoy rape and enjoy being forced into having sex than did those who were "less likely to rape" to begin with. This indicates to us that exposure to violent pornography is not necessarily causing callous attitudes about rape but rather may reinforce and strengthen already existing beliefs and values. If aggressive pornography is not the cause of the negative attitudes, then it ought not be blamed for them.

What we have is a picture of violent pornography that is somewhat different from that drawn by the commission. We do not, as yet, know if the detrimental effects of watching pornography are long-lived or only fleeting. We do know that it is specifically the pornographic materials that depict women "enjoying" rape that are especially damaging, but it remains unclear whether all men are affected equally even by these bizarre scripts. Finally, it remains to be seen whether changes in attitudes about women and rape revealed in relatively small-scale tests have any applicability to rape and aggression in the real world.

There is some evidence from the work of Malamuth that these attitudes do have some relationship to real-world aggression, but again these are attitudes that people already have. The commission members were obviously aware of these issues. In fact, these conclusions, well-grounded in scientific research, are briefly summarized deep within their report, which makes it even more perplexing that they ignore the data in making their 92 recommendations.

Our major criticism of the report and its authors, however, has to do with a subject that has been glossed over in the commission's 1,960-page report. The commission has ignored the inescapable conclusion that it is violence, whether or not accompanied by sex, that has the most damaging effect upon those who view it, hear it, or read about it. This is an extremely important distinction, with direct relevance to the work of the commission, because it has implications far beyond violent pornography and pornography in general.

Sexual violence and depictions of women "desiring" rape are not limited to X-rated films, books and magazines. In the popular film *The Getaway,* for example, one of the robbers kidnaps a woman (portrayed by Sally Struthers) and her husband. He rapes the woman, but she is portrayed as a willing participant. Struthers' character becomes the kidnapper's girlfriend and the two of them taunt her husband until he finally commits suicide. The woman then willingly continues with the assailant. Far from being consigned to dingy X-rated theaters, this film, originally produced in 1972 and shown in cinemas all over the country, is still shown occasionally on commercial television.

Malamuth and Check tried to determine whether the mildly explicit sexual violence in *The Getaway* and in *Swept Away,* another film with similar content, influenced viewers' attitudes toward women and rape. When the researchers questioned college students who saw both films and students who saw nonviolent films or no films at all, they found that the men who saw violent movies more readily accepted interpersonal violence and more frequently believed that women enjoy rape.

In another study we did with Berkowitz, men saw different versions of a film. The first version contained a scene of sexual aggression in which a woman is tied up, threatened with a gun and raped. The second version contained only the violent parts of the scene, with the sexually explicit rape omitted. The third version contained only the sexually explicit rape scene with the violence deleted.

The most callous attitudes about rape and the largest percentage of subjects indicating some likelihood of raping or using force were found among those men who had seen only the violent coercion. Subjects who saw the X-rated version without violence scored the lowest on both measures, and those who saw both the explicit sex and the violence scored somewhere in between.

Taken together, these studies strongly suggest that violence against women need not occur in a pornographic or sexually explicit context to have a negative effect upon viewer attitudes and behavior. But even more importantly, it must be concluded that violent images, rather than sexual ones, are most responsible for people's attitudes about women and rape.

As should be obvious to anyone with a television set, the mass media contain an abundance of such nonsexually explicit images and messages. These ideas about rape are so pervasive in our culture that it is myopic to call them the exclusive domain of violent pornography. In fact, one would not have to search much farther than the local 7-Eleven to find numerous bloody murder mysteries in detective magazines that reinforce this point.

And this is where we have our strongest disagreement with the Commission on Pornography. Granted that the charter of the group was to examine the pernicious effects of pornography on society. Granted also that the time, money and other resources of the commission were limited. But it seems appropriate to note that if the commissioners were looking for the most nefarious media threat to public welfare, they missed the boat. The most clear and present danger, well documented by the social science literature, is all violent material in our society, whether sexually explicit or not, that promotes violence against women. Let us hope that the next commission will provide a better example by disentangling sexuality from violence, therefore yielding more useful conclusions.

---

## REFLECTING ON MEANING

1. What problems with the government commission's report on pornography do Donnerstein, Linz, and Penrod cite? What are the report's "serious errors of commission"? What is its "serious error of omission"? What is the difference between these two kinds of error?

2. A significant part of the essay looks at whether violent images in pornography are on the increase. What do the authors conclude on this question? How do their conclusions illuminate the findings of the commission's report? How important do you think these conclusions are in general? Why?

3. What is the connection that the authors make between violent pornography and aggression toward women? What do the studies on pornography and behavior that they survey suggest? What themes in pornography seem to be linked closely to aggression? What do studies on popular films containing "mildly explicit sexual violence" suggest? In what ways does the cause-effect relationship that these authors suggest differ from that suggested by the commission's report?

## EXPLORING RHETORICAL STRATEGIES

1. In their introduction the authors inform their audience that their studies were among those cited in the commission's final report in 1986. In what ways does this circumstance help them establish credibility? How does this fact encourage you to respond to their criticisms of the report?

2. Before turning their attention to popular films, the authors summarize the points they have made so far. Beyond providing a summary, what function does this recapitulating paragraph serve? How does it facilitate readers' understanding of the material already covered and that to be addressed?

3. What evidence do Donnerstein, Linz, and Penrod offer to support their criticism of the commission's report? Do you find their evidence convincing? Why or why not?

# A First Amendment Junkie

SUSAN JACOBY

*Susan Jacoby's perspective on pornography places the controversy firmly within the context of First Amendment issues. Jacoby argues that censorship of pornography clearly violates First Amendment rights and that "the impulse to censor places no faith in the possibilities of democratic persuasion."*

It is no news that many women are defecting from the ranks of civil libertarians on the issue of obscenity. The conviction of Larry Flynt, publisher of *Hustler* magazine—before his metamorphosis into a born-again Christian—was greeted with unabashed feminist approval. Harry Reems, the unknown actor who was convicted by a Memphis jury for conspiring to distribute the movie *Deep Throat,* has carried on his legal battles with almost no support from women who ordinarily regard themselves as supporters of the First Amendment. Feminist writers and scholars have even discussed the possibility of making common cause against pornography with adversaries of the women's movement—including opponents of the equal rights amendment and "right-to-life" forces.

All of this is deeply disturbing to a woman writer who believes, as I always have and still do, in an absolute interpretation of the First Amendment. Nothing in Larry Flynt's garbage convinces me that the late Justice Hugo L. Black was wrong in his opinion that "the Federal Government is without any power whatsoever under the Constitution to put any type of burden on free speech and expression of ideas of any kind (as distinguished from conduct)." Many women I like and respect tell me I am wrong; I cannot remember having become involved in so many heated discussions of a public issue since the end of the Vietnam War. A feminist writer described my views as those of a "First Amendment junkie."

Many feminist arguments for controls on pornography carry the implicit conviction that porn books, magazines and movies pose a greater threat to women than similarly repulsive exercises of free speech pose to other offended groups. This conviction has, of course, been shared by everyone—regardless of race, creed or sex—who has ever argued in favor of abridging the First Amendment. It is the argument used by some Jews who have withdrawn their support from the American Civil Liberties Union because it has defended the right of American Nazis to march through a community inhabited by survivors of Hitler's concentration camps.

If feminists want to argue that the protection of the Constitution should not be extended to *any* particularly odious or threatening form of speech, they have a reasonable argument (although I don't agree with it). But it is ridiculous to suggest that the porn shops on 42d Street are more disgusting to women than a march of neo-Nazis is to survivors of the extermination camps.

The arguments over pornography also blur the vital distinction between expression of ideas and conduct. When I say I believe unreservedly in the First Amendment, someone always comes back at me with the issue of "kiddie porn." But kiddie porn is not a First Amendment issue. It is an issue of the abuse of power—the power adults have over children—and not of obscenity. Parents and promoters have no more right to use their children to make porn movies than they do to send them to work in coal mines. The responsible adults should be prosecuted, just as adults who use children for back-breaking farm labor should be prosecuted.

Susan Brownmiller, in *Against Our Will: Men, Women and Rape,* has described pornography as "the undiluted essence of anti-female propaganda." I think this is a fair description of some types of pornography, especially of the brutish subspecies that equates sex with death and portrays women primarily as objects of violence.

The equation of sex and violence, personified by some glossy rock record album covers as well as by *Hustler,* has fed the illusion that censorship of pornography can be conducted on a more rational basis than other types of censorship. Are all pictures of naked women obscene? Clearly not, says a friend. A Renoir nude is art, she says, and *Hustler* is trash. "Any reasonable person" knows that.

But what about something between art and trash—something, say, along the lines of *Playboy* or *Penthouse* magazines? I asked five women for their reactions to one picture in *Penthouse* and got responses that ranged from "lovely" and "sensuous" to "revolting" and "demeaning." Feminists, like everyone else, seldom have rational reasons for their preferences in erotica. Like members of juries, they tend to disagree when confronted with something that falls short of 100 percent vulgarity.

In any case, feminists will not be the arbiters of good taste if it becomes easier to harass, prosecute and convict people on obscenity charges. Most of the people who want to censor girlie magazines are equally opposed to open discussion of issues that are of vital concern to women: rape, abortion, menstruation, contraception, lesbianism—in fact, the entire range of sexual experience from a woman's viewpoint.

Feminist writers and editors and film makers have limited financial resources: Confronted by a determined prosecutor, Hugh Hefner will fare better than Susan Brownmiller. Would the Memphis jurors who convicted Harry Reems for his role in *Deep Throat* be inclined to take a more positive view of paintings of the female genitalia done by sensitive feminist artists? *Ms.* magazine has printed color reproductions of some of those art works; *Ms.* is already banned from a number of high school libraries because someone considers it threatening and/or obscene.

Feminists who want to censor what they regard as harmful pornography have essentially the same motivation as other would-be censors: They want to use the power of the state to accomplish what they have been unable to achieve in the marketplace of ideas and images. The impulse to censor places no faith in the possibilities of democratic persuasion.

It isn't easy to persuade certain men that they have better uses for $1.95 each month than to spend it on a copy of *Hustler*? Well, then, give the men no choice in the matter.

I believe there is also a connection between the impulse toward censorship on the part of people who used to consider themselves civil libertarians and a more general desire to shift responsibility from individuals to institutions. When I saw the movie *Looking for Mr. Goodbar,* I was stunned by its series of visual images equating sex and violence, coupled with what seems to me the mindless message (a distortion of the fine Judith Rossner novel) that casual sex equals death. When I came out of the movie, I was even more shocked to see parents standing in line with children between the ages of 10 and 14.

I simply don't know why a parent would take a child to see such a movie, any more than I understand why people feel they can't turn off a television set their child is watching. Whenever I say that, my friends tell me I don't know how it is because I don't have children. True, but I do have parents. When I was a child, they did turn off the TV. They didn't expect the Federal Communications Commission to do their job for them.

I am a First Amendment junkie. You can't OD on the First Amendment, because free speech is its own best antidote.

## REFLECTING ON MEANING

1. Jacoby makes a distinction between the "expression of ideas and conduct," arguing that "kiddie porn" is very different from adult pornography. What is the distinction? According to Jacoby, why is kiddie porn an "issue of the abuse of power"? What is her assumption about power in relationships between women and men? Do you agree or disagree with this assumption? Why?
2. What point is Jacoby making when she frames the pornography debate as "art" versus "trash"? Are feminists, as she suggests, attempting to become "arbiters of good taste" when they object to pornography? To what extent can pornography be construed as an issue of aesthetics?
3. Does Jacoby think that all images—even violent ones—should be protected by the First Amendment? Does she define what she means by such terms as *pornography, erotica,* and *obscenity*? To what degree does her stand on the issue rest on her definition of these terms? To what extent does your stand rest on the way you define these terms?

## EXPLORING RHETORICAL STRATEGIES

1. How appropriate is the analogy Jacoby makes between drug addiction and her unqualified support for the First Amendment? What effect does her reiteration of this analogy have in her final sentence? What implications does the analogy suggest?
2. Jacoby criticizes not only the idea of censorship but advocates of censorship as well—especially feminists. To what extent does her argument rely on establishing feminists as an opposing faction, one whose views are wrong? How does she use this conception of feminists as a strategy to advance her argument and to manipulate your response to the issue?
3. What persona does Jacoby present in this essay? What strategies does she employ to construct this persona? Is it effective?

# Chapter 13

# ABORTION

## A Defense of Abortion

JUDITH JARVIS THOMSON

*A professor of philosophy, Judith Jarvis Thomson argues that abortion is not necessarily morally wrong even if the fetus is considered human. Published in 1971, this ground-breaking essay has been hailed as a brilliant example of philosophical argumentation from a feminist point of view.*

Most opposition to abortion relies on the premise that the fetus is a human being, a person, from the moment of conception. The premise is argued for, but, as I think, not well. Take, for example, the most common argument. We are asked to notice that the development of a human being from conception through birth into childhood is continuous; then it is said that to draw a line, to choose a point in this development and say "before this point the thing is not a person, after this point it is a person" is to make an arbitrary choice, a choice for which in the nature of things no good reason can be given. It is concluded that the fetus is, or anyway that we had better say it is, a person from the moment of conception. But this conclusion does not follow. Similar things might be said about the development of an acorn into an oak tree, and it does not follow that acorns are oak trees, or that we had better say they are. Arguments of this form are sometimes called "slippery slope arguments"—the phrase is perhaps self-explanatory—and it is dismaying that opponents of abortion rely on them so heavily and uncritically.[1]

I am inclined to agree, however, that the prospects for "drawing a line" in the development of the fetus look dim. I am inclined to think also that we shall probably have to agree that the fetus has already become a human person well before birth. Indeed, it comes as a surprise when one first learns how early in its life it begins to acquire human characteristics. By the tenth week, for example, it already has a face, arms and legs, fingers and toes; it has internal organs, and brain activity is detectable.[2] On the other hand, I think that the premise is false, that the fetus is not a person from the moment of conception. A newly fertilized ovum, a newly implanted clump of cells, is no more a person than an acorn is an oak tree. But I shall not discuss any of this. For it seems to me to be of great interest to ask what happens if, for the sake of argument, we allow the premise. How, precisely, are we supposed to get from there to the conclusion that abortion is morally impermissible? Opponents of abortion commonly spend most of their time establishing that the fetus is a person, and hardly any time explaining the step from there to the impermissibility of abortion. Perhaps they think the step too simple and obvious to require much comment. Or perhaps instead they are simply being economical in argument. Many of those who defend abortion rely on the premise that the fetus is not a person, but only a bit of tissue that will become a person at birth; and why pay out more arguments than you have to? Whatever the explanation, I suggest that the step they take is neither easy nor obvious, that it calls for closer examination than it is commonly given, and that when we do give it this closer examination we shall feel inclined to reject it.

I propose, then, that we grant that the fetus is a person from the moment of conception. How does the argument go from here? Something like this, I take it. Every person has a right to life. So the fetus has a right to life. No doubt the mother has a right to decide what shall happen in and to her body; everyone would grant that. But surely a person's right to life is stronger and more stringent than the mother's right to decide what happens in and to her body, and so outweighs it. So the fetus may not be killed; an abortion may not be performed.

It sounds plausible. But now let me ask you to imagine this. You wake up in the morning and find yourself back to back in bed with an unconscious violinist. A famous unconscious violinist. He has been found to have a fatal kidney ailment, and the Society of Music Lovers has canvassed all the available medical records and found that you alone have the right blood type to help. They have therefore kidnapped you, and last night the violinist's circulatory system was plugged into yours, so that your kidneys can be used to extract poisons from his blood as well as your own. The director of the hospital now tells you, "Look, we're sorry the Society of Music Lovers did this to you—we would never have permitted it if we had known. But still, they did it, and the violinist now is plugged into you. To unplug you would be to kill him. But never mind, it's only for nine months. By then he will have recovered from his ailment, and can safely be unplugged from you." Is it morally incumbent on you to accede to this situation? No doubt it would be very nice of you if you did, a great kindness. But do you *have* to accede to it? What if it were not nine months, but nine years? Or longer still? What if the director of the hospital says, "Tough luck, I agree, but you've now got to stay in bed, with the violinist plugged into you, for the rest of your life. Because remember this. All persons have a right to life, and violinists are persons. Granted you have a right to decide what happens in and to your body, but a person's right to life outweighs your right to decide what happens in and to your body. So you cannot ever be unplugged from him." I imagine you would regard this as outrageous, which suggests that something really is wrong with the plausible-sounding argument I mentioned a moment ago.

In this case, of course, you were kidnapped; you didn't volunteer for the operation that plugged the violinist into your kidneys. Can those who oppose abortion on the ground I mentioned make an exception for a pregnancy due to rape? Certainly. They can say that persons have a right to life only if they didn't come into existence because of rape; or they can say that all persons have a right to life, but that some have less of a right to life than others, in particular, that those who came into existence because of rape have less. But these statements have a rather unpleasant sound. Surely the question of whether you have a right to life at all, or how much of it you have, shouldn't turn on the question of whether or not you are the product of a rape. And in fact the people who oppose abortion on the ground I mentioned do not make this distinction, and hence do not make an exception in case of rape.

Nor do they make an exception for a case in which the mother has to spend the nine months of her pregnancy in bed. They would agree that would be a great pity, and hard on the mother; but all the same, all persons have a right to life, the fetus is a person, and so on. I suspect, in fact, that they would not make an exception for a case in which, miraculously enough, the pregnancy went on for nine years, or even the rest of the mother's life.

Some won't even make an exception for a case in which continuation of the pregnancy is likely to shorten the mother's life;

they regard abortion as impermissible even to save the mother's life. Such cases are nowadays very rare, and many opponents of abortion do not accept this extreme view. All the same, it is a good place to begin: a number of points of interest come out in respect to it.

1. Let us call the view that abortion is impermissible even to save the mother's life "the extreme view." I want to suggest first that it does not issue from the argument I mentioned earlier without the addition of some fairly powerful premises. Suppose a woman has become pregnant, and now learns that she has a cardiac condition such that she will die if she carries the baby to term. What may be done for her? The fetus, being a person, has a right to life, but as the mother is a person too, so has she a right to life. Presumably they have an equal right to life. How is it supposed to come out that an abortion may not be performed? If mother and child have an equal right to life, shouldn't we perhaps flip a coin? Or should we add to the mother's right to life her right to decide what happens in and to her body, which everybody seems to be ready to grant—the sum of her rights now outweighing the fetus' right to life?

The most familiar argument here is the following. We are told that performing the abortion would be directly killing[3] the child, whereas doing nothing would not be killing the mother, but only letting her die. Moreover, in killing the child, one would be killing an innocent person, for the child has committed no crime, and is not aiming at his mother's death. And then there are a variety of ways in which this might be continued. (1) But as directly killing an innocent person is always and absolutely impermissible, an abortion may not be performed. Or, (2) as directly killing an innocent person is murder, and murder is always and absolutely impermissible, an abortion may not be performed.[4] Or, (3) as one's duty to refrain from directly killing an innocent person is more stringent than one's duty to keep a person from dying, an abortion may not be performed. Or, (4) if one's only options are directly killing an innocent person or letting a person die, one must prefer letting the person die, and thus an abortion may not be performed.[5]

Some people seem to have thought that these are not further premises which must be added if the conclusion is to be reached, but that they follow from the very fact that an innocent person has a right to life.[6] But this seems to me to be a mistake, and perhaps the simplest way to show this is to bring out that while we must certainly grant that innocent persons have a right to life, the theses in (1) through (4) are all false. Take (2), for example. If directly killing an innocent person is murder, and thus is impermissible, then the mother's directly killing the innocent person inside her is murder, and thus is impermissible. But it cannot seriously be thought to be murder if the mother performs an abortion on herself to save her life. It cannot seriously be said that she *must* refrain, that she *must* sit passively by and wait for her death. Let us look again at the case of you and the violinist. There you are, in bed with the violinist, and the director of the hospital says to you, "It's all most distressing, and I deeply sympathize, but you see this is putting an additional strain on your kidneys, and you'll be dead within the month. But you have to stay where you are all the same. Because unplugging you would be directly killing an innocent violinist, and that's murder, and that's impermissible." If anything in the world is true, it is that you do not commit murder, you do not do what is impermissible, if you reach around to your back and unplug yourself from that violinist to save your life.

The main focus of attention in writings on abortion has been on what a third party may or may not do in answer to a request from a woman for an abortion. This is in a way understandable. Things being as they are, there isn't much a woman can safely do to abort herself. So the question asked is what a third party may do, and what the mother may do, if it is mentioned at all, is deduced, almost as an afterthought, from what it is concluded that third parties may do. But it seems to me that to treat the matter in this way is to refuse to grant to the mother that very status of person which is so firmly insisted on for the fetus. For we cannot simply read off what a person may do from what a third party may do. Suppose you find yourself trapped in a tiny house with a growing child. I mean a very tiny house, and a rapidly growing child—you are already up against the wall of the house and in a few minutes you'll be crushed to death. The child on the other hand won't be crushed to death; if nothing is done to stop him from growing he'll be hurt, but in the end he'll simply burst open the house and walk out a free man. Now I could well understand it if a bystander were to say, "There's nothing we can do for you. We cannot choose between your life and his, we cannot be the ones to decide who is to live, we cannot intervene." But it cannot be concluded that you too can do nothing, that you cannot attack it to save your life. However innocent the child may be, you do not have to wait passively while it crushes you to death. Perhaps a pregnant woman is vaguely felt to have the status of house, to which we don't allow the right of self-defense. But if the woman houses the child, it should be remembered that she is a person who houses it.

I should perhaps stop to say explicitly that I am not claiming that people have a right to do anything whatever to save their lives. I think, rather, that there are drastic limits to the right of self-defense. If someone threatens you with death unless you torture someone else to death, I think you have not the right, even to save your life, to do so. But the case under consideration here is very different. In our case there are only two people involved, one whose life is threatened, and one who threatens it. Both are innocent: the one who is threatened is not threatened because of any fault, the one who threatens does not threaten because of any fault. For this reason we may feel that we bystanders cannot intervene. But the person threatened can.

In sum, a woman surely can defend her life against the threat to it posed by the unborn child, even if doing so involves its death. And this shows not merely that the theses in (1) through (4) are false; it shows also that the extreme view of abortion is false, and so we need not canvass any other possible ways of arriving at it from the argument I mentioned at the outset.

2. The extreme view could of course be weakened to say that while abortion is permissible to save the mother's life, it may not be performed by a third party, but only by the mother herself. But this cannot be right, either. For what we have to keep in mind is that the mother and the unborn child are not like two tenants in a small house which has, by an unfortunate mistake, been rented to both: the mother *owns* the house. The fact that she does adds to the offensiveness of deducing that the mother can do nothing from the supposition that third parties can do nothing. But it does more than this: it casts a bright light on the supposition that third parties can do nothing. Certainly it lets us see that a third party who says "I cannot choose between you" is fooling himself if he thinks this is impartiality. If Jones has found and fastened on a certain coat, which he needs to keep him from freezing, but which Smith also needs to keep him from freezing, then it is not impartiality that says "I cannot choose between you" when Smith owns the coat. Women have said again and again "This body is *my* body!" and they have reason to feel angry, reason to feel that it has been like shouting into the wind. Smith, after all, is hardly likely to bless us if we say to him, "Of course it's your coat, anybody would grant that it is. But no one may choose between you and Jones who is to have it."

We should really ask what it is that says "no one may choose" in the face of the fact that the body that houses the child is the mother's body. It may be simply a failure to appreciate this fact. But it may be something more interesting, namely the sense that one has a right to refuse to lay hands on people, even where it would be just and fair to do so, even where justice seems to require that somebody do so. Thus justice might call for somebody to get Smith's coat back from Jones, and yet you have a right to refuse to be the one to lay hands on Jones, a right to refuse to do physical violence to him. This, I think, must be granted. But then what should be said is not "no one may choose," but only "*I* cannot choose," and indeed not even this, but "*I* will not *act*," leaving it open that somebody else can or should, and in particular that anyone in a position of authority, with the job of securing people rights, both can and should. So this is no difficulty. I have not been arguing that any given third party must accede to the mother's request that he perform an abortion to save her life, but only that he may.

I suppose that in some views of human life the mother's body is only on loan to her, the loan not being one which gives her any prior claim to it. One who held this view might well think it impartiality to say "I cannot choose." But I shall simply ignore this possibility. My own view is that if a human being has any just, prior claim to anything at all, he has a just, prior claim to his own body. And perhaps this needn't be argued for here anyway, since, as I mentioned, the arguments against abortion we are looking at do grant that the woman has a right to decide what happens in and to her body.

But although they do grant it, I have tried to show that they do not take seriously what is done in granting it. I suggest the same thing will reappear even more clearly when we turn away from cases in which the mother's life is at stake, and attend, as I propose we now do, to the vastly more common cases in which a woman wants an abortion for some less weighty reason than preserving her own life.

3. Where the mother's life is not at stake, the argument I mentioned at the outset seems to have a much stronger pull. "Everyone has a right to life, so the unborn person has a right to life." And isn't the child's right to life weightier than anything other than the mother's own right to life, which she might put forward as ground for an abortion?

This argument treats the right to life as if it were unproblematic. It is not, and this seems to me to be precisely the source of the mistake.

For we should now, at long last, ask what it comes to, to have a right to life. In some views having a right to life includes having a right to be given at least the bare minimum one needs for continued life. But suppose that what in fact *is* the bare minimum a man needs for continued life is something he has no right at all to be given? If I am sick unto death, and the only thing that will save my life is the touch of Henry Fonda's cool hand on my fevered brow, then all the same, I have no right to be given the touch of Henry Fonda's cool hand on my fevered brow. It would be frightfully nice of him to fly in from the West Coast to provide it. It would be less nice, though no doubt well meant, if my friends flew out to the West Coast and carried Henry Fonda back with them. But I have no right at all against anybody that he should do this for me. Or again, to return to the story I told earlier, the fact that for continued life that violinist needs the continued use of your kidneys does not establish that he has a right to be given the continued use of your kidneys. He certainly has no right against you that *you* should give him continued use of your kidneys. For nobody has any right to use your kidneys unless you give him such a right; and nobody has the right against you that you shall give him this right—if you do allow him to go on using your kidneys, this is a kindness on your part, and not something he can claim from you as his due. Nor has he any right against anybody else that *they* should give him continued use of your kidneys. Certainly he had no right against the Society of Music Lovers that they should plug him into you in the first place. And if you now start to unplug yourself, having learned that you will otherwise have to spend nine years in bed with him, there is nobody in the world who must try to prevent you, in order to see to it that he is given something he has a right to be given.

Some people are rather stricter about the right to life. In their view, it does not include the right to be given anything, but amounts to, and only to, the right not to be killed by anybody. But here a related difficulty arises. If everybody is to refrain from killing that violinist, then everybody must refrain from doing a great many different sorts of things. Everybody must refrain from slitting his throat, everybody must refrain from shooting him—and everybody must refrain from unplugging you from him. But does he have a right against everybody that they shall refrain from unplugging you from him? To refrain from doing this is to allow him to continue to use your kidneys. It could be argued that he has a right against us that *we* should allow him to continue to use your kidneys. That is, while he had no right against us that we should give him the use of your kidneys, it might be argued that he anyway has a right against us that we shall not now intervene and deprive him of the use of your kidneys. I shall come back to third-party interventions later. But certainly the violinist has no right against you that *you* shall allow him to continue to use your kidneys. As I said, if you do allow him to use them, it is a kindness on your part, and not something you owe him.

The difficulty I point to here is not peculiar to the right to life. It reappears in connection with all the other natural rights; and it is something which an adequate account of rights must deal with. For present purposes it is enough just to draw attention to it. But I would stress that I am not arguing that people do not have a right to life—quite to the contrary, it seems to me that the primary control we must place on the acceptability of an account of rights is that it should turn out in that account to be a truth that all persons have a right to life. I am arguing only that having a right to life does not guarantee having either a right to be given the use of or a right to be allowed continued use of another person's body—even if one needs it for life itself. So the right to life will not serve the opponents of abortion in the very simple and clear way in which they seem to have thought it would.

4. There is another way to bring out the difficulty. In the most ordinary sort of case, to deprive someone of what he has a right to is to treat him unjustly. Suppose a boy and his small brother are jointly given a box of chocolates for Christmas. If the older boy takes the box and refuses to give his brother any of the chocolates, he is unjust to him, for the brother has been given a right to half of them. But suppose that, having learned that otherwise it means nine years in bed with that violinist, you unplug yourself from him. You surely are not being unjust to him, for you gave him no right to use your kidneys, and no one else can have given him any such right. But we have to notice that in unplugging yourself, you are killing him; and violinists, like everybody else, have a right to life, and thus in the view we are considering just now, the right not to be killed. So here you do what he supposedly has a right you shall not do, but you do not act unjustly to him in doing it.

The emendation which may be made at this point is this: the right to life consists not in the right not to be killed, but rather in the right not to be killed unjustly. This runs a risk of circularity, but never mind: it would enable us to square the fact that the violinist has a right to life with the fact that you do not act unjustly toward him in unplugging yourself, thereby killing him. For if you do not kill him unjustly, you do not violate his right to life, and so it is no wonder you do him no injustice.

But if this emendation is accepted, the gap in the argument against abortion stares us plainly in the face: it is by no means enough to show that the fetus is a person, and to remind us that all persons have a right to life—we need to be shown also that killing the fetus violates its right to life, i.e., that abortion is unjust killing. And is it?

I suppose we may take it as a datum that in a case of pregnancy due to rape the mother has not given the unborn person a right to the use of her body for food and shelter. Indeed, in what pregnancy could it be supposed that the mother has given the unborn person such a right? It is not as if there were unborn persons drifting about the world, to whom a woman who wants a child says "I invite you in."

But it might be argued that there are other ways one can have acquired a right to the use of another person's body than by having been invited to use it by that person. Suppose a woman voluntarily indulges in intercourse, knowing of the chance it will issue in pregnancy, and then she does become pregnant; is she not in part responsible for the presence, in fact the very existence, of the unborn person inside her? No doubt she did not invite it in. But doesn't her partial responsibility for its being there itself give it a right to the use of her body?[7] If so, then her aborting it would be more like the boy's taking away the chocolates, and less like your unplugging yourself from the violinist—doing so would be depriving it of what it does have a right to, and thus would be doing it an injustice.

And then, too, it might be asked whether or not she can kill it even to save her own life: If she voluntarily called it into existence, how can she now kill it, even in self-defense?

The first thing to be said about this is that it is something new. Opponents of abortion have been so concerned to make out the independence of the fetus, in order to establish that it has a right to life, just as its mother does, that they have tended to overlook the possible support they might gain from making out that the fetus is *dependent* on the mother, in order to establish that she has a special kind of responsibility for it, a responsibility that gives it rights against her which are not possessed by any independent person—such as an ailing violinist who is a stranger to her.

On the other hand, this argument would give the unborn person a right to its mother's body only if her pregnancy resulted from a voluntary act, undertaken in full knowledge of the chance a pregnancy might result from it. It would leave out entirely the unborn person whose existence is due to rape. Pending the availability of some further argument, then, we would be left with the conclusion that unborn persons whose existence is due to rape have no right to the use of their mothers' bodies, and thus that aborting them is not depriving them of anything they have a right to and hence is not unjust killing.

And we should also notice that it is not at all plain that this argument really does go even as far as it purports to. For there are cases and cases, and the details make a difference. If the room is stuffy, and I therefore open a window to air it, and a burglar climbs in, it would be absurd to say, "Ah, now he can stay, she's given him a right to the use of her house—for she is partially responsible for his presence there, having voluntarily done what enabled him to get in, in full knowledge that there are such things as burglars, and that burglars burgle." It would be still more absurd to say this if I had had bars installed outside my windows, precisely to prevent burglars from getting in, and a burglar got in only because of a defect in the bars. It remains equally absurd if we imagine it is not a burglar who climbs in, but an innocent person who blunders or falls in. Again, suppose it were like this: people-seeds drift about in the air like pollen, and if you open your windows, one may drift in and take root in your carpets or upholstery. You don't want children, so you fix up your windows with fine mesh screens, the very best you can buy. As can happen, however, and on very, very rare occasions does happen, one of the screens is defective; and a seed drifts in and takes root. Does the person-plant who now develops have a right to the use of your house? Surely not—despite the fact that you voluntarily opened your windows, you knowingly kept carpets and upholstered furniture, and you knew that screens were sometimes defective. Someone may argue that you are responsible for its rooting, that it does have a right to your house, because after all you *could* have lived out your life with bare floors and furniture, or with sealed windows and doors. But this won't do—for by the same token anyone can avoid a pregnancy due to rape by having a hysterectomy, or anyway by never leaving home without a (reliable!) army.

It seems to me that the argument we are looking at can establish at most that there are *some* cases in which the unborn person has a right to the use of its mother's body, and therefore some cases in which abortion is unjust killing. There is room for much discussion and argument as to precisely which, if any. But I think we should sidestep this issue and leave it open, for at any rate the argument certainly does not establish that all abortion is unjust killing.

5. There is room for yet another argument here, however. We surely must all grant that there may be cases in which it would be morally indecent to detach a person from your body at the cost of his life. Suppose you learn that what the violinist needs is not

nine years of your life, but only one hour: all you need do to save his life is to spend one hour in that bed with him. Suppose also that letting him use your kidneys for that one hour would not affect your health in the slightest. Admittedly you were kidnapped. Admittedly you did not give anyone permission to plug him into you. Nevertheless it seems to me plain you *ought* to allow him to use your kidneys for that hour—it would be indecent to refuse.

Again, suppose pregnancy lasted only an hour, and constituted no threat to life or health. And suppose that a woman becomes pregnant as a result of rape. Admittedly she did not voluntarily do anything to bring about the existence of a child. Admittedly she did nothing at all which would give the unborn person a right to the use of her body. All the same it might well be said, as in the newly emended violinist story, that she ought to allow it to remain for that hour—that it would be indecent in her to refuse.

Now some people are inclined to use the term "right" in such a way that it follows from the fact that you ought to allow a person to use your body for the hour he needs, that he has a right to use your body for the hour he needs, even though he has not been given that right by any person or act. They may say that it follows also that if you refuse, you act unjustly toward him. This use of the term is perhaps so common that it cannot be called wrong; nevertheless it seems to me to be an unfortunate loosening of what we would do better to keep a tight rein on. Suppose that box of chocolates I mentioned earlier had not been given to both boys jointly, but was given only to the older boy. There he sits, stolidly eating his way through the box, his small brother watching enviously. Here we are likely to say "You ought not to be so mean. You ought to give your brother some of those chocolates." My own view is that it just does not follow from the truth of this that the brother has any right to any of the chocolates. If the boy refuses to give his brother any, he is greedy, stingy, callous—but not unjust. I suppose that the people I have in mind will say it does follow that the brother has a right to some of the chocolates, and thus that the boy does act unjustly if he refuses to give his brother any. But the effect of saying this is to obscure what we should keep distinct, namely the difference between the boy's refusal in this case and the boy's refusal in the earlier case, in which the box was given to both boys jointly, and in which the small brother thus had what was from any point of view clear title to half.

A further objection to so using the term "right" that from the fact that A ought to do a thing for B, it follows that B has a right against A that A do it for him, is that it is going to make the question of whether or not a man has a right to a thing turn on how easy it is to provide him with it; and this seems not merely unfortunate, but morally unacceptable. Take the case of Henry Fonda again. I said earlier that I had no right to the touch of his cool hand on my fevered brow, even though I needed it to save my life. I said it would be frightfully nice of him to fly in from the West Coast to provide me with it, but that I had no right against him that he should do so. But suppose he isn't on the West Coast. Suppose he has only to walk across the room, place a hand briefly on my brow—and lo, my life is saved. Then surely he ought to do it, it would be indecent to refuse. Is it to be said "Ah, well, it follows that in this case she has a right to the touch of his hand on her brow, and so it would be an injustice in him to refuse?" So that I have a right to it when it is easy for him to provide it, though no right when it's hard? It's rather a shocking idea that anyone's rights should fade away and disappear as it gets harder and harder to accord them to him.

So my own view is that even though you ought to let the violinist use your kidneys for the one hour he needs, we should not conclude that he has a right to do so—we would say that if you refuse, you are, like the boy who owns all the chocolates and will give none away, self-centered and callous, indecent in fact, but not unjust. And similarly, that even supposing a case in which a woman pregnant due to rape ought to allow the unborn person to use her body for the hour he needs, we should not conclude that he has a right to do so; we should conclude that she is self-centered, callous, indecent, but not unjust, if she refuses. The complaints are no less grave; they are just different. However, there is no need to insist on this point. If anyone does wish to deduce "he has a right" from "you ought," then all the same he must surely grant that there are cases in which it is not morally required of you that you allow that violinist to use your kidneys, and in which he does not have a right to use them, and in which you do not do him an injustice if you refuse. And so also for mother and unborn child. Except in such cases as the unborn person has a right to demand it—and we were leaving open the possibility that there may be such cases—nobody is morally *required* to make large sacrifices, of health, of all other interests and concerns, of all other duties and commitments, for nine years, or even for nine months, in order to keep another person alive.

6. We have in fact to distinguish between two kinds of Samaritan: the Good Samaritan and what we might call the Minimally Decent Samaritan. The story of the Good Samaritan, you will remember, goes like this:

> A certain man went down from Jerusalem to Jericho, and fell among thieves, which stripped him of his raiment, and wounded him, and departed, leaving him half dead.
>
> And by chance there came down a certain priest that way; and when he saw him, he passed by on the other side.
>
> And likewise a Levite, when he was at the place, came and looked on him, and passed by on the other side.
>
> But a certain Samaritan, as he journeyed, came where he was; and when he saw him he had compassion on him.
>
> And went to him, and bound up his wounds, pouring in oil and wine, and set him on his own beast, and brought him to an inn, and took care of him.
>
> And on the morrow, when he departed, he took out two pence, and gave them to the host, and said unto him, "Take care of him; and whatsoever thou spendest more, when I come again, I will repay thee."
>
> (Luke 10:30–35)

The Good Samaritan went out of his way, at some cost to himself, to help one in need of it. We are not told what the options were, that is, whether or not the priest and the Levite could have helped by doing less than the Good Samaritan did, but assuming they could have, then the fact they did nothing at all shows they were not even Minimally Decent Samaritans, not because they were not Samaritans, but because they were not even minimally decent.

These things are a matter of degree, of course, but there is a difference, and it comes out perhaps most clearly in the story of Kitty Genovese, who, as you will remember, was murdered while thirty-eight people watched or listened, and did nothing at all to help her. A Good Samaritan would have rushed out to give direct assistance against the murderer. Or perhaps we had better allow that it would have been a Splendid Samaritan who did this, on the ground that it would have involved a risk of death for himself. But the thirty-eight not only did not do this, they did not even trouble to pick up a phone to call the police. Minimally Decent Samaritanism would call for doing at least that, and their not having done it was monstrous.

After telling the story of the Good Samaritan, Jesus said "Go, and do thou likewise." Perhaps he meant that we are morally required to act as the Good Samaritan did. Perhaps he was urging people to do more than is morally required of them. At all events it seems plain that it was not morally required of any of the thirty-eight that he rush out to give direct assistance at the risk of his own life, and that it is not morally required of anyone that he give long stretches of his life—nine years or nine months—to sustaining the life of a person who has no special right (we were leaving open the possibility of this) to demand it.

Indeed, with one rather striking class of exceptions, no one in any country in the world is *legally* required to do anywhere near as much as this for anyone else. The class of exceptions is obvious. My main concern here is not the state of the law in respect to abortion, but it is worth drawing attention to the fact that in no state in this country is any man compelled by law to be even a Minimally Decent Samaritan to any person; there is no law under which charges could be brought against the thirty-eight who stood by while Kitty Genovese died. By contrast, in most states in this country women are compelled by law to be not merely Minimally Decent Samaritans, but Good Samaritans to unborn persons inside them. This doesn't by itself settle anything one way or the other, because it may well be argued that there should be laws in this country—as there are in many European countries—compelling at least Minimally Decent Samaritanism.[8] But it does show that there is a gross injustice in the existing state of the law. And it shows also that the groups currently working against liberalization of abortion laws, in fact working toward having it declared unconstitutional for a state to permit abortion, had better start working for the adoption of Good Samaritan laws generally, or earn the charge that they are acting in bad faith.

I should think, myself, that Minimally Decent Samaritan laws would be one thing, Good Samaritan laws quite another, and in fact highly improper. But we are not here concerned with the law. What we should ask is not whether anybody should be compelled by law to be a Good Samaritan, but whether we must accede to a situation in which somebody is being compelled—by nature, perhaps—to be a Good Samaritan. We have, in other words, to look now at third-party interventions. I have been arguing that no person is morally required to make large sacrifices to sustain the life of another who has no right to demand them, and this even where the sacrifices do not include life itself; we are not morally required to be Good Samaritans or anyway Very Good Samaritans to one another. But what if a man cannot extricate himself from such a situation? What if he appeals to us to extricate him? It seems to me plain that there are cases in which we can, cases in which a Good Samaritan would extricate him. There you are, you were kidnapped, and nine years in bed with that violinist lie ahead of you. You have your own life to lead. You are sorry, but you simply cannot see giving up so much of your life to the sustaining of his. You cannot extricate yourself, and ask us to do so. I should have thought that—in light of his having no right to the use of your body—it was obvious that we do not have to accede to your being forced to give up so much. We can do what you ask. There is no injustice to the violinist in our doing so.

7. Following the lead of the opponents of abortion, I have throughout been speaking of the fetus merely as a person, and what I have been asking is whether or not the argument we began with, which proceeds only from the fetus' being a person, really does establish its conclusion. I have argued that it does not.

But of course there are arguments and arguments, and it may be said that I have simply fastened on the wrong one. It may be said that what is important is not merely the fact that the fetus is a person, but that it is a person for whom the woman has a special kind of responsibility issuing from the fact that she is its mother. And it might be argued that all my analogies are therefore irrelevant—for you do not have that special kind of responsibility for that violinist, Henry Fonda does not have that special kind of responsibility for me. And our attention might be drawn to the fact that men and women both *are* compelled by law to provide support for their children.

I have in effect dealt (briefly) with this argument in section 4 above; but a (still briefer) recapitulation now may be in order. Surely we do not have any such "special responsibility" for a person unless we have assumed it, explicitly or implicitly. If a set of parents do not try to prevent pregnancy, do not obtain an abortion, and then at the time of birth of the child do not put it out for adoption, but rather take it home with them, then they have assumed responsibility for it, they have given it rights, and they cannot *now* withdraw support from it at the cost of its life because they now find it difficult to go on providing for it. But if they have taken all reasonable precautions against having a child, they do not simply by virtue of their biological relationship to the child who comes into existence have a special responsibility for it. They may wish to assume responsibility for it, or they may not wish to. And I am suggesting that if assuming responsibility for it would require large sacrifices, then they may refuse. A Good Samaritan would not refuse—or anyway, a Splendid Samaritan, if the sacrifices that had to be made were enormous. But then so would a Good Samaritan assume responsibility for that violinist; so would Henry Fonda, if he is a Good Samaritan, fly in from the West Coast and assume responsibility for me.

8. My argument will be found unsatisfactory on two counts by many of those who want to regard abortion as morally permissible. First, while I do argue that abortion is not impermissible, I do not argue that it is always permissible. There may well be

cases in which carrying the child to term requires only Minimally Decent Samaritanism of the mother, and this is a standard we must not fall below. I am inclined to think it a merit of my account precisely that it does *not* give a general yes or a general no. It allows for and supports our sense that, for example, a sick and desperately frightened fourteen-year-old schoolgirl, pregnant due to rape, may *of course* choose abortion, and that any law which rules this out is an insane law. And it also allows for and supports our sense that in other cases resort to abortion is even positively indecent. It would be indecent in the woman to request an abortion, and indecent in a doctor to perform it, if she is in her seventh month, and wants the abortion just to avoid the nuisance of postponing a trip abroad. The very fact that the arguments I have been drawing attention to treat all cases of abortion, or even all cases of abortion in which the mother's life is not at stake, as morally on a par ought to have made them suspect at the outset.

Secondly, while I am arguing for the permissibility of abortion in some cases, I am not arguing for the right to secure the death of the unborn child. It is easy to confuse these two things in that up to a certain point in the life of the fetus it is not able to survive outside the mother's body; hence removing it from her body guarantees its death. But they are importantly different. I have argued that you are not morally required to spend nine months in bed, sustaining the life of that violinist; but to say this is by no means to say that if, when you unplug yourself, there is a miracle and he survives, you then have a right to turn round and slit his throat. You may detach yourself even if this costs him his life; you have no right to be guaranteed his death, by some other means, if unplugging yourself does not kill him. There are some people who will feel dissatisfied by this feature of my argument. A woman may be utterly devastated by the thought of a child, a bit of herself, put out for adoption and never seen or heard of again. She may therefore want not merely that the child be detached from her, but more, that it die. Some opponents of abortion are inclined to regard this as beneath contempt—thereby showing insensitivity to what is surely a powerful source of despair. All the same, I agree that the desire for the child's death is not one which anybody may gratify, should it turn out to be possible to detach the child alive.

At this place, however, it should be remembered that we have only been pretending throughout that the fetus is a human being from the moment of conception. A very early abortion is surely not the killing of a person, and so is not dealt with by anything I have said here.

## NOTES

1. I am very much indebted to James Thomson for discussion, criticism, and many helpful suggestions.
2. Daniel Callahan, *Abortion: Law, Choice and Morality* (New York, 1970), p. 373. This book gives a fascinating survey of the available information on abortion. The Jewish tradition is surveyed in David M. Feldman, *Birth Control in Jewish Law* (New York, 1968), Part 5; the Catholic tradition in John T. Noonan, Jr., "An Almost Absolute Value in History." In *The Morality of Abortion,* ed. John T. Noonan, Jr. (Cambridge, Mass., 1970).
3. The term "direct" in the arguments I refer to is a technical one. Roughly, what is meant by *direct killing* is either killing as an end it itself, or killing as a means to some end; for example, the end of saving someone else's life. See note 6, below, for an example of its use.
4. Cf. *Encyclical Letter of Pope Pius XI on Christian Marriage,* St. Paul Editions (Boston, n.d.), p. 32: "however much we may pity the mother whose health and even life is gravely imperiled in the performance of the duty allotted to her by nature, nevertheless what could ever be a sufficient reason for excusing in any way the direct murder of the innocent? This is precisely what we are dealing with here." Noonan (*The Morality of Abortion,* p. 43) reads this as follows: "What cause can ever avail to excuse in any way the direct killing of the innocent? For it is a question of that."
5. The thesis in (4) is in an interesting way weaker than those in (1), (2), and (3): they rule out abortion even in cases in which both mother *and* child will die if the abortion is not performed. By contrast, one who held the view expressed in (4) could consistently say that one needn't prefer letting two persons die to killing one.
6. Cf. the following passage from Pius XII, *Address to the Italian Catholic Society of Midwives:* "The baby in the maternal breast has the right to life immediately from God.—Hence there is no man, no human authority, no science, no medical, eugenic, social, economic or moral 'indication' which can establish or grant a valid juridical ground for a direct deliberate disposition of an innocent human life, that is a disposition which looks to its destruction either as an end or as a means to another end perhaps in itself not illicit.—The baby, still not born, is a man in the same degree and for the same reason as the mother" (quoted in Noonan, *The Morality of Abortion,* p. 45).
7. The need for a discussion of this argument was brought home to me by members of the Society for Ethical and Legal Philosophy, to whom this paper was originally presented.
8. For a discussion of the difficulties involved, and a survey of the European experience with such laws, see *The Good Samaritan and the Law,* ed. James M. Ratcliffe (New York, 1966).

## REFLECTING ON MEANING

1. Thomson suggests that one's position on abortion cannot logically follow from one's position on whether the fetus is a person. What does she mean? According to Thomson, how are both anti-abortionists and pro-choice advocates guilty of not thinking through their positions logically?
2. Thomson's argument centers on a comparison between the fetus and a violinist plugged into the reader's body. To what extent do you agree that the fetus has no more right to use its mother's body without her authorization than the violinist has to use your kidneys without your permission? Is the analogy appropriate in all cases? Why or why not? To what extent does it work to illustrate the argument for each view Thomson identifies, beginning with the "extreme view"?
3. Thomson does not argue that abortion is morally right in all cases. In what situations does she think it would be wrong? Does the law address this issue in other situations? How does the Good Samaritan analogy help her clarify the moral and legal dimensions of these situations?

## EXPLORING RHETORICAL STRATEGIES

1. Thomson defuses the gender politics of abortion—the fact that only women face pregnancy—by making the violinist's host gender-neutral. Also, she personalizes the issue by suggesting that the violinist is plugged into the reader, who, of course, may be either male or female. How do both of these strategies help her advance her thesis? Why do you think it was important for her to avoid the gender aspect of the issue? Why do you think she personalized the violinist analogy?
2. The violinist analogy serves as the core of the discussion, but Thomson freely makes use of other analogies throughout her essay. How does the use of analogy help neutralize the emotional aspects of the abortion issue? In what ways is it a useful strategy for argumentation? What are its limitations?
3. From the elaborate and sophisticated argument that Thomson weaves, what can you deduce about her audience and purpose? To whom is she addressing her essay? What evidence supports your deduction?

# Abortion and the Conscience of the Nation

## RONALD REAGAN

*In this address delivered during his first term as president, Ronald Reagan urges forward legislation that would restrict the abortion rights granted by the Supreme Court's decision in* Roe v. Wade *in 1973. Reagan argues that the issue is not when life begins but "whether to affirm and protect the sanctity of all human life."*

The tenth anniversary of the Supreme Court decision in *Roe v. Wade* is a good time for us to pause and reflect. Our nationwide policy of abortion-on-demand through all nine months of pregnancy was neither voted for by our people nor enacted by our legislators—not a single state had such unrestricted abortion before the Supreme Court decreed it to be national policy in 1973. But the consequences of this judicial decision are now obvious: Since 1973, more than 15 million unborn children have had their lives snuffed out by legalized abortions. That is over ten times the number of Americans lost in all our nation's wars.

Make no mistake, abortion-on-demand is not a right granted by the Constitution. No serious scholar, including one disposed to agree with the Court's result, has argued that the framers of the Constitution intended to create such a right. Shortly after the *Roe v. Wade* decision, Professor John Hart Ely, now Dean of Stanford Law School, wrote that the opinion "is not constitutional law and gives almost no sense of an obligation to try to be." Nowhere do the plain words of the Constitution even hint at a "right" so sweeping as to permit abortion up to the time the child is ready to be born. Yet that is what the Court ruled.

As an act of "raw judicial power" (to use Justice White's biting phrase), the decision by the seven-man majority in *Roe v. Wade* has so far been made to stick. But the Court's decision has by no means settled the debate. Instead, *Roe v. Wade* has become a continuing prod to the conscience of the nation.

Abortion concerns not just the unborn child, it concerns every one of us. The English poet, John Donne, wrote: " . . . any man's death diminishes me, because I am involved in mankind; and therefore never send to know for whom the bell tolls; it tolls for thee."

We cannot diminish the value of one category of human life—the unborn—without diminishing the value of all human life. We saw tragic proof of this truism last year when the Indiana courts allowed the starvation death of "Baby Doe" in Bloomington because the child had Down's Syndrome.

Many of our fellow citizens grieve over the loss of life that has followed *Roe v. Wade.* Margaret Heckler, soon after being nominated to head the largest department of our government, Health and Human Services, told an audience that she believed abortion to be the greatest moral crisis facing our country today. And the revered Mother Teresa, who works in the streets of Calcutta ministering to dying people in her world-famous mission of mercy, has said that "the greatest misery of our time is the generalized abortion of children."

Over the first two years of my Administration I have closely followed and assisted efforts in Congress to reverse the tide of abortion—efforts of Congressmen, Senators and citizens responding to an urgent moral crisis. Regrettably, I have also seen the massive efforts of those who, under the banner of "freedom of choice," have so far blocked every effort to reverse nationwide abortion-on-demand.

Despite the formidable obstacles before us, we must not lose heart. This is not the first time our country has been divided by a Supreme Court decision that denied the value of certain human lives. The *Dred Scott* decision of 1857 was not overturned in a day, or a year, or even a decade. At first, only a minority of Americans recognized and deplored the moral crisis brought about by denying the full humanity of our black brothers and sisters; but that minority persisted in their vision and finally prevailed. They did it by appealing to the hearts and minds of their countrymen, to the truth of human dignity under God. From their example, we know that respect for the sacred value of human life is too deeply engrained in the hearts of our people to remain forever suppressed. But the great majority of the American people have not yet made their voices heard, and we cannot expect them to—any more than the public voice arose against slavery—*until* the issue is clearly framed and presented.

What, then, is the real issue? I have often said that when we talk about abortion, we are talking about two lives—the life of the mother and the life of the unborn child. Why else do we call a pregnant woman a mother? I have also said that anyone who doesn't feel sure whether we are talking about a second human life should clearly give life the benefit of the doubt. If you don't know whether a body is alive or dead, you would never bury it. I think this consideration itself should be enough for all of us to insist on protecting the unborn.

The case against abortion does not rest here, however, for medical practice confirms at every step the correctness of these moral sensibilities. Modern medicine treats the unborn child as a patient. Medical pioneers have made great breakthroughs in treating the unborn—for genetic problems, vitamin deficiencies, irregular heart rhythms, and other medical conditions. Who can forget George Will's moving account of the little boy who underwent brain surgery six times during the nine weeks before he was born? Who is the *patient* if not that tiny unborn human being who can feel pain when he or she is approached by doctors who come to kill rather than to cure?

The real question today is not when human life begins, but, *What is the value of human life?* The abortionist who reassembles the arms and legs of a tiny baby to make sure all its parts have been torn from its mother's body can hardly doubt whether it is a human being. The real question for him and for all of us is whether that tiny human life has a God-given right to be protected by the law—the same right we have.

What more dramatic confirmation could we have of the real issue than the Baby Doe case in Bloomington, Indiana? The death of that tiny infant tore at the hearts of all Americans because the child was undeniably a live human being—one lying helpless before the eyes of the doctors and the eyes of the nation. The real issue for the courts was *not* whether Baby Doe was a human being. The real issue was whether to protect the life of a human being who had Down's Syndrome, who would probably be mentally handicapped, but who needed a routine surgical procedure to unblock his esophagus and allow him to eat. A doctor testified to the presiding judge that, even with his physical problem corrected, Baby Doe would have a "nonexistent" possibility for a "minimally adequate quality of life"—in other words, that retardation was the equivalent of a crime deserving the death penalty. The judge let

Baby Doe starve and die, and the Indiana Supreme Court sanctioned his decision.

Federal law does not allow federally assisted hospitals to decide that Down's Syndrome infants are not worth treating, much less to decide to starve them to death. Accordingly, I have directed the Departments of Justice and HHS to apply civil rights regulations to protect handicapped newborns. All hospitals receiving federal funds must post notices which will clearly state that failure to feed handicapped babies is prohibited by federal law. The basic issue is whether to value and protect the lives of the handicapped, whether to recognize the sanctity of human life. This is the same basic issue that underlies the question of abortion.

The 1981 Senate hearings on the beginning of human life brought out the basic issue more clearly than ever before. The many medical and scientific witnesses who testified disagreed on many things, but not on the *scientific* evidence that the unborn child is alive, is a distinct individual, or is a member of the human species. They did disagree over the *value* question, whether to give value to a human life at its early and most vulnerable stages of existence.

Regrettably, we live at a time when some persons do *not* value all human life. They want to pick and choose which individuals have value. Some have said that only those individuals with "consciousness of self" are human beings. One such writer has followed this deadly logic and concluded that "shocking as it may seem, a newly born infant is not a human being."

A Nobel Prize winning scientist has suggested that if a handicapped child "were not declared fully human until three days after birth, then all parents could be allowed the choice." In other words, "quality control" to see if newly born human beings are up to snuff.

Obviously, some influential people want to deny that every human life has intrinsic, sacred worth. They insist that a member of the human race must have certain qualities before they accord him or her status as a "human being."

Events have borne out the editorial in a California medical journal which explained three years before *Roe v. Wade* that the social acceptance of abortion is a "defiance of the long-held Western ethic of intrinsic and equal value for every human life regardless of its stage, condition, or status."

Every legislator, every doctor, and every citizen needs to recognize that the real issue is whether to affirm and protect the sanctity of all human life, or to embrace a social ethic where some human lives are valued and others are not. As a nation, we must choose between the sanctity of life ethic and the "quality of life" ethic.

I have no trouble identifying the answer our nation has always given to this basic question, and the answer that I hope and pray it will give in the future. America was founded by men and women who shared a vision of the value of each and every individual. They stated this vision clearly from the very start in the Declaration of Independence, using words that every schoolboy and schoolgirl can recite:

> We hold these truths to be self-evident, that all men are created equal, that they are endowed by their Creator with certain unalienable rights, that among these are life, liberty, and the pursuit of happiness.

We fought a terrible war to guarantee that one category of mankind—black people in America—could not be denied the inalienable rights with which their Creator endowed them. The great champion of the sanctity of all human life in that day, Abraham Lincoln, gave us his assessment of the Declaration's purpose. Speaking of the framers of that noble document, he said:

> This was their majestic interpretation of the economy of the Universe. This was their lofty, and wise, and noble understanding of the justice of the Creator to His creatures. Yes, gentlemen, to all His creatures, to the whole great family of man. In their enlightened belief, nothing stamped with the divine image and likeness was sent into the world to be trodden on. . . . They grasped not only the whole race of man then living, but they reached forward and seized upon the farthest posterity. They erected a beacon to guide their children and their children's children, and the countless myriads who should inhabit the earth in other ages.

He warned also of the danger we would face if we closed our eyes to the value of life in any category of human beings:

> I should like to know if taking this old Declaration of Independence, which declares that all men are equal upon principle and making exceptions to it where will it stop. If one man says it does not mean a Negro, why not another say it does not mean some other man?

When Congressman John A. Bingham of Ohio drafted the Fourteenth Amendment to guarantee the rights of life, liberty, and property to all human beings, he explained that *all* are "entitled to the protection of American law, because its divine spirit of equality declares that all men are created equal." He said the rights guaranteed by the amendment would therefore apply to "any human being." Justice William Brennan, writing in another case decided only the year before *Roe v. Wade,* referred to our society as one that "strongly affirms the sanctity of life."

Another William Brennan—not the Justice—has reminded us of the terrible consequences that can follow when a nation rejects the sanctity of life ethic:

> The cultural environment for a human holocaust is present whenever any society can be misled into defining individuals as less than human and therefore devoid of value and respect.

As a nation today, we have *not* rejected the sanctity of human life. The American people have not had an opportunity to express their view on the sanctity of human life in the unborn. I am convinced that Americans do not want to play God with the value of human life. It is not for us to decide who is worthy to live and who is not. Even the Supreme Court's opinion in *Roe v. Wade* did not explicitly reject the traditional American idea of intrinsic worth and value in all human life; it simply dodged this issue.

The Congress has before it several measures that would enable our people to reaffirm the sanctity of human life, even the smallest and the youngest and the most defenseless. The Human Life Bill expressly recognizes the unborn as human beings and accordingly protects them as persons under our Constitution. This bill, first introduced by Senator Jesse Helms, provided the vehicle for the Senate hearings in 1981 which contributed so much to our understanding of the real issue of abortion.

The Respect Human Life Act, just introduced in the 98th Congress, states in its first section that the policy of the United States is "to protect innocent life, both before and after birth." This bill, sponsored by Congressman Henry Hyde and Senator Roger Jepsen, prohibits the federal government from performing abortions or assisting those who do so, except to save the life of the mother. It also addresses the pressing issue of infanticide which, as we have seen, flows inevitably from permissive abortion as another step in the denial of the inviolability of innocent human life.

I have endorsed each of these measures, as well as the more difficult route of constitutional amendment, and I will give these initiatives my full support. Each of them, in different ways, attempts to reverse the tragic policy of abortion-on-demand imposed by the Supreme Court ten years ago. Each of them is a decisive way to affirm the sanctity of human life.

We must all educate ourselves to the reality of the horrors taking place. Doctors today know that unborn children can feel a touch within the womb and that they respond to pain. But how many Americans are aware that abortion techniques are allowed today, in all 50 states, that burn the skin of a baby with a salt solution, in an agonizing death that can last for hours?

Another example: two years ago, the *Philadelphia Inquirer* ran a Sunday special supplement on "The Dreaded Complication." The "dreaded complication" referred to in the article—the complication feared by doctors who perform abortions—is the *survival* of the child despite all the painful attacks during the abortion procedure. Some unborn children *do* survive the late-term abortions the Supreme Court has made legal. Is there any question that these victims of abortion deserve our attention and protection? Is there any question that those who *don't* survive were living human beings before they were killed?

Late-term abortions, especially when the baby survives, but is then killed by starvation, neglect, or suffocation, show once again the link between abortion and infanticide. The time to stop both is now. As my Administration acts to stop infanticide, we will be fully aware of the real issue that underlies the death of babies before and soon after birth.

Our society has, fortunately, become sensitive to the rights and special needs of the handicapped, but I am shocked that physical or mental handicaps of newborns are still used to justify their extinction. This Administration has a Surgeon General, Dr. C. Everett Koop, who has done perhaps more than any other American for handicapped children, by pioneering surgical techniques to help them, by speaking out on the value of their lives, and by working with them in the context of loving families. You will not find his former patients advocating the so-called "quality of life" ethic.

I know that when the true issue of infanticide is placed before the American people, with all the facts openly aired, we will have no trouble deciding that a mentally or physically handicapped baby has the same intrinsic worth and right to life as the rest of us. As the New Jersey Supreme Court said two decades ago, in a decision upholding the sanctity of human life, "a child need not be perfect to have a worthwhile life."

Whether we are talking about pain suffered by unborn children, or about late-term abortions, or about infanticide, we inevitably focus on the humanity of the unborn child. Each of these issues is a potential rallying point for the sanctity of life ethic. Once we as a nation rally around any one of these issues to affirm the sanctity of life, we will see the importance of affirming this principle across the board.

Malcolm Muggeridge, the English writer, goes right to the heart of the matter: "Either life is always and in all circumstances sacred, or intrinsically of no account; it is inconceivable that it should be in some cases the one, and in some the other." The sanctity of innocent human life is a principle that Congress should proclaim at every opportunity.

It is possible that the Supreme Court itself may overturn its abortion rulings. We need only recall that in *Brown v. Board of Education* the court reversed its own earlier "separate-but-equal" decision. I believe if the Supreme Court took another look at *Roe v. Wade,* and considered the real issue between the sanctity of life ethic and the quality of life ethic, it would change its mind once again.

As we continue to work to overturn *Roe v. Wade,* we must also continue to lay the groundwork for a society in which abortion is not the accepted answer to unwanted pregnancy. Pro-life people have already taken heroic steps, often at great personal sacrifice, to provide for unwed mothers. I recently spoke about a young pregnant woman named Victoria, who said, "In this society we save whales, we save timber wolves and bald eagles and Coke bottles. Yet, everyone wanted me to throw away my baby." She has been helped by Sav-a-life, a group in Dallas, which provides a way for unwed mothers to preserve the human life within them when they might otherwise be tempted to resort to abortion. I think also of House of His Creation in Coatesville, Pennsylvania, where a loving couple has taken in almost 200 young women in the past ten years. They have seen, as a fact of life, that the girls are *not* better off having abortions than saving their babies. I am also reminded of the remarkable Rossow family of Ellington, Connecticut, who have opened their hearts and their home to nine handicapped adopted and foster children.

The Adolescent Family Life Program, adopted by Congress at the request of Senator Jeremiah Denton, has opened new opportunities for unwed mothers to give their children life. We should not rest until our entire society echoes the tone of John Powell in the dedication of his book, *Abortion: The Silent Holocaust,* a dedication to every woman carrying an unwanted child: "Please believe that you are not alone. There are many of us that truly love you, who want to stand at your side, and help in any way we can." And we can echo the always-practical woman of faith, Mother Teresa, when she says, "If you don't want the little child, that unborn child, give him to me." We have so many families in America seeking to adopt children that the slogan "every child a wanted child" is now the emptiest of all reasons to tolerate abortion.

I have often said we need to join in prayer to bring protection to the unborn. Prayer and action are needed to uphold the sanctity of human life. I believe it will not be possible to accomplish our work, the work of saving lives, "without being a soul of prayer." The famous British Member of Parliament, William Wilberforce, prayed with his small group of influential friends, the "Clapham Sect," for *decades* to see an end to slavery in the British empire. Wilberforce led that struggle in Parliament, unflaggingly, because he believed in the sanctity of human life. He saw the fulfillment of his impossible dream when Parliament outlawed slavery just before his death.

Let his faith and perseverance be our guide. We will never recognize the true value of our own lives until we affirm the value in the life of others, a value of which Malcolm Muggeridge says: ". . . however low it flickers or fiercely burns, it is still a Divine flame which no man dare presume to put out, be his motives ever so humane and enlightened."

Abraham Lincoln recognized that we could not survive as a free land when some men could decide that others were not fit to be free and should therefore be slaves. Likewise, we cannot survive as a free nation when some men decide that others are not fit to live and should be abandoned to abortion or infanticide. My Administration is dedicated to the preservation of America as a free land, and there is no cause more important for preserving that freedom than affirming the transcendent right to life of all human beings; the right without which no other rights have any meaning.

---

## REFLECTING ON MEANING

1. What is the definition of human life that Reagan assumes in this essay? What qualifies as "life," according to Reagan? In shaping your response, consider his reference to fetuses that "feel a touch within the womb" and "respond to pain." Why would "one writer" whom Reagan cites assert that "a newly born infant is not a human being"? To what extent are the definitions of life and of human being a matter of biology? To what extent might either term be defined by culture?

2. Reagan shifts the abortion debate away from the question of when life begins by articulating it as an opposition between those who uphold the "sanctity of life" and those who uphold the "quality of life." What is the essence of this dichotomy? Does this opposition direct attention away from a more central issue? If so, how?

3. Why does Reagan bolster his argument by referring to the founders of our country? Why does he state that "nowhere do the plain words of the Constitution even hint at a 'right' " like abortion? What is the significance of trying to determine what the founders of the United States intended?

## EXPLORING RHETORICAL STRATEGIES

1. Reagan begins his essay by aligning himself with the people he is speaking to—the American public. For example, he speaks of "our nationwide policy," "our people," and "all our nation's wars." However, the meaning of the possessive pronoun *our* subtly shifts when it changes to *we* and *us,* the corresponding personal pronouns: "Despite the formidable obstacles before us, we must not lose heart." How does Reagan's use of pronouns shift? What makes this an effective rhetorical strategy?

2. Reagan's attempts to identify himself with the American people and to align them on his side of the issue also allows him to establish "good guy" and "bad guy" categories. Who are the "influential people" who "want to deny that every human life has intrinsic, sacred worth"? Who are the people who "have already taken heroic steps, often at great personal sacrifice"? In what ways does this strategy influence your reading of the argument?

3. Reagan peppers his language with colloquial diction, such as when he suggests that some people may want to determine if a baby is "up to snuff" before allowing it to live. Can you find other instances of this kind of diction? How effective is it? How does it help him establish a certain persona?

# Putting Women Back into the Abortion Debate

ELLEN WILLIS

*Is the crux of the abortion issue a matter of determining if fetuses are human beings? Ellen Willis's response to the question is an emphatic no. Willis argues that the abortion debate is not a "human life issue" but a "feminist issue." The key question, she asserts, is not "Are fetuses the moral equivalent of born human beings?" but "Can it be moral, under any circumstances, to make a woman bear a child against her will?"*

Some years ago I attended a New York Institute for the Humanities seminar on the new right. We were a fairly heterogeneous group of liberals and lefties, feminists and gay activists, but on one point nearly all of us agreed: the right-to-life movement was a dangerous antifeminist crusade. At one session I argued that the attack on abortion had significance far beyond itself, that it was the linchpin of the right's social agenda. I got a lot of supporting comments and approving nods. It was too much for Peter Steinfels, a liberal Catholic, author of *The Neoconservatives,* and executive editor of *Commonweal.* Right-to-lifers were not all right-wing fanatics, he protested. "You have to understand," he said plaintively, "that many of us see abortion as a *human life issue.*" What I remember best was his air of frustrated isolation. I don't think he came back to the seminar after that.

Things are different now. I often feel isolated when I insist that abortion is, above all, a *feminist issue.* Once people took for granted that abortion was an issue of sexual politics and morality. Now, abortion is most often discussed as a question of "life" in the abstract. Public concern over abortion centers almost exclusively on fetuses; women and their bodies are merely the stage on which the drama of fetal life and death takes place. Debate about abortion—if not its reality—has become sexlessly scholastic. And the people most responsible for this turn of events are, like Peter Steinfels, on the left.

The left wing of the right-to-life movement is a small, seemingly eccentric minority in both "progressive" and antiabortion camps. Yet it has played a critical role in the movement: by arguing that opposition to abortion can be separated from the right's antifeminist program, it has given antiabortion sentiment legitimacy in left-symp and (putatively) profeminist circles. While left antiabortionists are hardly alone in emphasizing fetal life, their innovation has been to claim that a consistent "prolife" stand involves opposing capital punishment, supporting disarmament, demanding government programs to end poverty, and so on. This is of course a leap the right is neither able nor willing to make. It's been liberals—from Garry Wills to the Catholic bishops—who have supplied the mass media with the idea that prohibiting abortion is part of a "seamless garment" of respect for human life.

Having invented this counter-context for the abortion controversy, left antiabortionists are trying to impose it as the only legitimate context for debate. Those of us who won't accept their terms and persist in seeing opposition to abortion, antifeminism, sexual repression, and religious sectarianism as the real seamless garment have been accused of obscuring the issue with demagoguery. Last year *Commonweal*—perhaps the most important current forum for left antiabortion opinion—ran an editorial demanding that we shape up: "Those who hold that abortion is immoral believe that the biological dividing lines of birth or viability should no more determine whether a developing member of the species is denied or accorded essential rights than should the biological dividing lines of sex or race or disability or old age. This argument is open to challenge. Perhaps the dividing lines are sufficiently different. Pro-choice advocates should state their reasons for believing so. They should meet the argument on its own grounds. . . ."

In other words, the only question we're allowed to debate—or the only one *Commonweal* is willing to entertain—is "Are fetuses the moral equivalent of born human beings?" And I can't meet the argument on its own grounds because I don't agree that this is the key question, whose answer determines whether one supports abortion or opposes it. I don't doubt that fetuses are alive, or that they're biologically human—what else would they be? I do consider the life of a fertilized egg less precious than the well-being of a woman with feelings, self-consciousness, a history, social ties; and I think fetuses get closer to being human in a moral sense as they come closer to birth. But to me these propositions are intuitively self-evident. I wouldn't know how to justify them to a "nonbeliever," nor do I see the point of trying.

I believe the debate has to start in a different place—with the recognition that fertilized eggs develop into infants inside the bodies of women. Pregnancy and birth are active processes in which a woman's body shelters, nourishes, and expels a new life; for nine months she is immersed in the most intimate possible relationship with another being. The growing fetus makes considerable demands on her physical and emotional resources, culminating in the cataclysmic experience of birth. And childbearing has unpredictable consequences; it always entails some risk of injury or death.

For me all this has a new concreteness: I had a baby last year. My much-desired and relatively easy pregnancy was full of what antiabortionists like to call "inconveniences." I was always tired, short of breath; my digestion was never right; for three months I endured a state of hormonal siege; later I had pains in my fingers, swelling feet, numb spots on my legs, the dread hemorrhoids. I had to think about everything I ate. I developed borderline glucose intolerance. I gained 50 pounds and am still overweight; my shape has changed in other ways that may well be permanent. Psychologically, my pregnancy consumed me—though I'd happily bought the seat on the roller coaster, I was still terrified to be so out of control of my normally tractable body. It was all bearable, even interesting—even, at times, transcendent—because I wanted a baby. Birth was painful, exhausting, and wonderful. If I hadn't wanted a baby it would only have been painful and exhausting—or worse. I can hardly imagine what it's like to have your body and mind taken over in this way when you not only don't look forward to the result, but positively dread it. The thought appalls me. So as I see it, the key question is "Can it be moral, under any circumstances, to make a woman bear a child against her will?"

From this vantage point, *Commonweal*'s argument is irrelevant, for in a society that respects the individual, no "member of the species" in *any* stage of development has an "essential right" to make use of someone else's body, let alone in such all-encompassing fashion, without that person's consent. You can't make a case against abortion by applying a general principle about everybody's human rights; you have to show exactly the opposite—that the relationship between fetus and pregnant woman is an exception, one that justifies depriving women of their right to bodily integrity. And in fact all antiabortion ideology rests on the premise—acknowledged or simply assumed—that women's unique capacity to bring life into the world carries with it a unique obligation; that women cannot be allowed to "play God" and launch only the lives they welcome.

Yet the alternative to allowing women this power is to make them impotent. Criminalizing abortion doesn't just harm individual women with unwanted pregnancies, it affects all women's sense of themselves. Without control of our fertility we can never envision ourselves as free, for our biology makes us constantly vulnerable. Simply because we are female our physical integrity can be violated, our lives disrupted and transformed, at any time. Our ability to act in the world is hopelessly compromised by our sexual being.

Ah, sex—it does have a way of coming up in these discussions, despite all. When pressed, right-to-lifers of whatever political persuasion invariably point out that pregnancy doesn't happen by itself. The leftists often give patronizing lectures on contraception (though some find only "natural birth control" acceptable), but remain unmoved when reminded that contraceptives fail. Openly or implicitly they argue that people shouldn't have sex unless they're prepared to procreate. (They are quick to profess a single standard—men as well as women should be sexually "responsible." Yes, and the rich as well as the poor should be allowed to sleep under bridges.) Which amounts to saying that if women want to lead heterosexual lives they must give up any claim to self-determination, and that they have no right to sexual pleasure without fear.

Opposing abortion, then, means accepting that women must suffer sexual disempowerment and a radical loss of autonomy relative to men: if fetal life is sacred, the self-denial basic to women's oppression is also basic to the moral order. Opposing abortion means embracing a conservative sexual morality, one that subordinates pleasure to reproduction: if fetal life is sacred, there is no room for the view that sexual passion—or even sexual love—for its own sake is a human need and a human right. Opposing abortion means tolerating the inevitable double standard, by which men may accept or reject sexual restrictions in accordance with their beliefs, while women must bow to them out of fear . . . or defy them at great risk. However much *Commonweal*'s editors and those of like mind want to believe their opposition to abortion is simply about saving lives, the truth is that in the real world they are shoring up a particular sexual culture, whose rules are stacked against women. I have yet to hear any left right-to-lifers take full responsibility for that fact or deal seriously with its political implications.

Unfortunately, their fuzziness has not lessened their appeal—if anything it's done the opposite. In increasing numbers liberals and leftists, while opposing antiabortion laws, have come to view abortion as an "agonizing moral issue" with some justice on both sides, rather than an issue—however emotionally complex—of freedom versus repression, or equality versus hierarchy, that affects their political self-definition. This above-the-battle stance is attractive to leftists who want to be feminist good guys but are uneasy or ambivalent about sexual issues, not to mention those who want to ally with "progressive" factions of the Catholic church on Central America, nuclear disarmament, or populist economics without that sticky abortion question getting in the way.

Such neutrality is a way of avoiding the painful conflict over cultural issues that continually smolders on the left. It can also be a way of coping with the contradictions of personal life at a time when liberation is a dream deferred. To me the fight for abortion has always been the cutting edge of feminism, precisely because it denies that anatomy is destiny, that female biology dictates women's subordinate status. Yet recently I've found it hard to focus on the issue, let alone summon up the militance needed to stop the antiabortion tanks. In part that has to do with second-round weariness—do we really have to go through all these things twice?—in part with my life now.

Since my daughter's birth my feelings about abortion—not as a political demand but as a personal choice—have changed. In this society, the difference between the situation of a childless woman and of a mother is immense; the fear that having a child will dislodge one's tenuous hold on a nontraditional life is excruciating. This terror of being forced into the sea-change of motherhood gave a special edge to my convictions about abortion. Since I've made that plunge voluntarily, with consequences still unfolding, the terror is gone; I might not want another child, for all sorts of reasons, but I will never again feel that my identity is at stake. Different battles with the culture absorb my energy now. Besides, since I've experienced the primal, sensual passion of caring for an infant, there will always be part of me that does want another. If I had an abortion today, it would be with conflict and sadness unknown to me when I had an abortion a decade ago. And the antiabortionists' imagery of dead babies hits me with new force. Do many women—left, feminist women—have such feelings? Is this the sort of "ambivalence about abortion" that in the present atmosphere slides so easily into self-flagellating guilt?

Some left antiabortionists, mainly pacifists—Juli Loesch, Mary Meehan, and other "feminists for life"; Jim Wallis and various writers for Wallis's radical evangelical journal *Sojourners*—have tried to square their position with concern for women. They blame the prevalence of abortion on oppressive conditions—economic injustice, lack of child care and other social supports for mothers, the devaluation of childrearing, men's exploitative sexual behavior and refusal to take equal responsibility for children. They disagree on whether to criminalize abortion now (since murder is intolerable no matter what the cause) or to build a long-term moral consensus (since stopping abortion requires a general social transformation), but they all regard abortion as a desperate solution to desperate problems, and the women who resort to it as more sinned against than sinning.

This analysis grasps an essential feminist truth: that in a male-supremacist society no choice a woman makes is genuinely free or entirely in her interest. Certainly many women have had abortions they didn't want or wouldn't have wanted if they had any plausible means of caring for a child; and countless others wouldn't have gotten pregnant in the first place were it not for inadequate contraception, sexual confusion and guilt, male pressure, and other stigmata of female powerlessness. Yet forcing a woman to bear a child she doesn't want can only add injury to insult, while refusing to go through with such a pregnancy can be a woman's first step toward taking hold of her life. And many women who have abortions are "victims" only of ordinary human miscalculation, technological failure, or the vagaries of passion, all bound to exist in any society, however utopian. There will always be women who, at any given moment, want sex but don't want a child; some of these women will get pregnant; some of them will have abortions. Behind the victim theory of abortion is the implicit belief that women are always ready to be mothers, if only conditions are right, and that sex for pleasure rather than procreation is not only "irresponsible" (i.e., bad) but something men impose on women, never something women actively seek. Ironically, left right-to-lifers see abortion as always coerced (it's "exploitation" and "violence against women"), yet regard motherhood—which for most women throughout history has been inescapable, and is still our most socially approved role—as a positive choice. The analogy to the feminist antipornography movement goes beyond borrowed rhetoric: the antiporners, too, see active female lust as surrender to male domination and traditionally feminine sexual attitudes as expressions of women's true nature.

This Orwellian version of feminism, which glorifies "female values" and dismisses women's struggles for freedom—particularly sexual freedom—as a male plot, has become all too familiar in recent years. But its use in the abortion debate has been especially muddleheaded. Somehow we're supposed to leap from an oppressive patriarchal society to the egalitarian one that will supposedly make abortion obsolete without ever allowing women to see themselves as people entitled to control their reproductive function rather than be controlled by it. How women who have no power in this most personal of areas can effectively fight for power in the larger society is left to our imagination. A "New Zealand feminist" quoted by Mary Meehan in a 1980 article in *The Progressive* says, "Accepting short-term solutions like abortion only delays the implementation of real reforms like decent maternity and paternity leaves, job protection, high-quality child care, community responsibility for dependent people of all ages, and recognition of the economic contribution of childminders"—as if these causes were progressing nicely before legal abortion came along. On the contrary, the fight for reproductive freedom is the foundation of all the others, which is why antifeminists resist it so fiercely.

As "profile" pacifists have been particularly concerned with refuting charges of misogyny, the liberal Catholics at *Commonweal* are most exercised by the claim that antiabortion laws violate religious freedom. The editorial quoted above hurled another challenge at the proabortion forces:

> It is time, finally, for the pro-choice advocates and editorial writers to abandon, once and for all, the argument that abortion [*sic*] is a religious "doctrine" of a single or several churches being imposed on those of other persuasions in violation of the First Amendment. . . . Catholics and their bishops are accused of imposing their "doctrine" on abortion, but not their "doctrine" on the needs of the poor, or their "doctrine" on the arms race, or their "doctrine" on human rights in Central America. . . .
>
> The briefest investigation into Catholic teaching would show that the church's case against abortion is utterly unlike, say, its belief in the Real Presence, known with the eyes of faith alone, or its insistence on a Sunday obligation, applicable only to the faithful. The church's moral teaching on abortion . . . is for the most part like its teaching on racism, warfare, and capital punishment, based on ordinary reasoning common to believers and nonbelievers. . . .

This is one more example of right-to-lifers' tendency to ignore the sexual ideology underlying their stand. Interesting, isn't it, how the editorial neglects to mention that the church's moral teaching on abortion jibes neatly with its teaching on birth control, sex, divorce, and the role of women. The traditional, patriarchal sexual morality common to these teachings is explicitly religious, and its chief defenders in modern times have been the more conservative churches. The Catholic and evangelical Christian churches are the backbone of the organized right-to-life movement and—a few

Nathansons and Hentoffs notwithstanding—have provided most of the movement's activists and spokespeople.

Furthermore, the Catholic hierarchy has made opposition to abortion a litmus test of loyalty to the church in a way it has done with no other political issue—witness Archbishop O'Connor's harassment of Geraldine Ferraro during her vice-presidential campaign. It's unthinkable that a Catholic bishop would publicly excoriate a Catholic officeholder or candidate for taking a hawkish position on the arms race or Central America or capital punishment. Nor do I notice anyone trying to read William F. Buckley out of the church for his views on welfare. The fact is there is no accepted Catholic "doctrine" on these matters comparable to the church's absolutist condemnation of abortion. While differing attitudes toward war, racism, and poverty cut across religious and secular lines, the sexual values that mandate opposition to abortion are the bedrock of the traditional religious world view, and the source of the most bitter conflict with secular and religious modernists. When churches devote their considerable political power, organizational resources, and money to translating those values into law, I call that imposing their religious beliefs on me—whether or not they're technically violating the First Amendment.

Statistical studies have repeatedly shown that people's views on abortion are best predicted by their opinions on sex and "family" issues, not on "life" issues like nuclear weapons or the death penalty. That's not because we're inconsistent but because we comprehend what's really at stake in the abortion fight. It's the anti-abortion left that refuses to face the contradiction in its own position: you can't be wholeheartedly for "life"—or for such progressive aspirations as freedom, democracy, equality—and condone the subjugation of women. The seamless garment is full of holes.

---

## REFLECTING ON MEANING

1. The heart of Willis's argument is that the abortion debate is increasingly being articulated in a way that misses the central point. According to Willis, what is the crucial point that makes abortion a "feminist issue"? Do you agree or disagree that the focus of the debate has been off center? Why?

2. Willis claims that the abortion issue "affects all women's sense of themselves." What does she mean? According to Willis, what are the social, political, and personal consequences of anti-

abortion legislation for women? In what way, in her view, are antiabortionists not talking "simply about saving lives," but about "shoring up a particular sexual culture, whose rules are stacked against women"?

3. What is the "Orwellian version of feminism" that Willis describes? Why does she say that it "glorifies 'female values' and dismisses women's struggles for freedom—particularly sexual freedom—as a male plot"? What does this version of feminism have to do with the abortion issue?

## EXPLORING RHETORICAL STRATEGIES

1. Willis castigates those who, she says, have "supplied the mass media with the idea that prohibiting abortion is part of a 'seamless garment' of respect for human life." What is the significance of this metaphor? How does she reinforce it in her conclusion?
2. In several instances Willis tells about her own experiences and feelings—for instance, her pregnancy and her changing views on abortion since having a child. What function do these sections of the essay serve? Do they help Willis advance her main point? Why or why not?
3. What is the tone of Willis's argument? Do you think that it would help her persuade conservative antiabortionists to reconsider their point of view? Why or why not? Whom do you think she is hoping to reach in this essay? What is her purpose in this piece of writing?

# The Ambivalence of Abortion

LINDA BIRD FRANCKE

*While abortion continues to be a topic of public controversy and debate, Linda Bird Francke offers a personal perspective on the issue. In this narrative she tells about the emotions that having an abortion created in her.*

We were sitting in a bar on Lexington Avenue when I told my husband I was pregnant. It is not a memory I like to dwell on. Instead of the champagne and hope which had heralded the impending births of the first, second and third child, the news of this one was greeted with shocked silence and Scotch. "Jesus," my husband kept saying to himself, stirring the ice cubes around and around, "Oh, Jesus."

Oh, how we tried to rationalize it that night as the starting time for the movie came and went. My husband talked about his plans for a career change in the next year, to stem the staleness that fourteen years with the same investment-banking firm had brought him. A new baby would preclude that option.

The timing wasn't right for me either. Having juggled pregnancies and child care with what freelance jobs I could fit in between feedings, I had just taken on a full-time job. A new baby would put me right back in the nursery just when our youngest child was finally school age. It was time for *us*, we tried to rationalize. There just wasn't room in our lives now for another baby. We both agreed. And agreed. And agreed.

How very considerate they are at the Women's Services, known formally as the Center for Reproductive and Sexual Health. Yes, indeed, I could have an abortion that very Saturday morning and be out in time to drive to the country that afternoon. Bring a first morning urine specimen, a sanitary belt and napkins, a money order or $125 cash—and a friend.

My friend turned out to be my husband, standing awkwardly and ill at ease as men always do in places that are exclusively for women, as I checked in at nine A.M. Other men hovered around just as anxiously, knowing they had to be there, wishing they weren't.

No one spoke to each other. When I would be cycled out of there four hours later, the same men would be slumped in their same seats, locked downcast in their cells of embarrassment.

The Saturday morning women's group was more dispirited than the men in the waiting room. There were around fifteen of us, a mixture of races, ages and backgrounds. Three didn't speak English at all and a fourth, a pregnant Puerto Rican girl around eighteen, translated for them.

There were six black women and a hodgepodge of whites, among them a T-shirted teenager who kept leaving the room to throw up and a puzzled middle-aged woman from Queens with three grown children.

"What form of birth control were you using?" the volunteer asked each one of us. The answer was inevitably "none." She then went on to describe the various forms of birth control available at the clinic, and offered them to each of us.

The youngest Puerto Rican girl was asked through the interpreter which she'd like to use: the loop, diaphragm, or pill. She shook her head "no" three times. "You don't want to come back here again, do you?" the volunteer pressed. The girl's head was so low her chin rested on her breastbone. "*Sí,*" she whispered.

We had been there two hours by that time, filling out endless forms, giving blood and urine, receiving lectures. But unlike any other group of women I've been in, we didn't talk. Our common denominator, the one which usually floods across language and economic barriers into familiarity, today was one of shame. We were losing life that day, not giving it.

The group kept getting cut back to smaller, more workable units, and finally I was put in a small waiting room with just two other women. We changed into paper bathrobes and paper slippers, and we rustled whenever we moved. One of the women in my room was shivering and an aide brought her a blanket.

"What's the matter?" the aide asked her. "I'm scared," the woman said. "How much will it hurt?" The aide smiled. "Oh, nothing worse than a couple of bad cramps," she said. "This afternoon you'll be dancing a jig."

I began to panic. Suddenly the rhetoric, the abortion marches I'd walked in, the telegrams sent to Albany to counteract the Friends of the Fetus, the Zero Population Growth buttons I'd worn, peeled away, and I was all alone with my microscopic baby. There were just the two of us there, and soon, because it was more convenient for me and my husband, there would be one again.

How could it be that I, who am so neurotic about life that I step over bugs rather than on them, who spend hours planting flowers and vegetables in the spring even though we rent out the house and never see them, who make sure the children are vaccinated and inoculated and filled with vitamin C, could so arbitrarily decide that this life shouldn't be?

"It's not a life," my husband had argued, more to convince himself than me. "It's a bunch of cells smaller than my fingernail."

But any woman who has had children knows that certain feeling in her taut, swollen breasts, and the slight but constant ache in her uterus that signals the arrival of a life. Though I would march myself into blisters for a woman's right to exercise the option of motherhood, I discovered there in the waiting room that I was not the modern woman I thought I was.

When my name was called, my body felt so heavy the nurse had to help me into the examining room. I waited for my husband to burst through the door and yell "stop," but of course he didn't. I concentrated on three black spots in the acoustic ceiling until they grew in size to the shape of saucers, while the doctor swabbed my insides with antiseptic.

"You're going to feel a burning sensation now," he said, injecting Novocain into the neck of the womb. The pain was swift and severe, and I twisted to get away from him. He was hurting my baby, I reasoned, and the black saucers quivered in the air. "Stop," I cried. "Please stop." He shook his head, busy with his equipment. "It's too late to stop now," he said. "It'll just take a few more seconds."

What good sports we women are. And how obedient. Physically the pain passed even before the hum of the machine signaled that the vacuuming of my uterus was completed, my baby sucked up like ashes after a cocktail party. Ten minutes start to finish. And I was back on the arm of the nurse.

There were twelve beds in the recovery room. Each one had a gaily flowered draw sheet and a soft green or blue thermal blanket. It was all very feminine. Lying on these beds for an hour or more were the shocked victims of their sex, their full wombs now stripped clean, their futures less encumbered.

It was very quiet in that room. The only voice was that of the nurse, locating the new women who had just come in so she could monitor their blood pressure, and checking out the recovered women who were free to leave.

Juice was being passed out, and I found myself sipping a Dixie cup of Hawaiian Punch. An older woman with tightly curled bleached hair was just getting up from the next bed. "That was no goddamn snap," she said, resting before putting on her miniskirt and high white boots. Other women came and went, some walking out as dazed as they had entered, others with a bounce that signaled they were going right back to Bloomingdale's.

Finally then, it was time for me to leave. I checked out, making an appointment to return in two weeks for an IUD insertion. My husband was slumped in the waiting room, clutching a single yellow rose wrapped in a wet paper towel and stuffed into a Baggie.

We didn't talk the whole way home, but just held hands very tightly. At home there were more yellow roses and a tray in bed for me and the children's curiosity to divert.

It had certainly been a successful operation. I didn't bleed at all for two days just as they had predicted, and then I bled only moderately for another four days. Within a week my breasts had subsided and the tenderness vanished, and my body felt mine again instead of the eggshell it becomes when it's protecting someone else.

My husband and I are back to planning our summer vacation and his career switch.

And it certainly does make more sense not to be having a baby right now—we say that to each other all the time. But I have this ghost now. A very little ghost that only appears when I'm seeing something beautiful, like the full moon on the ocean last weekend. And the baby waves at me. And I wave at the baby. "Of course, we have room," I cry to the ghost. "Of course, we do."

---

## REFLECTING ON MEANING

1. Why are Francke and her husband disturbed by her pregnancy? What reasons do they each have for not wanting to have a child? Do you find their concerns reasonable? Why or why not?
2. Consider the following passage, and explain how it illustrates the conflict between Francke's intellectual and abstract feminist philosophy and the concrete experience of having an abortion:

   > I began to panic. Suddenly the rhetoric, the abortion marches I'd walked in, the telegrams sent to Albany to counteract the Friends of the Fetus, the Zero Population Growth buttons I'd worn, peeled away, and I was all alone with my microscopic baby.

3. *Ambivalence* is the word Francke uses to describe her feelings. In what ways is she ambivalent about her abortion? Is she saying that she would not have an abortion were she to relive her experience? Why or why not? What is she saying?

## EXPLORING RHETORICAL STRATEGIES

1. Francke's opening paragraphs take us from a bar to a telephone call to a women's health center. What is the effect of these concrete situations in Francke's telling of her story? What is the effect of the abrupt transition from the conversation between Francke and her husband to the phone call?
2. What is the tone that Francke adopts in telling about her experience? Can you identify shifts of voice in the essay—places where her tone seems to change? How do her concluding paragraphs change the tone of the essay?
3. Francke tells in great detail about the other women she encountered at the health center. Why does she do this? How does this section of the essay help her transcend the relating of her own personal experience? How does it place the abortion issue in a larger context?

# TAKING A STAND

## QUESTIONS FOR CONSIDERATION

1. This part highlights several public issues that have become feminist causes: comparable worth, pornography, and abortion. What makes these issues of special concern to feminists? To what extent are they gender issues? Select one of these issues, summarize the views of the appropriate authors on these questions, and explain your own point of view. Is the issue a gender issue by definition and, thus, of special concern to feminists? Or, perhaps, does the issue transcend gender politics?
2. The essays by Krauthammer and by Amott and Matthaei put forth opposing viewpoints on the issue of comparable worth. Which essay presents the more reasonable argument? Compare and contrast both arguments, analyze them to determine how they are constructed, and evaluate them for effectiveness. Consider especially how successfully each argument refutes the opposition viewpoint.
3. Do you think comparable worth legislation will effectively address inequities in the wages of women and men? Can you think of a more feasible or effective way to solve this problem? Summarize the strengths and weaknesses of the comparable worth plan, and argue that it is or is not a feasible way to bridge the income gap between the sexes. Propose an alternate solution by refining the current comparable worth plan or by designing another system that you think will work better.
4. Brownmiller, Donnerstein, Linz, and Penrod, and Jacoby examine the effects of pornography and discuss attempts to ban it in the United States. What is pornography? How do these authors define it? In what ways do their definitions concur or diverge? To what extent do their stands on this issue derive from their definitions of pornography? After considering the views of these authors, construct your own definition of pornography and argue that it should or should not be banned.
5. The essays by Thomson, Reagan, Willis, and Francke range over the spectrum of views on the abortion issue. Do these authors agree on any points? What common assumptions and beliefs do they share, if any? At what points do their arguments diverge? Consider the viewpoints they assert, and attempt to negotiate a middle ground on which all can agree. How successfully can you do this? What problems do you encounter? Why?
6. Thomson and Reagan expound very different kinds of arguments to support their views on abortion. Consider the extent

to which their essays illuminate each other. What appeals does each author make? What evidence do they use to support their beliefs? How would each respond to the other's argument? Analyze each argument and evaluate its soundness both as a logical argument and as a rhetorically effective argument.

6. What is your stand on the abortion issue? Summarize the viewpoints of at least two authors and explain how your position differs. Argue that your viewpoint is more reasonable.

# Part VI

## Sexism and the Status of Women

Besides the emotional or psychological by-products of sexism—such as feelings of inferiority, helplessness, and lowered self-esteem—discrimination produces serious, concrete consequences for many women, especially for those competing for careers in a male-dominated workplace. Simply because of their sex, women are often victims of unfair pay and promotion practices, forced to accept menial jobs and lower pay than their male counterparts. Part VI looks at how sexual discrimination affects women in the workplace and in society at large and produces debilitating social powerlessness.

Various kinds of discrimination are addressed by the authors of the first group of essays. Susan Fraker shows that despite the apparent advances of women in business and industry, few are given the opportunity to hold senior management positions. Diana Pearce reveals one of the most serious consequences of discrimination: the huge number of women, especially black women, forced to live in degrading poverty. Philip Goldberg adds a surprising twist by arguing that many women see their own sex as inferior and thus discriminate against other women.

The extent of the humiliating powerlessness many women face daily is the focus of the next four selections. According to Brigid Brophy, women are still oppressed by a male-dominated society, even though their oppression is no longer as obvious as it was. Claiming that powerlessness "corrupts women's hearts," Ellen Goodman discusses the health of women in clerical positions. The prominent economist John Kenneth Galbraith analyzes how women serve not their own needs but those of the dominant economic interests in the United States. Finally, Diane Johnson explores the ultimate form of discrimination and powerlessness: rape.

Although the authors represented in Part VI acknowledge that some advances have been made in curbing economic discrimination against women, several suggest that this progress may be more apparent than real. Certainly the cumulative picture of powerlessness portrayed in these essays is a sobering indication of how much must yet be done before women and men will enjoy equal status in and out of the workplace.

# Chapter 14

# DISCRIMINATION

## Why Women Aren't Getting to the Top

SUSAN FRAKER

*Despite the number of women entering the work force and the success of those who have garnered entry- and middle-management positions, women have still not broken into the ranks of senior management. In this essay, Susan Fraker documents the scarcity of women in high-level executive positions, looks at possible reasons why they are not better represented in the upper ranks of businesses, and makes some suggestions for the future.*

Ten years have passed since U.S. corporations began hiring more than token numbers of women for jobs at the bottom rung of the management ladder. A decade into their careers, how far up have these women climbed? The answer: not as far as their male counterparts. Despite impressive progress at the entry level and in middle management, women are having trouble breaking into senior management. "There is an invisible ceiling for women at that level," says Janet Jones-Parker, executive director of the Association of Executive Search Consultants Inc. "After eight or ten years, they hit a barrier."

The trouble begins at about the $75,000 to $100,000 salary level, and seems to get worse the higher one looks. Only one company on *Fortune*'s list of the 500 largest U.S. industrial corporations has a woman chief executive. That woman, Katharine Graham of the Washington Post Co. (No. 342), readily admits she got the job because her family owns a controlling share of the corporation.

More surprising, given that women have been on the ladder for ten years, is that none currently seems to have a shot at the top rung. Executive recruiters, asked to identify women who might become presidents or chief executives of *Fortune* 500 companies, draw a blank. Even companies that have women in senior management privately concede that these women aren't going to occupy the chairman's office.

Women have only four of the 154 spots this year at the Harvard Business School's Advanced Management Program—a prestigious 13-week conclave to which companies send executives they are grooming for the corridors of power. The numbers aren't much better at comparable programs at Stanford and at Dartmouth's Tuck School. But perhaps the most telling admission of trouble comes from men at the top. "The women aren't making it," confessed the chief executive of a *Fortune* 500 company to a consultant. "Can you help us find out why?"

All explanations are controversial to one faction or another in this highly charged debate. At one extreme, many women—and some men—maintain that women are the victims of blatant sexism. At the other extreme, many men—and a few women—believe women are unsuitable for the highest managerial jobs: they lack the necessary assertiveness, they don't know how to get along in this rarefied world, or they have children and lose interest in—or time for—their careers. Somewhere in between is a surprisingly large group of men and women who see "discrimination" as the major problem, but who often can't define precisely what they mean by the term.

The discrimination they talk about is not the simple-minded sexism of dirty jokes and references to "girls." It is not born of hatred, or indeed of any ill will that the bearer may be conscious of. What they call discrimination consists simply of treating women differently from men. The notion dumbfounds some male managers. You mean to say, they ask, that managerial women don't want to be treated differently from men in any respect, and that by acting otherwise—as I was raised to think only decent and gentlemanly—I'm somehow prejudicing their chances for success? Yes, the women respond.

"Men I talk to would like to see more women in senior management," says Ann Carol Brown, a consultant to several *Fortune* 500 companies. "But they don't recognize the subtle barriers that stand in the way." Brown thinks the biggest hurdle is a matter of comfort, not competence. "At senior management levels, competence is assumed," she says. "What you're looking for is someone who fits, someone who gets along, someone you trust. Now that's subtle stuff. How does a group of men feel that a woman is going to fit? I think it's very hard."

The experience of an executive at a large Northeastern bank illustrates how many managerial women see the problem. Promoted to senior vice president several years ago, she was the first woman named to that position. But she now believes it will be many years before the bank appoints a woman executive vice president. "The men just don't feel comfortable," she says. "They make all sorts of excuses—that I'm not a banker [she worked as a consultant originally], that I don't know the culture. There's a smoke screen four miles thick. I attribute it to being a woman." Similarly, 117 to 300 women executives polled recently by UCLA's Graduate School of Management and Korn/Ferry International, an executive search firm, felt that being a woman was the greatest obstacle to their success.

A common concern among women, particularly in law and investment banking, is that the best assignments go to men. "Some departments—like sales and trading or mergers and acquisitions—are considered more macho, hence more prestigious," says a woman at a New York investment bank. "It's nothing explicit. But if women can't get the assignments that allow them to shine, how can they advance?"

Women also worry that they don't receive the same kind of constructive criticism that men do. While these women probably overestimate the amount of feedback their male colleagues receive, even some men acknowledge widespread male reluctance to criticize a woman. "There are vast numbers of men who can't do it," says Eugene Jennings, professor of business administration at Michigan State University and a consultant to a dozen large companies. A male banking executive agrees: "A male boss will haul a guy aside and just kick ass if the subordinate performs badly in front of a client. But I heard about a woman here who gets nervous and tends to giggle in front of customers. She's unaware of it and her boss hasn't told her. But behind her back he downgrades her for not being smooth with customers."

Sometimes the message that has to be conveyed to a woman manager is much more sensitive. An executive at a large company says he once had to tell a woman that she should either cross her legs or keep her legs together when she sat. The encounter was obviously painful to him. "She listened to me and thanked me and expressed shock at what she was doing," he recalls, with a touch of agony in his voice. "My God, this is something only your mother tells you. I'm a fairly direct person and a great believer in equal opportunity. But it was damn difficult for me to say this to a woman whom I view to be very proper in all other respects."

Research by Anne Harlan, a human resource manager at the Federal Aviation Administration, and Carol Weiss, a managing associate of Charles Hamilton Associates, a Boston consulting firm, suggests that the situation doesn't necessarily improve as the number of women in an organization increases. Their study, conducted at the Wellesley College Center for Research on Women and completed in 1982, challenges the theory advanced by some experts that when a corporation attained a "critical mass" of executive women—defined as somewhere between 30% and 35%—job discrimination would vanish naturally as men and women began to take each other for granted.

Harlan and Weiss observed the effects of different numbers of women in an organization during a three-year study of 100 men and women managers at two Northeastern retailing corporations. While their sample of companies was not large, after their results were published, other companies said they had similar experiences. Harlan and Weiss found that while overt resistance drops quickly after the first few women become managers, it seems to pick up again as the number of women reaches 15%. In one company they studied, only 6% of the managers were women, compared with 19% in the second company. But more women in the second company complained of discrimination, ranging from sexual harassment to inadequate feedback. Could something other than discrimination—very different corporate cultures, say—have accounted for the result? Harlan and Weiss say no, that the two companies were eminently comparable.

Consultants and executives who think discrimination is the problem tend to believe it persists in part because the government has relaxed its commitment to affirmative action, which they define more narrowly than some advocates do. "We're not talking about quotas or preferential treatment," says Margaret Hennig who, along with Anne Jardim, heads the Simmons College Graduate School of Management. "That's stupid management. We just mean the chance to compete equally." Again, a semantic chasm separates women and men. Women like Hennig and Jardim think of affirmative action as a vigorous effort on the part of companies to ensure that women are treated equally and that sexist prejudices aren't permitted to operate. Men think the term means reverse discrimination, giving women preferential treatment.

Legislation such as the Equal Employment Opportunity Act of 1972 prohibits companies from discriminating against women in hiring. The laws worked well—indeed, almost too well. After seven or eight years, says Jennings of Michigan State, the pressure was off and no one pushed hard to see that discrimination was eliminated in selecting people for senior management. Jennings thinks the problem began in the latter days of the Carter Administration, when the economy was lagging and companies worried more about making money than about how their women managers were doing. The Reagan Administration hasn't made equal opportunity a priority either.

What about the belief that women fall behind not because of discrimination, but because they are cautious, unaggressive, and differently motivated than men—or less motivated? Even some female executives believe that women derail their careers by choosing staff jobs over high-risk, high-reward line positions. One woman, formerly with a large consumer goods company and now president of a market research firm, urges women to worry less about sexism and more about whether the jobs they take are the right route to the top. "I spent five years thinking the only reason I didn't become a corporate officer at my former company was because of my sex," she says. "I finally had to come to grips with the fact that I overemphasized being a woman and underemphasized what I did for a living. I was in a staff function—the company didn't live and die by what I did."

Men and women alike tend to believe that because women are raised differently they must manage differently. Research to support this belief is hard to come by, though. The women retail managers studied by Harlan and Weiss, while never quarterbacks or catchers, had no trouble playing on management teams. Nor did they perform less well on standardized tests measuring qualities like assertiveness and leadership. "Women don't manage differently," Harlan says flatly.

In a much larger study specifically addressing management styles, psychologists Jay Hall and Susan Donnell of Teleometrics International Inc., a management training company, reached the same conclusion. They matched nearly 2,000 men and women managers according to age, rank in their organization, kind of organization, and the number of people they supervised. The psychologists ran tests to assess everything from managerial philosophies to the ability to get along with people, even quizzing subordinates on their views of the boss. Donnell and Hall concluded, "Male and female managers do not differ in the way they manage the organization's technical and human resources."

Data on how women's expectations—and therefore, arguably,

their performance—may differ from men's are more confusing. Stanford Professor Myra Strober studied 150 men and 26 women who graduated from the Stanford Business School in 1974. When she and a colleague, Francine Gordon, polled the MBAs shortly before graduation, they discovered that the women had much lower expectations for their peak earnings. The top salary the women expected during their careers was only 60% of the men's. Four years later the ratio had fallen to 40%.

Did this mean that women were less ambitious or were willing to take lower salaries to get managerial jobs? Strober doesn't think so. She says a major reason for the women's lower salary expectations was that they took jobs in industries that traditionally pay less, but which, the women thought, offered opportunities for advancement. Almost 20% of the women in her sample went into government, compared with 3% of the men. On the other hand, no women went into investment banking or real estate development, which each employed about 6% of the men. Strober points out, however, that investment banking and big-time real estate were all but closed to women in the early 1970s. "One way people decide what their aspirations are," she says, "is to look around and see what seems realistic. If you look at a field and see no women advancing, you may modify your goals."

Some of what Mary Anne Devanna found in her examination of MBAs contradicts Strober's conclusions. Devanna, research coordinator of the Columbia Business School's Center for Research in Career Development, matched 45 men and 45 women who graduated from the Columbia Business School from 1969 to 1972. Each paired man and woman had similar backgrounds, credentials, and marital status. The starting salaries of the women were 98% of the men's. Using data collected in 1980, Devanna found a big difference in the salaries men and women ultimately achieved, though. In manufacturing, the highest paying sector, women earned $41,818 after ten years vs. $59,733 for the men. Women in finance had salaries of $42,867 vs. $46,786 for the men. The gap in the service industries was smallest: $36,666 vs. $38,600. She then tested four hypotheses in seeking to explain the salary differences: (1) that women are less successful because they are motivated differently than men, (2) that motherhood causes women to divert attention from their careers, (3) that women seek jobs in low-paying industries, and (4) that women seek types of jobs—in human resources, say—that pay less.

Devanna found no major differences between the sexes in the importance they attached to the psychic or monetary rewards of work. "The women did not expect to earn less than the men," she says. Nor did she find that motherhood led women to abandon their careers. Although several women took maternity leaves, all returned to work full time within six months. Finally, Devanna found no big differences in the MBAs' choice of industry or function, either when they took their first jobs or ten years later.

Devanna concluded that discrimination, not level of motivation or choice of job, accounted for the pay differences. Could the problem simply have been performance—that the women didn't manage as well as men? Devanna claims that while she couldn't take this variable into account specifically, she controlled for all the variables that should have made for a difference in performance—from family background to grades in business school.

In their discussions with male executives, researchers like Devanna hear a recurrent theme—a conviction that women don't take their careers seriously. Even though most female managers were regarded as extremely competent, the men thought they would eventually leave—either to have children or because the tensions of work became too much. Both are legitimate concerns. A woman on the fast track is under intense pressure. Many corporate types believe that she gets much more scrutiny that a man and must work harder to succeed. The pressures increase geometrically if she has small children at home.

Perhaps as a result, thousands of women have careers rather than husbands and children. In the UCLA-Korn/Ferry study of executive women, 52% had never married, were divorced, or were widowed, and 61% had no children. A similar study of male executives done in 1979 found that only 5% of the men had never married or were divorced and even fewer—3%—had no children.

Statistics on how many women bear children and then leave the corporation are incomplete. Catalyst, a nonprofit organization that encourages the participation of women in business, studied 815 two-career families in 1980. It found that 37% of the new mothers in the study returned to work within two months; 68% were back after 4½ months; 87% in eight months. To a company, of course, an eight-month absence is a long time. Moreover, the 10% or so who never come back—most males are convinced the figure is higher—represent a substantial capital investment lost. It would be naive to think that companies don't crank this into their calculation of how much the women who remain are worth.

Motherhood clearly slows the progress of women who decide to take long maternity leaves or who choose to work part time. But even those committed to working full time on their return believe that they are sometimes held back—purposely or inadvertently. "Men make too many assumptions that women with children aren't free to take on time-consuming tasks," says Gene Kofke, director of human resources at AT&T. Karen Gonçalves, 34, quit her job as a consultant when she was denied challenging assignments after the birth of her daughter. "I was told clearly that I couldn't expect to move ahead as fast as I had been," she says. Later, when Gonçalves began working at the consulting firm of Arthur D. Little Inc. in Cambridge, Massachusetts, she intentionally avoided discussions of family and children: "I didn't keep a picture of my daughter in the office, and I would travel anywhere, no matter how hard it was for me."

Sometimes pregnancy is more of an issue for the men who witness it than for the women who go through it. Karol Emmerich, 35, now treasurer of Dayton Hudson Corp., was the first high-level woman at the department-store company to become pregnant. "The men didn't really know what to do," she recalls. "They were worried when I wanted to take three months off. But they wanted to encourage me to come back. So they promoted me to treasurer when I was seven months pregnant. Management got a lot of good feedback." Emmerich's experience would please Simmons Dean Anne Jardim, who worries that most organizations aren't doing enough to keep women who want to have children. "It's mind-boggling," she argues. "Either some of the brightest women in this country aren't going to reproduce or the companies are going to write off women in whom they have a tremendous investment."

To the corporation it may seem wasteful to train a woman and then be unable to promote her because she won't move to take the new job. The Catalyst study found that 40% of the men surveyed had moved for their jobs, vs. only 21% of the women. An argument can be made that an immobile executive is worth less to the corporation—and hence may be paid less.

Where women frequently do go is out of the company and into business for themselves. "When the achievements you want aren't forthcoming, it makes going out on your own easier," says a woman who has set up her own consultancy. "I was told I wouldn't make it into senior management at my bank. Maybe I just didn't have it. But the bank never found any woman who did. They were operating under a consent decree and they brought in a lot of women at the vice president level. Every single one of them left." Karen Gonçalves left Arthur D. Little to do part-time teaching and consulting when she was pregnant with her second child. "I didn't think I would get the professional satisfaction I wanted at ADL," she says.

From 1977 to 1980, according to the Small Business Administration, the number of businesses owned by women increased 33%, compared with an 11% increase for men—though admittedly the women's increase started from a much smaller base. While it's not clear from the numbers that women are entering the entrepreneurial ranks in greater numbers than they are joining corporations, some experts think so. "It's ironic," says Strober of Stanford. "The problem of the 1970s was bringing women into the corporation. The problem of the 1980s is keeping them there."

A few companies, convinced that women face special problems and that it's in the corporation's interest to help overcome them, are working hard at solutions. At Penn Mutual Life Insurance Co. in Philadelphia, where nearly half the managers are women, executives conducted a series of off-site seminars on gender issues and sex-role stereotypes. Dayton Hudson provides support (moral and financial) for a program whereby women in the company trade information on issues like personal financial planning and child care.

What women need most, the experts say, are loud, clear, continuing statements of support from senior management. Women have come a long way at Merck, says B. Lawrence Branch, the company's director of equal employment affairs, because Chairman John J. Horan insisted that their progress be watched. Merck has a program that identifies 10% of its women and 10% of minorities as "most promising." The company prepares a written agenda of what it will take for them to move to the next level. Progress upward may mean changing jobs or switching functions, so Merck circulates their credentials throughout the company. "We have a timetable and we track these women carefully," says Branch. Since 1979 almost 40% of the net growth in Merck's managerial staff has been women.

Sensitive to charges of reverse discrimination, Branch explains that Merck has for years singled out the best employees to make sure they get opportunities to advance. Women, he notes, were consistently underrepresented in that group. In his view the tracking program simply allows women to get into the competition with fast-track men. Others might not be so charitable. Any company that undertakes to do something on behalf of its managerial women leaves itself open to the charge that it too is discriminating—treating women and men differently.

What everyone may be able to agree on is that opening corporations to competition in the executive ranks is clearly good for performance and profits. But how can a company do this? It can try to find productive part-time work for all employees who want to work part time—even managers. It can structure promotions so that fewer careers are derailed by an absence of a few months or the unwillingness to relocate. It can make sure that the right information, particularly on job openings, reaches everyone. Perhaps most importantly, it can reward its managers for developing talent of all sorts and sexes, penalize them if they don't, and vigilantly supervise the process.

---

## REFLECTING ON MEANING

1. Fraker states that many people blame a vague kind of discrimination for the lack of women in senior management positions. What sort of discrimination does she mean? How is it manifested in the workplace? In what ways are women treated differently from men? How is this discrimination based not on the issue of competence but on the idea of "comfort"?
2. Fraker discusses the belief that women aren't suited for the demands of senior management. According to Fraker, who subscribes to this idea? What do such critics suggest about differences in men's and women's management styles? Are their suggestions borne out by the studies Fraker cites?
3. As Fraker points out, the number of women going into business for themselves is increasing. What does this trend suggest about businesses' responsiveness to women's needs? Why are corporations having a difficult time keeping the women they hire? What are Fraker's suggestions for making the corporate environment more responsive to women?

## EXPLORING RHETORICAL STRATEGIES

1. Fraker weaves a lot of data into her essay, but she manages to keep it interesting and easy to read. How does she do this?
2. What was Fraker's purpose in writing this essay? What purpose does her title imply? Does the essay deliver on its promise? Why or why not?
3. This selection was originally published in 1984 as an article in *Fortune* magazine. Based on Fraker's tone and the kind of information she provides, what can you surmise about her audience?

# The Feminization of Ghetto Poverty

## DIANA M. PEARCE

*Writing for the journal* Society, *Diana Pearce looks at the alarming increase of women who live at or below the poverty level. Pearce examines the special nature of poverty for women and concludes that black women especially are trapped in a double bind of gender and race.*

The "other America" is a changing neighborhood: men are moving out; women and their children are moving in. This dramatic change is not a reaction to recent fluctuations in the economy, but instead reflects long-term structural shifts both in the labor market and in marriage and childbearing practices. Today, three-quarters of the poor are women and children.

The poverty *rate* for female-headed households has remained steady over the past decade, with just under one-third of these families living in poverty. But because a significant number of male-headed households have left poverty, and because the number of households headed by women has increased, the proportion of *poor* families that are maintained by women has risen in the 1970s from 36 percent to more than 50 percent. Moreover, there is evidence that the trend is accelerating. Between 1969 and 1978, there was an annual net increase of 100,000 female-headed families in poverty, but in the two years between 1978 and 1980, the net increase each year was approximately 150,000. Furthermore, according to Reynolds Farley and Suzanne Bianchi, families headed by women have experienced a decline in economic status over the past two decades, with their average income dropping from 77 percent to 62 percent of the average income of white husband-and-wife families, and from 36 percent to 47 percent of black husband-and-wife families.

These trends are appearing even more strongly in the black community. Although the proportion of the poor who are black did not change during the 1970s, the proportion who were in families headed by women increased. Indeed, the decade of the seventies saw a dramatic shift of the burden of poverty among blacks from male-headed to female-headed families. The number of black families in poverty who were maintained by men declined by 35 percent, while the number maintained by women *increased* by 62 percent. In the course of one decade, black female-headed families increased from about one-half to three-fourths of all poor black families.

Some elements of the experience of being poor are common to all women; that is, they are a function of gender. Others, however, are the effect of race, though even these are experienced differently by men and women, as we shall see.

Though poor women share many characteristics in common with poor men (such as low education, lack of market-relevant job skills, or location in job-poor areas), the greater rates of poverty among women can be traced to two distinctly female causes. First of all, women who head their families often bear most or all of the economic burden of raising the children. Secondly, because of sex discrimination, occupational segregation in a segmented labor market, and sexual harassment, women who seek to support themselves and their families through paid work are disadvantaged in the labor market.

If a woman is married, even if she is employed outside the home, she shares substantially in the resources obtained by her husband. That transfer drops off dramatically when the parents no longer live together. In 1975, for example, only 25 percent of the women eligible actually received child support, and for more than half of those, the annual income from child-support payments was less than $1,500. If the parents were never married, the picture is even worse; only 5 percent of these fathers provide child support. Ironically, a woman is better off if her husband is dead, for widows are the best protected against income loss following the loss of a spouse and are therefore least likely to be poor. However, receipt of such transfers is unlikely to provide much of the bulwark against poverty; the average amount as of 1978 was about $1,800, and the duration is generally only a few years.

Accordingly, many women seek income through paid employment. For all too many, this goes against their lifelong expectations and preparations. Although it is true that most women today expect to work or have worked, sex-role socialization in general and vocational preparation in particular do not prepare women to be the *primary* breadwinner. Instead, the traditional emphasis has been on jobs, rather than careers, and on making job choices that emphasize flexibility and adaptability, rather than income potential. Thus, women faced with the necessity of being the sole source of support for themselves and their children are handicapped.

These handicaps are reinforced by a highly discriminatory labor market. Despite increased attention given this problem—including litigation and legislation—continuing high levels of *occupational segregation* of women stand in marked contrast to the decline of racial segregation in employment and education. Women who work full time continue to earn only 59 cents on the dollar earned by men who work full time. And while we do not know with precision the magnitude of the problem, it is increasingly evident that large numbers of women experience sexual harassment and thereby incur heavy economic, as well as personal, costs in lost recommendations, denied promotions, abrupt dismissals, and demotions.

## Being Black, Female, and Poor

The inequality experienced by women in the labor market has been conceptualized by some as confinement to the secondary sector of a dual labor market. According to the dual-economy theory, jobs and industries are readily divided into primary and secondary sectors, and this division is reinforced by barriers that make it difficult for workers to move from one sector to another. In the primary sector, jobs are characterized by good pay and fringe benefits, job security, a high degree of unionization, good working conditions, and due process in job rights. In contrast, the secondary sector includes work in marginal industries; these jobs are low-paying, often seasonal or sporadic, less likely to be unionized, and offer little protection against the vagaries of either the individual employer or the ups and downs of the marketplace.

The duality of the labor market is complemented and reinforced by a parallel duality in the welfare system. There is a primary welfare sector in which benefits are conferred as a right, often (but not always) because they have been "earned." One is not stigmatized by receipt of these benefits, nor must one demonstrate poverty or suffer degrading, detailed investigations of one's lifestyle. The benefits are more generous, often with minimum or national levels set by the federal government. Not only are benefit levels relatively generous, but one does not have to exhaust one's resources to qualify; nor are benefits reduced in proportion to other income. Examples of primary-welfare-sector benefits include unemployment compensation and social security.

In contrast, the secondary welfare sector is characterized by benefits that are much lower, on the average, and highly variable across states and even across localities within a state. Since such benefits are a privilege, not received by right, they may be revoked arbitrarily and for different reasons in different places. They may be, and usually are, reduced in proportion to other income. Receipt of welfare, in the eyes of the public and many recipients, is stigmatizing and demoralizing.

For those in the secondary sector of either the labor market or the welfare system, escape is difficult. This is especially so for women and minorities. For a variety of reasons, the welfare system and related training and jobs programs (such as WIN and CETA) do not overcome the labor-market barriers faced by women. For example, training is often for traditionally female occupations, such as clerical work or food service, occupations that do not pay wages adequate to support a woman and even one child. The stubborn obsession with getting women off welfare and into jobs as quickly as possible, with no attention to their special needs (e.g., for child care or fringe benefits that include adequate health insurance), has long-term results that are counterproductive. Those who accept or are forced to take economically marginal jobs in the secondary sector quickly find that they do not have access to the primary welfare sector when they lose or are laid off from these jobs. They are then forced to depend on impoverished secondary-welfare-sector programs. Thus, the interlocking secondary welfare system and secondary labor market reinforce a vicious circle of welfare dependency and marginal work.

Women and minorities are concentrated in the secondary welfare sector. As shown in Table 1, whereas men are slightly overrepresented and women underrepresented in the primary welfare sector, there is a severe sex discrepancy in the secondary sector. Less than half of white men receive secondary-sector benefits according to their proportion in the population, while three times the number of white women—and six times the number of black women—receive income from the secondary welfare sector according to their proportions in the population.

Many, of course, receive income from earnings as well as from transfer programs, but since the receipt of primary-sector benefits is strongly associated with previously held primary-sector *jobs*, the figures in Table 1 indicate implicitly the effect of differential participation not only in the primary and secondary welfare sectors, but also in the primary and secondary labor markets. (Theoretically, one could receive income from primary as well as from secondary welfare programs, but Census Bureau data show that few actually do.)

**Table 1**
**Primary Versus Secondary Welfare Sectors, 1978**

| | *All Household Heads* | | *Primary Sector*[a] | | *Secondary Sector*[b] | |
|---|---|---|---|---|---|---|
| | *Percentage* | *Poverty Rate* | *Percentage* | *Poverty Rate* | *Percentage* | *Poverty Rate* |
| Men[c] | | | | | | |
| White | 79.2 | 4.7 | 81.5 | 4.0 | 30.2 | 35.7 |
| Black | 6.2 | 11.8 | 7.3 | 7.2 | 10.1 | 36.9 |
| Subtotal | 85.4 | 5.3 | 88.8 | 4.3 | 40.3 | 36.1 |
| Women[d] | | | | | | |
| White | 10.4 | 23.5 | 8.9 | 10.4 | 28.7 | 66.8 |
| Black | 4.2 | 50.6 | 2.3 | 32.3 | 30.9 | 75.8 |
| Subtotal | 14.6 | 31.4 | 11.2 | 15.1 | 59.6 | 71.2 |
| Total | 100.0 | | 100.0 | 5.5 | 100.0 | 67.7 |

[a]Includes unemployment and workmen's compensation, veterans' benefits
[b]Includes all types of cash public assistance (aid to families with dependent children, general assistance, etc.)
[c]Both male-only and husband-and-wife households
[d]Female householder, no husband
*Source:* U.S. Census Bureau, *Characteristics of the Population Below the Poverty Level: 1978,* Series P-60, No. 124

If one compares poverty rates across gender and race categories, several conclusions suggest themselves. First, the poverty rate for those receiving benefits (and perhaps, also, earnings) in the secondary sector (67.7%) is more than eleven times the rate for those in the primary sector (5.5%). Second, within each sector, the poverty rates are greater for blacks than for whites, and greater for women than for men; but the gender differentials are greater than the racial ones. In this connection, the differences in poverty rates between black and white men within each sector are quite small, whereas there is a substantial added disadvantage to being both black and female. The "double" disadvantage experienced by black women is actually, in quantitative terms, a geometrically increasing "quadruple" disadvantage.

## Special Effects

It is clear from the data that although much of the economic gulf is accounted for by gender, black women experience considerable further disadvantages associated with race. These disadvantages can be grouped into three areas for purposes of discussion: trends in racial desegregation in various areas, demographic trends, and welfare programs.

Considerable occupational desegregation has been experienced by both men and women. This has meant an exodus from extremely low-paying jobs (often irregular and part-time), particularly in household service, that have been race/sex "occupational ghettoes." But because *sex* segregation levels, which have always been higher than those of race, have remained quite high, and because the wages of women have remained at less than 60 percent of men's wages, black men have benefited more from the racial desegregation of occupations than black women. Thus, statistics purporting to show that black women are closing the gap on white women faster than black men are on white men are misleading. The use of white women as a benchmark is inappropriate, for it eliminates the effects of gender. If one compares the progress of black men and black women to that of white men, then at present rates black men will catch up to white men in 35 years, but it will take black women 135 years to achieve occupational parity with white men.

In other areas, there have been parallel developments. For example, as Robert Crain and Rita Mehard have pointed out, school desegregation has opened up opportunities for black students of both sexes and, therefore, has resulted in increased achievement levels. Continued sex segregation of vocational programs, however, has the consequence of channeling women students into lower-paying occupations. For obvious economic reasons, housing desegregation has been experienced disproportionately by two-parent, two-income black families. In sum, racial desegregation has had a much greater impact on families with a male householder.

More than 40 percent of black families, and more than 50 percent of those with children, are headed by a single parent (almost all of whom are women). This is partly related to high divorce rates, but several other factors have contributed to the growth of single-parent homes. One of these is the high ratio of out-of-wedlock births—now at about 55 percent for blacks. Many of these children are born to teenagers. Black women tend to marry or remarry at lower rates than white women, and they tend to remain single longer if they do marry. This is, in part, because of a shortage of black men of marriageable age. For example, the ratio (in the resident population) of black women to men ages 20 to 49 is 1.16 (the white ratio is 1.01); in other words, there are sixteen "extra" black women for every hundred black men.

This imbalance in the sex ratio is the result of several factors, including higher levels of suicide and homicide among black men and an incredible incarceration rate for young black men—phenomena that are directly related to very high levels of poverty, underemployment, and unemployment. While it is true that *being a single parent* causes poverty, it is also clear that the widespread poverty among young black men, and their less-than-cheerful prospects for future economic stability, is an important *cause* of the formation of single-parent households among blacks. The converse also holds, so that marriage is as much the result of economic security, well-being, and upward mobility as it is the cause of economic well-being among families. In this connection, Farley and Bianchi find that the black community is not becoming polarized along traditional class lines (such as occupation or education), but that there is a polarization along *marital-status* lines. Two-parent families are increasing their economic status while families headed by women become poorer, opening up a different kind of schism in black America.

All of the factors noted above play a part in the racial differences seen in patterns of welfare use. Keeping in mind that these differences are relative, and that there is high degree of overlap among the factors, I will briefly examine some of the differences between white and black women who are welfare recipients.

White women tend more often to be divorced (as opposed to being single or separated). They also tend to come to welfare with more resources (including education, work experience, and even ownership of a house and/or a more favorable residential location vis-à-vis job opportunities. On the other hand, white women are also less likely to be employed and are more likely to go on welfare as a result of the loss of a husband's earnings. Because of this combination of more immediate need and yet greater "long-run" resources, white women not only tend to be on welfare for shorter periods of time, they are also more fully dependent during the time that they are on welfare. In contrast, more black women come to welfare as a result of unemployment and underemployment. Whereas white women often leave welfare because they have obtained a job or remarried (or both), black women are less likely to find a job—at least one providing sufficient income to support themselves and their family—and are less likely to marry or remarry.

In sum, white women tend more often to use welfare for shorter periods of time, even though welfare accounts for most (if not all) of their income while they are on welfare. Black women who head households, in contrast, are more likely to use welfare for longer periods of time, but in conjunction with earnings and other sources of income (e.g., child support), and are less likely to be totally dependent upon welfare, particularly over a period of years. Again, it should be remembered that these racial differences are relative. It should be emphasized, too, that the differences between women householders who use welfare and those that do not are not all that great. Data reported by Martin Rein and Lee Rainwater show that among those who were heavily dependent on welfare over a seven-year period, almost 30 percent of annual income came from earnings, while among low-income families who did not use welfare during that period, about 70 percent of annual income came from earnings. Phillip AuClaire estimates that about 58 percent of the annual income of long-term welfare recipients who were also employed came from earnings.

## The Workhouse Without Walls

Black women experience quantitatively more poverty than either black men or white women, no matter what the circumstances or income source. But there is also an important qualitative difference not made explicit by the above discussion. The various causes of white women's poverty can be traced back to a single, fundamental source—sexism, perpetuated mainly by white men. Only in a sexist society can the breakup of a marriage actually improve the economic well-being of the father, cause the mother and children to suffer a large drop in economic status, and permit most fathers to provide little or no support to their children. The low wages afforded women of equal education and experience cannot be explained away as anything except sex discrimination. The poverty of black women, in contrast, is related to more complex factors. Black men are rarely in the position of employers and, therefore, are hardly able to determine the wage scales of women vis-à-vis men. And for many black men, their own high rates of unemployment and low income make the question of sharing income with their children and their children's mothers moot. Thus, in addition to the sources of poverty experienced by all women—the economic burden of children, labor-market discrimination and duality, a welfare system that provides penurious benefits and no training/support system—black women experience directly and, through black men, indirectly, the effects of racial discrimination.

A further qualitative difference experienced by black women is that their poverty has a more permanent, or at least, indefinite quality. They, of course, bear the burden of poverty in the black community, a community that as a whole has long had much more poverty than the white community. Thus, because of the greater economic resources in the white community, white women stand a much greater chance of leaving poverty through marriage than black women. Black women are more likely to experience what I have called the "workhouse without walls," in which they support themselves through a combination of earnings, welfare, child support, and other transfers, whether concurrently or serially.

It is evident that, within the black community, there is a growing gulf between two-parent, two-earner families and families headed by women. It is also clear that the high unemployment rates among black youth which contribute to the formation of single-parent families, together with the sexism in the labor/welfare system which locks women householders into poverty, are resulting in increasing proportions of black children being born into and/or growing up in families that must struggle every day with poverty.

---

## REFLECTING ON MEANING

1. What are the characteristics of poor men? Of poor women? What two gender-based causes of poverty among women does Pearce identify? In what ways do women's expectations handicap them on the job market? How does the job market discriminate against women? How does it reinforce their socioeconomic status?
2. What is the dual-economy theory? How is this duality reflected in the welfare system? According to Pearce, in what ways do "the interlocking secondary welfare system and secondary labor market reinforce a vicious circle of welfare dependency and marginal work"? Do you agree with her perspective? Why or why not?
3. What are the different forms of poverty that white and black women experience? What distinct disadvantages do black women suffer? How do gender and race intersect to make their situation even more troublesome?

## EXPLORING RHETORICAL STRATEGIES

1. At the beginning of her essay, Pearce alludes to the "other America" as a "changing neighborhood." What is the "other America"? What does this label tell you about her audience? Who is her audience? Why does she refer to the other America as a neighborhood?

2. What is the main idea of Pearce's essay? How do you know?
3. What is the function of the statistics Pearce provides? Is her interpretation of them reasonable? Why or why not?

# Are Women Prejudiced Against Women?

PHILIP GOLDBERG

*Most people would agree that men perceive and evaluate women and men differently—such is the basis for claims of discrimination and sexism. Professor of psychology Philip Goldberg argues, however, that women do the same—that "women* do *consider their own sex inferior." In the following essay, Goldberg describes and reports on an experiment that led him to this conclusion, a study in which women evaluated identical articles attributed to hypothetical male and female authors.*

"Woman," advised Aristotle, "may be said to be an inferior man."

Because he was a man, Aristotle was probably biased. But what do women themselves think? Do they, consciously or unconsciously, consider their own sex inferior? And if so, does this belief prejudice them against other women—that is, make them view women, simply because they *are* women, as less competent than men?

According to a study conducted by myself and my associates, the answer to both questions is Yes. Women *do* consider their own sex inferior. And even when the facts give no support to this belief, they will persist in downgrading the competence—in particular, the intellectual and professional competence—of their fellow females.

Over the years, psychologists and psychiatrists have shown that both sexes consistently value men more highly than women.

Characteristics considered male are usually praised: those considered female are usually criticized. In 1957 A. C. Sheriffs and J. P. McKee noted that "women are regarded as guilty of snobbery and irrational and unpleasant emotionality." Consistent with this report, E. G. French and G. S. Lesser found in 1964 that "women who value intellectual attainment feel they must reject the woman's role"—intellectual accomplishment apparently being considered, even among intellectual women, a masculine preserve. In addition, ardent feminists like Simone de Beauvoir and Betty Friedan believe that men, in important ways, are superior to women.

Now, is this belief simply prejudice, or are the characteristics and achievements of women really inferior to those of men? In answering this question, we need to draw some careful distinctions.

## Different or Inferior?

Most important, we need to recognize that there are two distinct dimensions to the issue of sex differences. The first question is whether sex differences exist at all, apart from the obvious physical ones. The answer to this question seems to be a unanimous Yes—men, women, and social scientists agree that, psychologically and emotionally as well as physically, women *are* different from men.

But is being different the same as being inferior? It is quite possible to perceive a difference accurately but to value it inaccurately. Do women automatically view their differences from men as *deficiencies*? The evidence is that they do, and that this value judgment opens the door to anti-female prejudice. For if someone (male or female) concludes that women are inferior, his perceptions of women—their personalities, behavior, abilities, and accomplishments—will tend to be colored by his low expectations of women.

As Gordon W. Allport has pointed out in *The Nature of Prejudice,* whatever the facts about sex differences, anti-feminism—like any other prejudice—*distorts perception and experience.* What defines anti-feminism is not so much believing that women are inferior, as allowing that belief to distort one's perceptions of women. More generally, it is not the partiality itself, but the distortion born of that partiality, that defines prejudice.

Thus, an anti-Semite watching a Jew may see devious or sneaky behavior. But, in a Christian, he would regard such behavior only as quiet, reserved, or perhaps even shy. Prejudice is self-sustaining: It continually distorts the "evidence" on which the prejudiced person claims to base his beliefs. Allport makes it clear that anti-feminism, like anti-Semitism or any other prejudice, consistently twists the "evidence" of experience. We see not what is there, but what we *expect* to see.

The purpose of our study was to investigate whether there is real prejudice by women against women—whether perception itself is distorted unfavorably. Specifically, will women evaluate a professional article with a jaundiced eye when they think it is the work of a woman, but praise the same article when they think its author is a man? Our hypotheses were:

- Even when the work is identical, women value the professional work of men more highly than that of women.
- But when the professional field happens to be one traditionally reserved for women (nursing, dietetics), this tendency will be reversed, or at least greatly diminished.

Some 140 college girls, selected at random, were our subjects. One hundred were used for preliminary work; 40 participated in the experiment proper.

To test the second hypothesis, we gave the 100 girls a list of 50 occupations and asked them to rate "the degree to which you associate the field with men or with women." We found that law and city planning were fields strongly associated with men, elementary-school teaching and dietetics were fields strongly associated with women, and two fields—linguistics and art history—were chosen as neutrals, not strongly associated with either sex.

Now we were ready for the main experiment. From the professional literature of each of these six fields, we took one article. The articles were edited and abridged to about 1500 words, then combined into two equal sets of booklets. The crucial manipulation had to do with the authors' names—the same article bore a male name in one set of booklets, a female name in the other set. An example: If, in set one, the first article bore the name John T. McKay, in set two the same article would appear under the name Joan T. McKay. Each booklet contained three articles by "men" and three articles by "women."

The girls, seated together in a large lecture hall, were told to read the articles in their booklets and given these instructions:

> "In this booklet you will find excerpts of six articles, written by six different authors in six different professional fields. At the end of each article you will find several questions. . . . You are not presumed to be sophisticated or knowledgeable

in all the fields. We are interested in the ability of college students to make critical evaluations. . . ."

Note that no mention at all was made of the author's sexes. That information was contained—apparently only by coincidence—in the authors' names. The girls could not know, therefore, what we were really looking for.

At the end of each article were nine questions asking the girls to rate the articles for value, persuasiveness, and profundity—and to rate the authors for writing style, professional competence, professional status, and ability to sway the reader. On each item, the girls gave a rating of from 1 (highly favorable) to 5 (highly unfavorable).

Generally, the results were in line with our expectations—but not completely. In analyzing these results, we used three different methods: We compared the amount of anti-female bias in the different occupational fields (would men be rated as better city planners, but women as better dieticians?); we compared the amount of bias shown on the nine questions that followed each article (would men be rated more competent, but women as more persuasive?); and we ran an overall comparison, including both fields and rating questions.

Starting with the analysis of bias by occupational field, we immediately ran into a major surprise. (See the table below.) That there is a general bias by women against women, and that it is strongest in traditionally masculine fields, was clearly borne out. But in other fields the situation seemed rather confused. We had expected the anti-female trend to be reversed in traditionally feminine fields. But it appears that, even here, women consider themselves inferior to men. Women seem to think that men are better at *everything*—including elementary-school teaching and dietetics!

Scrutiny of the nine rating questions yielded similar results. On all nine questions, regardless of the author's occupational field, the girls consistently found an article more valuable—and its author more competent—when the article bore a male name. Though the articles themselves were exactly the same, the girls felt that those written by the John T. McKays were definitely more impressive, and reflected more glory on their authors, than did the mediocre offerings of the Joan T. McKays. Perhaps because the world has accepted female authors for a long time, the girls were willing to concede that the female professionals' writing styles were not *far* inferior to those of men. But such a concession to female competence was rare indeed.

Statistical analysis confirms these impressions and makes them

**Law: A Strong Masculine Preserve**

| | *Mean* | |
|---|---|---|
| *Field of Article* | *Male* | *Female* |
| Art History | 23.35 | 23.10 |
| Dietetics | 22.05 | 23.45 |
| Education | 20.20 | 21.75 |
| City Planning | 23.10 | 27.30 |
| Linguistics | 26.95 | 30.70 |
| Law | 21.20 | 25.60 |

These are the total scores the college girls gave to the six pairs of articles they read. The lowest possible score—9—would be the most favorable; the highest possible score—54—the most critical. While male authors received more favorable ratings in all occupational fields, the differences were statistically significant only in city planning, linguistics, and—especially—law.

more definite. With a total of six articles, and with nine questions after each one, there were 54 points at which comparisons could be drawn between the male authors and the female authors. Out of these 54 comparisons, three were tied, seven favored the female authors—and the number favoring the male authors was 44!

Clearly, there is a tendency among women to downgrade the work of professionals of their own sex. But the hypothesis that this tendency would decrease as the "femaleness" of the professional field increased was not supported. Even in traditionally female fields, anti-feminism holds sway.

Since the articles supposedly written by men were exactly the same as those supposedly written by women, the perception that the men's articles were superior was obviously a distortion. For reasons of their own, the female subjects were sensitive to the sex of the author, and this apparently irrelevant information biased their judgments. Both the distortion and the sensitivity that precedes it are characteristic of prejudice. Women—at least these young college women—are prejudiced against female professionals and, regardless of the actual accomplishments of these professionals, will firmly refuse to recognize them as the equals of their male colleagues.

Is the intellectual double-standard really dead? Not at all—and if the college girls in this study are typical of the educated and presumably progressive segments of the population, it may not even be dying. Whatever lip service these girls pay to modern ideas of equality between men and women, their beliefs are staunchly traditional. Their real coach in the battle of the sexes is not Simone de Beauvoir or Betty Friedan. Their coach is Aristotle.

---

## REFLECTING ON MEANING

1. According to Goldberg, what is prejudice? How does it influence perception? What does he mean when he says that it "consistently twists the 'evidence' of experience"?
2. Goldberg makes a distinction between believing that women and men are different and believing that their differences necessarily make one gender inferior to the other. What does he mean? How do people come to believe that differences are deficiencies?
3. What were the goals of the study Goldberg conducted? What questions was he trying to answer? How was the study carried out? What were the results? What was the "major surprise" that Goldberg discovered in the data? Do you agree with his overall conclusions? Why or why not?

## EXPLORING RHETORICAL STRATEGIES

1. In his introduction and conclusion, Goldberg makes allusions to Aristotle, Simone de Beauvoir, and Betty Friedan. What do these allusions tell you about his intended audience? How do they help him advance his thesis?
2. Goldberg occasionally takes a tone of astonishment and surprise. How does he convey these emotions? How do they affect his tone in other sections of the essay? Given his conclusions, in what ways is this tone appropriate or inappropriate?
3. The format of Goldberg's essay conforms largely to the conventions of reports in the social sciences. On the basis of this essay, can you determine what those conventions are?

# Chapter 15

# SOCIAL POWERLESSNESS

## Women: Invisible Cages

BRIGID BROPHY

*Despite a seeming consensus that women are no longer bound by gender-based social hierarchies, argues Brigid Brophy, they are not really free; rather, they simply* "look *free.*" *They are "like the animals in a modern zoo," imprisoned behind bars even more pernicious because they are invisible.*

All right, nobody's disputing it. Women are free. At least, they *look* free. They even feel free. But in reality women in the western, industrialised world today are like the animals in a modern zoo. There are no bars. It appears that cages have been abolished. Yet in practice women are still kept in their place just as firmly as the animals are kept in their enclosures. The barriers which keep them in now are invisible.

It is about forty years since the pioneer feminists, several of whom were men, raised such a rumpus by rattling the cage bars—or created such a conspicuous nuisance by chaining themselves to them—that society was at last obliged to pay attention. The result was that the bars were uprooted, the cage thrown open: whereupon the majority of the women who had been held captive decided they would rather stay inside anyway.

To be more precise, they *thought* they decided; and society, which can with perfect truth point out "Look, no bars," *thought* it was giving them the choice. There are no laws and very little discrimination to prevent western, industrialised women from voting, being voted for or entering the professions. If there are still comparatively few women lawyers and engineers, let alone women presidents of the United States, what are women to conclude except that this is the result either of their own free choice or of something inherent in female nature?

Many of them do draw just this conclusion. They have come back to the old argument of the anti-feminists, many of whom were women, that women are unfit by nature for life outside the cage. And in letting this old wheel come full cycle women have fallen victim to one of the most insidious and ingenious confidence tricks ever perpetrated.

In point of fact, neither female nature nor women's individual free choice has been put to the test. As American Negroes have discovered, to be officially free is by no means the same as being actually and psychologically free. A society as adept as ours has become at propaganda—whether political or commercial—should know that "persuasion," which means the art of launching myths and artificially inducing inhibitions, is every bit as effective as force of law. No doubt the reason society eventually agreed to abolish its anti-woman laws was that it had become confident of commanding a battery of hidden dissuaders which would do the job just as well. Cage bars are clumsy methods of control, which excite the more rebellious personalities inside to rattle them. Modern society, like the modern zoo, has contrived to get rid of the bars without altering the fact of imprisonment. All the zoo architect needs to do is run a zone of hot or cold air, whichever the animal concerned cannot tolerate, round the cage where the bars used to be. Human animals are not less sensitive to social climate.

The ingenious point about the new-model zoo is that it deceives both sides of the invisible barrier. Not only can the animal not see how it is imprisoned; the visitor's conscience is relieved of the unkindness of keeping animals shut up. He can say "Look, no bars round the animals," just as society can say "Look, no laws restricting women" even while it keeps women rigidly in place by zones of fierce social pressure.

There is, however, one great difference. A woman, being a thinking animal, may actually be more distressed because the bars of her cage cannot be seen. What relieves society's conscience may afflict hers. Unable to perceive what is holding her back, she may accuse herself and her whole sex of craven timidity because women have not jumped at what has the appearance of an offer of freedom. Evidently quite a lot of women have succumbed to guilt of this sort, since in recent years quite an industry has arisen to assuage it. Comforting voices make the air as thick and reassuring as cotton wool while they explain that there is nothing shameful in not wanting a career, that to be intellectually unadventurous is no sin, that taking care of home and family may be personally "fulfilling" and socially valuable.

This is an argument without a flaw: except that it is addressed exclusively to women. Address it to both sexes and instantly it becomes progressive and humane. As it stands, it is merely anti-woman prejudice revamped.

That many women would be happier not pursuing careers or intellectual adventures is only part of the truth. The whole truth is that many *people* would be. If society had the clear sight to assure men as well as women that there is no shame in preferring to stay non-competitively and non-aggressively at home, many masculine neuroses and ulcers would be avoided, and many children would enjoy the benefit of being brought up by a father with a talent for the job instead of by a mother with no talent for it but a sense of guilt about the lack.

But society does nothing so sensible. Blindly it goes on insisting on the tradition that men are the ones who go out to work and adventure—an arrangement which simply throws talent away. All the home-making talent which happens to be born inside male bodies is wasted; and our businesses and governments are staffed quite largely by people whose aptitude for the work consists solely of their being what is, by tradition, the right sex for it.

The pressures society exerts to drive men out of the house are very nearly as irrational and unjust as those by which it keeps women in. The mistake of the early reformers was to assume that men were emancipated already and that therefore reform need ask only for the emancipation of women. What we ought to do now is go right back to scratch and demand the emancipation of both sexes. It is only because men are not free themselves that they have found it necessary to cheat women by the deception which makes them appear free when they are not.

The zones of hot and cold air which society uses to perpetuate its uneconomic and unreasonable state of affairs are the simplest and most effective conceivable. Society is playing on our sexual vanity. Just as the sexual regions are the most vulnerable part of the body, sexuality is the most vulnerable part of the Ego. Tell a man that he is not a real man, or a woman that she is not one hunderd percent woman and you are threatening both with not being attractive to the opposite sex. No one can bear not to be attractive to the opposite sex. That is the climate which the human animal cannot tolerate.

So society has us all at its mercy. It has only to murmur to the man that staying at home is a feminine characteristic, and he will be out of the house like a bullet. It has only to suggest to the woman that logic and reason are the province of the masculine mind, whereas "intuition" and "feeling" are the female *forte,* and she will throw her physics textbooks out of the window, barricade herself into the house and give herself up to having wishy-washy poetical feelings while she arranges the flowers.

She will, incidentally, take care that her feelings *are* wishy-washy. She has been persuaded that to have cogent feelings, of the kind which really go into great poems (most of which are by men), would make her an unfeminine woman, a woman who imitates men. In point of fact, she would not be imitating men as such, most of whom have never written a line of great poetry, but poets, most of whom so far happen to be men. But the bad logic passes muster with her because part of the mythology she has swallowed ingeniously informs her that logic is not her *forte.*

Should a woman's talent or intelligence be so irrepressible that she insists on producing cogent works of art or watertight meshes of argument, she will be said to have "a mind like a man's." This is simply current idiom; translated, it means "a good mind." The use of the idiom contributes to an apparently watertight proof that all good minds are masculine, since whenever they occur in women they are described as "like a man's."

What is more, this habit of thought actually contributes to perpetuating a state of affairs where most good minds really do belong to men. It is difficult for a woman to *want* to be intelligent when she has been told that to be so will make her like a man. She inclines to think an intelligence would be as unbecoming to her as a moustache; and many women have tried in furtive privacy to disembarrass themselves of intellect as though it were facial hair.

Discouraged from growing "a mind like a man's," women are encouraged to have thoughts and feelings of a specifically feminine tone. For society is cunning enough not to place its whole reliance on threatening women with blasts of icy air. It also flatters them with a zone of hot air. The most deceptive and cynical of its blandishments is the notion that women have some specifically feminine contribution to make to culture. Unfortunately, as culture had already been shaped and largely built up by men before the invitation was issued, this leaves women little to do. Culture consists of reasoned thought and works of art composed of cogent feeling and imagination. There is only one way to be reasonable, and that is to reason correctly; and the only kind of art which is any good is good art. If women are to eschew reason and artistic imagination in favour of "intuition" and "feeling," it is pretty clear what is meant. "Intuition" is just a polite name for bad reasoning, and "feeling" for bad art.

In reality, the whole idea of a specifically feminine—or, for the matter of that, masculine—contribution to culture is a contradiction of culture. A contribution to culture is not something which could not have been made by the other sex—it is something which could not have been made by any other *person*. Equally, the notion that anyone, of either sex, can create good art out of simple feeling, untempered by discipline, is a philistine one. The arts are a sphere where women seem to have done well; but really they have done *too* well—too well for the good of the arts. Instead of women sharing the esteem which ought to belong to artists, art is becoming smeared with femininity. We are approaching a philistine state of affairs where the arts are something which it is nice for women to take up in their spare time—men having slammed out of the house to get on with society's "serious" business, like making money, administering the country and running the professions.

In that "serious" sphere it is still rare to encounter a woman. A man sentenced to prison would probably feel his punishment was redoubled by indignity if he were to be sentenced by a woman judge under a law drafted by a woman legislator—and if, on admission, he were to be examined by a woman prison doctor. If such a thing happened every day, it would be no indignity but the natural course of events. It has never been given the chance to become the natural course of events and never will be so long as women remain persuaded it would be unnatural of them to want it.

So brilliantly has society contrived to terrorise women with this threat that certain behavior is unnatural and unwomanly that it has left them no time to consider—or even sheerly observe—what womanly nature really is. For centuries arrant superstitions were accepted as natural law. The physiological fact that only women can secrete milk for feeding babies was extended into the pure myth that it was women's business to cook for and wait on the entire family. The kitchen became woman's "natural" place because, for the first few months of her baby's life, the nursery really was. To this day a woman may suspect that she is unfeminine if she can discover in herself no aptitude or liking for cooking. Fright has thrown her into such a muddle that she confuses having no taste for cookery with having no breasts, and conversely assumes that nature has endowed the human female with a special handiness with frying pans.

Even psycho-analysis, which in general has been the greatest benefactor of civilisation since the wheel, has unwittingly reinforced the terrorisation campaign. The trouble was that it brought with it from its origin in medical therapy a criterion of normality instead of rationality. On sheer statistics every pioneer, genius and social reformer, including the first woman who demanded to be let out of the kitchen and into the polling booth, is abnormal, along with every lunatic and eccentric. What distinguishes the genius from the lunatic is that the genius's abnormality is justifiable by reason or aesthetics. If a woman who is irked by confinement to the kitchen merely looks round to see what other women are doing and finds they are accepting their kitchens, she may well conclude that she is abnormal and had better enlist her psycho-analyst's help towards "living with" her kitchen. What she ought to ask is whether it is rational for women to be kept to the kitchen, and whether nature really does insist on that in the way it insists women have breasts. And in a far-reaching sense to ask that question is much more normal and natural than learning to "live with" the handicap of women's inferior social status. The normal and natural thing for human beings is not to tolerate handicaps but to reform society and to circumvent or supplement nature. We don't learn to live minus a leg: we devise an artificial limb.

That, indeed, is the crux of the matter. Not only are the distinctions we draw between male nature and female nature largely arbitrary and often pure superstition: they are completely beside the point. They ignore the essence of *human* nature. The important question is not whether women are or are not less logical by nature than men, but whether education, effort and the abolition of our illogical social pressures can improve on nature and make them (and, incidentally, men as well) *more* logical. What distinguishes human from any other animal nature is its ability to be unnatural. Logic and art are not natural or instinctive activities: but our nature includes a propensity to acquire them. It is not natural for the human body to orbit the earth; but the human mind has a natural adventurousness which enables it to invent machines whereby the body can do so. There is, in sober fact, no such creature as a natural man. Go as far back as they will, the archaeologists cannot come on a wild man in his natural habitat. At his most primitive, he has already constructed himself an artificial habitat, and decorated it not by a standardised instinctual method, as birds build nests, but by individualised—that is, abnormal—works of art or magic. And in doing so he is not limited by the fingers nature gave him; he has extended their versatility by making tools.

Civilisation consists not necessarily in defying nature but in making it possible for us to do so if we judge it desirable. The higher we can lift our noses from the grindstone of nature, the wider the area we have of choice; and the more choices we have freely made, the more individualised we are. We are at our most civilised when nature does not dictate to us, as it does to animals and peasants, but when we can opt to fall in with it or better it. If modern civilisation has invented methods of education which make it possible for men to feed babies and for women to think logically, we are betraying civilisation itself if we do not set both sexes free to make a free choice.

---

## REFLECTING ON MEANING

1. The author's contention that women are not free hinges on a crucial distinction: "to be officially free," Brophy states, "is by no means the same as being actually and psychologically free." What does she mean? Do you agree that women are free only in an "official" sense? Why or why not?

2. According to Brophy, what is the effect of this hidden imprisonment on women? In what ways does it alter their conceptions of themselves? What kind of emotional toll does it take on them? How does society reinforce the gender roles that create this situation? In what ways are men, too, subject to gender-role pressures that "are very nearly as irrational and unjust"? Why does Brophy qualify this comparison?

3. Brophy claims that society holds women powerless by encouraging them to be "feminine" and by propagating "the notion that women have some specifically feminine contribution to make to culture." In what ways are women urged to be feminine? How does society advance the notion that women's contributions are different from men's?

4. "Not only are the distinctions we draw between male nature and female nature largely arbitrary and often pure superstition: they are completely beside the point. They ignore the essence of *human* nature." What does Brophy mean by this assertion? Do you agree or disagree? Why?

## EXPLORING RHETORICAL STRATEGIES

1. The analogy of the caged animal is a powerful device at work throughout the essay. How does Brophy expand on this analogy

in the course of the selection? Is it an appropriate analogy? Why or why not?

2. Brophy opens her essay in this way: "All right, nobody's disputing it. Women are free. At least, they *look* free. They even feel free." What does this opening suggest about the attitude she expects her audience to have on women's freedom? How does she seem to think her audience will react to her views?

3. "She inclines to think an intelligence would be as unbecoming to her as a moustache; and many women have tried in furtive privacy to disembarrass themselves of intellect as though it were facial hair." What is particularly appropriate about this analogy? What concrete image does it create? How does the word *furtive* add to the image?

---

# The Higher Economic Purposes of Women

## JOHN KENNETH GALBRAITH

*A professor of economics at Harvard University, John Kenneth Galbraith examines the role of women in maintaining and increasing economic growth in the United States. Arguing that women serve "the needs of the dominant economic interest"—that is, the "large corporation"—he concludes that women must "see that they serve purposes which are* not *their own" before "they can serve purposes which* are *their own."*

In the nineteen-fifties, for reasons that were never revealed to me, for my relations with academic administrators have often been somewhat painful, I was made a trustee of Radcliffe College. It was not a highly demanding position. Then, as now, the college had no faculty of its own, no curriculum of its own and, apart from the dormitories, a gymnasium and a library, no academic plant of its own. We were a committee for raising money for scholarships and a new graduate center. The meetings or non-meetings of the trustees did, however, encourage a certain amount of reflection on the higher education of women, there being no appreciable distraction. This reflection was encouraged by the mood of the time at Harvard. As conversation and numerous formal and informal surveys reliably revealed, all but a small minority of the women students felt that they were a failure unless they were firmly set for marriage by the time they got their degree. I soon learned that my fellow trustees of both sexes thought this highly meritorious. Often at our meetings there was impressively solemn mention of our responsibility, which was to help women prepare themselves for their life's work. Their life's work, it was held, was care of home, husband and children. In inspired moments one or another of my colleagues would ask, "Is there anything so important?"

Once, and rather mildly, for it was more to relieve tedium than to express conviction, I asked if the education we provided wasn't rather expensive and possibly also ill-adapted for these tasks, even assuming that they were combined with ultimate service to the New Rochelle Library and the League of Women Voters. The response was so chilly that I subsided. I've never minded being in a minority, but I dislike being thought eccentric.

It was, indeed, mentioned that a woman should be prepared for what was called a *second* career. After her children were raised and educated, she should be able to essay a re-entry into intellectual life—become a teacher, writer, researcher or some such. All agreed that this was a worthy, even imaginative design which did not conflict with *basic* responsibilities. I remember contemplating but censoring the suggestion that this fitted in well with the common desire of husbands at about this stage in life to take on new, younger and sexually more inspiring wives.

In those years I was working on the book that eventually became *The Affluent Society*. The task was a constant reminder that much information solemnly advanced as social wisdom is, in fact, in the service of economic convenience—the convenience of some influential economic interest. I concluded that this was so of the education of women and resolved that I would one day explore the matter more fully. This I have been doing in these last few years, and I've decided that while the rhetorical commitment of women to home and husband as a career has been weakened in the interim, the economic ideas by which they are kept persuaded to serve economic interests are still almost completely intact. Indeed, these ideas are so generally assumed that they are very little discussed.

Women are kept in the service of economic interests by ideas that they do not examine and that even women who are professionally involved as economists continue to propagate, often with some professional pride. The husband, home and family that were celebrated in those ghastly Radcliffe meetings are no longer part of the litany. But the effect of our economic education is still the same.

Understanding of this begins with a look at the decisive but little-perceived role of women in modern economic development and at the economic instruction by which this perception is further dulled.

The decisive economic contribution of women in the developed industrial society is rather simple—or at least it so becomes once the disguising myth is dissolved. It is, overwhelmingly, to make possible a continuing and more or less unlimited increase in the sale and use of consumer goods.

The test of success in modern economic society, as all know, is the annual rate of increase in Gross National Product. At least until recent times this test was unquestioned; a successful society was one with a large annual increase in output, and the most successful society was the one with the largest increase. Even when the social validity of this measure is challenged, as on occasion it now is, those who do so are only thought to be raising an interesting question. They are not imagined to be practical.

Increasing production, in turn, strongly reflects the needs of the dominant economic interest, which in modern economic society, as few will doubt, is the large corporation. The large corporation seeks relentlessly to get larger. The power, prestige, pay, promotions and perquisites of those who command or who participate in the leadership of the great corporation are all strongly served by its expansion. That expansion, if it is to be general, requires an expanding or growing economy. As the corporation became a polar influence in modern economic life, economic growth became the accepted test of social performance. This was not an accident. It was the predictable acceptance of the dominant economic value system.

Economic growth requires manpower, capital and materials for increased production. It also, no less obviously, requires increased consumption, and if population is relatively stable, as in our case, this must be increased per-capita consumption. But there is a further and equally unimpeachable truth which, in economics at least, has been celebrated scarcely at all: just as the production of goods and services requires management or administration, so does their consumption. The one is no less essential than the other. Management is required for providing automobiles, houses, clothing, food, alcohol and recreation. And management is no less required for their possession and use.

The higher the standard of living, that is to say the greater the consumption, the more demanding is this management. The larger the house, the more numerous the automobiles, the more elaborate the attire, the more competitive and costly the social rites involving food and intoxicants, the more complex the resulting administration.

In earlier times this administration was the function of a menial servant class. To its great credit, industrialization everywhere liquidates this class. People never remain in appreciable numbers in personal service if they have alternative employment. Industry supplies this employment, so the servant class, the erstwhile managers of consumption, disappears. If consumption is to continue and expand, it is an absolute imperative that a substitute administrative force be found. This, in modern industrial societies, is the function that wives perform. The higher the family income and the greater the complexity of the consumption, the more nearly indispensable this role. Within broad limits the richer the family, the more indispensably menial must be the role of the wife.

It is, to repeat, a vital function of economic success as it is now measured. Were women not available for managing consumption, an upper limit would be set thereon by the administrative task involved. At some point it would become too time-consuming, too burdensome. We accept, without thought, that a bachelor of either sex will lead a comparatively simple existence. (We refer to it as the bachelor life.) That is because the administrative burden of a higher level of consumption, since it must be assumed by the individual who consumes, is a limiting factor. When a husband's income passes a certain level, it is expected that his wife will be needed "to look after the house" or simply "to manage things." So, if she has been employed, she quits her job. The consumption of the couple has reached the point where it requires full-time attention.

Although without women appropriately conditioned to the task there would be an effective ceiling on consumption and thus on production and economic expansion, this would not apply uniformly. The ceiling would be especially serious for high-value products for the most affluent consumers. The latter, reflecting their larger share of total income—the upper 20 percent of income recipients received just under 42 percent of all income in 1977—account for a disproportionate share of total purchases of goods. So women are particularly important for lifting the ceiling on this kind of consumption. And, by a curious quirk, their doing so opens the way for a whole new range of consumer products—washing machines, dryers, dishwashers, vacuum cleaners, automatic furnaces, sophisticated detergents, cleaning compounds, tranquilizers, pain-relievers—designed to ease the previously created task of managing a high level of consumption.

Popular sociology and much associated fiction depict the extent and complexity of the administrative tasks of the modern diversely responsible, high-bracket, suburban woman. But it seems likely that her managerial effectiveness, derived from her superior education, her accumulating experience as well as her expanding array of facilitating gadgetry and services, keeps her more or less abreast of her increasingly large and complex task. Thus the danger of a ceiling on consumption, and therefore on economic expansion, caused by the exhaustion of her administrative capacities does not seem imminent. One sees here, more than incidentally, the economic rationale, even if it was unsuspected for a long time by those involved, of the need for a superior education for the upper-bracket housewife. Radcliffe prepared wives for the higher-income family. The instinct that this required superior intelligence and training was economically sound.

The family of higher income, in turn, sets the consumption patterns to which others aspire. That such families be supplied with intelligent, well-educated women of exceptional managerial competence is thus of further importance. It allows not only for the continued high-level consumption of these families, but it is important for its demonstration effect for families of lesser income.

That many women are coming to sense that they are instruments of the economic system is not in doubt. But their feeling finds no support in economic writing and teaching. On the contrary, it is concealed, and on the whole with great success, by modern neoclassical economics—the everyday economics of the textbook and classroom. This concealment is neither conspiratorial nor deliberate. It reflects the natural and very strong instinct of economics for what is convenient to influential economic interest—for what I have called the convenient social virtue. It is sufficiently successful that it allows many hundreds of thousands of women to study economics each year without their developing any serious suspicion as to how they will be used.

The general design for concealment has four major elements:

First, there is the orthodox identification of an increasing consumption of goods and services with increasing happiness. The greater the consumption, the greater the happiness. This proposition is not defended; it is again assumed that only the philosophically minded will cavil. They are allowed their dissent, but, it is held, no one should take it seriously.

Second, the tasks associated with the consumption of goods are, for all practical purposes, ignored. Consumption being a source of happiness, one cannot get involved with the problems in managing happiness. The consumer must exercise choice; happiness is maximized when the enjoyment from an increment of expenditure for one object of consumption equals that from the same expenditure for any other object or service. As all who have ever been exposed, however inadequately, to economic instruction must remember, satisfactions are maximized when they are equalized at the margin.

Such calculation does require some knowledge of the quality and technical performance of goods as well as thought in general. From it comes the subdivision of economics called consumer economics; this is a moderately reputable field that, not surprisingly, is thought especially appropriate for women. But this decision-making is not a burdensome matter. And once the decision between objects of expenditure is made, the interest of economics is at an end. No attention whatever is given to the effort involved in the care and management of the resulting goods.[1]

The third requisite for the concealment of women's economic role is the avoidance of any accounting for the value of household work. This greatly helps it to avoid notice. To include in the Gross National Product the labor of housewives in managing consumption, where it would be a very large item which would increase as consumption increases, would be to invite thought on the nature of the service so measured. And some women would wonder if the service was one they wished to render. To keep these matters out of the realm of statistics is also to help keep them innocuously within the sacred domain of the family and the soul. It helps sustain the pretense that, since they are associated with consumption, the toil involved is one of its joys.

The fourth and final element in the concealment is more complex and concerns the concept of the household. The intellectual obscurantism that is here involved is accepted by all economists, mostly without thought. It would, however, be defended by very few.

The avowed focus of economics is the individual. It is the

individual who distributes her or his expenditures so as to maximize satisfactions. From this distribution comes the instruction to the market and ultimately to the producing firm that makes the individual the paramount power in economic society. (There are grave difficulties with this design, including the way in which it reduces General Motors to the role of a mere puppet of market forces, but these anomalies are not part of the present story.)

Were this preoccupation with the individual pursued to the limit, namely to the individual, there would be grave danger that the role of women would attract attention. There would have to be inquiry as to whether, within the family, it is the husband's enjoyments that are equalized and thus maximized at the margin. Or, in his gallant way, does he defer to the preference system of his wife? Or does marriage unite only men and women whose preference schedules are identical? Or does marriage make them identical?

Investigation would turn up a yet more troublesome thing. It would be seen that, in the usual case, the place and style of living accord with the preferences and needs of the member of the family who makes the money—in short, the husband. Thus, at least partly, his titles: "head of the household," "head of the family." And he would be seen to have a substantial role in decisions on the individual objects of expenditure. But the management of the resulting house, automobile, yard, shopping and social life would be by the wife. It would be seen that this arrangement gives the major decisions concerning consumption extensively to one person and the toil associated with that consumption to another. There would be further question as to whether consumption decisions reflect with any precision or fairness the preferences of the person who has the resulting toil. Would the style of life and consumption be the same if the administration involved were equally shared?

None of these questions gets asked, for at precisely the point they obtrude, the accepted economics abruptly sheds its preoccupation with the individual. The separate identities of men and women are merged into the concept of the household. The inner conflicts and compromises of the household are not explored; by nearly universal consent, they are not the province of economics. The household, by a distinctly heroic simplification, is assumed to be the same as an individual. It thinks, acts and arranges its expenditures as would an individual; it is so treated for all purposes of economic analysis.

That, within the household, the administration of consumption requires major and often tedious effort, that decisions on consumption are heavily influenced by the member of the household least committed to such tasks, that these arrangements are extremely important if consumption is to expand, are all things that are thus kept out of academic view. Those who study and those who teach are insulated from such adverse thoughts. The concept of the household is an outrageous assault on personality. People are not people; they are parts of a composite or collective that is deemed somehow to reflect the different or conflicting preferences of those who make it up. This is both analytically and ethically indefensible. But for concealing the economic function of women even from women it works.

One notices, at this point, an interesting convergence of economics with politics. It has long been recognized that women are kept on political leash primarily by urging their higher commitment to the family. Their economic role is also concealed and protected by submerging them in the family or household. There is much, no doubt, to be said for the institution of the family. And it is not surprising that conservatives say so much.

In modern society power rests extensively on persuasion. Such reverse incentives as flogging, though there are law-and-order circles that seek their revival, are in limbo. So, with increasing affluence, is the threat of starvation. And even affirmative pecuniary reward is impaired. For some, at least, enough is enough—the hope for more ceases to drive. In consequence, those who have need for a particular behavior in others resort to persuasion—to instilling the belief that the action they need is reputable, moral, virtuous, socially beneficent or otherwise good. It follows that what women are persuaded to believe about their social role and, more important, what they are taught to overlook are of prime importance in winning the requisite behavior. They must believe that consumption is happiness and that, however onerous its associated toil, it all adds up to greater happiness for themselves and their families.

If women were to see and understand how they are used, the consequence might be a considerable change in the pattern of their lives, especially in those income brackets where the volume of consumption is large. Thus, suburban life sustains an especially large consumption of goods, and, in consequence, is especially demanding in the administration required. The claims of roofs, furniture, plumbing, crabgrass, vehicles, recreational equipment and juvenile management are all very great. This explains why unmarried people, regardless of income, favor urban living over the suburbs. If women understood that they are the facilitating instrument of this consumption and were led to reject its administration as a career, there would, one judges, be a general return to a less demanding urban life.

More certainly there would be a marked change in the character of social life. Since they are being used to administer consumption, women are naturally encouraged to do it well. In consequence, much social activity is, in primary substance, a competitive display of managerial excellence. The cocktail party or dinner party is, essentially, a fair, more refined and complex than those at which embroidery or livestock are entered in competition but for the same ultimate purpose of displaying and improving the craftsmanship or breed. The cleanliness of the house, the excellence of the garden, the taste, quality and condition of the furnishings and the taste, quality and imagination of the food and intoxicants and the deftness of their service are put on display before the critical eye of those invited to appraise them. Comparisons are made with other exhibitors. Ribbons are not awarded, but the competent administrator is duly proclaimed a good housekeeper, a gracious hostess, a clever manager or, more simply, a really good wife. These competitive social rites and the accompanying titles encourage and confirm women in their role as administrators and thus facilitators of the high levels of consumption on which the high-production economy rests. It would add measurably to economic understanding were they so recognized. But perhaps for some it would detract from their appeal.

However, the more immediate reward to women from an understanding of their economic role is in liberalizing the opportunity for choice. What is now seen as a moral compulsion—the diligent and informed administration of the family consumption—emerges as a service to economic interests. When so seen, the moral compulsion disappears. Once women see that they serve purposes which are *not* their own, they will see that they can serve purposes which *are* their own.

## NOTES

1. There is a branch of learning—home economics or home science—that does concern itself with such matters. This field is a nearly exclusive preserve of women. It has never been accorded any serious recognition by economists or scholars generally; like physical education or poultry science, it is part of an academic underworld. And home economists or home scientists, in their natural professional enthusiasm for their subject matter and their natural resentment of their poor academic status, have sought to elevate their subject, homemaking, into a thing

of unique dignity, profound spiritual reward, infinite social value as well as great nutritional significance. Rarely have they asked whether it cons women into a role that is exceedingly important for economic interest and also highly convenient for the men and institutions they are trained to serve. Some of the best home economists were once students of mine. I thought them superbly competent in their commitment to furthering a housewifely role for women.

---

## REFLECTING ON MEANING

1. According to Galbraith, what is the contribution of women to the economy of the United States? In what ways do they facilitate production? Who served this function in an earlier time? How does women's role differ from that of men?

2. How is the role of women as "instruments of the economic system" concealed? In what ways is the "convenient social virtue" invoked to keep them unaware of their role? According to Galbraith, how would women's lives change if they were conscious of the role they play in perpetuating the needs of interests not their own? Do you agree? Why or why not?

3. What point is Galbraith making when he asserts that "the separate identities of men and women are merged into the concept of the household"? What are the economic and political effects of this merging for women? How do the institutions of family and household contribute to the economic and political oppression of women? Why don't they bring about the same for men?

## EXPLORING RHETORICAL STRATEGIES

1. Galbraith begins his essay by recollecting his days as a trustee at Radcliffe College, when he began to reflect on the economic interests that women serve. Other than as an account of the origin of his later speculation on this issue, how does this retrospective function in his essay? How does Galbraith later connect it to his main idea?

2. Galbraith makes numerous assertions in arguing his case. What evidence does he provide to support these assertions? What kind of evidence would they require? Do you find them convincing? Why or why not?

3. What tone does Galbraith establish in this essay? How does he convey himself to his audience? How does he expect his audience to react to his views? This piece was originally published in 1974 in *Ms.* magazine. How would a more contemporary audience react to this essay? Is Galbraith's argument still worth making?

---

# Being a Secretary Can Be Hazardous to Your Health

ELLEN GOODMAN

---

*The columnist Ellen Goodman looks at the effect of powerlessness on the health of women in clerical positions. "It is powerlessness and not power that corrupts women's hearts," she asserts, "and clerical workers are the number one victims."*

They used to say it with flowers or celebrate it with a somewhat liquid lunch. National Secretaries Week was always good for at least a token of appreciation. But the way the figures add up now, the best thing a boss can do for a secretary this week is cough up for her cardiogram.

"Stress and the Secretary" has become the hottest new syndrome on the heart circuit.

It seems that it isn't those Daring Young Women in their Dress-for-Success Suits who are following men down the cardiovascular trail to ruin. Nor is it the female professionals who are winning their equal place in intensive care units.

It is powerlessness and not power that corrupts women's hearts. And clerical workers are the number one victims.

In the prestigious Framingham study, Dr. Suzanne Haynes, an epidemiologist with the National Heart, Lung, and Blood Institute, found that working women as a whole have no higher rate of heart disease than housewives. But women employed in clerical and sales occupations do. Their coronary disease rates are twice that of other women.

"This is not something to ignore," says Dr. Haynes, "since such a high percent of women work at clerical jobs." In fact, 35 percent of all working women, or 18 million of us, hold these jobs.

When Dr. Haynes looked into their private lives, she found the women at greatest risk—with a one in five chance of heart disease—were clerical workers with blue-collar husbands, and three or more children. When she then looked at their work lives, she discovered that the ones who actually developed heart disease were those with nonsupportive bosses who hadn't changed jobs very often and who had trouble letting their anger out.

In short, being frustrated, dead-ended, without a feeling of control over your life is bad for your health.

The irony in all the various and sundry heart statistics is that we now have a weird portrait of the Cardiovascular Fun Couple of the Office: The Type A Boss and his secretary. The male heart disease stereotype is, after all, the Type A aggressive man who always needs to be in control, who lives with a great sense of time urgency . . . and is likely to be a white-collar boss.

"The Type A man is trying to be in control. But given the way most businesses are organized there are, in fact, few ways for them to be in control of their jobs," says Dr. Haynes. The only thing the Type A boss can be in control of is his secretary who in turn feels . . . well, you get the picture. He's not only getting heart disease, he's giving it.

As if all this weren't enough to send you out for the annual three martini lunch, clerical workers are increasingly working for a new Type A boss: the computer.

These days fewer women are sitting in front of bosses with notepads and more are sitting in front of Visual Display Terminals. Word processors, data processors, microprocessors . . . these are the demanding, time-conscious new automatons of automation.

There is nothing intrinsically evil about computers. I am writing this on a VDT and if you try to take it away from me, I will break your arm. But as Working Women, the national association of office workers, puts it in their release this week, automation is increasingly producing clerical jobs that are de-skilled, downgraded, dead-ended and dissatisfying.

As Karen Nussbaum of the Cleveland office described it, the office of the future may well be the factory of the past. Work on computers is often reduced to simple, repetitive, monotonous tasks.

Workers are often expected to produce more for no more pay, and there are also reports of a disturbing trend to processing speed-ups and piece-rate pay, and a feeling among clerical workers that their jobs are computer controlled.

"It's not the machine, but the way it's used by employers," says Working Women's research director, Judith Gregory. Too often, automation's most important product is stress.

Groups, like Working Women, are trying to get clerical workers to organize in what they call "a race against time" so that computers will become their tools instead of their supervisors.

But in the meantime, if you are 1) a female clerical worker, 2) with a blue-collar husband, 3) with three or more children, 4) in a dead-end job, 5) without any way to express anger, 6) with a Type A boss, 7) or a Type A computer controlling your work day . . . *You better start jogging.*

---

## REFLECTING ON MEANING

1. In what ways are clerical workers, including secretaries, powerless? Why aren't women in management equally powerless? What surprising health statistics about these different groups of women does Goodman provide?

2. What does a clerical worker's boss have to do with the level of stress she experiences? How does her home situation also contribute?

3. According to Goodman, how are computers contributing to the dilemma of clerical workers? How do computers reinforce rather than alleviate the lack of control that clerical workers have?

## EXPLORING RHETORICAL STRATEGIES

1. What tone does Goodman adopt in this selection? What devices does she use to achieve it? How does such diction as "cough up for her cardiogram" reinforce her tone?

2. What is the effect of Goodman's concluding paragraph? What is she parodying with her inventory of "symptoms"? How does her conclusion extend the parody of her title?

3. What is the occasion for which Goodman composed this essay? What kind of essay might you normally expect to find in com-

memoration of such an occasion? How has Goodman seized the occasion for more thought-provoking purposes?

# Rape

## DIANE JOHNSON

*"No other subject," asserts Diane Johnson, "is regarded so differently by men and women as rape." Examining several recent book-length studies of rape, Johnson explores social myths about rape and society's complicity in perpetuating it.*

No other subject, it seems, is regarded so differently by men and women as rape. Women deeply dread and resent it to an extent that men apparently cannot recognize; it is perhaps the ultimate and essential complaint that women have to make against men. Of course men may recognize that it is wrong to use physical force against another person, and that rape laws are not prosecuted fairly, and so on, but at a certain point they are apt to say, "But what was she doing there at that hour anyway?" or "Luckily he didn't really hurt her," and serious discussion ceases.

Women sense—indeed, are carefully taught to feel—that the institution of rape is mysteriously protected by an armor of folklore, Bible tales, legal precedents, specious psychological theories. Most of all it seems protected by a rooted and implacable male belief that women want to be raped—which most women, conscientiously examining their motives, maintain they do not—or deserve to be raped, for violation of certain customs governing dress or behavior, a strange proposition to which women are more likely to accede.

While women can all imagine themselves as rape victims, most men know they are not rapists. So incidents that would be resented on personal grounds if happening to their "own" women do not have even the intrinsic interest for them of arguments on principle against military intervention in the political destiny of foreign nations, as in Vietnam, where the "rape" of that country was referred to in the peace movement and meant defoliation of crops. But unlike the interest in the political destiny of Vietnam, which greatly diminished when the danger to American males, via the draft, was eliminated, rape is an abiding concern to women.

Even if they don't think about it very much, most have incorporated into their lives routine precautions along lines prescribed by the general culture. From a woman's earliest days she is attended by injunctions about strangers, and warnings about dark streets, locks, escorts, and provocative behavior. She internalizes the lessons contained therein, that to break certain rules is to invite or deserve rape. Her fears, if not entirely conscious, are at least readily accessible, and are continually activated by a vast body of exemplary literature, both traditional and in the daily paper. To test this, ask yourself, if you are a woman, or ask any woman what she knows about Richard Speck, the Boston Strangler, and "that thing that happened over on ——— Street last week," and you will find that she has considerable rape literature by heart.

It seems important, in attempting to assess the value or seriousness of Susan Brownmiller's polemic on rape *(Against Our Will),* to understand that there are really two audiences for it, one that will know much of what she has to say already, and another that is ill equipped by training or sympathy to understand it at all. This likely accounts for a certain unevenness of tone, veering from indignation to the composed deployment of statistics in the manner of a public debater. It is not surprising that women began in the past few years by addressing their complaints about rape to one another, not to men, and one infers that the subject is still thought to be of concern only to women. It remains to be seen what if any rhetorical strategies will prove to be of value in enlisting the concern of men.

That rape is aggressive, hostile, and intended to exact female submission, and that it is the extreme expression of underlying shared masculine attitudes, is, I think, most women's intuition of the subject, even women who have not been raped but who have tacitly accepted that this is how men are. Women who have in fact been raped (more than 255,000 each year) are certain of it after the indifference, disbelief, and brutality of police, doctors, judges, jurors, and their own families. That the actual rapists, making examples of a few women, in effect frighten and control all women seems obvious, even inarguable.

What is left to be explained, though neither Brownmiller nor Jean MacKellar, in another recent book on rape (*Rape: The Bait and the Trap*), can satisfactorily explain it, is what this primal drama of domination and punishment is about, exactly. Both books communicate an impression of an escalating conflict, with the increasing collective force of female anger and indignation about rape not only effecting some changes in judiciary and police procedures and even, perhaps, in popular attitudes, but also effecting an increase in anxiety about the subject, exemplified by the obligatory rape scenes in current movies and best sellers. Perhaps it is even female anger that is effecting an increase in rape itself, as if, whatever is at stake in this ancient hostility, it is now the rapist who has his back to the wall.

It is not too extreme to say that Brownmiller's book is exceedingly distressing, partly because it is exceedingly discouraging; it is a history of the failure of legal schemes and social sciences to improve society, at least society as viewed from a female perspective; it is the history of the failure of the social sciences even to address themselves to the peculiar mystery of male aggression toward those weaker than themselves. This failure seems in turn to demonstrate the powerlessness of human institutions before the force of patently untrue and sinister myths, whose ability to reflect, but also to determine, human behavior seems invincible. The disobedient Eve, the compliant Leda, the lying wife of Potiphar are still the keys to popular assumptions about women.

But Brownmiller's book is also distressing in another way that wicked myths and scary stories are distressing, that is, because they are meant to be. Here in one handy volume is every admonitory rape story you were ever told, horrifying in the way that propaganda is horrifying and also titillating just in the way that publishers hope a book will be titillating. Brownmiller is trapped in the fallacy of imitative form, and by the duplicitous powers of literature itself to contain within it its own contradictions, so that the exemplary anecdotes from Red Riding Hood to Kitty Genovese to the Tralala scene in *Last Exit to Brooklyn* must appeal at some level to the instincts they illustrate and deprecate. The book may be criticized for an emotional tone that is apparently impossible to exclude from an effective work on a subject so inaccessible to rational analysis. Because rape is an important topic of a potentially sensational and prurient nature, it is too bad that the book is not a model of surpassing tact and delicacy, unassailable learning and scientific methodology. Instead it is probably the book that was needed on this subject at this time, and may in fact succeed where reticence has failed to legitimate the fundamental grievance of women against men.

Much of the book is devoted to an attempt to locate in history the reasons for rape, but inquiry here is fruitless because though history turns up evidence, it offers little explanation. One learns merely that rape has been with us from earliest times, that it is associated variously with military policy, with ideas of property and possession (to rape someone's wife was interpreted as the theft of something from him), with interracial struggles and complicated tribal and class polarities of all kinds (masters and slaves, cowboys and Indians), with intrasexual power struggles, as in the rape of young or weak men in prison by gangs of stronger ones, and within families, by male relatives of young girls or children.

None of these patterns is, except in one respect, wholly consistent with the others, but viewed together they induce a kind of dispirited resignation to natural law, from which are derived the supposed constants of human nature, maybe including rape. The respect in which violations of conquered women in Bangladesh and of Indian (or white) women in pioneer America, or of men in prison, are alike is that they all dramatize some authority conflict. In war between groups of males, women are incidental victims and prizes, but in the back of the car the dispute arises between a man and a woman on her own behalf. The point at issue seems to be "maistrye," as the Wife of Bath knew; and the deepest lessons of our culture have inculcated in both sexes the idea that he is going to prevail. This in turn ensures that he usually does, but the central question of why it is necessary to have male mastery remains unanswered, and perhaps unasked. Meantime, the lesson of history seems to elevate the right of the male to exact obedience and inflict punishment to the status of immutable law.

Anthropology seems to support this, too, despite Brownmiller's attempts to find a primitive tribe (the obligingly rape-free Arapesh) to prove otherwise. Rather inconsistently, she conjectures that the origin of monogamy lies in the female's primordial fear of rape and consequent willingness to attach herself to some male as his exclusive property. If this is so, it would be the only instance in which the female will has succeeded in dictating social arrangements. In any case, alternate and better hypotheses exist for the origin of the family, generally that it developed for the protection of the young. The insouciance of Brownmiller's generalizations invites cavil and risks discrediting her book, and with it her subject. Granting that a primitive tribe can be found to illustrate any social model whatever, one would like to know just what all the anthropological evidence about rape is. If rape is the primordial norm; if, as Lévi-Strauss says, women were the first currency; if male humans in a state of nature run mad raping, unlike chimpanzees, who we are told do not, is rape in fact aberrant? Perhaps it is only abhorrent.

It seems evident that whatever the facts of our nature, it is our culture that leads women in some degree to collaborate in their own rape, an aspect of the matter that men seem determined to claim absolves *them* from responsibility. Perhaps this is implicit in the assumptions about male power they are heir to. But every woman also inherits assumptions about female submission. In even the simplest fairy tale, the vaguely sexual content of the punishment needs no elaboration: every woman darkly knows what really happened to Red Riding Hood in the woods—and to Grandmother, too, for that matter. Most women do not go into the woods alone, but the main point is that the form of the prohibition as it is expressed in most stories is not "Do not go into the woods lest you be raped," but "Obey me by not going into the woods or you *will* be raped."

Thus the idea of sexual punishment for disobedience is learned very early, and is accepted. Who has done this to you, Desdemona? "Nobody; I myself, farewell," says Desdemona meekly as she dies. Everyone feels that Carmen, that prick-tease, is "getting what she deserves," poor Lucrece's suicide is felt to be both noble and tactful, maybe Anna Karenina's too. So if a woman is raped, she feels, besides outrage, deep guilt and a need to find out what she has done "wrong" to account for it, even if her sin is only one of omission; for example, concerned citizens in Palo Alto were told a few days ago that "Sometimes women are raped because of carelessness."

To the extent that a woman can convince a jury that she was neither careless nor seductive, her attacker may be found guilty and she may be absolved from guilt, but more often in rape trials something is found in her behavior to "account" for her fate. The point is that whatever the circumstances of a rape, social attitudes and legal processes at the present time make the victim guilty of her own rape. Even the most innocent victim is likely to be told by her mother, "I told you never to walk home alone," and this is sometimes the attitude of an entire population, as in Bangladesh, where thousands of raped wives were repudiated by their husbands.

The unfortunate rape victim is in some ways worse off the more "feminine," the better socialized, she is, for she will have accepted normal social strictures: do not play rough, do not make noise or hit. Then she will be judged at the trial of her attacker on the extent to which she has struggled, hit, bitten (though she would not be expected to resist an armed robber). Not to struggle is to appear to want to be raped. In the courtroom men pretend not to understand the extent to which cultural inhibitions prevent women from resisting male force, even moral force, though in the parking lot they seem to understand it very well.

In the practical world, who are the rapists, who are the raped, what is to be done? It is here that Brownmiller's account is most interesting and most disturbing. Both Brownmiller and MacKellar agree on the statistical particulars: the rape victim is most likely a teen-aged black girl but she may be a woman of any age, and she will know her attacker to some extent in about half of the cases. The rapist is the same sort of person as other violent offenders: young, uneducated, unemployed, likely black or from another deprived subculture; the rapist is *not* the shy, hard-up loner living with his mother, victim of odd obsessions; a quarter of all rapes are done in gangs or pairs.

The sociology of rapists has some difficult political implications, as Brownmiller, to judge from the care with which she approaches it, is well aware. She traces the complicated history of American liberalism and Southern racism which has led to the present pass, in which people who have traditionally fought for human freedom seem committed to obstructing freedom for women. Historically, she reminds us, the old left, and the Communist Party in particular,

> understood rape as a political act of subjugation only when the victim was black and the offender was white. White-on-white rape was merely "criminal" and had no part in their Marxist canon. Black-on-black rape was ignored. And black-on-white rape, about which the rest of the country was phobic, was discussed in the oddly reversed world of the Jefferson School as if it never existed except as a spurious charge that "the state" employed to persecute black men.

Meantime, circumstances have changed; folk bigotry, like folk wisdom, turns out to contain a half-truth, or grain of prescience; and the black man has taken to raping. Now

> the incidence of actual rape combined with the looming spectre of the black man as rapist to which the black man in the name of his manhood now contributes, must be understood as a control mechanism against the freedom, mobility, and aspirations of all women, white and black. The crossroads of racism and sexism had to be a violent meeting place. There is no use pretending it doesn't exist.

It is at this crossroad that the problem appears most complex and most insoluble. Not only rapists, but also people more suavely disguised as right-thinking, like the ACLU and others associated with the civil-rights movement, still feel that protection of black men's rights is more important than injustice to women, whether white or black. Black men and white women are in effect pitted against one another in such a way as to impede the progress of both groups, and in particular to conceal and perpetuate the specific victimization of black women. Various studies report that blacks do up to 90 percent of rapes, and their victims are 80 to 90 percent black women, who now must endure from men of their own race what they historically had to endure from whites. A black girl from the ages of ten to fifteen is twelve times more likely than others to be a victim of this crime.

In this situation, which will win in the long run, sexism or racism? Who are the natural antagonists? It seems likely, on the evidence, that sexism, being older, will prevail.

The MacKellar/Amir book, a short, practical manual about rape, something to be used perhaps by jurors or counselors, gives a picture of the crime and of the rapist which is essentially the same as Brownmiller's. But MacKellar's advice, when compared with Brownmiller's, is seen to be overlaid by a kind of naive social optimism. What can women do? They can avoid hitchhiking; they can be better in bed: "if women were less inhibited with their men the sense of depravity that their prudishness inspires might be reduced," as if it were frustrated middle-class husbands who were out raping; authorities can search out those "many youngsters warped by a brutish home life [who] can still be recuperated for a reasonably good adult life if given therapy in time"; "Education. Education helps to reduce rape."

Maybe. But does any evidence exist to suggest that any of this would really help? Brownmiller has found none, but I suppose she would agree with MacKellar that for America's violent subcultures we must employ "the classical remedies of assimilating the people in these subcultures, economically and socially, in opportunities for education, jobs, and decent housing," and change the fundamental values of American society. "As long as aggressive, exploitive behavior remains the norm, it can be expected that individuals will make these errors and that the weaker members of society will be the victim."

Until aggressive, exploitive behavior is not the norm, a few practical measures are being suggested. The LEAA study, MacKellar, and Brownmiller are all in favor of prosecuting rape cases and of punishing rapists. Brownmiller feels the punishment should suit the crime, that it should be made similar to penalties for aggravated assault, which it resembles. MacKellar feels that the penalty should fit the criminal: "a nineteen-year-old unemployed black with a fourth-grade education and no father, whose uptight, superreligious mother has, after a quarrel, kicked him out of the home, should not be judged by the same standard nor receive the same kind of sentence as a white middle-aged used-car salesman, twice divorced, who rapes a girl he picks up at a newsstand during an out-of-town convention." She does not, by the way, say who should get the stiffer sentence, and I can think of arguments either way.

Both agree that corroboration requirements and courtroom questions about a victim's prior sexual history should be eliminated, and in this the government-sponsored study for the Law Enforcement Assistance Administration (*Rape and Its Victims*) also agrees. At present the established view holds that whether or not a raped girl is a virgin or is promiscuous is germane to the issue of whether a forced act of sexual intercourse has occurred in a given case. This reflects the ancient idea that by violating male standards of female chastity, a woman forfeits her right to say no.

The LEAA study found that prosecutors' offices in general were doing little to urge the revision of outdated legal codes, and that the legal system is in fact impeding reform. It observes (in a nice trenchant style that makes better reading than most government reports) that

> since rapists have no lobby, the major opposition to reform measures can be expected from public defenders, the defense bar in general, and groups, such as the American Civil Liberties Union, that are vigilant with respect to the rights of criminal defendants.

The conclusion one cannot help coming to is that whatever is to be done about rape will have to be done by women primarily. Brownmiller feels that law enforcement must include 50 percent women. She finds it significant that whereas male law-enforcement authorities report 15 to 20 percent of rape complaints to be "unfounded," among the ones they actually bother to write down, women investigators find only 2 percent of such reports to be unfounded, exactly the number of unfounded reports of other violent crimes. Apparently the goal of male-female law enforcement is not without its difficulties; women police officers in Washington, D.C., recently have complained that their male patrol-car partners are attempting to force them to have sexual intercourse.

Since these women are armed with service revolvers, we may soon see an escalation of what appears to be the Oldest Conflict.

MacKellar and the LEAA report both favor some sort of rape sentencing by degree, as in murder, with rape by a stranger constituting first-degree rape, and third degree taking cognizance of situations in which the victim may be judged to have shared responsibility for initiating the situation that led to the rape—for instance, hitchhiking. This is a compromise that would be unacceptable to feminist groups who feel that a woman is no more responsible for a rape under those circumstances than a man would be thought to be who was assaulted in the same situation.

It is likely that the concept of penalty by degree, with its concession to history, will prevail here, but one sees the objection on principle. While men continue to believe that men have a right to assert their authority over women by sexual and other means, rape will continue, and this in turn suggests two more measures. One is control of pornography, which Brownmiller argues is the means by which the rape ethic is promulgated. In spite of objections about censorship and about the lack of evidence that pornography and violence are related, Brownmiller's argument here is a serious one. She also feels that women should learn self-defense, if only to give them increased self-confidence and awareness of their bodies. But it is easy to see that this is yet another way in which the female might be made to take responsibility for being raped. If a women learns karate and is raped anyway, the question will become, why hadn't she learned it better?

Surely the definition of civilization is a state of things where the strong refrain from exercising their advantages over the weak. If men can be made to see that the abolition of sexual force is necessary in the long-term interest of making a civilization, then they may cooperate in implementing whatever measures turn out to be of any use. For the short term, one imagines, the general effect of female activism about rape will be to polarize men and women even more than nature has required. The cooperation of state authorities, if any, may ensue from their perception of rape, especially black-on-white rape, as a challenge to white male authority (as in the South). This in turn may produce an unlikely and ominous coalition of cops and feminists, and the generally severer prosecution and sentencing which we see as the current response to other forms of violent crime. But do we know that rapists will emerge from the prisons—themselves centers of homosexual rape—any less inclined to do it again?

Meantime, one feels a certain distaste for the congratulatory mood surrounding proposed law-enforcement reforms devoted entirely to making the crime less miserable for the victim while denying or concealing the complicity of so many men in its perpetuation. This implies a state of things worthy of a society described by Swift.

---

## REFLECTING ON MEANING

1. What are the social myths about rape that Johnson identifies? What is the "rooted and implacable male belief" that she describes? What is the "strange proposition" that women as well as men seem to subscribe to? According to Johnson, why is rape an "abiding concern to women" but not to men? Why is it an emotional issue for women but not for men?

2. Johnson maintains that women learn early the "lessons" of rape—"that to break certain rules is to invite or deserve rape." What does she mean? What lessons do women learn? Johnson also asserts that "every woman also inherits assumptions about female submission." How do these assumptions about submission reinforce the lessons society conveys about the "rules" of rape? How do women come to accept the "idea of sexual punishment for disobedience"?

3. What is rape, according to Johnson? Where does she supply this definition? Why does she cast it in terms of "domination and punishment"? In what ways is it punishment? For what? What are the social and cultural attitudes that the act of rape makes concrete?

## EXPLORING RHETORICAL STRATEGIES

1. Johnson suggests that Brownmiller's book might be criticized "for an emotional tone that is apparently impossible to exclude from an effective work on a subject so inaccessible to rational analysis." To what degree does her own essay transcend such an emotional tone? Is an emotional tone necessarily a negative thing? Why or why not?

2. Throughout her essay, Johnson alludes to women in myth and literature: Eve, Leda, Potiphar, the wife of Bath, Desdemona, Carmen, Anna Karenina—even Little Red Riding Hood. Why does she do this? What do these allusions tell you about the kind

of knowledge she expects her audience to have? What kind of audience did she have in mind as she composed this essay?

3. This essay is an example of a genre known as the review essay, an essay that not only summarizes and evaluates several books on a specific topic but that expresses the review writer's own views on the topic. What views does Johnson hold on rape? How does she distinguish them from her views on the books she is reviewing?

# TAKING A STAND
## QUESTIONS FOR CONSIDERATION

1. In this part many authors argue that women remain powerless despite recent advances in civil rights and changing social attitudes. What are the concrete manifestations of powerlessness that they see? Taken together, do their essays provide a convincing case that women are indeed powerless? Is their collective assessment of women's status valid? In exploring this issue, consider especially the essays by Brophy, Pearce, and Johnson.

2. Several authors claim that women themselves actually reinforce their powerlessness because society teaches them to do so. What are the various means by which society encourages women to internalize their sense of powerlessness? To what extent is such social propaganda a vital force at work on both women and men? Consider Galbraith's and Brophy's definitions of persuasion; Johnson's views on myth and the lesson of sexual punishment for disobedience; and Goldberg's allusions to Aristotle.

3. What is prejudice? Discrimination? Are the two terms synonymous? Analyze the meanings of these terms for at least three authors and construct your own definitions. Consider Goldberg's examination of prejudice, Fraker's discussion of the vague discrimination that career women face, Pearce's views on "occupational segregation" and Johnson's examination of rape.

4. What are the roles of home and family in reinforcing women's powerlessness? What insights into this question does Galbraith provide? What implications does Goodman suggest? In shaping your response to this question, you may also wish to consider the historical perspectives of Charlotte Perkins Gilman and John Stuart Mill in Part II and Deborah Fallows's opposing viewpoint in Part IV.

5. What kind of treatment do women receive in the various systems and institutions that make up our society? How are they rendered powerless by, for example, the corporate world, organized religion, and the economic, welfare, and justice systems? You may find the essays by Fraker, Johnson, Goodman, Galbraith, and Pearce helpful. For a historical perspective, review the selections by Mary Daly, Charlotte Perkins Gilman, and Pope Pius XI in Part II.

6. A recurrent analogy in this and other parts of the text is the comparison between women's powerlessness and imprisonment or slavery. Why do authors who write about gender issues make

extensive use of such analogies? How do these analogies allow them to explore connections between gender and race? Do their analogies differ in significant ways? In this part consider Pearce's "workhouse without walls" and Brophy's "invisible cages." You may also want to look at the essays by John Stuart Mill (Part II), Margaret Sanger ("Birth Control," Part II), and Simone de Beauvoir ("The Married Woman," Part IV).

# Part VII

## Additional Readings

# Life Behind the Veil

CHERRY LINDHOLM
and CHARLES LINDHOLM

The bazaar teems with activity. Pedestrians throng the narrow streets, wending past donkey carts, cyclists, and overloaded vehicles. Vendors haggle in the dark doorways of their shops. Pitiful beggars shuffle among the crowds, while bearded religious mendicants wander about, their eyes fixed on a distant world.

Drifting among the mobs of men are, here and there, anonymous figures hidden beneath voluminous folds of material, who float along like ships in full sail, graceful, mysterious, faceless, instilling in the observer a sense both of awe and of curiosity. These are the Moslem women of the Middle East. Their dress is the customary *chador,* which they wear when obliged to leave the privacy of their homes. The *chador* is but one means by which women maintain their *purdah,* the institution of female seclusion, which requires that women should remain unseen by men who are not close relatives and strikes Westerners as so totally foreign and incomprehensible.

Sometimes the alien aspect is tempered with a touch of Western familiarity. A pair of plastic sunglasses may gleam from behind the lace that covers the eyes, or a platform shoe might peep forth from beneath the hem of the flowing *chador.* Nevertheless, the overall presence remains one of inscrutability and is perhaps the most striking image of Middle Eastern societies.

We spent nine months in one of the most strict of all the *purdah* societies, the Yusufzai Pakhtun of the Swat Valley in the North-West Frontier Province of Pakistan. ("Pakhtun" is the designation preferred by the tribesmen, who were generally called Pathans in the days of the British *raj.)*

We had come to the Swat Valley after a hair-raising ride on a rickety bus from Peshawar over the 10,280-foot Malakand Pass. Winston Churchill came this way as a young war correspondent attached to the Malakand Field Force in 1897. As we came into the valley, about half the size of Connecticut, we passed a sign that said WELCOME TO SWAT. We were fortunate to have entrée into the community through a Swati friend we had made eight years before. In Swat, women are secluded inside the domestic compound except for family rituals, such as marriage, circumcision, and funerals, or visits to saints' tombs. A woman must always be in the protective company of other women and is never allowed out alone. It tells a great deal about the community that the word for husband in Pakhto, the language of the Pakhtun, is *khawund,* which also means God.

However, as everywhere, rules are sometimes broken or, more frequently, cleverly manipulated. Our Pakhtun host's stepmother, Bibi, an intelligent and forceful woman, was renowned for her tactics. Once, when all the females of the household had been forbidden to leave the compound to receive cholera inoculations at the temporary clinic next door, Bibi respectfully bowed her head and assured the men they could visit the mosque with easy minds. Once the men had gone, she promptly climbed the ladder to the flat roof and summoned the doctor to the door of her compound. One by one, the women extended their bare arms through the doorway and received their shots. Later, Bibi could honestly swear that no woman had set foot outside the compound walls.

Despite such circumventions, *purdah* is of paramount importance in Swat. As one Pakhtun proverb succinctly states: "The woman's place is in the home or the grave." Years ago in Swat, if a woman broke her *purdah,* her husband might kill her or cut off her nose as punishment and as a means of cleansing his honor. If a woman is caught alone with an unrelated man, it will always be assumed that the liaison is sexual, and public opinion will oblige her husband to shoot her, even if he does not desire her death; to go unavenged is to be known henceforth as *begherata,* or man without honor. As such, he would no longer have the right to call himself Pakhtun.

A shameless woman is a threat to the whole society. Our host remembered witnessing, thirty years ago when he was a child, the entire village stoning an adultress. This punishment is prescribed by Islamic law, though the law requires there be four witnesses to the sexual act itself to establish guilt. Nowadays, punishments for wifely misdemeanors have become less harsh, though adulterous wives are still killed.

In the rural areas, poorer families generally cannot maintain *purdah* as rigorously as their wealthier neighbors, for often the wife must help her husband in the fields or become a servant. Nevertheless, she is required to keep her hair covered at all times and to interact with men to a minimum. Here again, the rules are sometimes flouted, and a poor woman might entice a man with her eyes or even, according to village men who claimed personal experiences, become more aggressive in her seductive attempts and actually seize a man in a deserted alleyway and lure him into her house. Often, the man is persuaded. Such a woman will accept money from her lover, who is usually a man from a wealthy family. Her husband is then a *begherata,* but some men acquiesce to the situation because of the money the wife is earning or because of fear of the wife's socially superior and more powerful lover. But most poor men, and certainly all the elite, keep their women under strict control.

In the Islamic Middle East, women are viewed as powerful and dangerous beings, highly sexual and lacking in personal discipline and discrimination. In Middle Eastern thought, sexual intercourse itself, though polluting, lacks the same negative connotations it has in the West. It has always been believed that women have sexual climaxes, and there is no notion of female frigidity. Male impotence, however, is well-documented, and some middle-aged and even young men admitted to us that they had lost their interest in women. Sometimes, though rarely, a young bridegroom will find himself incapable of consummating his marriage, either because he finds his bride unattractive or because he has been previously enchanted by a male lover and has become impotent in a heterosexual relationship. Homosexuality has never been seen as aberrant in the Middle East. As a famous Afghan saying humorously declares: "A woman is for bearing children, a boy is for pleasure, but ecstasy is a ripe watermelon!" However, with Western influence, homosexuality in the Middle East is now less overt. But even when it was common and open, the man was still expected to marry and produce children.

Men must marry, though women are regarded as a chaotic and anarchic force. They are believed to possess many times the sexual desire of men and constitute a potential threat to the family and the family's honor, which is based in large measure on the possession and control of women and their excessive and dangerous sexuality.

Among the Pakhtun of Swat, where the male-female relation is one of the most hostile in the Middle East, the man avoids showing affection to his wife, for fear she will become too self-confident and will begin to assert herself in ways that insult his position and honor. She may start by leaving the compound without his permission and, if unchecked, may end by bringing outside men into the house for sexual encounters, secure in the knowledge that her husband, weakened by his affection for her, will not take action. This course of events is considered inevitable by men and women alike and was illustrated by a few actual cases in the village where we lived.

Women are therefore much feared, despite the pronouncements of male supremacy. They must be controlled, in order to prevent their alarming basic natures from coming to the fore and causing dishonor to their own lineages. *Purdah* is generally described as a system that serves to protect the woman, but implicitly it protects the men and society in general from the potentially disruptive actions of the powerful female sex.

Changes are occurring, however, particularly in the modern urban centers. The educated urban woman often dispenses with the *chador,* replacing it with a simple length of veiling draped over the head or across the shoulders; she may even decide to adopt modest Western dress. The extent of this transformation will depend partly upon the attitude of the community in which she lives.

In the urban centers of the stricter *purdah* regions the public display of *purdah* is scrupulous, sometimes even more striking than that of the tribal village. Behind the scenes, though, the city-dwelling woman does have more freedom than she would have in the village. She will be able to visit not only relatives but friends without specific permission from her husband, who is out at work all day. She may, suitably veiled, go shopping in the bazaar, a chore her husband would have undertaken in the village. On the whole, the city woman will have a great deal more independence, and city men sometimes lament this weakening of traditional male domination.

The urbanized male may speak of the custom-bound tribesmen (such as the Swat Pakhtun, the Bedouin nomads of Saudi Arabia or the Qashqai herdsmen of Iran) as country bumpkins, yet he still considers their central values, their sense of personal pride, honor, and autonomy, as cultural ideals and views the tribesmen, in a very real way, as exemplars of the proper mode of life. Elite families in the cities proudly emphasize their tribal heritage and sometimes send their sons to live for a year or so with distant tribal cousins, in order to expose them to the tribesman's integrity and moral code. The tribesman, on the other hand, views his urbanized relatives as weak and womanly, especially with reference to the slackening of *purdah* in the cities. Though the *purdah* female, both in the cities and in the tribal areas, rarely personifies the ideal virtues of silence, submission, and obedience, the concept of *purdah* and male supremacy remains central to the male identity and to the ideology of the culture as a whole.

The dynamic beneath the notion of male supremacy, the institution of *purdah,* and the ideology of women's sexual power becomes apparent when one takes an overall view of the social structure. The family in the Middle East, particularly in the tribal regions, is not an isolated element; kinship and marriage are the underlying principles that structure action and thought. Individuals interact not so much according to personal preference as according to kinship.

The Middle Eastern kinship system is known to anthropologists as a segmentary-lineage organization; the basic idea is that kinship is traced through one line only. In the Middle East, the system is patrilineal, which means that the male line is followed, and all the links through women are ignored. An individual can therefore trace his relationship to any other individual in the society and know the exact genealogical distance between them; i.e., the distance that must be traced to reach a common male ancestor. The system obliges men to defend their patrilineal relatives if they are attacked, but if there is no external force threatening the lineage, then men struggle against one another according to the principle of genealogical distance. This principle is nicely stated in a famous Middle Eastern proverb: "I against my brothers; my brothers and I against my cousins; my cousins, my brothers, and I against the world." The cousins in question are of course patrilineal.

Within this system, women appear to have no role, though they are the units of reproduction, the mothers of the sons who will carry on the patriline. Strange as it may seem, this is the core contradiction of the society: The "pure" patriline itself is actually descended from a woman. This helps explain the exaggerated fear of women's promiscuity and supposedly voracious sexuality. In order to protect the patriline, women must be isolated and guarded. Their sexuality, which threatens the integrity of the patriline, must be made the exclusive property of their husbands. Women, while being absolutely necessary for the perpetuation of the social order, are simultaneously the greatest threat to it.

The persistent denigration of women is explained by this core contradiction. Moslem society considers women naturally inferior in intelligence and ability—childlike, incapable of discernment, incompetent to testify in court, prey to whims and fancies. In tribal areas, women are prohibited from inheritance, despite a Koranic injunction, and in marriage they are purchased from their fathers like a commodity. Were woman not feared, these denials of her personhood would be unnecessary.

Another unique element of Middle Eastern culture is the prevalence of marriage with the father's brother's daughter. In many areas, in fact, this marriage is so favored that a boy must give explicit permission to allow his patrilineal female cousin to marry elsewhere. This peculiar marriage form, which is found nowhere else in the world, also serves to negate the woman by merging her lineage with that of her husband, since both are members of the same patriline (indeed, are the offspring of brothers). No new blood enters, and the sanctity of the patriline is steadily maintained.

However, this ploy gives rise to other problems: Cousin marriage often divides the brothers rather than uniting them. Although the bride-price is usually reduced in such marriages, it is always demanded, thus turning the brothers into opponents in a business negotiation. Furthermore, giving a woman in Swat carries an implication of inferiority; historically, victors in war took women from the vanquished. Cousin marriage thus renders the brothers' equality questionable. Finally, the young couple's fights will further alienate the brothers, especially since such marriages are notoriously contentious. This is because patrilineal male cousins are rivals for the common grandfather's inheritance (in fact, the Swati term for fathers' brother's son is *tarbur,* which also means enemy), and a man who marries his patrilineal cousin is marrying the sister of his lifelong opponent. Her loyalty is with her brother, and this is bound to cause frequent disputes.

Though the girl is treated like goods, she does not see herself as such. The fundamental premise of tribal life is the equality of the various landed families. There are very few hierarchies in these societies, and even the leaders are often no more than first among equals. Within this system, which has been described as a nearly perfect democracy, each *khan* (which means landowner and literally translates as king) family sees itself as superior to all others. The girls of the household feel the same pride in their lineage as their brothers and cannot help but regard their husbands' families through jaundiced eyes. The new bridge is prepared to defend the honor of her family, even though they have partially repudiated her by negotiating the marriage. Her identity, like that of a man, rests on her lineage pride, which she will fight to uphold. The husband, meanwhile, is determined to demonstrate his domination and mastery, since control of women is the nexus of a man's sense of self-respect.

Hostility is thus built into marriage by the very structure of the society, which pits every lineage against every other in a never-ending contest to maintain an equilibrium of power within this markedly egalitarian culture. The hostility of the marriage bond is evident from its beginnings. The reluctant bride is torn from her cot in her family's house and ensconced on a palanquin that strongly resembles a bier. The war drums that announce the marriage procession indicate the nature of the tie, as does the stoning of the palanquin by the small boys of the village as it is carried through the dusty streets. When the bride arrives at her new husband's house, his family triumphantly fires their rifles into the air. They have taken a woman! The young wife cowers in her veils as she is prodded and poked curiously by the females of the husband's house who try to persuade her to show her face. The groom himself is nowhere to be seen, having retreated to the men's house in shame. In three days, he will creep to her room and consummate the marriage. Taking the virginity of the bride is a highly charged symbolic act, and in some areas of the Middle East the display of the bloody nuptial sheet to the public is a vital part of the wedding rite. Breaking the hymen demonstrates the husband's possession of his wife's sexuality. She then becomes the most junior adult in the household, subordinate to everyone, but, most especially, under the heavy thumb of her mother-in-law.

The household the bride enters will be that of her husband's father, since the system, as well as being patrilineal, is also patrilocal. She will be surrounded by his relatives and will be alone with her husband only at night. During the day he will pay no attention to her, for it is considered shameful for a man to take note of his wife in front of others, particularly his father and mother. Within the compound walls, which shield the household from the rest of the world, she is at the mercy of her new family.

Life within the compound is hardly peaceful. Wives squabble among themselves, and wives who have built a power base by having sons even quarrel with the old matriarch, their mother-in-law. This is usually a prelude to a couple moving out of the house into their own compound, and husbands always blame their wives for the breakup of the extended family, even though they, too, will be glad to become the masters of their own homes and households.

But the worst fights among women are the fights between women married to the same man. Islam permits polygamous marriage, and legally a man may have four wives. Not all men are financially able to take more than one wife, but most men dream of marrying again, despite the Swati proverb that says, "I may be a fool, but not so much of a fool as the man with two wives." Men who can afford it often do take a second wife. The reason is not sexual desire, for wives do not mind if their husbands have liaisons with prostitutes or promiscuous poor women. Rather, the second wife is brought in to humiliate an overly assertive first wife. Bringing in a second wife is a terrible insult; it is an expression of contempt for the first wife and her entire lineage. The insult is especially cutting in Swat, where divorce is prohibited (though it is permitted in the Koran) and where a disliked wife must either endure her lot or retreat to her family's house and a life of celibacy. Small wonder then that households with two wives are pits of intrigue, vituperation, and magical incantation, as each wife seeks to expel the other. The Koran says a man should only practice polygamy if he is sure he can treat each wife equally; the only man we met who was able to approximate this ideal was a man who never went home. He spent his time in the men's house, talking with his cronies and having his meals sent to him.

The men's house is the best-built structure in any village, along with the mosque, which is also prohibited to women. It is a meeting place for the clan, the center for hospitality and refuge, and the arena for political manipulation. This is where the visitors will be received, surrounded by men who gossip, doze, or clean their rifles. Here, the guest might well imagine that women do not even exist. Only the tea and food that is sent over from the compound nearby tell him of the women working behind the walls.

Formerly, in Swat, most men slept in the men's house, visiting their wives secretly late at night and returning before daybreak. But now only a few elders and some ne'er-do-well youths live permanently in the elegant, aging buildings. Sometimes, however, a man may be obliged to move to the men's house for a few days if his wife makes his home too uncomfortable, for women too have their own weapons in the household battles. Arguments may flare up over almost anything: the husband buying a rotten piece of meat or forgetting to bring home a length of material, the wife ruining some curd or gossiping too much with a neighbor. The wife may then angrily refuse to cook, obliging the husband to retreat to the men's house for food. The man's weapon in fights is violence, while the woman can withdraw domestic services at will.

In the early days of a marriage, when the bride is new to the household and surrounded by her husband's people, she may be fairly meek. But when her status has improved as a result of producing sons, she will become more aggressive. Her lacerating tongue is renowned, and she will also begin to fight back physically as well as verbally. Finally, her exasperated husband may silence her with a blow from a heavy stick he keeps for that purpose. No shame is attached to beating one's wife, and men laugh about beatings they have administered. The women themselves, though they decry their men's brutality, proudly display their scars and bruises, characterizing a neighbor who is relatively gentle to his wife as "a man with no penis."

The older a women gets, the more powerful and fearless she becomes. She is aided by her sons who, though respecting their father, regard him as an obstacle to their gaining rights in land. The old man, who gains his stature from his landholding, is always reluctant to allot shares to his grown sons. Furthermore, the sons' ties of affection are much stronger with the mother. The elderly father, who is generally ten or fifteen years older than his wife, is thus surrounded by animosity in his own house. The situation of the earlier years has reversed itself, and the wife, who began alone and friendless, gains allies in her old age, while the husband becomes isolated. Ghani Khan, a modern Pakhtun writer, has described the situation well: "The Pakhtun thinks he is as good as anyone else and his father rolled into one and is fool enough to try this even with his wife. She pays for it in her youth, and he in his old age."

But many women do not live to see their triumph. In northern Swat, for every 100 women over the age of sixty there are 149 men, compared to the more equal 100 to 108 ratio below sixty. The women are worn out by continual childbearing, breast feeding, and a lack of protein. Though fertile in places, the Swat valley is heavily overpopulated with an estimated 1 million people, and survival is always difficult. The diet consists chiefly of bread, rice, seasonal vegetables, and some dairy products. Meat is a rarity and goes to the men and boys as a matter of course. They perpetuate the patrilineal clan and must survive, while women can always be replaced. The lives of men are hard, but the lives of women are harder, as witnessed by their early deaths.

In this environment, people must learn to be tough, just as they must learn to fit the structure of the patrilineal system. Child rearing serves both functions.

The birth of a boy in Swat is greeted by rejoicing, while the birth of a girl is an occasion for gloom. But the first few years for both sexes are virtually identical. Like most Middle Easterners, the Swatis practice swaddling, binding the baby tightly so that it is immobilized. Ostensibly, this is to help the baby sleep and prevent it from blinding itself with its flailing hands, but anthropologists have hypothesized that swaddling actually serves to develop a certain character type: a type which can withstand great restraint but which also tends to uncontrolled bursts of temper. This hypothesis fits Swat, where privation and the exigencies of the social structure demand stoicism, but where violent temper is also useful. We often saw Swati children of all ages lose themselves in tantrums to coerce their parents, and such coercion was usually successful. Grown men and women as well are prone to fits of temper, and this dangerous aspect makes their enemies leery of pressing them too hard.

Both sexes are indoctrinated in the virtues of their family and its lineage. In marital fights this training is obvious, as both partners heatedly assert, "Your ancestor was nothing, and mine was great!" At a man's death his sister, not his wife, is his chief mourner. And if a woman is killed it is her brother, not her husband, who avenges her.

Child training in Swat produces strong characters. When they give affection, they give it wholeheartedly, and when they hate, they hate bitterly. The conditions under which they live are cruel and cramped, and they respond with cruelty and rigidity in order to survive. But at the same time, the people are able to bear their hard lives with pride and dignity.

# The Contrived Postures of Femininity

## SUSAN BROWNMILLER

I was taught to sit with my knees close together, but I don't remember if I was given a reason. Somewhere along the way I heard that boys like to look up girls' skirts and that it was our job to keep them from seeing our panties, but I didn't put much stock in this vicious slur. "Put your knees together" seemed to be a rule of good posture like "Sit up straight," and nothing more. As with other things that became entrenched in my mind as unquestionably right and feminine, when I thought about it later on I could see an aesthetic reason. The line of a skirt did seem more graceful when the knees weren't poking out in different directions. Slanting them together was the way to avoid looking slovenly in a chair. (Sitting with legs crossed became an acceptably feminine posture only after skirts were shortened in the 1920s.)

Bending over to pick up a piece of paper was fraught with the danger of indecent exposure during the sixties miniskirt era, and like other women who believed minis looked terrifically dashing when we stepped along the street, I had to think twice, compose myself, and slither down with closed knees if I dropped something. A breed of voyeurs known as staircase watchers made their appearance during this interesting time. Slowly it dawned on me that much of feminine movement, the inhibited gestures, the locked knees, the nervous adjustments of the skirt, was a defensive maneuver against an immodest, vulgar display that feminine clothing flirted with in deliberate provocation. My feminine responsibility was to keep both aspects, the provocative and the chaste, in careful balance, even if it meant avoiding the beautifully designed open stairway in a certain Fifth Avenue bookshop.

But why did I think of vulgarity when the focal point at issue—I could no longer deny the obvious—was my very own crotch? And why did I believe that if I switched to trousers, the problem would be magically solved?

Spreading the legs is a biologically crucial, characteristically female act. Not only does the female have the anatomical capacity to stretch her legs further apart than the average male because of the shape of her pelvis, but a generous amount of leg spread is necessary to the act of sexual intercourse, to the assertive demand for pleasure, and to the act of giving birth. There may have been a time in history when this female posture was celebrated with pride and joy—I am thinking of the Minoan frescoes on Crete where young women are shown leaping with ease over the horns of a charging bull (the sexual symbolism of the woman and the bull has been remarked upon by others)—but in civilization as we know it, female leg spread is identified with loose, wanton behavior, pornographic imagery, promiscuity, moral laxity, immodest demeanor, and a lack of refinement. In other words, with qualities that the feminine woman must try to avoid, even as she must try to hint that somewhere within her repertoire such possibilities exist.

There is nothing hidden about the male sexual organ. It is a manifest presence; the legs need not spread to reveal it, nor are they usually positioned as wide apart as the female's to accomplish the sexual act. But while copulation and other genital activity require a generous spread of the thighs in order for a woman to achieve her pleasure, in the feminine code of behavior she is not supposed to take the initiative out of her own desire.

The ideology of feminine sexual passivity relies upon a pair of closed thighs more intently than it does upon speculative theories of the effects of testosterone on the libido, aggression, and the human brain. Open thighs acknowledge female sexuality as a positive, assertive force—a force that is capable of making demands to achieve satisfaction.

Students of Japanese history know that Samurai warriors trained their daughters in the use of weapons to give them the requisite skill to commit hara-kiri when faced with disgrace. As part of the training, girls were taught how to tie their lower limbs securely so they would not embarrass themselves and their families by inadvertently assuming an immodest position in the agony of death. Traditional Japanese etiquette pays close attention to the rules of modest posture for women. In the classic squat position for eating, men are permitted to open their knees a few inches for comfort but women are not. Men may also sit cross-legged on the floor, but women must kneel with their legs together.

Studies by the psychologist Albert Mehrabian show that, despite evidence of superior anatomical flexibility and grace, women are generally less relaxed than men. Mehrabian proposes that attitudes of submissiveness are conveyed through postures of tension. In his analysis of body language among high and low status males, high-ranking men are more relaxed in their gestures in the presence of subordinates. Not surprisingly, men of all ranks generally assume more relaxed postures and gestures when communicating with women.

Today's customary restraints on women's bodily comportment are broadly defined by fingertips and heels, a pocketbook on the shoulder, and a schooled inhibition against spreading the knees. In addition, as the French feminist Colette Guillaumin has noted, women are physically burdened by what she calls "diverse loads," the habitual signs of chief responsibility for the domestic role—children on the arm, their food and toys in hand, and a bag of groceries or shirts from the dry cleaner's hugged to the chest. Rarely does a woman experience the liberty of taking a walk with empty hands and arms swinging free at her sides. So rare is this, in fact, that many women find it physically unnerving when they do. Unaccustomed to the freedom, they are beset by worries that some needed belonging, some familiar presence (a purse, a shopping bag?) has been forgotten.

Small, fluttery gestures that betray nervousness or a practiced overanimation are considered girlishly feminine and cute. Toying with a strand of hair, bobbing the head, giggling when introduced, pulling the elbows in close to the body, and crossing the legs in a knee and ankle double twist are mannerisms that men studiously avoid.

Jewelry plays a subtle role in delineating masculine and feminine gestures. To drum one's fingers on the table is an aggressive expression of annoyance and is conspicuously unfeminine, but to fidget with a necklace or twist a ring is a nonthreatening way of dissipating agitation. Clutching protectively at the throat is not restricted to females, but corresponding masculine gestures are to loosen the collar and adjust the necktie, actions which indicate some modicum of control.

Quaint postures that throw the body off balance, such as standing on one leg as if poised for flight, or leading from the hips in a debutante slouch, or that suggest a child's behavior (the stereotypic sexy secretary taking dictation while perched on the boss's knee), fall within the repertoire of femininity that is alien, awkward, and generally unthinkable as a mode of behavior for men. Reclining odalisque-style, such a shocker thirty years ago when Truman Capote posed in this manner for a book jacket, is a classic feminine tableau of eroticized passivity with an established tradition in art.

Of course, feminine movement was never intended for solo performance. Vine-clinging, lapdog-cuddling, and birdlike perching require a strong external support. It is in order to appeal to men that the yielded autonomy and contrived manifestations of helplessness become second nature as expressions of good manners and sexual goodwill. For smoother interaction between the sexes, the prevailing code of masculine action demands a yielding partner to gracefully complete the dance.

Nancy Henley, psychologist and author of *Body Politics* (Prentice-Hall), has written, "In a way so accepted and so subtle as to be unnoticed even by its practitioners and recipients, males in couples will often literally push a woman everywhere she is to go—the arm from behind, steering around corners . . . crossing the street."

In this familiar *pas de deux,* a woman must either consent to be led with a gracious display of good manners or else she must buck and bristle at the touch of the reins. Femininity encourages the romance of compliance, a willing exchange of motor autonomy and physical balance for the protocols of masculine protection. Steering and leading are prerogatives of those in command. Observational studies of who touches whom in a given situation show that superiors feel free to lay an intimate, guiding hand on those with inferior status, but not the reverse. "The politics of touch," a concept of Henley's, operates instructively in masculine-feminine relations.

Henley was the first psychologist to connect the masculine custom of shepherding an able-bodied woman through situations that do not require physical guidance with other forms of manhandling along a continuum from petty humiliation (the sly pinch, the playful slap on the fanny) to the assaultive abuses of wife-beating and rape. This is not to say that the husband who steers his wife to a restaurant table with a paternal shove is no different from the rapist, but rather to suggest that women who customarily expect to have their physical movements directed by others are poorly prepared by their feminine training to resist unwanted interference or violent assault. Fear of being judged impolite has more immediate reality for many women than the terror of physical violation.

To be helped with one's coat, to let the man do the driving, to sit mute and unmoving while the man does the ordering and picks up the check—such trained behavioral inactivity may be ladylike, gracious, romantic and flirty, and soothing to easily ruffled masculine feathers, but it is ultimately destructive to the sense of the functioning, productive self. The charge that feminists have no manners is true, for the history of manners, unfortunately for those who wish to change the world, is an index of courtly graces addressed toward those of the middle classes who aspire to the refinements of their betters, embodied in the static version of the cared-for, catered-to lady of privilege who existed on a rarefied plane above the mundane reality of strenuous labor. When a feminist insists on opening a door for herself, a simple act of physical autonomy that was never an issue for servants, field and factory workers, and women not under the protection of men, her gesture rudely collides with chivalrous expectations, for manly action requires manifest evidence of a helpless lady in order to demonstrate courtly respect.

The psychology of feminine movement, as we know and practice its provocative airs and graces, is based on the premise that direct acts of initiative and self-assertion are a violation of the governance of male-female relations, if not of nature itself. In place of forthright action we are offered a vision so exquisitely romantic and sexually beguiling that few care to question its curious imagery of limitations: a Venus de Milo without arms, a mermaid without legs, a Sleeping Beauty in a state of suspended animation with her face upturned, awaiting a kiss.

# Sexual Politics: A Manifesto for Revolution

KATE MILLETT

When one group rules another, the relationship between the two is political. When such an arrangement is carried out over a long period of time it develops an ideology (feudalism, racism, etc.). All historical civilizations are patriarchies: their ideology is male supremacy.

Oppressed groups are denied education, economic independence, the power of office, representation, an image of dignity and self-respect, equality of status, and recognition as human beings. Throughout history women have been consistently denied all of these, and their denial today, while attenuated and partial, is nevertheless consistent. The education allowed them is deliberately designed to be inferior, and they are systematically programmed out of and excluded from the knowledge where power lies today—e.g., in science and technology. They are confined to conditions of economic dependence based on the sale of their sexuality in marriage, or a variety of prostitutions. Work on a basis of economic independence allows them only a subsistence level of life—often not even that. They do not hold office, are represented in no positions of power, and authority is forbidden them. The image of woman fostered by cultural media, high and low, then and now, is a marginal and demeaning existence, and one outside the human condition—which is defined as the prerogative of man, the male.

Government is upheld by power, which is supported through consent (social opinion), or imposed by violence. Conditioning to an ideology amounts to the former. But there may be a resort to the latter at any moment when consent is withdrawn—rape, attack, sequestration, beatings, murder. Sexual politics obtains consent through the "socialization" of both sexes to patriarchal policies. They consist of the following:

1. the formation of human personality along stereotyped lines of sexual category, based on the needs and values of the master class and dictated by what he would cherish in himself and find convenient in an underclass: aggression, intellectuality, force and

efficiency for the male; passivity, ignorance, docility, "virtue," and ineffectuality for the female.
2. the concept of sex role, which assigns domestic service and attendance upon infants to all females and the rest of human interest, achievement and ambition to the male; the charge of leader at all times and places to the male, and the duty of follower, with equal uniformity, to the female.
3. the imposition of male rule through institutions: patriarchal religion, the proprietary family, marriage, "The Home," masculine oriented culture, and a pervasive doctrine of male superiority.

A Sexual Revolution would bring about the following conditions, desirable upon rational, moral and humanistic grounds:

1. the end of sexual repression—freedom of expression and of sexual mores (sexual freedom has been partially attained, but it is now being subverted beyond freedom into exploitative license for patriarchal and reactionary ends).
2. Unisex, or the end of separatist character-structure, temperament and behavior, so that each individual may develop an entire—rather than a partial, limited, and conformist—personality.
3. re-examination of traits categorized into "masculine" and "feminine," with a total reassessment as to their human usefulness and advisability in both sexes. Thus if "masculine" violence is undesirable, it is so for both sexes, "feminine" dumb-cow passivity likewise. If "masculine" intelligence or efficiency is valuable, it is so for both sexes equally, and the same must be true for "feminine" tenderness or consideration.
4. the end of sex role and sex status, the patriarchy and the male supremacist ethic, attitude and ideology—in all areas of endeavor, experience, and behavior.
5. the end of the ancient oppression of the young under the patriarchal proprietary family, their chattel status, the attainment of the human rights presently denied them, the professionalization and therefore improvement of their care, and the guarantee that when they enter the world, they are desired, planned for, and provided with equal opportunities.
6. Bisex, or the end of enforced perverse heterosexuality, so that the sex act ceases to be arbitrarily polarized into male and female, to the exclusion of sexual expression between members of the same sex.
7. the end of sexuality in the forms in which it has existed historically—brutality, violence, capitalism, exploitation, and warfare—that it may cease to be hatred and become love.

8. the attainment of the female sex to freedom and full human status after millennia of deprivation and oppression, and of both sexes to a viable humanity.

# Racism and Feminism

## BELL HOOKS

I am a black woman. I attended all-black public schools. I grew up in the south where all around me was the fact of racial discrimination, hatred, and forced segregation. Yet my education as to the politics of race in American society was not that different from that of white female students I met in integrated high schools, in college, or in various women's groups. The majority of us understood racism as a social evil perpetuated by prejudiced white people that could be overcome through bonding between blacks and liberal whites, through militant protest, changing of laws or racial integration. Higher educational institutions did nothing to increase our limited understanding of racism as a political ideology. Instead professors systematically denied us truth, teaching us to accept racial polarity in the form of white supremacy and sexual polarity in the form of male dominance.

American women have been socialized, even brainwashed, to accept a version of American history that was created to uphold and maintain racial imperialism in the form of white supremacy and sexual imperialism in the form of patriarchy. One measure of the success of such indoctrination is that we perpetuate both consciously and unconsciously the very evils that oppress us. I am certain that the black female sixth grade teacher who taught us history, who taught us to identify with the American government, who loved those students who could best recite the pledge of allegiance to the American flag was not aware of the contradiction; that we should love this government that segregated us, that failed to send schools with all black students supplies that went to schools with only white pupils. Unknowingly she implanted in our psyches a seed of the racial imperialism that would keep us forever in bondage. For how does one overthrow, change, or even challenge a system that you have been taught to admire, to love, to believe in? Her innocence does not change the reality that she was teaching black children to embrace the very system that oppressed us, that she encouraged us to support it, to stand in awe of it, to die for it.

That American women, irrespective of their education, economic status, or racial identification, have undergone years of sexist and racist socialization that has taught us to blindly trust our knowledge of history and its effect on present reality, even though that knowledge has been formed and shaped by an oppressive system, is nowhere more evident than in the recent feminist movement. The group of college-educated white middle and upper class women who came together to organize a women's movement brought a new energy to the concept of women's rights in America. They were not merely advocating social equality with men. They demanded a transformation of society, a revolution, a change in the American social structure. Yet as they attempted to take feminism beyond the realm of radical rhetoric and into the realm of American life, they revealed that they had not changed, had not undone the sexist and racist brainwashing that had taught them to regard women like themselves as Others. Consequently, the Sisterhood they talked about has not become a reality, and the women's movement they envisioned would have a transformative effect on American culture has not emerged. Instead, the hierarchical pattern of race and sex relationships already established in American society merely took a different form under "feminism": the form of women being classed as an oppressed group under affirmative action programs further perpetuating the myth that the social status of all women in America is the same; the form of women's studies programs being established with all-white faculty teaching literature almost exclusively by white women about white women and frequently from racist perspectives; the form of white women writing books that purport to be about the experience of American women when in fact they concentrate solely on the experience of white women; and finally the form of endless argument and debate as to whether or not racism was a feminist issue.

Every women's movement in America from its earliest origin to the present day has been built on a racist foundation—a fact which in no way invalidates feminism as a political ideology. The racial apartheid social structure that characterized 19th and early 20th century American life was mirrored in the women's rights movement. The first white women's rights advocates were never seeking social equality for all women; they were seeking social equality for white women. Because many 19th century white women's rights advocates were also active in the abolitionist movement, it is often assumed they were anti-racist. Historiographers and especially recent feminist writing have created a version of American history in which white women's rights advocates are presented as champions of oppressed black people. This fierce romanticism has informed most studies of the abolitionist movement. In contemporary times there is a general tendency to equate abolitionism with a repudiation of racism. In actuality, most white abolitionists, male and female, though vehement in their anti-slavery protest, were totally opposed to granting social equality to black people. Joel Kovel, in his study *White Racism: A Psychohistory,* emphasizes that the "actual aim of the reform movement, so nobly and bravely begun, was not the liberation of the black, but the fortification of the white, conscience and all."

It is a commonly accepted belief that white female reformist empathy with the oppressed black slave, coupled with her recognition that she was powerless to end slavery, led to the development of a feminist consciousness and feminist revolt. Contemporary historiographers and in particular white female scholars accept the theory that the white women's rights advocates' feelings of solidarity with black slaves were an indication that they were anti-racist and were supportive of social equality of blacks. It is this glorification of the role white women played that leads Adrienne Rich to assert:

> . . . It is important for white feminists to remember that—despite lack of constitutional citizenship, educational deprivation, economic bondage to men, laws and customs forbidding women to speak in public or to disobey fathers, husbands, and brothers—our white foresisters have, in Lillian Smith's words, repeatedly been "disloyal to civilization" and have "smelled death in the word 'segregation,' " often defying patriarchy for the first time, not on their own behalf but for the sake of black men, women, and children. We have a strong anti-racist female tradition despite all efforts by the white patriarchy to polarize its creature-objects, creating dichotomies of privilege and caste, skin color, and age and condition of servitude.

There is little historical evidence to document Rich's assertion that white women as a collective group or white women's rights advocates are part of an anti-racist tradition. When white women reformers in the 1830s chose to work to free the slave, they were motivated by religious sentiment. They attacked slavery, not racism. The basis of their attack was moral reform. That they were not demanding social equality for black people is an indication that they remained committed to white racist supremacy despite their anti-slavery work. While they strongly advocated an end to slavery, they never advocated a change in the racial hierarchy that allowed their caste status to be higher than that of black women or men. In fact, they wanted that hierarchy to be maintained. Consequently, the white women's rights movement which had a lukewarm beginning in earlier reform activities emerged in full force in the wake of efforts to gain rights for black people precisely because white women wanted to see no change in the social status of blacks until they were assured that their demands for more rights were met.

White women's rights advocate and abolitionist Abby Kelly's comment, "We have good cause to be grateful to the slave for the benefit we have received to ourselves, in working for him. In striving to strike his irons off, we found most surely, that we were manacled ourselves," is often quoted by scholars as evidence that white women became conscious of their own limited rights as they worked to end slavery. Despite popular 19th century rhetoric, the notion that white women had to learn from their efforts to free the slave of their own limited rights is simply erroneous. No 19th century white woman could grow to maturity without an awareness of institutionalized sexism. White women did learn via their efforts to free the slave that white men were willing to advocate rights for blacks while denouncing rights for women. As a result of negative reaction to their reform activity and public effort to curtail and prevent their anti-slavery work, they were forced to acknowledge that without outspoken demands for equal rights with white men they might ultimately be lumped in the same social category with blacks—or even worse, black men might gain a higher social status than theirs.

It did not enhance the cause of oppressed black slaves for white women to make synonymous their plight and the plight of the slave. Despite Abby Kelly's dramatic statement, there was very little if any similarity between the day-to-day life experiences of white women and the day-to-day experiences of the black slave. Theoretically, the white woman's legal status under patriarchy may have been that of "property," but she was in no way subjected to the de-humanization and brutal oppression that was the lot of the slave. When white reformers made synonymous the impact of sexism on their lives, they were not revealing an awareness of or sensitivity to the slave's lot; they were simply appropriating the horror of the slave experience to enhance their own cause.

The fact that the majority of white women reformers did not feel political solidarity with black people was made evident in the conflict over the vote. When it appeared that white men might grant black men the right to vote while leaving white women disenfranchised, white suffragists did not respond as a group by demanding that all women and men deserved the right to vote. They simply expressed anger and outrage that white men were more committed to maintaining sexual hierarchies than racial hierarchies in the political arena. Ardent white women's rights advocates like Elizabeth Cady Stanton who had never before argued for women's rights on a racially imperialistic platform expressed outrage that inferior "niggers" should be granted the vote while "superior" white women remained disenfranchised. Stanton argued;

> If Saxon men have legislated thus for their own mothers, wives and daughters, what can we hope for at the hands of Chinese, Indians, and Africans? . . . I protest against the enfranchisement of another man of any race or clime until the daughters of Jefferson, Hancock, and Adams are crowned with their rights.

White suffragists felt that white men were insulting white womanhood by refusing to grant them privileges that were to be granted black men. They admonished white men not for their sexism but for their willingness to allow sexism to overshadow racial alliances. Stanton, along with other white women's rights supporters, did not want to see blacks enslaved, but neither did she wish to see the status of black people improved while the status of white women remained the same.

Animosity between black and white women's liberationists was not due solely to disagreement over racism within the women's movement; it was the end result of years of jealousy, envy, competition, and anger between the two groups. Conflict between black and white women did not begin with the 20th century women's movement. It began during slavery. The social status of white women in America has to a large extent been determined by white people's relationship to black people. It was the enslavement of African people in colonized America that marked the beginning of a change in the social status of white women. Prior to slavery, patriarchal law decreed white women were lowly inferior beings, the subordinate group in society. The subjugation of black people allowed them to vacate their despised position and assume the role of a superior.

Consequently, it can be easily argued that even though white men institutionalized slavery, white women were its most immediate beneficiaries. Slavery in no way altered the hierarchical social status of the white male but it created a new status for the white female. The only way that her new status could be maintained was through the constant assertion of her superiority over the black woman and man. All too often colonial white women, particularly those who were slave mistresses, chose to differentiate their status from the slave's by treating the slave in a brutal and cruel manner. It was in her relationship to the black female slave that the white woman could best assert her power. Individual black slave women were quick to learn that sex-role differentiation did not mean that the white mistress was not to be regarded as an authority figure. Because they had been socialized via patriarchy to respect male authority and resent female authority, black women were reluctant to acknowledge the "power" of the white mistress. When the enslaved black woman expressed contempt and disregard for white female authority, the white mistress often resorted to brutal punishment to assert her authority. But even brutal punishment could not change the fact that black women were not inclined to regard the white female with the awe and respect they showed to the white male.

By flaunting their sexual lust for the bodies of black women and their preference for them as sexual partners, white men successfully pitted white women and enslaved black women against one another. In most instances, the white mistress did not envy the black female slave her role as sexual object; she feared only that her newly acquired social status might be threatened by white male sexual interaction with black women. His sexual involvement with black women (even if that involvement was rape) in effect reminded the white female of her subordinate position in relationship to him. For he could exercise his power as racial imperialist and sexual imperialist to rape or seduce black women, while white women were not free to rape or seduce black men without fear of punishment. Though the white female might condemn the actions of a white male who chose to interact sexually with black female slaves, she was unable to dictate to him proper behavior. Nor could she retaliate by engaging in sexual relationships with enslaved or free black men. Not surprisingly, she directed her anger and rage at the enslaved black women. In those cases where emotional ties developed between white men and black female slaves, white mistresses would go to great lengths to punish the female. Severe beatings were the method most white women used to punish black female slaves. Often in a jealous rage a mistress might use disfigurement to punish a lusted-after black female slave. The mistress might cut off her breast, blind an eye, or cut off another body part. Such treatment naturally caused hostility between white women and enslaved black women. To the enslaved black woman, the white mistress living in relative comfort was the representative symbol of white womanhood. She was both envied and despised—envied for her material comfort, despised because she felt little concern or compassion for the slave woman's lot. Since the white woman's privileged social status could not exist if a group of women were present to assume the lowly position she had abdicated, it follows that black and white women would be at odds with one another. If the white woman struggled to change the lot of the black slave woman, her own social position on the race-sex hierarchy would be altered.

Manumission did not bring an end to conflicts between black and white women; it heightened them. To maintain the apartheid structure slavery had institutionalized, white colonizers, male and female, created a variety of myths and stereotypes to differentiate the status of black women from that of white women. White racists and even some black people who had absorbed the colonizer's mentality depicted the white woman as a symbol of perfect womanhood and encouraged black women to strive to attain such perfection by using the white female as her model. The jealousy and envy of white women that had erupted in the black woman's consciousness during slavery was deliberately encouraged by the dominant white culture. Advertisements, newspaper articles, books, etc., were constant reminders to black women of the difference between their social status and that of white women, and they bitterly resented it. Nowhere was this dichotomy as clearly demonstrated as in the materially privileged white household where the black female domestic worked as an employee of the white family. In these relationships, black women workers were exploited to enhance the social standing of white families. In the white community, employing domestic help was a sign of material privilege and the person who directly benefited from a servant's work was the white woman, since without the servant she would have performed domestic chores. Not surprisingly, the black female domestic tended to see the white female as her "boss," her oppressor, not the white male whose earnings usually paid her wage.

Throughout American history white men have deliberately promoted hostility and divisiveness between white and black women. The white patriarchal power structure pits the two groups against each other, preventing the growth of solidarity between women and ensuring that women's status as a subordinate group under patriarchy remains intact. To this end, white men have supported changes in the white woman's social standing only if there exists another female group to assume that role. Consequently, the white patriarch undergoes no radical change in his sexist assumption that woman is inherently inferior. He neither relinquishes his dominant position nor alters the patriarchal structure of society. He is, however, able to convince many white women that fundamental changes in "woman's status" have occurred because he has successfully socialized her, via racism, to assume that no connection exists between her and black women.

Because women's liberation has been equated with gaining privileges within the white male power structure, white men—and not women, either white or black—have dictated the terms by which women are allowed entrance into the system. One of the terms male patriarchs have set is that one group of women is granted privileges that they obtain by actively supporting the oppression and exploitation of other groups of women. White and black women have been socialized to accept and honor these terms, hence the fierce competition between the two groups; a competition that has always been centered in the arena of sexual politics, with white and black women competing against one another for male favor. This competition is part of an overall battle between various groups of women to be the chosen female group.

The contemporary move toward feminist revolution was continually undermined by competition between various factions. In regards to race, the women's movement has become simply another arena in which white and black women compete to be the chosen female group. This power struggle has not been resolved by the formation of opposing interest groups. Such groups are symptomatic of the problem and are no solution. Black and white women have for so long allowed their idea of liberation to be formed by the existing status quo that they have not yet devised a strategy by which we can come together. They have had only a slave's idea of freedom. And to the slave, the master's way of life represents the ideal free lifestyle.

Women's liberationists, white and black, will always be at odds with one another as long as our idea of liberation is based on having the power white men have. For that power denies unity, denies common connections, and is inherently divisive. It is woman's acceptance of divisiveness as a natural order that has caused black and white women to cling religiously to the belief that bonding across racial boundaries is impossible, to passively accept the notion that the distances that separate women are immutable.

**Credits** *(continued)*

Pages 23–29. Prudence Mackintosh, from "Masculine/Feminine" in *Thundering Sneakers,* 1977. Reprinted by permission of The Wendy Weil Agency, Inc. Copyright © 1974–1981 by Prudence Mackintosh.

Pages 31–37. Dorothy L. Sayers, from *Unpopular Opinions,* Harcourt Brace Jovanovich, Inc., 1947. Reprinted by permission of David Higham Associates, Ltd.

Pages 39–54. Lucy Gilbert and Paula Webster, from *Bound by Love.* Copyright © 1982 by Lucy Gilbert and Paula Webster. Reprinted by permission of Beacon Press.

Pages 56–59. Alan Alda, "What Every Woman Should Know About Men," *Ms.* Magazine, October 1975. © 1975, Alan Alda, all rights reserved. Reprinted by permission.

Pages 60–66. Herb Goldberg, from *The Hazards of Being Male,* NAL, 1976.

Pages 68–72. Harold Rosenberg, "Masculinity: Style and Cult," *Vogue,* November 1967. Courtesy *Vogue.* Copyright © 1967 by The Condé Nast Publications Inc.

Pages 74–84. Marc Feigen Fasteau, from *The Male Machine.* Copyright 1974. McGraw-Hill Publishing Company. Reprinted by permission.

Pages 86–89. Noel Perrin, "The Androgynous Male," *The New York Times,* February 5, 1984. Copyright © 1984 by The New York Times Company. Reprinted by permission.

Pages 90–99. Edmund White, "Sexual Culture," *Vanity Fair,* 1983. Reprinted by permission.

Pages 101–107, 344–350. Simone de Beauvoir, from the Introduction and Chapter XVI of *The Second Sex* by Simone de Beauvoir, translated by H. M. Parshley. Copyright 1952 by Alfred A. Knopf, Inc. Reprinted by permission of the publisher.

Pages 108–124. Naomi Weisstein, "Psychology Constructs the Female." Copyright Naomi Weisstein, 1971. Reprinted by permission.

Pages 126–136, 542–546. Susan Brownmiller, "Emotion" and excerpts from "Movement" in *Femininity,* 1983. Copyright © 1984 by Susan Brownmiller. Reprinted by permission of Linden Press, a division of Simon & Schuster, Inc.

Pages 137–143, 299–312. Gloria Steinem, "Sisterhood" and "Men and Women Talking," from *Outrageous Acts and Everyday Rebellions.* Copyright © 1983 by Gloria Steinem, © 1984 by East Toledo Productions, Inc. Reprinted by permission of Henry Holt and Company, Inc.

Pages 151–156. Plato, from Book V of *The Republic,* translated by A. D. Lindsay. E. P. Dutton and Company, 1957. Reprinted by permission of J. M. Dent and Everyman's Library.

Pages 158–161. Mary Daly, excerpted from "Social Attitudes Towards Women." Reprinted with permission of Charles Scribner's Sons, an imprint of Macmillan Publishing Company, from *Dictionary of the History of Ideas,* Philip P. Wiener, Editor in Chief. Volume IV, pp. 523–525. Copyright © 1973 by Charles Scribner's Sons.

Pages 163–167. Pope Pius XI, from "On Christian Marriage: Encyclical Letter Casti Connubii," from *The Church and the Reconstruction of the Modern World,* Terence P. McLaughlin. Copyright © 1957 by T. P. McLaughlin. Reprinted by permission of Doubleday, a division of Bantam, Doubleday, Dell Publishing Group, Inc.

Pages 168–175. Dorothy Gies McGuigan, "To Be a Woman and a Scholar." Reprinted with permission from *LSA* (Fall 1978), The University of Michigan.

Pages 212–224. Charlotte Perkins Gilman, from *Women and Economics,* edited by Carl N. Degler 1966. Introduction and notes © 66 Carl N. Degler 133076-6. Originally published by Small, Maynard and Co. Reprinted by permission from HarperCollins Publishers.

Pages 225–231. Margaret Sanger, excerpt from "Awakening and Revolt," in *My Fight for Birth Control,* 1931. Reprinted by permission.

Pages 232–235. Margaret Sanger, "Birth Control—A Parents' Problem or Woman's?" from *Woman and the New Race,* 1920. Reprinted by permission.

Pages 236–241. Virginia Woolf, "Professions for Women," from *The Death of the Moth and Other Essays.* Copyright 1942 by Harcourt Brace Jovanovich, Inc. and renewed 1970 by Marjorie T. Parson, Executrix. Reprinted by permission of the publisher.

Pages 247–258. Casey Miller and Kate Swift, from *The New York Times,* April 16, 1972. Copyright © "One Small Step for Genkind," by Casey Miller and Kate Swift. All rights reserved.

Pages 259–270. Alleen Pace Nilsen, "Sexism in English: A 1990s Update." Copyright © Alleen Pace Nilsen, 1990. Reprinted by permission.

Pages 272–286. Casey Miller and Kate Swift, from *Words and Women.* Copyright © 1976 by Casey Miller and Kate Swift. Used by permission of Doubleday, a division of Bantam, Doubleday, Dell Publishing Group, Inc.

Pages 287–290. Cyra McFadden, "In Defense of Gender," *The New York Times,* August 2, 1981. Copyright © 1981 by The New York Times Company. Reprinted by permission.

Pages 292–298. Robin Lakoff, "You Are What You Say," *Ms.* Magazine, July 1974. Reprinted by permission.

Pages 319–326. Matina Horner, "Fail: Bright Woman." Reprinted with permission from *Psychology Today* Magazine. Copyright © 1969 (PT Partners, L.P.).

Pages 328–335. Adrienne Rich, "Taking Women Students Seriously," from *On Lies, Secrets, and Silence: Selected Prose 1966–1978.* Reprinted by permission of the author and W. W. Norton & Company, Inc. Copyright © 1979 by W. W. Norton & Company, Inc.

Pages 341–343. Judy (Syfers) Brady, "I Want a Wife," *Ms.* Magazine, December 1979. Reprinted by permission.

Pages 351–354. Rick Greenberg, "Escaping the Daily Grind for Life as a House Father." Reprinted by permission of Rick Greenberg.

Pages 356–364. Deborah Fallows, "Why Mothers Should Stay Home," *The Washington Monthly,* January 1982. Reprinted with permission from *The Washington Monthly.* Copyright by The Washington Monthly Company, 1611 Connecticut Avenue, N.W., Washington, D.C. 20009, (202) 462-0128.

Pages 365–368. Nancy Friday, from "Mother Love" in *My Mother/Myself.* Copyright © 1977, 1987 by Nancy Friday. Used by permission of Dell Books, a division of Bantam, Doubleday, Dell Publishing Group, Inc.

Pages 370–381. Betty Rollin, "Motherhood: Who Needs It?" *Look* Magazine, September 1970. Copyright © 1970 by Betty Rollin. Reprinted by permission of the author.

Pages 382–386. Lindsy Van Gelder, "Marriage as a Restricted Club," *Ms.* Magazine, February 1984. Reprinted by permission of the author.

Pages 393–401. Teresa Amott and Julie Matthaei, "Comparable Worth, Incomparable Pay." Copyright © *Radical America,* Vol. 18, no. 5, 1984. Reprinted by permission.